Evolution and Growth of China's Wholesale Industry since 1978

EVOLUTION AND GROWTH OF CHINA'S WHOLESALE INDUSTRY SINCE 1978

Ma Longlong

Enrich Professional Publishing

Published by

Enrich Professional Publishing (S) Private Limited
16L, Enterprise Road,
Singapore 627660
Website: www.enrichprofessional.com
A Member of Enrich Culture Group Limited

Hong Kong Head Office:
1/F., Lemmi Center, 50 Hoi Yuen Road, Kwun Tong, Kowloon, Hong Kong, China

Beijing Office:
Rm 1108A, Culture Plaza, No. 59 Zhongguancun St., Haidian District, Beijing, China

Translated by Li Ling and Yang Mifen

ISBN (Hardback) 978-981-4298-40-7
ISBN (ebook) 978-981-4298-41-4 (pdf)
978-981-4298-65-0 (epub)

Enrich Professional Publishing is an independent globally minded publisher focusing on the economic and financial developments that have revolutionized new China. We aim to serve the needs of advanced degree students, researchers, and business professionals who are looking for authoritative, accurate and engaging information on China.

Printed in Hong Kong

Contents

Foreword

With the overall economic restructuring in China, the reform and development of the circulation system in China has also gone through 30 years of twists and turns.

It is the initial desire and ultimate goal of the three decades of reform and development of the circulation system in China to push forward the integration of the domestic market and the international market, introduce foreign capital, and promote the internationalization process in the field of circulation.

In the first few years of the reform and opening up, it has been found that the circulation of wholesale commodities refers to not only that in the domestic market, but also that in the international market. That is, it involves the circulation of all wholesale commodities, and the sum of the circulation of domestic wholesale commodities and that of international wholesale commodities.

That's because during the entire process of commodity circulation, not all wholesale commodities are distributed on the domestic market. Some of them are imported before being traded and wholesaled domestically. For imported consumer goods, they have to be put into retail from being wholesaled on the domestic market. Others may be traded domestically, and exported through domestic wholesale before being traded domestically in the importing countries. Therefore, the circulation of wholesale commodities in China may simply refer to the domestic circulation of wholesale commodities, or the continued circulation of China's wholesale commodities by other countries in their wholesale commodity circulation, or the continued the circulation of wholesale commodities of other countries by China in its circulation of wholesale commodities.

Foreign traders are wholesalers. Marx once said that importers and exporters were a kind of wholesalers. Exporters exported means of subsistence for consumption in the form of finished products, under which circumstance they were called wholesalers. Such wholesalers only played an intermediate role in the reproduction process, facilitating the transfer of products to retailers before enabling such products to enter the field of consumption from retailers. Or when such wholesalers exported raw materials, semi-products, ancillary materials, machines and labor tools, under which circumstance they played an intermediate role in the exchange among producers, being W-G or G-W in different situations, i.e. commercial capital being turned into currency capital or currency capital being turned into commercial capital. Therefore, exporters were more or less the same as wholesalers in nature, so were importers and exporters. Therefore, the wholesale trade is not limited to domestic wholesale, but includes foreign trade, which is the experience got by China in its three decades of reform and development of wholesale commodity circulation.

In the reform and opening up, China has to not only expand foreign trade, but also connect domestic and foreign capital flows. In particular, it has to attract foreign capital into domestic construction in order to promote the development of the wholesale trade. Opening up wider to the outside world is totally necessary in the field of circulation. However, in view of the position of the wholesale trade which is more important than that of the retail trade, China must be prudent when introducing foreign capital. It is a big issue closely related to not only the successful establishment of an open and controllable market in China, but also the protection of an independent national market and the establishment of a unified national market.

Internationalization of the wholesale trade is an inevitable demand of a developed commodity economy. Specifically, it is necessary for economically-developed countries to globalize their unified domestic markets before becoming the integral parts of the global market in terms of international division of labor. The trend of global market integration enables the wholesale trade in the domestic market to be inseparable from the international trade in the global market. Wholesale trade in the domestic market falls into three categories in general: pure domestic wholesale or being domestic wholesale-led; domestic wholesale being integrated with foreign trade; and pure foreign trade or being foreign trade-led. The latter two forms of wholesale trade touches upon internationalization, which requires enterprises engaged in such forms of wholesale trade to have to take part in the great circulation of the global market based on the international division of work.

Domestic and foreign trades in China have long been separated, which hasn't be fundamentally changed even up to now, yet must be completely changed if China intends to achieve industrialization and modernization. Separating the domestic and foreign trades with executive power will prevent the market needed in the industrialization and modernization from developing stronger. In reality, the global market is changing rapidly; and as the domestic wholesale trade, international trade is becoming a powerful driving force for the development of the economy. International trade is undergoing profound changes: the trade in goods not only keeps expanding, but also increasingly goes global; trade liberalism and protectionism co-exist and play their roles alternately; and transnational companies are developing rapidly, all of which requires the internationalization of the domestic wholesale trade.

Domestic and foreign markets have to be integrated during the internationalization of the wholesale trade. Since opening up and domestic reform must be coordinative with each other, domestic economic operations must be consistent with international practices. Only in so doing could domestic and foreign trades get developed in a coordinative way. The integration of the domestic and foreign markets includes that in commodities, services, capital, legal protection and a number of other aspects. Without the integration of commodity markets, it would be hard to solve the integration in other aspects, because the commodity market is the basis of the market system and domestic and foreign wholesale takes the greatest part of tangible trade. In integrating the domestic and foreign wholesale trades, financial issues, fiscal issues, taxation issues, price issues, as well as such issues concerning business entities, corporate system, operating mechanism, method of trading, logistics, business and industry associations, macroeconomic regulation, etc. must be well handled. Only by well handling or solving the above-mentioned issues could the internationalization of the wholesale trade be achieved smoothly. It calls for continuing the institutional reform in the domestic and foreign wholesale trades. Besides, it is found that adhering to opening up, achieving the internationalization of the wholesale trade, and trying to solve the problem of integrating domestic and foreign markets as soon as possible doesn't mean that China should overlook the protection of its national economy. China insists on moderately opening up the domestic market, including the wholesale market, under the premise of protecting its national industries in order to attract foreign investments and introduce advanced technologies.

Integrating the domestic market with foreign markets and internationalizing the wholesale trade don't mean that it is not necessary to protect the promising, but immature sections of the domestic economy. On the contrary, even the national economy has to seriously treat the issue of "foreign goods". Faced with the challenges of "the three types of foreign-funded" enterprises, in whether the "resumption of its GATT status" or the accession to the WTO, China must gradually reduce its import tariffs before reaching the general level of import tariffs of developing countries. It calls for China to remove the barrier of high tariffs on some Chinese goods, which requires it to improve the qualities of its national industries and agricultural products, diversify varieties, and reduce the cost before competing with the "foreign goods" on the market.

Experience in the reform and development of the circulation of wholesale commodities over the past three decades has proven repeatedly that a unified domestic market should in the first place a vast and independent national market needed in the industrialization. Without such a market, effective and positive participation in the international division of work and the entry into the global market will be out of the question. However, in order to thoroughly complete the construction of such a market, trades that represent the interests of the new-type social and economic forces, mainly referring to the wholesale trades, have to be the pioneers. The problem is that large Chinese enterprises engaged in domestic wholesale and foreign trade are still unclear about their historic missions, and that the government policy on circulation has failed to play its due role in such aspect. In the domestic market, foreign investors have abundant capital, many of which receive low-interest loans from the Chinese Government and enjoy the preferential policies provided by the Chinese Government. However, the Chinese wholesale traders encounter various difficulties, especially the financial difficulty, putting them at a disadvantage in market competitions. A sharp, yet must be addressed problem has to be put forward here. That is, priority must be given to supporting the national commerce and wholesale trade if China intends to develop its national economy and the wholesale trade. It is the true support. Only with a strong and great market capable of controlling the domestic market and protecting the national economy internally, as well as participating in international competitions and meeting the demands for achieving the modernization externally could the wholesale trade be counted as the truly internationalized wholesale trade.

It's been the focus of debate as for the fate and position of the wholesale trade for 30 years. The two waves of "the theory of wholesale being useless" in Japan and the reform of the wholesale trade thus stirred were worth considering. During the 1960s, the Japanese manufacturers serialized Japan's circulation section through national ads and the brand strategy of investing in new products before mastering part of the initiative and controlling wholesale enterprises from price, stocking and sales regions, etc. Representative industries included household appliances, automobiles, cosmetics, cameras, stationery, cleaning supplies, etc. Of which, the most representative enterprises were Matsushita Electric Industrial Company and Kao Corporation. Due to the establishment of the mass production system, the center of circulation gradually shifted from the advantages of the wholesale traders to those of the manufacturers. Local wholesale traders were selected, regrouped and adapted by capable brand manufacturers, leading to the first wave of "the theory of wholesale being useless". Since the 1970s, modern types of operation such as large supermarket chains and chain stores have been developing fast before gradually grasping the initiative of circulation. Targeting at manufacturers' circulation serialization and exclusive prices, modern large retailers confronted manufacturers through such powerful weapons as their own brands, the large mass production system and efficient logistics distribution centers. A poster child would be the 7-11 convenient stores. Through the network of the circulation information, large retailers succeeded in holding the position superior to that of the suppliers and began to exercise the centralization and logistics functions of wholesale traders' in tradition, leading to another wave of "the theory of wholesale being useless" that edged out wholesale traders.

To conform to the objective needs of the commodity circulation law, the wholesale trade in Japan took "transforming from the previous production agents to retail and purchasing agents" as its strategic target, and boldly stepped up their role change into purchasing agents through such strategies as strengthening informationization, enhancing their logistics functions, and carrying out retail supports, thus promoting the overall reorganization of the wholesale industry. The report entitled *The 21st Century-oriented Ideas of the Circulation* issued by the Japanese Ministry of International Trade and Industry has made "retail support" one of the most important directions of the reform and development of the retail industry and set a series of incentive systems.

The good news is that after three decades of reform and opening up, various forms of wholesale operation apart from the traditional wholesale by distributors have appeared in China, including the direct supply and wholesale by the manufacturers, which is not limited to means of production, but also includes articles for daily use, farm and agricultural products; the wholesale by agents or brokers; the wholesale by the third-party logistics enterprises, which carries out supply chain management and helps supply raw materials and standard parts to manufacturers, including the sales of products; and the supply and wholesale by dispatching centers, which delivers goods to all units in the society, including small stores, etc.

Various forms of wholesale operations have adapted to the rapid development of the manufacturing industry in China. Over the three decades of reform and opening up, "Made in China" has ruled the world. The output value of more than 100 products, including those produced by transnational companies in China, has succeeded in ranking No.1 around the world; and the three world-level manufacturing districts-the Pearl River Delta, the Yangtze River Delta and the Bohai Rim have been established. Such a huge output value calls for a corresponding circulation industry, which has to be undertaken by the wholesale industry of course. It is undoubtedly a historical choice, answering the question on the fate of the wholesale industry objectively.

Experience in the past three decades shows that various forms of wholesale businesses have also meet the requirement of small and medium-sized enterprises on market supply. A lot of fields in China are low in industrial concentration ratio. Most enterprises in such fields, including the fields of production and circulation, are small in size. The output value of the small and medium-sized enterprises accounts for half of that of the national economy, while over 90% of the total retail sales of consumer goods are contributed by 99% of the small and medium-sized circulation enterprises in China. Direct trade between the numerous retail businesses and the same numerous production enterprises is unimaginable. Therefore, it is the best choice to buy/sell and stock in bulk through the wholesale trade.

Various forms of wholesale operations have also met the objective need of diversified consumption demands. The long established dual-layered economic structure in China and the income gap between urban and rural areas and among different regions have led to different consumption levels and behaviors, making it impossible for manufacturers to supply goods directly for tens of millions of retail enterprises, or for the retail enterprises to login each manufacturer's website to see if it needs their products. In term of saving the transaction costs, the wholesale industry in China is more than just promising.

A newly-emerged thing in the circulation field in China in the past three decades since the reform and opening up is the formation and development of the wholesale markets. The volume of commodity circulation of such markets as Hanzheng Street in Wuhan, Yiwu in Zhejiang Province, the Lotus Pond market in Cheng Du, Tai He in Anhui Province and a number of other markets has all exceeded tens of billions of RMB each year. Many of them have developed into famous large-scale, professional and global centers of commodity circulation that go beyond national boundaries. Wholesale markets are featured by cheap products, individual operators and stores, small sizes, flexible prices, as well as being based on small retailers and individual consumers with low and middle-level incomes. Major sellers in the wholesale market could be divided into three types: large enterprises who usually take the wholesale market as one of the supplements to their main sales channels; capable operators who customize or buy out a brand before selling on the market the products under the brand; small and medium-sized enterprises whose products are daily necessities and who take the wholesale market as the major sales channel. The phenomenon of following suit in the wholesale market is very serious. The life cycles of products are short. For small and medium-sized enterprises featured by the shortage of capital, operating flexibility and quick reactions, making use of the wholesale market before achieving rapid product distribution and penetration is often an effective strategy for striding over the threshold of starting an undertaking.

Wholesale markets once played an important role in pushing forward the reform of the commodity circulation system and the construction of the commodity market in China, and are still with great vitality today. Wholesale markets are closely related to and extensively adapt to the level of economic development in China, as well as the physical living standards of the Chinese people. In a fairly long period to come, wholesale markets will maintain certain space for survival and growth. Together with other new means of circulation, wholesale markets play an important role in advancing the modernization of commodity circulation in China. Meanwhile, seen from other countries, establishing a modern commodity circulation system relying on the wholesale markets is very popular in major developing countries, including South Africa, Turkey, Egypt, India, etc. Even in the Western developed countries, Wal-Mart and Carrefour are not the only two retailers. Their commodity circulation systems are also composed of various forms of circulations and various types of trades in goods, and have respective customer groups. Numerous dealers and traders gathering in wholesale markets have set up a huge network of commercial operations, which is a very valuable business resource. Of course, there are a lot of problems in the wholesale markets, such as the much-heard integrity crisis, fake commodities, etc. However, these problems are not wholesale markets-specific, but popular in the process of establishing and improving the market economy. What needs to be discussed is not when to rectify or how to ban the wholesale markets, but how to constantly improve the technical contents of such markets, greatly intensifying the informationalized construction of such markets, highlighting the brands and characteristics of professional services, and better adapting the wholesale markets to modern industrial production.

Is the wholesale market a backward business pattern? Does it develop only in townships or underdeveloped regions as a supplement of the modern pattern of circulation in cities or areas with prosperous economy? The reality in China is that the more developed the region is, the more developed the local wholesale market will be. Marx had long noticed that beyond the organization specialized in commodity circulation, i.e. the wholesale trade, there was the wholesale market, an organization playing the role of distribution centers and serving for commodity circulation. On the basis of comprehensive markets, such wholesale markets will develop into professional wholesale markets. Professional wholesale markets are trading markets set up to meet the large amounts of supply and demand of a certain commodity. Therefore, it is not true that all commodities would have their professional trading markets. Marx said that only large amounts of consumables (only the market for grains, and that for tea, sugar and coffee are of economic significance, the market for wines and that for alcohols may be counted in to some extent) or products used as industrial raw materials such as the markets for crude wool, silk, wood and metals. Further, wholesale markets could be divided into wholesale markets in places of origin, those in places for sales and those in the transitional areas. Marx also said that main markets for such diversified products were formed in each and all centers. All such locations became centers because of the import-export relationship or they themselves being the centers of some production or direction suppliers. Reviewing relevant dissertations of Marx helps us understand the nature and role of the wholesale market in a comprehensive and correct way.

Wholesale is not only related to the smoothness of commodity circulation, but also very influential in the mutual adaptation and matching of the aggregate supply and demand. Due to the movements of speculative capital in the wholesale field, especially after the credit system and futures markets integrated commercial capital with financial capital, the influence of wholesale on the macro-economy will be multiplied, or even lead to economic crises or undermine social stability. In the Asian financial crisis broken out during 1997–1998 and the global economic and financial crisis starting since 2007, volatility in the sector of wholesale and financial market disturbances interacted with each other and mutually reinforced before severely damaging the productive forces and greatly lowering people's living standards. Therefore, the circulation of wholesale commodities must be understood and recognized at the height of national economic security.

Looking back, we have to admit that during the past three decades since it launched the reform and opening up, China has encountered a great number of problems in developing the wholesale commodity circulation and reforming its wholesale system, and that many of the problems haven't been solved completely. Is wholesale really useful? How should people view commercial wholesale? What should the pattern of ownership be like in the field of wholesale commodity circulation? How to give full play to the due role of wholesale in China's economic growth and process of industrialization and modernization? How to adapt to the development of the commodity economy, industrialization and the process of modernization before gradually setting up the industrial and organizational system needed by the socialized and modernized mass production? What kind of macroeconomic regulation should be carried out by the state in order to ensure that the market institution will play its essential role in regulating the entire economic operation in a correct and comprehensive way?, etc. No answers to the above questions have been found. Currently, many problems exist in developing the wholesale commodity circulation and reforming the wholesale system, including serious losses of the wholesale trade, backward material and technological foundations of the wholesale commodity circulation, intensified local protectionism, chaotic market circulation orders and severe government intervention in some places, and the lack of economic power in macro-economic regulation. The reality indicates that problems existing in the wholesale field are extremely complicated. More efforts are needed in order to explore and study such problems in a fundamental and strategic way. It is a systematic engineering with a long way ahead. To achieve the established development goal and complete the two changes in the pattern of economic growth and economic restructuring, China must fundamentally explore the problems existing in the wholesale circulation field in the long run, which is not only the requirement of reform, but also that of the development of the times.

By summing up the experience obtained in the reform and opening up of the wholesale field over the past three decades, we have noticed that there is much room for improvement in related theoretical and practical studies.

In-depth researches are needed

Over the past three decades, most economic theorists in China have focused on the commodity market mechanism and market system and level, while few of them have probed into the internal structure, the operating mechanism and the development process of the market and circulation, nor distinguished the development levels of the market and circulation of economically-developed countries and some developing countries like China, as well as the national conditions of China in this aspect. In the aspect of market and circulation, great interest has been in the financial market and the circulation of securities and less attention has been paid to the commodity market and circulation of commodities. To them, it seems that questions in such aspect are irrelevant to economic development and institutional reform, and no theoretical questions deserve their notice. Even when they did do researches on commodity circulation, most of them focused on the trading of futures, but ignoring commodity circulation on the cash markets. As a result, those studying wholesale commodity circulation have been limited to business economic theorists and commodity circulation authorities.

In addition, existing difficulties and problems in the field are a burden on the researches on wholesale commodity circulation. Few researches are based on fundamental and long-term problems, affecting the discussion over theoretical questions. Too much attention being given to studying related policies has brought about a series of problems in this complicated field, making it a mess. Though reasonable, many countermeasures are not targeting at the wholesale trade as a whole, but the outstanding problems concerning the overall economy, making it hard to put them into practice, or making positive results. For example, industrial production organizations could develop self-marketing wholesale when necessary. However, there are requirements on the size of the self-marketing wholesale, or whether a substantial or major part of such organizations should be put under commercial and professional wholesale. It depends on whether the self-marketing could save social labors, increase economic efficacy, and whether the self-marketing violates the objective rules on social division of labor. However, there is this tendency of expanding self-marketing blindly in reality, which is actually closely related to the uncompleted institutional reform of the national economy. Due to the backward production, serious losses and excessive redundant enterprise employees, manufacturers could not only hold a large number of surplus staffs, but also make up for the insufficient production benefits with the profits obtained through circulation before offsetting production losses. Therefore, though business professional wholesale formed in the development of social division of work has its existence and development basis, some industrial producers may also expand self-marketing blindly by leaving aside professional business wholesale regardless of all possible conditions, leading to social losses. It can be seen that the problem of expanding self-marketing blindly by producers is hard to be solved if China does not focus on the overall economy, or solve the low efficiency of state-owned industrial organizations and the hidden unemployment of such organizations while creating conditions for wholesale, or is limited by wholesale itself. In view of this, wholesale must be put into the overall economic development and the overall situation of the entire economic system before being studied fundamentally and in the long run. Or it would be impossible to solve the problems in the wholesale field thoroughly.

Global studies must be carried out

In the studies of the problems existing in wholesale commodity circulation in the past three decades, Chinese theorists have failed to focus on the overall situation of the wholesale trade, but put too much emphasis on business, especially finding the way out for state-owned wholesale businesses. Priority was given to studying how to maintain and give play to the leading role of state-owned commerce in the initial 10 or more years, then how to help the state-owned wholesale trade get rid of the plight of operators, the slide and losses of economic benefits in the latter stage, which was undoubtedly the specific demonstration of studying the problem based on current politics before looking for countermeasures. However, as for state-owned wholesale businesses, studies were not made comprehensively, but focused on three separated parts according to administrative management, namely agricultural products, means of subsistence and means of production. In the strict sense, of related studies, the three systems of grains, commerce, and goods and materials have long been the mainstream, while other systems such as cotton and various cash crops, tobacco monopoly and medicines have been the branches. Though combining the characteristics of individual systems is favorable for exploring problems, it neglects the studies and explorations of the wholesale totality, thus is not conducive to solving the problems in the wholesale field in general.

Besides, studies on the problems existing in wholesale commodity circulation focus more on domestic wholesale trade, but neglect the integration of domestic and foreign wholesale trades and fail to study such problems by making full use of the two markets and resources. So there must be limitations. For example, such studies overlook the influence of foreign trade and foreign capital on the domestic wholesale business and limit the activities of enterprises engaged in the wholesale trade to the domestic market. It is closely related to the limitations of the existing institutions. However, seen from the development of the commodity economy, the process of industrialization and the construction of the market economic system have been separated. Such separation of domestic trade from foreign trade has to be broken. In economically-developed countries, domestic and foreign trades are not separated. For example, conglomerates in Japan control not only the exports, but also the domestic wholesale trade. Therefore, when studying the problems existing in the wholesale trade, we are required to further emancipate the mind and explore new ideas.

Studies on countermeasures must be synchronized with theoretical studies

Studies on the problems existing in wholesale commodity circulation in the past three decades have focused on finding the way out in the aspect of institutional reform, but paid less attention to how to adapt to the development of the market economy and the industrialization process before constructing and developing the wholesale circulation industry and constantly enhancing the role of wholesale in economic development. Even if it is a problem relating to economy, it would be analyzed and explored from the angle of institutional reform. For example, discussions on the economic plight of state-owned wholesale enterprises being one of the conditions that hinder institutional reform are relatively more in number, but studies on how to deepen the institutional reform to help state-owned wholesale enterprises get rid of their plight as soon as possible and display their due functions are relatively fewer. For another example, China has popularized the forms of organizations and movements of wholesale commodity circulation in the modernization process as the target patterns in the institutional reform, only to fail to notice that such forms of organizations and movements are the results of commodity circulation, even the entire economic development. Since they are actually the results got in the development of the productive forces, their appearance, existence and development to a higher height are conditional. Not any single form or pattern adopted or popularized could be applicable and popular under all circumstances and get reform results. Actually, economic development and institutional reform are the premise of each other and mutually-conditional. Economic development is the ultimate goal. Though institutional reform could clear up a road for economic development and plays a decisive role, whether the reform is feasible and how to reform have to be based on economic conditions and the level of economic development. Whether the reform is right or whether the road is through is judged by whether the reform serves economic development. Therefore, economic development determines institutional reforms. It in nature reflects the basic law that productivity determines production relations, that the summation of production relations-the economic relation-determines the superstructure, that the superstructure has to serve the economic foundation, and that the production relations have to adapt to productivity before facilitating the development of productivity. Therefore, it is not right to confuse the concrete forms of economic development with those of institutional reforms, or take and publicize some specific forms of economic development as the concrete goal of institutional reform. Or it would lead to misunderstanding and obstacles for studying the wholesale problem in a comprehensive and systematic way.

In addition, current studies on wholesale commodity circulation focus more on how to establish and intensify government macro-management, but less on how to give play to the regulatory role of the market mechanism, how to speed up cultivating the wholesale market and how to give play to the role of economic entities on the wholesale market. Therefore, studies on economic operation seem more inadequate. There has been a notion very popular in the recent several decades, that is, it seems that under the modern market economy, the market mechanism has stopped playing the role of regulating the entire social economy extensively as analyzed by traditional classic economics, and government regulation takes the dominant position and shows a growing trend. After analyzing a variety of market economies, someone believed that comparing with that in the United States, Britain, France and Germany, the government-led market economy of Japan conforms more to the situation in China. Influenced by such a viewpoint, real economic studies, including on the wholesale field, showed a tendency of paying more attention to how to regulate the wholesale market and carry out studies on administrative intervention.

Taking an overall look at the reform of wholesale commodity circulation in China in the past three decades since the reform and opening up, we believe that it is really an arduous task to fundamentally solve the problems existing in wholesale commodity circulation in China, requiring scholars and practitioners to make long-term common efforts. It is a historic mission that we should undertake. To move on based on the established achievements made by predecessors, China needs to study and overcome the above-mentioned tendencies to be improved, pay attention to studying the market, commodity circulation and wholesale trade theories while keeping studying theories on the market economy, carry out symptomatic analyses and the current researches on countermeasures on top of closely combining the existing difficulties and problems, and highlighting studies on fundamental, long-term and overall problems, trying to find out theoretical basis for solving the problems. It is also needed to jump out of the small circle of the wholesale trade and state-owned wholesale trade while paying certain attention to them, turn to studying holistic, fundamental, long-term problems of great significance to the overall situation, and turn to studying the common and unified process of domestic and foreign wholesale commodity circulations while studying the problems of the domestic wholesale trade. Focusing on studying institutional reforms has to be got rid of and turned to studying the dialectical relationship between economic development and institutional reforms; and the focus on the reform of the wholesale system has to be turned to developing the wholesale commodity circulation and promoting the development of the productive forces. Relations between the government, the market, and wholesale commodity circulation have to be dealt with correctly. In the relations where market growth dominates and market cultivation supplements, focus should be shifted to studying how the wholesale commodity circulation forms, changes, operations and develops under the conditions of the market economy, and how should the government serve economic development through the macro-regulation of the wholesale field under the conditions of market cultivation.

The market economy is a kind of system of social and economic operations, under which the production, distribution and consumption in the society are all commercialized. Within the framework of such a system, all economic activities have to be realized through the market and circulation. Such a stage featured by a highly-developed commodity economy is the expected market economy. Of course, what China pursues is the market economy of socialist nature based on the public ownership.

In market and commodity circulation, wholesale commodity circulation holds a core position. In the open macro-system of the market economy, wholesale connects with production, retail and consumption; the structure and functions of wholesale commodity circulation play a special linkage role in the operation of the overall macro-economy; and normal operation of the market economy has to be supported by a developed wholesale commodity circulation system. This special position and role of commodity circulation have determined the complexity and significance of carrying out studies on problems existing in wholesale.

Over the past three decades since the reform and opening up, China has experienced a tough process of explorations in its reform of the wholesale commodity circulation, in which there were both successes and failures. Generally speaking, people haven't been very clear about how to reconstruct the objectives and methods of the wholesale commodity circulation system consistent with the socialist market economy in China; reform measures already taken are transitional and provisional; and systematic studies on shaping a brand-new wholesale commodity circulation system under the current conditions of the market economy aren't sufficient. Theorists have published a lot of books on the problems existing in wholesale in the past decade, many of whom put forward useful and far-sighted views. However, most of these books are limited to studying how to help state-owned wholesale trade organizations get rid of recurring plights, but few discusses the problems existing in wholesale commodity circulation from the angle of the overall economic development and the reform of the economic system. This book, based on absorbing previous research accomplishments, thoroughly elaborates the problems existing in wholesale commodity circulation in the past three decades since the reform and opening up in a comprehensive way at a certain theoretical height and from a variety of angles such as their past, present and future development. This book is featured by discussing the start-up and development process of wholesale commodity circulation in the past three decades since the reform and opening up, as well as the wholesale trade organization and operation. Though some elaboration and discussions are not profound enough limited by time, length and the collection of materials, making such a great number of comprehensive analyses of the various problems existing in wholesale commodity circulation is something having never been done before, and a pioneering achievement which provided theoretical and empirical frameworks for the reference of subsequent in-depth studies.

Since it is a pioneering job to make systematic studies on the problems existing in wholesale commodity circulation, the author adheres to the following principles in terms of choosing research methods. Firstly, being led by the basic theories of the Marxist economics while absorbing and learning from related theories of western economic schools before integrating them and forming the theoretical basis of the book; Marxist classical writers inspected and explained the appearance, form and role of wholesale while studying the market and commodity circulation, the combination of which formed the basic thought of Marxist classical writers on problems existing in wholesale commodity circulation; of which, some incisive views and discussions become the starting point of the in-depth studies made in this book. Of course, theories on regional and international trades and location theories in Western economics are of great referential significance to our studies on wholesale commodity circulation. Secondly, making analyses and studies by combining history with reality; the author carries out detailed studies on the development of wholesale trade at different stages and, based on analyzing related materials, summarizes and generalizes the rules of popular significance in the field of wholesale commodity circulation at different development stages. Since the logics of historic development are more or less the same as the development orbit of human mind, such a method could testify the results of theoretical studies on the one hand while providing ideas for empirical studies of the real situation of wholesale commodity circulation on the other. Thirdly, focusing on studying countermeasures while analyzing theories, the history and the status quo in a comprehensive way, trying to provide more valuable opinions on the subsequent reforms of the economic system, and the development of wholesale commodity circulation in China.

1 Chapter

Overall Review of the Wholesale Trade in the Three Decades of Reform and Opening up

It's been 30 years since China launched the reform and opening up policy at the Third Plenary Session of the 11th CPC (Communist Party of China) National Congress in 1978, during which the Chinese economy has maintained a rapid and steady development, the economic aggregate of China has kept expanding, and the scale of market circulation has been extended constantly. Meanwhile, the wholesale trade in China showed a tendency of changes and development which was closely related to the social and economic environment. The influence of the wholesale trade on economic development became increasingly prominent. In this chapter, the author will review the reform of the wholesale trade in China over the past three decades, present the achievements made, and point out existing problems before explaining the necessity and inevitability of the existence of the wholesale trade based on China's national conditions.

Reform Course of the Wholesale Trade

Reform of the wholesale trade refers to adjusting and innovating certain aspects and links in the wholesale trade in which the production relations fail to keep up with the requirement of the development of productivity and the superstructure doesn't conform to the situation of economic foundation, either, in order to further perfect and develop the wholesale system. It has also been the main content of the reform of the wholesale trade in China since the Third Plenary Session of the 11th CPC National Congress. Reform of the wholesale trade has been carried out by closely combining the macroeconomic restructuring in China. As the economic restructuring in China was advanced from the planned economy to being planned economy-led with the supplements of market regulations to the planned commodity economy and to the socialist market economy that has been applied till now, the reform course of the wholesale trade in China could be divided into the following three stages:

The first stage: adjustment of the wholesale pattern (1978–1991)

Adjustment of the wholesale pattern refers to turning the original "three fixeds" (fixed supply areas, fixed supply objects and fixed pricing range) into "three varieties and one less", that is, establishing an open-minded wholesale system featured by "a variety of economic sectors, a variety of operational modes, a variety of circulation channels, and less links" before organizing commodity circulation. On the one hand, it was the requirement on adapting the simplified economic sectors, operational modes and circulation channels brought about by reforming the traditional wholesale system, and on solving the problem of too many vertical links, on the other hand, it aimed at adapting to the commodity economy put forward at the Third Plenary Session of the 12th CPC National Congress.

Reform background

After China completed the socialist transformation of agriculture, handicrafts and the capitalist industry and commerce in 1956, its socialist wholesale trade got rid of the past backward, chaotic and abnormal state before developing rapidly and establishing, from small to large, coarse, and to fine, in a top-down manner, a wholesale system with three levels of wholesale centers as the mainstay, underwriting and purchasing industrial products at standard prices, and allocating and distributing commodities to all commercial undertakings based on the "three fixeds". In the early days of the People's Republic of China, the establishment of such a frame was of theoretical and practical significance. By organizing commodity distribution and throughput, the state-owned wholesale trade under the control of socialism competed with enemies and the bourgeoisie, effectively cracked down upon speculation, hoarding and cornering and other capitalist activities, and achieved great successes on the economic front, playing an important role in regulating the national commodity circulation, stabilizing commodity prices, guaranteeing production, and satisfying the living needs of the general public. Under the particular conditions at the time, commerce being controlled by the Central Government was of historic necessity, playing an effective role in recovering the economy in the early days of the People's Republic of China. However, the said highly-centralized commodity distribution system under the direct control of state organs was hierarchical with too many regulations, restrictions and regional protectionism, leading to increasingly stagnant commodity circulation. In particular, at times of dramatic social and economic changes, faced with production expansion and the diversification of demands, wholesale establishments failed to do in-depth work, and commodity varieties couldn't meet consumer demands, resulting in untimely supply. Meanwhile, in rural areas, the combination of wholesales establishments with supply and marketing cooperatives was not close enough, so a great number of commodities couldn't be seen in rural areas, causing serious sellout. The traditional wholesale trade with the "three fixeds" as the main content had far lagged behind of the situation, and adjustment of the wholesale pattern became imminent.

Reform contents

At the Third Plenary Session of the 11th CPC National Congress held in 1978, the Communist Party of China proposed to construct the socialism with Chinese characteristics, raising the curtain of the socialist reform and opening a new page for the reform of the wholesale trade as well. After 1978, China began to pay more and more attention to its commercial circulation system, restored the State Administration for Industry and Commerce and the Ministry of Food while each province in China restored their respective provincial companies, properly centralizing the administration authorities. In July 1979, the National Department of Commerce Directors Seminar was held, proposing to dismantle and merge First-level wholesale centers and well adjusting Second-level wholesale centers by economic region. In September 1980, the Third Plenary Session of the Fifth National People's Congress confirmed the four modes of purchasing and selling, namely state monopoly for purchasing and selling, planned purchase, subscription and selective purchasing before making the decision to implement them since 1981. In 1982, the Ministry of Commerce and the Ministry of Light Industry issued a joint notice, announcing to add wholesale and retail on the commissioned basis to the above-mentioned four modes of purchasing and selling. Before long, based on wholesale and retail on the commissioned basis, China developed the joint management and purchase by industry and commerce. The co-existence of the aforesaid six modes of purchasing and selling was the specific demonstration of the market structure combining planned regulation with market regulation. It pushed forward the development of production and the expansion of the size of circulation and intimated the relations between production and marketing. Reform of the wholesale trade in those several years stayed on confirming the various forms of wholesale. It was not until the State Council of China forwarded, in 1984, *Report of the Ministry of Commerce concerning Several Problems Existing in the Current Reform of the Commercial System in Urban Areas in China* and took urban reform as the core of the reform of the economic system that China truly began to make major adjustments of its wholesale pattern. Adjustment of the wholesale pattern since 1984 mainly had the following two contents: firstly, reform of the three levels of wholesale of industrial products for daily use, in which the First-level wholesale centers of industrial products for daily use set by the Ministry of Commerce in Shanghai, Tianjin and Guangzhou were transferred under the control of respective local city; Second-level provincial wholesale centers were also transferred to respective local city, and merged with municipal wholesale companies to form municipal enterprises; and the setting of state-owned commercial wholesale companies within the same industry in the same city according to administrative levels was not allowed; secondly, the change of the layered price markdown existing inside the then commerce into price by lot or coordinated price based on the wholesale market quotation. In the early days of the adjustment, the depressed productive forces released enormous energies, contributing to the great development of the wholesale trade. However, with the hyper-normal development of the wholesale trade, the wholesale market became chaotic. In 1988, China put forward the working guideline of adjusting the economic environment, rectifying the economic order, and deepening the reform in an all-round manner at the Third Plenary Session of the 13th CPC National Congress held in 1988. In 1989, China issued Guo Fa (1989) No. 74 document entitled *Opinions on Further Clearing Up and Rectifying Various Commercial Wholesale Companies*, determining to further clear up and rectify commercial wholesale companies, combine with the overall deepening of the reform of the commodity circulation system, further perfect the commercial wholesale system featured by open channels and less links and with state-run commercial and supply and marketing cooperatives as the mainstay, construct a normal commodity circulation order, and achieve the healthy development of the planned commodity economy.

Reform measures

According to different highlights of each stage, specific reform measures could also be divided into three stages:

(1) 1978–1983: adjusting the policy on commodity purchasing and selling within the overall framework led by the planned economy. Major measures taken in this period included: 1) replacing the centralized purchase and contracted marketing of industrial products and the unified purchasing of farm and sideline products by the state according to fixed quotes with various modes of purchasing and selling that conformed to market rules; 2) breaking the wholesale system featured by "three fixeds" and expanding the autonomy of enterprises' in management; 3) breaking the situation of exclusive sales by state-owned commercial enterprises, relaxing the right of management over the wholesale of part of small articles, and allowing the free trade of each and all market entities. Though China failed to set market orientations when implementing the above-mentioned reforms, it did strengthen market regulation in an objective way. In particular, the smash of the wholesale system featured by "three fixeds" shook the foundation of the distributive and the closed old system, creating conditions for the reform featured by "three varieties and one less".

(2) 1984–1988: carrying out the "Three varieties and one less" reform while constructing the "socialist planned commodity economy". Specific measures included: 1) in the aspect of circulation channels, reforming the multi-layered wholesale system featured by the three-level wholesale centers set up in accordance with administrative regions, and setting up wholesale institutions centered with different economic regions; 2) in the aspect of the ownership structure, allowing collective, individual and privately-run commercial enterprises to engage in wholesale businesses and breaking the pattern of exclusive operations by state-owned commercial wholesale enterprises through single channels; 3) in the aspect of types of operation, breaking the exclusive commercial operation, allowing industrial wholesale and the existence of professional operation, mixed operation, exclusive operation and joint operation. Serial reforms targeting at the wholesale commercial system promoted the formation of the new commodity circulation system and ensured the activeness, prosperity and stability of the urban and rural markets over the years.

(3) 1989–1991: rectifying the wholesale order. In the reform in the early days, since China focused too much on "devolution of powers", but somewhat neglected the necessity of "regulation", such phenomena as setting up wholesale institutions randomly, wholesaling commodities beyond authorization, and reselling or trafficking commodities at higher prices could be found everywhere, leading to chaotic wholesale order. During 1989–1991, China began the reform aiming at taking under control the economic environment and rectifying the order of the wholesale trade, which further pushed forward the reform of "Three varieties and one less". Some measures in the reform of "Three varieties and one less" were taken hastily, thus laying a basis for crises of the wholesale system. However, generally speaking, the reform and development in the early days made the most obvious achievements in the most extensive areas, by the largest steps and at the fastest pace. In the early 1990s, an open wholesale pattern featured by multiple channels and less links was initially formed.

The second stage: establishment of the modern wholesale enterprise system (1992–1998)

Adjustments of the wholesale system and pattern in the previous stage played a role in promoting the development of the wholesale trade in the short run. However, due to excessive "devolution of powers" and an overly-high speed, there were hidden troubles in the development of the wholesale trade, which finally evolved into the chaos on the entire wholesale market. In 1992, the

Third Plenary Session of the 14th CPC National Congress was held, turning the focus of the reform of the wholesale system to establishing a modern wholesale enterprise system under the conditions of the market economy.

Reform background

Adjustment of the wholesale pattern with "three varieties and one less" as the main contents in the previous more than ten years had brought vitality to the wholesale field. However, too much instead of appropriate attention was paid to the multi-channel form, leading to chaotic wholesale order. Though China rectified the wholesale order in the later period of the reform, and somewhat improved market order, it had by no means taken the path of orderly competitions. In particular, the disorderly competitions led by inappropriate development of collective and individual wholesale businesses had reduced the operational scale of state-owned wholesale enterprises, and caused serious slide of the economic benefits of the wholesale commerce. Some large and medium-sized wholesale enterprises used to be profitable began to suffer losses one after another. The wholesale trade was faced with a grave situation. Firstly, the costs of the wholesale trade rose. Secondly, "chain debts" appeared in a recurrent way, leading to corporate profits being unable to be truly realized. Though China tried to clear up "chain debts" by increasing loans to large and medium-sized enterprises and resuming settlement through collection and acceptance, effects were not significant. Moreover, due to the sluggish market, most wholesale enterprises adopted delayed payment or aftermarket payment as the methods of settlement, leading to a great amount of capital being tied up in the settlement link. Loans in arrears made a great part of the sales income of a wholesale enterprise nominal and book income. What's more, enterprises had to pay interests on the loans in arrears. Thirdly, under the pressure of multi-channel competitive sales, the gross interest rate of wholesale reduced. Since the marketing of industrial products had no clear links, nor did it adhere to equivalent prices with commercial products, some industrial products were even dumped at prices lower than the cost prices of commercial products, to maintain their operational scale, most commercial enterprises engaged in wholesale had to promote their products by increasing rebates, surrendering part of their profits, lowering down prices, etc., leading to a lowered level of profits. In one word, reform of the wholesale trade in the past only targeted at the disadvantages of the old system, and focused on adjusting the ownership structure and transforming the organizational form and operational method of the wholesale trade, thus failing to thoroughly solve the problems concerning the driving force, decision-making, adjustment and restraint of the wholesale trade in the society, or fundamentally change the entire wholesale trade in terms of the setting of wholesale institutions, organizational scale, operational modes and measures. The transformation and variation of the wholesale enterprises lagged far behind the dramatic changes of the external economic environment.

Reform contents

At the 14th CPC National Congress held in 1992, China clarified that the objective of its reform of economic system was to establish a socialist market economic system. On July 23, 1992, the State Council of China issued *Regulations of the State Council on the Transformation of the Operational Mechanism of State-owned Industrial Enterprises,* defining, in clear-cut terms, the objectives of the transformation of the operational mechanism by state-owned industrial enterprises, pointing out that enterprises should adopt to the requirements of the market economy and become commodity production and business units capable of independent management, self-development and self-constraining, and of assuming sole responsibility for their own profits and losses. The trials of share-holding enterprises launched on the basis of over 200 state-owned enterprises included wholesale enterprises. It was not until 1993 that the construction of modern wholesale enterprises was truly proposed. *Decision of the Central Committee of the Communist Party of China on Several Problems Concerning the Construction of the Socialist Market Economic System* adopted at the Third Plenary Session of the 14th CPC National Congress provided in clear-cut terms that "Constructing modern corporate system is an inexorable requirement for developing socialized mass production and the market economy, as well as the direction of the reform of state-owned enterprises in China." While thoroughly implementing the *Measures for the Implementation of Changing Their Operational Mechanisms by Commercial Enterprises Owned by the Whole People, Measures for the Implementation of Changing Their Operational Mechanisms by Material Supply Enterprises Owned by the Whole People, Notice on the Several Opinions on Pushing Forward the Reform of the Operational Mechanism of Supply and Marketing Cooperatives,* domestic trade departments at all levels and foreign trade enterprises carried out new explorations. State-owned wholesale trade carried out reforms boldly and decisively, tried modernized operational modes and management tools, positively transformed their operational mechanisms, boosted up their strength, and established modern wholesale enterprises system. For example, in 1994, enterprises engaged in the circulation of the means of production set up a number of materials enterprise groups, and large-scale enterprise groups engaged in wholesale circulation appeared. In 1996, the Ministry of Domestic Trade selected 50 large-scale commercial enterprise groups as key liaison enterprises, opening up and revitalizing small circulation enterprises by merging, allying, selling, dividing, auctioning, and contracting them, or making them state-owned and private-run, or implementing the shareholding cooperative system in them, ensuring value maintenance and appreciation of state-owned assets.

Reform measures

From the angle of reform conditions, reform in this stage touched upon: reform of the external environment and that of the internal environment of wholesale enterprises. Reform of the wholesale enterprises' external environment included: 1) canceling the provision that state-owned wholesale commerce withheld income and business taxes from individual and privately-run commerce, and advocating equal competitions; 2) reducing the interest rate on loans; 3) supplementing enterprises' discretionary funds; 4) clearing up numerous apportions and inspections, alleviating the burdens of state-run commerce; 5) launching the reform of the share-holding system, establishing the modern corporate system, and reconstructing the ownership structure so as to enable enterprises to become legal entities and major market competitors capable of independent operation, the assumption of their own profits and losses, self-development and self-constraint, changing "tanks" into "drains". Reform of the wholesale enterprises' internal environment included: 1) taking the road of joining together and establishing enterprise groups such as chain-store operations and comprehensive companies by allying industrial and commercial enterprises, wholesale enterprises with wholesale enterprises, wholesale enterprises with retail enterprises; 2) improving staffs' qualities; 3) adopting a variety of organizational forms, including agents (manufacturer agent, retail agent, commission agent, import-export agent), brokers, large-scale stockroom-style supermarkets, wholesale with limited functions (such as warehouse wholesale, wholesale delivery, mail-order wholesale) and chain-store wholesale, etc.; 4) reconstructing the functions of state-owned wholesale enterprises: transforming to being multi-functional (trade, storage and delivery, financing and information), to being economic (state-owned wholesale enterprises with weaker strength could develop into wholesalers with limited functions), to general agents and exclusive distributors, to logistics centers, and to comprehensive companies, strengthening the service function. All in all, it aimed at transforming wholesale enterprises into modern enterprises featured by "clearly-defined property rights, well-defined rights and liabilities, separation of government functions and enterprise management and scientific management" by adjusting external and internal conditions.

The third stage: rectification and reorganization of the wholesale trade (1999 to present)

Reform of the wholesale enterprises, especially the state-owned sector of the wholesale trade in the previous stage, was somewhat effective. Wholesale enterprises have begun to see their own bettered business performances and connect with modern enterprises rapidly. However, with time, reform of the wholesale trade has encountered bottlenecks. It became difficult to further release the productive forces when production enterprises, foreign-funded enterprises and chain retail stores began to get engaged in the wholesale trade in various forms and divide the market share of wholesale trade. In particular, faced with the pressure of competitions, some small enterprises are stuck in business difficulties.

Reform background

Reform of the wholesale trade in the early days which adapted to the market economic system improved the wholesale system to a certain degree and helped establish the enterprise operational mechanism initially. However, with the deepening of the reform of the socialist market economic system and the globalization brought about by WTO, the wholesale trade encounters the greatest shock ever. Outside wholesale enterprises, large retailers and manufacturers foray into the wholesale trade before extruding it. In particular, the opening up of the wholesale trade to foreign capital has even intensified competitions. Inside wholesale enterprises, reform in the past was not complete. Though the old system has had its day, reform of the new modern corporate system is developing slowly. Wholesale enterprises are still in transition and the primary stage. They couldn't even guarantee their own survival and development, let alone facing challenges. Challenges from the external and internal environments have led to the shrinkage of the wholesale trade. Specifically, the functions of the wholesale link have become weakened and the market share of wholesale has been reduced. Rectification and reorganization of the wholesale trade in China according to concurrent conditions since 1999 will still be the focus of the reform of the wholesale trade in the future.

Reform content

Rectification and reorganization of the wholesale trade refer to a series of strategic repositioning targeting at the problems existing in the wholesale trade. By reforming the modern corporate system in the previous stage, till the end of 1999, most small and medium-sized enterprises engaged in domestic trade had adopted joint-stock partnership, or become state-owned, yet privately-run, or carried out leasing and contract operations; and 90% of them had achieved restructuring. However, in the competition of various forms of ownerships, such enterprises were relatively weak. In 2000, reform of wholesale enterprises got deepened. On the one hand, state-owned assets withdrew from the wholesale trade in a selective way, but on the other hand, wholesale enterprises enhanced their strengths through M & A and reorganization, achieving the combination among strong ones. In 2001, reform of enterprises engaged in state-owned commerce was initially completed. State-owned assets held or controlled shares in promising large and medium-sized enterprises. Meanwhile, the combination of large commercial enterprise groups helped release the vitality of wholesale enterprises. As for the entry of foreign capital into the wholesale trade, China issued *Measures on Launching Trials of Foreign-invested Commercial Undertakings* in June 1999, making clear-cut provisions on foreign-invested commercial wholesale trade for the first time. The formal implementation of *Measures on the Management of Foreign-invested Commercial Fields* since June 1, 2004 has signified the normal opening up of the wholesale trade to the outside world, as well as the entry of the foreign-invested wholesale trade into the stage of standardized management.

Reform measures

Measures for rectifying and reorganizing the wholesale trade in this stage have touched upon the following several aspects: system, namely strengthening legislation, further deepening the reform of the wholesale enterprises, and establishing a new-type perfect wholesale circulation system governed by laws and regulations; types of operation, namely taking comprehensive business services as the direction on the basis of China's accession to the WTO, and enhancing the services for the manufacturing and retailing industries and expanding such functions as trade, storage and delivery, financing and information by ways of commissioned processing, commission agent, brand agent, franchise operation, franchising, professional distribution or joint- or chain-operation with industrial production and retail enterprises; forms of organization, namely continuing setting up professional wholesale enterprises, distributors, exclusive distributors, general agents, wholesale markets, etc.; more importantly, positively promoting the transformation of the wholesale trade to new types of operation such as distribution centers and comprehensive business companies; capital structure, namely vigorously developing wholesale enterprises composed of the state-owned, collective, individual, privately-run, joint-stock economic sectors following the principles of market competitions, enabling the ownership structure of the wholesale trade in China to be more diversified and internationalized in the future; mode of trade, namely introducing e-commerce and other modern advanced technologies. What deserves special attention is that China has to vigorously push forward the chain management led by the wholesale commerce and that qualified large commercial enterprises are suggested to develop into leading enterprises with certain controlling capabilities before playing an active role in the entire supply chain.

All in all, as can be seen from the development orbit of the wholesale trade, the process of the reform of the wholesale trade is a never-ending circulation process of denying, recognizing and denying again the wholesale trade. In this round of reform, denial of the wholesale trade has stimulated reforms. Reform at the first stage eliminated the restraining factors being not contributive to the development of the productive forces, pushing forward the development of the wholesale trade. At the later stage of the reform, hidden and deep-seated problems in the wholesale trade which were unable to meet the requirements of developing the productive forces exposed themselves, inducing a new round of wholesale negativism before a new round of reforms. In this recurrent process, reform of the wholesale trade zigzags between reorganizations and denials.

Achievements Made and Problems Existing in the Reform of the Wholesale Trade

Looking back at the history of reforming the wholesale trade in China in the past three decades, we could sketch a grand historic scenario, or specifically, an extensive, profound and great change from unified purchase and distribution to free circulation, from direct control to indirect regulation, from the unification of state-owned and collective enterprises to being led by privately-run enterprises, from the single type of operation to various types of operation. Reflections of the great change in the development of the wholesale trade include both monumental achievements and a great number of problems.

Achievements of the reform of the wholesale trade

With the baptism in the past three decades, the wholesale trade in China has made an unprecedented expansion. More and more entities have been engaged in the wholesale trade. Commodities in the circulation of the wholesale trade have become greater and greater in number. Operational performances of wholesale enterprises have been greatly improved. The wholesale market system has been gradually standardized. The wholesale system has been more and more legalized. Specifically, achievements having been made in the reform of the wholesale trade are reflected as follows:

Rapid expansion of the wholesale trade

In the past three decades of reform, the Chinese economy has gradually entered a stage of rapid development; the size of circulation has been enlarged rapidly; and the wholesale trade has been presenting a trend of accelerated growth. Indicators that best reflect the size of the wholesale trade are the number of the wholesale institutions and the turnover of wholesale commodities.

Steady increase in the number of wholesale institutions

Size of the wholesale trade is firstly reflected by the total number of wholesale institutions. The more such institutions are, the larger the size of the wholesale trade will be. In 1992, the number of public commercial institutions was 14,214 thousand, being 9.4 times larger than that in 1978, up 56% annually. The number of units engaged in industrial activities was 19,515 in 1998 and 60,884 in 2006, registering an average annual growth rate of 21.2%. The number of business corporations engaged in the wholesale trade was 16,945 in 1998 and 29,046 in 2007, registering an average annual growth rate of 7.1%. In addition, the number of practitioners in wholesale institutions can also reflect the size of the wholesale trade. Such number was 7,774 thousand in 1978 and 31,990 thousand in 1992, expanding 4.1 times and presenting an average annual growth rate of 20.7%. The number of practitioners in wholesale enterprises above the designated size was 2,544 thousand in 1999 and 2,496 thousand in 2007, reducing only 2%. Under the premise that both the number of the business corporations engaged in the wholesale trade and that of the units engaged in industrial activities have increased, the number of practitioners in wholesale enterprises reduced, indicating not only the increase in the number of wholesale enterprises, but also the improvement of the efficiency of wholesale enterprises.

Fast growth of the wholesale turnover

The turnover of wholesale commodities is another important indicator that reflects the size of the wholesale trade. The larger the size of wholesale trade is, the greater the turnover of wholesale commodities will be. Seen from the total value of commodities purchased, that of the trades owned by the whole people reached RMB 173.97 billion in 1978, which was later increased to RMB 1,232.23 billion in 1993, registering an average annual growth rate of 38%. The total value of commodities of the wholesale and retail trade in China was RMB 3,093.63 billion in 1994 and 3,854.97 billion in 1996, increasing by 24.6%. The total value of wholesale commodities above the designated size was RMB 2,044.23 billion in 1999 and 10,483.25 billion in 2007, expanding by four times within simply nine years. As for the net domestic sales, we could also see the development and growth of the size of the wholesale trade. Net domestic sales were RMB 187.22 billion in 1978, and increased to 1,282.5 billion in 1993, increasing by 5.8 times. The total sales of wholesale and retail commodities during 1994–1996 increased from RMB 3,317.81 billion to 4,254.69 billion, up 28.2%. The total sales of wholesale commodities above the designated size increased from RMB 2,205.58 billion in 1999 to 10,562 billion in 2007, increasing by nearly four times.

Improvement of the operational performances and structural optimization of wholesale enterprises

Development of the wholesale trade doesn't simply mean the expansion of the total quantity, but also the improvement of quality. Specifically, it is reflected by the improvement of the organizational and performance levels, as well as the optimization of the industrial and ownership structures.

Rapid growth and significant improvement of the operational performances of the wholesale trade

In terms of the organizational efficiency of wholesale enterprises, the operational performance of wholesale enterprises has improved significantly. The income of wholesale enterprises above the designated size from main businesses was RMB 2,009.99 billion in 1999, which was later increased to RMB 9,544.08 in 2007, up 374.8% in total and 41.7% annually. Though the cost of main businesses increased by 376.9% from 1999–2007, the profits of main businesses increased from RMB 74.04 billion in 1999 to 633.61 billion in 2007, up 755.8% in total and 84% annually, being was far higher than the annual growth rate of the former. As for the assets of profits of main businesses of wholesale enterprises above the designated size, the total value was RMB 3,869.77 billion in 2007, up altogether 166.1% comparing with RMB 1,454.04 billion in 1998 and 18.4% annually on the average. Liabilities of main businesses of wholesale enterprises above the designated size reached RMB 2,745.28 billion, up 130.9% comparing with RMB 1,189.1 billion in 1998 in total and 14.5% annually on the average. The growth rate of assets was far higher than that of liabilities.

Great development momentum and brilliant achievements of wholesale enterprises above the designated size

Through M & A, reorganization and reformation, groups of wholesale enterprises got rid of the past state of being "small, separated and barely satisfactory" and grew into large-scale circulation enterprises with certain capabilities. In 1992, of the top 100 wholesale enterprises in China, none of the top four enterprises had more than RMB 100 million of sales revenue. Added together, the aggregate sales revenue of the top four enterprises reached RMB 1.764 million, which was negligible comparing with RMB 1,073.68 billion, the social sales volume of business commodities. The sales volume of the top four wholesale enterprises in China in 2007, namely PetroChina Company Limited Northeast Marketing Company, Sinopec Corp.-East China Company, Sinopec Corp.-North China Company and Sinopec Corp.-South China Company, all exceeded RMB 100 million in 2007. Added together, their sales volume reached RMB 614.87 million. Such large wholesale enterprises played a leading role in guiding industrial development.

Optimized and constantly upgraded wholesale structure

Structure of the wholesale trade in China has been optimized and upgraded constantly. In 1999, the sales revenue of wholesale of food, drinks and tobacco products accounted for the largest proportion, reaching 28.0%, or nearly 1/3 of the total sales revenue of the wholesale trade. Of which, the sales of wholesale of tobacco products accounted for the largest proportion, being 17.2% of the total and valuing RMB 379.55 billion. It was followed by the wholesale of oil and petrol products, the sales volume of which reached RMB 321.55 billion, accounting for 14.6%. The sales of wholesale of drugs and medical instruments accounted for 4.6%; the sales of wholesale of automobile, motorcycle and accessories accounted for 57%; and the sales of wholesale of agricultural and animal products accounted for 2.9%. Till 2007, the sales of wholesale of minerals, building materials and chemical products replaced those of food, drinks and tobacco products before taking the greatest part, accounting for 55%

of the total sales volume of the wholesale trade. While the sales of wholesale of food, drinks and tobacco products reduced to about 11% of the total; the sales of wholesale of drugs and medical instruments, automobiles, motorcycle and accessories maintained basically stable, being about 4%. Upgrading of the structure of the wholesale trade reflects the accelerated modernization process and the constant improvement of the consumption level, as well as the constant improvements of the consumption structure of urban and rural residents.

With the deepening of the marketing economy and the reform of the wholesale system, the ownership structure of wholesale enterprises has also undergone substantial changes. The pattern of a variety of ownerships developing side by side and multi-layered market entities competing against each other has already formed. Wholesale entities become more and more diversified and privatized, further activating the market. Prior to the reform and opening up, state-owned and collective wholesale enterprises dominated the market, the sales volume of which accounted for more than 98% of the total social sales of all wholesale enterprises. Seen from statistical figures, the number of state-owned and collective economic institutions practicing independent accounting accounted for 97% of the total number of enterprises engaged in wholesale and retail; the number of outlets accounted for 94%; and the proportion of individual economy was only 0.2%. With the separation of administration from enterprise management and that of the ownership from the right of management, especially after the reform touched upon the tenure system, fundamental changes happened to the ownership structure of business operators of wholesale enterprises. According to National Bureau of Statistics of China, the sales revenue of the private sector of the wholesale trade accounted for as high as 20% of the total sales revenue of the wholesale trade in 2007, being close to that of the state-owned sector of the wholesale trade which was 26%. Sales revenue of the foreign-invested sector of the wholesale trade accounted for 8.8%. The privately-run sector instead of state-owned and collective sectors of the wholesale trade became dominant. Competitions among various entities were in full swing.

Remarkable achievements in constructing the wholesale markets

Wholesale market is the type of consumer goods wholesale dealing that develops the fastest and has the greatest influence since the reform and opening up. Significant achievements have been made during the construction of the wholesale markets.

Brisk market supply and demand

The wholesale market has achieved a rapid development from scratch. The total number of wholesale markets was 2,418 in 1999 before increasing to 7,394 in 2001, up 205.8%. What's more noteworthy is that the business volume of the wholesale markets increased by 1,762.6% during 1999–2001, the growth rate of which had far greater than that of the number of the wholesale markets, fully demonstrating the vigorous market demands in China and the improvement of the performance of the wholesale markets. Of the wholesale markets, the number of agricultural products wholesale markets increased from 1,858 in 1999 to 4,351 in 2001, up 134.2%, and the business volume increased by 1,431.1%; that of industrial products wholesale markets grew from 560 in 1992 to 2,380 in 2001, up 325%, the business volume of which grew at a rate of over 1,500%. Comparing the growth rate of the agricultural products wholesale markets with that of industrial products wholesale markets, we could easily see the acceleration of the industrialization process and the upgrading of the consumption structure in China. In particular, after entering the 21st century, a group of large and influential wholesale markets have emerged in China, the number, stands, business area and turnover of which kept increasing. Wholesale markets each valuing more than RMB 100 million was 1,734 in total, with 1,235,070 stands, 70.51 million square meters of business area, as well as RMB 1,545.09 billion of the total turnover in 2002; till 2007, the number of wholesale markets each valuing more than RMB 100 million was 2,366 in total, with 1,674,768 stands, 150.687 million square meters of business area and a total RMB 3587.15 billion of the total turnover, up 36.5%, 35.6%, 113.7% and 132.2%, respectively, indicating that the process of scale development of the Chinese wholesale markets has sped up.

Standardized market order and perfect market functions

As wholesale markets keep developing and expanding, their business area keeps increasing, and investment entities keep diversified, China has managed its wholesale markets in an increasingly standardized way. The gradual amelioration of the market order has provided a good environment for commodity transactions. Meanwhile, functions of wholesale markets have been given full play to and perfected step by step. Certain attention has been given to displaying various market functions such as commodity transaction and distribution, price formation and discovery, settlement, risk dispersion, information collection, processing and publication, comprehensive services, etc., enabling wholesale markets to play an important role in rationally allocating commodity resources in the society.

Gradually perfection of the wholesale system

The wholesale system is a collection of the systems about, and ways and methods of specifically organizing, managing and regulating the wholesale trade. To put it simple, it refers to the organization and legal system that maintain the operation of the wholesale trade. Along with the economic restructuring in China, organizational and management departments of the wholesale trade have been gradually clarified; the mode of operation of the wholesale trade has been led by market allocation of resources instead of government regulation and reform; and the mode of operation of the wholesale trade has become gradually legalized.

Centralization of various administrative organs

The traditional wholesale system featured by fixed supply objects, fixed rebate rate and fixed ranges of pricing has been gradually improved to the new-type wholesale circulation system under the regulation of laws. The improvement of the new-type wholesale system governed by law couldn't be achieved without the government playing a role therein. Its outstanding reflection was the gradual transformation of government administration. Various administrative management departments of the wholesale trade were centralized. During the 1980s, commercial administrative organs underwent a number of reforms. The Ministry of Grains, the Ministry of Commerce, the Ministry of Materials and the Ministry of Domestic Trade stepped down from the stage of history in succession, and the national system of supply and marketing cooperatives were no longer government organs. The new Ministry of Commerce set up in the early 2003 began to carry out unified management, breaking the long separated management of domestic and foreign trades.

Direct government macroeconomic regulation measures being changed into indirect

At the same time of the reform of the wholesale trade institutions, the macroeconomic regulation measures carried out by the government adapted to market demands gradually, and became indirect regulation led by legal and economic means and supplemented by administrative means instead of being fully led by administrative means. Through a series of measures such as reduction, rectification and power devolution, enterprises got rid of direct government intervention and gradually became economic entities capable of independent operation, self-development, and of assuming sole responsibility for their own profits and losses. Practice has proven that government's changing its function of taking part in commodity allocation and distribution directly is conducive to separating administration from corporate management, to mobilizing enterprises' enthusiasm in active production and operation, to activating market transactions, to giving play to the positive role of the market mechanism in regulating market supply and demand, to improving the efficiency of commodity circulation, to prospering the commodity market, and to contributing to the construction of clean, honest and incorruptible government departments.

Gradual perfection of the legal system

China has developed, revised and ameliorated a series of laws, regulations and administrative management systems in order to standardize commodity wholesale and circulation. Such laws, regulations and systems play a basic role in China's setting up of a fair, standardized, orderly and efficient market environment. China has eliminated the old management mode of planned economy in the reform of its wholesale system on the one hand while exploring and studying the construction of the legal system up to the requirements of the socialist market economy. The deeper the transformation of the wholesale system and the closer the distance to the realization of the new system is, the more the requirements on a sound legal system will be. A new legal system refers to not only the results, but also the guarantee of the reform, in view of which the construction of a legal system is called the most important link in the reform of the economic system and market construction.

Enhanced role of the market in resource allocation

Reform of the economic system in China is in nature a market-oriented reform that has been pushed forward along the route of "the market mechanism playing an essential role in resource allocation". Under the guidance of such principle, in the reform of its wholesale system, China gradually reduced direct government intervention and expanded the ratio and scope of the market mechanism in the wholesale trade. When regulating commodity supply and demand, the government firmly grasped those commodities crucial for the national economy and people's livelihood. During the 1990s, China implemented the "provincial governor's assuming responsibility for local grain production" and the "city mayor's assuming responsibility for local food supply", and established a commodity reserves system at both central and local levels concerning important commodities such as grain and cotton, guaranteeing domestic market stability. For other commodities, the Chinese Government gave full play to the role of the market in resource allocation and carried out indirect regulation with economic means like fiscal, taxation and currency policies.

Problems existing in the reform of the wholesale trade

After three decades of reform, wholesale circulation has formed a diversified pattern; enterprises engaged in the wholesale trade have been linked with modern enterprise; and the wholesale system has become more market-oriented. It is safe to say that the wholesale trade in China has been improved, standardized and legalized at both macro- and micro-levels. However, since the Chinese economic system is in a transformation period, so is the reform of the wholesale system, a number of management modes are not so mature and many problems need to be improved and solved. Such problems could be seen from the following four aspects:

(1) Reform measures are transitional and provisional, not systematic. Recalling the three decades of reform and opening up, a lot of policies, laws and regulations implemented in the reform of the wholesale trade were developed at the demands of a specific period, so they are provisional and transitional. People haven't figured it out as for how to reconstruct the goals and methods of the wholesale commodity circulations system adaptive to the socialist market economy in China. By taking transitional and provisional reform measures, China has failed to study, in a systematic way, the problems existing in the brand-new wholesale commodity circulation system under the current conditions of the market economy. In the development of the wholesale trade, a master plan is still in short; development goals are not clear; inter-department separation, industrial monopoly and barriers among regions still exist; and there is this lack of a unified management authority, thus a nationally unified great market is still far away.

(2) Reform achievements depend on policies, and enterprises' autonomy plays a limited role. Though China has transformed the originally highly-centralized wholesale system into a modern wholesale system featured by various ownerships, modes of operations and multiple forms of market economic conditions, thoughts of the traditional planned system of wholesale enterprises still exist extensively, since the reform based on the original planned economic system has been developed for three decades, and lasted shorter than the development of the traditional wholesale system. Therefore, there will be a variety of open or secret competitions focusing on the reservation

of the wholesale system. Totally-open small and medium-sized individual wholesale enterprises are small in size and weak in market control, so entities of the wholesale system are mainly wholly state-owned or state-controlled large wholesale enterprises. Though they are seemingly profitable, they get profits mainly on privileges. Each of the policies, laws and regulations corresponds to a vested interest. Every policy change is at the mean time a kind of interest adjustment. Reform of rectifying the wholesale order during 1986–1991 was a very good demonstration.

(3) Reform of the state-owned wholesale enterprises is of great difficulty. Small and medium-sized wholesale enterprises haven't withdrawn completely from the state-owned sector of the economy. It is obvious that their mechanism transformation and system innovation are insufficient, that their economic benefits are low, that their collectivization development is slow, that they have heavy historic burdens, and that their market competitiveness and risk-resistance capacity are weak. The government's capability of macroeconomic regulation that adapts to the conditions of the market economy is still weak. The setting of commodity market circulation management institutions is not rational enough, or capable of meeting the requirements of the market economy. Problems such as overstaffing market circulation management institutions, overlapping functions, separated policies haven't been solved, and the government's mode of management hasn't been thoroughly transformed. Irregular management behaviors, department monopoly, regional segregation, local protectionism and inconsistent policies still exist. Great changes have happened to the economic system, the circulation policies and market environment in China since it launched the reform and opening up. Despite of the series of related reforms in recent years, the wholesale trade in China hasn't been fundamentally changed in terms of institutional setting, the overall size of organizations, management mode and means in general, and the change in the direction of the wholesale trade in China lags behind the dramatic changes in the external economic environment.

(4) The legal system for the market economy hasn't been fully established. Legal construction focusing on the wholesale trade and the market is relatively backward, and some laws haven't been formally released. It is popular that government departments release mutually constraining administrative regulations, or law enforcement officials fail to act in accordance with the law or enforce the law in a strict way, or it is hard for law enforcement officials to act by the law.

Fate of the Wholesale Trade

With the deepening of the reform of the wholesale circulation, the original pattern of wholesale circulation in China has been broken, yet the new pattern adaptive to the new environment in the 21st century hasn't been formed. The leading position of the wholesale trade in the past keeps weakening in front of the multiple pressures from upstream manufacturers, downstream retail enterprises and foreign capital. Full-time wholesalers, the central link of the circulation system and market network in the past, have gradually lost fixed commodity, channel and market resources. The wholesale trade shrinks gradually. In view of this, a lot of people doubt the necessity for the wholesale trade to continue exist, putting forward the "theory of wholesale being useless" to deny the wholesale trade.

Though "wholesale shrinkage" has become an accomplished fact in face of the above-mentioned external and internal stresses, it simply indicates that the wholesale trade needs to be deepened and furthered, but doesn't mean that it is useless and should never exist. On the contrary, the wholesale trade plays an important role in national economy. Its existence is necessary, which is determined by the national conditions of China. Seen from the functions of the wholesale trade itself, wholesale is irreplaceable.

National conditions of China make it necessary the existence of the wholesale trade

Development of the wholesale trade is, first of all, based on certain national conditions. The wholesale trade must be consistent with China's national conditions. National conditions of China are manifold, the specific influence of which on the wholesale trade has the following several characteristics: relatively large economic aggregate; in face of economic restructuring; great differences in local productive forces; significant dual-layered characteristics; and low organizational levels of industrial and commercial enterprises. Though the traditional wholesale trade in China is faced with challenges, it still has great development space under the specific background of national conditions at the present stage, and will continue playing an indispensable role in the system of commodity markets in China in a fairly long time.

Economic transformation, the need for expanding domestic demand

The wholesale trade used to be viewed as the end of the industrial chain, failing to attract enough attention. Nowadays, more and more people have argued that instead of being the "end of the industrial chain", modern circulation is the "pioneer" or the locomotive that pulls economic growth. The position of the wholesale trade as the leading industry is unshakable in the entire economic system. According to the data of developed countries in recent years, the added value of the wholesale trade accounts for 14.1% of the total GDP in China. The added value of the wholesale trade accounts for as high as 19.7% and 20.5%, respectively, of the total GDP in Singapore and the United States. The wholesale trade also plays a prominent role in driving China's economic growth. Statistics show that in 2004, GDP in China increased by 13.2% year on year, of which commerce (wholesale, retail, hotels and restaurants) contributed to 1.61%. Development of the social economy must rely on the strong role of the circulation trade therein. The wholesale trade is necessary in China because: 1) China boasts a population of 1.3 billion, having a great consumer base. Even if low-growth income or level of consumption would form an enormous consumer market; 2) the Chinese economy presents a sustained and rapid growth; the level of consumption keeps increasing; consumer demands are diversified and individualized, which will all increase the operational cost of the retail commerce, calling for logistics or distribution organizations with the wholesale function to provide, for retailers or people with diversified demands, a wide range of qualified commodities with low logistics costs; 3) the wholesale trade is a base industry for China to construct a harmonious society. Generally, a harmonious society covers three aspects: effective satisfaction of the residents' consumer demands; effective guarantee of the residents' consumption safety; and effective promotion of social employment, all of which can't be achieved without the development of the wholesale trade.

Dual-layered economy with distinguished features, the requirement on scattered demands

The dualistic urban-rural structure in China has determined the relatively low level of consumption in rural areas. The dualistic economic structure of wholesale in rural and urban areas has led to a great difference between the level of wholesale in coastal areas in East China and that in Central and West China. The income gap between residents of urban and rural areas and among different regions further leads to inconsistent consumption levels and behaviors. Influenced by cultural, social, personal and psychological factors, consumers' behaviors show personalized and diversified characteristics, which make it more difficult to meet their demands. Diversified choices made by consumers themselves require manufacturers to produce more diversified commodities or services with more comprehensive specifications on the one hand, while requiring retail enterprises to provide corresponding commodity portfolios on the other hand, enhancing the demands for wholesale enterprises to distribute, allocate and sort out commodities. In addition, even if the production and retail trades could meet consumers' diversified demands, it would be impossible for a manufacturer to supply goods directly to each of millions of retail enterprises, or for a retail enterprise to login the website of each of the manufacturers whose products it needs. For both sides, transaction costs are high. With its advantages in the fast delivery system featured by "small quantity, multiple varieties and high frequency", the wholesale trade could meet consumers' demands rapidly. All of the above-mentioned have enabled the Chinese wholesale trade to continue developing. In particular, modern commerce does not see limited development space in terms of its scale and chain patterns, nor is it economic in rural areas due to the vast territory with a sparse population. Wholesale trade is especially indispensable for separated and small-scale individual businesses. Li Xihua, a famous economist, believes that the entry into China of foreign-funded enterprises with their capital, scale and technical advantages, will indeed seriously threaten the Chinese wholesale trade. However, it should also be noticed that such development takes some time. China has a vast territory with unbalanced regional economic development. Even with more technical forces, foreign investors will still be limited by geological and natural conditions. So there is still development space for the Chinese wholesale trade, which will not be crashed in front of China's accession to the WTO.

Small and medium-sized production and retail enterprises being the mainstay, the requirement of a low organizational level

Current conditions of the production and retail trades in China have also determined that there is room for the existence of wholesale trade. The existence of an enormous number of small and scattered manufacturers and retailers in China is the objective demand for the existence of the wholesale trade. Though the trend of getting expanded and centralized is significant among manufacturing and retailing enterprises, which presents a serious challenge for wholesale enterprises, seen from the entire market, both the production and the retail sectors are featured by low level of industrial concentration and relatively small sizes. Small and scattered manufacturers and retail enterprises are still in the majority. In terms of complete machines, the largest fridge and washing machine manufacturer in China has an annual scale of production of about two million sets, while the global production of washing machines of HP Company had already reached 1.74 million sets in 1999. An HP factory of fully-automated washing machine in the United States can manufacture as many as three million sets of washing machines within a single year. In terms of key component manufacturing, the largest compressor plant in China could manufacture only 2.5 million sets of compressors a year, while the annual production capability of Embraco Group reaches 23 million sets. Large domestic manufacturers in China being such case, let alone those small and medium-sized enterprises. In the retail sector, over 99% of the total retail sales of consumer goods in China in 2004 were realized by 99% of the small and mediums-sized circulation enterprises. Put in a global context, all Chinese circulation enterprises are small and medium-sized. Under such circumstances, if a manufacturer trades with a great number of retail enterprises directly or a retail enterprise trades with a great number of manufacturers directly, it would demand for the devotion of certain manpower and materials, causing a heavy burden to small enterprises. What's more, it is not economic, either. Over 90% of the small and medium-sized manufacturers and 97% of the small and medium-sized retail enterprises in China cannot develop without wholesale trade. Therefore, mass sales and purchase through wholesale is the best choice. The existence of a large number of small and scattered manufacturers and retailers has provided broad space for the existence and development of wholesale enterprises.

Need for the development of special industries

Though specialty retailers are reducing in number, seen from the industry itself, the reduced part of retailers are mainly engaged in the aspect of the means of production. Due to its large consumer demands and the fact that a great part of the products could reach consumers without warehouse facilities in marketing, reduced demand for wholesale is inevitable. However, in terms of the means of subsistence, the demand for wholesale is still large, especially in some special industries. For example, production of agricultural products (like fruits, vegetables, native products and traditional Chinese medicinal materials) and that of small articles of daily use are not that concentrated. Such products are sold in many provinces, even across China, during which a great number of trafficking wholesalers and peddlers are needed to link production with consumer demands.

International experience proofs the existence space of the wholesale trade

"The theory of wholesale being useless" is not consistent with China's basic national conditions or the experience of countries each with a developed market such as the United States and Japan. International experience has denied such theory and confirmed that the wholesale trade is still the fastest developing industry in commerce.

Industrial self-marketing, retail, self-purchase cannot replace wholesale

In some economically-developed countries like the United States and Western Europe, manufacturers do wholesale businesses; large retailers have internal wholesale systems; and independent wholesalers are reducing in number, the ratio of which is not great enough to replace the wholesale trade. Take the United States for example, the sales volume of wholesale departments (which may be seen as the self-marketing of production departments) accounted for about 35% of the total sales volume of manufacturers in the United States during the 1960s. In different years, proportions of commercial wholesale and industrial self-marketing grew side by side, but at about 10:7. What's more, not only industry and the retail trade seize wholesale markets, but also wholesalers have got involved in the fields of industry and the retail trade. A trend of small wholesalers joining together or stimulating retailers to form alliance or separated chains to deal with integrated agricultural, industrial and commercial organizations. Led by comprehensive companies, the business volume of independent wholesalers has far exceeded that of industrial self-marketing. Seen from the above analyses, in economically-developed countries, the number of independent wholesalers has somewhat reduced. However, it is not the result of one-sided expansion of industrial self-marketing, but that of industrial and commercial combination and of the increase in wholesale and retail unities, the reflection of high capital concentration, the demonstration of enhanced control of related department by monopoly capital; and the expansion of combination, fixation and integration, but not the demonstration of purely expanding industrial self-marketing and reducing wholesale commerce.

Rise of the absolute value of the size of the wholesale trade

The status of the wholesale trade once went down in developed countries, leading to the "theory of wholesale being useless". However, in the long run, the wholesale trade keeps expanding, indicating the unshakable status of the wholesale trade. Take the United States for example; wholesale organizations in the United States were in the plight in 1939, the average sales volume of which reduced to the historical low in 1949. However, since 1987 when Clinton began to take office, under the premise of a stable and high-speed economic growth, the wholesale trade has also been showing a strong growth momentum, and the average sales of wholesale has been growing rapidly. Currently, about 90% of the daily industrial consumer goods, 20% of the industrial means of production and most agricultural products are sold through wholesale. Since 1993, the ratio of its wholesale sales to its GDP has kept increasing (see Table 1.1), being 8.1% in 2001, up 1.3% year on year; and up 26.6% comparing with that in 1993. Moreover, professional wholesale still accounts for a high proportion in the wholesale field, being 60% in terms of business volume and 70–80% in terms of personnel. It indicates that wholesale circulation led by independent wholesalers is becoming more and more influential and powerful in commodity circulation and that wholesale organizations begin to revive in the United States.

Table 1.1. Wholesale trade value and its ratio to the GDP in the U.S.

Items	1993	1995	1997	1999	2001
Value of wholesale items (1 billion USD)	452.4	483.0	584.1	708.6	748.7
GDP (1 billion USD)	7,063	7,544	8,160	8,859	9,215
Ratio (%)	6.4	6.4	7.2	8.0	8.1

Source: US Census Bureau, 2002 Economic Census Statistical Abstract of the US. 2002.

The situation in Japan is more or less the same. Since the 1990s, the wholesale commerce in Japan has been shrinking on the whole; and both large and small enterprises, their scale of operation and number of stores has showed a declining tendency. To protect its own survival space, the Japanese wholesale commerce underwent a structural adjustment and policy change cored with its own reforms. After a period of M & A and reorganization, full-time wholesalers had become the main force of wholesale commerce. Of which, small and medium-sized wholesale enterprises each with less than 100 staffs accounted for 99.3%, practitioners accounted for 84.5%, and annual sales volume accounted for 62.1% of the wholesale trade in general. However, large wholesale commercial institutions each with more than 100 staffs were only a few in number, accounting for 0.7% of all wholesale commercial institutions in Japan, 15.5% of all in terms of practitioners and 37.9% of all in terms of annual sales volume. In France, the proportion of independent wholesalers reduced substantially during the 1960s and 1970s, which was somewhat improved since 1975. In 1987, there were about 80,000 wholesale outlets across France, of which the sales volume of commercial wholesalers still accounted for over

50% of the total sales volume of wholesale, reaching 1,780 billion francs. To survive and develop, French wholesalers are taking professional, united and modern measures to re-set their primary position in the wholesale trade. In Singapore, a small, but economically-developed city country, wholesalers have always held the central position of the wholesale trade. Most of them are Chinese. They purchase commodities from import agents before selling them to retailers. With flexible sizes of batches, they are doing the business in a flexible way. Wholesalers even have professional sales force, fixed sales channels and relatively stable customers. Take a general look at the development of the national wholesale trade, we could see that the wholesale trade was once shrunk, yet showed a trend of stable growth through various indicators after readjustment. What's more, wholesale organizations have always been the central link of the commodity circulation system, holding a pivotal position in the circulation field.

Functions of wholesale in itself determine the indispensability of the wholesale trade

Wholesale refers to all of the other trading behaviors, in the field of commodity circulation beyond the acts of purchase and sale with commodity capital as the medium and directly related to the personal consumption of different social members-humans. That is, wholesale means all trading behaviors among producers, operators, and between producers and operators in the field of commodity circulation, which are differentiated from the trading behaviors between producers (or operators) and consumers. Of economic nature, it doesn't mean the trading behaviors aiming at meeting immediate consumption needs, but those aiming at meeting the needs of production and consumption, and commodity circulation. Though the two are both trading behaviors, wholesale is different from retail. Retail involves activities directly connected to individual consumers, while wholesale refers to other trading behaviors, namely activities closely related to production, production consumers and production operators. Seen from the economic characteristics of wholesale activities in themselves, we could see that wholesale has two significant characteristics: resale transactions and credit transactions. In particular, characteristics of wholesale and resale transactions determine that wholesale institutions serve as the middlemen of manufacturers and users in the process of commodity circulation. Its functions in distributing commodities, regulating supply and demand, delivering information in a cost-effective way, processing circulation, logistics, circulation finance, sharing risks, and providing sales supports meet the needs of social division of work. It has a wide interface with retail outlets, as well as special technologies such as purchasing and wholesaling commodities. In particular, the application and popularization of information and network technologies since the 1990s have enhanced the display of wholesale, enabling wholesale to effectively serve industry and other forms of commerce. What's more, the wholesale trade has enjoyed scale economics in distribution, presenting high distribution efficiency. Capable wholesale enterprises could develop to being multi-functional, providing comprehensive and high-quality services for manufacturers and retailers. Basic functions of modern wholesale enterprises mainly include: trading, that is, allocating commodities in small batches to retailers after purchasing commodities from manufacturers according to market demands; storage, that is, solving the space and time contradictions between commodity production and distribution through warehousing and transportation, trying hard to reduce the inventory of manufacturers and retailers; financing, that is, providing financial assistance to manufacturers and retailers directly or indirectly; and information function, that is, providing market information and consultation services to manufacturers and retailers, etc.

Challenges faced by the wholesale trade are also opportunities

Though the manufacturing trade vigorously builds the self-marketing system, while the wholesale trade enhances chain-orientation, they are not always effective in the process of vertical integration. Most retail stores are limited by insufficient venue, inconvenient transportation, distribution shortage, small sizes of wholesale and small profit margins, making industrial self-marketing, the combination of production and sales and other emerging forms unable to replace the wholesale trade. Firstly, small manufacturers, limited by financial and material resources, are unable to set up a department or institution for direct sales independently. Secondly, even if with abundant financial resources, manufacturers prefer increasing production investments to investing capital into costly distribution channels when making decisions. Thirdly, since many retailers operate various commodities, they don't want to deal directly with individual companies from the angle of saving and reducing transaction cost. To improve efficiency, manufacturers and retailers begin to get rid of the pattern of being "large and all-inclusive" or "being small and all-inclusive" and introduce the concept of social work division into the enterprise. Keeping core businesses and "outsourcing" non-core businesses has become the choice of many enterprises. Current development of the logistics and information technologies will not replace the wholesale trade. But by reducing the asymmetry of production and demand using information technologies, it enables the wholesale trade to improve the circulation efficiency and reduces the cost of circulation by integrating the logistics industry, providing a better technical platform and development space for the wholesale trade and creating conditions for the transformation of wholesale to the third-party logistics. It is estimated that in the future 10 years, 1/3 of the value of international trade will be realized through the network. The emergence of e-commerce has provided a brand-new idea and pattern for the wholesale of major commodities (including means of production and subsistence). All commodities suitable for bulk wholesales could effectively extend the trading radius, expand the trading circle, speed up the trading process, and reduce the cost of trading through e-commerce.

All in all, shrinkage of the wholesale trade doesn't mean that wholesale is useless. National conditions, international experience and the functions of the wholesale trade itself have all determined the necessity of the existence of the wholesale trade. In addition, whether the wholesale trade could save cost and improve efficiency is crucial for its survival. In the long run, socialized mass production could definitely become special. Specialization will definitely call for the wholesale trade, which is the requirement on improving the efficiency. As long as there exists socialized mass production based on socialized work division, and there are various structural contradictions between mass production and mass consumption, there will be the necessity for the existence of the wholesale trade. The more developed the market economy is, the more prominent the necessity will be.

2

Chapter

Growth and Contribution of the Wholesale Trade

In the past three decades since the reform and opening up, the wholesale trade in China has kept expanding, and its contribution to the economic and social development of China has been strengthened constantly. In 2007, the wholesale trade realized an added value of RMB 41.78 billion, accounting for 6.9% of the total output value in China and becoming one of the most important pillar industries for the development of the national economy.

Growth of the Wholesale Trade

In the three decades of reform and opening up, the wholesale trade has undergone different stages of reform and development, making great achievements. In this section, the author will describe the growth process of the wholesale trade from such angles as the basic information of the wholesale trade, sales volume and financial level and scale. Data herein are from *China Commerce and External Economic Statistics: 1952–1988, China Business Yearbook (1988–1992), Market Statistical Yearbook of China (1993–2004)* and *China Trade and External Economic Statistical Yearbook*. Of which, the statistical criteria during 1999–2007 were limited to the wholesale trade above the designated size. Wholesale enterprises above the designated size refer to those enterprises each with over RMB 20 million of annual sales volume and more than 20 practitioners.

Rapid development after the launch of the reform (1978–1984)

After the Third Plenary Session of the 11th CPC National Congress pointed out the way ahead for the Chinese wholesale trade, development of the wholesale trade entered a phase of rapid development along with the reform and opening up. The development scale of the wholesale trade during this period is analyzed below from the total number of the wholesale institutions, and that of practitioners and its growth rate (see Fig. 2.1 and Fig. 2.2).

Wholesale institutions

Number of wholesale institutions showed a steady growth in this phase. Of which, the year 1979 saw the fastest growth of the wholesale institutions, which was 16.5%; and the year 1982 saw the lowest growth of the wholesale institutions, which was close to zero. Till 1984, wholesale institutions gained rapid growth again, with the growth rate being 12.7%. With six years of development, the total number of wholesale institutions had grown to 239 thousand in 1984, being 80 thousand plus more than that in 1978.

Fig. 2.1. Number of the wholesale institutions (1978–1984)

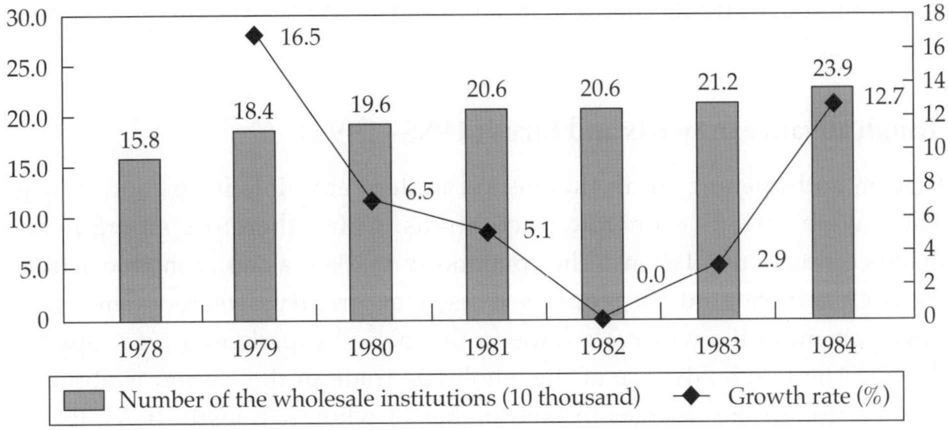

Fig. 2.2. Number of wholesale practitioners (1978–1984)

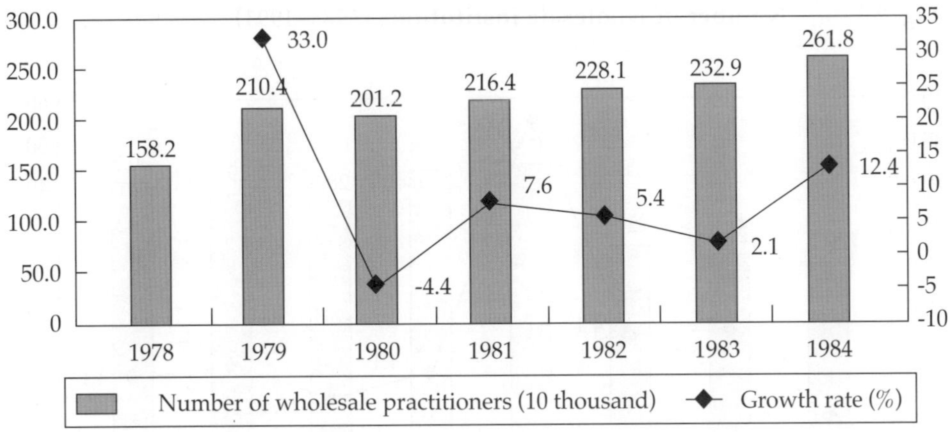

Wholesale practitioners

The same as the growth of the number of wholesale institutions, wholesale practitioners grew fastest in number in 1979 at a rate of 33%, while slowest in 1980 at -4.4%, indicating a decrease trend. After that, the number of wholesale practitioners got a relatively steady development. Till 1984, the number of wholesale practitioners had reached 2.618 million, being 1 million plus more than that in 1978.

Seen from the figures on the development of and changes in the wholesale institutions and number of practitioners, the wholesale trade in this phase was relatively steady, showing a growing trend. Development of the wholesale trade is closely related to the reform of the commodity economy, especially that of the wholesale system in the same phase. Of which, reform policies on the commodity circulation system launched in 1984 served as the greatest promoting force.

Tough advance in twists and turns (1985–1992)

Reform and opening up in this period underwent violent ups and downs. There were serious economic fluctuations. China therefore strengthened macroeconomic regulations. The commodity market, as an economic activity most closely related to people's lives, was greatly affected. Therefore, development of the wholesale trade in this period experienced great ups and downs. The tough advance of the wholesale trade in this period is observed below through the changes in the number of wholesale institutions, that of practitioners and the growth rate (see Fig. 2.3).

Fig. 2.3. Number of wholesale institutions (1985–1991)

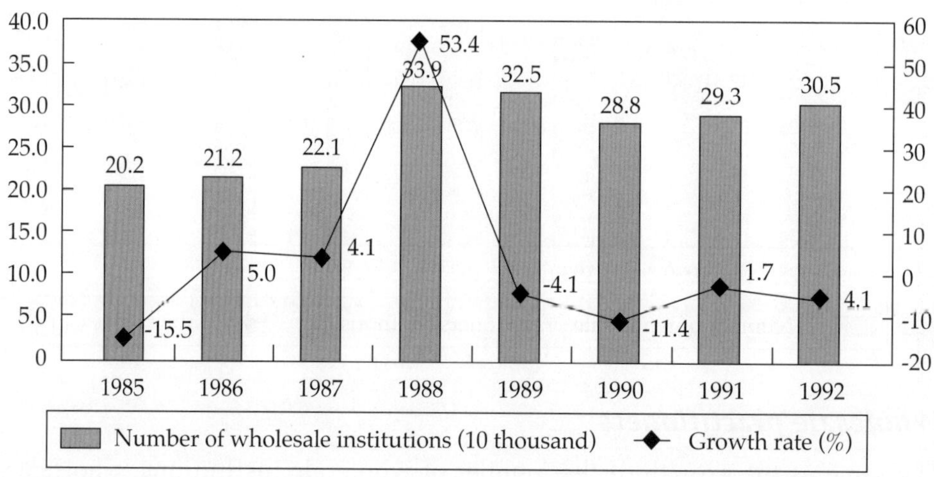

Wholesale institutions

It can be seen from Fig. 2.3 that the number of wholesale institutions in this period grew in a wave-like way, which could be seen more clearly from the growth rate of the number of wholesale institutions. Compared with that in 1984, the number of wholesale institutions reduced by 15% in 1985, and maintained a steady growth during 1985–1987. In 1988, since the statistics then included the number of wholesale institutions and practitioners in the entire society, while previous statistics were simply the number of wholesale institutions and practitioners of the commercial system, growth rate of wholesale institutions and practitioners became prominent, reaching 53.4%. Since then, wholesale institutions reduced gradually in number, of which the fall in 1990 was the greatest, reaching 11.4%. Till 1992, the number of wholesale institutions was 305 thousand, down 34 thousand than that in 1988. Major reason for the decline of the number of wholesale institutions was the business difficulties faced by the wholesale trade. Due to the extraordinary development of the wholesale trade at the previous stage, market order of the wholesale trade was chaotic and the effectiveness of operation of the wholesale trade dropped significantly. Therefore, local governments all cleared up and rectified local wholesale enterprises carefully.

Wholesale practitioners

As can be seen from Fig. 2.4, comparing with that in Fig. 2.3, the number column of wholesale practitioners in this period was relatively stable and its range of variation was not as fierce as that of wholesale institutions. In view of the same statistical reasons, the number of wholesale practitioners in 1988 was prominent, reaching 17.9% before returning to be steady. Compared with the changes in the number of wholesale institutions, the stable development of wholesale practitioners was mainly thanks to institutional M & A. Reform and merger of state-owned wholesale enterprises in this period led to the reduction of the number of wholesale institutions, not significant reduction of the number of wholesale practitioners.

Fig. 2.4. Number of wholesale practitioners (1985–1992)

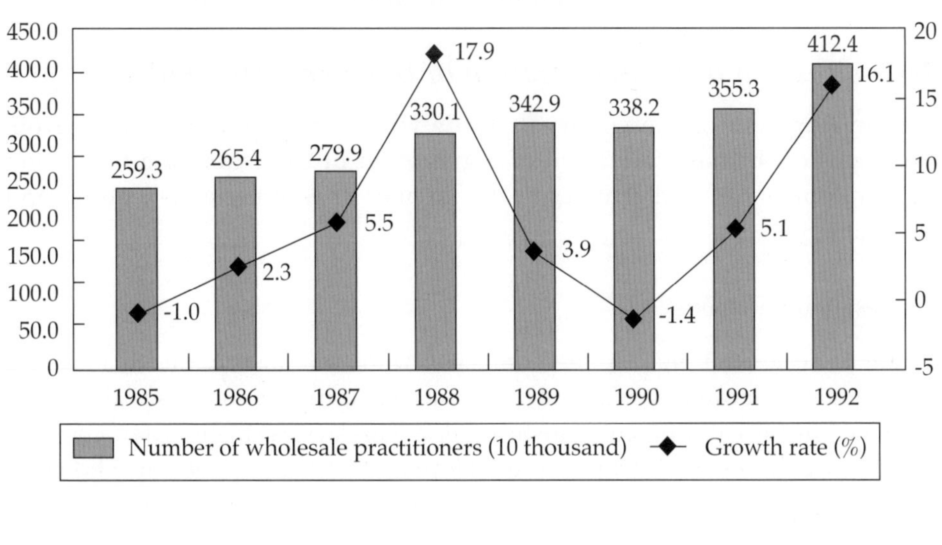

It could be seen from the above analysis that development of and changes in the fundamental state of the wholesale trade was consistent with the development trend of the wholesale trade, leading to disturbances. However, the wholesale trade was developing on the whole. In particular, the number of wholesale practitioners in 1992 exceeded that in 1989, showing an irresistible development momentum.

Rapid development in twists and turns (1993–1997)

The wholesale trade was faced with a severe situation in this period: unbalanced market supply structure and heavy stockpile of some commodities. In the transition to the socialist market economy, some enterprises failed to meet the requirements of the new economic situation or grasp market information, thus were unable to produce readily marketable products. What's more, the influence of administrative intervention on the production and circulation fields existed from time to time; local protectionism kept causing troubles; a great number of projects were launched blindly without prior market investigation and scientific appraisals; and the phenomenon of redundant construction projects was serious, aggravating structural imbalance in market supply. Faced with such a situation, under the leadership of the CPC Central Committee and the State Council of China, reforms of grains, cottons, fertilizers and other important commodities were launched smoothly; the system for important commodity reserves was initially set up; the macroeconomic regulation capability of China got strengthened; laws and regulations on market circulation got improved gradually; and great achievements were made in market construction. The wholesale trade hence entered the stage of rapid development.

The development situation of the wholesale trade in face of conditions of a severe market environment is analyzed in details below from the angles of the basic registration and sales revenue of the wholesale trade in detail.

Basic situation of the registration of the wholesale trade

The development of the wholesale trade will be analyzed as follows from the angles of the basic situation of registration of the wholesale trade, and the development of and changes in the number of wholesale institutions and practitioners.

Wholesale institutions

As can be seen from Fig. 2.5, the number of wholesale institutions in 1993 was small, mainly because it was independent accounting enterprises that were calculated in 1993 at different statistic criteria. However, statistic criteria became unified after 1993. Seen from the development of the number of wholesale institutions during 1994–1996, it increased rapidly in this period at a rate of above 10% every year, even 39% in 1994. The market of consumer goods grew rapidly, too. In the aspect of policies, the 14th CPC Central Committee built the socialist market economic system before opening up a wider road for the development of the commodity economy.

Fig. 2.5. Number of wholesale institutions (1992–1996)

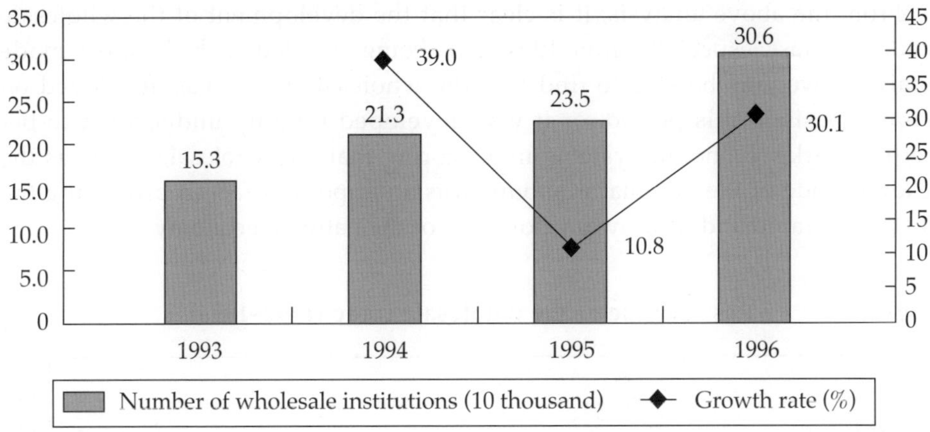

Wholesale practitioners

As could be seen from Fig. 2.6, wholesale practitioners grew rapidly in this period, the growth rate of which exceeded 50% in 1994. Till 1996, wholesale practitioners reached 13.09 million in number, being more than doubled than that in 1992.

Fig. 2.6. Number of wholesale practitioners (1993–1996)

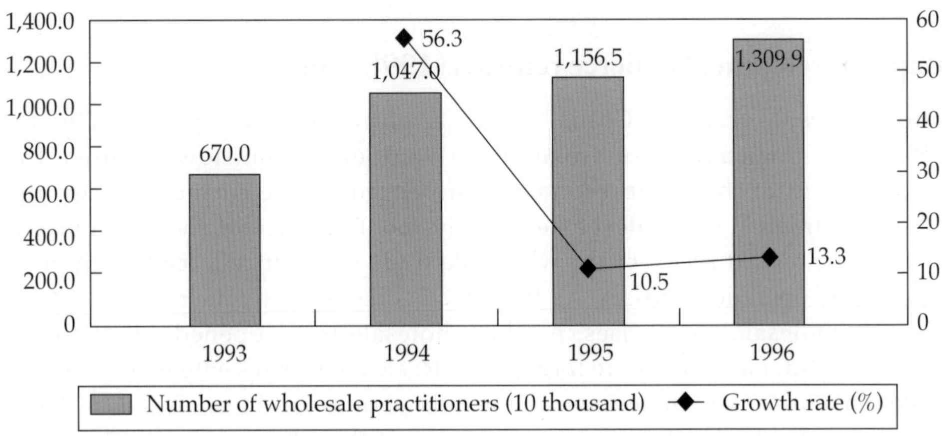

Sales volume of the wholesale trade

It can be seen from Fig. 2.7 that the sales revenue of the wholesale trade in this period got improved greatly at an extremely high speed. Its growth in 1993 was extraordinary comparing with that in 1994, being 1.5 times greater. The sales volume kept increasing during 1994–1996. Till 1996, the sales revenue of the wholesale trade increased by 2.5 times than that in 1992, and nearly RMB 550 billion comparing with that in 1994, showing a rapid scale expansion.

From the above analysis, it is clear that the development of the wholesale trade was fast, especially after 1994. This being coupled with the afore-made analyses, we may be able to find that the wholesale trade was developed on a weak basis in this period, or it was developed toughly under a yet-to-be-perfect market economic system, underscoring that the wholesale trade, as the leading trade of the national economy, was an important fact in promoting the sustained, rapid and healthy development of the national economy.

Fig. 2.7. Sales revenue of the wholesale trade (1992–1996)

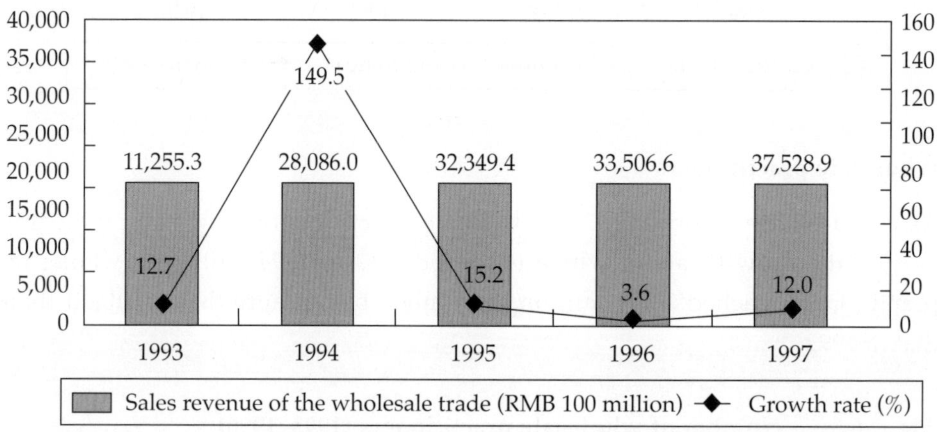

Rapid development in fierce reforms (1998–2007)

The wholesale trade in China was in revolution in this period. During 1997–1999, financial crises broke out in Southeast Asia, slowing down the development of the world economy. Influenced by the financial crises, the wholesale trade in China developed slowly, too. In particular, the development of the state-owned sector of the wholesale trade was difficult, leading to great amounts of operational losses. All these factors had sped up the reform of state-owned wholesale enterprises. As the wholesale trade opened wider to the outside world, more and more foreign wholesale enterprises entered China. The development of the wholesale trade in this period will be analyzed in detail in terms of the basic situation of registration of the wholesale trade above the designated size, the sales revenue, assets and liabilities and the scale of profits. Since statistics in 1997 and 1998 failed to collect data on the basic situation of the wholesale trade, we could only analyze the basic development of the wholesale trade during 1999–2002. Statistical criteria on the basic situation of the wholesale trade in this period were wholesale institutions above the designated size.

Basic situation of the registration of the wholesale trade above the designated size

Development of the wholesale trade in this period will be observed through such indicators as the number of business corporations engaged in the wholesale trade, the number of industrial establishments and practitioners.

Wholesale business corporations

Changes in the number of business corporations engaged in the wholesale trade above the designated size showed that the wholesale trade began to fall into recession since 2000 on the whole before beginning to flourish again in 2004 (see Fig. 2.8). In 2000, the number of business corporations engaged in the wholesale trade above the designated size dropped by 6% comparing with that in 1999. The number of business corporations engaged in the wholesale trade above the designated size was only 14,937 in 2003, reducing by nearly 1,500 comparing with that in 1999. The unexpected emergence of the sector of the wholesale trade above the designated size in 2004 should be taken into consideration from the following two aspects: firstly, the statistical criteria; in 2004, China launched a national economic census, in which a lot of enterprises below the designated size were revealed, before making data alignment to statistics; secondly, China lowered the threshold on the entry into the wholesale trade after its accession to the WTO, so the number of business corporations engaged in the wholesale trade grew rapidly. From the data during 2005–2007, it could be seen that the number of business corporations above the designated size engaged in the wholesale trade was a lot more than that prior to 2003, fully demonstrating the rapid development of the wholesale trade in China after China's accession to the WTO.

Wholesale practitioners

Comparing the number of business corporations above the designated size engaged in the wholesale trade and that of wholesale practitioners, we may find that during 1999–2004, development of the wholesale trade above the designated size was sluggish; practitioners engaged in wholesale trade above

Fig. 2.8. Number of business corporations above the designated size engaged in the wholesale trade (1999–2007)

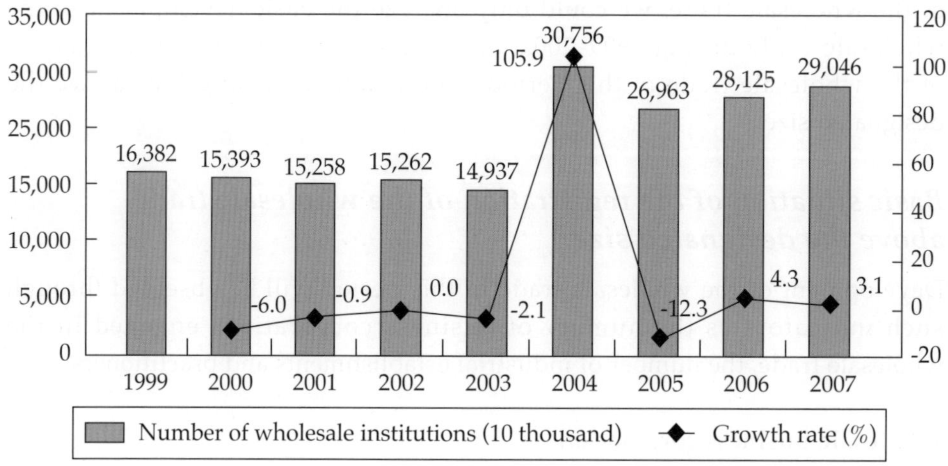

the designated size showed a declining tendency, even reduced by 14.5%, being a lot more than the reduced number of business corporations above the designated level engaged in the wholesale trade (see Fig. 2.9). The great difference could be explained from the following two aspects: firstly, collapse of enterprises; a wholesale enterprise involved a lot of practitioners, so the reduction of wholesale practitioners would be definitely more than that of wholesale enterprises, and the fall would be greater; secondly, business merger; enterprises carried out M & A and reorganization in order to improve their competitiveness, during which a lot of wholesale practitioners would choose to leave the trade. The abnormal growth of the number of wholesale practitioners in 2004 was due to the same reasons for the changes in the number of business corporations engaged in the wholesale trade over the same year. From Fig. 2.9, it could be seen that changes in the number of wholesale practitioners were small since 2005 before showing a substantial increase in 2007. The number of business corporations engaged in the wholesale trade had maintained a steady growth rate since the significant decline in 2005.

Respective proportion of wholesale institutions and practitioners in the wholesale trade and related changes

It can be seen from Fig. 2.10 that the proportion of the number of business corporations engaged in the wholesale trade and that of wholesale practitioners both showed a declining tendency. Of the former proportion, it reduced from 54% in 1999 to 36% in 2007, down 18% within nearly a decade. Of which, it dropped the fastest in 2004 at a rate of 16%. Correspondingly, the proportion of the retail trade in the wholesale and retail trade increased. The wane and wax of the wholesale and retail trade was exactly one of the results of the economic development, upgrading of the consumption structure, innovation and accelerated growth of the retail trade in recent years.

Fig. 2.9. Number of wholesale practitioners (1999–2007)

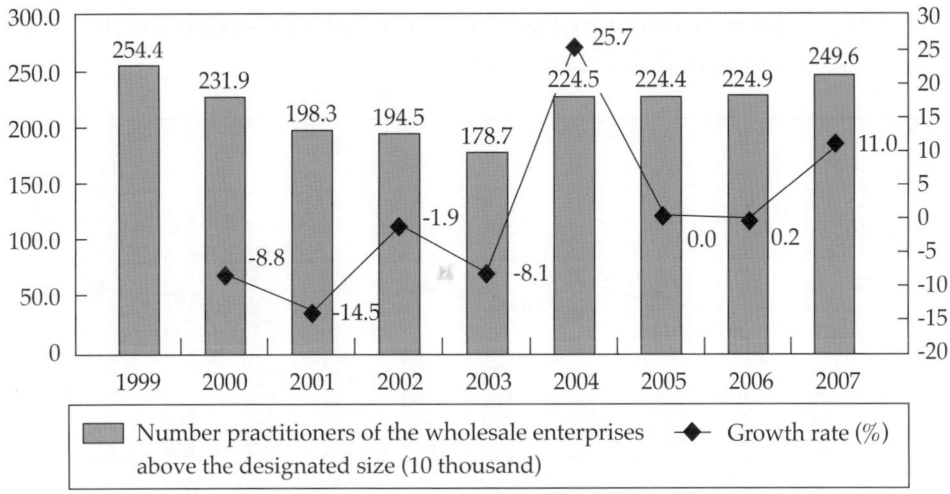

Fig. 2.10. Respective proportion of the wholesale business corporations above the designated size and the wholesale practitioners (1999–2007)

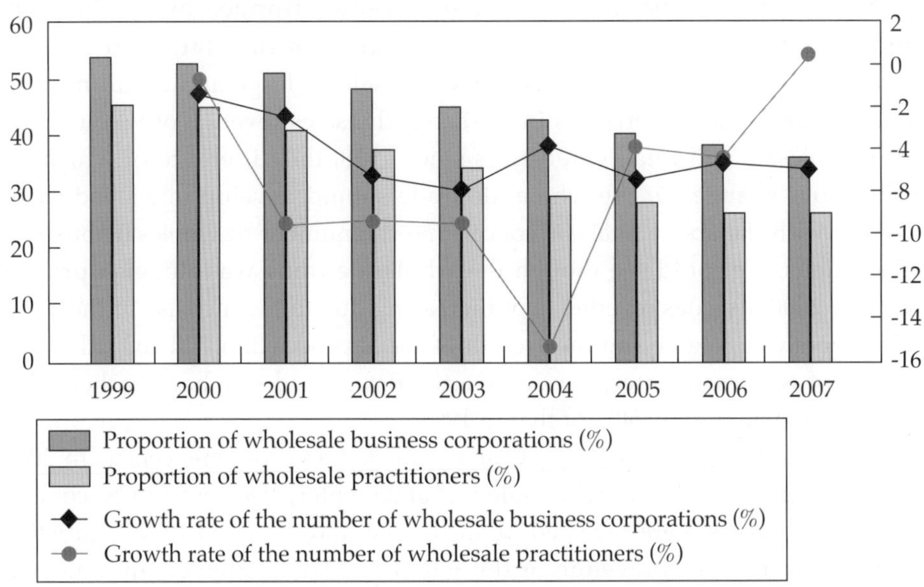

Sales revenue of the wholesale enterprises above the designated size

It could be seen from Fig. 2.11 that the wholesale trade maintained a steady development in this period. Due to the national economic census launched in 2004, many statistical data changed abnormally. Therefore, analysis of Fig. 2.11 will be divided into two stages.

Fig. 2.11. Sales revenue of the wholesale enterprises above the designated size (1998–2007)

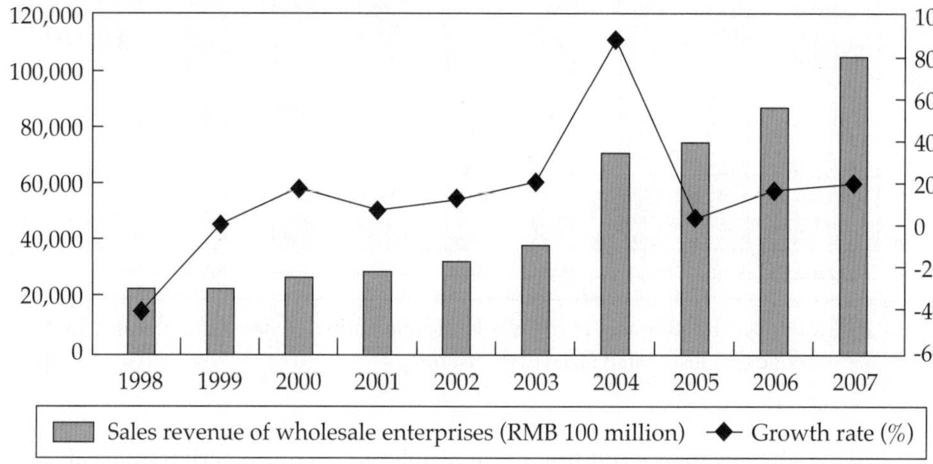

The first stage (1998–2003): the sales revenue dropped by 40% in 1998, which was thought to be caused by the change in the statistical criteria. China calculated the sales revenue of wholesale of large and medium-sized wholesale and retail enterprises in 1997, but the sales revenue of wholesale of those wholesale and retail enterprises since 1998, the difference of which led to the above change. Or the wholesale trade should develop in a steady way. Together with the above analysis concerning the number of wholesale business corporations, we could see though the wholesale trade was sluggish prior to and after 2000, its sales revenue kept increasing due to the increase in the social and economic aggregate and the growth of social production. Till 2002, the sales revenue of wholesale enterprises above the designated size had reached RMB 3,159.2 billion, up nearly 50% of that in 1998.

The second stage (2004–2007): China launched an economic census in 2004, in which a great number of wholesale and retail enterprises used to be covered for various reasons were revealed, repositioned and included in the statistical materials, so the sales revenue of the wholesale trade showed an abnormal growth in 2004. Excluding the factor of statistical criteria, the development of the sales revenue of wholesale enterprises above the designated size was steady in this period. Since 2004, along with the entry of the foreign capital into the Chinese wholesale trade on a large scale, the sales revenue of the wholesale trade in China had been greatly improved. Till 2007, it reached RMB 10,436.27 billion, up 20% year on year and being significantly higher than the growth of the GDP of the wholesale and retail trade. Such a high-speed growth was greatly related to the overheated development of the national economy in 2007 and the excessive liquidity in the field of consumption. How to enable the circulation industry, especially the wholesale trade industry to play its leading role in national economy and guiding the national economy to develop in a healthy and coordinated way became an important subject faced by the wholesale trade.

Financial position of the wholesale establishments above the designated size

By analyzing the state of financial development of the wholesale trade, we could get a clearer understanding of the entire wholesale trade. Analysis of the financial state mainly refers to the size of assets, liabilities and profits of the wholesale trade. Such indicators reflect the overall size of the wholesale trade fundamentally.

Size of assets

The size of assets of the wholesale trade kept expanding in this period, which was especially significant since 2004. The growth of the size of assets of the wholesale trade reached 56.4% in 2004, and maintained a two-digit figure in 2006 and 2007 (see Fig. 2.12). Comparatively speaking, the size of assets of the wholesale trade during 1998–2001 changed little. Growth of the asset size of the wholesale trade was the same as the trend of rapid development of the national economy in the twenty-first century.

Size of liabilities

As shown in Fig. 2.13, the liabilities of the wholesale trade in this period kept increasing. However, comparing with the changes in the asset size, it was more fluctuating. The same as the size of assets of the wholesale establishments in 2004, which expanded significantly, the growth rate of liabilities reached 50.2%. In 2007, the total liabilities of the wholesale trade had exceeded RMB 2.5 trillion.

Liabilities grew along with the expansion of assets. As for the increase brought about by the national economic census, the abnormal growth of liabilities in 2004 was also caused by the development of the wholesale trade in the same period. However, the asset-liability ratio changed little, even dropped. The same ratio of the wholesale establishments above the designated size was 72.5% in 2004, but 75.5% in 2003.

Fig. 2.12. Size of assets of wholesale establishments above the designated size (1999–2007)

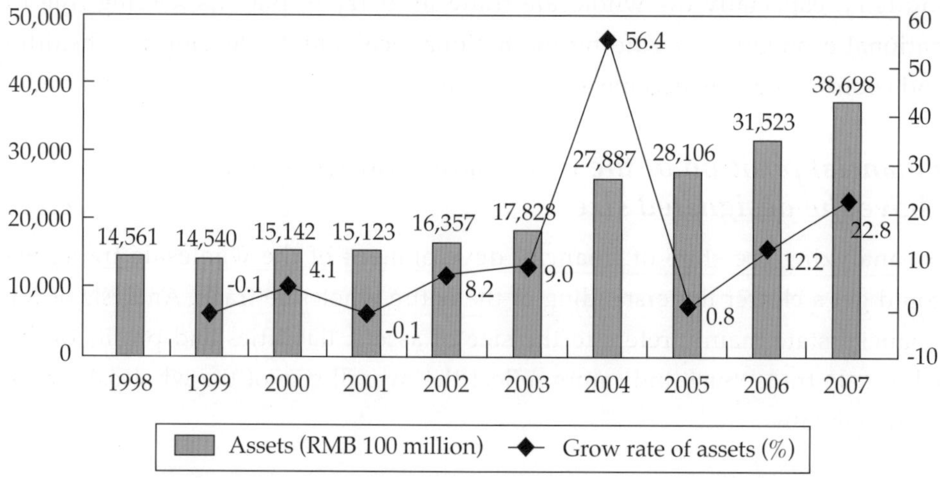

Fig. 2.13. Scale of liabilities of the wholesale establishments above the designated size (1999–2007)

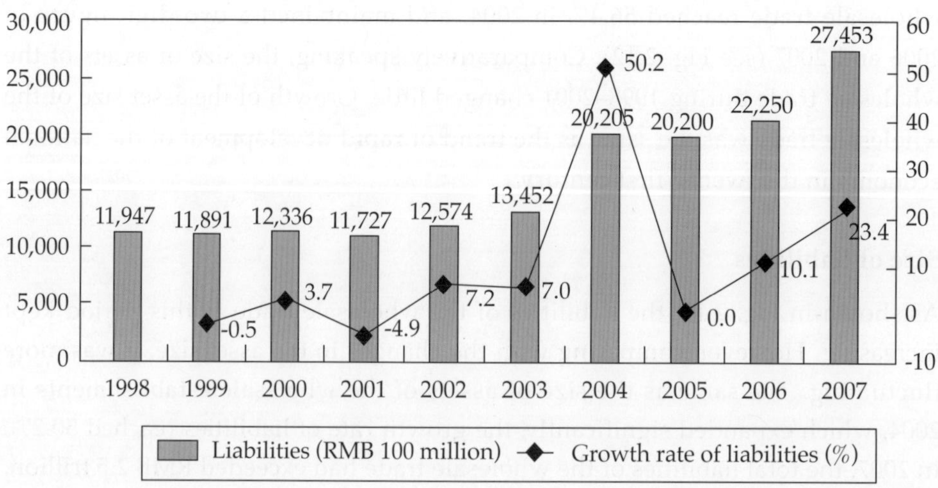

Size of profits

Seen from the total profits of the wholesale establishments above the designated size and their growth, the changing tendencies of the size of assets and the size of liabilities of the wholesale trade were the same. Total profits of the wholesale industry increased by 177.3% in 2004, making a great breakthrough in terms of industrial profits (see Fig. 2.14).

Fig. 2.14. Size of profits of the wholesale establishments above the designated size (1999–2007)

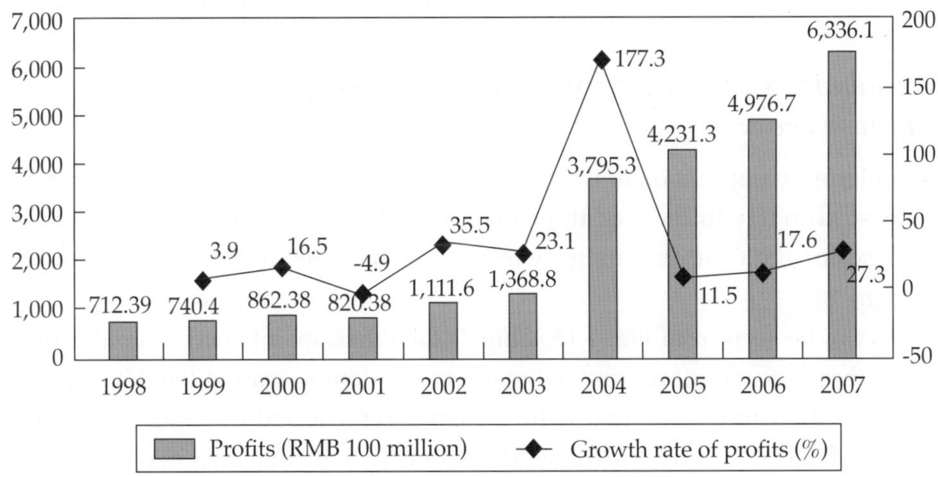

From the analysis of the financial position of the wholesale trade, it could be seen that wholesale establishments above the designated size maintained a relatively steady development during 1998–2003. After 2004, the development of all wholesale establishments above the designated size got improved. The consistency of the three indicators reflected the real development situation of the wholesale trade in China.

To sum up, the wholesale trade had made a significant progress in the three decades of reform and opening up. As the leader of the national economy and the center of commodity circulation, the wholesale trade contributed greatly to China's national economy and commerce, which will be elaborated in the following two sections.

Contributions to the national economy by the wholesale trade in the three decades of reform

Gross Domestic Product (GDP) is an indicator that measures the economic aggregate. The reform and opening up of China underwent three decades of development during 1978–2008, during which China saw earth-shaking changes, the significant improvement of the livelihood of the Chinese people, and the radical changes in the life and fate of each family and individual. GDP is the most convincing in measuring a country's comprehensive economic strength. The development of the national economy is the premise and guarantee of the development of the wholesale trade, while the development of the wholesale trade is conducive to the development of the national economy. The rapid growth of China's GDP, the significant improvement of its industrial structure and the amelioration of its people's livelihood since the reform and opening up are all closely related to the rapid development of the wholesale trade.

Tremendous development of and changes in the Chinese economy

A preliminary impression of the tremendous development of and changes in the Chinese economy in the past three decades will be got by phased and detailed analyses of the GDP and its growth rate in the three decades of reform and opening up.[1]

As can be seen from Fig. 2.15, China's GDP had maintained a rapid growth in the three decades of reform and opening up, demonstrating the development speed of the Chinese economy. In the early reform and opening up in 1978, China's GDP was only RMB 364.52 billion, which then had exceeded RMB 20,000 billion in 2006 and reached RMB 24,661.9 billion in 2007, presenting an average annual growth of 9.7%. In 2007, China's GDP had risen to the world's No. 4 from the world's No. 13, following the United States, Japan and Germany. With the increase of China's GDP, everything in China underwent earth-shaking changes.

The average annual growth rate of China's GDP in the three decades of reform and opening up was 9.7%, being far higher than the annual growth rate of the global economy over the same period which was 3.3%. It indicates that China's ability to create wealth was stronger and stronger and the accumulation of social wealth became faster and faster. It could be seen clearly from the growth curve that the growth of GDP wasn't all the way smooth, but experienced great ups and downs. Its growth during 1978–1990 encountered great setbacks, since when the growth rate of GDP has showed a steady development state.

Reasons for the ups and downs of the economic development will be analyzed through historical facts of the economy.

Fig. 2.15. China's GDP and its growth rate in the three decades of reform and opening up (1978–2007)

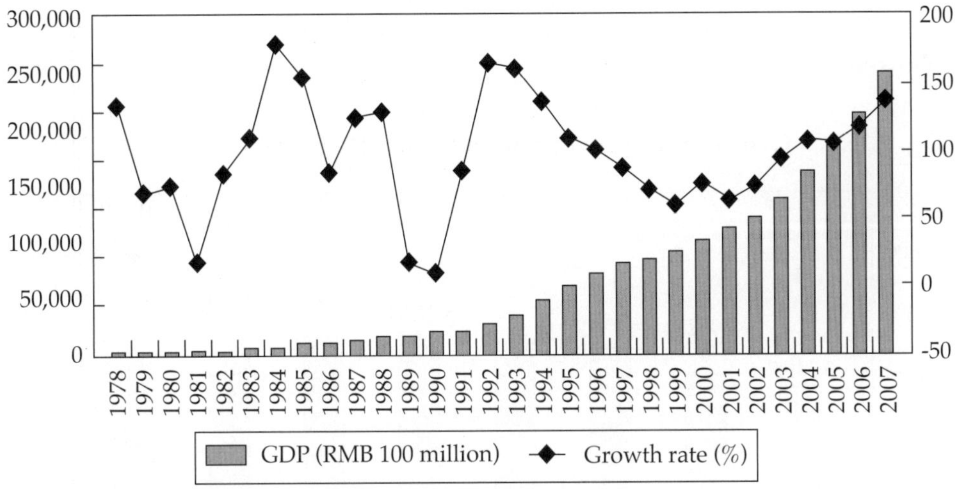

From the launch of the reform and opening up to the end of the Sixth Five-year Plan period (1978–1985)

In December 1978, the Communist Party of China decided to shift its focus of work to economic construction at the Third Plenary Session of the 11th CPC Central Committee and developed the policy of reform and opening up, opening a window for the then China. The enthusiasm of the Chinese people in developing the economy was mobilized top down, and China saw an enthusiasm of "going all out and advancing quickly". Rapid economic growth was achieved in 1978 in China, with the growth rate reaching 11.7%. The decline in the growth rate during 1979–1981 was in line with the rules of economic development, because it took some time for economic growth to be digested.

The growth rate of GDP in China during 1982–1985 showed a tendency of rapid rise, because China intensified its reform efforts. In September 1982, the Communist Party of China proposed to "thoroughly implement the principle of taking the planned economy as the mainstay and market regulation as the supplement" at its 12th National Congress. In October 1984, it was pointed out that the socialist economy was "a planned commodity economy based on the public ownership" at the Third Plenary Session of the 12th CPC National Congress, enabling the Chinese economy to develop at a high speed. Influenced by the Third Plenary Session of the 12th CPC National Congress, the Chinese economy grew rapidly in 1985 and the growth rate of China's GDP reached 12.9% (see Fig. 2.16). However, there were a number of unstable factors involved in the development. The strategic objective of doubling the total industrial and agricultural output by the end of the 21st century which was formally determined at the 12th CPC National Congress rendered local governments to compete with each other, leading to economic overheat in the several years that followed.

Fig. 2.16. GDP and its growth rate in China (1978–1984)

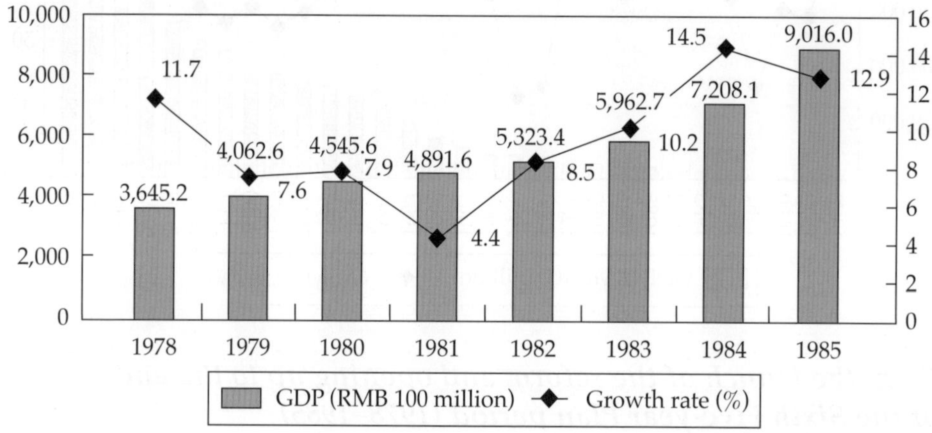

National economy during the Seventh Five-year Plan period (1986–1990)

The peak of GDP growth in this period appeared in 1987 and 1988, being at a rate over 11%; and the trough appeared in 1990, being 3.9%. The overall GDP growth rate presented unstable characteristics, too. Fierce fluctuations of the GDP increase in this period, along with high inflation, were influenced profoundly by policies. Downturn of the GDP growth rate in 1986 was the digestion of the relatively rapid growth rate in the previous stage. At the 13th CPC National Congress held in October 1987, it was pointed out that "the system of the socialist planned commodity economy should be a system of the internal unification of the planned and market economies", greatly promoting the development of the national economy. In 1988, the "No. 1 Document" of the CPC Central Committee stopped focusing on the issue of agriculture, shifted to the macro-economy, and confirmed the profitable growth of the Chinese economy in 1987. In such an atmosphere, central and local government leaders were encouraged, in the mid-1988, pulled by various factors, money supply grew rapidly, even at a rate of over 30%, indicating subtle signs of inflation. To curb sudden inflation, the Chinese Government adopted tightened fiscal and monetary policies at the end of 1988. Till 1989, the growth rate of GDP in China began to slide, slumping to the lowest ebb once again in 1990 (see Fig. 2.17).

Fig. 2.17. GDP and its growth rate in China (1986–1990)

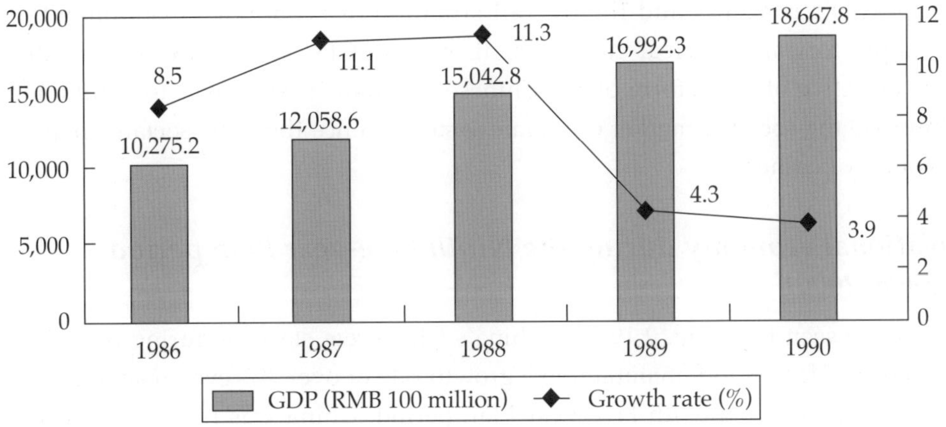

Fig. 2.18. GDP and its growth rate in China (1991–1995)

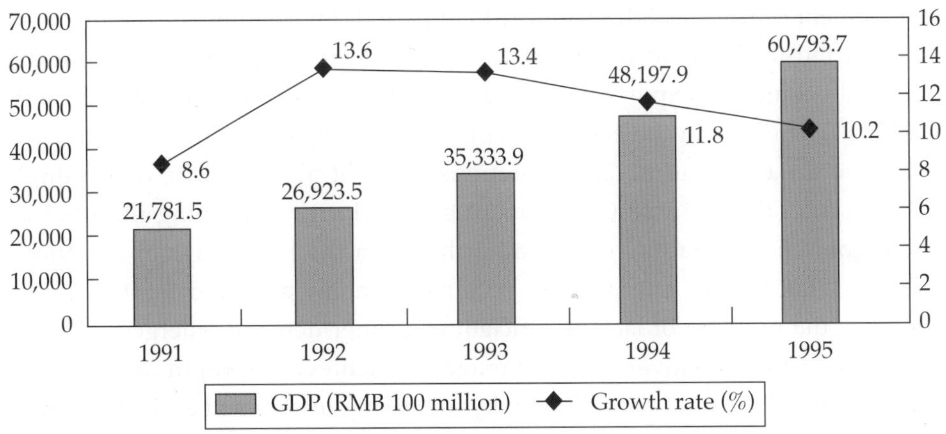

National economy during the Eighth Five-year Plan period (1991–1995)

The reform and opening up in China was promoted at the fastest speed during the Eighth Five-year Plan period, being the fastest of all countries around the world over the same period. The average annual growth rate of GDP reached 12%, showing a high-speed steady development. It was also a period of the fastest economic growth and least economic fluctuations since the foundation of the People's Republic of China (see Fig. 2.18). The 8th Five-year Plan period was developed against the background of the rapid growth of China's national economy and the rectification of the economic environment during the 1980s, aiming at establishing an economic system that integrated the planned economy with market regulation. However, the speech made by Deng Xiaoping during his inspection of South China in 1992 and the convening of the 14th CPC

National Congress in October in the same year contributed to the great changes in people's concepts and the overall situation of economic development. It was put forward, in clear-cut terms, at the 14th CPC National Congress, that the objective of the reform of the Chinese economic system was to "build and improve the socialist market economic system". Since then, the socialist market economy boomed.

National economy during the Ninth Five-year Plan period (1996–2000)

It can be seen from Fig. 2.19 that China's GDP grew steadily during the Ninth Five-year Plan period, maintaining a growth rate of over 7%, even reaching 9.7% in 1996. Entering the 9th Five-year Plan period, China was faced with severe domestic and foreign situations in its economic development: domestically, a relatively high inflation rate appeared due to the rapid social and economic development during the 8th Five-year Plan period; internationally, the financial crisis started in Thailand in 1997 spread and affected the entire Asia quickly, greatly shocking the exports, foreign capital utilization and economic growth of China. Therefore, in the early days of the 9th Five-year Plan period, to curb and solve the outstanding contradictions brought about by the overly-high inflation rate, the Chinese Government gave priority to curbing inflation in macroeconomic regulation; on the other hand, in the latter days of the Ninth Five-year Plan period, after China's national economy achieved "soft landing" smoothly, the problem of lacking efficient consumer demand emerged. In view of this, the Chinese Government managed to achieve the rapid and healthy development of the national economy by increasing investment and stimulating consumption.

Fig. 2.19. GDP and its growth rate in China (1996–2000)

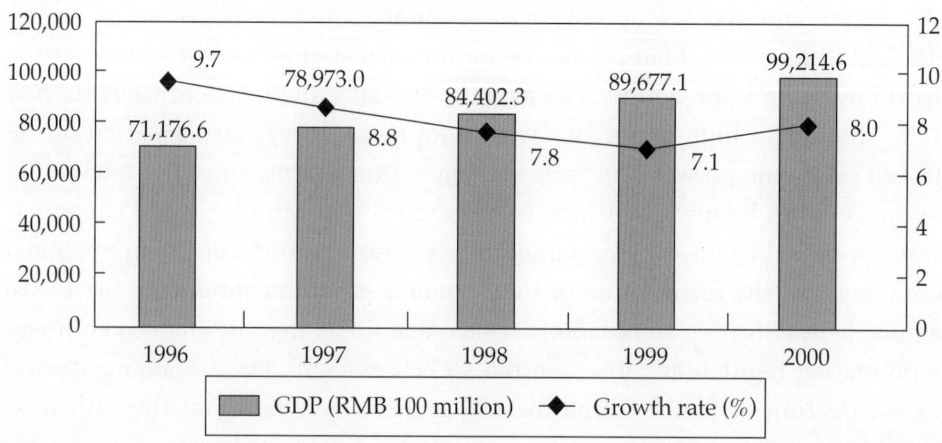

Development period in the twenty-first century (2001 to present)

The GDP growth rate in China has showed a new round of growth momentum and a state of steady development since 2001 (see Fig. 2.20). After entering the 21st century, China provided in its 10th Five-year Plan that the government should no longer dominate resource allocation, and that the market should play its essential role in resource allocation. With the development of the market economy, the macroeconomic control and regulatory capability of the Communist Party of China and the Chinese Government over the national economy as the whole has been improved significantly. In the report to its Sixteenth national congress, the Communist Party of China proposed to deepen the understanding of the rules of the socialist market economy, give full play to the fundamental role of the market in resource allocation, improve the basic economic system and market system, and deepen fiscal, financial and other institutional reforms. In October 2003, the Third Plenary Session of the 16th CPC National Congress adopted the *Decision of the Central Committee of the Communist Party of China on Several Issues concerning the Improvement of the System of the Socialist Market Economy*, putting forward, in clear-cut terms, the objectives, tasks, guiding ideology and principles of improving the system of the socialist market economy. In 2007, the Communist Party of China pointed out, in its report to the 17th CPC National Congress, that the key to achieve the future objectives of economic development was to make great progresses in transforming the mode of economic development and improving the system of the socialist market economy. The correct guiding ideology and principles of the Communist Party of China has enabled the Chinese economy to be particularly strong in this period and capable of withstanding trials and hardships, and achieved a steady development in a not-brisk global economic environment.[2]

Fig. 2.20. GDP and its growth rate in China (2001–2007)

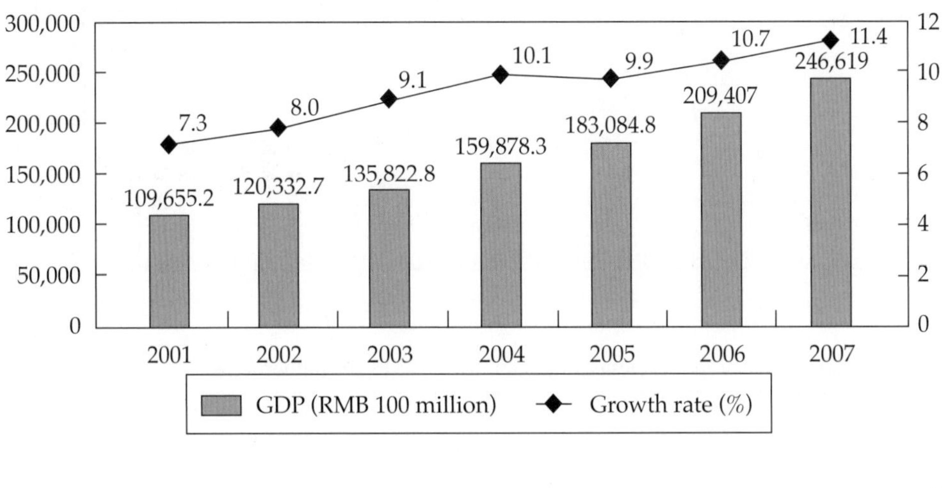

Status and contribution of the wholesale trade in the national economy

In the history of business development, the emergence of the wholesale trade was a natural result of the requirement on extending and intensifying commodity circulation, and effectively distributing commodities in circulation, and necessary division of social specialty carried out in accordance with the rules of the average rate of profits. With the development of the national economy, the wholesale trade, as the main part of the circulation industry, is playing a more and more important leading role.[3]

Status and contribution of the added value of the wholesale trade in and to the national economy

Since the statistic criteria on the added value of the wholesale trade was unavailable, and the development of the wholesale trade was closely related to and highly identical with the development of the entire industry, the added value of the wholesale and retail trade[4] is adopted here to observe its economic status.

Added value of the wholesale and retail trade

As shown in Fig. 2.21, significant progresses had been made in the wholesale and retail trade during the three decades of reform and opening up in China. The added value of the wholesale and retail trade increased from RMB 1,816.95 billion to 24.23 billion in 1978, increasing by 74 times.

Fig. 2.21. Added value and its growth rate of the wholesale and retail trade (1978–2007)

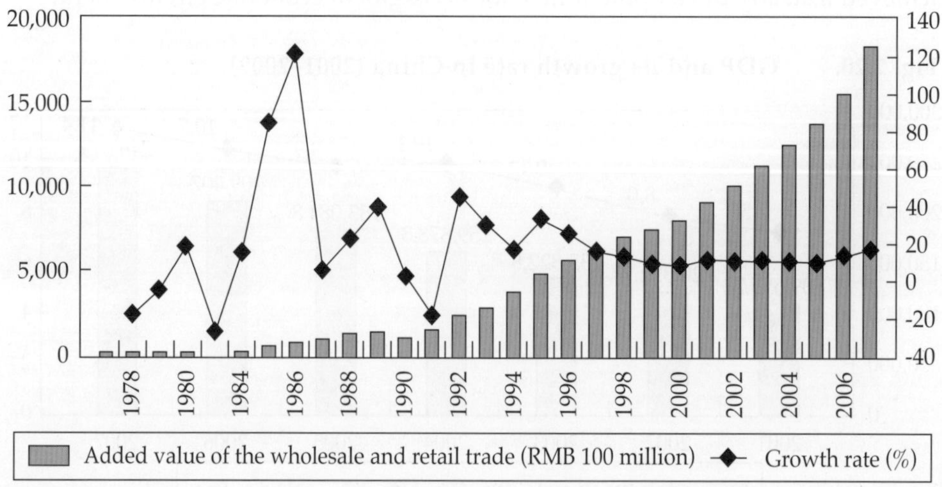

Seen from the changing trend of the growth rate, that of the added value of the wholesale and retail trade and that of GDP have been similar. From the early days of the reform and opening up to the convening of the 14th CPC National Congress, changes in the growth rate were great, the peak of which appeared in 1985, reaching 120%. The two significant troughs appeared in 1982 and 1990, respectively. Since 1994, the growth rate of the added value of the wholesale and retail trade has become very stable, varying between 10–20%. Though the growth rate shows a declining tendency, the total amount of the added value of the wholesale and retail trade has kept increasing, which is consistent with the process and tendency of the development of the wholesale trade analyzed in the previous section. In particular, the appearance of the peak and troughs of the growth rate is closely related to and highly consistent with the concurrent macroeconomic situation and the restructuring of the commercial economy.

Status of the wholesale and retail trade in the national economy

Firstly, it can be seen from Fig. 2.22 that the proportion of the added value of the wholesale and retail trade in GDP kept increasing before being maintained at 8% since the 1990s. Referring to Fig. 2.21, we can see that the proportion of the added value of the wholesale and retail trade was highly coincident with the development of GDP. Both had experienced great fluctuations prior to the 1990s, namely in the early days of the reform and opening up, but showed a high degree of stability entering the 1990s.

Fig. 2.22. Ratio of the added value of the wholesale and retail trade to GDP (1978–2007)

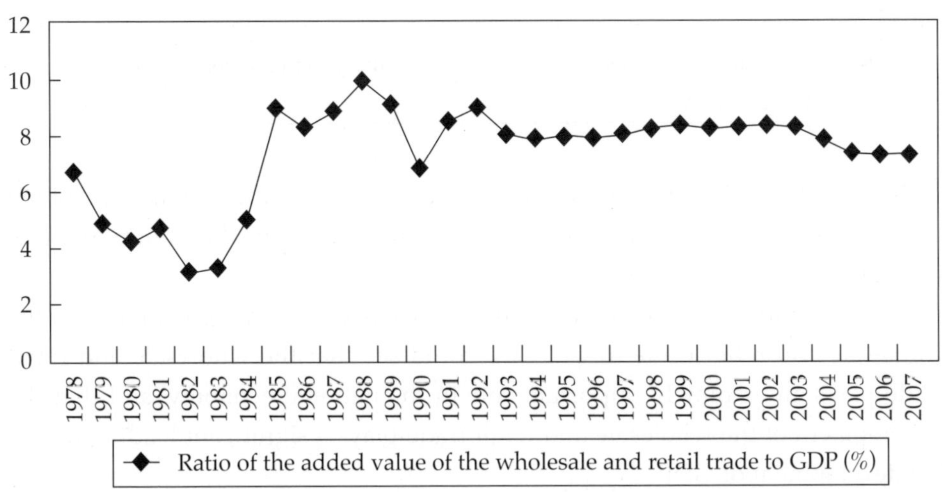

Degree of contribution of the wholesale and retail trade to the national economy

Seen from Fig. 2.23, the contribution rate had fluctuated greatly prior to 1992, then became relatively steady in the latter part of the 1990s, the growth trend of which was very similar to that of GDP on the whole, indicating a high goodness of the contribution rate of the wholesale and retail trade to the national economy and the growth rate of GDP. In addition, the contribution rate of the wholesale and retail trade to the national economy had an amplification effect on the GDP growth rate. A tiny fluctuation of GDP corresponded to a high contribution rate of the wholesale and retail trade. When the GDP growth rate was high, the contribution rate of the wholesale and retail trade would be even higher; when the GDP growth rate reduced, the contribution rate of the wholesale and retail trade would reduce more, which demonstrates once again the role of the wholesale and retail trade in leading the national economy.

Fig. 2.23. Contribution of the added value of the wholesale trade to GDP

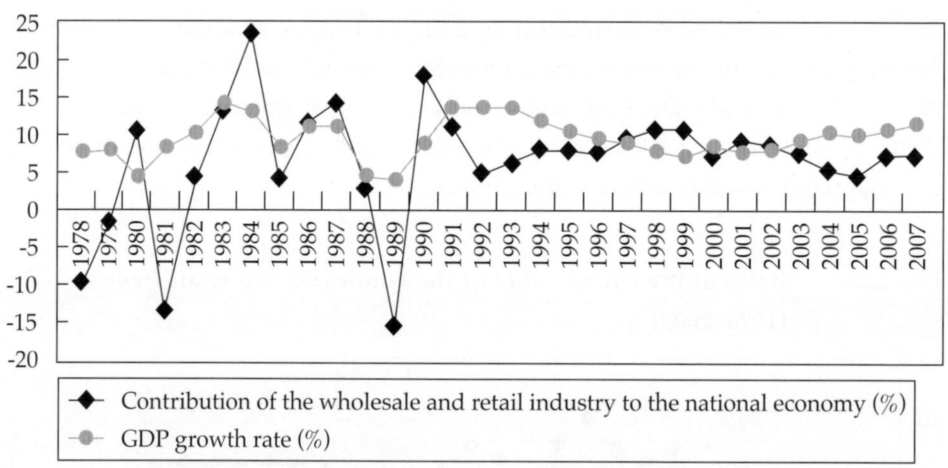

Note: Industrial contribution rate refers to the ratio of the incremental added value of respective industry and the increment of GDP. In this figure, the rate was calculated at the current year price.

From the ratio of the wholesale and retail trade to and the contribution of the wholesale and retail trade to GDP, we could see that the wholesale and retail trade plays an extremely important role in the national economy, and that the development of the wholesale and retail trade plays a significant leading role in the development of GDP.

Status and contribution of the added value of the wholesale trade in and to the tertiary industry

The wholesale trade connects manufacturers with retailers and plays an important role in the smooth circulation of commodities. The author will investigate the status of the wholesale trade, an important sub-industry of the tertiary industry, below and its contribution to the tertiary industry. Since the added value of the wholesale trade hasn't been calculated separately, the added value of the wholesale and retail trade will be adopted to investigate the development trend of the wholesale trade.

Status of the added value of the wholesale and retail trade in the tertiary industry

From Fig. 2.24, we can see that the ratio of the wholesale and retail trade kept declining, having been maintained at 20% gradually since the 1990s. Referring to the figure about the ratio of the added value of the wholesale and retail trade to the national GDP, we may find that the ratio of the added value of the wholesale trade in the tertiary industry to the GDP of the tertiary industry and that in the national GDP presented a high goodness. Both had experienced great fluctuations prior to the 1990s, namely in the early days of the reform and opening up, but showed a high degree of stability entering the 1990s.

Fig. 2.24. Respective ratio of all trades of the tertiary industry to the GDP of the tertiary industry (1978–2007)

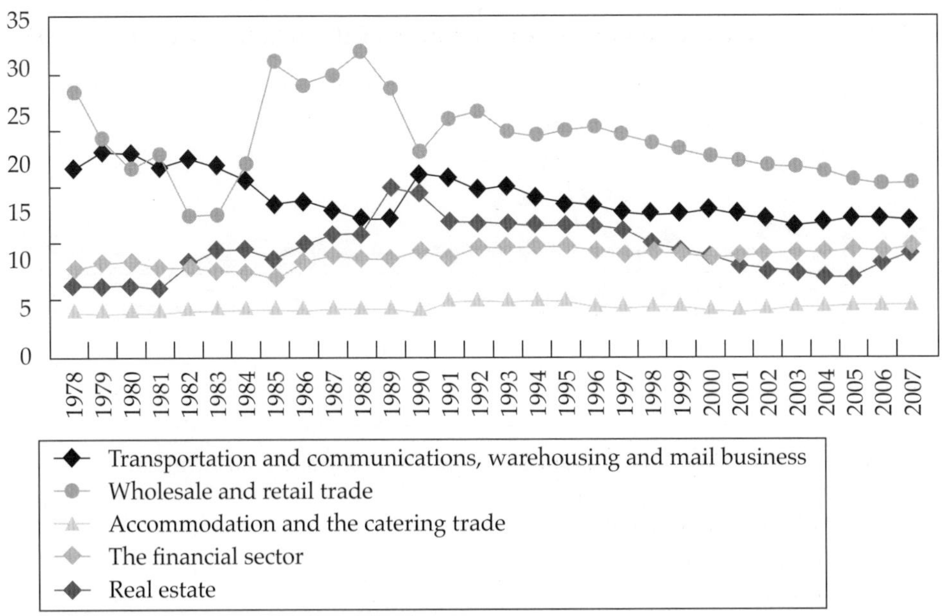

Comparing with that of other trades of the tertiary industry, the proportion of the added value of the wholesale and retail trade in the GDP of the tertiary industry in the early and later days of the reform and opening up was undoubtedly the highest of all. From the perspective of the proportion fluctuation, it can be seen that the goodness between the added value of the wholesale and retail trade and the GDP growth rate was higher than that of other trades. That is to say, during the previous two waves of economic fluctuations in China, the wholesale and retail trade was greatly influenced, leading to significant fluctuations, too. Since 1991, as the Chinese economy became more and more stable, the development of all trades, including the wholesale and retail trade, and the respective ratio of their added value to the GDP became more and more steady, too.

Contribution of the added value of the wholesale and retail trade to the tertiary industry

From the contribution rates of different trades listed in Fig. 2.25, as far as the tertiary industry is concerned, the contribution rate of the wholesale and retail trade was of great fluctuation, making it one of the most fluctuating trades therein. What's different was that the average contribution rate of the wholesale and retail trade to the tertiary industry was close to 20%, being the highest of that of all trades. It fully demonstrated that the wholesale and retail trade was the leading trade of the tertiary industry, the development level of which fully represented the development level of the tertiary industry.

Fig. 2.25. Contribution of the added value of the wholesale trade to GDP

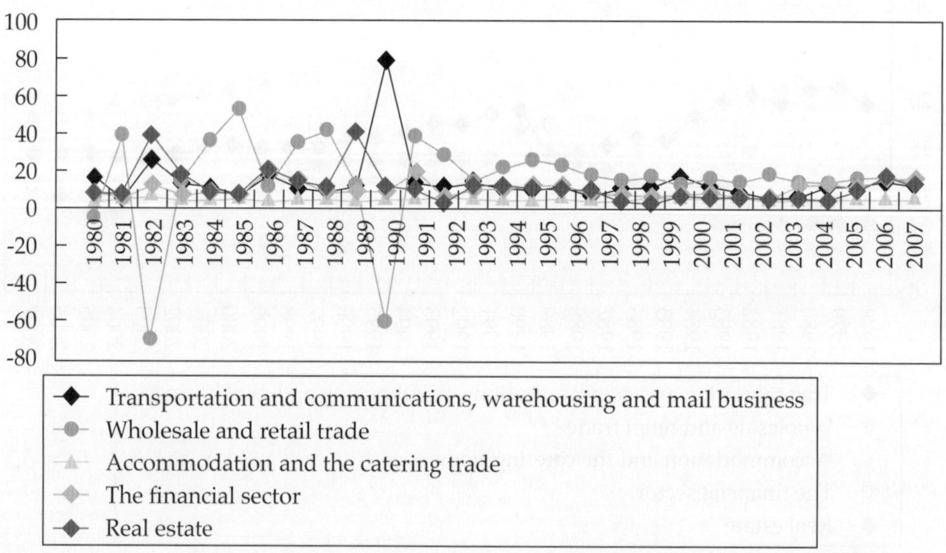

Therefore, the wholesale and retail trade played an important role in the tertiary industry, the rapid development of which led the development of the tertiary industry. Paying attention to the development of the wholesale and retail trade is the only way of accelerating the development of the tertiary industry.

National status and contribution of the wholesale trade employment

In a populous nation like China, economic development is inseparable from the employment of the working people. Comparatively, the efficiency of rural labor force is low; industries and the building trade have low requirements on the quality of labor force; and the tertiary industry has relatively greater superiority. On the one hand, its technical content is high; on the other hand, it creates a higher value. What's more, the tertiary industry has an enormous potential for absorbing a large number of labor force. 30 years of development has also proven that the tertiary industry, including the wholesale and retail trade, is an important force that guarantees the labor force in China to get employed. The status in and contribution to the national team of employees of the number of wholesale and retail employees is investigated as follows through year-end number of on-post staff and workers.[5]

Number of year-end on-post staff and workers in the wholesale and retail trade

It can bee seen clearly from Fig. 2.26 that number of year-end on-post staff and workers in the wholesale and retail trade changed in a significantly phased way: 1985–1992; 1993–1997 and 1998–2007. Since data changed in a consistent way, it can be predicted that the statistic criteria changed. During 1985–1992, the number of year-end on-post staff and workers in the wholesale and retail trade showed a tendency of steady development, increasing from 15.755 billion in 1985 to 19.464 million in 1992, maintaining a growth rate of about 3%. It reached the highest point in 1988, being 4.3%. During 1993–1997, the number of year-end on-post staff and workers in the wholesale and retail trade showed a declining tendency, falling from 18.33 million in 1994 to 17.74 million in 1997, the annual declining rate of which was 1%. In 1998, since the number of on-post staff and workers of the wholesale and retail enterprises above the designated size was calculated, the same number changed greatly. It can be seen from Fig. 2.26 that during 1998–2007, the number of on-post staff and workers of the wholesale and retail enterprises below the designated size kept reducing, from 12.56 million in 1998 to 4.794 million in 2007, being a great fall.

Fig. 2.26. China's GDP and its growth rate in the three decades of reform and opening up (1978–2007)

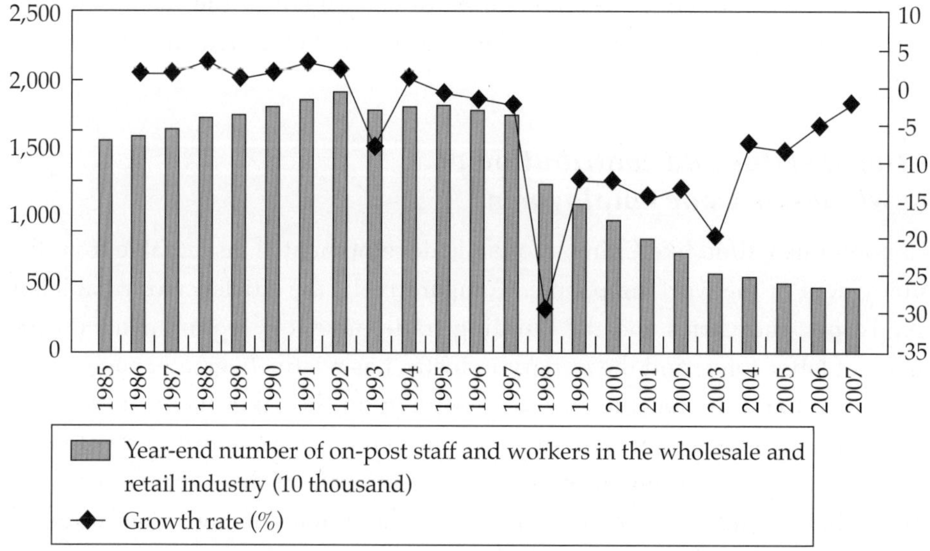

It can be seen from the above development tendency of the GDP of the wholesale and retail trade that the wholesale and retail trade kept expanding. Therefore, the main reason for the reduction of the number of employees in the wholesale and retail trade in the same period was thought to be the introduction of advanced operational and management technologies, which enabled the wholesale and retail trade to focus on controlling the cost. In particular, the application of various advanced automated technologies enabled the wholesale and retail enterprises to expand without requiring more practitioners.

National status of the employees of the wholesale and retail trade

From Fig. 2.27, it can be seen that changes in the ratio of the year-end number of on-post staff and workers in the wholesale and retail trade to the national total were consistent with those in the ratio of the year-end number of on-post staff and workers in the wholesale and retail trade, and could also be divided into 3 stages: 1985–1992, 1993–1997 and 1998–2007. The ratio was very stable in the previous 2 stages, maintaining at over 12%, but began to keep dropping since 1998, falling from 10% in 1998 to 4.2% in 2007.

Comparing with that of other trades of the tertiary industry, the proportion of the year-end number of staff and workers in the wholesale and retail trade had begun to be lower than that of transportation and communications, warehousing and mail businesses, but still higher than that of the financial trade and the real estate trade.

Fig. 2.27. Ratio of the year-end number of staff and workers in the tertiary industry to the national total year-end number of staff and workers (1985–2007)

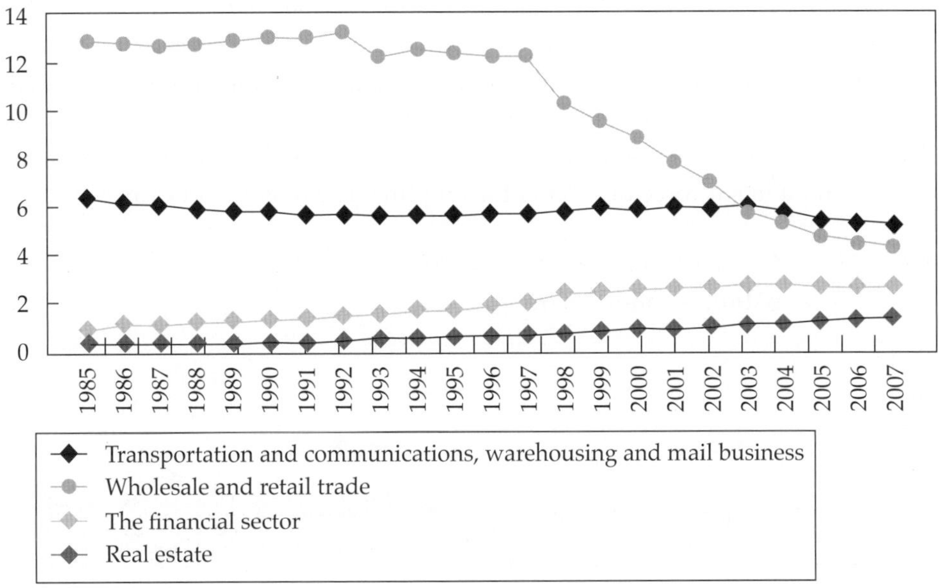

Besides the change in the statistical criteria, the continued declining of the number of the staff and workers of the wholesale and retail trade was also an important reason for the changes in the year-end number of on-post staff and workers in the wholesale and retail trade.

Contribution of the employed people in the wholesale and retail trade to national employment

From Fig. 2.28, we can see that of the trades of the tertiary industry, the change in the employment contribution rate of the wholesale and retail trade was the greatest of all. First of all, prior to 2003, the employment contribution rate of the wholesale and retail trade was higher than that of other trades, which even reached 45.7% in 2002. After 2003, due to the adoption of new industrial standards, its contribution rate to national employment was negative, which even reached -49% in 2004. Since then, the number of staff and workers maintained relatively stable, and the absolute value of its negative contribution rate to national employment became increasingly smaller.

It is clear that the contribution rates of different trades to national employment would change, too, only on a small scale. Changes in the respective year-end number of on-post staff and workers in each and all trades were closely related to the then development of the national economy, development policies and situation of the trade. For example, due to the development of the real estate business in 2004, its contribution rate jumped.

Both the proportion and the contribution rate of the year-end number of on-post staff and workers in the wholesale and retail trade kept declining, yet the trade was highly labor-intensive. With the further development of the wholesale and retail trade, it will need more labor force to provide services for consumers. Therefore, the considerable amount of posts created by the wholesale and retail trade is still a major force in solving the employment pressure of China.

Fig. 2.28. Contribution rate of all trades of the tertiary industry to national employment

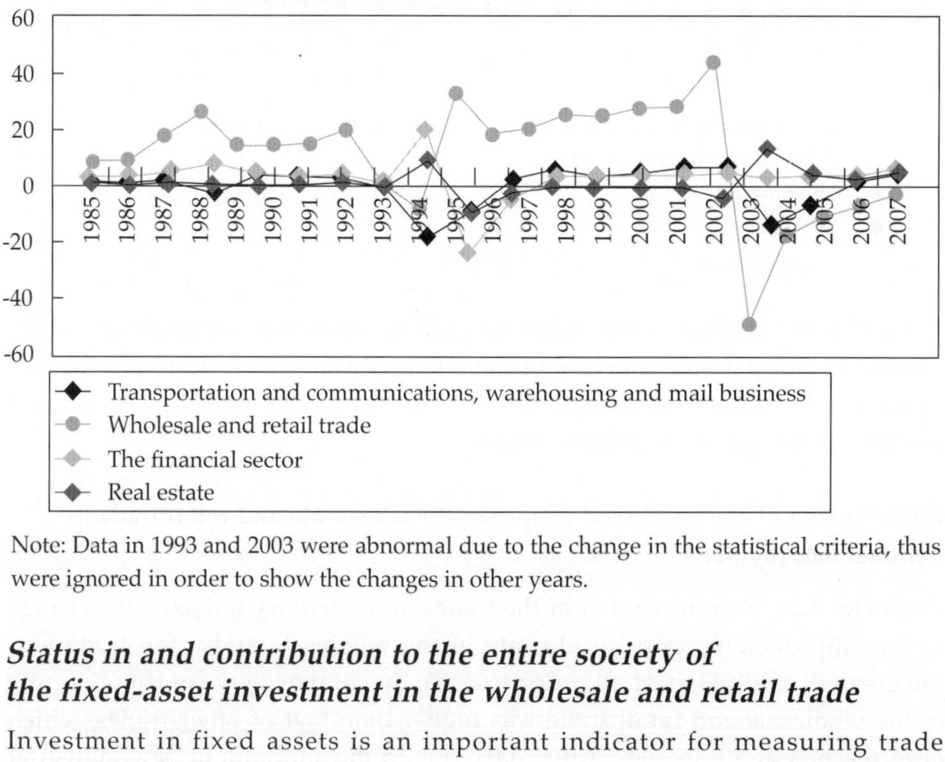

Note: Data in 1993 and 2003 were abnormal due to the change in the statistical criteria, thus were ignored in order to show the changes in other years.

Status in and contribution to the entire society of the fixed-asset investment in the wholesale and retail trade

Investment in fixed assets is an important indicator for measuring trade development. The status, contribution and development scale of the wholesale trade in the national economy will be investigated through the ratio of the fixed-asset investment in the wholesale and retail trade to the total social investment in fixed assets.

Fixed-asset investment in the wholesale and retail trade

As shown in Fig. 2.29, the fixed-asset investment in the wholesale and retail trade grew significantly during 1996–2007, increasing from RMB 53 billion in 1996 to 288 billion in 2007, increasing by more than four times. In terms of the development trend of its growth rate, the fixed-asset investment in the wholesale and retail trade developed slowly before 2004, the growth rate of which was about 10%, even dropped by 12.5%. However, it had begun a new round of growth at a rate of over 25% since 2004, being accelerated.

Fig. 2.29. Total social investment in fixed assets of the wholesale and retail trade (1996–2007)

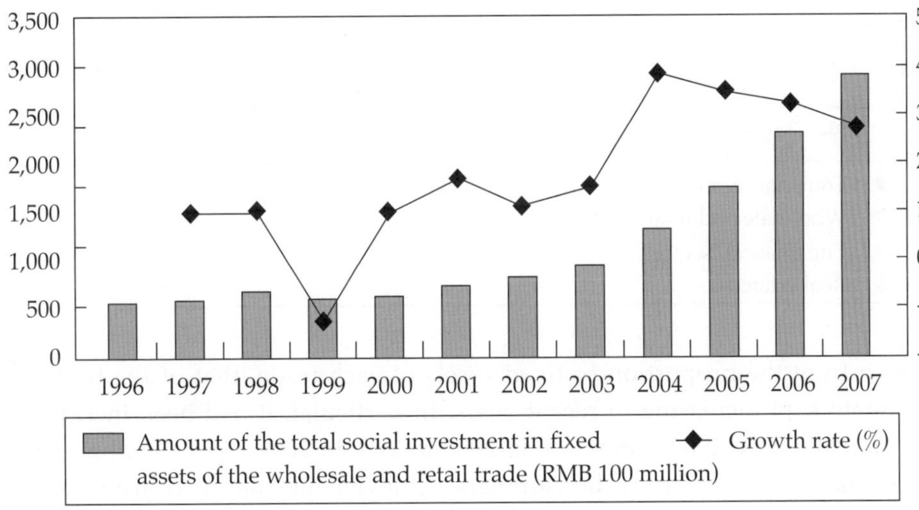

There was a close relationship between the growth trend of the fixed assets of the wholesale and retail trade and the reduction of the requirements for foreign capital to enter the Chinese wholesale and retail trade after China's accession to the WTO. Apart from the accelerated entry of foreign capital into the Chinese market, various domestic investors also increased their investment in the wholesale and retail trade, expecting for the wholesale and retail market shares. What's more, the size of capital investment made by foreign-invested enterprises was relatively large, improving the investment in fixed assets of the wholesale and retail trade.

Social status of the fixed-asset investment in the wholesale and retail trade

As shown in Fig. 2.30, the ratio of the total social fixed assets of the wholesale and retail trade to the nationwide fixed assets was very stable, fluctuating at about 2% during 1996–2007, to the highest percentage of 2.3% in 1997 and the lowest percentage of 1.7% in 2003.

Fig. 2.30. Ratio of the fixed-asset investment in each trade of the tertiary industry to nationwide fixed-asset investment (1996–2007)

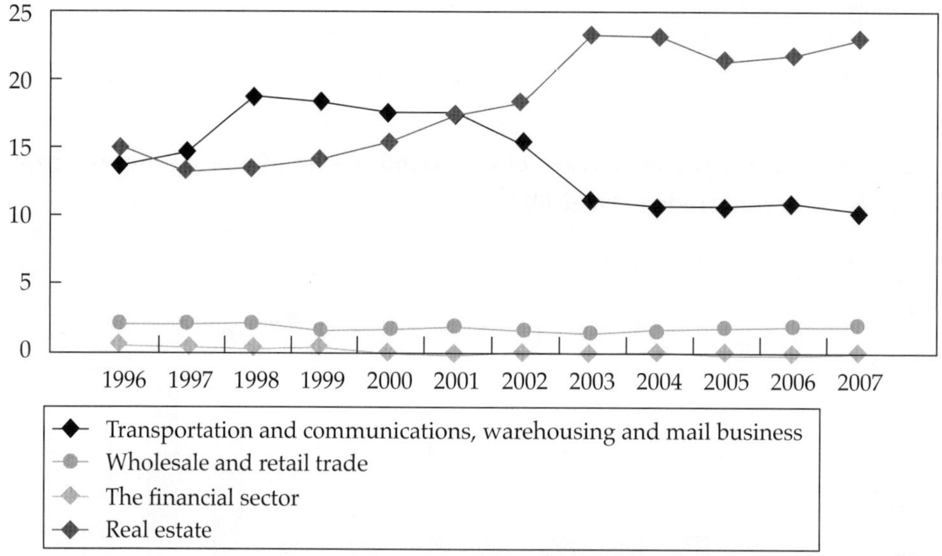

Seen from the proportion of fixed assets of each trade, that of the trade of real estate kept increasing in recent years. In particular, it had been increasing very quickly since 2000, from 16% in 2000 to 24% in 2007, up 8% within eight years, making a significant development achievement; that of transportation and communications, warehousing and mail business showed evident development stages and kept declining; and that of the financial trade was even lower. To sum up, the wholesale and retail trade held a relatively stable position in the construction of fixed assets of different sectors.

Contribution of the investment in fixed assets of the wholesale and retail trade to the entire society

As shown in Fig. 2.31, the contribution rate of the fixed-asset investment in the wholesale and retail trade to the nationwide fixed assets was not high, but even negative sometimes. It reflected the growth stability of the fixed assets of the wholesale and retail trade on the one hand, and demonstrated that the nature of the wholesale and retail trade had determined its small demand for investment in fixed assets on the other hand.

Comparatively, the contribution rate of the fixed-asset investment in the real estate trade was the greatest and most fluctuating of the four trades listed, which was consistent with the development situation of the real estate trade; that of transportation and communications, warehousing and mail business was generally great, yet fluctuating; while that of the financial trade and of the wholesale and retail trade were similar. Clearly, trades each with larger investment in fixed assets had higher contribution rates, yet were very fluctuating.

Therefore, the wholesale trade held an important position in the national economy, and its contribution to the GDP kept increasing. Since it is highly labor-intensive, it is an important way of solving the problem of employment in China. Moreover, seen from the growth trend of fixed assets, the fixed assets of the wholesale trade kept increasing, too. The wholesale trade is thus the leading trade of the national economy, playing an irreplaceable role in the development of the national economy.

Fig. 2.31. National contribution rate of the fixed-asset investment in all trades of the tertiary industry (1997–2007)

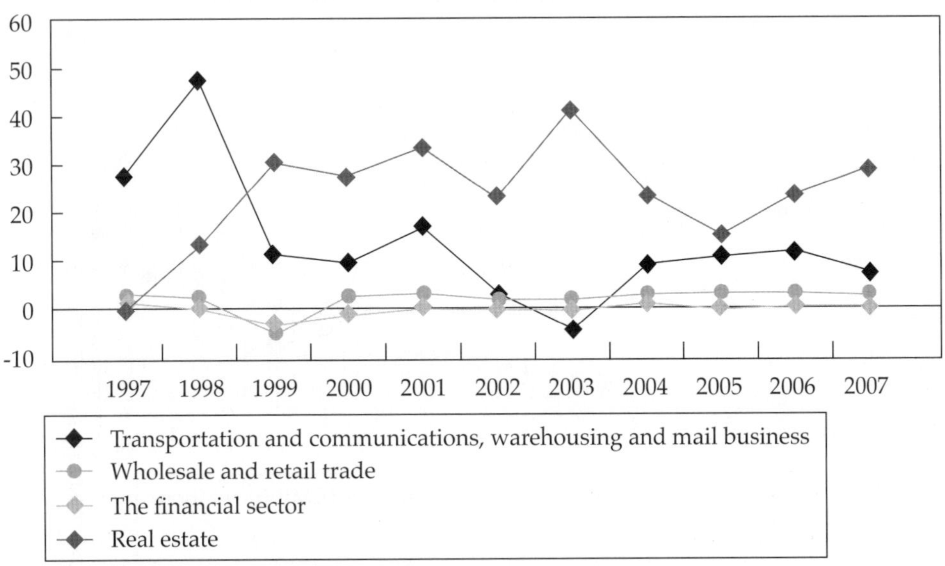

Contribution of the Wholesale Trade to Commerce

Commerce, consisting of wholesale commerce and retail commerce, used to be put under the most rigid management during the planned economy period. Though with the most significant features of the planned economy, commerce is the field in which China firstly launched the reform and opening up policy in the new period. With three decades of baptism of the reform and opening up, the Chinese commerce has achieved an enormous development and witnessed profound changes.

Development of the Chinese commerce in the three decades of reform and opening up

Firstly, the development of the Chinese commerce in the three decades of reform and opening up will be observed through the total volume of retail sales of social consumables.[6]

It can be seen clearly from Fig. 2.32 that the total volume of retail sales of social consumables, a direct reflector of the size of commerce, was increasing on the whole. It was RMB 155.9 billion in 1978 before growing to RMB 8,921 billion in 2007, increasing by 56.2 times at an average annual growth rate of over 15%. However, there were great changes in the increase, showing distinct stages. The development process and characteristics of the commerce in different stages will be analyzed below in accordance with historical facts, then a preliminary analysis of the reasons.

Fig. 2.32. Total volume of retail sales of social consumables (1978–2007)

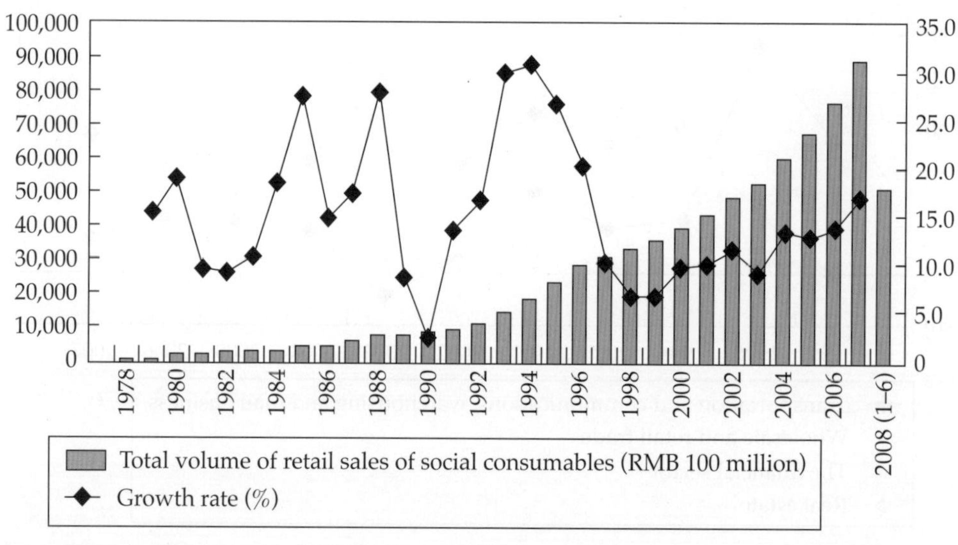

From the initial launch of the reform and opening up to the end of the Sixth Five-year Plan period (1978–1985)

The period during 1978–1985 saw the early transformation of the commercial economic departments in China into commercial enterprises, as well as the completion of the construction during the 6th Five-year Plan period. Reforms during this period focused on the rural areas. Since the reform objectives of the circulation system of agricultural products hadn't be clarified and commercial departments in many places were still in exploration, reform of commercial enterprises was blind. Commercial enterprises in Shenzhen Special Economic

Zone, a district in the frontier of reform, took the lead in carrying out the reform, having a significant demonstrative effect on other places in China.

As shown in Fig. 2.33, the total volume of retail sales of social consumables was developing steadily in this period. There was a greater increase or, to be more specifically, an explosive increase, in commerce in 1980, because China set up special economic zones in Guangdong province and Fujian province in that year, releasing the long depressed commodity circulation. However, such increase was often overdrawn in advance, laying a basis for the declining of the growth rate of commerce in the year that followed.

Fig. 2.33. Number of wholesale practitioners (1978–1984)

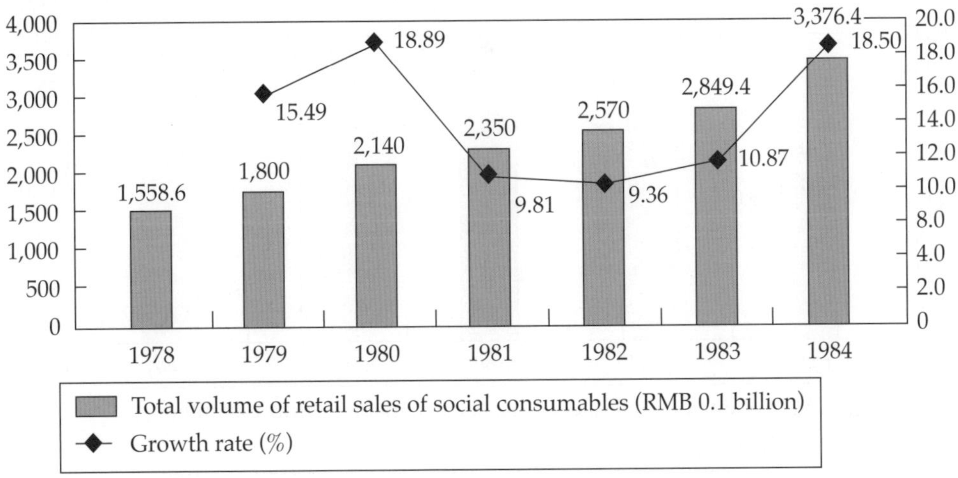

The period during 1982–1985 witnessed the continue increase in the growth rate of the total amount of retail sales of social consumables. Such abnormal increase in commerce was caused by the deepening of the reform of the circulation system on the one hand: in 1984, China began to launch trials of expanding the right of management of state-owned commercial enterprises, the two-step "substitution of tax payment for profit delivery", the contracting system, the leasing system, and the breaking of the traditional circulation system featured by "three fixeds", contributing to the enthusiasm of social commodity transactions; and by the price reform over the same period on the other hand: the implementation of the dual-track system of the means of production in 1984, the full liberalization of prices of agricultural and sideline products and light industrial products in January 1985, the transfer of some powers of the central authorities to local authorities, and the implementation of the "overall rationing system" by local finances had led to a serious expansion of the purchasing power of social groups, promoting the rapid growth of the total amount of retail sales of social consumables.

National economy during the 17th Five-year Plan period (1986–1990)

Economic restructuring in China entered a turbulent period in development during 1986–1990. This period, an extraordinary history in the process of reform and opening up in China, witnessed the initial victory and repeated setbacks.

Radical changes in the growth rate showed that it was a period of great turbulences: the growth rate reached 28% in 1988 and dropped to 2.5% in 1990 (see Fig. 2.34).

Fig. 2.34. Total volume of retail sales of social consumables (1986–1990)

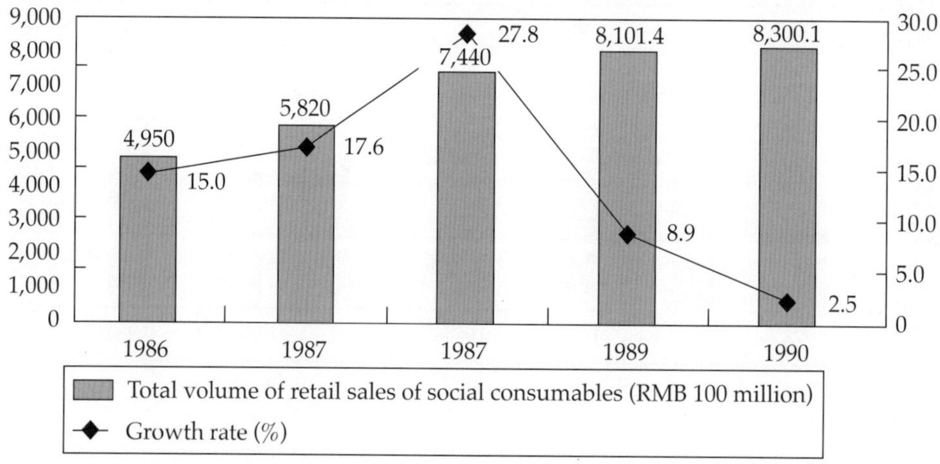

The growth of the total volume of retail sales of social consumables accelerated significantly during 1986–1987, being higher than not only the growth rate of the number of commercial practitioners and the total commercial capital, but also that of the national economy, commodity market and people's livelihood.

In 1988, due to the overheating economy and excessive demand, inflation accelerated significantly, prices rose greatly, and market fluctuations became more and more frequent. Various commercial reforms and the self-construction causes continued developing throughout the year, and the total volume of retail sales of social consumables grew in an abnormal way. The year-round volume of retail sales of social consumables reached RMB 744 billion, up 27.8% year on year, which was not only the highest of all since the foundation of the People's Republic of China, but also far higher than the growth rate of the per capita disposable income for subsistence of urban and rural residents (22.2%) and that of the per capita net income of rural residents (17.7%). In 1989, influenced by the demand inertia in the first half of the year, sales of most commodities were still prosperous, yet the growth rate was reduced significantly year on year. In the process of furthering the control and rectification and deepening reforms, China adopted a series of major measures such as controlling the economic aggregate, timely adjusting the degree of economic tightening, and positively improving the economic structure, greatly influencing the growth rate of the total volume of retail sales of social consumables, up only 2.5% year on year and being more or less the same over the previous year allowing for price rises.

During the Eighth Five-year Plan period (1991–1995)

It was during this period that the 14th CPC National Congress was held. Encouraged by the important speech made by Deng Xiaoping during his inspection of South China and the spirit of the 14th CPC National Congress, reform and opening up and economic construction in China entered a new phase of accelerated development. The domestic market was stable and prosperous, reforms were intensified, outstanding achievements were made in all fields of work, and the Chinese commerce presented a gratifying situation on the whole.

During this period, the growth of the total volume of retail sales of social consumables was extraordinary, at a high rate of over 10%, which even reached 30.5% in 1994.

In 1991, the domestic market continued showing a tendency of stable growth, and the total volume of retail sales of social consumables grew in a balanced way at a rate of 13.4%. Encouraged by the important speech made by Deng Xiaoping during his inspection of South China in 1992 and the spirit of the 14th CPC National Congress, the Chinese people further emancipated their mind, changed past concepts, sped up the reform, and widened the opening up to the outside world, contributing to the new progresses made in commodity circulation. It was in 1993 that the circulation industry withstood tests and accelerated development in a complicated market environment, and that major reforms of the commodity circulation system were launched. Therefore, the year 1993 marked the entry of the Chinese circulation reform and development into a new stage. In 1994, the consumer goods market showed a development trend of becoming flourishing. The year-round total volume of retail sales of social consumables reached RMB 1,862.29 billion, up 30.5% over the previous year. The great development momentum continued in 1995 when the year-round total volume of retail sales of social consumables reached RMB 2,361.38 billion, up 27% over the previous year (see Fig. 2.35).

Fig. 2.35. Total volume of retail sales of social consumables (1991–1995)

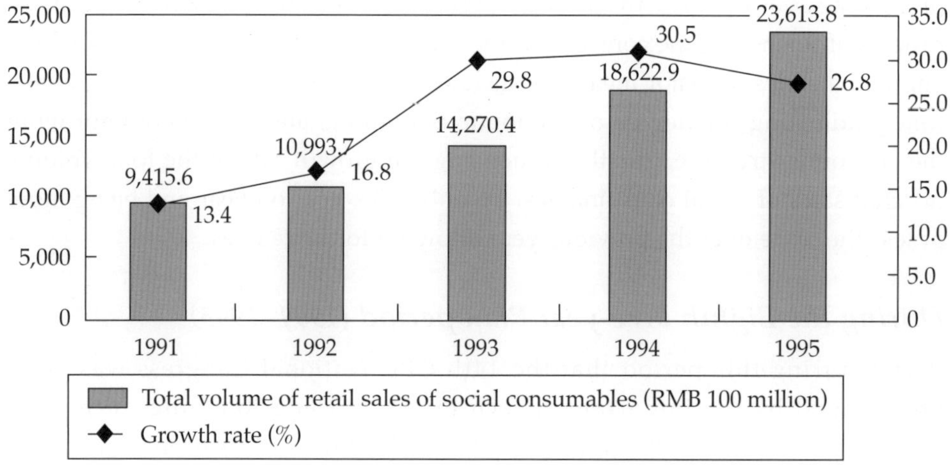

During the Ninth Five-year Plan period (1996–2000)

The total volume of retail sales of social consumables kept growing steadily during this period, yet at a declining rate. The situation of the domestic commodity market was fine, the market was prosperous, both purchasing and marketing were brisk, the commodity price was stable, the growth rate dropped, and the elimination of fake commodities had also achieved periodical results.

Growth rate of the total volume of retail sales of social consumables plummeted over the previous stage. Apart from reaching 20.1% in 1996 due to the continuation of the growth inertia in the previous stage, the same growth rate was below 10% in other years.

In view of the domestic and foreign economic situations, major task in this period was to take under control inflation and maintain a steady development. After intensifying the implementation of the macroeconomic regulation measures in 1996, Chin saw a good situation of "high-growth and low-inflation" national economy. However, the growth of the sales of the consumer goods market slowed down. Though a few commodities were fast-selling, the consumption of most commodities wasn't prosperous. In 1998, the total volume of retail sales of social consumables reached 3,337.8 billion RMB, a nominal growth of 6.8% over the previous year. The growth rate dropped 3.4%. In face of the increasingly fierce competitions on the consumer goods market, having sales became one of the main competitive methods among businesses and manufacturers. Though influenced by the spread of the Asian financial crises, the world economic recession and the reduction of the domestic demand, the Chinese commodity market was still in the interval of smooth operation on the whole. In 1999, the Central Government of China took such measures as adopting positive fiscal policies, increasing fiscal expenditures, improving the income of low-income urban and rural residents, issuing additional national debts, and intensifying the construction of infrastructures, greatly stimulating the increase in consumer demands. To further expanding domestic demand, China issued a series of new policies to stimulate consumption in 2000, including lowering the deposit and lending rates for the seventh time, collecting interest tax, promoting credit consumption, and cleaning up and eliminating the belated policies on curbing consumption during inflation, which all promoted the consumer goods market to revive. The total volume of retail sales of social consumables hence increased significantly, the growth rate of which reached 9.7% (see Fig. 2.36).

Fig. 2.36. Total volume of retail sales of social consumables (1996–2000)

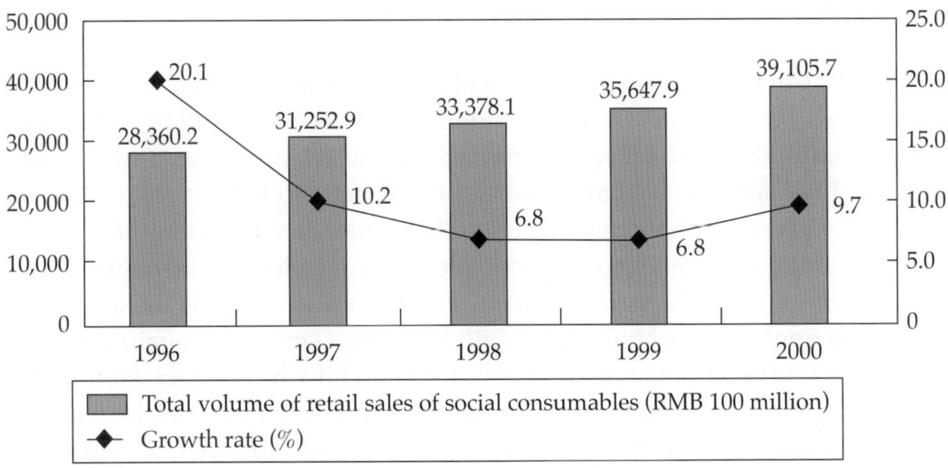

Development period in the 21st century (2001 to present)

It is a key period for China to construct the socialist market economy in a comprehensive way. The stable and rapid development of the national economy has stimulated the equally stable and rapid development of the commodity market. Under a series of policies on and measures for expanding domestic demands, the total volume of retail sales of social consumables has been moving forward steadily, the growth rate of which somewhat rises over the previous several years. Commodity market operation in this period is mainly credited to positive fiscal policies.

Apart from being 9.1% in 2003 under the influence of "SARS", the growth rate of the total amount of retail sales of social consumables in other years has been maintained above 10%, which even reached 16.8% (see Fig. 2.37).

Fig. 2.37. Total volume of retail sales of social consumables (2001–2007)

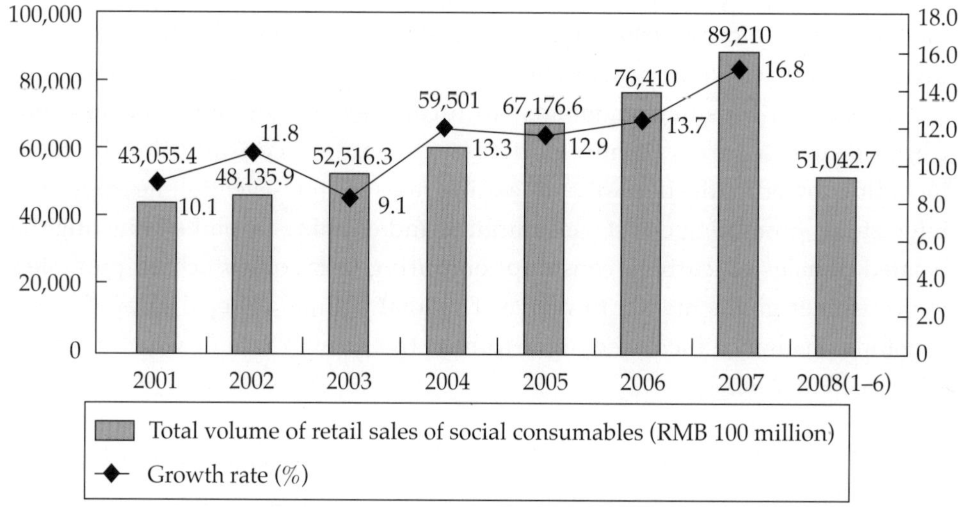

In 2001, China increased the salaries of public servants for twice, the amount of which was 30% greater. It began to double the salaries of public servants in the very last month of each year, improved the subsistence allowances of urban and rural residents, and accelerated the construction of the system of social securities, greatly enhancing consumers' confidence and strengthening the potential of the consumer goods market for achieving a high growth throughout the year. In addition, a series of major good news since 2001, including the success in applying for holding the 29th Olympic Games, the qualification of the men's football for the next round of game and China's accession to the WTO, have all brought about enormous business opportunities for various businesses. In 2002, the 16th CPC National Congress was held, at which the objective of improving the socialist market economy was established, injecting a strong force for the development of the commodity economy in China. A new round of economic development began in 2003, during which investment, production and exports all presented a tendency of rapid growth; the market demand for means of production was flourishing; and sales of autos, steel and metal, petroleum products, coals and rubber became hot, all contributing to the prosperity of the commodity market. In 2004, China fulfilled its commitments made by it at its accession to the WTO by liberalizing the restrictions on the entry of foreign capital into the Chinese wholesale trade, increasing the external pressures of competition of the circulation industry, and promoting the social circulation industry to develop fast. In 2005, the CPC Central Committee highlighted the important role of circulation in the outline of its 11th Five-year Plan. The Chinese economy developed in a steady and rapid way during

2006–2007. In particular, the prosperity of the capital market effectively promoted the consumption on the consumer goods market, contributing to the rise of the total volume of retail sales of social consumables to a new historic high.

To sum up, the development of commerce in China hasn't been always smooth, but gone through twists and turns, even reversals in the three decades of reform and opening up. However, it is undeniable that significant achievements have been made in developing the commerce, especially enlarging the size of commodity circulation, pushing the Chinese commerce to a new height and making important contribution to the development and progress of the Chinese economy and society and the overall advance of the reform and opening up.

Status in and contribution to commerce of the wholesale trade

Commerce consists of many trades. Generally, it involves the wholesale trade and the retail trade that are engaged in the organization of commodity operations, as well as the catering trade and the lodging trade that mainly provide labor forces. Since the reform and opening up, different trades of commerce have shown different development states. Some develop slowly, while others develop quickly. The entire industrial structure has been optimized along with economic restructuring. Of which, the wholesale trade accounts for a large proportion in commerce, and plays an irreplaceable role. The status of the wholesale trade in commerce will be analyzed below from such aspects as the sales volume of the wholesale and retail trade, the year-end number of on-post staff and workers in the wholesale trade, the fixed-asset investment in the wholesale trade, etc.

Status in and contribution to commerce of the sales volume of the wholesale trade

Since the sales volume of the wholesale trade was not calculated independently, the development trend of the wholesale trade in commerce is hereby investigated using the total volume of retail sales of social consumables of the wholesale and retail trade.

Total volume of retail sales of social consumables of the wholesale and retail trade

As can be see from Fig. 2.38, the wholesale and retail trade grew rapidly, being RMB 7,367.6 billion more in 2007 comparing with that in 1978, being 54 times greater. Comparing with the changes in the total volume of retail sales of social consumables, the total volume of retail sales of social consumables of the wholesale and retail trade was highly fitted with that of the entire society, both with fluctuations in the same years. Seen from the changes in the growth rate of the total volume of retail sales of social consumables of the wholesale and retail trade, it wasn't always smooth in the 30 years of reform and opening up, but went through a lot of ups and downs. In particular, prior to 1997, the growth rate of the total volume of retail sales of social consumables of the wholesale and retail trade had been very great, which even reached 37.5% in 1993 after falling to 2% in 1990. In addition, the same growth rate was very similar to that of GDP, fully demonstrating the judgment that the wholesale and retail trade is the leading trade of the national economy.

Fig. 2.38. Total volume of retail sales of social consumables (1978–2007)

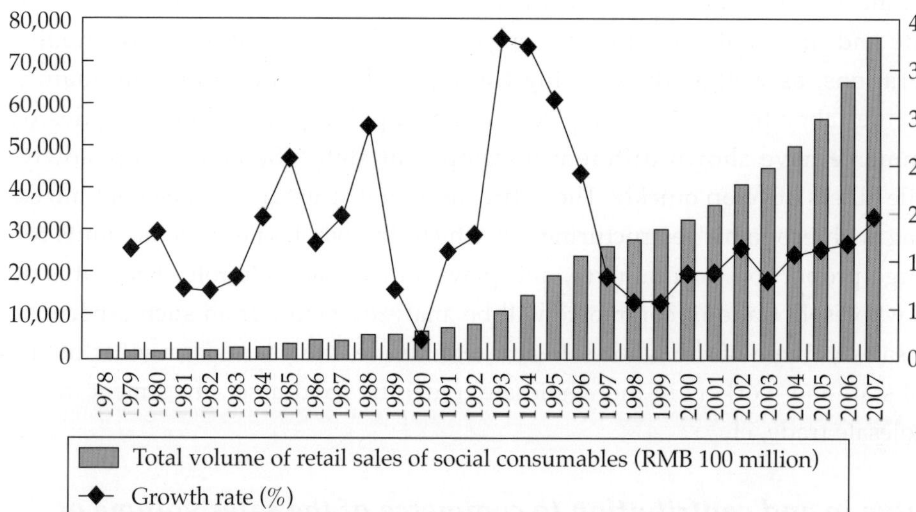

Status of the total volume of retail sales of social consumables of the wholesale and retail trade in commerce

As can be seen from Fig. 2.39, comparing with that of other trades, the ratio of the sales volume of the wholesale and retail trade to the total volume of retail sales of social consumables held an absolute leading position and was the mainstay of commerce. It reached the peak in 1978, being 87.5%; and dropped to the lowest point in 1992, being 72%. What's more, from Fig. 2.39, it could be seen that the ratio of the wholesale and retail trade to the total volume of retail sales of social consumables was stable. In particular, after the 14th CPC National Congress, it rose instead of being reduced, showing a great development potential. Therefore, seen from the trades of commodity circulation, the wholesale trade still possessed many elements of social circulation, having an important influence on the trade of commodity circulation.

Fig. 2.39. Ratios of the total volumes of retail sales of social consumables of different trades to commerce (1978–2007)

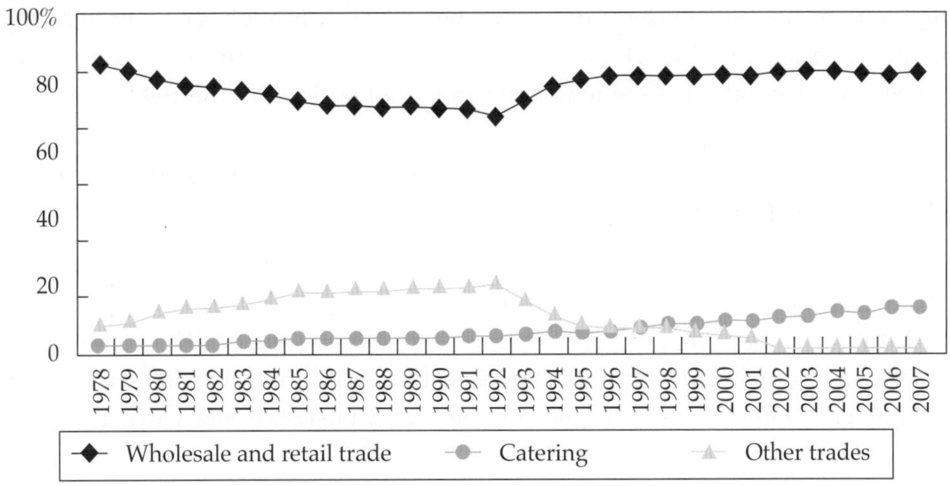

Fig. 2.40. Contribution rate of the total volume of retail sales of social consumables of the wholesale and retail trade to commerce (1979–2007)

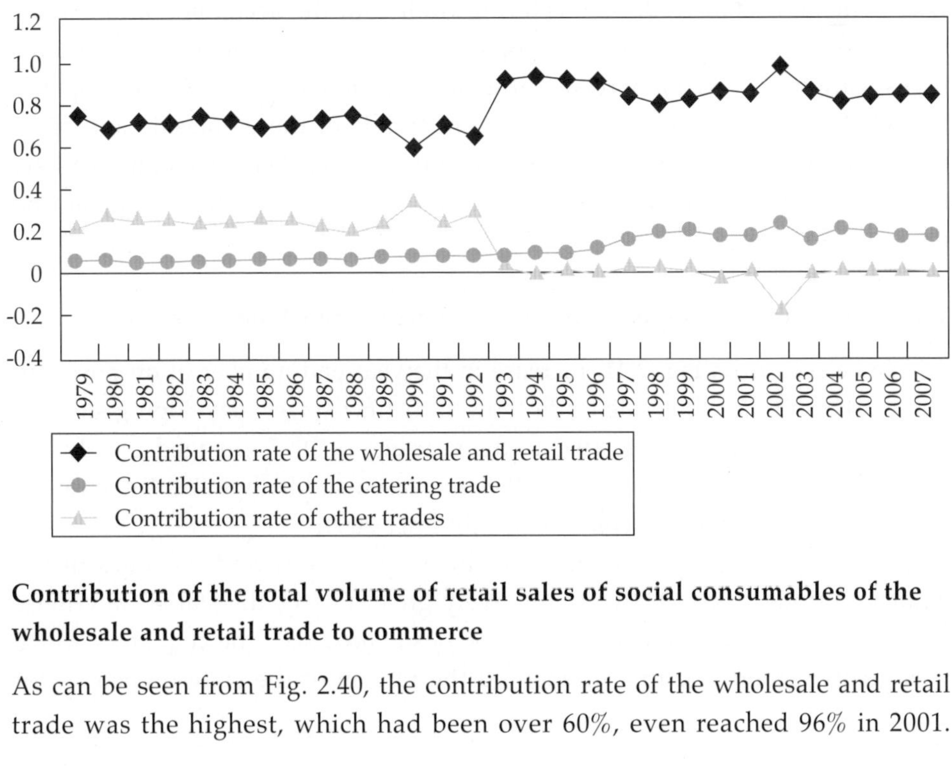

Contribution of the total volume of retail sales of social consumables of the wholesale and retail trade to commerce

As can be seen from Fig. 2.40, the contribution rate of the wholesale and retail trade was the highest, which had been over 60%, even reached 96% in 2001.

From the large curves of fluctuations, we can see that the contribution rate of the wholesale and retail trade to commerce wasn't always the same. Such contribution rate had been about 70% prior to 1990, but declined to 60% after the great fluctuations in 1990, 1991 and 1992. Nevertheless, entering the 1990s, the wholesale and retail trade ushered in a new spring before developing at a high speed. Its contribution rate to commerce broke through 80% before being maintained above 80%, which was consistent with the reform measures and development situation of the wholesale and retail trade since the 1990s.

Status in and contribution to commerce of the employment in the wholesale trade

In terms of the proportion of the sales volume, that of the wholesale trade held an irreplaceable and absolute leading position in commerce. The proportion of employment and that of sales volume were closely related. The commercial status and contribution of the wholesale trade is hereby verified using the commercial status of the year-end number of on-post staff and workers in the wholesale trade.

Since the year-end number of on-post staff and workers in commerce only referred to that of the wholesale and retail trade and the classified wholesale trade and retail trades prior to 2003, and began to consist of that of the wholesale and retail trade, the catering trade and the accommodation trade, the wholesale and retail trade is adopted here to replace commerce before the investigation of the commercial status of the number of employed people in the wholesale trade and the development trends of the wholesale and retail trade. The year-end number of on-post staff and workers in commerce here refers to the year-end number of on-post staff and workers in the wholesale and retail trade.

Year-end number of on-post staff and workers in the wholesale trade

As can be seen from Fig. 2.41, increase in the year-end number of on-post staff and workers in the wholesale trade showed distinct stages: developing steadily, with a slight increase during 1993 to the year-end of 1997; changed greatly and showed a declining tendency since 1998; increased suddenly in 2001, the rate of which reached 20%; then increased rapidly since 2004.

Changes in the year-end number of on-post staff and workers in the wholesale trade since 1998 were relatively great. Firstly, the statistical criteria were wholesale establishments above the designated size, the change of which was great. Secondly, China intensified the reform of the state-owned sector of the wholesale trade since 1998, leading to the unemployment of enormous amounts of staff and workers. Thirdly, the operational and management technologies in the wholesale trade were improved. In particular, wholesale enterprises above the designated size had become stronger economically and were capable of introducing advanced technologies and carrying out automated management, thus better controlled staff cost. In addition, with the development of other trades of the tertiary industry, a large part of the labor force had shifted from the traditional wholesale commerce to other trades, leading to the declining in the year-end number of on-post staff and workers in the wholesale trade objectively. As can also be seen in Fig. 2.41, the growth rate of the year-end number of on-post staff and workers in the wholesale trade kept rising after 2004, which was greatly related to the revival of the wholesale trade in recent years. Great amounts of foreign capital and the establishment of the private sector of the wholesale trade increased the number of wholesale practitioners, at least reduced the declining rate.

Fig. 2.41. Year-end number of on-post staff and workers in the wholesale trade and its changes (1993–2007)

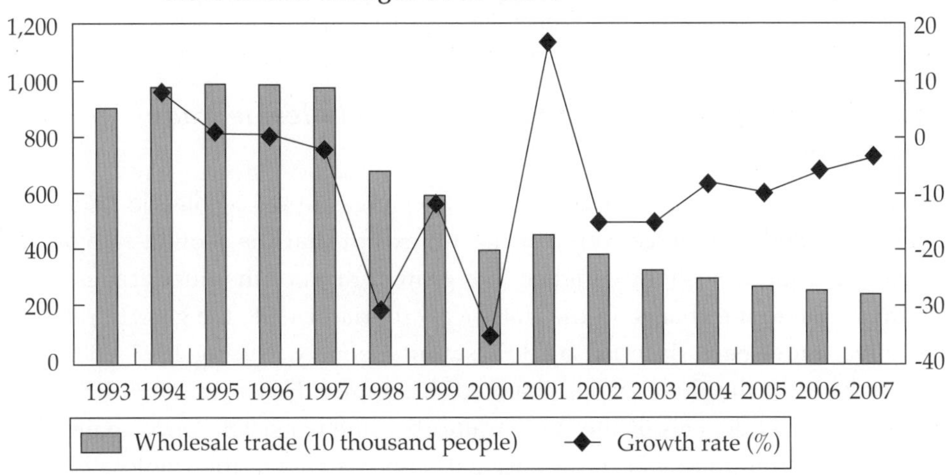

Status of the employment in the wholesale trade in commerce

As can be seen from Fig. 2.42, though the year-end number of on-post staff and workers kept reducing, its ratio to the year-end number of on-post staff and workers in the wholesale and retail trade was usually over 50%, even reached 57% in many years. Though reduced to 49% in 2000, the proportion was soon recovered to 57% in 2001 steadily. Since 2003, it showed a declining tendency, dropping by 1% almost each year. Till 2007, it had declined to 51%. Changes in the proportion of the year-end number of on-post staff and workers in the wholesale and retail trade demonstrated the wane and wax of the development of the wholesale trade and the retail trade. In particular, there was this trend of the retail trade developing faster than the wholesale trade after China's accession to the WTO.

Fig. 2.42. Commercial proportion of the respective year-end number of on-post staff and workers in the wholesale trade and the retail trade (1993–2007)

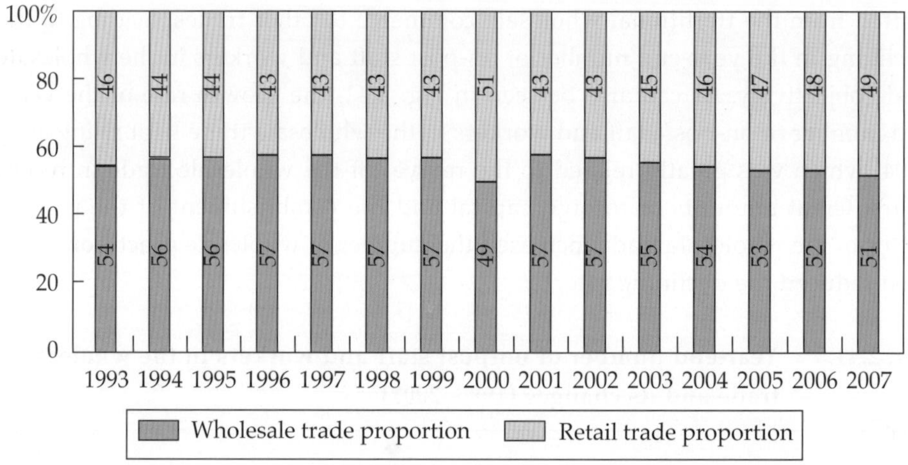

Contribution of the employment in the wholesale trade to commerce

As can be seen from Fig. 2.43, prior to 1998, changes in the wholesale trade, the retail trade and commerce were consistent, except that the growth rate of the wholesale trade was slightly higher. The growth rates of the three trades were positive. Due to the change in the statistical criteria in 1998, the growth rates of the three trades each dropped by 30% simultaneously. During 1998–2002, the growth rates of the three trades changed differently. However, after 2002, the development tendencies of the three trades became consistent once again. The fall of the year-end number of on-post staff and workers in the wholesale trade was relatively great.

As can be seen from the analysis of the respective growth rate of the three during 1998–2003, the volatility of the growth rate of the year-end number of on-post staff and workers in the wholesale trade was far greater than that of commerce, yet presented a high consistence with the latter. Comparatively, the volatility of the growth rate of the year-end number of on-post staff and workers in the retail trade was small, fully demonstrating that changes in the number of people employed in commerce were mainly caused by those in the number of people employed in the wholesale trade. Starting from 2003, there was a better goodness between the growth rate of the year-end number of on-post staff and workers in the retail trade and that in commerce, indicating that the growth rate of the number of people employed in commerce was influenced by the retail trade. It also reflected that both the wholesale and the retail trades have been developing fast since China's accession to the WTO. However, the development speed of the wholesale trade has been slightly slower than that of the retail trade in terms of the employed people absorbed.

Fig. 2.43. Growth rate of the respective year-end number of on-post staff and workers in the wholesale trade, the retail trade and commerce (1994–2007)

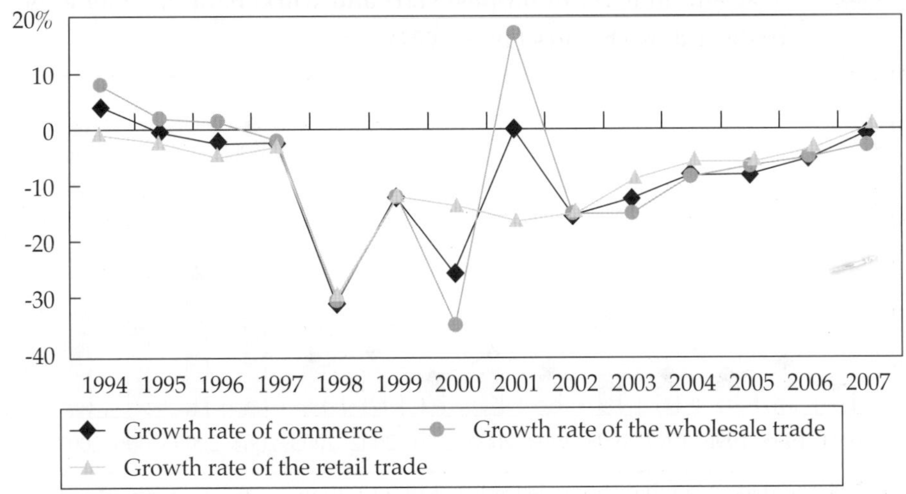

Note: Since the year-end number of on-post staff and workers in the wholesale trade, that in the retail trade and that in commerce all kept declining, the changes in the growth rate of the year-end number of on-post staff and workers is hereby used to investigate the contribution of the wholesale trade to the employment in commerce.

Status in and contribution to commerce of the fixed-asset investment in the wholesale trade

Investment in fixed assets reflects the development speed and scale of a trade. The status in and contribution to commerce of the wholesale trade will be observed using the absolute value of the fixed-asset investment in the wholesale trade, the ratio of fixed-asset investment to commerce, as well as the growth rate of the fixed-asset investment.[7]

Fixed assets of the wholesale trade

As shown in Fig. 2.44, fixed-asset investment in the wholesale trade increased enormously during 1994–2007, increasing from RMB 11.8 billion in 1994 to 119.5

billion in 2007, being nearly 10 times greater. However, the growth rate of fixed-asset investment changed a lot. Fixed-asset investment grew extremely slowly, even negatively (in 1996 and 2001) prior to 2004, but began to grow quickly after that, reaching 119% in 2004, then 50% in 2005. The changes were consistent with the fact that a great number of wholesale enterprises had been established since 2004 which would definitely promote the growth of fixed-asset investment in the wholesale trade. Moreover, the foreign-invested sector of the wholesale trade grew rapidly and was capable of making fixed-asset investment with ample capital.

Fig. 2.44. Year-end number of on-post staff and workers in the wholesale trade and its changes (1993–2007)

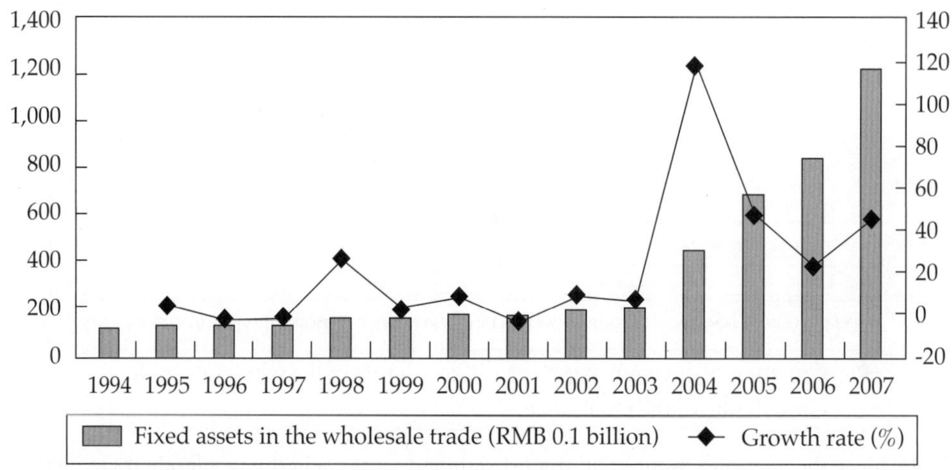

Status of the fixed assets in the wholesale trade in commerce

It can be seen from Fig. 2.45 that during 1994–2000, the ratio of fixed-asset investment in the wholesale trade to the wholesale and retail trade kept increasing, reached the highest point of 68% in 2000, began to decline all the way to 40% in 2004, and kept rising since then. Till 2007, the ratio of fixed-asset investment in the wholesale trade to the wholesale and retail trade was 47%.

As can be seen from the ratio of fixed-asset investment in the wholesale trade to commerce, comparing with that of the retail trade, the fixed-asset construction of the wholesale trade began to slow down since 2000, which was a result of the retail trade's keeping expanding its scope of business and creating new types of operation in recent years. However, the ratio of fixed-asset investment in the wholesale trade to that of the national total kept rising all the way since 2005, reflecting the reviving trend of the Chinese wholesale trade after China's accession to the WTO.

Fig. 2.45. Ratio of fixed-asset investment in the wholesale trade to commerce (1994–2007)

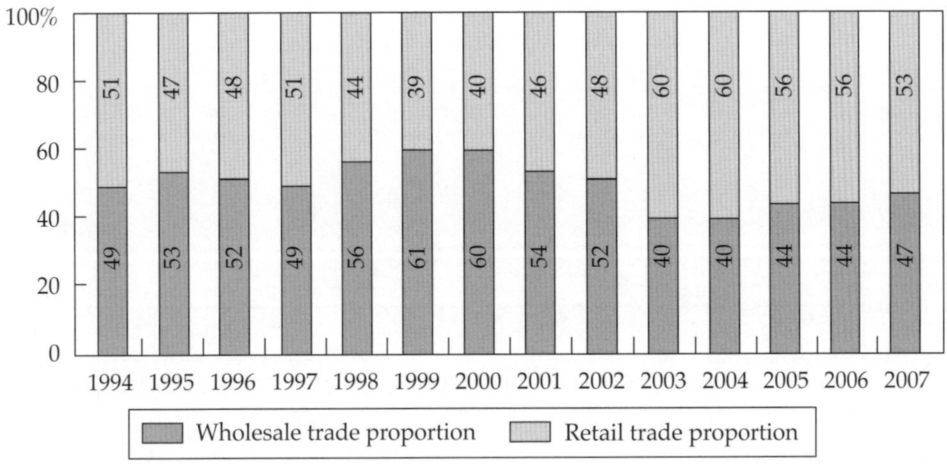

Note: Fixed-asset investment in commerce here refers to fixed-asset investment in the wholesale and retail trade.

Contribution of fixed-asset investment in the wholesale trade to commerce

As shown in Fig. 2.46, the growth rates of fixed assets in commerce, the wholesale trade and the retail trade all changed greatly. During 1995–1999, the range of variation of the three was relatively small, except that the growth rate of the fixed assets in the wholesale trade was slightly higher than that of the retail trade. During 2000–2004, the fixed assets in the retail trade grew faster than those in the wholesale trade, and the difference between the two was greater than that in the previous stage. Since 2004, the growth rate of the fixed assets in the wholesale trade began to exceed that of the retail trade once again, while that of commerce were in between and relatively close to that of the retail trade.

As can also be seen from the description of data, the fixed-asset investment in the wholesale trade and that in the retail trade during the 10 years from 1994–2003 were developing in a wane and wax way. With the development of the retail trade, many retail establishments bypassed many wholesale organizations before purchasing commodities directly from manufacturers, leading to a slight declining in the growth rate of fixed-asset investment in the wholesale trade under the expansion of the retail trade. However, since 2004, fixed assets in the wholesale trade began to grow at a rate even higher than that of the retail trade, from which we can see another accelerated development of the Chinese wholesale trade after China's accession to the WTO.

Fig. 2.46. Growth rates of fixed assets in the wholesale trade, the retail trade and commerce (1995–2007)

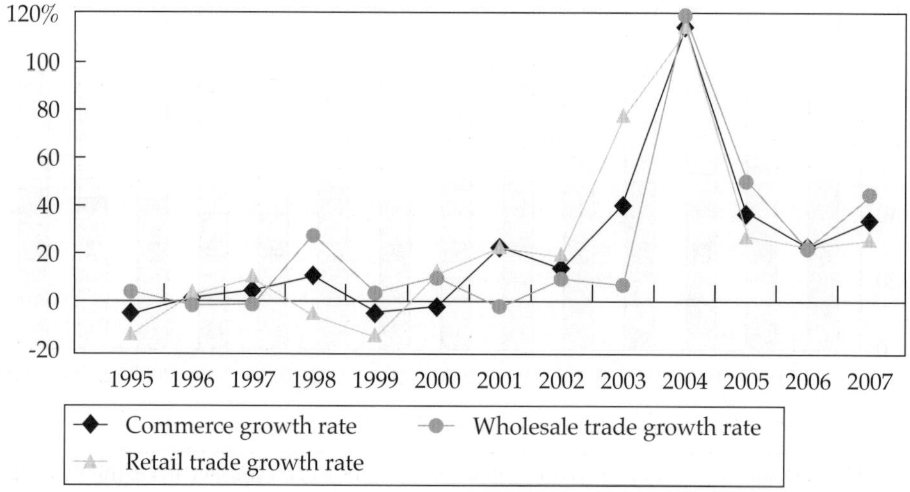

The wholesale trade plays an irreplaceable role in developing commerce. With the development of the national economy, it will play an increasingly greater role. Therefore, fixed-asset investment in the wholesale trade should never be ignored.

It can be seen from the above analysis that of the wholesale and retail trade, wholesale accounts for a larger proportion and holds an important position in commerce, playing a crucial role in developing commerce. Denying the necessity of the existence of the wholesale trade is the denial of and department from the rules of commodity circulation, which could only lead to great chaos to the production and circulation orders of the entire society. In this sense, well solving the problems existing in the wholesale trade is a very important step in reforming and developing commodity circulation in China.

3
Chapter

Evolution of the Wholesale Industrial Organizations

Under the planned economic system, China set up three levels of wholesale centers and implemented the "three fixeds (fixed supply areas, fixed supply objects and fixed pricing range)" way of distribution. But such way of wholesale has been completely eliminated since the reform and opening up. What has replaced it is the exploration of various types of wholesale operations and operational methods. With the development of the market economy, competitions among wholesale enterprises became more and more fierce. In particular, after China opened up the wholesale trade, domestic wholesale enterprises had to face the pressure of external competitions, leading to great changes in the market structure, market behaviors and market performance of the wholesale trade. The industrial concentration of the wholesale trade kept declining and policy-based barriers for the entry and withdrawal of enterprises gradually reduced. What replaced them and continued playing their role were structural barriers, such as of the scale economy, the amount of capital required, and the cost and expenses, as well as strategic barriers. Reduction of the barriers against the entry into the wholesale trade enabled a great number of enterprises to try to enter the wholesale trade, while aggravated market competitions also forced many enterprises to withdraw. Phenomena such as developing the superior and weeding out the inferior, and M & A appeared among enterprises. As healthy market competitions were intensified, market performance was greatly improved, so were the profitability, solvency, progressive capability and operational capability of wholesale enterprises. The improvement of market performance in turn influenced market structure and corporate behaviors. Wholesale organizations evolved in the constant changes of such market structure, market behaviors and market performances. In this chapter, the author will measure and analyze the market structure, behaviors (entry and exit) and performances of the wholesale trade, and explore related development rules based on related data in the three decades of reform and opening up.[1]

Concentration Ratio of the Wholesale Markets

The concentration ratio of the wholesale markets mainly reflects the degree of market monopoly and competitions in the wholesale trade. It is the most commonly used measurement for the competitiveness and monopoly of the wholesale trade. The wholesale trade centralization is slightly lower than that of other industries (e.g. traditional industries) on the whole, because there are various types of operation in the wholesale trade. Even if there are some large enterprises on the market, small enterprises still hold a large market share. In this section, the author will reflect the overall development trend of the wholesale market structure in China at the macro-level by measuring the wholesale market concentration.

Measurement of the wholesale market concentration

Great development of the wholesale markets in China has been achieved since the reform and opening up, leading to changes in the wholesale market structure which is reflected by the rise or declining in the wholesale market concentration. Next, the author will select such indicators as CR_4[2] and CR_8[3] to make a specific measurement and observe the changes in the wholesale market structure in China since the reform and opening up.

In the early days of the reform and opening up, institutional barriers against the entry into the Chinese wholesale trade were relatively high since China hadn't launched the reform of its circulation system. Most wholesale enterprises then were large-scale state-owned enterprises, so the market concentration was very high. With the advance of the reform and opening up and the reform of the circulation system in China, institutional barriers against the entry into the wholesale market became lessened, investors became gradually diversified, market competitions became more and more fierce, and market concentration reduced accordingly. The concentration and changing trends of the wholesale markets in China since 1992 are shown below in Fig. 3.1.

Fig. 3.1. Wholesale market concentration in China (1992–2007)

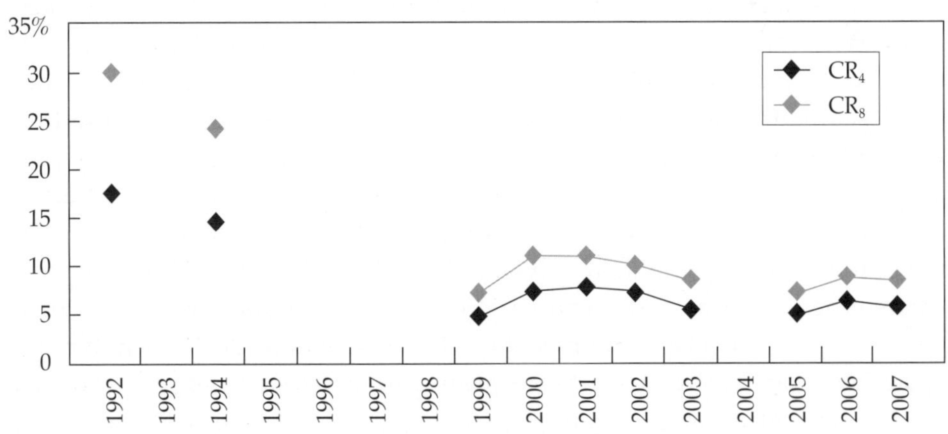

It can be seen from Fig. 3.1 and Table 3.1 that the wholesale market concentration in China kept declining. CR_4 was 17.65% in 1992, and reduced to 5.89% in 2007 (which was limited to the market concentration of wholesale establishments above the designated size, that of the entire wholesale trade would be lower); CR_8 was 30.12% in 1992, and reduced to 8.34% in 2007, declining nearly 2/3.

Table 3.1. The concentration ratio of wholesale markets in China (1992–2007)

Year	Total sales volume of t he wholesale trade (RMB 100 million)	Total sales volume of the top 4 large-scale wholesale enterprises in China (RMB 100 million)	Total sales volume of the top 8 large-scale wholesale enterprises in China (RMB 100 million)	CR_4 (%)	CR_8 (%)
1992	9,998.3	1,763.1	3,008.2	17.65	30.12
1994	28,086.0	4,117.6	6,815.0	14.66	24.26
1999	22,055.8	1,085.7	1,537.2	4.92	6.97
2000	25,977.9	1,908.0	2,753.6	7.34	10.60
2001	28,131.1	2,243.7	3,071.4	7.98	10.92
2002	31,591.9	2,315.5	3,159.5	7.33	10.00
2003	37,974.3	2,142.4	3,245.0	5.64	8.55
2005	74,921.3	3,916.9	5,314.6	5.23	7.09
2006	86,834.8	5,624.0	7,673.1	6.48	8.84
2007	104,362.7	6,148.7	8,706.4	5.89	8.34

The wholesale market concentration was relatively high throughout 1992, because the market economic reform in China was still at the initial stage; many types of operation were under development instead of being fully developed; and the wholesale trade was led mainly by large state-owned wholesale enterprises. High wholesale market concentration at the time was understandable. After the subsequent speech made by Deng Xiaoping during his inspection of South China in 1992 and the setting of the objective of establishing the socialism market economy, the market economic reform in China was launched in a thorough way. A great number of private enterprises entered the wholesale trade, and various types of operation of the wholesale trade were fully developed. Competitions between and inside different types of operation became increasingly fierce, leading to the reduction of the wholesale market concentration. For example, commercial wholesale was maintained in the reform of the original state-owned wholesale, but were composed more of other capital, especially private capital. For another example, the commodity wholesale market is the fastest developing and most influential type of consumer goods wholesale in China since the reform and opening up. Builders of the wholesale market are diversifying, including villages, township governments, other economic entities, local governments at all levels, state-owned and collective enterprises and various types of social capital.

Wholesale establishments set up by private capital kept increasing in number since 1992. The widespread existence of the private sector of the economy made competitions of such kind very intense and led to the declining of market concentration. There were other types of operation in the wholesale trade such as agents and wholesale in the retail trade. As for agents, they were at the initial stage in commodity wholesale, thus were far from being mature. Large agents hadn't been developed greatly. As for wholesale in the retail trade, it was simply a field of wholesale in the retail trade. It would not expand in itself. Since various types of operation in the wholesale trade also led to intense competitions, the market was segregated into small parts. It was hard to form relatively large wholesale enterprises, which was one of the reasons for the declining of the wholesale market concentration.

Changing trends of the wholesale market concentration since 1999 are shown in Fig. 3.2.

Fig. 3.2. Wholesale market concentration in China (1999–2007)

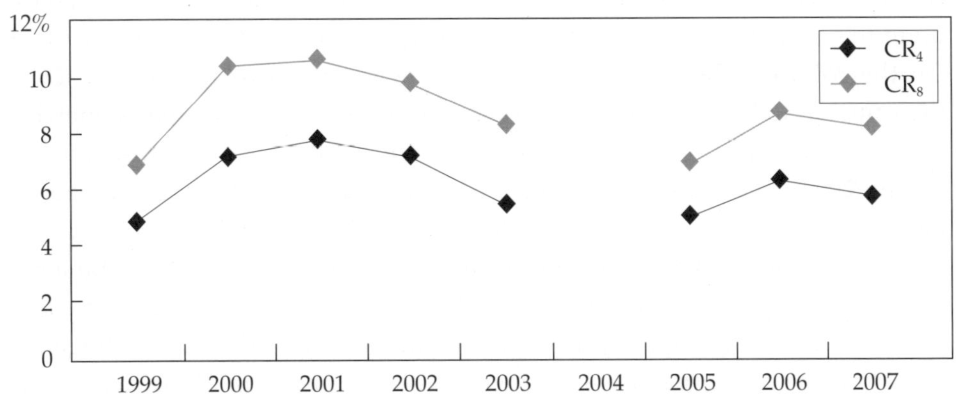

Fig. 3.2. reflects the changing trends of the wholesale market concentration in China since 1999 in a more detailed way. Apart from the reasons mentioned above, the reform and opening up of the Chinese wholesale trade also had a significant influence on the wholesale trade concentration. Specifically, China restricted the opening up of the wholesale trade to the outside world, yet opened up the retail trade to the outside world. To enter China, many foreign enterprises engaged in both wholesale and retail, leading to the increase in competition elements in the wholesale trade. However, the method of engaging in both wholesale and retail wasn't the main type of operation of the wholesale trade after all, so it failed to help form large-scale foreign-invested wholesale enterprises, leading to the continuous declining of the wholesale market

concentration in the same period. CR_4 and CR_8 reduced from 17.65% and 30.12%, respectively, in 1992 to 4.92% and 6.97%, respectively, in 1999. During 1999–2003, encouraged by the positive results made in opening up the retail trade, the State Council of China approved to issue *Experimental Measures for Commercial Enterprises with Foreign Investment*, allowing, for the first time, Beijing, Shanghai, Tianjin and Chongqing each to launch a trial of Sino-foreign joint venture commercial wholesale enterprise, but such trials should never be held by foreign businessmen. Prior to 2001, China opened up joint-stock wholesale enterprises. In 2001, Marubeni Corporation from Japan joined hands with Shanghai No. 1 Department Store before establishing the first joint-stock clothing wholesale market, being the pioneer in setting up joint-stock wholesale markets in China. Since the opening up of the wholesale trade had rendered domestic enterprises to face the enormous pressures brought about by the entry of foreign capital, domestic enterprises, especially some large-scale wholesale enterprises rectified and reformed themselves, improved their operation, management and competitiveness in order to face the challenges of foreign capital. Since it was only joint-stock enterprises that were allowed to be opened up in this period, it didn't cause too great competitions to domestic enterprises. On the contrary, the market share of domestic enterprises increased. Over the same period, the wholesale market concentration in China got somewhat improved, being maintained at about 7% (CR_4) and 10% (CR_8), respectively, during 2000–2002. From the end of 2003 to December 11, 2004, China opened up its wholesale market to the outside world. In 2004, it approved to establish 11 foreign-invested wholesale enterprises. Since December 11, 2004, China has fully opened up its commodity trading market, opening up the trading of steel, publications and agricultural materials. From January to June 2005, altogether 186 wholesale enterprises were approved to be established in China, accounting for 75.9% of the total number of newly-approved enterprises. After the opening up, foreign-invested wholesale trade brought large-scale domestic wholesale markets under tremendous pressures of competition; the market was segregated once again; market shares of a number of large-scale wholesale enterprises in China began to reduce under the pressure of competitions. Therefore, industrial concentration of the wholesale trade in this period was declining, too. It had been maintained at about 5% (CR_4) and 8% (CR_8), respectively.

Bain classified the market structure into several types (see Table 3.2) in accordance with market concentration (with CR_4 and CR_8 as the main standards)

The wholesale market concentration in China was 5.89% (CR_4), being far lower than 30%; and 8.34% (CR_8), being far lower than 40% in 2007. Even if the market concentration was high in 1992, CR_4 was 17.65% and CR_8 was 30.12%, respectively, being far lower than 30% and 40%, respectively. Therefore, according to Bain's criteria on market classification, the wholesale market structure in China was competition-based. However, it is not right to hence deny that some enterprises in local markets held great market shares, and that monopolistic competitions existed in local markets. Take the wholesale of automobiles in China for example. In 2001, the sales volume of wholesale of automobiles in China was RMB 133 billion. Of which, the top four auto enterprises with the largest contribution of sales included Shanghai Volkswagen Sales Co., Ltd. with a contribution of RMB 42.7 billion, JMC Auto Sales Inc. with a contribution of RMB 3.3 billion, Zhejiang Kangqiao Auto Industry and Trade Group with a contribution of RMB 2.2 billion, and Hebei Auto Co., Ltd. with a contribution of RMB 2.1 billion. The total market share of the above top 4 auto enterprises, namely CR_4, was 37.82%, indicating that the wholesale market structure in China had no longer been competition-based, but become Oligopoly-led Type V. It also reflected that as a circulation trade, the wholesale trade is special in terms of market concentration. That is, great differences existed among various types of operation, various categories of businesses and various regions. Therefore, certain attention should be paid to the whole and the characteristics of different types of operation, various categories of businesses and various regions when making specific comments on the wholesale market concentration.

Table 3.2. Bain's classification of market structures

	CR_4 (%)	CR_8 (%)
Oligopoly-led Type I	$85 \leq CR_4$	-
Oligopoly-led Type II	$75 < CR_4 \leq 85$	$85 \leq CR_8$
Oligopoly-led Type III	$50 < CR_4 \leq 75$	$75 \leq CR_8 < 85$
Oligopoly-led Type IV	$35 < CR_4 \leq 50$	$45 \leq CR_8 < 75$
Oligopoly-led Type V	$30 < CR_4 \leq 35$	$40 \leq CR_8 < 45$
Competition-based	$CR_4 \leq 30$	$CR_8 \leq 40$

Comparison of the wholesale market concentration with the market concentration of other industries

A vertical analysis of the changing trends of the wholesale market concentration in China was made in the temporal dimension. Now, the wholesale market concentration will be analyzed through an inter-industrial comparison. Since certain difficulties existed in collecting related data, CR_8 of the industrial concentration of 37 industries in China in 1995 is to be taken as the example in the comparison. Though data on market concentration were not mentioned in the above analysis, considering that 1994 was immediately before 1995 and data in these 2 years were highly comparable, indicators in 1994 and 1995 will be compared below at the same level.

In 1995, the CR_8 of nonmetal mineral products industry, the industry with the lowest market concentration, was 2.5%; and that of the petroleum and natural gas extraction industry, the industry with the highest market concentration, was 76.8% (see Table 3.3 for details). CR_8 of the wholesale trade over the same period was 24.26%. There were altogether 10 industries, namely the top 10 industries in the leftmost column of Table 3.3, whose market concentration was higher than that of the wholesale trade. It will be found through careful observation that industries each with a higher market concentration than the wholesale market in 1995 were all featured by strong natural monopoly, such as the petroleum and natural gas extraction industry, petroleum processing and coking, gas production and supply, etc., or by strong administrative monopoly, such as tobacco supply, tap water production and supply. Some industries were featured by both natural monopoly and administrative monopoly. Therefore, the wholesale market concentration in China was higher than the industrial market concentration in 1994. It was mainly because though China had launched the reform of the circulation system in 1994, state-owned or state-held large-scale wholesale enterprises still held the leading position during this period. The total market shares of the top a few large enterprises were extremely high. Though private and individual wholesale enterprises got engaged in, they were small in size and far from being comparable with large state-owned wholesale enterprises, leading to the wholesale market concentration being higher than that of most manufacturing industries over the same period.

Table 3.3. Industrial concentration of 37 industries in China in 1995 (CR_8)

Product Name	CR_8 (%)	Product Name	CR_8 (%)	Product Name	CR_8 (%)
Petroleum and Natural Gas Extraction	76.8	Smelting and Pressing of Nonferrous Metals	14.7	Nonmetal Minerals Mining and Dressing	5.9
Petroleum Processing and Coking	44.8	Electronic and Communications Equipment Manufacturing	14.7	Timber Processing & Bamboo, Cane, Palm Fiber and Straw Products	5.7

(Con'd)

Product Name	CR_8 (%)	Product Name	CR_8 (%)	Product Name	CR_8 (%)
Electricity, Steam, Hot Water Production and Supply	39.0	Logging and Transport of Timber and Bamboo	13.5	Food Processing	5.4
Chemical Fiber Manufacturing	37.6	Pharmaceutical Industry	11.8	Furniture Manufacturing	5.4
Tobacco Processing	37.0	Manufacturing of Raw Chemical Materials & Chemical Products	11.3	Papermaking and Paper Products	5.3
Gas Production and Supply	37.0	Food Manufacturing	9.9	Printing and Record Medium Reproduction	5.1
Rubber Manufacturing	32.7	Manufacturing of Electric Equipment and Machinery	8.8	Metal Products Manufacturing	4.6
Smelting and Pressing of Ferrous Metals	30.2	Beverage Manufacturing	8.6	Garments and other Fiber Products Manufacturing	3.8
Tap Water Production and Supply	24.8	Stationery, Educational and Sports Goods Manufacturing	8.1	Leather, Furs, Down and Related Products Manufacturing	2.9
Mining and Dressing of Ferrous Metals	24.5	Manufacturing of Instruments, Meters, Cultural and Office Machinery	7.8	Textile Industry	2.8
Transport Equipment	20.9	Plastic Products Manufacturing	6.7	Non-metal Mineral Products Manufacturing	2.5
Manufacturing Coal Mining and Refining	20.4	Manufacturing of General Purpose	6.5		

(Con'd)

Product Name	CR_8 (%)	Product Name	CR_8 (%)	Product Name	CR_8 (%)
Nonferrous Metals Mining and Dressing	15.9	EquipmentSpecial Purpose Equipment Manufacturing	6.2		

Source of data: Jin Yongsheng. *Studies on the Organizational Innovation of the Circulation Industry in China*. Beijing: Capital University of Economics & Business Press. 2004, p45.

However, it was temporary. It can be seen from the above analysis that wholesale market concentration in China in the 21st century dropped significantly over that in the first half of the 1990s. Of which, CR_8 of the market concentration of wholesale establishments above the designated size was only 8.34% in 2007, that of the entire wholesale trade was even lower. CR_{10} of the market concentration of the steel industry over the same year was 36.79%, and that of industries featured by administrative monopoly or natural monopoly was even higher. Therefore, the market concentration of industries was higher than that of the wholesale trade. The phenomenon was directly related to the characteristics of the two industries. Specifically speaking, traditional industries, especially the extraction of petroleum and natural gas and iron and steel industries, highlight the scale economy and would usually require large-scale single enterprises. Enterprises engaged in such industries extend their sizes and concentrate economic resources by increasing production and merging, leading to a high market concentration. It is even true in some industries with complete natural monopoly. Belonging to the circulation industry, the wholesale trade does not need a great amount of production cost and its scale economy is not that significant, too. Plus, there are different types of operation in the wholesale trade, including commercial wholesale agencies, merchant manufacturers, retail wholesalers, wholesale through the wholesale markets and other types of wholesale institutions. Fierce competitions exist among different types of operation, leading to a relatively low market concentration of all wholesale establishments.

Size of Wholesale Organizations

The same as industrial concentration, the size of wholesale enterprises also determines market structure. In a certain sense, the history of the wholesale trade is a history of constant innovations of the wholesale organizations and size expansion of wholesalers. Size extension of wholesalers is the inevitable trend of socioeconomic development, also one of the inevitable choices of wholesalers in pursuing profit increase and achieving scale economy. In this section, the author will investigate the level and scale of industrial organizations of the wholesale trade in China based on data since the reform and opening up.

Level of the size of wholesale organizations

Study on the size of wholesale organizations is mainly based on input and output. Input of wholesale enterprises includes assets, agencies and practitioners, reflecting the concentration of factors of production inside the enterprise. Seen from the angle of output, the sales volume of an enterprise also reflects the expansion of enterprise scale. To reflect the level of systematization of the wholesale trade, the author will, from the angles of input and output, select the average asset size of the wholesale trade, the average number of employees in wholesale trade and the average sales of the wholesale trade as indicators.

Size of wholesale organizations from the angle of input

Size of wholesale organizations will be demonstrated in the analysis of the changes in the average assets of the wholesale trade and the average number of employees in the wholesale trade.

The average size of assets of the wholesale trade

It can be seen from Fig. 3.3 that despite the significant declining fluctuation of the average size of assets of the wholesale trade in 2004, the overall trend was on the rise. The average size of assets of wholesale enterprises was RMB 133.44 million in 2007, up 50.3% over that in 1999 which was RMB 88.758 million. Besides being closely related to the improvement of the market environment, the supports of related policies, the expansion of the size of wholesale enterprises are also intimately related to the reform and development of the wholesale trade itself. With the advance of the market economic reform, wholesale enterprises also launched reforms. A great number of wholesale enterprises, especially large-scale wholesale enterprises implemented the share-holding system positively, improved corporate governance and the market mechanism, established a sound board decision-making mechanism, strengthened the internal management and incentive systems, and made efforts to transform to the modern corporate system. Many wholesale enterprises went public before financing by issuing stocks or securities, further enlarging their size of assets. In addition, with the development of the logistics industry and the improvement of logistics infrastructures, development of the wholesale trade had obtained a better foundation. Wholesale enterprises themselves also introduced more advanced technologies and modes of management, and expand themselves by developing the superior and weeding out the inferior in market competitions, M & A, reorganization, etc., thus the size of single wholesale enterprises had showed a trend of constant expansion since 1999. However, a great declining of 24.0% appeared in 2004 mainly due to the invest enthusiasm during the year and the sharp increase in the number of wholesale enterprises, especially some small-size privately-run wholesale enterprises. Therefore, though the size of assets of the wholesale trade in 2004 witnessed a substantial increase in 2004, the average size of assets of the wholesale enterprises decreased. Of the newly-established wholesale enterprises, especially the small privately-run wholesale enterprises had to compete with not only the former enterprises, but also foreign-invested enterprises entering China because of the reform and opening up. For the lack of competitive advantages, many of such small wholesale enterprises closed down or were merged by other large enterprises one after another in the following year, leading to the drop in the number of enterprises. Single size of enterprises extended and basically recovered to the size prior to 2004. With the development in 2006 and 2007, the size of single wholesale enterprises kept expanding. In 2007, the average assets of wholesale enterprises reached RMB 133.44 million.

Fig. 3.3. Average size of assets of wholesale establishments above the designated size (1997–2007)

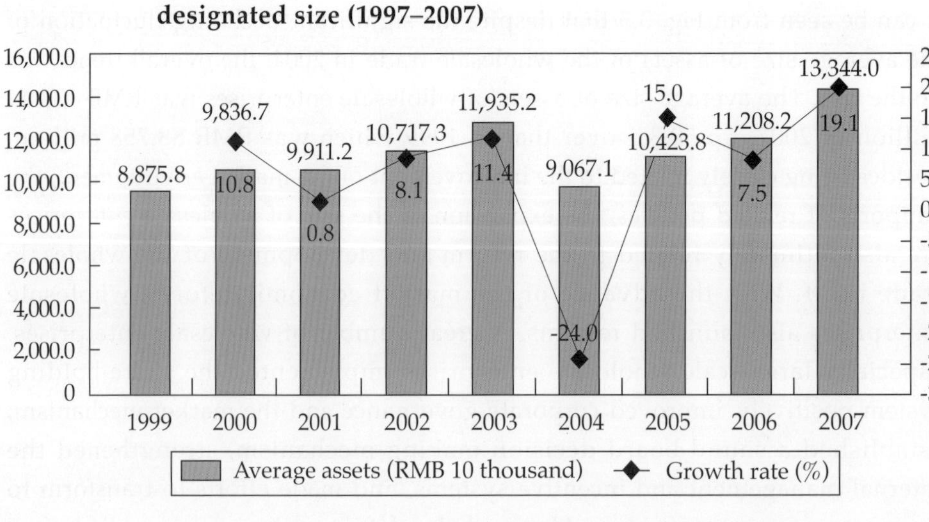

The average number of employees in the wholesale trade

As can be seen from Fig. 3.4, change in the average number of employees in the wholesale trade during 1978–1992 was not great, being about 10. However, it reached 13.5 in 1992 and reduced to 9.4 in 1987. The overall trend was slow growth with occasional slight fluctuations. In 1992, it reached to the largest number. It can be seen from the above description that the size of single wholesale enterprise was small and composed of about 10 employees, indicating the existence of decentralization of industrial organizations. There were many reasons for the relatively high average cost of wholesale enterprises and the lack of scale economy. Economic development was backward in the then China, organizational progress of the wholesale trade was slow, plus the equally backward technologies and management, the extension of the size of single wholesale enterprises encountered certain technical barriers and the level of organization was relatively low. With the advance of reform and opening up, the level of economic development in China was constantly improved, too, and the size of single wholesale enterprises kept extending. Fig. 3.5 lists out the average number of employees in the wholesale trade since 1999, reflecting the organizational progress of the wholesale trade since the end of the 20th century.

Fig. 3.4. Overview of the development of the average number of employees in the wholesale trade in China (1978–1992)

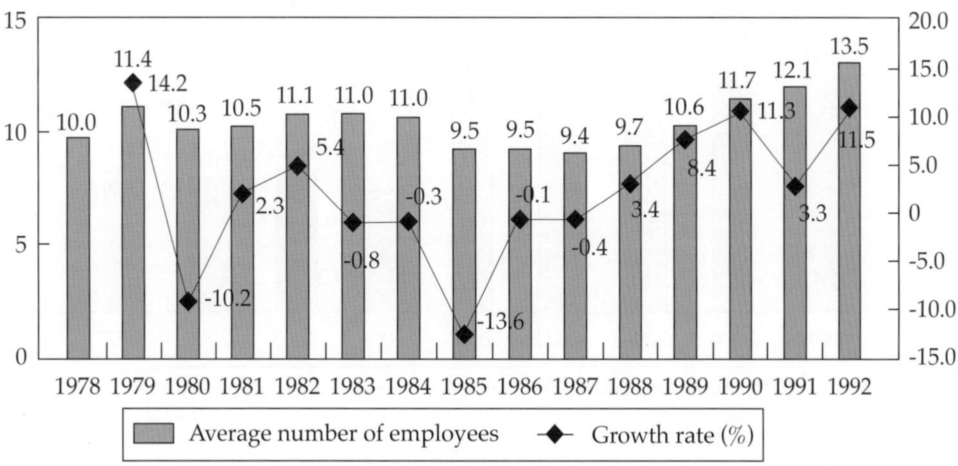

As can be seen from Fig. 3.5, the average number of employees in wholesale enterprises had shown a significant declining trend since 1999. In particular, in 2004, it dropped by 39%, from 119.6 employees/enterprise in 2003 to 73.0 employees/enterprise. Though a trend of growth appeared after 2005, the number was still far lower than that prior to 2004. Moreover, it showed a declining trend once again in 2006. However, the average size of assets of wholesale enterprises showed a trend of growth. Therefore, the declining of the average number of employees in wholesale enterprises wasn't caused by the reduction of their sizes. The two quite opposite changes rightly indicated the constant improvement of the organizational level of the wholesale trade in China. The modernization drive of the wholesale trade greatly accelerated. With the constant development of modern technologies, wholesale enterprises are paying more and more attention to introducing advanced technologies and strengthening the construction of modernization. Many wholesale enterprises have set their own information system before carrying out operations using modernized information management system and electronic network monitoring system, achieving computerized and automated operations, management and financial processing, and greatly saving the cost of manpower. Enterprises' modernization and informationization will definitely lead to the replacement of manpower by technologies, greatly saving enterprises' cost of manpower and facilitating the improvement of the enterprises' performances.

Fig. 3.5. Overview of the development of the average number of employees in the wholesale trade in China (1999–2007)

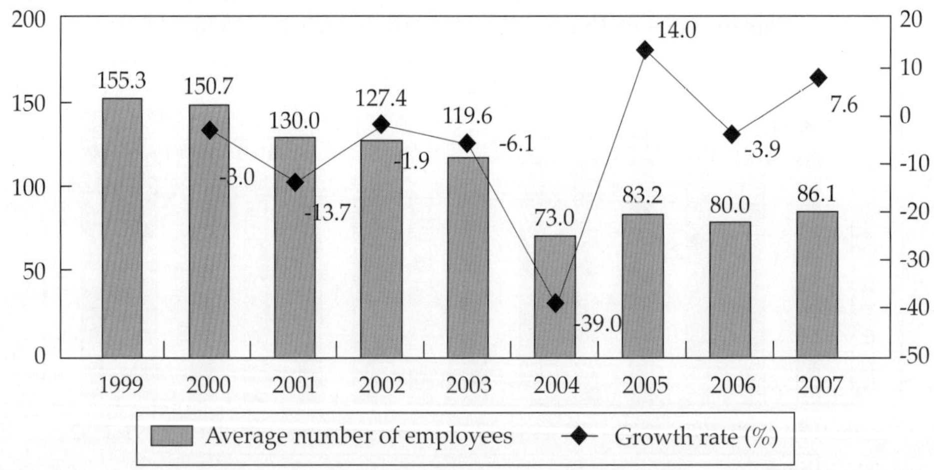

Size of the wholesale trade from the angle of output

The size of wholesale organizations has been demonstrated from the angle of input. Now the author will investigate the size of wholesale organizations from the average sales volume of enterprises before further demonstrating and explaining the level of wholesale organizations.

Average sales volume of the wholesale trade

As the same as the above analysis of the size and level of the wholesale trade on the whole from the angle of output, the analysis of the size of single wholesale enterprises will also be carried out in 2 stages according to different statistical criteria. Let's check the situation during 1994–1996 (see Fig. 3.6).

Fig. 3.6. Average sales of commodities of the wholesale trade in China (1994–1996)

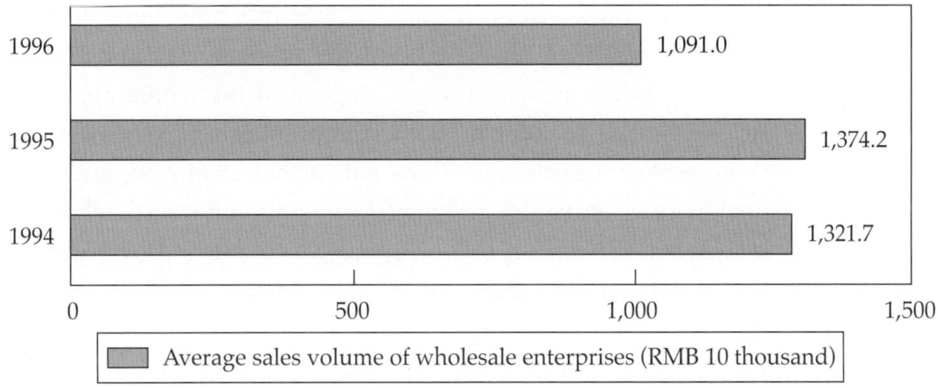

It can be seen from Fig. 3.6 that the average sales volume of wholesale enterprises during 1994–1996 was above RMB 10 million. Of which, that in 1995 was RMB 13.742 million, up 4.0% comparing with that in 1994 (RMB 13.217 million); and RMB 10.91 million in 1996, down 20.6% over 1995.

As the objective of the market economy became further established, the role of the market in resource allocation kept strengthened. Each and all wholesale enterprises, to get an upper hand in market competitions, adopted various measures one after another to strengthen their management and operation, expand their sizes, and enhance the scale economy. The expansion of the sizes of enterprises brought about the constant increase in their business volumes, and the growth momentum of the sales of commodities. However, with the advance of the market reform, policy barriers against the entry into the wholesale trade became lessened and a great number of enterprises surged, leading to fiercer competitions and the reduction of market shares held by each and all enterprises. The average sales volume of enterprises dropped in 1996.

Average sales of wholesale establishments above the designated size

Take a look at the situation after 1999, since it was the indicators related to wholesale enterprises above the designated size in China that were calculated in 1999, the average sales of commodities of wholesale establishments were significantly higher than the data during 1994–1996. Though the two were calculated at different criteria and not directly comparable, the size of wholesale establishments above the designated size could reflect the size and level of the entire wholesale trade to some extent.

As can be seen from Fig. 3.7, the average sales of commodities of the wholesale establishments during 1999–2007 were growing, up 156.9% from RMB 134.634 million in 1999 to RMB 345.867 million in 2007. The constant extension of the size of single wholesale enterprises in China indicated the improvement of their organizational level and the increasingly maturity of their development. In particular, with the opening up of the wholesale trade, under the pressure of having to compete with foreign-invested enterprises, the overall level of wholesale enterprises in China got further improved, and most large wholesale enterprises above the designated size adopted the shareholding system and other advanced forms of organizations. Constant improvements of the operational, management and technical levels of such enterprises coupled with the increasingly perfect construction of infrastructure in China and the development of logistics and other supportive industries facilitated the further expansion of the volume of commodity sales of wholesale enterprises. The average sales of commodities of the wholesale trade had reached RMB 345.867 million in 2007. Of course, another exception could be seen clearly from Fig. 3.7, namely the significant drop in the average sales of wholesale enterprises in 2004. It can be seen from the above analysis that the total sales volume of the wholesale trade increased significantly in 2004. However, the growth rate of the number of wholesale enterprises was even more significant, market competitions were fiercer, and the market share of each enterprise became smaller. As a result, the average sales of commodities of wholesale enterprises in 2004 dropped over the previous year.

The situation of wholesale enterprises above the designated size didn't represent the overall situation of all wholesale enterprises in China. As a matter of fact, there was a clear trend of polarization of wholesale enterprises in China during this period. On the one hand, large-scale wholesale enterprises were more and more standardized, modernized and internationalized, but on the other hand, a great number of small, low-level and traditional wholesale enterprises failed to get upgraded, thus were faced with more and more serious challenges, and stuck in plights before closing down in fierce market competitions. Consequently, the scale of single wholesale enterprises became larger and larger, while small enterprises showed an opposite trend.

Fig. 3.7. Average sales of commodities of wholesale establishments above the designated size (1999–2007)

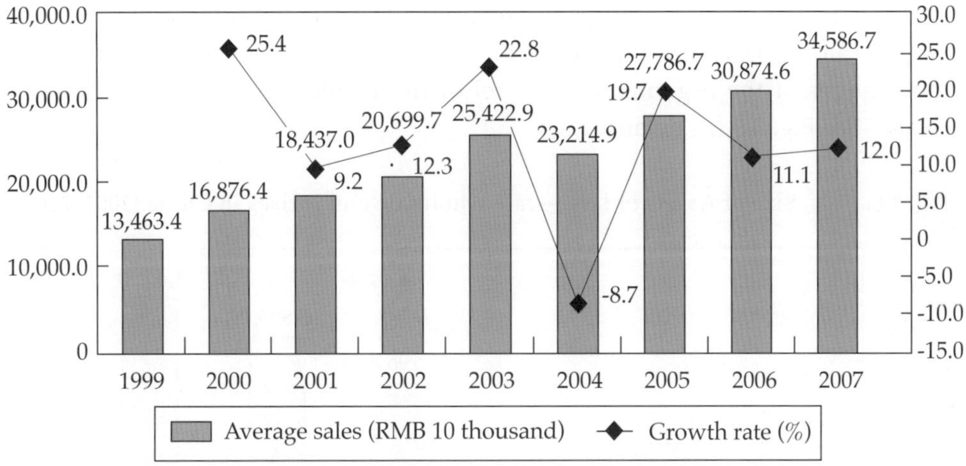

Organizational size and level of large wholesale enterprises

Large wholesale enterprises are the core force of the wholesale trade. Since the reform and opening up, with the development of the market economy and the improvement of the market competition system, the overall scale of the wholesale trade got developed greatly, and the development of large wholesale enterprises advanced by leaps and bounds in China. Related indicators of the top 50 largest wholesale enterprises in China are selected to describe the scale of large wholesale enterprises. According to the statistical criteria of the medium and large wholesale enterprises in *China Statistical Yearbook*, The top 50 largest enterprises chosen are the top 50 wholesale enterprises in terms of the sales of commodities in China. Since data available were mainly during 2001–2007, description and analysis of the scale of large wholesale enterprises in these several years were made.

Size of assets of large-scale enterprises

It can be seen from Fig. 3.8 that the total amount of assets of large-scale wholesale enterprises was increasing on the whole, up 127.4% from RMB 149.65 billion in 2001 to RMB 340.3 billion in 2007. In particular, it increased by 254.3% during 2003–2005 at a great rate. Though such indicator was unavailable in 2004 for statistical reasons, it could also be inferred that the great growth of the overall amount of assets of large-scale wholesale enterprises should appear in 2004. The year 2003 was special, in which the size of assets of large-scale wholesale enterprises was RMB 61.98 billion, down 56.3% comparing with

RMB 141.7 billion in 2002. In the two years that followed its sharp increase in 2004 and 2005, the size of assets maintained a sustained and steady expansion at a growth rate of 29.0% and 20.1%, respectively. From the ratio of the assets of larges-scale wholesale enterprises to the total assets of all wholesale enterprises, the changes of the organizational level of the wholesale trade could be seen clearly. See Fig. 3.9 for details.

Fig. 3.8. Size of Assets of large-scale wholesale enterprises in China (2001–2007)

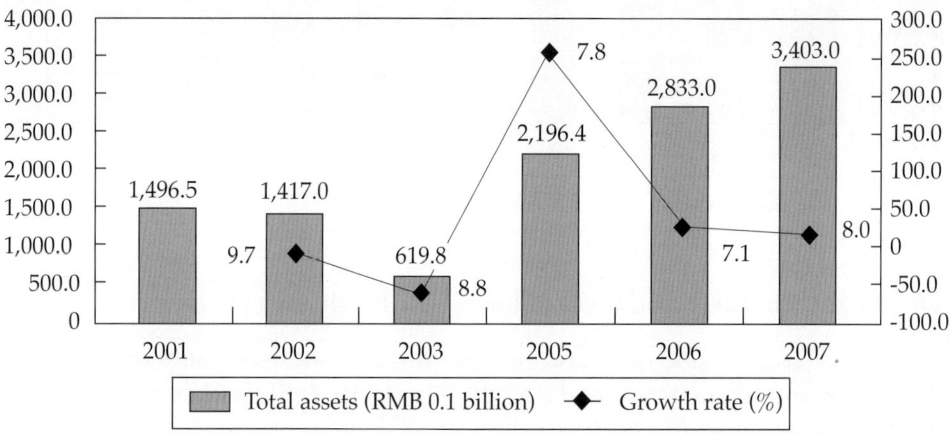

Fig. 3.9. Proportion of the assets of large-scale wholesale enterprises in China (2001–2007)

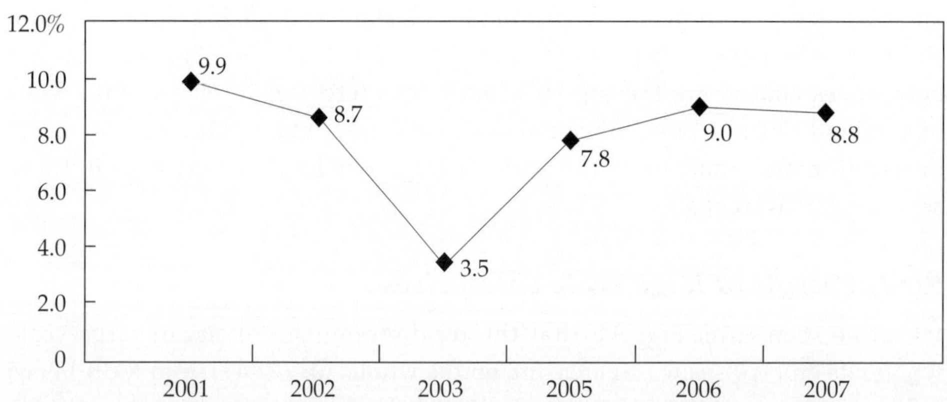

As can be seen from Fig. 3.9, the ratio of the assets of the top 50 large-scale wholesale enterprises to the total assets of wholesale enterprises above the designated size was at about 8% and 9% in all those years expect 2003, showing little changes. The same ratio was only 3.5% in 2003, being absolutely consistent with the sudden drop in the total assets in 2003. Subsequently, with the rise of the size of assets of large-scale wholesale enterprises, the same ratio rose correspondingly. Development trends of asset size and the proportion of assets of large-scale wholesale enterprises indicated that the development of the wholesale trade was not only the expansion of the overall amount, but also constant structural optimizations. The degree of decentralization of the wholesale trade was reduced gradually, and the concentration of the wholesale trade kept rising.

Sales volume of large wholesale enterprises

Let's now see the size of large-scale wholesale enterprises from the angle of output.

From Fig. 3.10, it can be seen that the sales volume of commodities of the top 50 largest wholesale enterprises kept increasing from RMB 368.82 billion in 1999 to RMB 2,002.83 billion in 2007, up 443.0%. Of which, the growth rate in 2005 was the greatest of all, up 65.1% over that in 2003, being the same as the asset size. The same as assets, though such indicator in 2004 was unavailable, it could also be inferred that great growth appeared in 2004. In the two years that followed, the sales volume of large-scale enterprises grew steadily at 28.3% and 26.9%, respectively.

Fig. 3.10. Sales volume of large-scale wholesale enterprises in China (1999–2007)

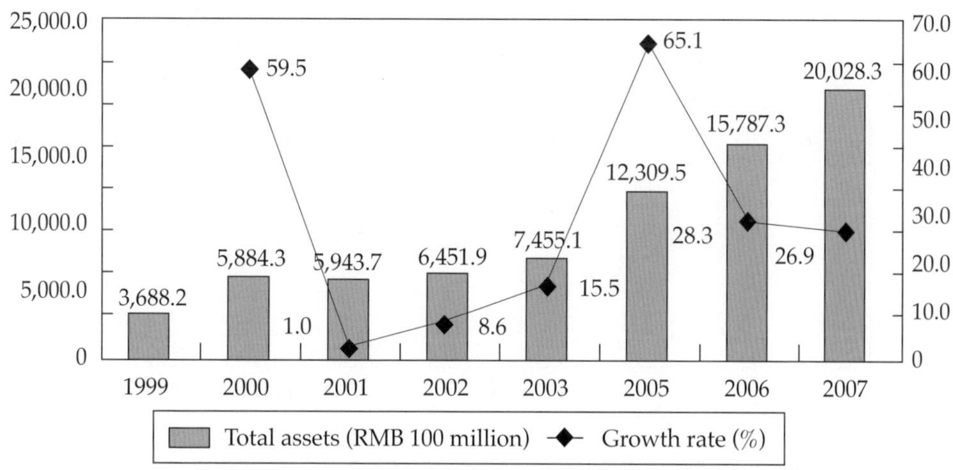

Changes in the proportion of the sales volume of large-scale wholesale enterprises to the sales volume of wholesale enterprises above the designated size were as follows:

It can be seen from Fig. 3.11 that the ratio of the sales volume of the top 50 largest wholesale enterprises in China to that of the entire wholesale trade was relatively high. It was 19.4% on the average during 1999–2007, the fluctuation range of which was not very great. Between the highest percentage of 22.7% in 2000 and the lowest percentage of 16.4% in 2005, there was this difference of 6.3%. It indicated that large-scale wholesale enterprises grew really fast, that the wholesale market concentration was relatively high, that the role of large-scale wholesale enterprises in leading and stimulating the development of the entire wholesale trade was extremely significant, and that large-scale wholesale enterprises had a strong control over the market. It was also the result of developing the superior and weeding out the inferior through market competitions, M & A and reorganization. On the other hand, the higher the proportion of large-scale wholesale enterprises, the higher the wholesale market concentration, the lower the competitiveness of the market, and the higher the oligopoly. Along with the profound influence of the development of large-scale wholesale enterprises on the market structure were changes in the corporate behaviors and market performance of such enterprises. Therefore, it is very necessary to reflect the industrial organization of the entire wholesale trade by the size of large-scale wholesale enterprises.

Fig. 3.11. Proportion of the sales volume of commodities of large-scale wholesale enterprises in China (1999–2007)

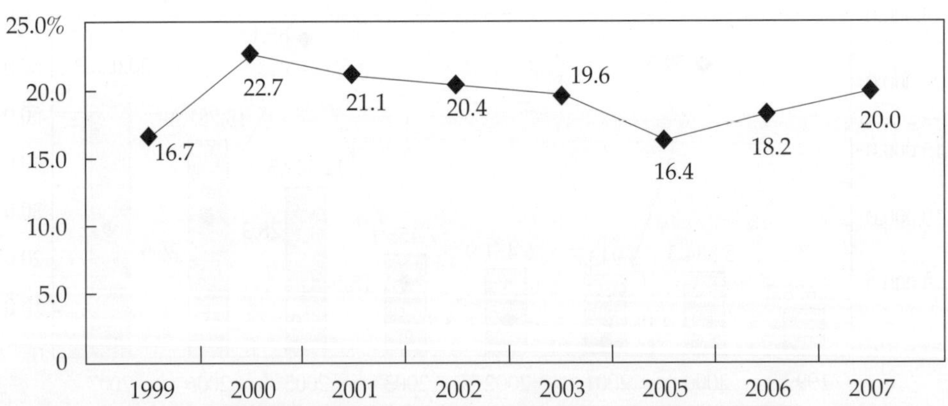

Entry into and Exit from the Wholesale Trade

As has mentioned in the first section, entry and exit is one of the most important factors that determines market structure, then market performance. Entry and exit of enterprises is an effective form, in the process of which the market mechanism plays its role in enabling the optimal allocation of resources. In this section, the author will investigate the level of market competitions and market structure by analyzing the main barriers against the entry into and exit from the wholesale trade in China in different stages since the reform and opening up.

Entry and exit of wholesale institutions

The number of institutions in the wholesale trade or that of enterprises in the wholesale trade is a reflection of the scale of the wholesale trade, changes in which could reflect the overall situation of entry into and exit from the wholesale trade in the concurrent year, thus influencing the wholesale market concentration and market performance. Since the reform and opening up, policy barriers against the entry into the wholesale trade were relaxed gradually. Generally speaking, the number of institutions entering the wholesale trade was greater than that of institutions exiting from the wholesale trade, leading to the aggregation of market competitions and the reduction in industrial concentration while influencing market performance. The overall entry and exit situation of the wholesale trade will be investigated through the changes in the number of wholesale institutions. Let's firstly check the changes in the number of wholesale institutions during 1978–1992 (see Fig. 3.12).

Fig. 3.12. Overview of the entry and exit of wholesale institutions (1979–1992)

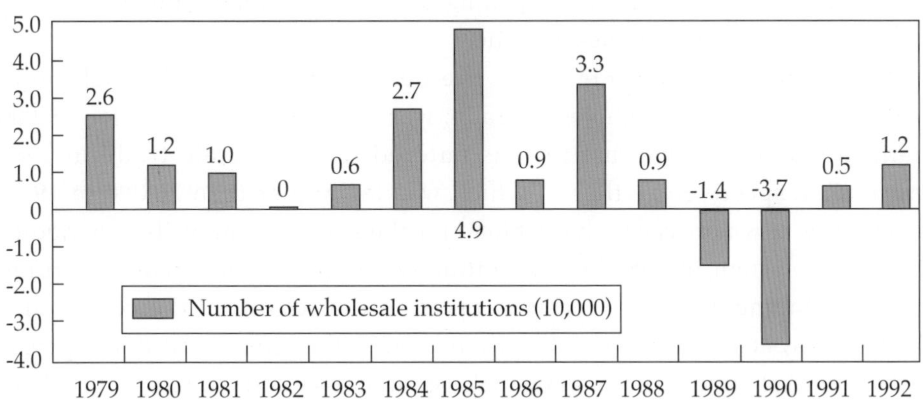

As can be seen from Fig. 3.12, the overall number of wholesale institutions in China seemed to keep increasing during 1978–1996. During the period, new enterprises entered and original enterprises exited from the wholesale trade each year. Specific numbers were as shown in the nature column in Fig. 3.12. Generally speaking, except for 1989 and 1990 when wholesale institutions reduced by 14,000 and 37,000 in number, respectively, and the exits were greater than the entries, the number of institutions entering the wholesale trade in other years was greater than that exiting from the wholesale trade. The total number of institutions in the wholesale trade was increasing.

Under the conditions of the planned economy, there were mainly 3 levels of wholesale centers in China and the "three fixeds" (fixed supply areas, fixed supply objects and fixed pricing range) mode of distribution was in use. In this period, main investment entities in the wholesale trade were state-owned; policy barriers against the entry into the wholesale trade were forceful. It was difficult for some privately-run, individual and other business entities to enter into the wholesale trade, so the whole market concentration was relatively high and the market structure was less competitive. The wholesale trade was basically dominated by large-scale state-owned or state-held wholesale enterprises. After 1978, China began to implement the reform and opening up policy and launched the reform of the circulation system. While keeping strengthening state-owned commerce, China began to actively develop collective commerce, resumed and developed individual commerce, opened up the village fair trade, and expanded industrial self-marketing, helping form once again the circulation system featured by various types of economies and a multiple of circulation channels. The wholesale trade ushered in a spring of development. Privately-run and individual enterprises began to enter the wholesale trade one after another. Reduction of such policy barriers led to the results listed in Fig. 3.12. In the initial year of reform and opening up in 1979, a total number of 26,000 institutions entered the wholesale trade.

As can be seen from Fig. 3.12, the next period, during which more institutions entered the wholesale trade, was after 1984. In particular, 49,000 institutions and 33,000 institutions entered the wholesale trade in 1985 and 1987, respectively, either of which was far higher than 26,000 in 1979. Specifically, it was because that China launched the reform of its commodity circulation system in 1984 before gradually endowing the circulation trade with development space. Measures taken in the reform of the commodity circulation system which were directly related to the reform and development of the wholesale trade were mainly making vigorous efforts to reform the state-owned wholesale enterprises and weakening the direct government control of the wholesale circulation. By enlarging the operational autonomy, determining the "substitution of tax payment for profit delivery" in two steps, and adopting the contract system and the shareholding system along with the adjustment of the organizational systems of state-owned wholesale enterprises, the former promoted enterprises to transform in the direction of new entities featured by independent profits and operation. While specifically, the latter measure was reflected in the constant reduction of the commodity varieties under the planning and management of local governments at all levels, the replacement of state monopoly in the purchase and marketing of industrial products and the unified and fixed state purchasing of agricultural and sideline products with the sale on credit that was in line with market rules, the elimination of the restrictions of fixed purchase and sale relations, the permission of free trade among various market entities, the increasing role of the pricing mechanism in wholesale activities, and the opening up of the wholesale trade to the non-state-owned sector of the economy. The reform resulted in the further relaxation of the wholesale trade by the state. Policy barriers were even more reduced. Plus, the Chinese economy achieved a great development since the reform and opening up. Due to the long existence of policy barriers in the circulation trade, especially the wholesale trade, market competitions were not fierce. Coupled with greater profit margins, many investment entities, lured and driven by profits, made investments and entered the wholesale trade when policy barriers were further reduced.

The total number of wholesale institutions was reduced in 1989 and 1990. The number of those exiting from the wholesale trade was larger than that of institutions entering the wholesale trade. Mainly, it was because that with the reduction of policy barriers against the entry into the wholesale trade in China, a great number of wholesale institutions flocked in. Yet some of such institutions were not truly qualified for entering the wholesale trade, leading to a certain degree of chaos, excessive market competitions and many unfair competitions. In 1990, China cleared up and rectified wholesale institutions, and ordered unqualified wholesale institutions to close down before forcing such institutions to exit from the market. Actually, China raised the barriers against the entry into the wholesale trade, leading to the exit of many institutions from the wholesale trade. Of course, the political disturbance in 1989 influenced China's economic development to some extent, including the development of the wholesale trade. In addition, the source of the original data listed above changed somewhat in 1988 (which has been mentioned in Section II in this chapter), influencing the statistical results to some extent, too.

In 1992, the number of institutions entering the wholesale trade exceeded that exiting from the wholesale trade in China, the difference between which was 12,000 in number. Such phenomenon appeared mainly because that China had already got rid of the disturbance of the political turmoil in 1989, and the political situation in China has been stabled which created good conditions for economic development. Meanwhile in 1992, the famous speech made by Deng

Xiaoping during his inspection of South China gave insights to the relations between the planned economy and the market economy and that between socialism and capitalism, fully confirming the status and role of the market economy in socialist countries, promoting the reform of the market economy to get furthered, and future reducing the entry barriers against the wholesale trade. At the same time, the improvement of the economic situation had created more profitable chances for the wholesale trade. Investors made investments in the wholesale trade and a great number of institutions entered the wholesale trade once again.

That wholesale institutions poured into the market would intensify market competitions, reduce market concentration, and enable the market structure to become more fully competitive. Though specific data in this period were unavailable to measure the wholesale market concentration, the overall wholesale market concentration kept declining all the way based on the analysis in Section I in this chapter.

Let's check the entry and exit situation of the wholesale trade in 1995 and 1996.

As can be seen from Fig. 3.13, the number of institutions newly entering the wholesale trade in 1995 was 23,000 more than that exiting from the wholesale trade. The number of institutions newly entering the wholesale trade in 1996 was even greater, being 71,000. Or in other words, the number of institutions exiting from the wholesale trade in 1996 was even lower. From the overall situation of entry and exit in the above-mentioned two years, it could be seen that the barriers against the entry into the wholesale trade were relatively lower, that enterprises were free to enter or exit from the wholesale trade. Meanwhile, profits of the wholesale trade were high, playing a significant role in attracting outsiders. Specifically speaking, in 1994, the objective of establishing a socialist market economic system had been determined and the development of the market economy in China had entered a new stage. Due to equality and other features of the market economy, China gradually relaxed, even eliminated policy restrictions over the entry into the wholesale trade. Policy barriers against the entry into the market became lower and lower. Driven by high profits, various investment entities got involved in. Economic barriers such as the barrier of scale economy, that of cost expenses, technical barriers and the barrier of necessary amount of capital, were replacing policy-based barriers gradually. However, such barriers played a significant role only in large-scale enterprises. Therefore, small and medium-sized enterprises entered into the wholesale trade during this period without encountering much resistance. Meanwhile, active enterprises hadn't had better strategic behaviors to set up strategic entry barriers. The numbers of enterprises and that of wholesale practitioners kept increasing, inevitably leading to fiercer market competitions. Some enterprises with poor performance, low level of management and no competitive edge were forced to exit. Since the wholesale trade hadn't fully developed, the market space was relatively great and the profitability was relatively higher, too, the total number of enterprises entering the wholesale trade was far greater than that exiting from the wholesale trade, to say it generally. With the increase in the number of institutions entering the trade, market competitions became more and more fierce, leading to the reduction of market concentration. Just as mentioned in Section I in this chapter, CR_4, an indicator that reflects market concentration, reduced from 17.65% in 1992 to 14.66% in 1994; CR_8, another indicator that reflects market concentration, reduced from 30.12% in 1992 to 24.26% in 1994. Market structure became more and more competition-based.

Fig. 3.13. Overview of the entry and exit of wholesale institutions in 1995 and 1996

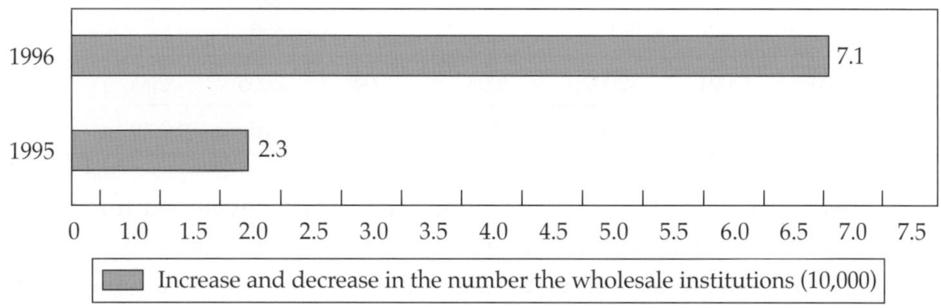

Since 1999, China began to make statistical investigations of wholesale enterprises above the designated size. Let's check the overall situation of the entry and exit of wholesale institutions in China since it entered the 21st century.

As can be seen from Fig. 3.14, quite different from the overall situation of the wholesale trade in the previous several stages, the overall situation in this stage was alternative. The total number of wholesale enterprises reduced 1,000 and the number of wholesale enterprises exiting from the wholesale trade was greater than that of entering wholesale enterprises in 2000; the number of wholesale enterprises exiting from the wholesale trade was still 100 greater than that of entering wholesale enterprises in 2001; both numbers were more or less the same in 2002; the number of enterprises entering the wholesale trade was slightly greater than that exiting from the wholesale trade in 2003; the number of enterprises entering the wholesale trade increased sharply, being 15,800 more than that of the enterprises exiting from the wholesale trade in 2004; opposite change appeared once again in 2005, yet at a relatively smaller rate; in the two years that followed, the number of enterprises entering the wholesale trade exceeded that of enterprises exiting from the wholesale trade. Of which, the maximum fluctuation appeared in 2004.

Fig. 3.14. Overview of the entry and exit of wholesale enterprises above the designated size (2000–2007)

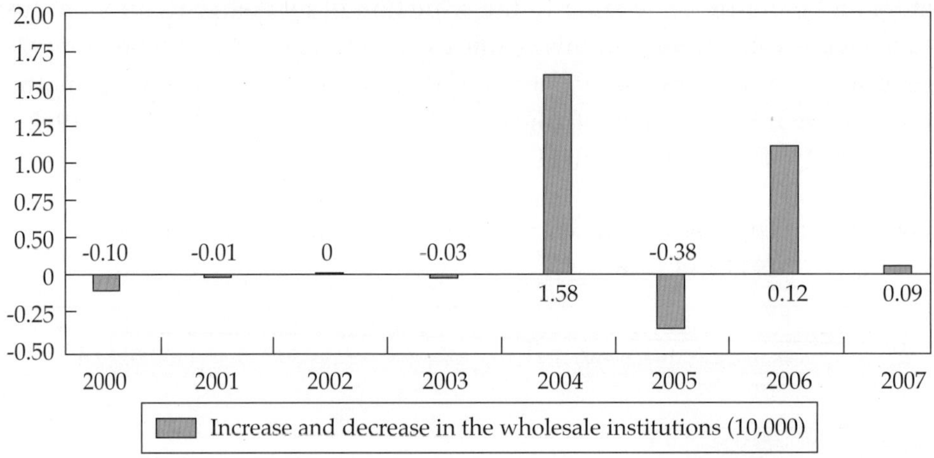

At this stage, since the market economy had been developed for quite a while and become relatively mature, policy barriers against the entry into the wholesale trade were no longer the main barriers for domestic investment entities, but replaced by economic barriers. Statistics in this stage were mainly about wholesale enterprises above the designated size instead of all. Wholesale enterprises above the designated size were large in scale and presented structural barriers against the entry, such as the barrier of scale economy and that of cost and expenses, technical barrier, differentiation barrier and the barrier of the necessary amount of capital, which were all barriers against new enters into the wholesale trade. Therefore, the entry and exit from the wholesale trade in this stage was mainly determined by the scale of such barriers. Meanwhile, since incumbent enterprises had already been large-scale enterprises above the designated size, which had advantages in many aspects. To prevent the entry of new enterprises, and avoid competitions and lowering down the profitability of the entire industry, they would definitely take advantage of their dominant position to set some strategic barriers against entry in order to prevent new enterprises from entering, such as filling market blanks as soon as possible, establishing their own advantages, seeking for collaborative defense, sending out warnings, and hunting for related policies, laws and regulations, etc. Similarly, wholesale enterprises exiting from the trade in this stage were mainly for the reason that they were primarily faced with high economic barriers instead of policy barriers under the traditional planned economy. For large-scale circulation enterprises, fixed (sunk) costs and other economic factors could have a great effect to prevent exit, because large-scale wholesale enterprises had higher asset specialty and fixed costs. That's why reasons for the entry and exit of wholesale enterprises in this stage were no longer as simple and direct as those in the previous several stages, but depended more on the characteristics of the wholesale trade, the overall situation of trade competitions, the profit margin, the ability of incumbent enterprises to set up strategic barriers, and the intensity of such barriers. So there were no specific rules on the entry and exit of wholesale enterprises in this stage. Instead, the entry and exit of wholesale enterprises in this stage developed along with the development of the above-mentioned factors.

Additionally, China began to open up its wholesale trade in this stage. For foreign-invested enterprises, to enter or exit from the wholesale trade would not only be influenced by the above-mentioned various barriers and factors, but also the policies made by China on opening up its wholesale trade. Most entering foreign-invested enterprises were with sufficient capital, advanced management and technologies, high-quality personnel, so for these enterprises, many structural barriers against the entry such as the barrier of the scale economy, that of cost and expenses, technical barrier, the barrier of the necessary amount of capital were not even barriers. On the contrary, policy barriers were primary barriers for them.

The above analysis couple with the history of opening up its wholesale trade by China makes it easy to explain why the number of entering wholesale enterprises increased sharply in 2004. Mainly, that's because policy barriers against the entry of foreign-invested enterprises into the Chinese wholesale trade were lowered. In the subsequent year, the number of entering enterprises into the wholesale trade was smaller than that of exiting from enterprises, but the number of wholesale enterprises above the designated size maintained high before showing an increase by a small margin in 2006 and 2007.

Entry and exit of wholesale practitioners

The entry and exit situation of the wholesale trade was investigated just now from the changes in the number of wholesale institutions. Next, another indicator which is highly related to wholesale institutions-the number of wholesale practitioners-will be adopted to analyze the entry and exit situation of the wholesale trade. The overall situation during 1978–1992 is as shown in Fig. 3.15.

Fig. 3.15. Entry and exit of wholesale practitioners (1979–1992)

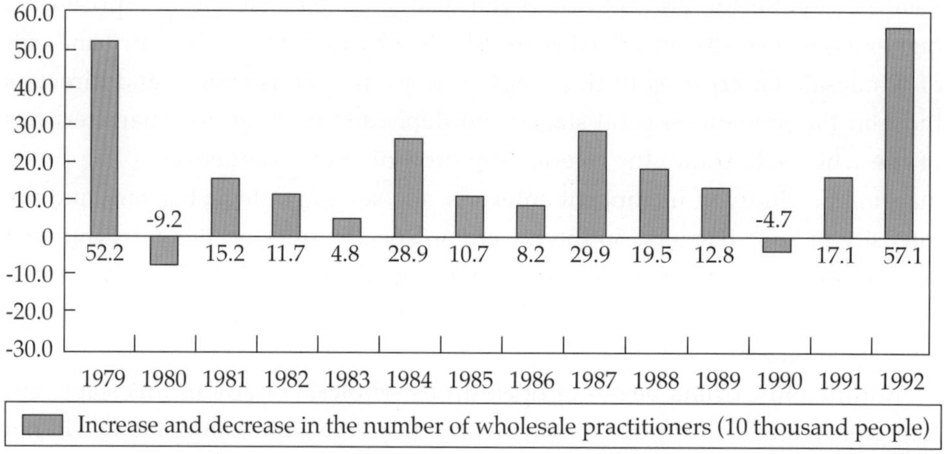

As can be seen from Fig. 3.15, similar to the changes in the number of wholesale institutions, the number of increased wholesale practitioners each year was greater than that of decreased practitioners except for 2 years. That is to say, new comers entered the wholesale trade constantly. Compared with the changes in the number of institutions in the wholesale trade mentioned above, the years in which more practitioners entered (exited) the wholesale trade were basically consistent with those in which more institutions entered (exited) the wholesale trade. Specifically, both the entering wholesale practitioners and the entering wholesale institutions were relatively more in number in 1979 and during 1984–1987; and those exiting from the wholesale trade were relatively more in number in 1990. In particular, for the wholesale trade in China which is more of a labor-intensive industry, increase in the number of wholesale institutions will sure bring about the expansion of personnel correspondingly. Therefore, changing trends of the two were basically consistent. Reasons for the entry and exit of wholesale institutions also apply to the changes in the entry and exit of wholesale practitioners. In some special years such as 1980, wholesale institutions increased 10,000 in number, namely the number of newly-entered institutions into the wholesale trade was 10,000 more than that of originally incumbent, yet exited institutions from the wholesale trade. Changes in the number of wholesale practitioners were opposite. 92,000 practitioners more exited from instead of entering the wholesale trade. After the policy barriers (against the entry into the wholesale trade) were lowered, many enterprises or other institutions entering the wholesale trade were privately- or individually-run, small and with fewer practitioners; while those institutions that exited from the wholesale trade were mostly large-scale state-owned wholesale institutions, the staff number of which was far greater than that of small wholesale institutions. It led to the quite opposite changing trends that institutions entering the wholesale trade were greater than those existing from the wholesale trade in terms of number, yet entering wholesale practitioners were far fewer than those exiting from the wholesale trade. In 1992, the difference between the number of entering wholesale institutions and that of exiting wholesale institutions was 12,000, resulting in the number of practitioners entering the wholesale trade being 571,000 more than that of practitioners exiting from the wholesale trade. In this period, policy barriers were the main barriers that influenced market entry. Economic barriers played a negligible role therein. In particular, as more and more practitioners entered the wholesale trade, the market concentration of some small and medium-sized enterprises kept reducing and the competitive features of the market structure kept strengthened.

Next, we will analyze the entry and exit of wholesale practitioners in 1995 and 1996, see Fig. 3.16.

Fig. 3.16. Entry and exit of wholesale practitioners in 1995 and 1996

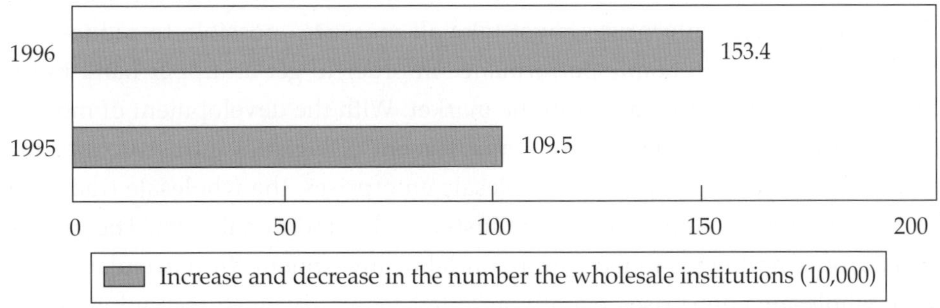

As can be seen from Fig. 3.16, the number of practitioners newly entered the wholesale trade in 1995 was 1.095 million more than that of practitioners exiting from the wholesale trade in the same year. The difference was even greater in 1996, being 1.534 million. Comparing with the entry and exit of wholesale institutions mentioned just now, the changing trends between the two were basically consistent. That is to say, the increase in the number of wholesale practitioners was mostly brought about by the increase in the number of wholesale enterprises, for the same reasons and for the lowering of the barriers against the entry into the wholesale trade in China. Specifically, it was caused by lowered and lessened policy barriers.

Since 1999, indicators concerning the wholesale trade calculated in *China Market Statistical Yearbook* and *China Trade and External Economic Statistical Yearbook* were mainly about wholesale enterprises above the designated size. Next, the entry and exit of practitioners in the wholesale establishments above the designated size in this period will be analyzed.

As can be seen from Fig. 3.17, the entry and exit of practitioners in the wholesale establishments above the designated size in this period was quite different from that in the previous several stages. In this period, more practitioners exited from other than entering the wholesale trade. In particular, 3.36 million more practitioners exited from other than entering the wholesale trade in 2000. It was mainly because employees of wholesale enterprises above the designated size were mainly calculated during this period. Such wholesale enterprises were relatively large. When entering the wholesale trade, they had to face some structural barriers and strategic barriers set by incumbent enterprises. Fierce market competitions existed among incumbent enterprises, enterprises having the potential for entering the wholesale trade, and between the two types of enterprises. At the same time, China had opened up its wholesale trade to the outside world, so domestic wholesale enterprises had to face enormous competitions with foreign-invested enterprises. Therefore, in such fierce competitions, both the originally incumbent enterprises and the newly entered enterprises must take all measures possible to reduce cost and improve their economic performance in order to get an upper hand in the competitions and occupy a seat in the market. With the development of modern communications technologies, the improvement of logistics infrastructure, and that of the management level of wholesale enterprises, the wholesale trade was no longer a simple labor-intensive industry in the traditional form. The growth of its profits no longer relied purely on labor investment. In particular, large-scale wholesale enterprises usually adopted more advanced technologies and modes of operations to replace human labors, saving labor cost while improving their efficiency. So China saw the results listed in Fig. 3.17. Of course, it was all about the situation of wholesale enterprises above the designated size that was calculated. The overall situation of the entire wholesale trade may not be the same.

Entry and exit of the assets of the wholesale trade

The entry and exit situation of the wholesale trade and the barriers existed therein have been investigated just now from the changes in the number of wholesale institutions and those in the number of wholesale practitioners. Next, the entry and exit of the assets of the wholesale trade will be adopted to analyze the entry and exit situation of the wholesale trade.

Fig. 3.17. Entry and exit of practitioners in the wholesale establishments above the designated size (2000–2007)

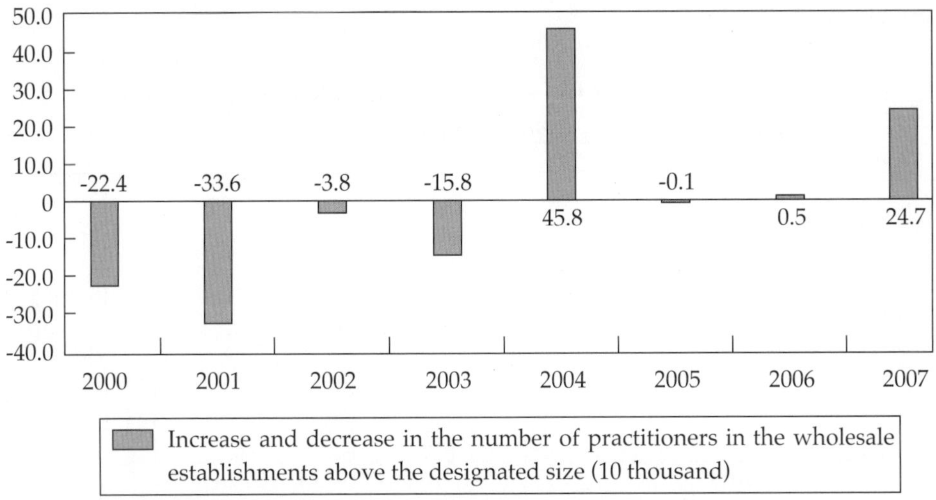

As can be seen from Fig. 3.18, the total assets of the wholesale trade were slightly reduced in 1999 and 2001, but increased in other years in this period. That is to say, the total assets newly entering the wholesale trade were higher than those exiting from the wholesale trade. In particular, in 2004 and 2007, the total amount of assets newly entering the wholesale trade was RMB 1,005.91 billion and RMB 717.47 billion, respectively, more than the total amount of assets exiting from the wholesale trade. It was consistent with the entry and exit of wholesale enterprises. Increase in the number of enterprises would be definitely accompanied with the increase in newly-entered assets, while the total assets that exited from the wholesale trade were not large in amount. It could be concluded that the market hadn't been fully developed and market competitions hadn't been fierce enough. Though the entry of new enterprises would intensify market competitions and share market profit margins, it was still profitable. Therefore, incumbent enterprises wouldn't adopt strong measures to stop the entry of new enterprises, or set high structural and policy barriers against the entry into the wholesale trade. In particular, since 2004, China has opened its wholesale trade wider to the outside world and greatly reduced policy barriers against the entry of foreign capital, enabling the amount of investment of foreign capital to grow significantly. It explains the sharp increase in the assets of the wholesale trade in 2004. Of course, the increased total assets were not necessarily invested by newly-entered wholesale enterprises, but may be created by incumbent enterprises through M & A or making additional investments. Based on the entry and exit of wholesale enterprises, it is safe to draw such a conclusion that a great part of the newly-added assets in this period were from investments by newly-entered enterprises. That is to say, market barriers against the entry into the wholesale trade were low in this period; market profit margins were great; and the competitiveness of the market structure was not very strong.

Fig. 3.18. Entry and exit of the assets of wholesale enterprises above the designated size (2000–2007)

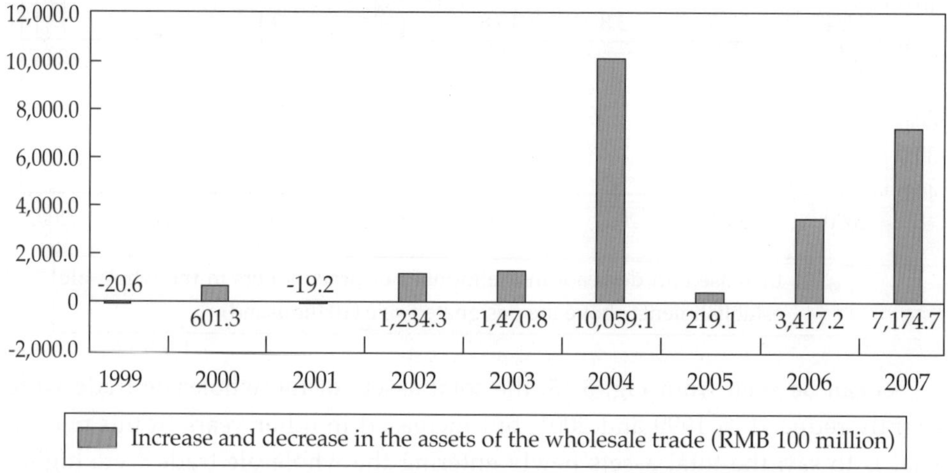

Level of Performance of the Wholesale Trade

Since the reform and opening up, the Chinese wholesale trade has achieved great development; the scale of industrial organization has kept expanding; and market performance has been improved significantly. The overall efficiency of the wholesale enterprises has been constantly improved. Specifically, their solvency, profitability, operational ability, ROA (return on assets) and sustainability have all improved. In this section, the author will describe and analyze the operational efficiency and performance indicator of the wholesale enterprises before reflecting the overall performance of the wholesale trade. In addition, based on such indicators as the wholesale market concentration and the entry and exit situation of the wholesale trade mentioned in the above several sections, the author will analyze the overall market structure, enterprise behaviors and market performance of the wholesale trade, as well as their interrelations.

Overall level of performance of the wholesale trade

With the changes in the wholesale market structure and enterprise behaviors since the reform and opening up, the market performance of the wholesale trade has also been in constant changes. Next, indicators of the performance of wholesale enterprises above the designated size will be analyzed and described to reflect the overall level of performance of the wholesale trade. Specifically, such indicators include the capacity for growth, operational capability, profitability and solvency.

The capacity for growth of the wholesale trade

The capacity for growth is an important measurement for the overall performance of an industry. Measurement of an industry's capacity for growth can reflect not only its current performance, but also its development potential in the future, playing a role in foreseeing the further development of an industry.

Growth momentum of the sales revenue

Since the reform and opening up, the sales revenue of the wholesale trade has been increasing all the way. In particular, entering the 21st century, the scale of the wholesale trade has been further expanded, and the sales revenue has been increased correspondingly. The growth rate of the wholesale trade in China was as shown in Fig. 3.19.

Fig. 3.19. Increase in the sales revenue of the wholesale trade (1999–2007)

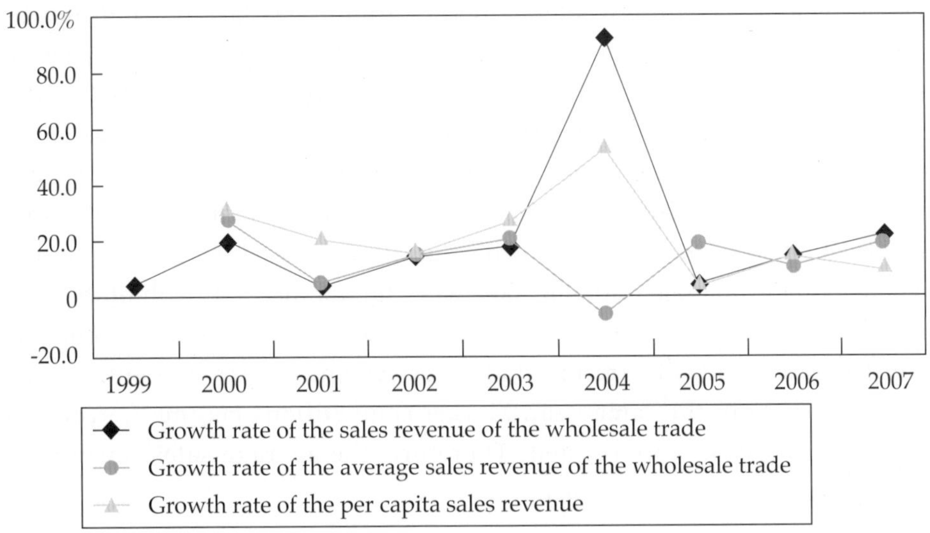

Seen from the growth rate of the sales revenue, apart from the growth rate of the average sales revenue of enterprises in 2004, the growth rate of the overall sales revenue of wholesale enterprises above the designated size, the average sales revenue of wholesale enterprises and that of the per capita sales revenue were all positive in other years during this period, indicating the smooth growth of the wholesale trade. However, the changing trends of the three indicators were not exactly consistent, but showed different characteristics. The growth rate of the total sales revenue was the most fluctuating of all, reaching the highest level of 92.9% in 2004 and the lowest level of simply 3.9% in 2001. The growth of the average sales revenue of the wholesale enterprises was once negative, falling by 6.3% in 2004. At its highest point, the growth rate of the average sales revenue of the wholesale enterprises was simply 28.1%. The highest growth rate of the per capita sales revenue appeared in 2004, being 53.5%; and the lowest of it appeared in 2005, being 4.2%.

It can be seen from the features of the three indicators that the growth rate of the total sales revenue of the wholesale trade was pretty much the same as that of the average sales revenue of wholesale enterprises. Therefore, a great part of the growth of the sales was created by newly-entered enterprises, not from the expansion of the size of original enterprises. Consequently, competitions in the wholesale trade were not that fierce. The entry of new enterprises wouldn't bring large-scale M & A with or the bankruptcy of original enterprises, but all enterprises, the old and the new, would segment market shares together. The profit margin of the wholesale trade was relatively large. The growth rate of the per capita sales revenue of the wholesale trade was greater than that of the sales revenue of the entire wholesale trade during 2000–2003. It could thus be concluded that the per capita efficiency of wholesale enterprises was improved. The phenomenon was caused by such reasons as the adoption of advanced technologies by wholesale enterprises, the increase in the per capita assets or the improvement of corporate governance, etc. From the above statistics, we can conclude that the primary reason for it was the constant reduction in the total number of wholesale practitioners, which greatly increased the per capita sales revenue of the wholesale trade. In 2004, with the significant growth of the total sales revenue of wholesale enterprises, the average sales revenue of wholesale enterprises reduced, illustrating that excessive enterprises had entered the wholesale trade in the same year. Market competitions became fiercer and market profits were apportioned. Therefore, the average sales revenue of wholesale enterprises didn't rise, but reduced.

Growth momentum of profits

The growth momentum of an enterprise not only depends on the growth of its revenue, but also its operational costs, management expenses and other factors. Profit is an indicator that includes all of these factors. So the growth momentum of an enterprise could be seen from the growth of its profits. See Fig. 3.20 for details.

Fig. 3.20. Growth of the profits of the wholesale trade (1999–2007)

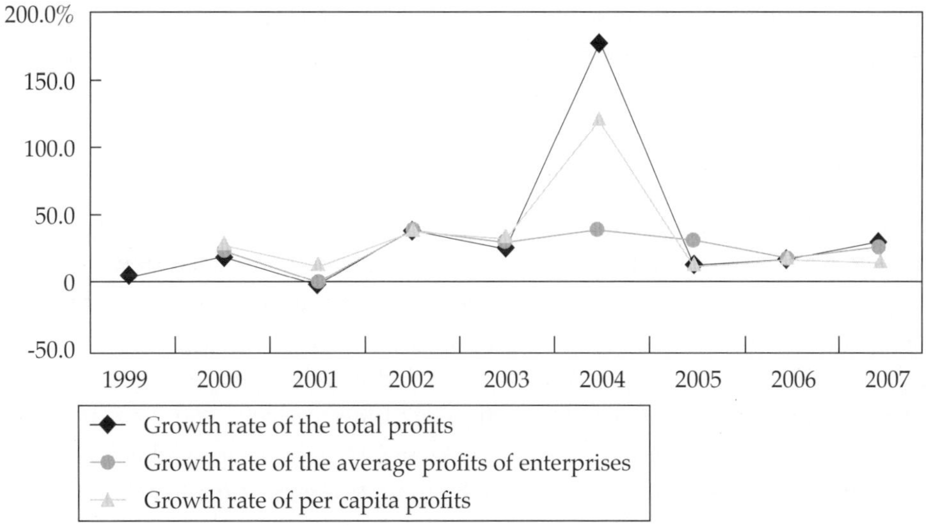

As can be seen from the figure, except for the year 2001 when both rates were negative, the total profits of wholesale enterprises above the designated size and that of the average profits of wholesale enterprises were positive in other years during this period. Of which, the growth rate of the total profits was the greatest in 2004, being 177.3% and reaching the historic high. The average profits of the wholesale enterprises in the same year didn't grow too much, which was consistent with the growth of the sales revenue of the industry. It illustrated that too many enterprises entered the wholesale trade in 2004, leading to fierce market competitions and apportioned average profits of enterprises. Different from the total profits and the average profits, the growth of the per capita profits kept positive at a great rate. Besides the increase in the total profits of enterprises, it was also contributed by the replacement of personnel with advanced technologies. It actually proved that the efficiency of the wholesale enterprises above the designated size kept improving.

All in all, the profits of the wholesale trade kept increasing, illustrating a good market performance of the wholesale trade. High market profits will attract more enterprises to enter the trade, further reducing the wholesale market concentration and strengthening the competitiveness of the market structure. In case of low barriers against the entry, the ultimate profits will reduce because of the entry of new enterprises.

Operational capability of the wholesale trade

The performance of an enterprise is not only reflected by its growth capacity in the future, but also its current operation. The operational capability of enterprises will be analyzed below on the basis of the turnover of total assets[4] of the wholesale enterprises above the designated size and the turnover of current assets[5].

Turnover of total assets

As shown by the statistical data in Fig. 3.21, the operational efficiency of the Chinese wholesale trade had been improved year by year since 1998. In 1998, the total assets turnover of the wholesale enterprises above the designated size was 1.32 times. After that, it kept climbing slightly. In 2004, the growth rate was high, reaching 2.84 times, up 44.2% over 2003. But it dropped in 2005 due to the great growth in 2004, down 14.9%, being 2.42 times. In 2006 and 2007, it began to grow again and finally reached 2.72 times in 2007. The process illustrated that the utilization rate of resources of the wholesale trade in China kept increasing, and that enterprises had better sales capabilities with less capital investment under the same conditions, conducive to improving the profitability of the wholesale trade.

Fig. 3.21. Total assets turnover of the wholesale trade (1998–2007)

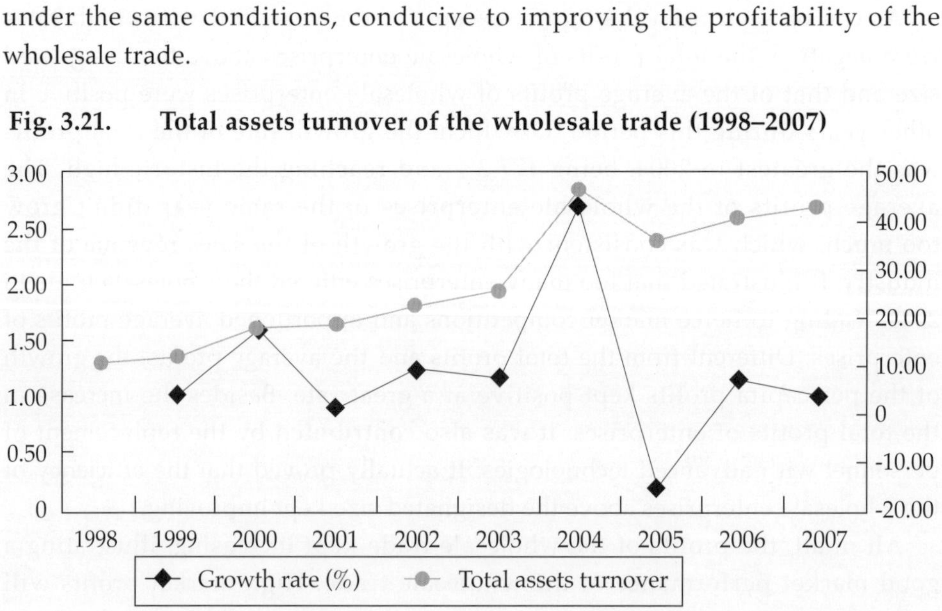

Current assets turnover

Total assets of the wholesale trade include not only current assets, but also fixed assets. Since fixed assets in themselves are with higher values and a lower rate of depreciation, the turnover of fixed assets is relatively slow. What's more, the wholesale trade belongs to the circulation sector. Compared with productive sectors, fixed-asset investments in the wholesale trade were relatively less. Therefore, current assets turnover of the wholesale trade could better reflect the utilization of resources by wholesale enterprises, and the sales and inventory disposal capabilities of such enterprises, thus could better reflect assets operation of the wholesale trade. Fig. 3.22 reflects the turnover of current assets of wholesale enterprises above the designated size during 1998–2007.

Fig. 3.22. Current assets turnover of the wholesale trade (1998–2007)

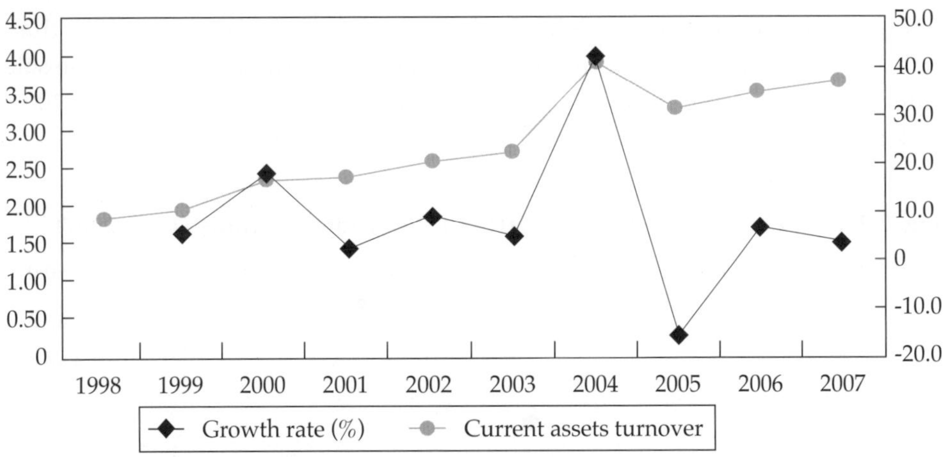

Except for 2005 when it dropped, current assets turnover had maintained a good growth momentum in other years during the same period. In particular, the current assets turnover in 2004 reached 3.85 times, up 42.5% over that in 2003. It was exactly for the excessive growth in 2004 that current assets turnover dropped in 2005 to 3.26 times, down 15.5%. In 2006 and 2007 that followed, it grew slightly. As can be seen in Fig. 3.21, comparatively, current assets turnover was greater than total assets turnover, mainly because that the turnover of fixed assets instead of the flow assets in the total assets was relatively slower. Yet the changing trend of current assets turnover and that of total assets turnover were consistent. Both grew significantly in 2004 and dropped in 2005 and both grew at a similar rate in other years. The constant improvement of the current assets turnover and that of the total assets turnover could illustrate the same thing, that is, the utilization rate of resources of the wholesale trade in China kept increasing; enterprises had better sales capabilities with less capital investment under the same conditions, conducive to improving the profitability of the wholesale trade.

Profitability of the wholesale trade

Profitability of the wholesale trade is an important measurement for the performance of wholesale enterprises. Main indicators of profitability chosen here are the rate of return on sales[6] and the return on assets (ROA)[7]. The higher the two rates, the higher the profitability of enterprises'.

The rate of return on sales

As can be seen from Fig. 3.23, the rate of return on sales of wholesale enterprises above the designated size was declining gradually during 1998–2001 before rising gradually during 2002–2007. It reached 6.6% in 2007, up 2.9% than 3.7%, the same rate in 1998. Of which, the rate of return on sales of wholesale enterprises above the designated size was 5.8% in 2004, up 43.8% over 2003, making 2004 the year with the greatest growth rate during the same period.

Fig. 3.23. The rate of return on sales of the wholesale trade (1998–2007)

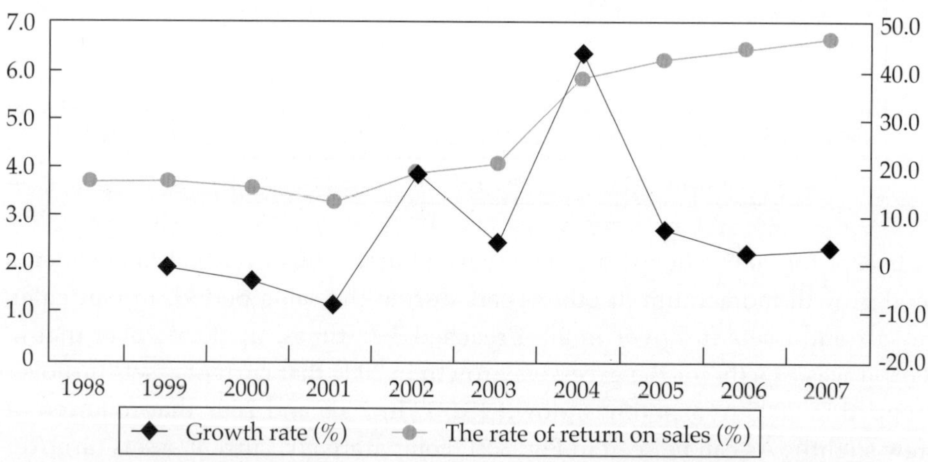

Changes in the rate of return on sales are closely related to mainly two indicators-sales profit and sales revenue. Under the premise of fixed sales revenue, if an enterprise could save various costs, reduction of enterprise expenses could help improve profits, then the profit margin. As can be seen from the above analysis of the total profits and revenue, as well as the growth rate, the total revenue and profits of wholesale enterprises above the designated size kept increasing, so the rate on return of sales was mainly determined by the growth rates of the two, showing enterprises' operations and the overall operation of the market. While the growth of profits depended mainly on the saving of all expenses, so the rate of return on sales was related to the changes in the overall market development, and to the measures taken by enterprises to reduce costs and expenses such as improving their management, adopting advanced technologies, and reducing practitioners.

On the whole, the rate of return on sales of the wholesale enterprises in China was on the rise, indicating that market operation of the wholesale trade in China was relatively better, that the operation of enterprises kept improving, and that the technical and management levels of wholesale enterprises had all improved.

Return on assets

It can be seen from Fig. 3.24 that the overall ROA of the wholesale enterprises above the designated size in China kept increasing during 1998–2007 from 4.9% in 1998 to 16.4% in 2007, up 13.5%. Of which, the same ROA was 13.6% in 2004, up 77.3% over 2003. The rising ROA of the wholesale trade in China illustrated that the profitability of the wholesale trade in China kept improving. On the one hand, it reflected the improvement of the operational management, technical level and personnel efficiency of wholesale enterprises, but on the other hand, it reflected that market structure of the wholesale trade in China was less competitive, and that the profit margin was relatively large, being very attractive to new enterprises.

Fig. 3.24. Return on assets of the wholesale trade (1998–2007)

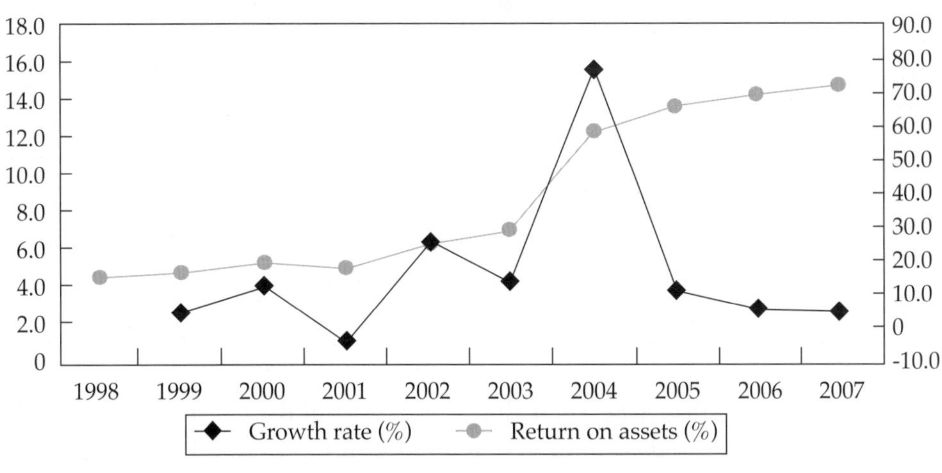

Taking an overall look at the changing trends of the performance of the wholesale trade in China, we can find that 2004 was a turning point of decisive significance in the development of the wholesale trade in China. Due to the acceleration of the opening up process of the wholesale trade in 2004, policy barriers against the wholesale trade in China became reduced greatly. At the same time, to face the approaching opening up of the wholesale trade in an all-round manner, government organs, industrial organizations and wholesale enterprises in China had all done a great deal of preparations and made significant achievements.

Solvency of wholesale enterprises

Indicator chosen to assess the long-term solvency of wholesale enterprises is the asset-liability ratio[8]. The asset-liability ratio reflects the comprehensive capacity of an enterprise of repaying its debts. The higher the ratio is, the poorer the enterprise' solvency will be, and vise versa. In addition, the asset-liability ratio, as an indicator, could also reflect enterprises' fund-raising capacity. Asset-liability ratio being too low illustrates that the enterprise fails to give full play to the role of financial leverage, which is not conducive to the rapid expansion of the enterprise's size. Therefore, it is not true that the lower the asset-liability ratio, the better.

Fig. 3.25. Asset-liability ratio of the wholesale trade (1998–2007)

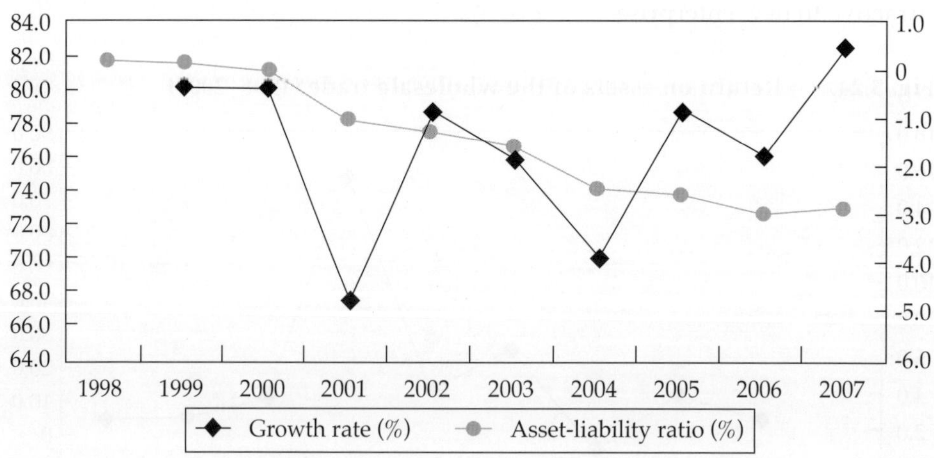

From Fig. 3.25, it can be seen that the asset-liability ratio of wholesale enterprises above the designated size had been maintained at somewhere below 83%, indicating a high solvency and fewer operational risks. Seen from the development trend, the asset-liability ratio was reducing gradually, from 82.0% in 1998 to 70.9% in 2007, down about 11%, indicating that the solvency of enterprises kept increasing and operational risks became increasingly smaller. On the other hand, reduction of the asset-liability ratio also demonstrated that wholesale enterprises failed to increase operational assets by issuing debts, and that the role of financial leverage failed to be fully displayed, which was unfavorable to the expansion of the size of wholesale enterprises in a faster way.

Performance levels of different sectors of the wholesale trade

The overall performance of the wholesale trade has been described and analyzed above. Since different sectors of the wholesale trade developed quite differently, the performance levels of different sectors of the wholesale trade will be investigated in detail and by ownership. Mainly the investigation will be made from operational capacity, profitability and insolvency.

Operational capacities of different sectors of the wholesale trade

The operational capacity of an enterprise is an important measurement for its performance. Since statistical data on different sectors of the wholesale trade were limited, total assets turnover is chosen here as the indicator. The total assets turnover of wholesale enterprises above the designated size is used to reflect the operational capacity of the wholesale trade.

Total assets turnover

As shown in Fig. 3.26, the total assets turnover of the privately-run and that of the foreign-invested sectors of the wholesale trade were higher than that of the state-owned and collective sectors of the wholesale trade. Total assets turnover of the privately-run sector of the wholesale trade was usually above 2.5 times, and that of the foreign-invested sector of the wholesale trade was above 1.5 times. Both turnovers even reached 3 times in 2001. Though the total assets turnover of the state-owned sector of the wholesale trade was lower than the privately-run and the foreign-invested sectors of the wholesale trade each year, it showed a growing trend, increasing from 1.38 times in 1999 to 2.24 times in 2007. However, total assets turnover of the collective sector of the wholesale trade had always been the lowest of the four, being below 2 times each year, even 1.5 times prior to 2003, fully reflecting the operational efficiencies of different sectors of the wholesale trade.

Fig. 3.26. Total assets turnover of each sector of the wholesale trade (1999–2007)

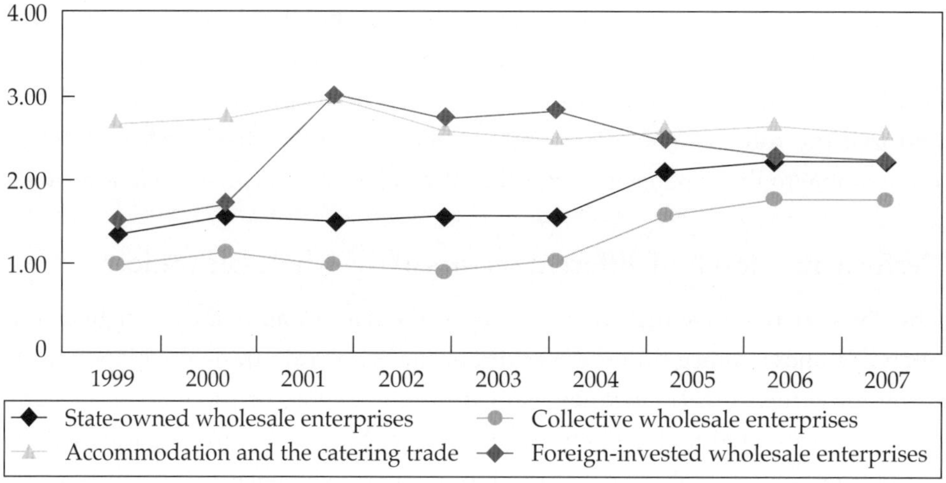

Fig. 3.27. Growth rate of the total assets turnover of each sector of the wholesale trade (2000–2007)

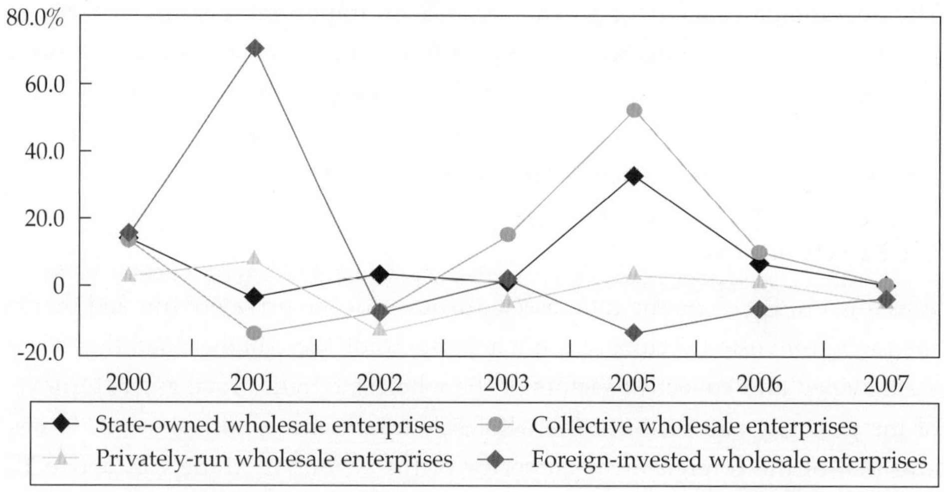

As shown in Fig. 3.27, the total assets turnovers of the foreign-invested and the collective sectors of the wholesale trade were the most fluctuating of all. Of which, the total assets turnover of the foreign-invested sector of the wholesale trade increased by 70% in 2001 before growing stably, even dropping slightly. The total assets turnover of the collective sector of the wholesale trade in 2000 was 14% higher that that in 1999, but 14% lower than that in 2001, and up 50% in 2005 over that in 2003. Comparatively, the total assets turnovers of the state-owned and the privately-run sectors of the wholesale trade fluctuated little.

The highest growth rate of the total assets turnover of the state-owned sector of the wholesale trade appeared in 2005, up 33% over that in 2003. Its range of fluctuation was below 20% in other years during the period. However, the range of fluctuation of the privately-run sector of the wholesale trade was even smaller, being below 10%.

Profitability of different sectors of the wholesale trade

The profitability of respective sector of the wholesale trade is an important measurement for the performances of different sectors of the wholesale trade. Here, main indicators of the profitability selected are still the rate of return on sales and the return on assets. The higher the two indicators are, the higher the profitability of the industry will be.

Fig. 3.28. Rate of return on sales of each sector of the wholesale trade (1999–2007)

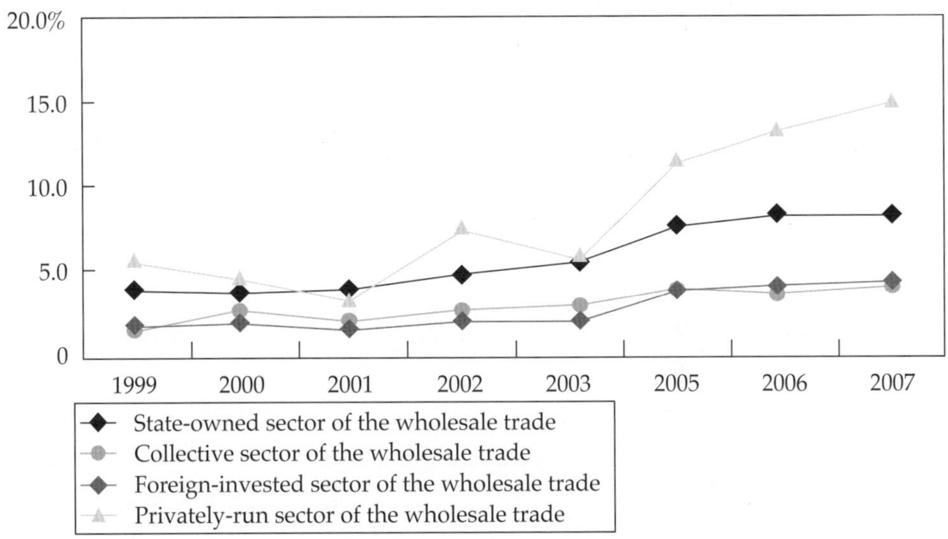

Rate of return on sales

As can be seen from Fig. 3.28, during 1999–2007, of the 4 different sectors of the wholesale trade, the foreign-invested sector of the wholesale trade saw the highest rate of return on sales, which was 14.8% at its highest point in 2007; the rate of return on assets of the state-owned sector of the wholesale trade ranked No. 2, reaching 8.3% in 2006 and 2007 at its highest point; and that of the privately-run sector of the wholesale trade and the collective sector of the wholesale trade were unstable and changing all the time in terms of ranking. Prior to 2005, the rate of return on sales of the collective sector of the wholesale trade was higher than that of the privately-run sector of the wholesale trade, but the rank conversed after 2005.

As can be seen from Fig. 3.29, during this period, the rates of return on sales of different sectors of the wholesale trade were all sometimes positive and sometimes negative. Of which, the rate of return on sales of the foreign-invested sector of the wholesale trade grew the fastest of all and fluctuated the most fiercely of all as well. Its growth rate reached the highest point of 122.6% in 2002, but fell significantly in 2003, grew significantly once again to reach 94.5% in 2005, then fell greatly before long. In addition, the range of fluctuation of the rate of return on sales of the privately-run sector of the wholesale trade was great, too. In particular, it reached 94.8% in 2005, being far higher than that in other years. Comparatively, the rates of return on sales of the state-owned and collective sectors of the wholesale trade grew steadily, being lower than 40% even at the highest point.

Fig. 3.29. Growth rate of the rate of return on sales of each sector of the wholesale trade (2000–2007)

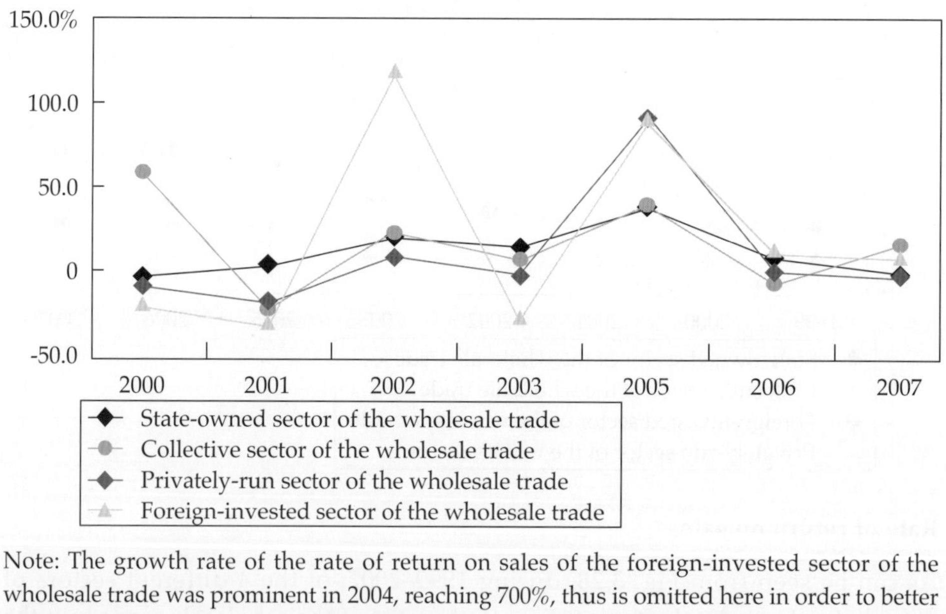

Note: The growth rate of the rate of return on sales of the foreign-invested sector of the wholesale trade was prominent in 2004, reaching 700%, thus is omitted here in order to better explain the changing trends of other data.

Return on assets

As can be seen from Fig. 3.30, the return on assets of different sectors of the wholesale trade were more or less the same prior to 2001, of which the return on assets of the privately-run sector and that of the state-owned sector of the wholesale trade were slightly higher than that of the collective sector and that of the foreign-invested sector of the wholesale trade. After 2002, differences between the return on assets of different sectors of the wholesale trade became significant. Of which, the foreign-invested sector of the wholesale trade had the highest return on assets, being far higher than that of other different sectors of the wholesale trade and being followed by the state-owned sector, the privately-run sector, and the collective sector of the wholesale trade. With time, the difference became greater and greater. In 2002, the highest return on assets (the foreign-invested sector of the wholesale trade) and the lowest return on assets (the collective sector of the wholesale trade) had a difference of 13.9%, which was further expanded to 26.5% in 2007.

Fig. 3.30. Return on assets of each sector of the wholesale trade (1999–2007)

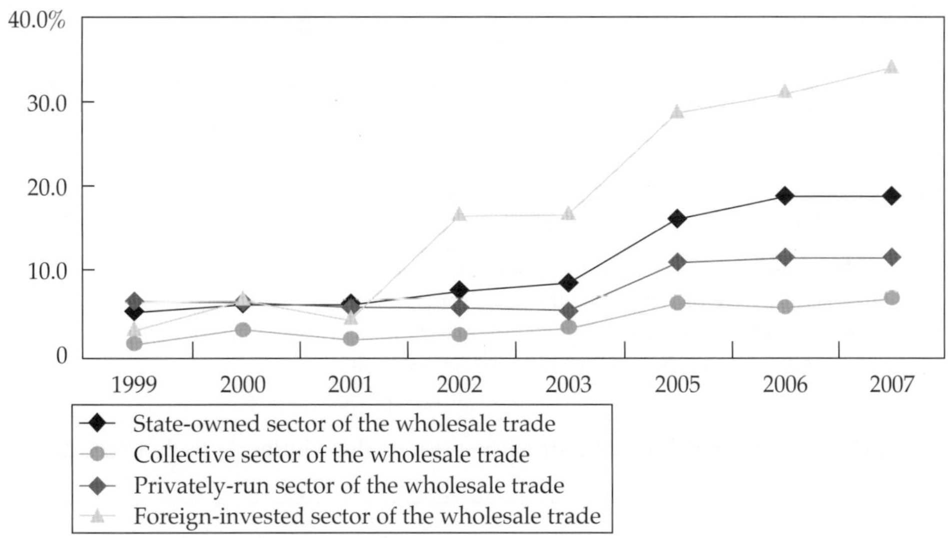

Let's check the specific growth rates of the return on assets of different sectors of the wholesale trade.

Changes in the return on assets of different sectors of the wholesale trade can be clearly observed from Fig. 3.31. Of which, the foreign-invested sector of the wholesale trade had the most fluctuating return on assets. After having a negative growth of 31.5% in 2001, the return on assets of the foreign-invested sector of the wholesale trade grew 257.4% in 2002, being far higher than its growth rate in other years and than that of other sectors of the wholesale trade in the same year. After its slump in 2003, the growth rate of the return on assets of the foreign-invested sector of the wholesale trade reached another peak in 2005, being 104.3%. The growth rate of return on assets of the collective sector of the wholesale trade fluctuated greatly, too, reaching 2 peaks in 2002 and 2005, respectively; and 2 ebbs in 2001 and 2006, respectively, being negative. Comparatively, fluctuations in the growth rate of the return on assets of the privately-run sector of the wholesale trade and that of the state-owned sector of the wholesale trade were relatively small, being stable in other years except for the peak in 2005.

Fig. 3.31. Growth rate of the return on assets of each sector of the wholesale trade (2000–2007)

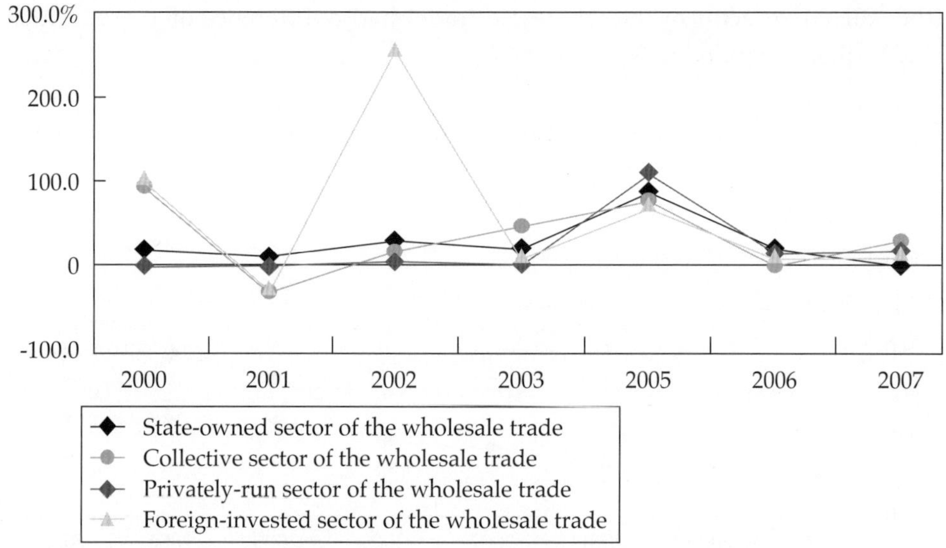

Fig. 3.32. Asset-liability ratio of each sector of the wholesale trade (1999–2007)

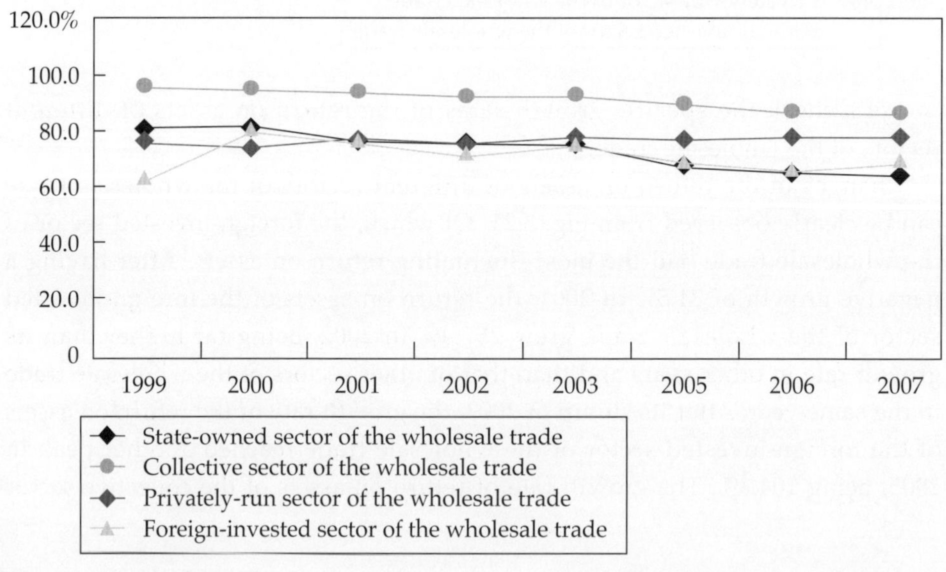

Solvency of different sectors of the wholesale trade

The asset-liability ratio is usually taken to investigate the solvency of different sectors of the wholesale trade. It can be seen from the description of the overall performance of the wholesale trade above that the solvency of the entire wholesale trade kept strengthened. See Fig. 3.32 for details.

The asset-liability ratio of the collective sector of the wholesale trade had been ranking the first among the four different sectors of the wholesale trade. Prior to 2003, the asset-liability ratio of the other three sectors of the wholesale trade was very close to one another, but after 2003, under the premise that the asset-liability ratio of the collective sector of the wholesale trade still ranked the first among the four, the asset-liability ratio of the privately-run sector of the wholesale trade grew significantly, being closer and closer to that of the collective sector of the wholesale trade and ranking the second of the four; that of the foreign-invested sector of the wholesale trade ranked the third of the four, being slightly higher than that of the state-owned sector of the wholesale trade. The higher the asset-liability ratio is, the poorer the solvency of an enterprise will be. Therefore, of the four different sectors of the wholesale trade, the state-owned sector of the wholesale trade had the best solvency of all, followed by the foreign-invested sector, then the privately-run sector and lastly the collective sector.

Specific growth rates are as follows.

Fig. 3.33. Growth rate of the asset-liability ratio of each sector of the wholesale trade (2000–2007)

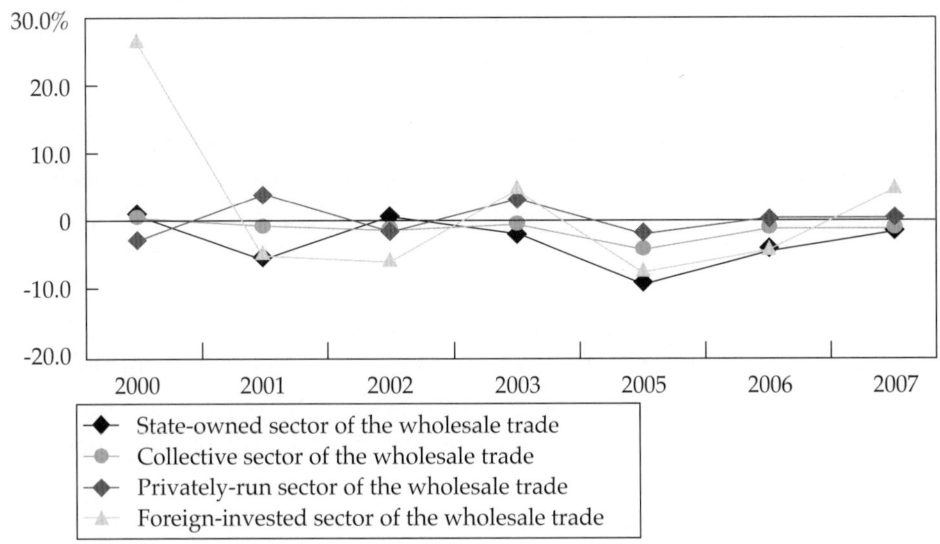

As can be seen from Fig. 3.33, of the asset-liability ratio of each sector of the wholesale trade, that of the foreign-invested sector was the most fluctuating of all, reaching the highest point of 26.5% in 2000, being nearly 30% higher than the lowest point in 2005; and that of the collective sector was the least fluctuating, falling slowly at the rate of about 1% in other years except for 2005 when it showed a significant fall along with other sectors of the wholesale trade. The asset-liability ratio of the privately-run sector and that of the foreign-invested sector were sometimes high and sometimes low, with frequent fluctuations, yet at lower rates.

From the above analysis of the performances of different sectors of the wholesale trade, we can see clearly the performance levels and development characteristics of different sectors of the wholesale trade.

(1) The state-owned sector of the wholesale trade ranked the second in terms of profitability. Its operational capability and solvency had been improved constantly. The overall performance of the state-owned sector of the wholesale trade was relatively high, mainly for the following several reasons: firstly, major measures aiming at helping the state-owned sector of the wholesale trade turn losses into profits adopted by China in 1998 had begun to play their roles, contributing to the improvement of the overall efficiency of the state-owned sector of the wholesale trade; secondly, the state-owned sector of the wholesale trade was forced to improve its competitiveness facing fierce competitions from their foreign counterparts, learn and introduce better modes of operation and management, and greatly improve their performances after China's accession to the WTO; finally, state policies provided the greatest supports for the state-owned sector of the wholesale trade. Though the dominant position of the state-owned sector of the wholesale trade had somewhat been weakened, but it hadn't completely lost. Therefore, it could still make better performance relying on its special position.

(2) The collective sector of the wholesale trade had the lowest level of performance on the whole in terms of the profitability, the operational capability and the solvency. It was closely related to the unclear property rights of the collective sector of the wholesale trade and the lack of effective supervision and incentive mechanisms.

(3) The privately-run sector of the wholesale trade stood out in terms of operational capability. Its total assets turnover was the highest of the four, which was closely related to the size of assets of the wholesale trade. The privately-run sector of the wholesale trade was flexible, capable of responding quickly to market signals.

(4) The foreign-invested sector of the wholesale trade had the highest level

of performance seen from the comprehensive assessment of its profitability, operational capabilities and solvency. In particular, its profitability, reflected as its rate of return on sales and return on assets, was far higher than that of other sectors of the wholesale trade. Reasons were indispensable from the strength of foreign-invested wholesale enterprises that had entered the Chinese wholesale trade. Such enterprises were all prestigious international enterprises having had rich experience in the wholesale trade, the most advanced management experience and modes of operations on the world, thus being capable of getting the highest profits with the lowest costs.

Levels of performances of the wholesale trade in different regions

The performances of the wholesale trade in 6 different regions in China will be analyzed in detail, mainly in terms of their profitability, operational capability and solvency with the purpose of getting the differences between the development efficiency of the wholesale trade in different regions in China.

Operational capability of the wholesale trade in different regions in China

The total assets turnover of the wholesale enterprises above the designated size will still be adopted here as the indicator to analyze the operational capability of wholesale enterprises.

As shown in Fig. 3.24, during 1999–2007, the total assets turnovers of the wholesale trade in different regions in China grew at different rates. In particular, they all showed a significant growth rate in 2005, meaning that the operational capabilities of the wholesale trade in different regions in China were enhanced constantly. Seen from the overall situation in this period, the total assets turnover of the wholesale trade in East China was the highest of all, followed by that of South Central China, then North China. That of Northeast China ranked the third prior to 2003, but grew significantly and exceeded that of East China before becoming the highest of all in 2005. Before 2007, the total assets turnover of the wholesale trade in Northwest China and that in Southwest China were basically the same. However, the total assets turnover of the wholesale trade in Northwest China showed a stunning growth rate all of sudden in 2007, ranking the second with 3.17 times. The difference between the highest and the lowest total assets turnovers of the wholesale trade in Northwest China was 0.85 times in 1999 and 1.32 times in 2007. It can be seen that the difference of the total assets turnover of the wholesale trade in different regions in China kept enlarging.

Fig. 3.34. Total assets turnover of the wholesale trade in different regions in China (1999–2007)

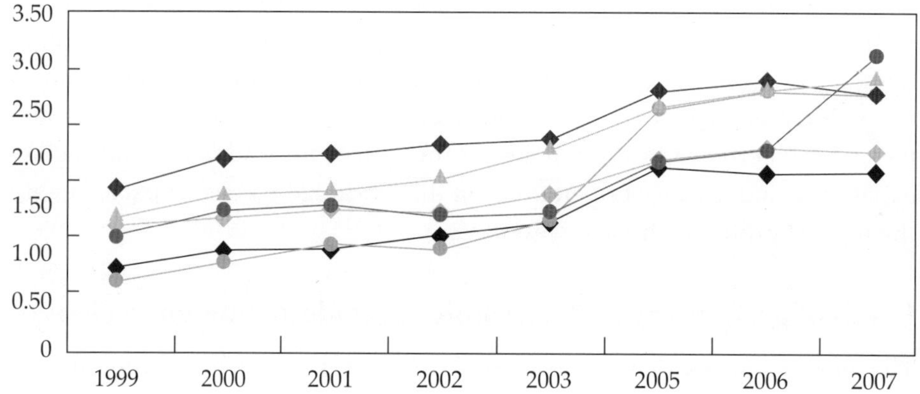

Year	1999	2000	2001	2002	2003	2005	2006	2007
North China	0.90%	1.09%	1.13%	1.23%	1.37%	1.92%	1.88%	1.90%
Northeast China	1.31%	1.50%	1.71%	1.64%	1.95%	3.08%	3.18%	3.22%
East China	1.75%	2.01%	2.08%	2.19%	2.22%	2.72%	2.82%	2.71%
South Central China	1.42%	1.61%	1.68%	1.81%	2.10%	2.54%	2.69%	2.83%
Southwest China	1.31%	1.42%	1.53%	1.45%	1.65%	1.96%	2.11%	2.04%
Northwest China	1.22%	1.48%	1.52%	1.43%	1.48%	2.00%	2.11%	3.07%

Profitability of the wholesale trade in different regions in China

The profitability of the wholesale trade in different regions is an important measurement for the performance of the wholesale trade in different regions. Main profitability indicators chosen here are still the rate of return on sales and the return on assets.

Rate of return on sales

As can be seen from Fig. 3.35, the rate of return on sales of wholesale enterprises in most regions in China all grew constantly, indicating the strengthened profitability of wholesale enterprises in different regions in China. Of which, the rate of return on sales of wholesale enterprises in Southwest China was far higher than that in other regions, ranking the first. It was followed by that in East China and South Central China, the two of which were close. The rate of return on sales of wholesale enterprises in East China was slightly higher before 2005, only to be replaced by that of wholesale enterprises in South Central China. Wholesale enterprises in Northeast China had the lowest rate of return on sales, which kept falling during 2000–2003. Though a growing trend appeared in 2005, it was still the lowest among the four. As for the difference between the highest and lowest rates, it was 4.9% in 1999 and 4.2% in 2007, showing a narrowed difference of the rates of return on sales of wholesale enterprises in all regions in China.

Fig. 3.35. Rate of return on sales of the wholesale trade in different regions in China (1999–2007)

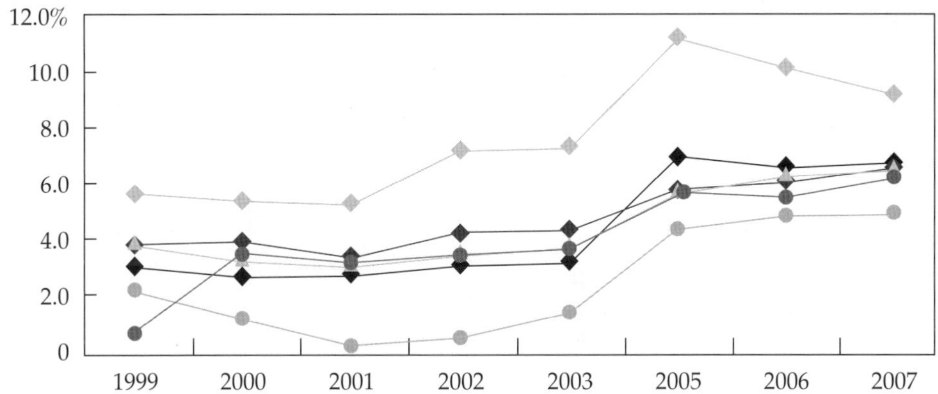

Year	1999	2000	2001	2002	2003	2005	2006	2007
North China	3.1%	2.9%	2.9%	3.2%	3.2%	7.0%	6.6%	6.8%
Northeast China	2.3%	1.4%	0.4%	0.6%	1.5%	4.4%	4.9%	5.0%
East China	3.9%	3.9%	3.6%	4.3%	4.5%	5.8%	6.2%	6.7%
South Central China	3.9%	3.4%	3.1%	3.7%	3.9%	5.8%	6.4%	6.3%
Southwest China	5.7%	5.5%	5.4%	7.1%	7.4%	11.2%	10.1%	9.2%
Northwest China	0.8%	3.6%	3.3%	3.5%	3.7%	5.7%	5.5%	6.1%

Return on assets

As can be seen from Fig. 3.36, the return on assets of wholesale enterprises in all regions in China was consistent with the rate of return on sales, that is, the return on assets of wholesale enterprises in most regions in China showed a growing tendency. However, the return on assets of wholesale enterprises in Southwest China was the highest, that in East China ranked the second, that in South Central China ranked the third, and that in Northeast China was the lowest of all. Different from the rate of return on assets, the return on assets of wholesale enterprises in Northeast China grew significantly by 352.9% in 2005, leaping over that in North China and Northwest China to rank No. 4. The growth rate of the return on assets of wholesale enterprises in Northwestern China was 61.9% in 2007, reaching 18.7% and being 0.1% lower than that of wholesale enterprises in Southwest China. As for the differences of the returns on assets of wholesale enterprises in all regions, the difference between the highest and lowest returns on assets of wholesale enterprises in China was 6.4% in 1999, which further fell to 5.9% in 2007. Coupled with the changes in the rate of return on sales, the profitability of wholesale enterprises in all regions was enhanced on the whole, and regional differences were narrowing down.

Fig. 3.36. Return on Assets of the wholesale trade in different regions (1999–2007)

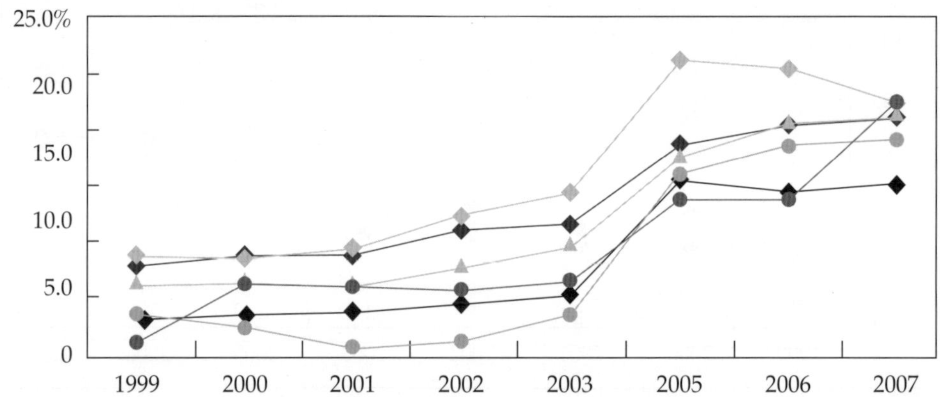

Year	1999	2000	2001	2002	2003	2005	2006	2007
North China	2.8%	3.1%	3.3%	3.9%	4.4%	13.4%	12.3%	12.9%
Northeast China	3.0%	2.0%	0.6%	1.0%	3.0%	13.5%	15.5%	15.9%
East China	6.8%	7.9%	7.5%	9.4%	9.9%	15.8%	17.4%	18.1%
South Central China	5.5%	5.4%	5.3%	6.6%	8.1%	14.8%	17.1%	17.7%
Southwest China	7.4%	7.8%	8.3%	10.3%	12.1%	21.9%	21.3%	18.8%
Northwest China	1.0%	5.3%	5.0%	5.0%	5.5%	11.5%	11.6%	18.7%

Solvency of the wholesale trade in different regions

The asset-liability ratio is the main indicator used in the investigation of the solvency of wholesale enterprises in different regions. From the above analysis of the overall performance of the wholesale trade, we can see that the overall solvency of the entire wholesale trade kept strengthened. See Fig. 3.37 for details.

Seen from the development trend, the asset-liability ratio in each region was falling. As for the ranking, wholesale enterprises in Northeast China had the highest asset-liability ratio, followed by Northwest China. After 2003, Southwest China had the lowest asset-liability ratio among all. As for regional differences, the difference between the highest asset-liability ratio (being 93%, in Northwest China) and the lowest (being 78%, in East China) was 15% in 1999.

In 2007, the same difference between the highest asset-liability ratio (being 78%, in Northeast China) and the lowest (being 61%, in Southwest China) was 17%. It is clear that the solvency of wholesale enterprises in all regions in China was enhanced, yet regional difference became greater and greater.

Fig. 3.37. Asset-liability ratio of wholesale enterprises in different regions (1999–2007)

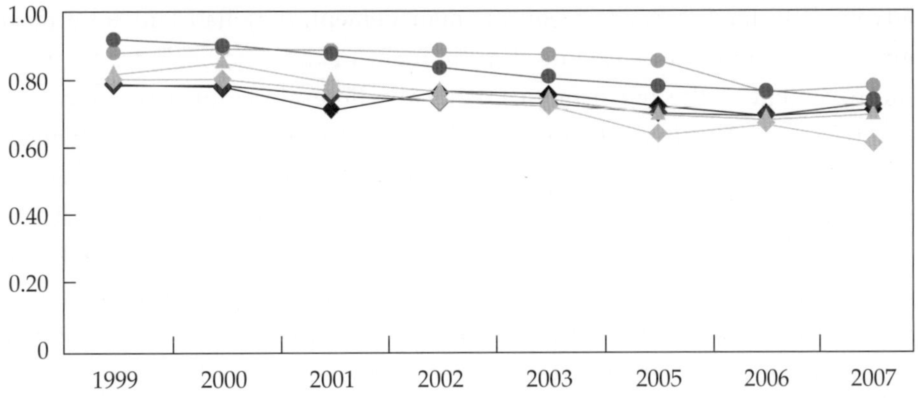

Year	1999	2000	2001	2002	2003	2005	2006	2007
North China	0.80	0.77	0.71	0.76	0.76	0.72	0.70	0.71
Northeast China	0.90	0.91	0.89	0.89	0.88	0.86	0.77	0.78
East China	0.78	0.78	0.75	0.73	0.72	0.70	0.70	0.72
South Central China	0.84	0.87	0.82	0.79	0.76	0.72	0.71	0.71
Southwest China	0.81	0.81	0.77	0.74	0.72	0.64	0.66	0.61
Northwest China	0.93	0.91	0.88	0.84	0.82	0.79	0.77	0.75

From the above analysis of the regional structure of the performances of the wholesale enterprises across China during this period, we can see that the operational capability, profitability and solvency of wholesale enterprises in all regions were increasing constantly, illustrating that the overall performance of the wholesale enterprises in all regions in China was on the rise, being consistent with the development trend of the wholesale trade as a whole. Of which, the profitability of wholesale enterprises in Southwest China was the highest of all. Mainly, it was because that the wholesale trade hadn't fully developed in Southwest China, wholesale enterprises were small in number, competitions were not fierce, and the wholesale market concentration was high. Low capacity for asset turnover illustrated that both asset and commodity circulations in Southwest China were slow. Low operational capability of the wholesale trade in Southwest China indicated from another angle that local wholesale trade hadn't fully developed and market competitions were not intense. As for wholesale enterprises in East China and South Central China, their profitability was second only to that of wholesale enterprises in Southwest China, but their capacity for asset turnover was the highest of all, and they had a strong solvency. Generally speaking, the level of their performance was the highest of all. Both regions are the most developed regions in China. With developed commerce, modernized circulation, improved market system, advanced technologies and scientific management, they had laid solid macro- and micro-foundations for the development of the wholesale trade and the improvement of the performance of local wholesale enterprises. Wholesale enterprises in Northeast China had the lowest profitability and solvency in China, and their capacity for asset turnover was not very high, either. Generally speaking, the level of performance of wholesale enterprises in Northeast China was the lowest among all of the six regions, which was inevitably related to the development history of the wholesale trade in Northeast China. Since the reform and opening up, Northeast China had always been the base of heavy industries in China whose industrial policies obviously tilt to the secondary industry and failed to pay enough attention to developing the tertiary industry. So the tertiary industry in Southeast China had been developing slowly, and the wholesale trade was no exception. That's why the overall performance level of wholesale enterprises in Northeast China was the lowest of all.

Performance levels of large-scale wholesale enterprises

The same as the large-scale enterprises selected in the previously three sections, large-scale wholesale enterprises here still refer to the top 50 wholesale enterprises in terms of the sales revenue. Due to limited statistics, we only describe the performance of large-scale enterprises since 1999 in detail. Specifically, their growth capacity will be reflected by the growth of their profits and increase in revenue; and their profitability will be investigated through the rate of return on assets.

The growth capacity of large-scale wholesale enterprises

The growth capacity of the wholesale enterprises above the designated size has been described and analyzed. The sales revenue and the growth rate of profits of large-scale wholesale enterprises will be adopted below to reflect the growth capacity of such enterprises and better analyze the level of performance of the wholesale trade in an all-round manner.

Growth rate of the sales revenue

he sales of the wholesale trade have been increasing since the reform and opening up. The overall sales, per capita sales revenue of wholesale enterprises and the average sales revenue have all been increasing. It was true for large-scale wholesale enterprises. See Fig. 3.38 for details of the sales revenue of large-scale wholesale enterprises.

As can be seen from Fig. 3.38, the growth rate of the sales revenue of each of the top 50 large-scale wholesale enterprises was all positive. That is to say, their sales kept increasing. However, the growth rate of the sales of the top 50 large-scale wholesale enterprises was greatly fluctuating, reaching the highest point of 65.1% in 2005 and the lowest point of 1.0% in 2001. Specific fluctuations were consistent with the aforesaid growth rate of sales of the wholesale trade as a whole. From the above range of fluctuations, it could be seen that the growth capacity of the sales revenue of large-scale wholesale enterprises was unstable and influenced by economic, political and legal factors. There were no significant rules to follow. However, the average growth of sales of the wholesale trade illustrated that the growth capacity of large-scale wholesale enterprises was relatively higher.

Fig. 3.38. Growth rate of the sales revenue of large-scale wholesale enterprises (2000–2007)

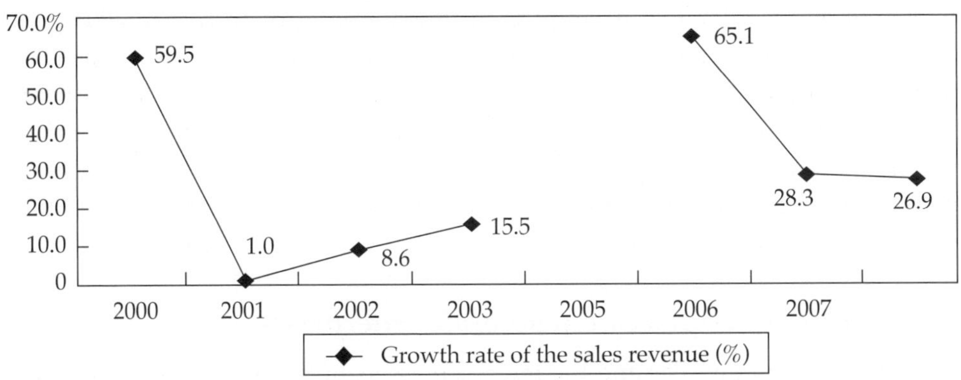

Growth rate of profits

As can be seen from the analysis of the overall performance of the wholesale enterprises above the designated size, during 1998–2007, the total profits, the per capita profits and the average profits of wholesale enterprises above the designated size all showed a growing trend. However, the growth of profits of large-scale wholesale enterprises showed a different trend. See Fig. 3.39 for details.

Fig. 3.39. Growth rate of profits of large-scale wholesale enterprises (2000–2007)

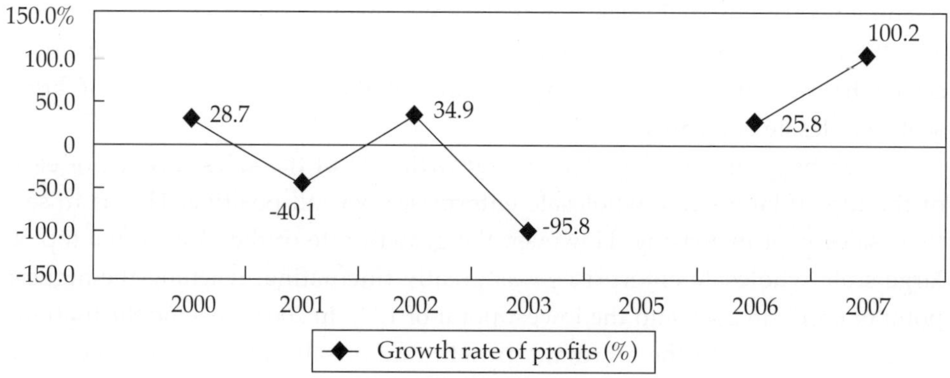

The growth rate of profits of the top 50 large-scale wholesale enterprises was sometimes positive and sometimes negative, illustrating the constant rises and falls, instability and great fluctuations of their profits. It reached the highest point in 2007, being 100.2%; and fell to the lowest point in 2003, being -95.8%. The overall growth rate of profits of the wholesale trade had never been this fluctuating. In particular, the great falls in 2001 and 2003, respectively, of the profits of the top 50 large-scale wholesale enterprises had never happened to the wholesale trade as a whole. Plus, data for 2004 were unavailable, thus it was unable to make a detailed description of the annual growth rate in 2004 and 2005. No law on the growth of profits of large-scale wholesale enterprises was there to follow. However, we can conclude from the surface that the capacity for profit growth of large-scale wholesale enterprises was unstable, and sometimes fell significantly, indicating that it was influenced by many factors such as market structure, changes in market concentration, enterprise behaviors and the political and legal factors, etc.

Profitability of large-scale wholesale enterprises

The rate of return on sales and the return on assets of the wholesale trade were growing all the way, indicating the constant improvement of the profitability of the wholesale trade as a whole. The profitability of large-scale wholesale enterprises was mainly reflected through the return on assets. See Fig. 3.40 for details.

It can be seen from Fig. 3.40 that the respective return on assets of the top 50 large-scale wholesale enterprises was positive, indicating that large-scale wholesale enterprises were profitable on the whole. However, the levels of profitability were quite different. Specifically, the return on assets reached the highest in 2007, being 16.1%, up 66.6% over the previous year; and fell to the lowest in 2003, being only 0.6%, down 90.4% over the previous year. Comparing with the overall situation of the wholesale trade, the return on assets of large-scale wholesale enterprises was more fluctuating. However, the profitability of such enterprises was improved constantly on the whole, from 4.6% in 2001 to 16.1% in 2007, up 11.5%, reflecting the improvement of the operational and management levels, technical level and personnel efficiency of large-scale wholesale enterprises and the acceleration of its modernization and standardization process.

Fig. 3.40. Returns on assets of large-scale wholesale establishments (2001–2007)

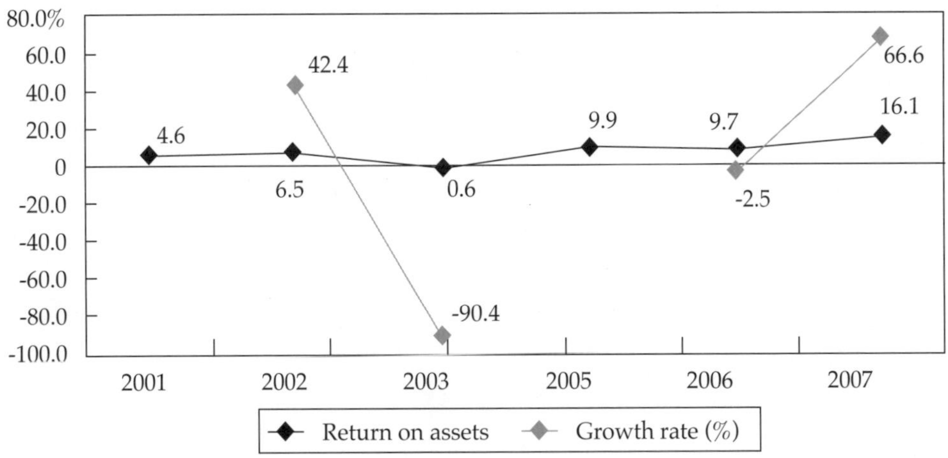

4

Chapter

Changes in the Structure of the Wholesale Trade

Since the reform and opening up, the wholesale trade has achieved great development and played an increasingly important role in commerce and the national economy in China. Along with industrial organization optimization, the wholesale trade has undergone changes in its structure. In this chapter, the author will investigate and analyze the regional structure, the ownership structure and the industrial structure of the wholesale trade in order to get rules of its development and changes.[1]

Development of and Changes in Different Sectors of the Wholesale Trade

The market-oriented reform launched in China since 1978 aimed at eliminating the disadvantages of the traditional planned economic system and enabling the market economic system to gradually play its essential role in resource allocation. The development of the wholesale trade which is closely related to the market has fully reflected such market-oriented features. Of which, the most representative of all is the rapid development of the non-public sector of the wholesale trade and the fierce changes in the ownership structure of the wholesale trade thus caused.

Basic information on the registration of different sectors of the wholesale trade

Basic information on the registration of different sectors of the wholesale trade includes the number of wholesale institutions, the number of outlets (industrial establishments) and practitioners. For the lack of statistical data, the statistics available are staged. Therefore, analysis of the basic information of different sectors of the wholesale trade will be made below by stage.

Initial stage of the reform and opening up (1978–1984)

At the stage, the forms of ownerships of the wholesale trade in China were mainly the state-owned sector of the wholesale trade, the collective sector of the wholesale trade and a few numbers of individual wholesalers. Objects of the reform in this stage were mainly the state-owned and collective wholesale enterprises, based on which the wholesale trade system left over from before the reform and opening up would be reformed.

State-owned and collective sectors of the wholesale trade

Reform of the state-owned and collective sectors of the wholesale trade experienced three stages during 1979–1984, namely:

(1) The trial of the responsibility system for operation during 1979–1981. In 1978, the Ministry of Commerce and the Ministry of Finance made a joint decision to improve and unify across China the proportion of profits retained of the state-owned sector of the wholesale trade, and provided that state finance would split the profits of such trades into 20–80% (namely 20% of such profits were required to be turned over to state finance, and the rest 80% may be retained by commerce). It created conditions for the reform and development of the wholesale trade. As of the end of 1981, more than 35,000 enterprises in 28 provinces, autonomous regions and municipalities had launched the trial of the responsibility system for operation, accounting for 1/3 of the state-owned wholesale enterprises across China.

(2) The trial of the operation contract responsibility system during 1982–1983. This reform aimed at solving the problem of combining enterprises' responsibilities, power and benefits and the problem of combining employees' responsibilities, power and salaries. Enterprises may be contracted by the state or by their staff and workers in order to solve the problem of enterprising getting equal treatments from the state regardless of their performances and staff and workers getting equal treatments from enterprises regardless of the work they had done, and to return the autonomy to enterprises themselves. However, for the limitations of social practices and awareness, the reform was pushed forward too quickly. A few enterprises had the tendency of harming consumer interests for the sole purpose of making profits, provoking strong repercussions. The reform encountered setbacks once again. Since the second half of 1983, China began to take the second step — "substitution of tax payment for profit delivery". It was not the profits, but the income tax (large and medium-sized enterprises still had to pay the regulatory tax) that was required from enterprises to be paid to the government. Profits of enterprises' were no longer contracted to the state.

(3) The trial of "change, transform, lease and sell" in 1984 in the reform. "Change" referred to change enterprises into being state-owned and collective-operated, and being capable of paying taxes according to regulations and assuming sole responsibility for their own profits and losses. "Transform" referred to change enterprises directly into being collective-owned, valuate the state-owned fixed assets at the concurrent value of the transformation,

and implement paid transfer and mortgage payments over the current assets allocated by the state. By "lease", it referred to lease some labor-based small shops engaged in catering, services, repair and overhauling to individual operators mainly through public bidding. By "sell", it meant that some small enterprises located in remote areas, with meager profits or suffering losses, as well as labor-based catering businesses were sold to individual operators or turned into a partnership through public auctions. According to statistics, as of the end of 1984, China had liberalized the operation of 58,060 small state-owned enterprises engaged in retail, catering and public services. Of which, 46,589 had been transformed into state-owned, yet collective-operated enterprises, 5,554 had been changed into partnership, and 5,917 had been leased to individual operators.[2]

During this period, state-owned and collective wholesale enterprises held an absolute leading position. Reform of the wholesale trade focused on the three levels of wholesale of manufactured goods for daily use. The reform simply touched upon the mode of wholesale operation, but failed to adjust the ownerships of the wholesale. Therefore, state-owned commercial wholesale enterprises were not only the mainstay, but also the backup force of commercial trade centers capable of playing a leading role in state-owned commerce.

Individual and privately-run sectors of the wholesale trade

At the end of the 1970s, the individual and privately-run sectors of the wholesale trade developed from scratch. Of the total sales of retail of social consumables in 1978, those of the non-public sector of the economy accounted for 2.1%.[3] Thanks to the improvement of the domestic economic situation brought about by the reform and opening up and the gradually relaxing policy environment, as of the first half of the 1980s, the individual sector of the Chinese economy recovered and developed soon, and the privately-run sector of the Chinese economy entered the initial stage, too.

In this period, the individual and privately-run sectors of the wholesale trade developed mainly in rural areas. The implementation of the household contract responsibility system in rural areas protected farmers' economic interests and democratic rights, and greatly stimulated farmers' enthusiasm and creativity, enabling the rural economy to develop rapidly after years of accumulation. Increase in farmers' income resulted in a substantial increase in their demands for means of agricultural production and social consumables. Coupled with the implementation of various economic construction-oriented policies of the Party and the Chinese Government, the individual and privately-run sectors of the wholesale trade which started from scratch showed a momentum of rapid development. The outlets of individual commerce reached 178,000 in 1978, then 7,281 thousand in 1984, up 39.9 times. The sales of retail increased from RMB 210 million to 32,370 million, up 153.1 times. According to the statistics of the State Administration for Industry and Commerce of the People's Republic of China, during 1981–1983, the total number, the number of practitioners, the amount of registered capital and the business income of small private businesses in rural areas increased by 3.38 times, 3.42 times, 8.18 times and 12.58 times, respectively.

As for the development routes of the individual and privately-run sectors of the wholesale trade in this period, most of such wholesale enterprises developed on their own based on their specific conditions and advantages and in a relaxing policy environment. Generally speaking, the development of the individual and privately-run sectors of the wholesale trade played a positive role in recovering the development of commerce in China. The public sector of the economy hadn't been weakened, but strengthened.[4]

The stage of the planned commodity economy (1985–1991)

During this period, the state-owned and collective sectors of the wholesale trade still held the dominant position. The privately-run sector of the wholesale trade achieved a certain degree of development. The details of the development of such sectors of the wholesale trade will be described below using the number of wholesale institutions and practitioners.

Number of wholesale institutions

Since data in this period were only about the number of wholesale institutions in the state-owned and collective sectors, and no statistics about the privately-run sector of the wholesale trade were available, the development of the privately-run sector of the wholesale trade can only be reflected by the number of private businesses. Let's firstly check the changes in the numbers of the state-owned and collective sectors of the wholesale trade.

As can be seen from Fig. 4.1, the number of state-owned wholesale businesses in China in 1990 fell nearly 40% over the previous two years. It didn't show a significant recovery until after 1992. Different from the changing trends of the number of state-owned wholesale businesses, the number of collective wholesale institutions during this period grew significantly. Though falling in 1990, too, it fell at a smaller rate than that of state-owned wholesale businesses, being simply 8.8%. However, the number of collective wholesale institutions in 1991 and 1992 exceeded that in 1988 and 1989, respectively. The difference between the state-owned wholesale businesses and the collective wholesale businesses in terms of number became increasingly smaller, which can be better reflected in Fig. 4.2.

Fig. 4.1. Numbers of the state-owned wholesale businesses and the collective wholesale businesses (1988–1992)

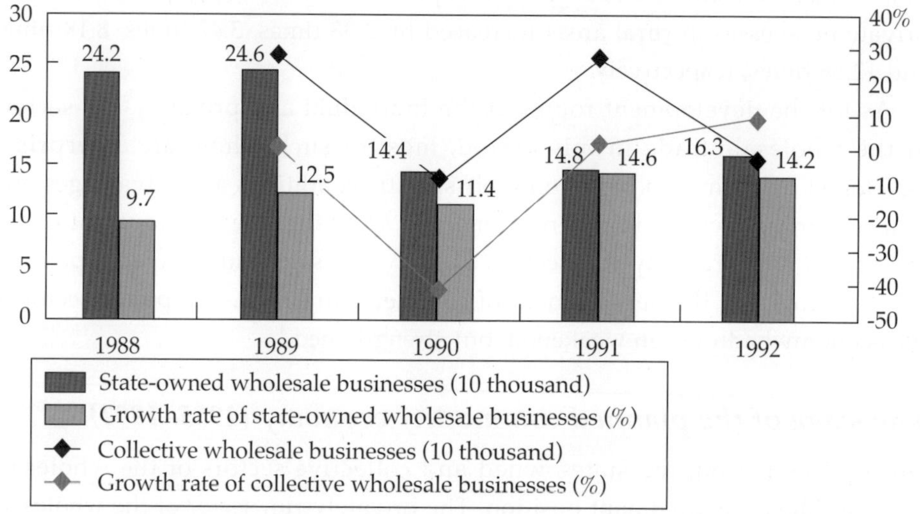

Fig. 4.2. Proportions of the state-owned wholesale businesses and the collective wholesale businesses (1988–1992)

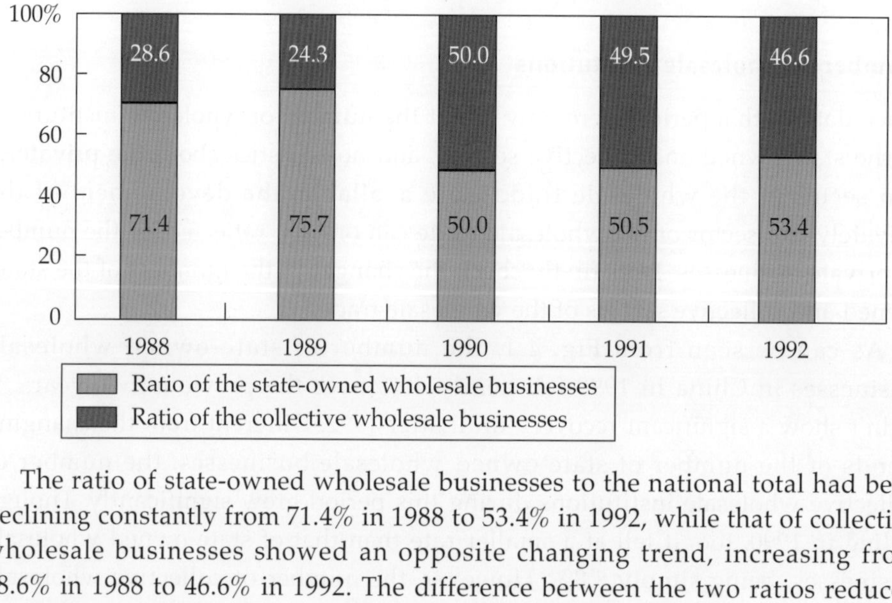

The ratio of state-owned wholesale businesses to the national total had been declining constantly from 71.4% in 1988 to 53.4% in 1992, while that of collective wholesale businesses showed an opposite changing trend, increasing from 28.6% in 1988 to 46.6% in 1992. The difference between the two ratios reduced from 42.8% in 1988 to 6.8% in 1992, being significantly reduced.

The development of the privately-run sector of the wholesale trade will be analyzed using the development of the number of private businesses.[5]

As can be seen from Fig. 4.3, the number of private businesses in China during this period grew in a fluctuating way: it grew very rapidly during 1984–1988, showing a positive growth momentum and reaching the highest point of 25.5% in 1985. However, the number reduced in 1989 when China intensified its macroeconomic control and cleared up and rectified its industry and commerce, and grew slowly after that to the level very close to that in 1988 before reaching 14.17 million in 1991.

Fig. 4.3. Changes in the number of private businesses (1984–1991)

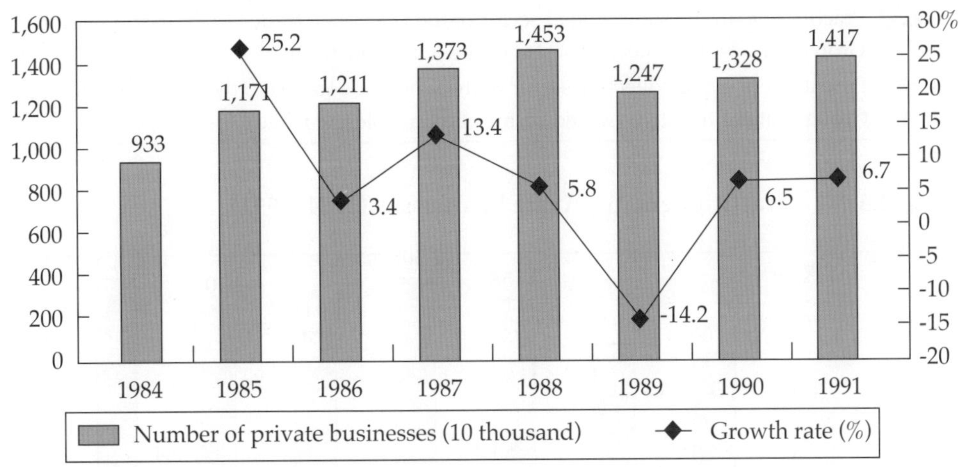

The number of practitioners

As can be seen from Fig. 4.4, practitioners in the state-owned sector of the wholesale trade showed a development momentum in fluctuations, reaching the greatest number of 3.014 million in 1989 and falling to the smallest number of 2.319 million in 1990, down 23.1%, though it recovered to 28.56 million in 1992. Practitioners in the collective sector of the wholesale trade didn't change much, showing a tendency of slow development and increasing from 11.39 million in 1989 to 12.69 million in 1992.

Comparing Fig. 4.4 with Fig. 4.3, we can see that there is a high goodness between the number of practitioners engaged in private businesses and that of private businesses, since private businesses were mainly small in size and many of them were family-run. As for the development trend, the number of practitioners in private businesses increased greatly from 13.04 million in 1984 to 23.08 million in 1991, being 10.04 million people more.

Fig. 4.4. Numbers of practitioners in the state-owned and collective sectors of the wholesale trade (1988–1992)

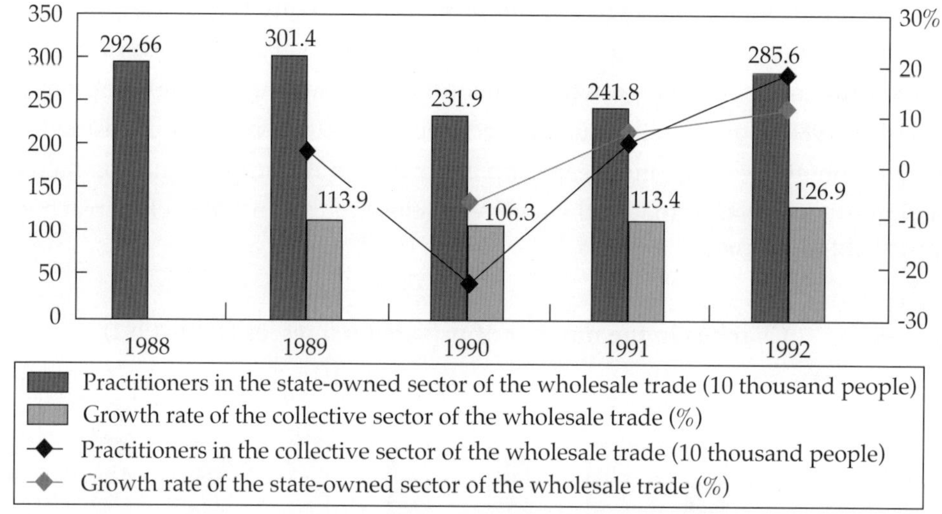

Fig. 4.5. Practitioners in private businesses (1984–1991)

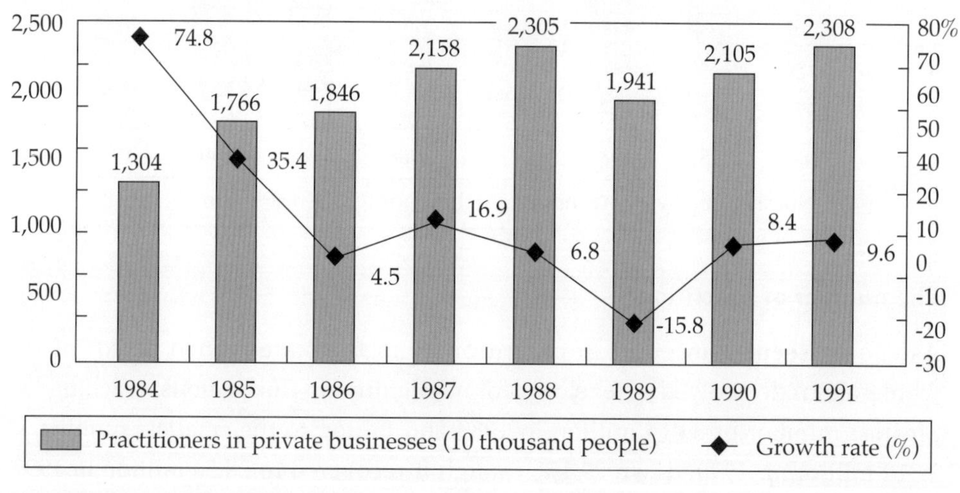

It can be seen from the basic situation of different sectors of the wholesale trade that the proportion of the number of state-owned wholesale institutions and that of the number of practitioners in state-owned wholesale institutions were still higher than 50%, illustrating the dominant position of the state-owned sector of the wholesale trade. However, the number of state-owned wholesale institutions and that of practitioners in state-owned wholesale institutions showed a tendency of great falls. The collective sector of the wholesale trade, in contrast, grew significantly, demonstrating that the dominance of the state-owned sector of the wholesale trade had no longer existed. It was mainly because that in April 1987, State Commission for Economic Restructuring, the Ministry of Commerce and the Ministry of Finance of China jointly issued *Report on the Opinions Concerning the Application for the Institutional Reform of the State-run Commerce and the Supply and Marketing Cooperatives*, shifting the focus of the reform of state-owned wholesale enterprises to how to improve enterprise vitality and profitability, and beginning to clear up and rectify some state-owned wholesale enterprises with poor performances or profitability, leading to the significant reduction of the number state-owned wholesale enterprises. To promote the reform of small enterprises in this period, the State Council of China approved, in May 1986, the *Report on the Several Issues Concerning the Commercial Restructuring in 1986* jointed issued by the State Commission for Economic Restructuring and the Ministry of Commerce, providing vigorous policy supports for small state-owned businesses to become state-owned, yet collective-run businesses, and promoting the development of the collective sector of the wholesale trade.

The privately-run sector of the wholesale trade achieved a great development in this period, too. In 1984, China began to reform its circulation system, eased market access, and allowed the existence of various market entities, enabling the privately-run sector of the wholesale trade to show a strong momentum of economic development. However, due to its weak foundation, the privately-run sector of the wholesale trade encountered many unfair treatments in the development process. That's why comparing with that of the state-owned sector and the collective sector of the wholesale trade, the proportion of the privately-run sector of the wholesale trade was negligible, and the public sector of the economy still held an absolute dominant position in this period.

The stage of rapid development of the market economy (1992–1997)

These five years was the interval between the convening the 14th CPC National Congress and that of the 15th CPC National Congress, as well as a period that witnessed the development of commodity economy in China after China had set up the socialist market economy. However, due to the influence of various domestic and international economies, the overall economic development in China advanced in fluctuations. It was a period during which the privately-run and the individual sectors of the economy developed greatly, yet the state-owned sector and the collective sector of the commerce encountered great difficulties in their development. Next, the basic situations of different sectors of the wholesale trade during these five years will be analyzed using the number of registered business corporations in different sectors of the wholesale trade, the number of outlets and practitioners.

The number of business corporations

As can be seen from Fig. 4.6, the numbers of business corporations in different sectors of the wholesale trade in this stage increased significantly. Of which, the number of business corporations in the state-owned sector of the wholesale trade increased from 97.2 thousand in 1994 to 116.8 thousand in 1996, being 19.6 thousand more; the number of business corporations in the collective sector of the wholesale trade increased from 99.3 thousand in 1994 to 134.6 thousand in 1996, being 35.3 thousand more and showing a growth rate greater than that of the state-owned sector of the wholesale trade. The number of privately-run wholesale enterprises grew to 43.2 thousand in 1996, being 4 times greater than that in 1994 and showing the greatest growing speed among all. Though foreign-invested wholesale enterprises grew only 200, it was a great progress. Compared with the previously several stages, there was a significant change listed in Fig. 4.6: the number of business corporations in the collective sector of the wholesale trade exceeded that in the state-owned sector of the wholesale trade and the difference between the two kept enlarging all the way, reaching 2,100 in 1994, then 17,800 in 1996.

Fig. 4.6. The number of business corporations in different sectors of the wholesale trade (1994–1996)

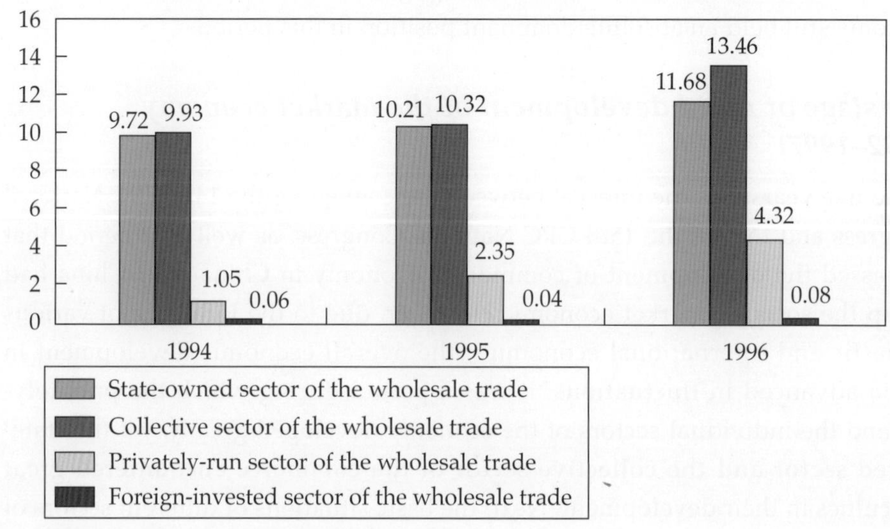

Number of outlets

As can be seen from Fig. 4.7, the development of the outlets of different sectors of the wholesale trade was greatly consistent with that of the numbers of business corporations mentioned above. The numbers of wholesale outlets in different sectors were all growing. Of which, the outlets in the privately-run sector of the wholesale trade grew the fastest of all, and those in the state-owned sector of the wholesale trade grew steadily. Both the absolute number and the growing speed of outlets in the collective sector of wholesale trade exceeded those in the state-owned sector of the wholesale trade, so did the absolute value of the state-owned sector of the wholesale trade. The number of outlets of the foreign-invested sector of the wholesale trade fell slightly in 1995, but showed a great increase in 1996, with the absolute number reaching 2,863.

Fig. 4.7. The number of business corporations in different sectors of the wholesale trade (1994–1996)

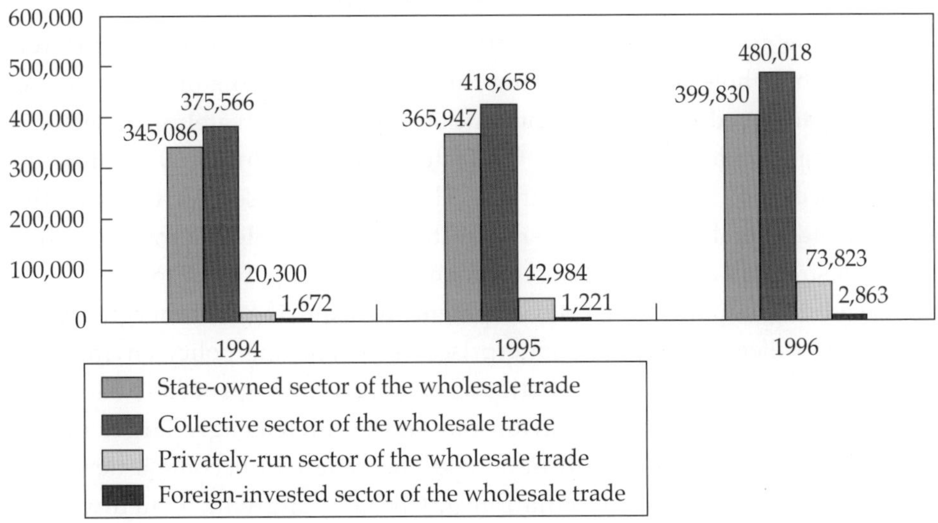

The number of practitioners

As can be seen from Fig. 4.8, the practitioners in the four sectors of the wholesale trade all grew substantially in this period. Of which, the number of practitioners in the privately-run sector of the wholesale trade grew from 171,000 in 1994 to 646,000 in 1996; that in the state-owned sector of the wholesale trade grew from 5.592 million in 1994 to 6.072 million in 1996; that in the collective sector of the wholesale trade increased nearly 600,000 within the 3 years; and that in the state-owned sector of the wholesale trade was far higher than that in the collective sector of the wholesale trade. The number of practitioners in the foreign-invested sector was the fastest of all, increasing from 15,900–51,100.

Fig. 4.8. The number of wholesale practitioners in different sectors (1994–1996)

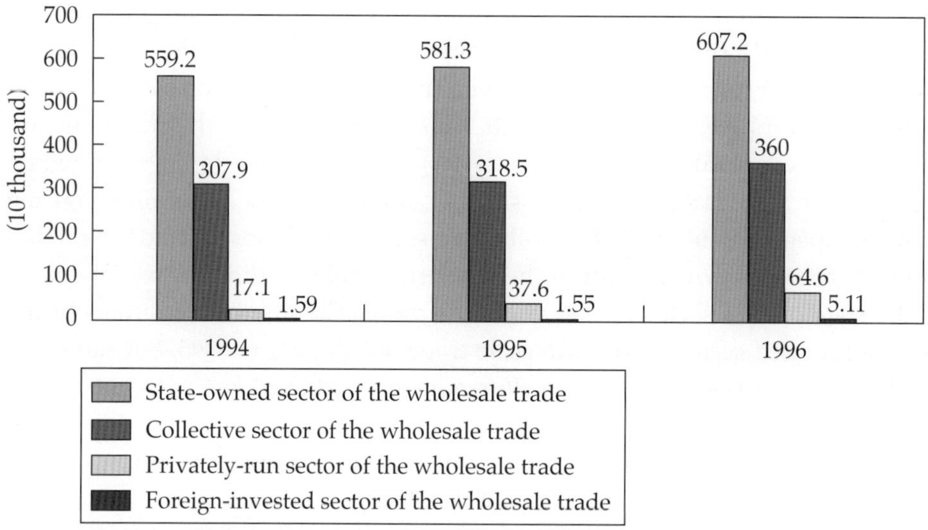

As can be seen from the description of the basic situations of different sectors of the wholesale trade during this period, all sectors of the wholesale trade had achieved great development, of which the privately-run sector of the wholesale trade developed at the fastest speed, followed by the foreign-invested sector of the wholesale trade. The primary reason for this was that both the individual and privately-run sectors of the wholesale trade in China had been strengthening since the reform and opening up, began to expand and embarked on the path of fast development by acquiring and merging state-owned and collective wholesale enterprises in the relaxing policy environment in 1992, showing such characteristics as a rapid growing speed, wide range of geological and industrial distribution and an increasingly larger market share. The individual sector of the wholesale trade had become a new force in the field of commodity circulation in China, along with which was the acceleration of the reform and opening up in China. That's why the foreign-invested sector of the wholesale trade also developed fast. Specifically, in July 1992, the Chinese Government announced to open up six cities, namely Beijing, Shanghai, Guangzhou, Tianjin, Dalian and Qingdao, and the retail business in five special economic zones, namely Shenzhen Special Economic Zone, Zhuhai Special Economic Zone, Shantou Special Economic Zone, Xiamen Special Economic Zone and Hainan Special Economic Zone. A great batch of large-scale multinational retail groups entered China, many of which also had a hand in the wholesale trade in the form of wholesale in retail while getting engaged in retail.

The absolute leadership of the state-owned and collective sectors of the wholesale trade wasn't shaken in this period. Though the proportions of the privately-run and individual sectors of the wholesale trade were still low, both developed fast. The common development of different sectors of the economy greatly enhanced the growth vigor of the wholesale trade.

The stage of all-round development of the market economy (1998–2007)

Since national statistics on the wholesale trade in this period were mainly about wholesale enterprises above the designated size, the basic situation of the wholesale trade above the designated size since 1998 will be analyzed below in detail.

The number of business corporations

As shown in Fig. 4.9, the dominant position of the number of wholesale enterprises above the designated size began to shift gradually from the state-owned sector of the wholesale trade to the privately-run sector of the wholesale trade. Prior to 2003, the state-owned sector of the wholesale trade had a relatively large number of business corporations, which even exceeded 10,000 in 1999, yet showed a declining trend. The privately-run sector of the wholesale trade, on the contrary, showed a growing momentum, with the number of business corporations increasing from 387 in 1999 to 13,673 in 2007. In 2005, the number of business corporations in the privately-run sector of the wholesale trade surpassed that in the state-owned sector of the wholesale trade. In addition, the number of collective wholesale enterprises in this stage reduced gradually, while that of foreign-invested wholesale enterprises kept increasing and surpassed the former in 2007.

Next, let's check the specific growth of the numbers of wholesale enterprises in different sectors.

As shown in Fig. 4.10, prior to 2003, the number of state-owned wholesale enterprises and that of collective wholesale enterprises kept decreasing, both at a rate of over 10%. Differently, the number of foreign-invested wholesale enterprises and that of privately-run wholesale enterprises kept growing rapidly, both at a rate of over 10%. After 2006, the development of various wholesale enterprises slowed down.

The proportions of the numbers of enterprises in different sectors of the wholesale trade are shown below:

As shown in Fig. 4.11, heights of columns in each chart reflect the sum of ratios of the above four categories of wholesale enterprises to the total number of wholesale enterprises. In the declining tendency, we can conclude that fixed-ownership wholesale enterprises apart from the above four categories of wholesale enterprises were increasing in number, indicating that the fixed-ownership sector of wholesale trade in China kept developing all the way.

Fig. 4.9. Numbers of business corporations in different sectors of the wholesale trade (1999–2007)

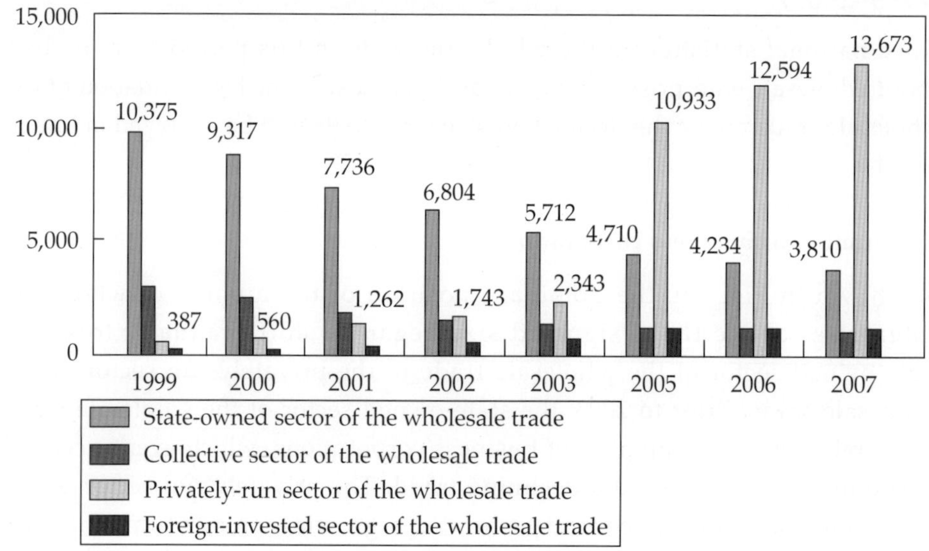

Fig. 4.10. Growth rates of the numbers of business corporations in different sectors of the wholesale trade (1999–2007)

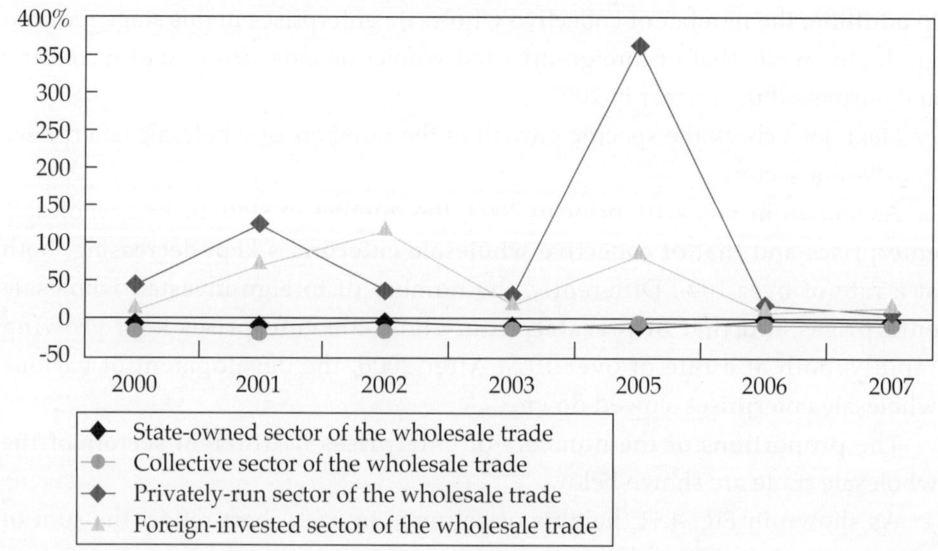

In addition, from the respective proportion of business corporations in each sector of the wholesale trade, we can see clearly that the number of business corporations in the state-owned sector of the wholesale trade kept declining, falling from 63.3% in 1999 to 13.1% in 2007. It illustrated that its absolute leadership had already gone. Differently, the number of business corporations in the privately-run sector of the wholesale trade kept increasing at a high speed. It had risen from 2.4% in 1999 to 47.1% in 2007, up 18.5 times. The proportion of foreign-invested wholesale enterprises grew slowly, but that of collective wholesale enterprises fell slowly. Till 2007, the former had obviously surpassed the latter.

Fig. 4.11. Proportions of the business corporations in different sectors of the wholesale trade above the designated level (1999–2007)

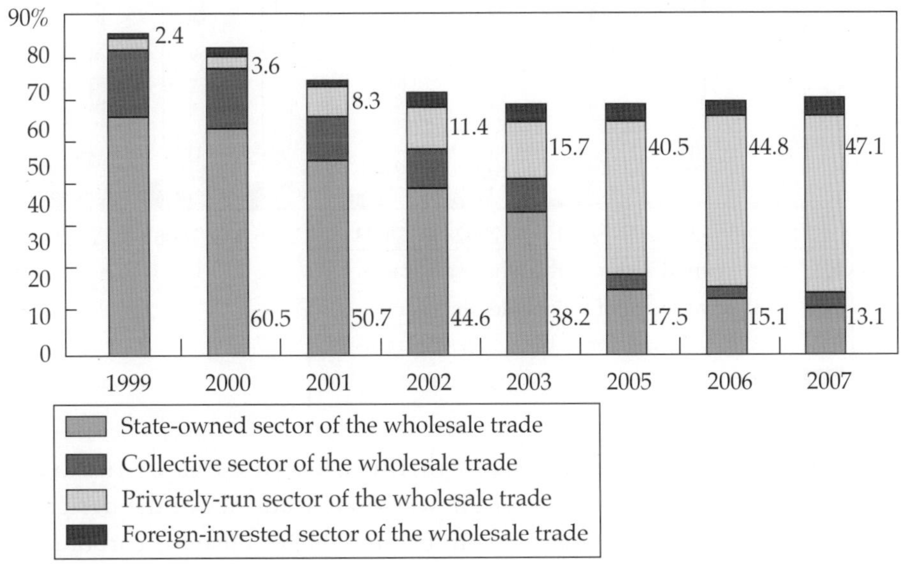

The number of industrial establishments

As shown in Fig. 4.12, during 1999–2003, the number of industrial establishments in the state-owned sector of the wholesale trade above the designated size kept falling, from 15,628 in 1999 to 10,029 in 2003, and that in the collective sector of the wholesale trade above the designated size fell from nearly 4,000 in 1999 to 1,898. However, the number of industrial establishments in the privately-run sector of the wholesale trade above the designated size kept increasing during this period from 391 to 1,991, being 4 times greater. The foreign-invested sector of the wholesale trade showed the same growth momentum. During 2005-2007, the numbers of industrial establishments in different sectors of the wholesale trade above the designated size all grew rapidly. In particular, that in the state-owned sector and privately-run sector of the wholesale trade grew the fastest among all. Changes in the number of industrial establishments in the collective sector of the wholesale trade above the designated size were the least of all. The number of industrial establishments in the foreign-invested sector of the wholesale trade above the designated size grew rationally.

Fig. 4.12. Numbers of industrial establishments in different sectors of the wholesale trade above the designated size (1999–2007)

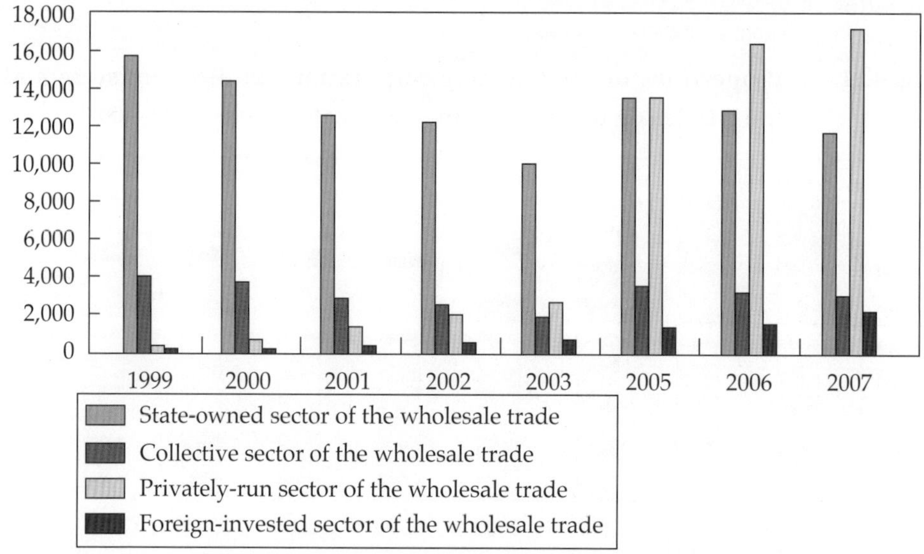

As shown in Fig. 4.13, changes in the growth rates of industrial establishments in different sectors of the wholesale trade above the designated size were consistent with the changes in the numbers of business corporations. The growth rates of industrial establishments in the state-owned and collective sectors of the wholesale trade above the designated size were negative prior to 2003, while those in the privately-run and foreign-invested sectors of the wholesale trade above the designated size were positive, and high. In 2005, industrial establishments in all sectors of the wholesale trade above the designated size grew significantly before becoming gradually stable.

The proportions of the numbers of industrial establishments in different sectors of the wholesale trade above the designated size are as follows:

As shown in Fig. 4.14, similar to the ratios of the numbers of business corporations (see Fig. 4.11), the ratios of the numbers of industrial establishments in different sectors of the wholesale trade to the total numbers of industrial establishments in the wholesale trade kept declining, reflecting the development of the mixed-ownership wholesale enterprises. Make a comparison among different sectors of the wholesale trade, we can find that the proportion of the number of industrial establishments in the state-owned sector of the wholesale trade above the designated size showed a declining tendency, falling from 65.9% in 1999 to 19.2% in 2007. Similarly, the proportion of the number of industrial establishments in the collective sector of the wholesale trade above the designated size declined, falling from 16.7% in 1999 to 5.0% in 2007. However, the proportion of the number of industrial establishments in the privately-run sector of the wholesale trade above the designated size kept rising, growing from 1.6% in 1999 to 28.2% in 2007, and that in the foreign-invested sector of the wholesale trade above the designated size kept rising, too, growing from 1% in 1999 to 3.4% in 2007, yet at a low rate.

Fig. 4.13. Growth rates of industrial establishments in different sectors of the wholesale trade above the designated size (1999–2007)

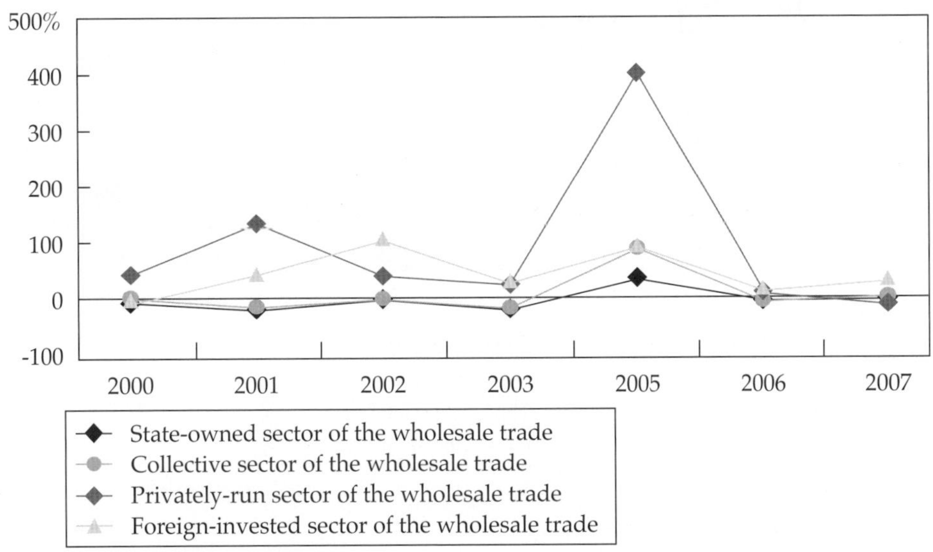

The number of practitioners

Though the number of business corporations and that of industrial establishments in the state-owned sector of the wholesale trade above the designated size were both surpassed by their corresponding counterparts in the privately-run sector of the wholesale trade in 2005, it is shown, in Fig. 4.15, that the number of practitioners in the state-owned sector of the wholesale trade held an absolute dominant position, which was still true as of 2007.

Seen from the development trends of different sectors of the wholesale trade, the numbers of practitioners in the state-owned sector of the wholesale trade and the collective sector of the wholesale trade kept falling, while those in the privately-run sector of the wholesale trade and the foreign-invested sector of the wholesale trade kept growing. From 1999–2007, practitioners in the state-owned sector of the wholesale trade fell from 1,699 thousand to about 670 thousand, those in the collective sector of the wholesale trade fell from 451 thousand to about 76 thousand, while those in the privately-run sector of the wholesale trade grew from 14 thousand to 489 thousand, and those in the foreign-invested sector of the wholesale trade grew from 10 thousand to 200 thousand (see Fig. 4.15). Development differences among the four sectors of the wholesale trade became smaller and smaller.

Fig. 4.14. Proportions of the numbers of industrial establishments in different sectors of the wholesale trade above the designated size (1999–2007)

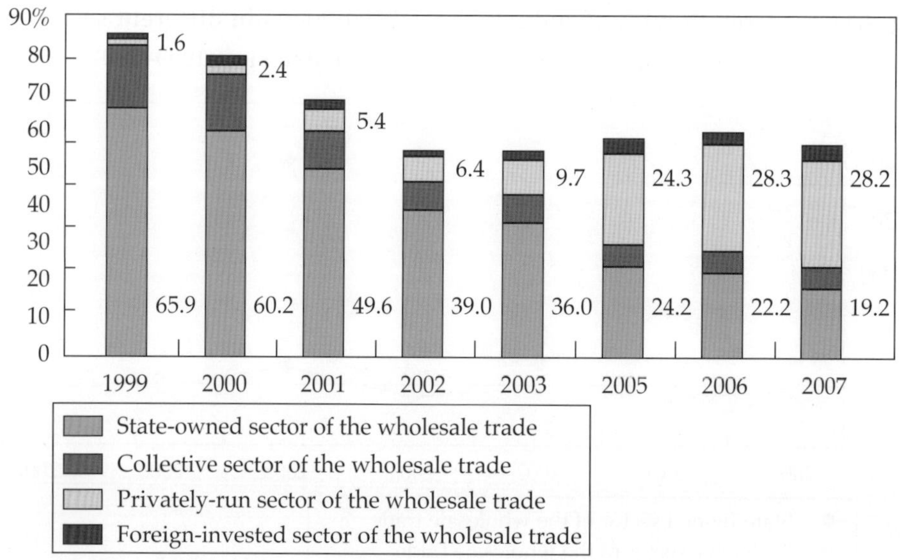

Specific growth was as follows:

As shown in Fig. 4.16, the number of practitioners grew the fastest in the privately-run sector of the wholesale trade at an extremely high rate. The growth rate exceeded 100% in 2001, then 250% in 2005; the growth rate of the number of practitioners in the foreign-invested sector of the wholesale trade ranked the second, being maintained at above 25%. In contrast, practitioners in the state-owned and collective sectors of the wholesale trade kept falling at the average annual rate of above 10%.

Seen from the absolute values of the proportions (see Fig. 4.17), the proportion of practitioners in the state-owned sector of the wholesale trade was higher than that in other respective sector of the wholesale trade. From it, we can see that the state-owned sector of the wholesale trade was relatively large in scale and with relatively more practitioners on the average. Conversely, the proportion of practitioners in the privately-run sector of the wholesale trade was significantly lower than that in other respective sector of the wholesale trade, indicating the small size of the privately-run sector of the wholesale trade and the small number of employees in a single enterprise, which was a significant feature of the privately-run sector of the wholesale trade in China.

Fig. 4.15. Practitioners in different sectors of the wholesale trade above the designated size (1999–2007)

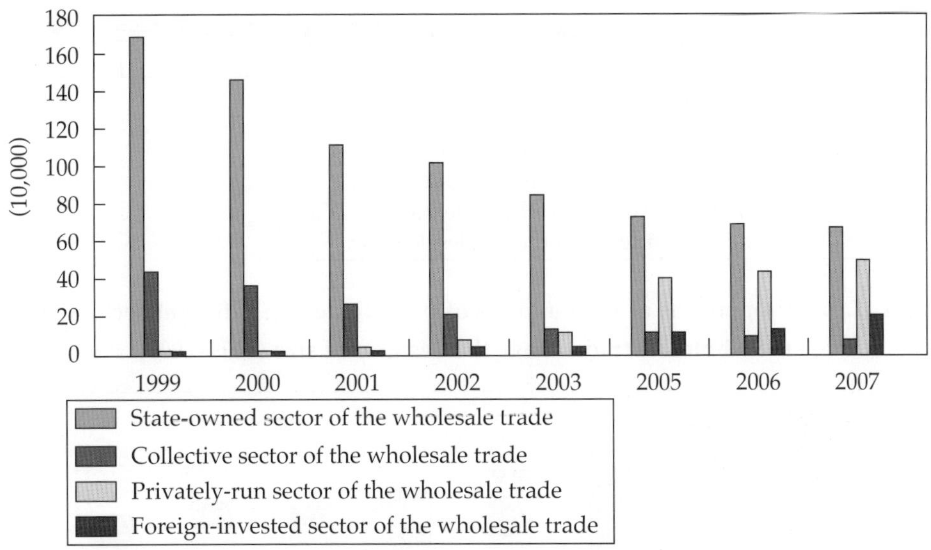

Seen from the development trend, the proportion of practitioners in the state-owned sector of the wholesale trade kept falling down from 67% in 1999 to 27% in 2007, but that in the privately-run sector of the wholesale trade kept rising from 1% in 1999 to 20% in 2007. The proportion of practitioners in the collective sector of the wholesale trade and that in the foreign-invested sector of the wholesale trade showed similar changing trends.

To sum up, it can be seen from the above analysis of the basic information on the registration of different sectors of the wholesale trade that both the state-owned and the collective sectors of the wholesale trade showed a clear shrinking trend, with the number of business corporations, practitioners and industrial establishments falling down; while the privately-run sector of the wholesale trade showed an opposite development trend, with the number of business corporations, practitioners and industrial establishments growing significantly. Such phenomenon appeared for an important reason: due to the

Fig. 4.16. Growth rate of the number of practitioners in different sectors of the wholesale trade above the designated size (1999–2007)

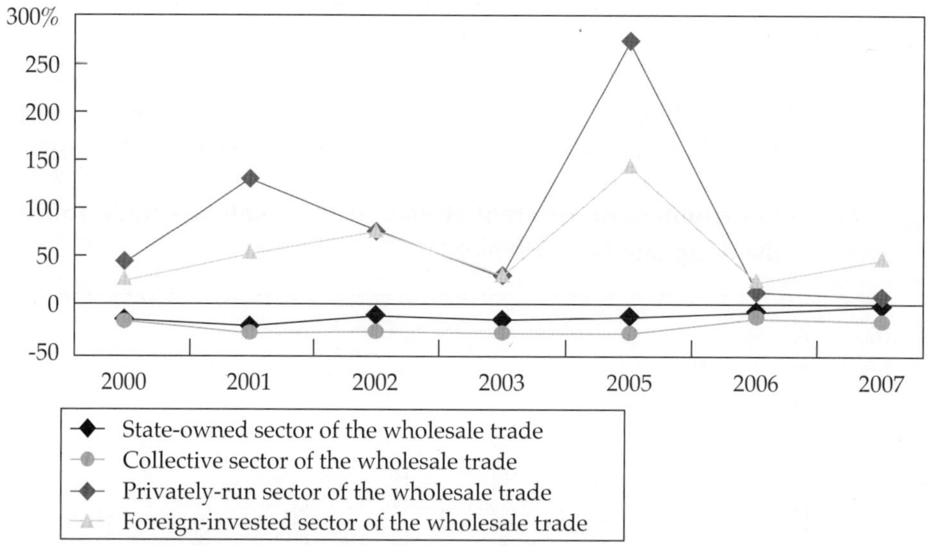

Fig. 4.17. Proportions of the numbers of practitioners in different sectors of the wholesale trade above the designated size (1999–2007)

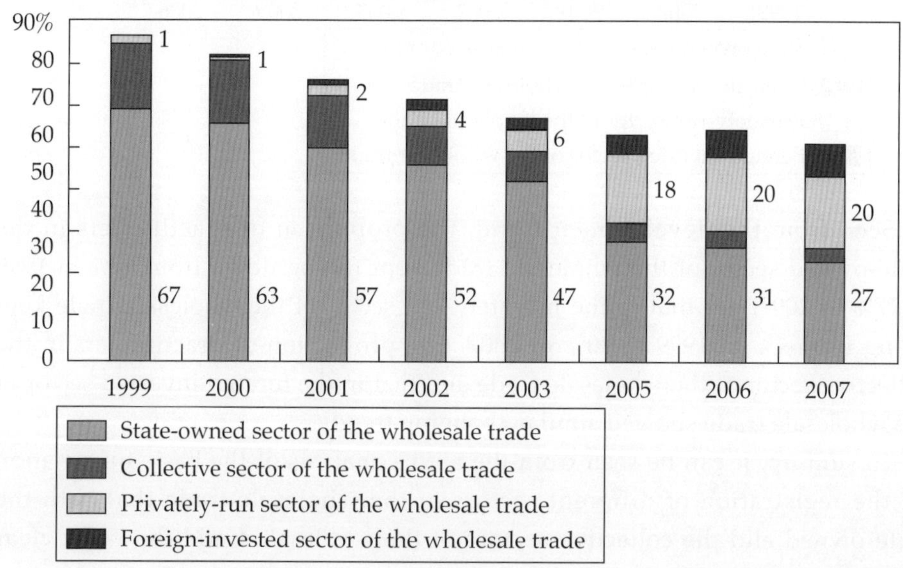

reform of the state-owned and collective sectors of the wholesale trade, many wholesale enterprises, especially those originally engaged in the collective sector of the wholesale trade, changed their nature before being leased or sold to individuals and becoming privately-run wholesale enterprises. The acceleration of the opening up of the wholesale trade in China contributed to the fast development of the foreign-invested sector of the wholesale trade. In addition, from the comparison between the number of practitioners and that of enterprises in the foreign-invested sector of the wholesale trade, it can be seen that most foreign-invested wholesale enterprises were large in size. It was because that the first foreign wholesalers entering China since the reform and opening up were large-scale multinational companies with world reputations. Compared with domestic wholesale enterprises, especially some privately-run wholesale enterprises, they had more advanced technologies and management experience, and absolute advantages in expanding their size and improving their competitiveness.

Sales of different sectors of the wholesale trade

The development scale and growing speed of the sales volume are one of the most direct reflections of the overall development of the wholesale trade. The sales volumes of different sectors of the wholesale trade will be described in detail in two stages.

Fig. 4.18. Sales volumes of different sectors of the wholesale trade (1994–1996)

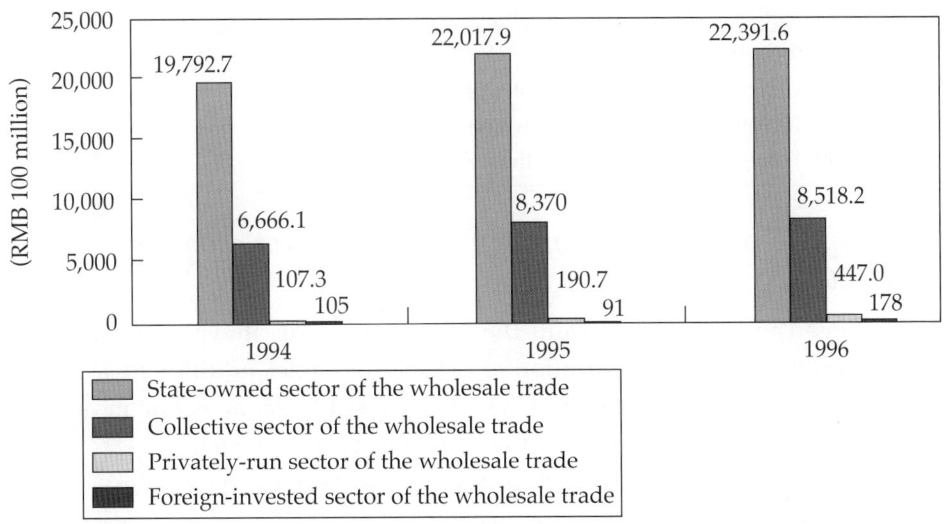

The stage of rapid development of the market economy (1992–1997)

As can be seen from the column chart of the sales volumes of different sectors of the wholesale trade (see Fig. 4.18), the sales volume of the state-owned sector of the wholesale trade still held a dominant position, followed by the collective sector. It was a result of the old wholesale system. However, with the advance of the reform of the wholesale system, China began to encourage the development of other sectors of the economy apart from the public sector of the economy, greatly benefiting the privately-run sector of the economy. The sales volume of the privately-run sector of the economy grew significantly, reaching 78% and 134%, respectively, in 1995 and 1996. Over the same period, the foreign-invested sector of the wholesale trade also developed greatly with the opening up of China, the sales volume of which was doubled in 1996 over that in 1995.

Fig. 4.19. Sales volume of each sector of the wholesale trade above the designated size (1998–2007)

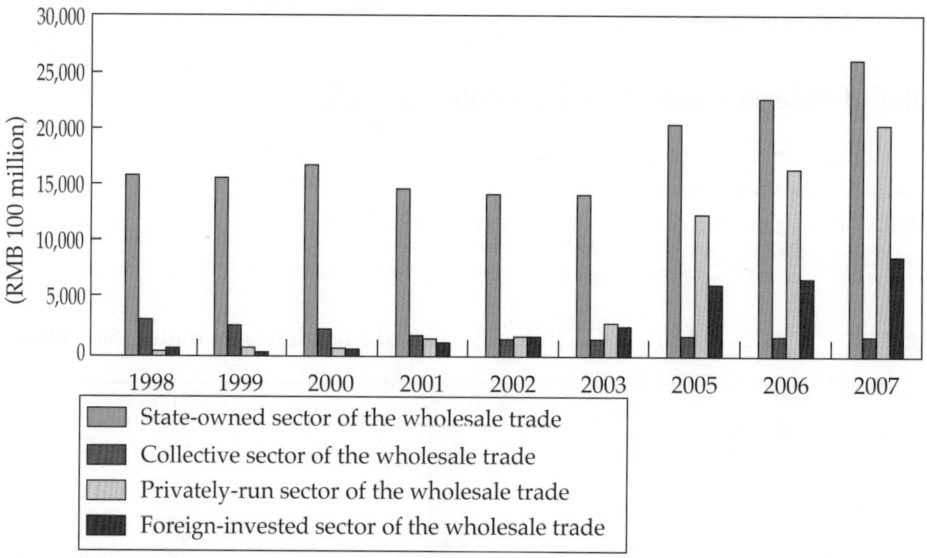

The stage of overall development of the market economy (1998–2007)

China began to take into account the wholesale trade above the designated size since 1998. Detailed description of the sales volumes of different sectors of the wholesale trade above the designated sizes will be made below in order to analyze the ownership structure of the wholesale trade in China.

As can be seen from Fig. 4.19, of the four sectors of the wholesale trade above the designated size, the state-owned sector of the wholesale trade had the greatest sales volume of all, showing a growing trend in fluctuations; that of the state-owned sector was at a rising stage during 1998–2000, began to slide during 2000–2003, and escalated since 2005. It can also be seen from Fig. 4.19 that the sales volume of the privately-run sector of the wholesale trade grew the fastest of all from RMB 16.1 billion in 1998 to 2,034.3 billion in 2007, increasing by 125 times within 10 years. In 2003, it replaced the sales volume of the collective sector of the wholesale trade before ranking the second of all. Though the sales volume of the foreign-invested sector of the wholesale trade didn't grow as fast as that of the privately-run sector of the wholesale trade, it developed significantly, increasing from RMB 28.9 billion in 1998 to 878.07 billion in 2007, being nearly 30-fold greater. Different from the above growing trend, the sales volume of the collective sector of the wholesale trade kept falling down from RMB 300.5 billion in 1999 to 166.1 billion in 2007, falling by nearly a half.

From the figure below (Fig. 4.20), it can be seen that during 1999–2007, both the privately-run and the foreign-invested sectors of the wholesale trade grew rapidly. In particular, the growth rate of the sales volume of the privately-run sector of the wholesale trade was above 50%, even reached 350% in 2005, while the growth rate of the foreign-invested sector of the wholesale trade reached 170% in the same year. Both the state-owned and collective sectors of the wholesale trade showed a trend of negative growth before 2005. In 2005, the growth rate of the sales volume of the state-owned sector of the wholesale trade reached 44%, and that of the collective sector of the wholesale trade reached 12%.

Fig. 4.20. Growth rate of the sales volume of each sector of the wholesale trade above the designated size (1999–2007)

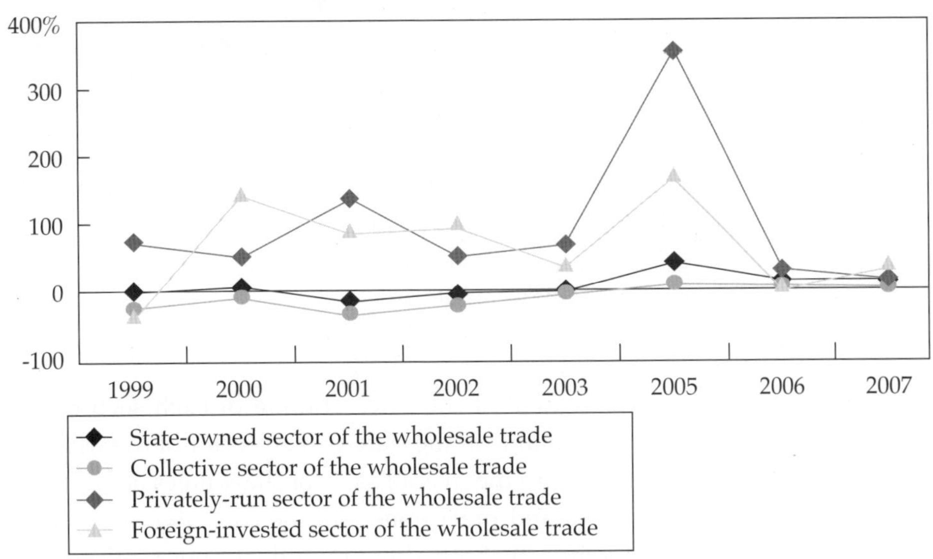

As can be seen from Fig. 4.21, the summation of the ratios of the sales volumes of the 4 sectors of the wholesale trade to the total sales of the wholesale trade kept falling down, fully reflecting the thriving development momentum of the mixed-ownership sector of the wholesale trade. Of which, the ratio of the sales volume of the state-owned sector of the wholesale trade to the total sales of wholesale of the society kept declining from 70% in 1998 to 26% in 2007, yet it still occupied a position of prominence comparing with that of other sectors of the wholesale trade, ranking the first among the four. The proportion of the sales volume of the privately-run sector of the wholesale trade rose quickly from 15% in 1998 to 20% in 2007. In particular, it had been maintained at above 20% since 2006. The proportion of the sales volume of the foreign-invested sector of the wholesale trade also grew really fast at a rate far higher than that of the proportion of the number of business corporations in the same sector which grew from 1% in 1998 to 8.8% in 2007. While the proportion of the sales of collective wholesale enterprises kept falling from 13.6% in 1998 to 1.7% in 2007.

Fig. 4.21. Proportion of the sales volume of each sector of the wholesales trade above the designated size (1999–2007)

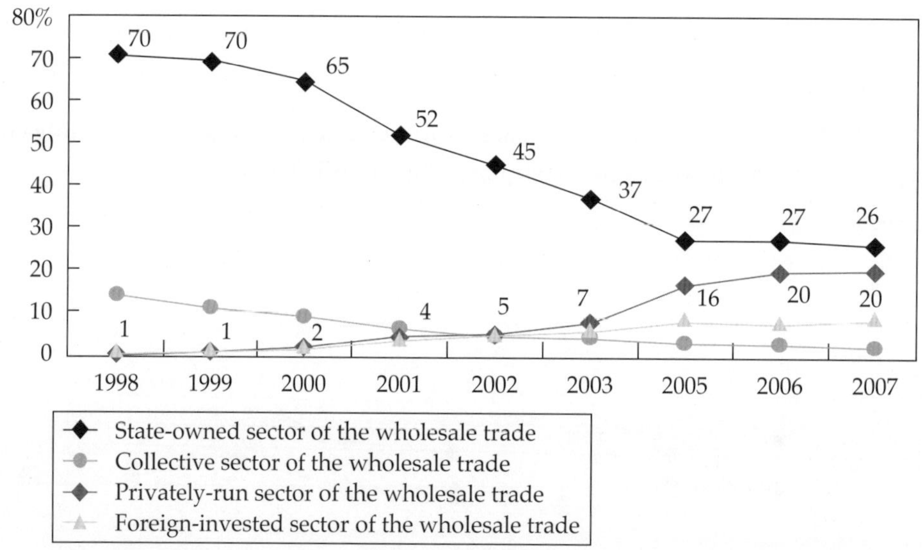

It can be seen from the growth of the sales volume of each sector of the wholesale trade that the sales volume of the state-owned sector of the wholesale trade kept growing, yet its ratio to the overall sales of the wholesale trade kept declining. The sales volume of and practitioners in the collective sector of the wholesale trade changed similarly, both showing a declining tendency. The ratio of the collective sector of the wholesale trade to the wholesale trade fell gradually, too. Differently, the sales and their proportions of the privately-run and foreign-invested sectors of the wholesale trade kept growing, which was consistent with the basic registration of different sectors of the wholesale trade having analyzed above. It is worth noticing that the absolute value of the sales volume of the state-owned sector of the wholesale trade was still the highest among all, holding the dominant position, though the proportion of the sales volume of the state-owned sector of the wholesale trade kept falling. It was in line with the requirement on building the socialist market economic system with the public ownership playing a dominant role and diverse forms of ownerships developing side by side.

Financial state of each sector of the wholesale trade

From the analysis of the financial state of each sector of the wholesale trade, we can get the development scale and operational efficiency of different sectors of the wholesale trade. Next, detailed analyses of the financial states of different sectors of the wholesale trade will be made using the following three indicators-assets, liabilities and the scale of profits.[6]

Fig. 4.22. Size of assets of each sector of the wholesale trade above the designated size (1999–2007)

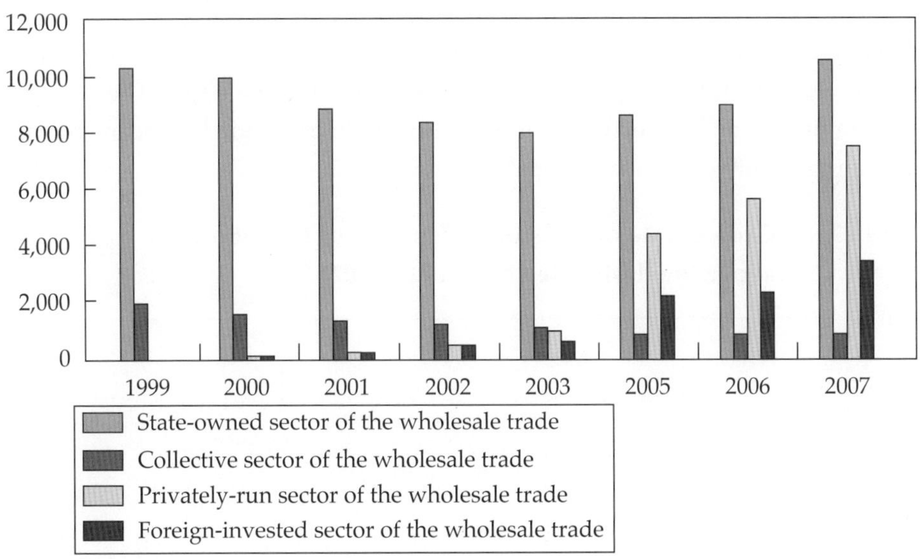

Size of assets

As can be seen from Fig. 4.22, since 1992, the asset size of the state-owned sector of the wholesale trade had been holding the dominant position and showing a growing trend in fluctuations. It increased by RMB 30.5 billion during 1999–2007. A big fluctuation appeared in 2003, in which the size of assets of the state-owned sector of the wholesale trade declined to a great extent, being RMB 800 billion in terms of the absolute value. Before 2003, the collective sector of the wholesale trade ranked the second among the four sectors in terms of the size of assets, only to show a declining trend, falling from RMB 196.92 billion in 1999 to 117.88 billion in 2003. After 2003, the collective sector of the wholesale trade ranked the bottom among the four different sectors of the wholesale trade. Till 2007, it had left only 90.96 billion RMB of assets. On the contrary, the privately-run and foreign-invested sectors of the wholesale trade grew rapidly in terms of the size of assets. As for the privately-run sector of the wholesale trade, its assets grew from RMB 9.03 billion in 1999 to 743.73 billion in 2007, increasing more than 80 times within just nine years, showing an amazing growth rate. The assets of the foreign-invested sector of the wholesale trade grew fast, too, from RMB 8.01 billion in 1999 to 354.63 billion in 2007.

Details on the growth are provided below:

As can be seen from Fig. 4.23, the growth rate of assets of each sector of the wholesale trade was highly consistent with the growth rate of their sales volumes. Of which, the privately-run sector of the wholesale trade had the highest growth rate of assets among all, which had been above 50%, even reached 310% in 2005. The foreign-invested sector of the wholesale trade developed fast, too, only to show a trend of development in twists and turns, with the growth rate being sometimes high and sometimes low. The assets of the state-owned and collective sectors of the wholesale trade had been showing a declining trend before achieving a positive growth in 2007.

Fig. 4.23. Growth rate of assts of each sector of the wholesale trade above the designated size (1999–2007)

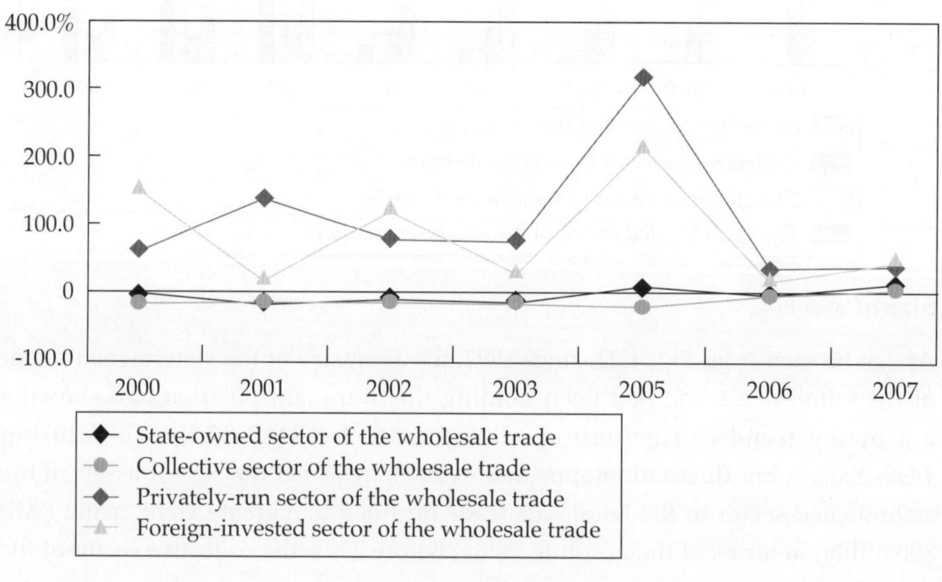

Let's now check the proportions of assets of different sectors of the wholesale trade.

It can be seen from Fig. 4.24 that the total assets illustrating the development of the mixed-ownership sector of the wholesale trade. As for specific proportions, the proportion of the assets of the state-owned sector of the wholesale trade still occupied the dominant position, only to show a significant declining tendency and a great fall, dropping from 70.2% in 1999 to 27.2% in 2007. Similarly, there was the collective sector of the wholesale trade, the proportion of assets of which fell from 13.5% in 1999 to 2.4% in 2007. The size of assets of the privately-run sector of the wholesale trade kept growing from less than 1% in 1999 to 19.2% in 2007, and that of the foreign-invested sector of the wholesale trade also rose from 0.6–9.2%.

Fig. 4.24. Proportion of the assets of each sector of the wholesale trade above the designated size (1999–2007)

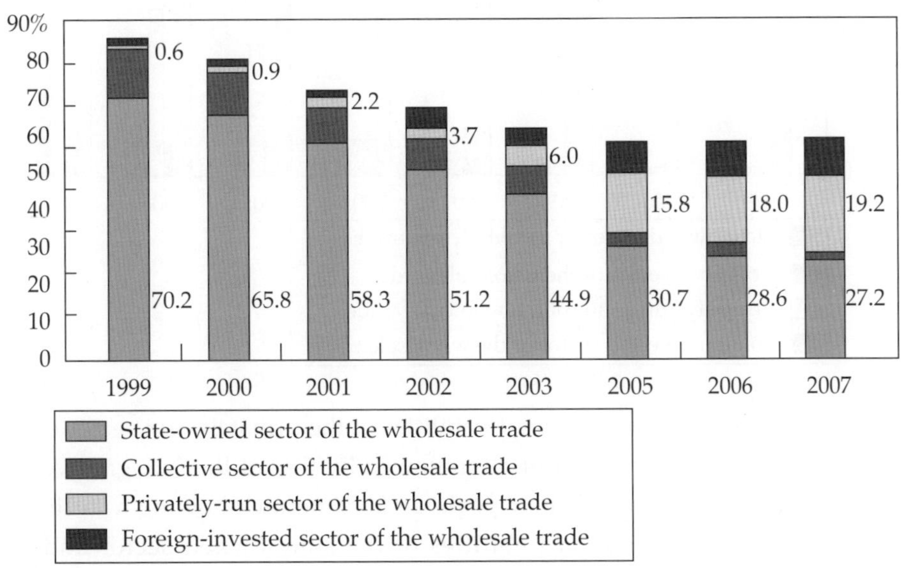

Scale of liabilities

By comparing the size of assets of different sectors of the wholesale trade above the designated size, we can see a high goodness between the size of assets and that of liabilities. The changing trends of different sectors of the wholesale trade were consistent: the liabilities of the state-owned assets had been the highest of all, only to show a declining tendency. Till 2007, the growth of the liabilities of state-owned assets became positive once again. The size of assets of the collective sector of the wholesale trade had been declining since 1999, falling from RMB 187.6 billion in 1999 to 78.2 billion RMB in 2007, down more than a half. While the liabilities of the privately-run sector of the wholesale trade kept growing before surpassing those of the collective sector of the wholesale trade and ranking the second among the four sectors in 2005 (see Fig. 4.25). The size of liabilities of the foreign-invested sector of the wholesale trade grew rapidly, too, from RMB 5.1 billion in 1999 to 247.4 billion in 2007. See Fig. 4.26 for specific information.

Fig. 4.25. Liabilities of different sectors of the wholesale trade above the designated size (1999–2007)

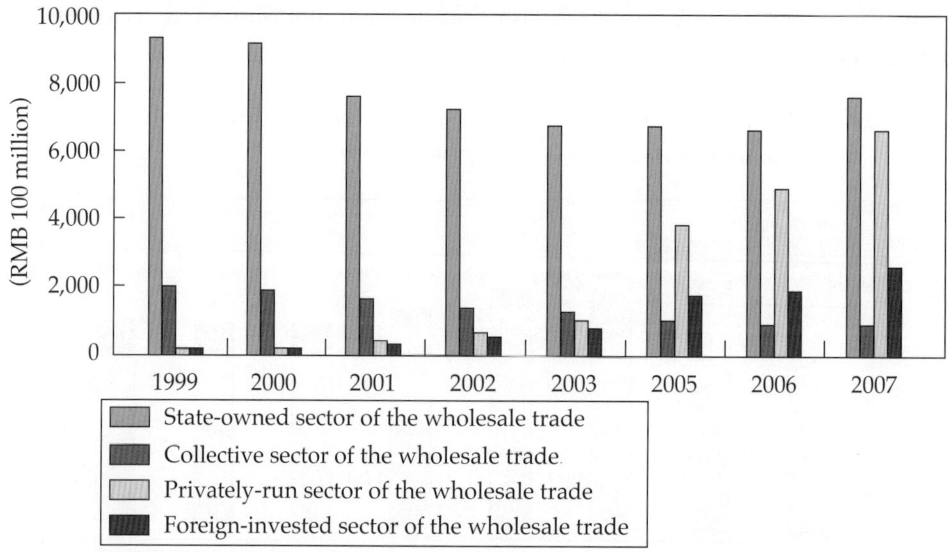

As can be seen, the growth rate of liabilities of the privately-run sector of the wholesale trade was the highest of all, followed by that of the foreign-invested sector, both of which reached their peaks in 2005 before showing a declining tendency. The growth rates of liabilities of the state-owned sector and the collective sector of the wholesale trade had been negative until 2007.

By comparing it with the figure of proportions of the asset sizes (see Fig. 4.24), the scales of liabilities and the proportions of the assets of different sectors of the wholesale trade were highly consistent. The proportion of liabilities of the state-owned sector of the wholesale trade was the highest of all, only to be under a declining state, falling from 69.9% in 1999 to 24.7% in 2007; that of the collective sector of the wholesale trade fell from 15.8% in 1999 to 2.8%; that of the privately-run sector of the wholesale trade grew from 0.6–21.2%; and that of the foreign-invested sector of the wholesale trade grew from 1–9% (see Fig. 4.27).

Fig. 4.26. Growth rate of the liabilities of each sector of the wholesale trade above the designated size (1999–2007)

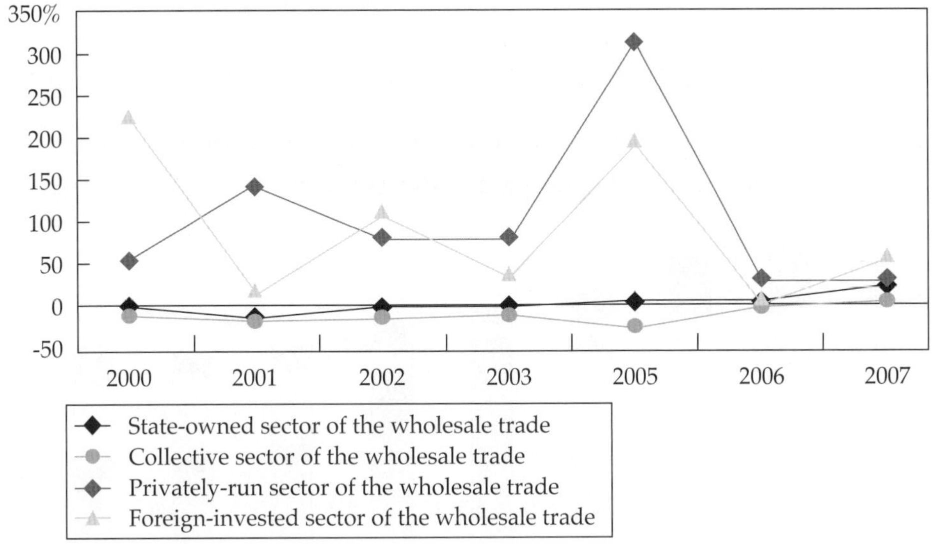

Profits from main businesses

As can be seen from Fig. 4.28, the profits of the state-owned sector of the wholesale trade were great in amount and relatively stable during 1999–2003, being somewhere between RMB 50 billion to 60 billion. The profits of the state-owned sector of the wholesale trade had been growing at a faster speed since 2003 before reaching RMB 140.4 billion in 2005, being more than doubled. The growing trend continued after that. Till 2007, the profits of the state-owned sector of the wholesale trade above the designated size had reached RMB 195 billion.

It can also be seen clearly from Fig. 4.28 that different from assets and liabilities, the absolute value of profits of the foreign-invested sector of the wholesale trade was greater than that of the privately-run sector of the wholesale trade and grew at a higher rate. To be more specific, the profits of the privately-run sector of wholesale trade grew from RMB 0.69 billion in 1999 to 119.9 billion in 2007, increasing by 200 times within nine years. Of the four sectors of the wholesale trade, the collective sector had the lowest growth rate of profits, which nearly remained the same within nine years and held the bottom among the four sectors of the wholesale trade.

From the growth rates of profits of different sectors of the wholesale trade, we can also see that the growing rates of profits of different sectors of the wholesale trade were quite different. Of which, the growth of profits of the privately-run sector of the wholesale trade and that of the foreign-invested sector of the wholesale trade fluctuated greatly. In particular, the growth rate of the sales profits of the privately-run sector of the wholesale trade reached the highest of 750% in 2005, yet was only 50% in 2000 at the lowest. The growths of the profits of the state-owned and collective sectors of the wholesale trade were stable and highly consistent.

Fig. 4.27. Proportion of the liabilities of each sector of the wholesale trade above the designated size (1999–2007)

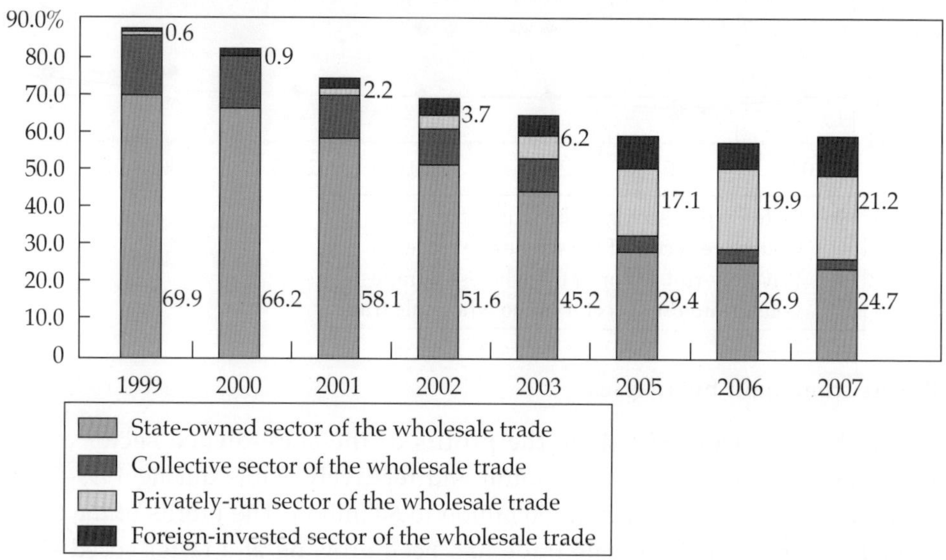

Fig. 4.28. Profits from main businesses of different sectors of the wholesale trade above the designated size (1999–2007)

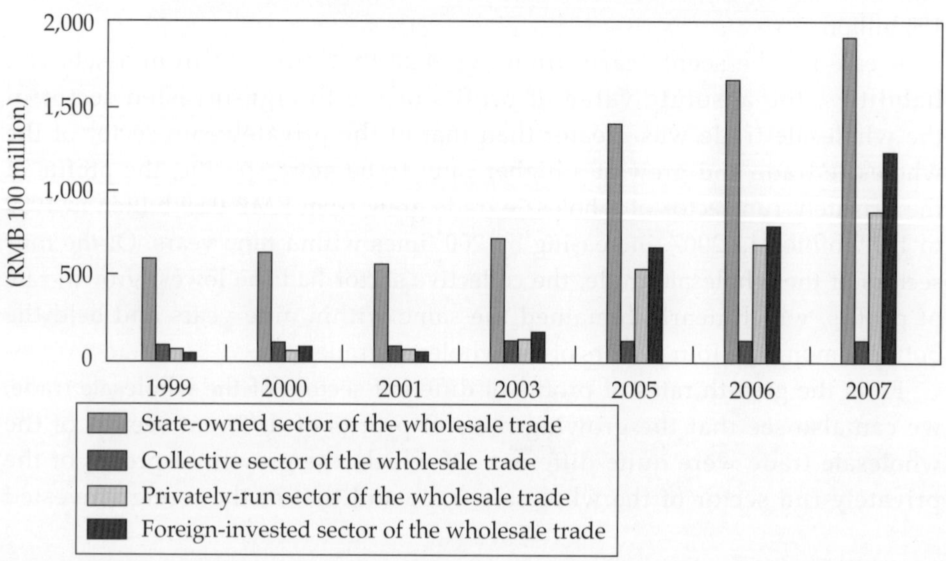

Fig. 4.29. Growth rate of the profits from main businesses of each sector of the wholesale trade above the designated size (1999–2007)

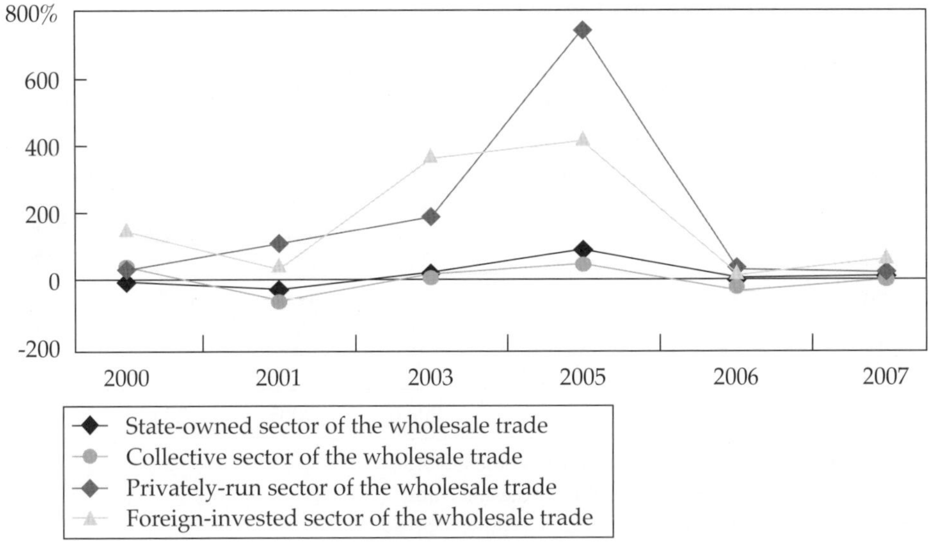

As can be seen from Fig. 4.30, the proportion of the profits of the state-owned sector of the wholesale trade ranked the first among that of the 3 sectors of the wholesale trade, only to show a declining trend, falling from 74.5% in 1999 to 30.8% in 2007. The proportion of the profits of the collective sector of the wholesale trade showed the same trend, falling from 4.3% in 1999 to 1.0% in 2007. The proportions of the sales profits of the privately-run and foreign-invested sectors of the wholesale trade increased gradually. Of which, the proportion of the sales profits of the foreign-invested sector of the wholesale trade grew the fastest of all, increasing from 0.9% in 1999 to 18.9% in 2007; that of the privately-run sector of the wholesale trade grew from 0.8% in 1999 to 13.5% in 2007.

Based on the above data analyses, it can be seen that financial states of different sectors of the wholesale trade were quite different from one another in this period. Specific reasons include:

(1) That the size of assets of the state-owned sector of the wholesale trade had been ranking the first among all was somewhat related to the solid foundation of and the control of state resources by the state-owned sector of the wholesale trade. However, the privately-run sector of the wholesale trade developed the fastest of all, which was closely related to the national encouragement of the development of the non-public economic sector. With the economic development in China, more and more capital was gathered in the hands of individuals, enabling individuals to have more chances to get engaged

Fig. 4.30. Ratio of the profits from main businesses of each sector of the wholesale trade above the designated size to the total profits of the wholesale trade (1999–2007)

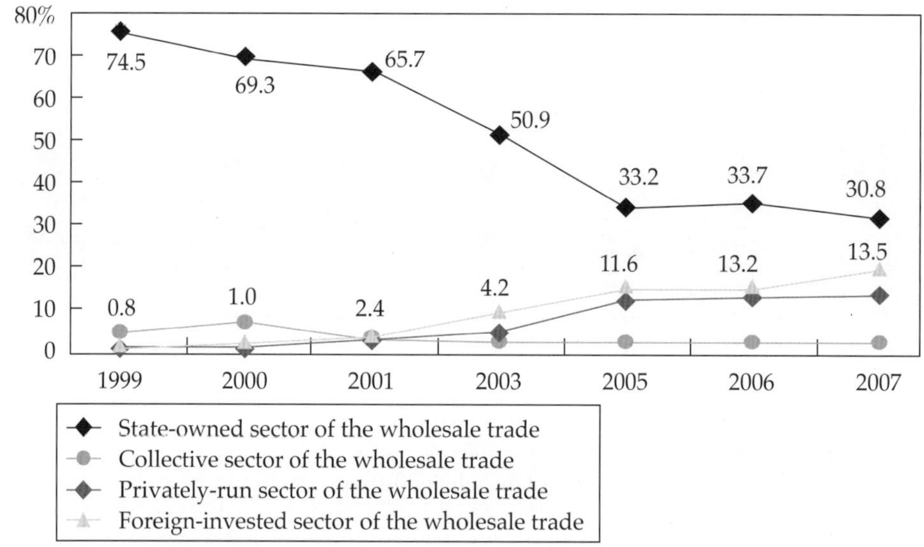

in the wholesale trade and get profits from it. The rapid expansion of the assets of the foreign-invested sector of the wholesale trade was intimately related to their own strength. Most foreign-invested wholesale enterprises entering China were multinational enterprises each with a world reputation. With abundant assets, they were able to support the development of their subsidiaries. During 1999–2003, the collective sector of the wholesale trade ranked the second among the four in terms of the size of assets, but due to poor management, it lagged behind, although it had a better capital foundation than the privately-run and foreign-invested sectors of the wholesale trade.

(2) Reasons for the differences between the growths of liabilities of different sectors of the wholesale trade were manifold. Firstly, there would be certain requirements on an enterprise's asset-liability ratio in order to ensure its solvency, which determined the existence of a positive correlation between its liabilities and assets. Under the premise that assets of the state-owed sector of the wholesale trade had shrunk, it was understandable that the liabilities of the state-owned sector of the wholesale trade grew negatively. That the total liabilities and growth rate of liabilities of the collective sector of the wholesale trade had always been maintained low was irrelevant to the assets of the collective sector of the wholesale trade. In addition, changes in the policies on different sectors of the wholesale trade were also reasons for the changes in the liabilities of different sectors of the wholesale trade. Liabilities of the foreign-

invested sector of the wholesale trade grew in a fluctuating way mainly because government policies on the foreign-invested sector of the wholesale trade changed greatly. Moreover, changes and fluctuations in the overseas economic environment (e.g. the exchange rate) would also have a direct influence on them.

(3) Profits of the privately-run sector of the wholesale trade grew at the fastest speed, since privately-run wholesale enterprises were small in size, thus they were capable of operating flexibly, better seizing market opportunities, and grasping profit opportunities. The rapid growth of profits of the foreign-invested sector of the wholesale trade was intimately related to the high operational efficiency of foreign-invested companies. Most foreign enterprises entering the Chinese wholesale trade had been operating for years in the international market, thus had accumulated rich experience in cost control and internal management. Therefore, they were capable of maintaining high-speed and stable growth of profits. Profits of the state-owned and collective sectors of the wholesale trade grew slowly, mainly because of the unclear property rights inside state-owned and collective wholesale enterprises, improper management, the lack of explicit incentive mechanisms and the low levels of operational efficiencies.

To sum up, it can be seen that great changes had happened to different sectors of the wholesale trade in the three decades of reform and opening up. The state-owned sector of the wholesale trade showed a trend of development in a shrinking way, the indicators of the basic registration, the sales volume and the financial indicators of which all showed a declining trend. Collective wholesale enterprises were small in number. In the reform, the proportion of collective wholesale enterprises didn't increase, but kept declining. In contrast, the privately-run and foreign-invested sectors of the wholesale trade developed rapidly, becoming the super-active main part of the wholesale trade on the wholesale commodities market in China. It was consistent with the reform of the market economic system in China. Changes in the ownership structure of the wholesale trade in China reflected China's reform of the market economic system, serving as a good reference for the economic restructuring in China.

Development Changes in the Wholesale Trade in Different Regions

Regional structure of the wholesale trade is composed of two aspects: on the one hand, it refers to the distribution ratio of the total social labor occupied by the wholesale trade in different regions, which not only reflects the size of the total social labor occupied by the wholesale trade in different regions, but also indicates the role of the total social labor in the distribution in different regions, and on the other hand, it refers to the distribution of the output value of the wholesale trade in different regions, which not only reflects the contribution of the wholesale trade to local economy in different regions, but also illustrates the role of the total social labor in the distribution in different regions.

In the analysis of the regional structure of the wholesale trade, we will analyze, in detail, the basic information, sales turnovers and financial states of the wholesale trade in East China, Central China and West China and the six major districts in order to get the characteristics of the regional structure of the wholesale trade in its development.

Regional structure of the wholesale trade in East China, Central China and West China

Economic developments in East China, Central China and West China are seriously unbalanced, enabling the development of the wholesale trade to show different features in East China, Central China and West China.[7] Next, the basic information (mainly including the number of business corporations, the number of outlets and the number of practitioners), the sales volumes and the financial states of the wholesale trade in East China, Central China and West China in the three decades of reform and opening up will be described in detail in order to explore the differences between the development of the wholesale trade in the above three major regions, with the purpose of finding out their features and reasons.

Basic information on the registration of the wholesale trade

Along with the reform of the circulation system since the reform and opening up, the wholesale trade in China has also achieved great development. In particular, after the 14th CPC National Congress initially set up the objective of building the socialist market economic system, the reform was accelerated and intensified, people's mind became more emancipated, and the development of the national economy of China became more active. Under such a situation, the commodity economy became flourishing gradually, and the wholesale trade achieved greater development. The development of the wholesale trade in different regions showed different features.

Fig. 4.31. Numbers of business corporations in East China, Central China and West China (1994–1996)

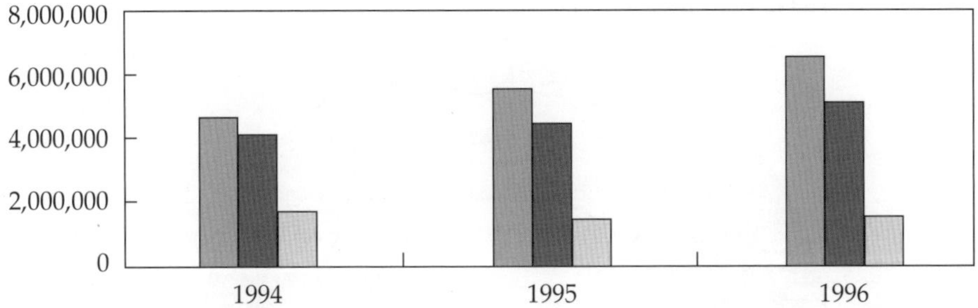

	1994	1995	1996
East China	4,706,408	5,370,076	6,384,326
Central China	4,143,623	4,603,625	5,017,609
West China	1,454,523	1,263,418	1,355,976

Number of business corporations

The number of business corporations is a basic reflection of the development of the wholesale trade. The growth of the number of business corporations in the wholesale trade during 1994–1996 was as shown in Fig. 4.31.

It can be seen that during 1994–1996, the number of wholesale business corporations in East China and Central China grew constantly. Though wholesale business corporations in West China somewhat fell, it didn't fall significantly. In terms of the total number of wholesale business corporations, that in East China was the most of all, being far higher than that in West China. Specific proportions of wholesale business corporations in three major regions are shown in Fig. 4.32 below.

As can be seen from Fig. 4.32, the number of wholesale business corporations in East China held an absolute dominant proportion, while that in West China had the lowest proportion among all. Seen from the changing trends, the proportion of wholesale business corporations in East China showed a growing trend, increasing from 55% in 1994 to 62% in 1996; that in Central China showed a declining trend, falling from 32% in 1994 to 27% in 1996; and that in West China also showed a declining trend, dropping from 13% to 12%, later to 11%.

China began to collect statistics on wholesale enterprises above the designated size after 1998. To reflect the development trend of and structural changes in the number of business corporations in East China, Central China and West China since 1998, the number of wholesale enterprises in each of the 3 major regions during this period will be described and analyzed below. See Fig. 4.33 for details.

Fig. 4.32. Proportions of wholesale business corporations in East China, Central China and West China (rings from inside to outside: 1994, 1995 and 1996)

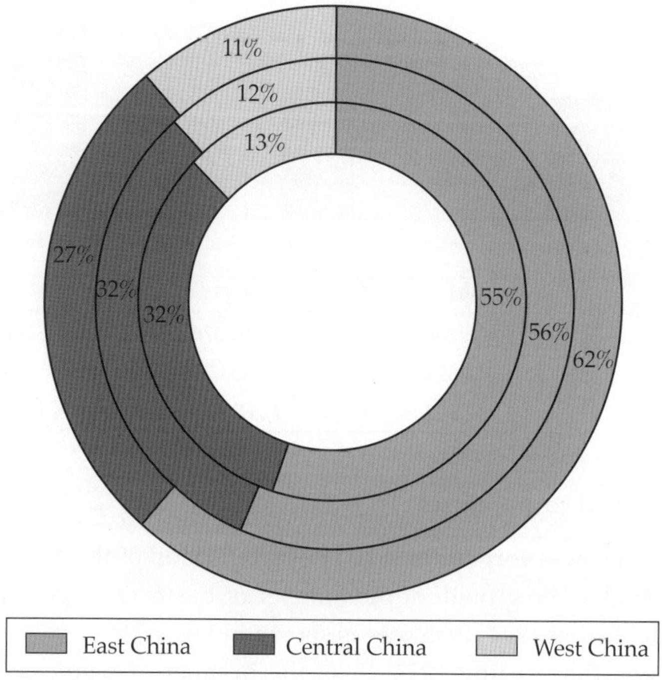

Fig. 4.33. Numbers of business corporations above the designated size in East China, Central China and West China (1998–2007)

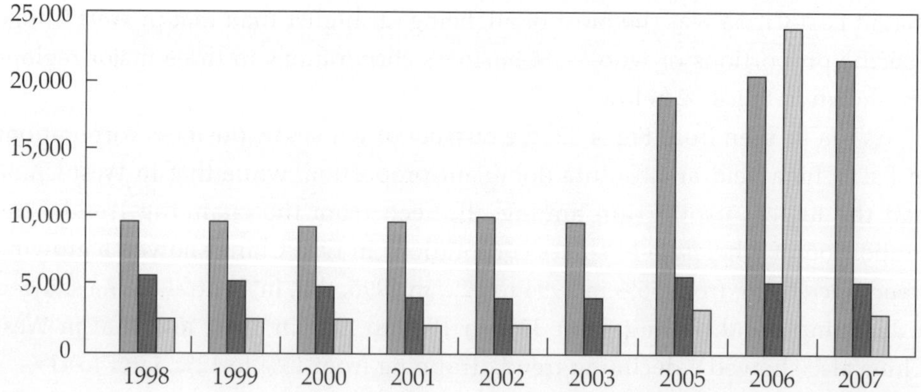

	1998	1999	2000	2001	2002	2003	2005	2006	2007
East China	9,633	9,629	9,093	9,578	9,748	9,533	18,594	20,324	21,468
Central China	5,495	4,972	4,546	4,070	3,882	3,708	5,668	5,227	5,294
West China	2,197	2,176	2,112	1,932	1,918	1,937	2,950	2,813	2,616

From Fig. 4.33, we can see that development of the wholesale trade in the three major regions was relatively stable during 1998–2003, seeing no big changes. However, due to the change in the statistical criteria during 2005–2007, the number of wholesale business corporations in each of the three major regions grew significantly in 2005 before continuing the trend of moderate growth. Of which, the number of business corporations above the designated size in East China was 1.5 times greater than the sum of that in West China and that in Central China during 1998–2005. The difference was further enlarged since 2005 to being nearly three times. The number of wholesale business corporations in Central China has always been twice greater than that in West China. Specific proportions in the three major regions are shown below in Fig. 4.34.

Fig. 4.34. Proportions of business corporations above the designated size in East China, Central China and West China (1998–2007)

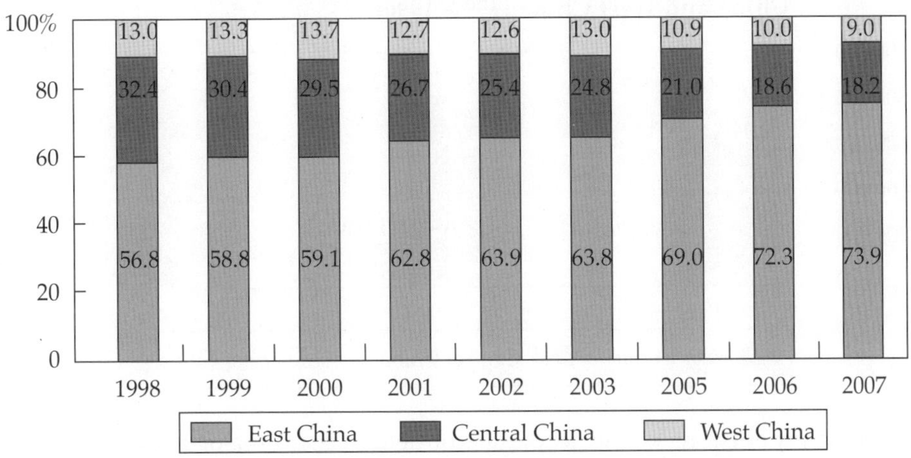

Seen from the respective proportion of business corporations in East China, Central China and West China, the proportion of business corporations in East China held an absolute dominance, being 56.8% at the lowest and 73.9% at the highest. It was followed by that in Central China, which ranged during 20–30%. The proportion of business corporations in West China was the lowest of all, being only about 10%. Seen from their development trends, the proportion of business corporations in East China kept increasing, while that in Central China and West China kept falling down, making the absolute dominance of that in East China more significant. From the above description, we can see that the development of the wholesale trade among the three major regions was extremely unbalanced, and the difference kept enlarging.

The number of wholesale outlets/industrial establishments

The respective growth of the numbers of wholesale enterprises in East China, Central China and West China has been described just now. Considering that an enterprise could set up a number of outlets, we hold that the number of outlets could better reflect the development of the wholesale trade. Next, a description and analysis of the numbers of wholesale outlets in these three major regions in China will be made.

As can be seen from Fig. 4.35, during 1994–1996, wholesale outlets in East China, Central China and West China all kept increasing. In 1996, the number of wholesale outlets in Central China reached 952,641, increasing by nearly 50% over that in 1994. Over the same period, the number of wholesale outlets in East China increased by about 250 thousand, up about 40%; and that in West China increased only about 50 thousand, the growth rate of which was about 30%.

Fig. 4.35. Numbers of wholesale outlets in East China, Central China and West China (1994–1996)

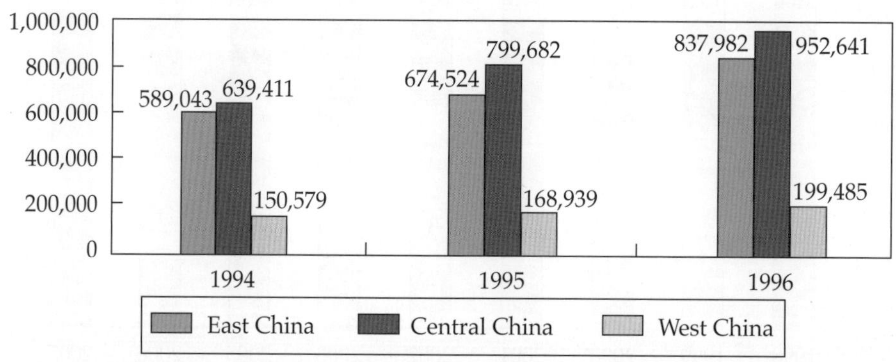

Specific proportions of the wholesale outlets in the 3 major regions were as shown below in Fig. 4.36.

As can be seen from Fig. 4.36, the proportion of wholesale outlets in Central China had always ranked the first among all, being above 45%. It was followed by that in East China, which was above 40%. The proportion of wholesale outlets in West China was the lowest of all, being about 10% only. As for the changing trend of such proportion, change in the proportion of wholesale outlets in East China was relatively small; that in Central China climbed somewhat, increasing by 1.7% from 1994–1996; and that in West China kept declining, falling 0.9% from 1994 to 1996. We can draw a similar conclusion from the development of wholesale outlets that the East China-Central China-West China regional structure of wholesale trade was extremely unbalanced, showing a widening tendency.

Fig. 4.36. Proportions of the wholesale outlets in East China, Central China and West China (1994–1996)

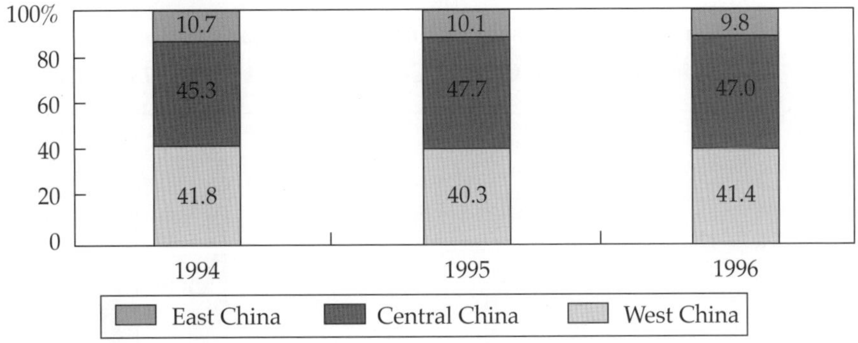

China didn't collect statistics on wholesale enterprises above the designated size until 1998, during which it adopted the same statistical indicators as those of wholesale outlets used several years before to measure the number of corporate wholesale establishments. The regional structure of the wholesale trade in China will be analyzed in the explanation of the numbers of corporate wholesale establishments in the three major regions in China since 1998.

As can be seen from Fig. 4.37, during 1998–2007, wholesale business corporations in East China, Central China and West China grew constantly in general. Of which, wholesale business corporations in East China grew the fastest of all in 2002, up nearly 35% year on year. After 2005, wholesale business corporations in the three major regions all grew significantly, since China carried out a census over its national economy in 2004 and greatly changed the statistical criteria. As can also be seen from Fig. 4.37, the difference among wholesale business corporations in East China, Central China and West China fluctuated with time: the number of wholesale business corporations in East China was 20% greater during 1998–2000, 1.5 times greater in 2001, and about twice greater in 2002 and 2003 than the sum of wholesale business corporations in Central China and West China. After 2005, the same difference began to narrow down. See the figure below for specific description of the difference among the three (see Fig. 4.38).

As can be seen from Fig. 4.38, the proportion of industrial establishments in East China was the highest of all, being more than half; that in Central China ranked the second, being somewhere between 20–30%; and that in West China was the lowest of all, being slightly more than 10%. Seen from their changing trends, the proportion of industrial establishments in East China and that in Central China sometimes rose and sometimes fell in a wane and wax way; and that in West China kept declining basically, falling from 16.4% in 1998 to 11.7%

in 2007, down 4.7%, and its difference with that in East China and Central China kept enlarging.

Fig. 4.37. Numbers of wholesale business corporations above the designated size in East China, Central China and West China (1998–2007)

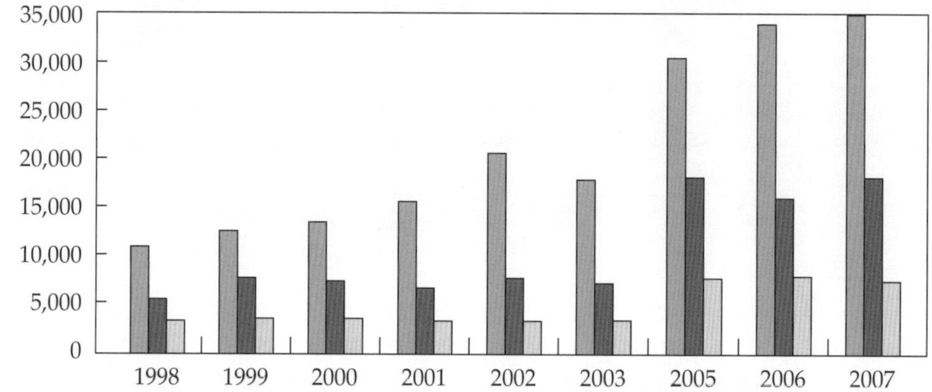

	1998	1999	2000	2001	2002	2003	2005	2006	2007
East China	10,897	12,632	13,362	15,410	20,321	17,608	30,187	33,870	34,986
Central China	5,206	7,553	7,087	6,421	7,516	6,961	17,924	15,749	18,024
West China	3,200	3,373	3,349	3,239	3,278	3,131	7,633	7,883	7,146

Fig. 4.38. Proportions of industrial establishments in the wholesale trade above the designated size in East China, Central China and West China (1998–2007)

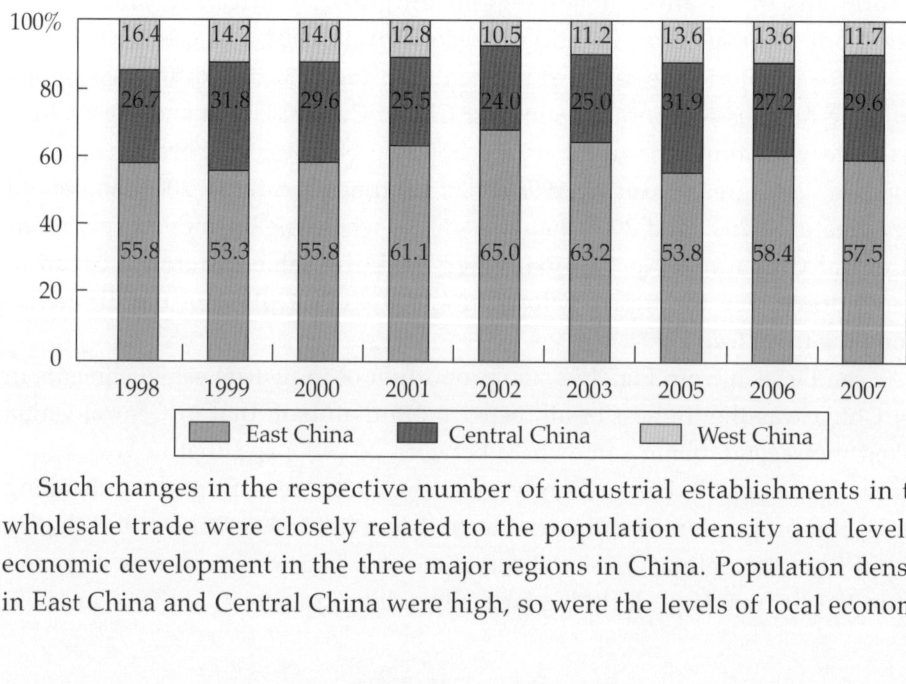

Such changes in the respective number of industrial establishments in the wholesale trade were closely related to the population density and level of economic development in the three major regions in China. Population density in East China and Central China were high, so were the levels of local economic development, so industrial establishments concentrated in East China and Central China; while West China had a vast territory with a sparse population, so industrial establishments were also sparse in number.

Fig. 4.39. Numbers of wholesale practitioners in East China, Central China and West China (1994–1996)

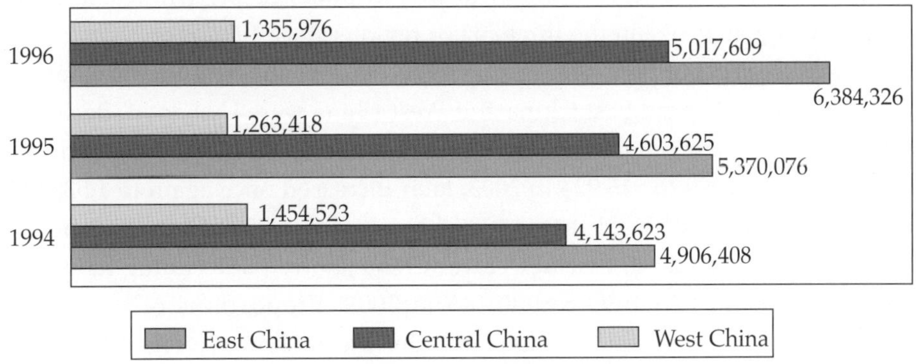

Fig. 4.40. Proportions of wholesale practitioners in East China, Central China and West China (1994–1996)

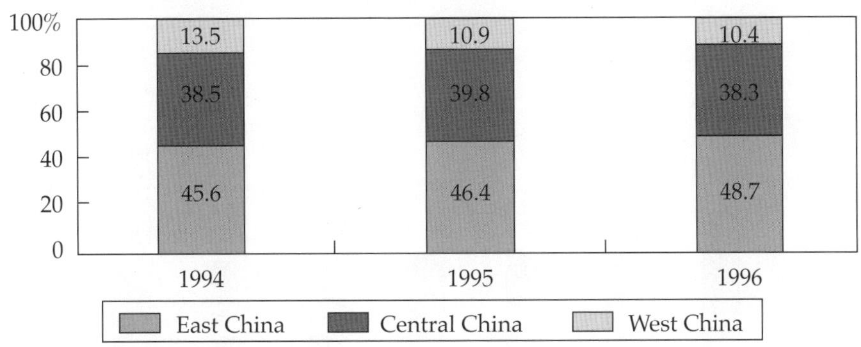

The number of practitioners

Fig. 4.39 shows the numbers of wholesale practitioners in the three major regions in China, seen from which, we can find that the number of practitioners in East China was the largest of all and developed the fastest of all, growing from more than 4.9 million in 1994 to 6.38 million in 1996, up 30.1%; and that the number of practitioners in West China was the smallest among all, even became negative with time, decreasing by 6.7% from 1994–1996.

Seen from their respective proportion, that in East China still held the dominant position, being very close to 50% (see Fig. 4.40); that in Central China ranked the second, being near 40%; and that in West China was the lowest among all, being a slightly more than 10%. Seen from their changing trends, that in East China kept growing, increasing by 3.1% from 1994 to 1996; that in Central China was relatively stable; and that in West China showed a significant declining trend, dropping 3.1% from 1994 to 1996. The conclusion thus drawn was the same as that drawn from above indictors: differences among the 3 major regions kept enlarging.

Let's now check the development of practitioners in the wholesale trade above the designated size in the three major regions since 1998.

As can be seen from Fig. 4.41, during 1999–2007, changes in the numbers of wholesale practitioners in East China and West China were U-shaped, declining first before rising. The number of wholesale practitioners in East China reduced from 1,273,959 in 1999 to 946,924 in 2003, later increased once again to 1,538,065 in 2007; that in West China fell from 325,129 in 1999 to 233,910 in 2002 before growing to 312,876 in 2007; that in Central China showed a declining tendency, falling from 883,624 in 1999 to 600,145 in 2007. Proportions of wholesale practitioners in the three major regions in China are as shown in Fig. 4.42.

Fig. 4.41. Practitioners in wholesale enterprises above the designated size in East China, Central China and West China (1998–2007)

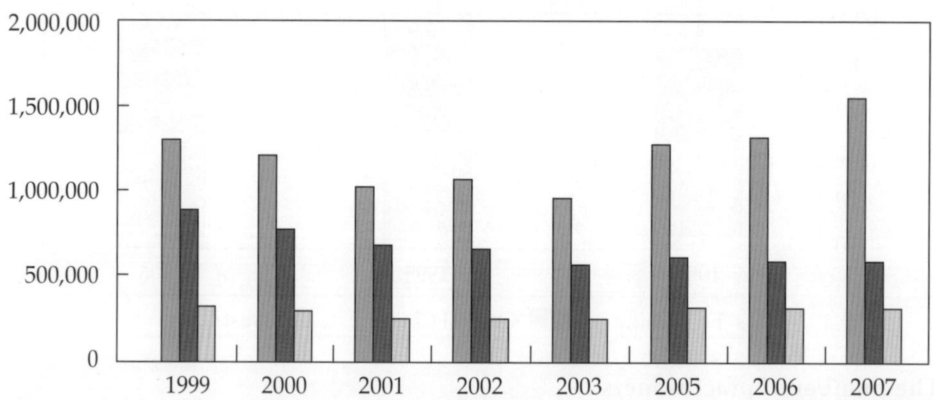

	1999	2000	2001	2002	2003	2005	2006	2007
East China	1,273,959	1,200,797	1,018,642	1,036,642	946,924	1,270,873	1,308,323	1,538,065
Central China	883,624	778,281	677,849	638,018	567,173	619,338	587,189	600,145
West China	325,129	288,292	245,903	233,910	237,829	308,780	310,375	312,876

As can be seen from Fig. 4.42, being consistent with the above several indicators, the proportion of wholesale practitioners in East China was the highest among all, being more than half; that in Central China ranked the second, being somewhere between 20–30%; and that in West China was the lowest of all, being slightly more than 10%. Seen from their changing trends, the proportion of wholesale practitioners in East China kept rising, being 11.5% up from 1999 to 2007; that in Central China kept declining, falling by 10.7% in 2007; and that in West China was not significant.

Fig. 4.42. Proportions of practitioners in wholesale enterprises above the designated size in East China, Central China and West China (1998–2007)

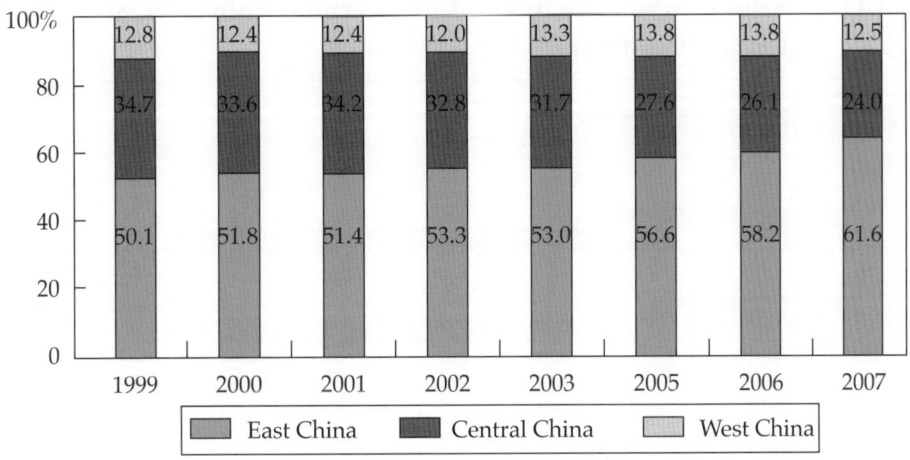

As can be seen from the analysis of the basic information on the wholesale trade, the development differences among wholesale enterprises in East China, Central China and West China kept enlarging, the more significant indicators of which included the number of business corporations and that of practitioners. It was because that the rapid economic development in East China had stimulated the rapid growth of the wholesale trade. Though with the supports of national policies, West China had a weak economic foundation and less developed commodity economy, thus the development of the wholesale trade in West China was unsatisfactory. The wholesale trade in Central China was fluctuating. In particular, local number of wholesale practitioners showed a declining trend, which was totally opposite to that in the other two regions. Fundamentally, it was caused by the outflow of population from Central China. Since Central China is close to East China, influenced by the magnetic field of the economic development in East China, many people left Central China for East China, leading to the reduction of population in Central China, and slowed development of local economy, including the wholesale trade.

Sales

The sales of wholesale reflect the development scale and situation of wholesale enterprises. Next, the changes in the structure of the wholesale trade in the three major regions in China will be further demonstrated by describing the sales of wholesale in East China, Central China and West China.

The sales of wholesale in East China, Central China and West China will be analyzed based on 2 stages (1994–1996 and 1998 to present). Let's check the sales of wholesale during 1994–1996.

Fig. 4.43. Sales of wholesale in East China, Central China and West China (1994–1996)

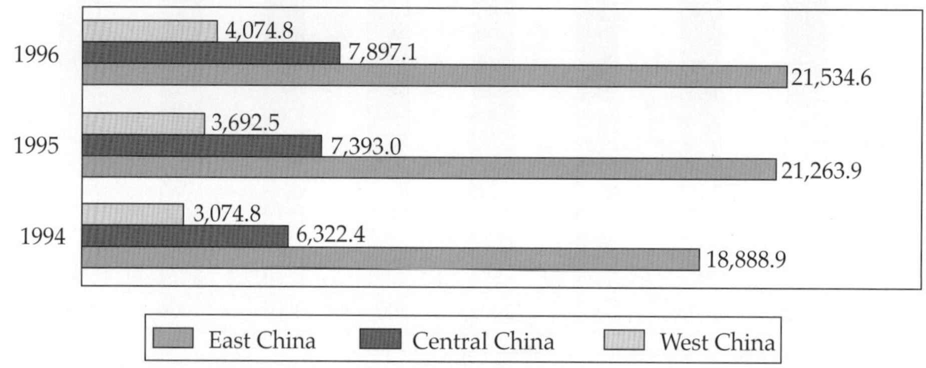

Fig. 4.44. Proportions of the sales of wholesale in East China, Central China and West China (1994–1996)

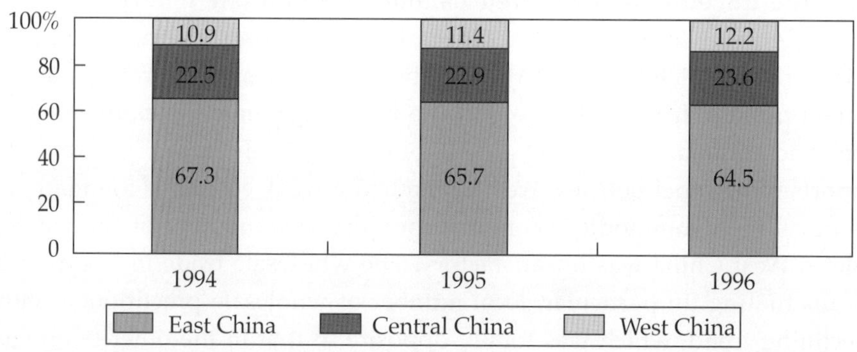

As can be seen from Fig. 4.43, during 1994–1996, the sales of wholesale in the three major regions in China all kept growing, of which wholesale sales grew by 14.0% in East China, 24.9% in Central China and 32.5% in West China. That in West China grew the fastest among all. Comparatively, the wholesale trade was more developed in East China than in the other two regions, and the sales of wholesale in East China were about twice greater than the sum of sales in the other two regions, showing great regional differences. Proportions of the sales of wholesale in different regions are shown below in Fig. 4.44.

As can be seen from Fig. 4.44, the sales of wholesale in East China held an absolute dominant position, accounting for more than 60% of the national total; the sales of wholesale in Central China ranked the second, accounting for 22–23% of the national total; and the proportion of the sales of wholesale in West China was the smallest, being a slightly more than 10%. Seen from the changing trends, the proportion of the sales of wholesale in East China kept declining, down 2.8% from 1994–1996; that in Central China and West China kept rising, up 1.1% and 1.3%, respectively.

It can be seen from the development of the wholesale trade in the previous stage that the development of local economies in East China, Central China and West China were extremely unbalanced. Fig. 4.45 shows the development of the wholesale trade during 1998–2007.

Fig. 4.45. Sales of the wholesale enterprises above the designated size in East China, Central China and West China (1998–2007)

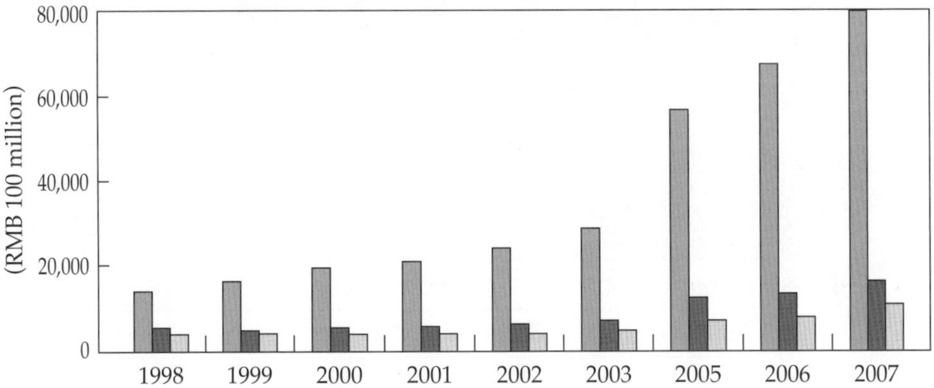

	1998	1999	2000	2001	2002	2003	2005	2006	2007
East China	13,453.9	15,385.9	18,190.7	20,279.9	23,332.3	27.868.4	56,599.4	67,091.7	80,233.9
Central China	4,412.4	4,143.5	4,910.2	5,005.8	5,463.9	6,518.1	11,963.1	12,316.4	15,571.6
West China	2,777.4	2,524.3	2,877.0	2,845.4	2,795.8	3,587.9	6,358.8	7,426.7	9,814.4

The sales of wholesale in East China, Central China and West China all kept growing during 1998–2007, the increase of which was 496.3% in East China, 252.9% in Central China and 253.4% in West China. The sales of wholesale in East China grew the fastest among all. Comparatively, the absolute value of the sales of wholesale in East China was the largest among all, which was even far higher than the sum of the sales of wholesale in Central and East China. The wholesale trade showed a stratified development in East China, Central China and West China, and the differences became greater and greater. Below are the ratios of the sales of wholesale in the three major regions to the national total sales of wholesale.[8]

As can be seen from Fig. 4.46, the proportion of the sales of wholesale in East China had the absolute advantage, reaching 77.3% at the highest; that in Central and West China was low. In particular, the proportion of the sales of wholesale in West China was only about 10%. Seen from the changing trends, the proportion of the sales of wholesale in East China rose by about 6% during 1999–2007. At the same time, the proportion of the sales of wholesale in Central China and that in West China fell. From the figure, we can see that economic development in China showed a trend of growing imbalance.

Fig. 4.46. Proportions of the sales of wholesale above the designated size in East China, Central China and West China (1998–2007)

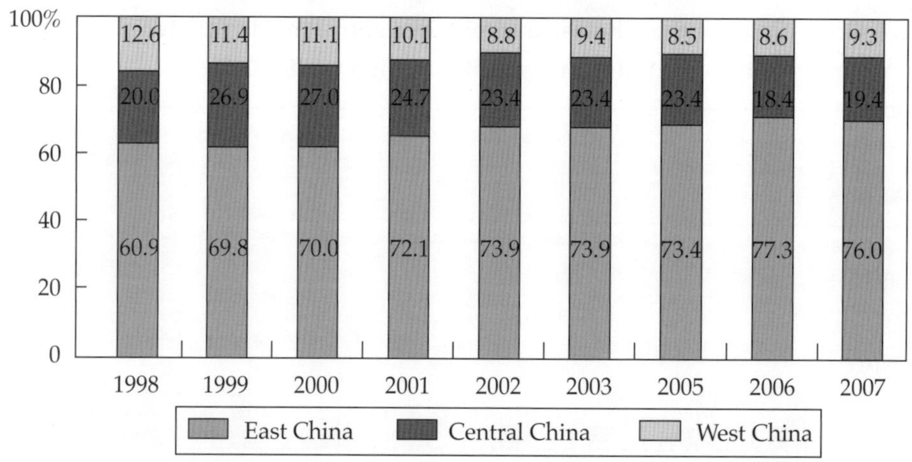

Characteristics of the East China-Central China-West China regional structure of the wholesale trade and reasons

Characteristics of the East China-Central China-West China regional structure of the wholesale trade

From the description and comparison of the numbers of wholesale enterprises, the numbers of wholesale outlets, the number of practitioners and the sales of the wholesale in East China, Central China and West China, we can draw such a conclusion that the East China-Central China-West China regional structure of the wholesale trade in China has the following three features:

(1) Development of the wholesale trade in East China holds a pivotal position in the development of the entire wholesale trade in China, the distribution of input and output elements of commodity wholesale in East China takes up large proportions in the national total. Specifically, the number of wholesale business

corporations, that of wholesale outlets and that of wholesale practitioners in East China account for roughly 3/5 of the national totals, showing a relatively high level of development.

(2) Development of the wholesale trade in China has an east-west stratified structure. Development of the wholesale trade in East China is significantly ahead of that in Central China which is slightly faster than that in West China.

(3) Wholesale enterprises in East China have this production efficiency and intensity which are far greater than those in Central China and West China. The number and level of development of wholesale outlets in East China are higher than those in Central and West China, playing a great role in improving the level of economic development and people's livelihood in East China.

Reasons for the formation of the characteristics of the East China-Central China-West China structure of the wholesale trade

Unbalanced development of the wholesale trade in China in different regions has profound historic and policy reasons. Since the third Plenary Session of the 11th CPC National Congress, profound changes have happened to the strategy of regional economic development in China, namely the strategy of balanced development has been changed into the strategy of unbalanced development. In December 1978, Comrade Deng Xiaoping put forward, for the first time, the new idea of unbalanced regional economic development in China. In September 1988, Deng Xiaoping generalized the relationship between the development of coastal areas and that of inland China into the thought of "Two Overall Situations" for the first time. Since the reform and opening up, China has shifted the focus on regional economic development to eastern areas. That's why it is often said that the rapid development of the wholesale trade in East China couldn't be achieved without its exceptional advantages:

(1) Advantageous national and economic conditions. Flat terrain, rich water resources, fertile land, long costal line and a developed transportation and communications system have all enabled East China to have a favorable foundation for economic development.

(2) High degree of opening up. In the modern history of economic development in China, east areas had been intimately connected to the outside world. After the reform and opening up, East China pioneered in China once again. A group of provinces such as Guangdong, Fujian and Shandong emerged suddenly in the mid- and late 1980s before beginning to take off in the 1990s with foreign advanced technologies and foreign capital.

(3) Sufficient capital supply. In the long process of economic development, East China has been able to have a stronger capability of accumulating capital and a higher efficiency in the use of funds than Central China and West China thanks to the relatively high per capita income and advanced technical and economic conditions. Coupled with the enhanced role of the market mechanism in the redistribution of national income and the financing of the entire society, East China enjoys greater freedom and has obtained great amounts of capital inflows based on the internal rules of the economy.[9]

Central China and West China lagged behind East China in terms of such factors, leading to the unbalanced distribution of local economic development and that of local development of the wholesale trade and promoting the features of the unbalanced distribution more prominent. Though China has made some favorable policies for the development of Central China and West China and paid special attention to the balanced development among different regions since 2000, the process of balanced development is long and it will need a longer time of accumulation for the local economic development in Central China and West China.

Six-region structure of the wholesale trade

The regional structure (East China, Central China and West China) of the wholesale trade in China has been analyzed above. Since such division of regions is relatively general, an analysis of a six-region structure will be made next in order to reflect the development situations of the wholesale trade in different regions in China in a more comprehensive way.[10] According to data available, the analysis below will be made based on two stages: 1994–1996 and 1998–2007.

Basic information on the registration of the wholesale trade

The same as the above analysis of the regional structure of the wholesale trade, basic indicators adopted here are still the number of wholesale business corporations, the number of practitioners and the number of outlets.

Number of wholesale business corporations

Seen on the whole, during 1994–1996, the number of wholesale enterprises in China grew from 212,494 to 306,235, up 44% within three years. Specific distributions were as shown in Fig. 4.47.

Fig. 4.47. Numbers of Wholesale business corporations in Six Regions (1994–1996)

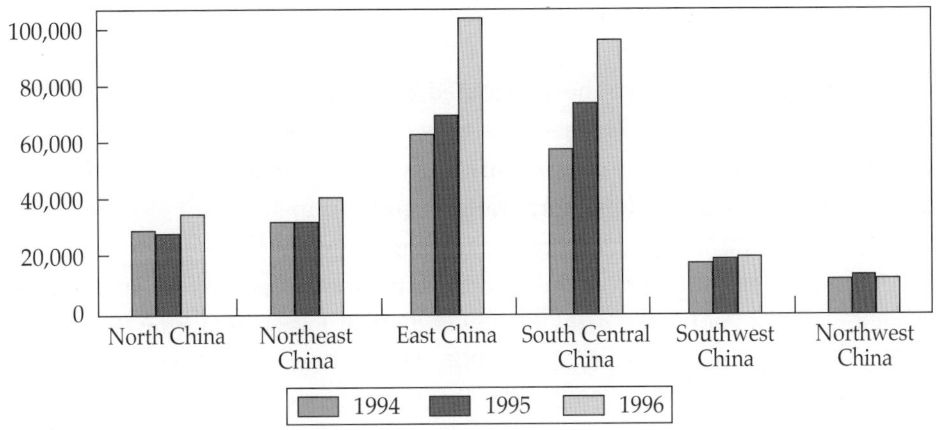

Fig. 4.48. Numbers of wholesale business corporations above the designated size in the 6 regions (1998–2007)

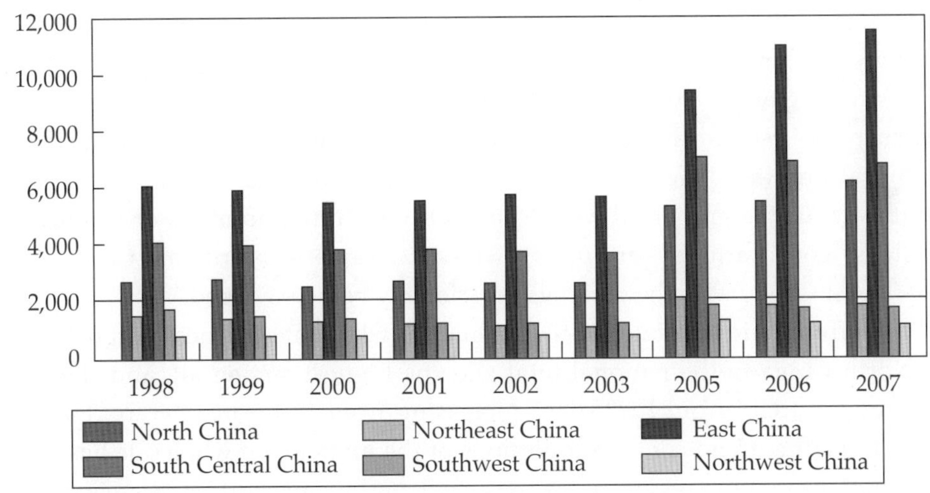

Seen from the growth of the number of wholesale business corporations, that in East China and that in South Central China were the highest among all. Of which, during 1994–1996, the number of wholesale enterprises in East China increased by nearly 40,578, up 65%; that in South Central China increased by nearly 37,365, up 65%; that in Southwest China and Northwest China didn't change and grew very slowly. Wholesale enterprises in Northwest China were 103 less from 1994–1996.

Seen from regional rankings, East China and South Central China had the largest number of wholesale business corporations among all, while Southwest and Northwest China had the least number of wholesale business corporations among all. What's more, rankings of the numbers of wholesale business corporations in the six regions didn't change over this period.

We have mentioned just now that China began to collect statistics on wholesale enterprises above the designated size since 1998. Seen from the total number, the numbers of wholesale business corporations above the designated size in the 6 regions had grown significantly during 1998–2007; and the total number of wholesale business corporations grew from 16,945 in 1998 to 29,046 in 2007. Specific information on the 6 regions is shown in Fig. 4.48.

As can be seen, numbers of the wholesale business corporations in each and all regions grew. As for the growing speed, that in East China grew the fastest of all, from 2,726 in 1998 to 6,205 in 2007. Though the growth rate slipped in 2001, it rallied to 4.89% in 2002. Wholesale business corporations in South Central China developed fast, too, increasing from 1,618 in 1998 to 2,176 in 2007. Wholesale business corporations in North China and Northeast China grew slowly and in a fluctuating way showed a falling tendency during 1999–2003 before grew slowly. Wholesale business corporations in Southwest China and Northwest China developed slowly without significant changes.

As for regional rankings, North China and South Central China had been ranking the first and the second in terms of the number of wholesale business corporations they each had, followed by North China, Northeast China, Southwest China and Northwest China. Of which, the numbers of wholesale business corporations were more or less the same in Northeast China and Southwest China, with the rankings occasionally being swapped.

Seen from ratio, the ratio of the number of wholesale business corporations in North China to the national total was the highest among all, and showed an growing trend from 1998–2007, increasing from 16.1% in 1998 to 21.4% in 2007. Changing trends of the proportions of the numbers of wholesale business corporations in other regions were consistent, and the proportions were more or less the same, being somewhere between 8–10%.

Number of outlets

The growth of wholesale enterprises in the six regions in this period has been analyzed just now. Next, let's check the number of outlets.

As shown in Fig. 4.49, the number of wholesale outlets grew the fastest in South Central China among all, increasing by 277 thousand during 1994–1996, up 63%; wholesale outlets in East China also increased by 165 thousand, up 38%. Other regions also developed to some extent in terms of the number of wholesale outlets, only to be at low rates.

Fig. 4.49. Numbers of wholesale outlets in the six regions (1994–1996)

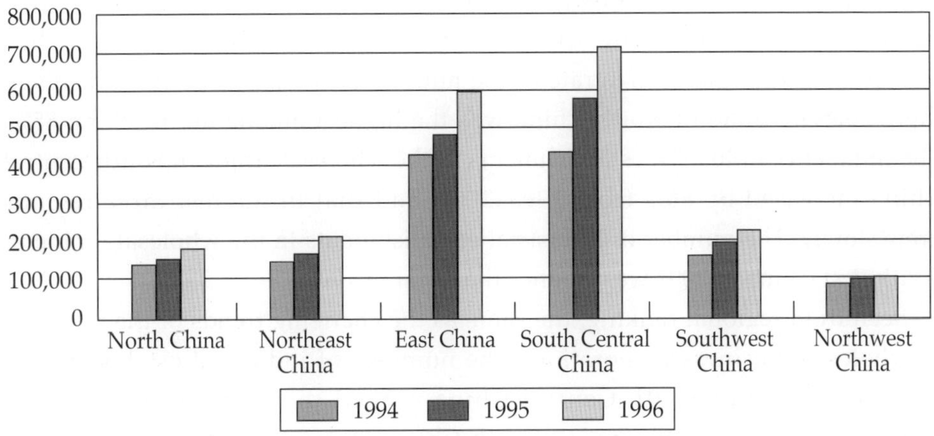

Fig. 4.50. Numbers of industrial establishments in the wholesale trade above the designated size in the six regions (1998–2007)

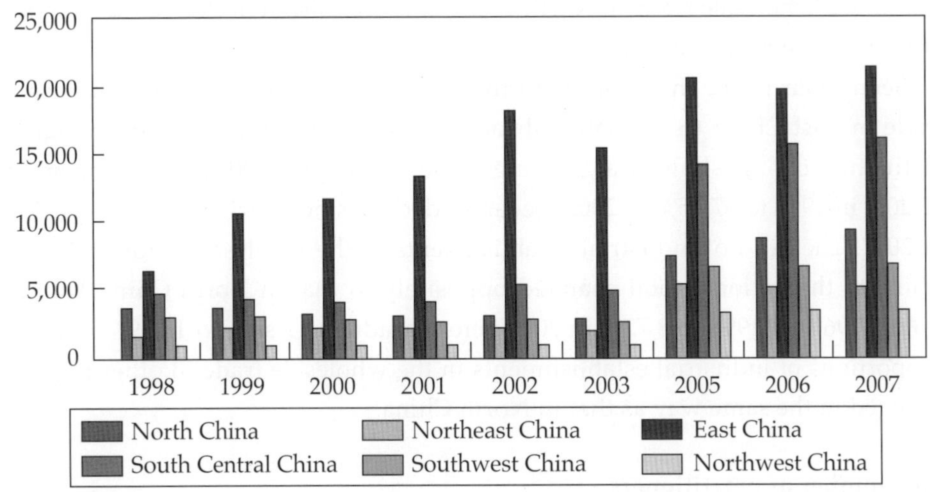

As for the rankings, comparing the numbers of wholesale business corporations and that of wholesale outlets in the 6 regions over the same period, we can see clearly that the champion and runner-up of the 6 regions in terms of the number of wholesale outlet swapped. South Central China leaped to No. 1, and East China leaped to No. 2 in terms of the number of wholesale outlets.

China began to collect statistics on wholesale enterprises above the designated size in 1998. Indicators of industrial establishments in the wholesale trade and those of the numbers of outlets were the same. During 1998–2007, the total number of industrial establishments in China grew from 19,515 in 1998 to 60,884 in 2007. The numbers of industrial establishments in the 6 regions also grew significantly. Details were as follows.

As shown in Fig. 4.50, the number of industrial establishments in the wholesale trade in East China grew from 6,283 in 1998 to 21,139 in 2007; that in North China increased by 3,479 within the same 10 years, being more than doubled. In 2005, the growth rate of the number of industrial establishments in the wholesale trade in North China was the highest among all, reaching 85%. The number of industrial establishments in the wholesale trade in South Central China increased by 66% from 1998–2007; and that in the rest three regions grew slowly. The number of industrial establishments in the wholesale trade in Southwest China in 2007 was smaller than that in 1998.

Seen from regional ranking, the same as the changing trends of the numbers of wholesale business corporations, the numbers of industrial establishments in East China and South Central China ranked the first and the second, respectively, followed by that in North China. Different from the numbers of the wholesale business corporations, the number of industrial establishments in Southwest China had been higher than that in Northeast China. The less developed wholesale trade in Northwest China was also reflected in the number of local industrial establishments.

Seen from ratio, the ratio of industrial establishments in the wholesale trade in East China to the national total was the highest among all, changing in fluctuations. It showed a growing trend from 1998–2002, increasing from 32.20% in 1998 to 57.45% in 2002, began to decline since 2003, and fell to 34.72% in 2007. The ratio of industrial establishments in the wholesale trade in North China to the national total changed oppositely to that in North China, falling from 17.96% in 1998 to 8.72% in 2002 before gradually rising to 15.09% in 2007. Proportions of industrial establishments in the wholesale trade in other regions changed in the same way as that in North China.

The number of practitioners

Comparing with the numbers of wholesale business corporations and the numbers of wholesale outlets in the six regions, the regional structure of wholesale practitioners in the six regions was more similar to that of the numbers of wholesale business corporations (see Fig. 4.51). As for their ranking in terms of practitioners, East China ranked the first, South Central China ranked the second, Southwest China and Northwest China ranked the fifth and the sixth, respectively. Seen from the growth rate, wholesale practitioners grew fast in East China and South Central China, stably with a slight decline in Northwest China, and slowly in the rest regions.

Fig. 4.51. Wholesale practitioners in the 6 regions (1994–1996)

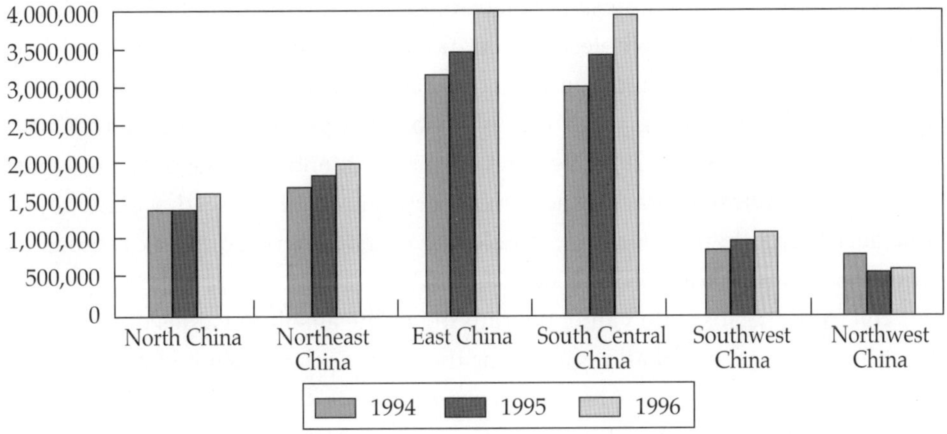

Fig. 4.52. Practitioners in the wholesale trade above the designated size in the 6 regions (1998–2007)

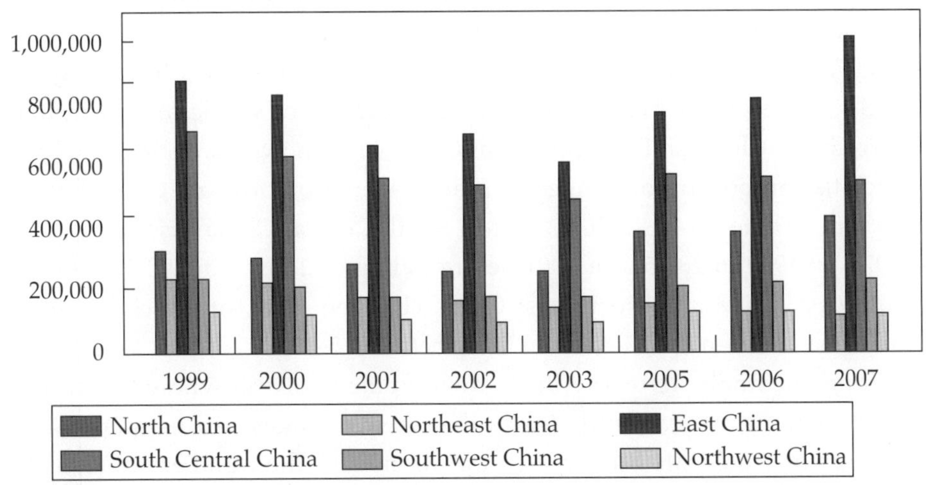

During 1998–2007, total wholesale practitioners in China fell to the smallest number of 1,787 thousand in 2003 before growing to the largest number of 2,496 thousand in 2007. Detailed development of wholesale practitioners in the six regions is shown in Fig. 4.52.

As shown in Fig. 4.52, it is clear that in the comparison of the numbers of wholesale business corporations and the umber of industrial establishments in the wholesale trade, fluctuations in the practitioners in the wholesale trade above the designated size in the six regions were not as fierce as those of the previous two indicators during 1999–2008. The wholesale practitioners in the six regions all showed a tendency of first decreasing then increasing.

Seen from the increment, comparing those in 1999 with those in 2007, it could be seen that only the wholesale practitioners in North China and East China were increased; that the wholesale practitioners in North China fluctuated, too, showed a rapid growth momentum after 2005, and exceeded 400,000 in 2007, up 31% over 1998. The growth rate of wholesale practitioners in East China had been negative since 1999, became 1% in 2003, and increased by 16% from 1999–2007. Wholesale practitioners in other regions all showed a tendency of first decreasing then increasing. Wholesale practitioners in the six regions all reduced in number form 1999–2007.

Seen from the absolute value, the ranking of the absolute values of wholesale practitioners in each and all regions was the same as the ranking of and changes in the numbers of wholesale business corporations in the six regions.

Seen from proportion, the proportions of wholesale practitioners in East Chin and North China both showed an increasing tendency. Of which, the ratio of wholesale practitioners in East China to the total number of wholesale practitioners in China was the highest among all, changing and fluctuating and showing a growing trend from 1998–2002. It rose from 34.40% in 1999 to 40.68% in 2007. The proportion of wholesale practitioners in North China grew from 12.98% in 1999 to 17.41% in 2007. The proportions of wholesale practitioners in Northeast China and South Central China each showed a declining trend, of which the proportion of wholesale practitioners in Northeast China fell from 9.58% in 1999 to 5.14% in 2007; that in South Central China rose slightly from 28.07% in 1999 to 28.35% in 2001 before falling to 22.13% in 2007; and that in Southwest China and Northwest China changed little, of which the former fluctuated between 8–10% and the latter between 5–6%.

From the analysis of the basic development of the wholesale trade in the six regions, we can find clearly that great changes had happened to the numbers of wholesale business corporations and the numbers of industrial establishments in the six regions, yet the proportions of wholesale practitioners in the 6 regions changed little. East China, North China and South Central China together held the absolute proportion in the entire wholesale trade in term of the three indicators, the sum of which usually surpassed 75%. It reflected the imbalanced development of the wholesale trade to a great extent. The differences of the regional structure could also be seen from the regional structure of the wholesale trade in East China, Central China and West China. It also demonstrated that the wholesale trade was one of the leading trades in economic development, as well as the first sign of economic development.

Sales

The levels of economic development in the six regions in China were quite different, so were the development levels of the wholesale trade in the same six regions. A more intuitive impression could be got from the changes in the sales of the wholesale trade. Therefore, we will make a detailed description over the growth of the sales of wholesale in the six regions. Let's check their growth during 1994–1997 first.

Fig. 4.53. Sales of wholesale in the 6 regions in China (1994–1997)

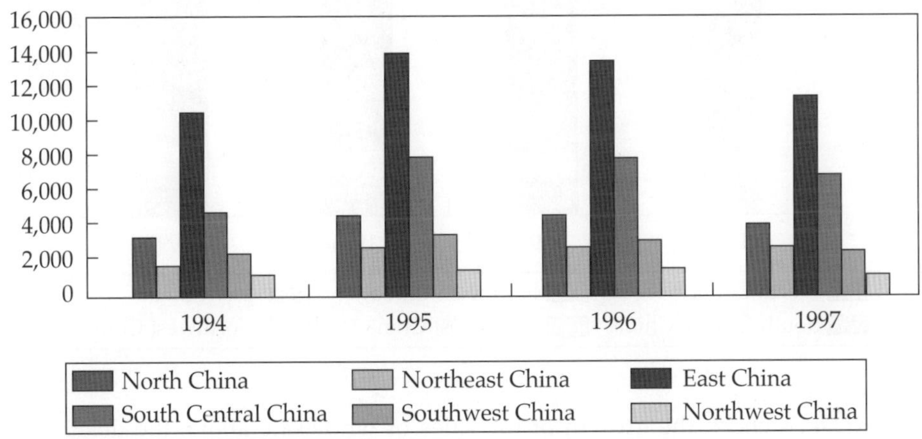

As can be seen clearly from Fig. 4.53, the sales of wholesale in the 6 regions were quite different from one another. The ranking of the six regions in terms of the sales of wholesale was relatively stable, being in an order of East China, South Central China, North China, Northeast China, Southwest China and Northwest China. Of which, the sales of wholesale in Northeast China and Southwest China were more or less the same, ranking the fourth and the fifth, respectively. Seen from the absolute value, the sales of wholesale in East China was 2.2 times, 3.1 times, 6.4 times, 4.3 times and 9.5 times greater, respectively, than the sales of wholesale in South Central China, North China, Northeast China, Southwest China and Northwest China, respectively, in 1994, which then became 1.7 times, 3.0 times, 4.68 times, 4.67 times and 9.5 times greater, respectively, in 1996. See the specific proportions in the figure below (see Fig. 4.54).

Seen from the respective proportion of the sales of wholesale in each of the six regions in China (see Fig. 4.54), it is clear that the respective ratio of the sales of wholesale in each of the six regions in China to the total sales hadn't change significantly. The ratio of the sales of wholesale in Northeast China to the national total sales of wholesale changed greatly, showing a growing trend. In contrast, the ratio of the sales of wholesale in Southeast China to the national total sales of wholesale showed a declining trend.

Fig. 4.54. Proportions of the sales of wholesale in the 6 regions in China (1994–1997)

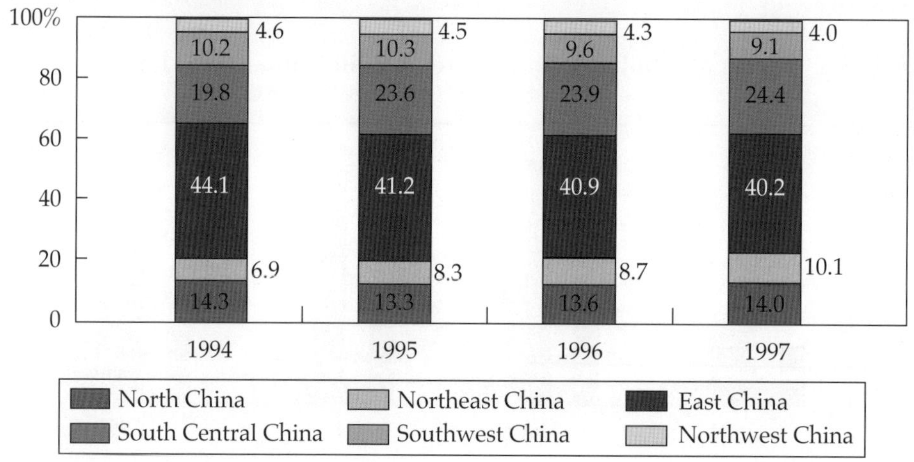

Next, let's check the growth of the sales of wholesale above the designated size in the six regions in China since 1999. See Fig. 4.55.

Fig. 4.55. Sales of wholesale above the designated size in the 6 regions in China (1999–2007)

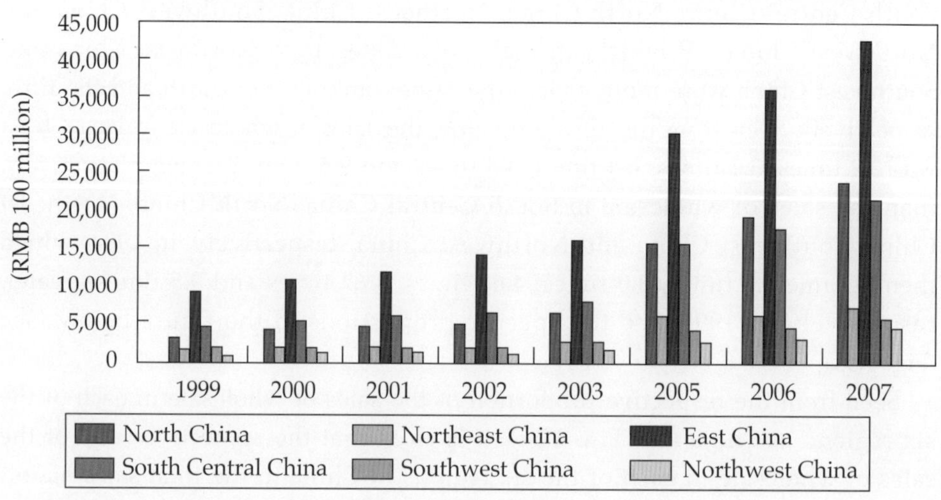

As can be seen from Fig. 4.55, the sales of wholesale in each of the six regions in China grew rapidly. Of which, the absolute value of the sales of wholesale in East China was the greatest of all, growing from RMB 942.4 billion in 1999 to 4,221.1 billion in 2007, being RMB 3,278.7 billion more and nearly twice greater than the sum of the sales of wholesale in Southwest and Northwest China.

The sales of wholesale in North China grew the fastest among all, increasing by nearly seven times within nine years, and ranking the second only to South Central China among the 6 regions. The sales of wholesale in Southwest China grew slowly, being only twice greater. It can also be seen from Fig. 4.55 that Northwest China showed a strong momentum of catching up with before surpassing Southwest China in terms of the sales of wholesale.

As can be seen from Fig. 4.56, the proportions of the sales of wholesale in the 6 regions hadn't changed much during 1999–2007. The sales of wholesale in North China grew the fastest of all, increasing from 15.2–22.3%; the sales of wholesale in Southwest China dropped the fastest of all, falling from 9.3–5.9%. The ratio the sales of wholesale in Northwest China kept increasing, showing a tendency of catching up with before surpassing that in Southwest China.

Fig. 4.56. Proportions of the sales of wholesale above the designated size in the six regions in China (1999–2007)

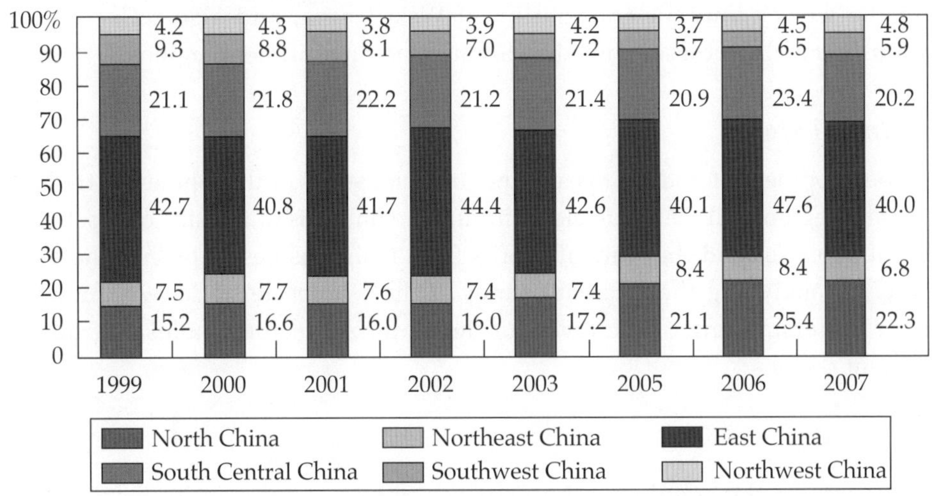

From the above analysis of the changes in the sales of wholesale in the six regions, it can be seen that the sales of wholesale in the six regions across China all kept growing in the second stage, illustrating the rapid development of the wholesale trade in this period.

Of which, the sales of wholesale in East China had been ranking the first in China. It is mainly because that East China has always been the most developed area in China, the effective consumer demands of local residents are the most flourishing among all. East China is also the forefront of the reform and opening up in China, the economic restructuring in which was among the first reforms and relatively complete. The opening up of the economic system has also promoted the rapid development of the wholesale trade in East China.

The sales of wholesale in North China grew fast, which may be directly related to the rapid economic development in North China. In particular, the Beijing-Tianjin region played an effective role in stimulating the economic development in surrounding areas, and local residents' disposable income grew constantly, increasing people's demands before making the sales of wholesale in North China leap to the second around China after 2005.

South Central China and Northeast China also developed fast. In particular, since China implemented the strategy of vigorously promoting the development of the old industrial areas in Northeast China and that of enabling Central China to grow, the sales of wholesale in these two regions had achieved a significant growth. Though the sales of wholesale in Northwest China and Southwest China kept growing, too, the difference between them and the sales of wholesale in the relatively developed East China and North China were enlarged constantly. It had much to do with the vast territory, yet sparse population, the inconvenience of transportation, the fragile eco-environment and the weak economic foundation of West China, and also reflected the seriously imbalanced economic development among different regions.

Financial states

The development of and changes in the financial states of the wholesale trade in different regions will be made clear through an analysis of the size of assets, the size of liabilities and the scale of profits from main businesses of the wholesale trade. By analyzing the financial states of the wholesale trade, we can get a better understanding of the levels of development of the wholesale trade in different regions.

Size of assets

The assets of the wholesale enterprises above the designated size kept increasing in China in this period, the national total of which increased from RMB 1,454.043 billion in 1999 to 3,869.771 billion in 2007. In particular, since 2002, the assets of the wholesale enterprises above the designated size in China had been growing faster and faster, the growth rate of which in 2007 was 22.76%. Respective growth of the assets of the wholesale enterprises above the designated size in the six regions in China is shown in Fig. 4.57.

Fig. 4.57. **Sizes of assets of the wholesale enterprises above the designated size in the six regions in China (1999–2007)**

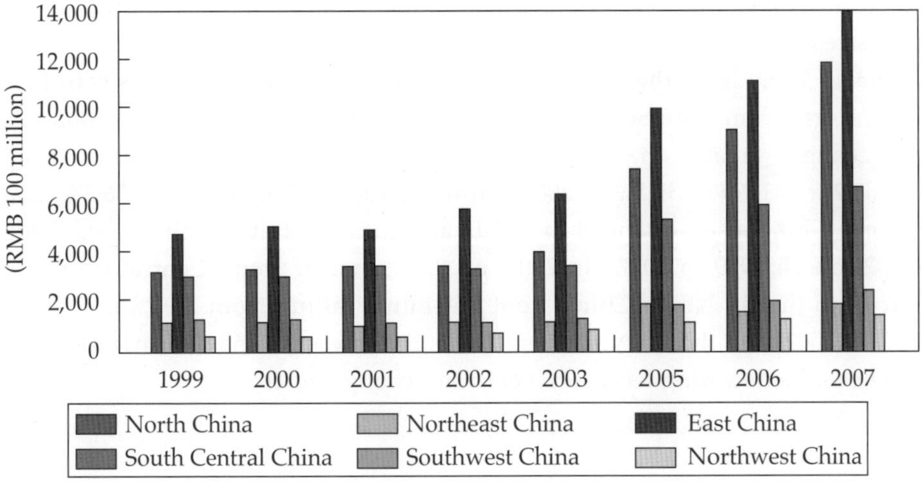

Fig. 4.58. **Proportions of assets of the wholesale enterprises above the designated size in the 6 regions (1999–2007)**

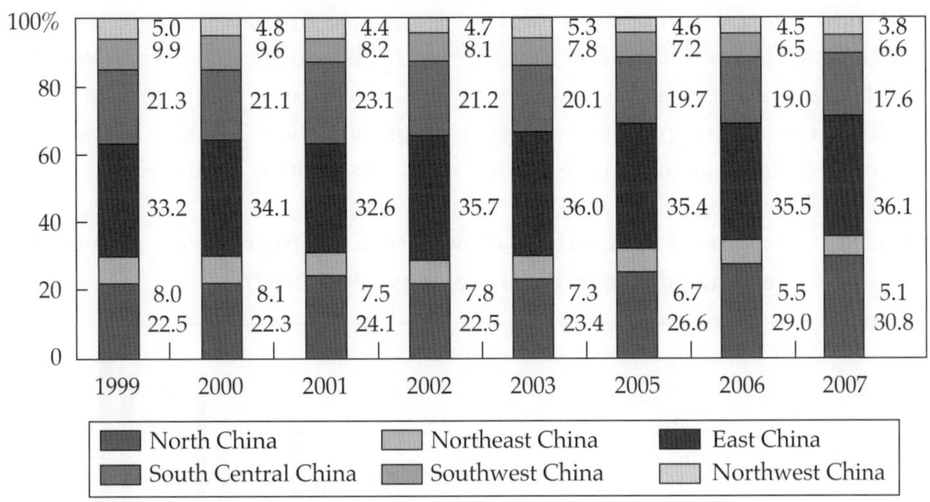

During 1999–2007, assets in the six regions all grew significantly. Seen from the absolute value, the absolute value of the assets of East China had been ranking the first among the six regions, increasing from RMB 483.12 billion in 1999 to 1,397.64 billion in 2007; that of the assets in North China increased from RMB 327.64 billion in 1999 to 1,191.14 billion in 2007, showing a growing trend during 2001–2007; that of the assets in Northeast China developed slowly, increasing from 1 RMB 17.0 billion in 1999 to 196.88 billion; that of the assets in Southwest China was relatively low and grew slowly, increasing from RMB 144.61 billion to 256.23 billion in 2007; that of the assets in South Central China and Northwest China were doubled within the nine years. Specific proportions of the sizes of assets of the six regions are shown below in Fig. 4.58.

During 1999–2007, the ratios of assets of the wholesale enterprises in East China, North China and South Central China to the total assets of the wholesale trade changed greatly: that in East China advanced in twists and turns, rising from 33.2% in 1999 to 35.7% in 2002 before fluctuating between 34.7–36.7%; that in North China also advanced in twists and turns, yet at a high speed, rising from 22.5% in 1999 to 30.8% in 2007, up 8.3%; that in South Central China, in contrast to that in North China, kept declining, falling from 21.3% in 1999 to 17.6% in 2007; and that in Northeast China, Southwest China, Northwest China also showed a declining tendency, yet didn't change much.

Size of liabilities

As shown in Fig. 4.59, of the total liabilities in each of the 6 regions, those in East China grew to some extent, but those in other regions didn't change much during 1999–2003. However, after 2005, liabilities in East China, North China and South Central China grew rapidly, but those in the rest regions didn't change much. Comparatively, there was a high goodness between sizes of liabilities and sizes of assets of the 6 regions. The size of assets in East China was the largest among all, so was its scale of liabilities. The size of assets in Northwest China was the smallest of all, so was its scale of liabilities.

Fig. 4.59. **Scales of liabilities of wholesale enterprises above the designated size in the six regions (1999–2007)**

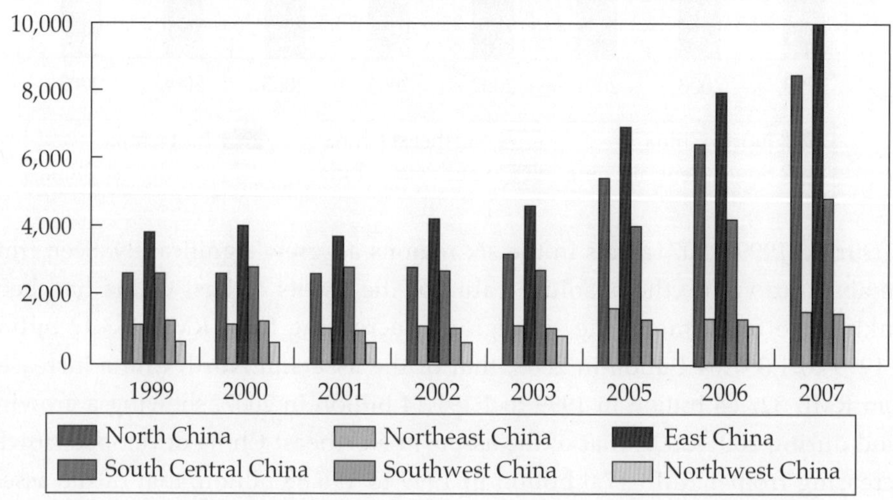

Fig. 4.60. **Proportions of the liabilities of the wholesale enterprises in the six regions (1999–2007)**

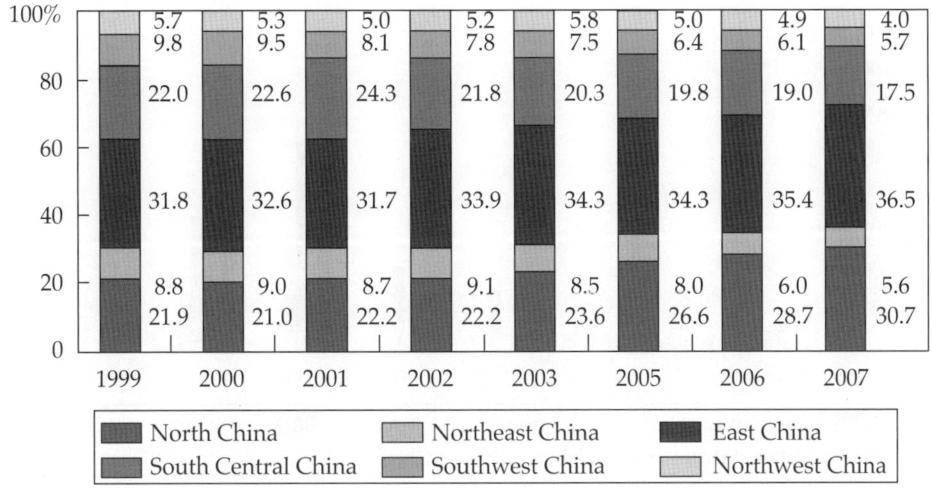

Let's check the proportions of the scales of liabilities of wholesale enterprises in the six regions in China (see Fig. 4.60).

As can be seen from the proportions of the sizes of assets of the wholesale trades each above the designated size in the six major regions (see Fig. 4.58), the changing trends of such proportions were completely the same as those of the sizes of assets of the same trades.

Profits from main businesses

As shown in Fig. 4.61, during 1999–2007, the profits from main businesses of the wholesale trades in the 6 regions all grew significantly, showing the same fluctuating trends. The growth rate of such profits was the highest of all in 2005, yet negative in 2000 and 2001.

Seen from the national total, the profits from main businesses of the wholesale enterprises in East China had been ranking the first among those in the six regions, growing from RMB 32.95 billion in 1999 to 252.7 billion in 2007. The profits from main businesses of the wholesale enterprises in North China caught up from behind, growing from RMB 9.1 billion in 1999 to 153.1 billion in 2007, surpassing those in South Central China in 2005 before ranking the second among the six regions. The ranking of those in other regions was the same as that of the numbers of wholesale business corporations in the six regions, which were South Central China, Northeast China and Northwest China in sequence in 2007. The proportions of profits from main businesses of the wholesale enterprises in the six regions are shown below in Fig. 4.62.

Fig. 4.61. Scales of the profits from main businesses of the wholesale trades each above the designated size in 6 regions (1999–2007)

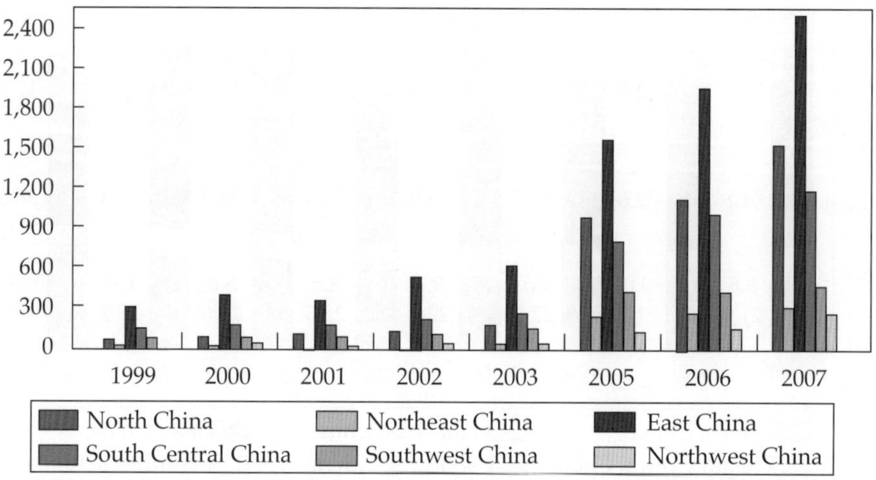

Fig. 4.62. Proportions of the profits from main businesses of the wholesale enterprises above the designated size in the six regions in China (1999–2007)

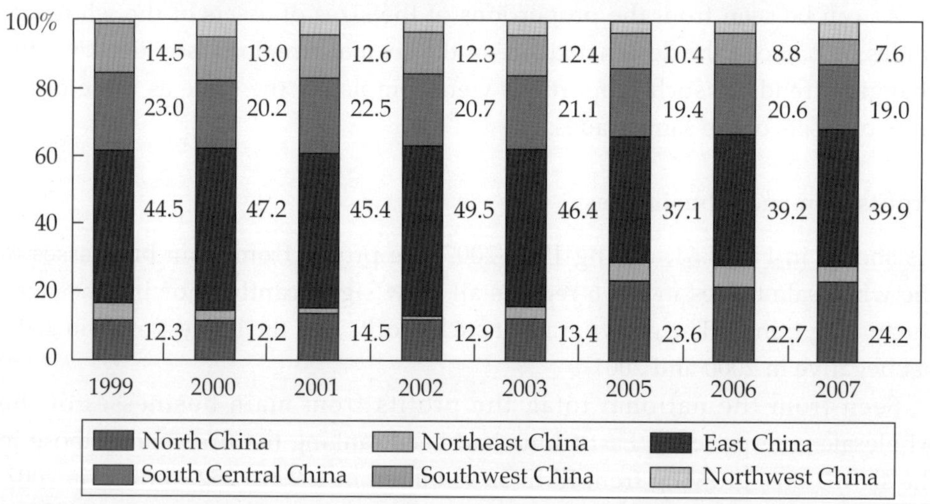

During 1999–2007, the profits from main businesses of the wholesale enterprises in the 6 regions in China to the national total didn't change much. Of which, the proportion of the profits from main businesses of the wholesale enterprises in East China was the greatest among all, reaching the peak of 49.5% in 2002 before showing a declining trend and falling to 39.9% in 2007.

The proportion of profits from main businesses of the wholesale enterprises in North China showed a growing trend and grew at a high speed, increasing from 12.3% in 1999 to 24.2% in 2007; that in Northeast China presented a trend of first decreasing then increasing, and was 5.0% in 2007, which was more or less the same as that in 1999. Though the same proportion in Northwest China was the lowest among all, it kept rising constantly, increasing from 1% in 1999 to 4.4% in 2007 at a high rate. The same proportion in South Central China didn't change significantly, being at about 20%; while that in Southwest China showed a declining tendency, falling from 14.5% in 1999 to 7.6% in 2007.

As can be seen from the analysis of the regional structure of the financial states of the wholesale trade, the wholesale trade in East China was the most developed, all indicators of which ranked the first among the 6 regions. Moreover, the absolute value of the wholesale trade in East China grew fast, too, yet its proportion showed a declining tendency. The wholesale trade grew the fastest in North China, enabling its ratio to show a growing trend. Growth of the wholesale trade in Northwest China was also significantly faster than that in Southwest China. From it, we can see the seriously imbalanced development of the wholesale trade in different regions.

Development and Changes in the Wholesale Enterprises in Different Economic Sectors

The industrial structure of the wholesale trade refers to the distribution ratio of the total social labor occupied by the wholesale sector in different economic sectors and the proportional relations among different economic sectors. As an important component of the entire structure of the wholesale trade, it plays a pivotal role in the pilot function of the wholesale trade.

The wholesale trade is composed of relatively more departments, existing in each department of the national economy. Since the reform and opening up, wholesale enterprises in different economic sectors have presented different development states, developing either slowly or rapidly. The entire industrial structure has been optimized constantly along with the economic restructuring. Next, the industrial structure of the wholesale trade will be described and analyzed from the basic information on the wholesale trade, the sales and the financial states of wholesale enterprises. Due to limited and phased statistical data on the wholesale trade, different economic sectors will be chosen to describe and analyze the changes in the industrial structure of the wholesale trade based on the changes in the statistical criteria in different development stages.

Basic information on the registration of wholesale enterprises in different economic sectors

Basic information on the registration of wholesale enterprises in different economic sectors includes the number of wholesale institutions (referred to as wholesale business corporations since 2001), the number of wholesale outlets (referred to as industrial establishments since 2001) and the number of wholesale practitioners. Basic information on the registration of wholesale enterprises in different economic sectors will be compared below based on the data available since the reform and opening up in order to get the development of and changes in the wholesale enterprises in different economic sectors in the 3 decades of reform and opening up.

The initial stage of the reform (1978–1992)

Limited by the availability of data, institutions engaged in the purchase and wholesale of agricultural and sideline products and their practitioners, and institutions engaged in the wholesale of industrial products and their practitioners are adopted here to describe the development of the wholesale trade in agriculture and in industry over this period.

Number of wholesale institutions

It can be seen clearly from Fig. 4.63 that the number of institutions engaged in the purchase and wholesale of agricultural and sideline products was greater than that engaged in the wholesale of industrial products, yet the growth rate of both was very fluctuating.

Seen from the absolute value of the number of wholesale institutions, the number of institutions engaged in the purchase and wholesale of agricultural and sideline products was on the rise during 1978–1988. It grew rapidly before reaching the highest point of 264 thousand in 1988, being more than doubled over that in 1978. After 1988, it began to fall. Till 1992, there were only 183 thousand such institutions left. As for the number of institutions engaged in the wholesale of industrial products, it grew from 37 thousand in 1978 to 121 thousand in 1992, being nearly tripled within 14 years. What's more, different from institutions engaged in the purchase and wholesale of agricultural and sideline products, the number of institutions engaged in the wholesale of industrial products fell in 1992, but it had soon recovered to the level of 1989 in 1991, even to a higher level in 1992, indicating that development of institutions engaged in the wholesale of industrial products was significantly faster than that of institutions engaged in the purchase and wholesale of agricultural and sideline products during this period.

Fig. 4.63. **Numbers of institutions engaged in the wholesale of agricultural and sideline products and in the wholesale of industrial products (1978–1992)**

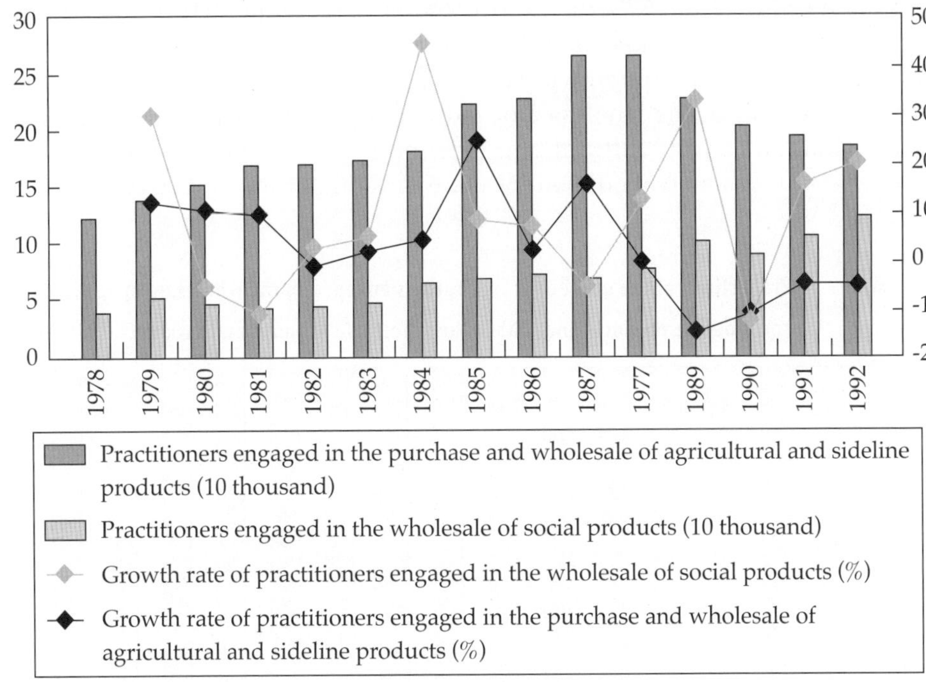

Seen from the growth rate, for institutions engaged in the purchase and wholesale of agricultural and sideline products, it was the first development peak for them during 1978–1981, during which their annual growth rate was over 10%. No significant change happened to such institutions during 1982–1984, and they developed steadily. However, during 1985–1989, the growth rate of them fluctuated greatly, showing two development peaks in 1985 and 1987, respectively; and one ebb in 1989. In 1985, the growth rate of the number of institutions engaged in the purchase and wholesale of agricultural and sideline products was the highest of all, increasing by 25% over the previous year. It grew be nearly 20% in 1987, but dropped by 14.4% in 1989. After that, institutions engaged in the purchase and wholesale of agricultural and sideline products showed a declining trend. As for institutions engaged in the wholesale of industrial products, we can see from Fig. 4.63 that they had two growth peaks over the same period in 1984 and 1989, respectively. In 1984, the growth rate was 44% over the previous year. In 1989 and 1988, it was 32%. Similarly, there were two significant ebbs over the same period in 1981 and 1990, respectively.

The number of institutions engaged in the wholesale of industrial products dropped by 10% in each of those two years.

As can be seen from the proportions of the two (see Fig. 4.64 for details), the proportion of institutions engaged in the purchase and wholesale of agricultural and sideline products to the total number of wholesale institutions in China kept falling down from 77% in 1978 to 60% in 1992, while that of institutions engaged in the wholesale of industrial products to the total number of wholesale institutions kept growing from 23% in 1978 to 40% in 1992, reflecting that development of the wholesale of industrial products was faster than that of the wholesale of agricultural and sideline products since the reform and opening up. It was an embodiment of the upgrading of the industrial structure in China.

Fig. 4.64. Proportions of the number of institutions engaged in the wholesale of agricultural and sideline products and that in the wholesale of industrial products (1978–1992)

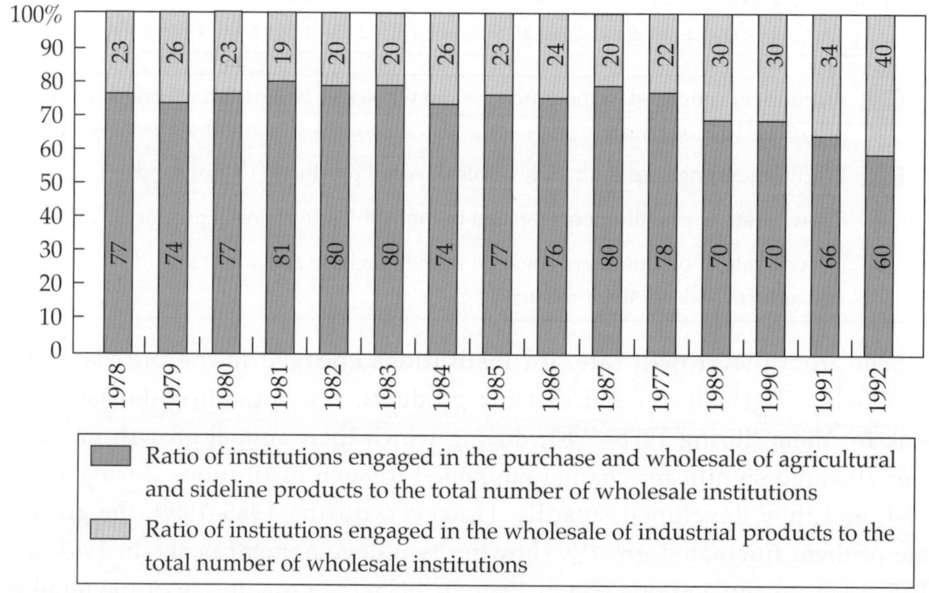

The number of practitioners

As shown in Fig. 4.65, compared with the changes in the numbers of wholesale institutions (see Fig. 4.63), practitioners, changes in practitioners and the existence of practitioners in institutions engaged in the wholesale of industrial products showed a high goodness with those of practitioners in institutions engaged in the purchase and wholesale of agricultural and sideline products. The number of practitioners engaged in the purchase and wholesale of agricultural and sideline products surpassed that in the wholesale of industrial products, the growth rates of both were fluctuating.

Fig. 4.65. Practitioners engaged in the purchase and wholesale of agricultural and sideline products and those in the wholesale of industrial products (1978–1992)

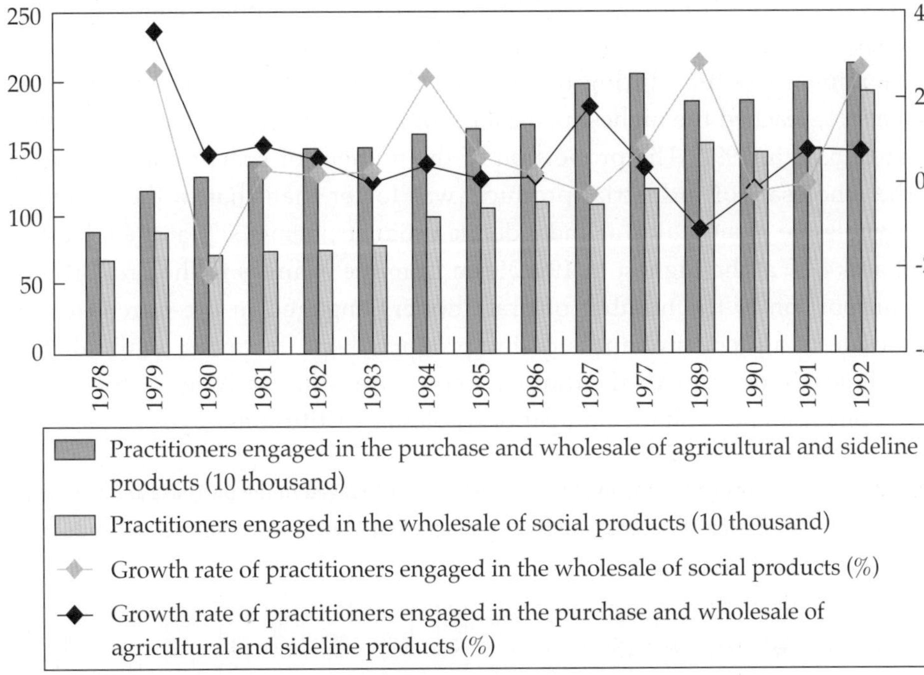

In terms of the absolute value, the number of practitioners in those institutions engaged in the purchase and wholesale of agricultural and sideline products was on the rise at a fast speed during 1978–1988 before reaching 2.104 million in 1988, being more than doubled over that in 1978 and becoming the highest point during this period. After 1988, the same number fell. Till 1992, it was only 2.172 million left. The number of practitioners in those institutions engaged in the wholesale of industrial products showed a growing trend, increasing from 697 thousand in 1978 to 1,952 thousand in 1992, being nearly doubled. Till 1992, the number of practitioners in those institutions engaged in the wholesale of industrial products and that in those institutions engaged in the purchase and wholesale of agricultural and sideline products were almost the same.

In terms of growth rate, the growth rate of the number of practitioners in those institutions engaged in agricultural and sideline products showed two significant peaks in this period: 1979 and 1987. In 1979, it reached 37.1%, showing an explosive growth; while in 1987, it grew by 18.5% over the previous year. In 1989, the number of practitioners in those institutions engaged in agricultural and sideline products fell by 10%; and that in institutions engaged in industrial products fluctuated greatly, showing four significant peaks and

1 ebb: its growth rate exceeded 25% in 1979, 1984, 1989 and 1992, while dropped 20% in 1980.

As can be seen from Fig. 4.66, the number of practitioners engaged in the purchase and wholesale of agricultural and sideline products had been holding the dominant position during this period, the proportion of which had been above 50%, reached the highest percentage of 72% in 1987, and fell to the lowest point of 53% in 1992. The proportion of the number of practitioners engaged in the wholesale of industrial products was lower than that in the purchase and wholesale of agricultural and sideline products, being 33% at the lowest in 1982 and 47% at the highest in 1992. Seen from the changes in the proportions, the proportion of the number of practitioners engaged in the purchase and wholesale of agricultural and sideline products kept declining, while that in the wholesale of industrial products kept increasing, showing a consistent development trend with the number of wholesale institutions.

Fig. 4.66. Proportions of the number of practitioners engaged in the purchase and wholesale of agricultural and sideline products and that in the wholesale of industrial products (1978–1992)

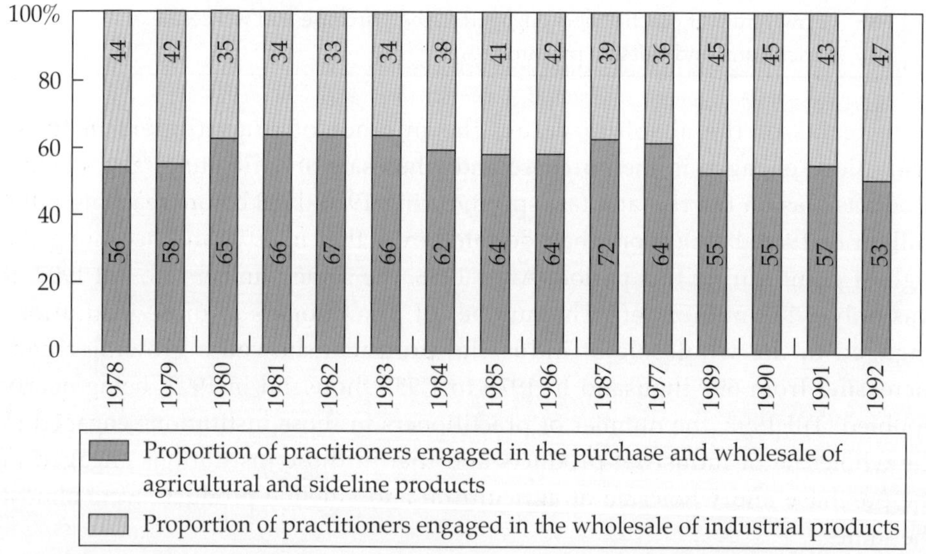

Development of and changes in the purchase and wholesale of agricultural and sideline products and the wholesale of industrial products during this period had much to do with the concurrent reform of the wholesale trade.

(1) Purchase and wholesale of agricultural and sideline products. During 1978–1988, development of institutions and practitioners engaged in the purchase and wholesale of agricultural and sideline products was credited to the

national reform of the policies on purchasing agricultural and sideline products. Since agricultural and sideline products were regional and highly seasonal, and many of them were fresh, China paid special attention to centering with distribution centers and carrying out multi-channel and less-link circulation to try to achieve direct connection between production and marketing as much as possible. After implementing the reform and opening up policy in 1978, China determined its basic policies on the wholesale and operation of agricultural and sideline products: 1) of the products under contract purchase or state order, the part being contracted or ordered should be purchased and operated by designated operational department of the state, while that unplanned part should be allowed to circulate freely; 2) the operational link of agricultural and sideline products was in counties. All agricultural and sideline products, as long as they could be operated in counties, should never be intervened by provincial and municipal governments, but directed transported and sold by counties; 3) positive attention should be paid to developing pool operations between agriculture and commerce, agriculture, industry and commerce, and between commerce, intimating the connections between the production and marketing areas, and exploring the integration of production, processing and sales. Apart from all or part of cotton, tobacco and other commodities being included in contracting purchase or put under state order, thus should be purchased and distributed by designated departments of China, other farm products were collected and distributed in a multi-channel and open way. The implementation of such policies promoted the increase in institutions engaged in the purchase and wholesale of agricultural and sideline products before stimulating the increase in the number of practitioners. The development of agricultural and sideline products in turn promoted the production and trading of farm products, making significant contributions to improving the livelihood of the vast people.

During 1989–1992, development of the wholesale of agricultural and sideline products in China became sluggish. Due to the excess market demand and soaring commodity prices during 1985–1988, relatively large market volatility appeared in 1988, contributing to a situation of "commodities being in short supply, commodity price soaring, market order being chaotic and consumers struggling for commodities" across China. After that, influenced by the macroeconomic regulation of the Central Government, development of agricultural and sideline products in China showed fluctuations; institutions engaged in the purchase and wholesale of agricultural and sideline products reduced gradually in number; and the number of practitioners fell, too. In 1989, China began to seriously clear up various types of companies, especially those established since the second half of 1986, including many institutions engaged in the purchase and wholesale of agricultural and sideline products, and strengthened the management over commodities that were immediately related to the livelihood of the Chinese people or of prominent supply-demand contradictions, including carrying out exclusive sales of fertilizers and pesticides, and carrying out unified management of rice by state-owned grain departments. With such measures, supply of important commodities such as agricultural and sideline products gradually returned to normal in 1991.

(2) The wholesale of industrial products. Since special attention was paid to the wholesale mechanism of industrial products for daily use in the reform of the wholesale trade, the wholesale of industrial products got developed rapidly over this period. Prior to the reform, wholesale enterprises of industrial products actually allocated commodities at all levels in accordance with administrative divisions and original provisions, and formed a closed market that allocated commodities horizontally. After 1979, many provinces in China pioneered in the reform, allowing grassroots wholesale and retail stores to purchase commodities across administrative regions, unplanned commodities to be purchased and marketed in and outside the province, and commodities manufactured and sold locally could be ordered directly from manufacturers by retail stores. In 1982, the State Council of China decided to break the dual-layered old system before implementing a new system, allowing the cross-administrative region and different levels of wholesale activities to develop rapidly. In 1983, the Ministry of Commerce put forward clearly that a supply-marketing relationship could be established among wholesale enterprises, wholesale and retail enterprises and between commercial and industrial enterprises, formally collapsing the old pattern of commodity supply by level. In 1984, approved by the State Council of China, the Ministry of Commerce launched a major reform once again over the wholesale system of industrial products for daily use, deciding to decentralize the wholesale enterprises under the governance of the Central Government or provincial governments to local cities, and integrate such wholesale enterprises with municipal-level wholesale enterprises before establishing a set of wholesale enterprises with specialties; stop establishing overlapped state-owned wholesale enterprises in the same economic sector in the same city according to administrative levels; and change the original price markdown to pricing by lot or negotiated pricing. The reform created important conditions for gradually establishing a system of industrial products for daily use featured by being city-based, open and networked.

In the process of reforming the old system of the wholesale of industrial products, China encouraged multi-channel wholesale, and allowed all operators of the state-owned, collective and individual enterprises to apply for dealing in wholesale in accordance with related policies and regulations. After 1986, after years of rectification and deepening of the reform, the circulation of industrial products was basically opened up, eliminating mandatory plans and management of commodities; price control was lifted and prices under state administration no longer existed; manufacturers and suppliers met directly, both enjoying greater autonomy thanks to multi-firm operation. Reform of the mechanism of the wholesale of industrial products pushed forward the development of the wholesale of all industrial products.

The establishment stage of the socialist market economy (1993–1997)

The five years during 1993–1997 witnessed a relatively rapid economic development after the convening of the 14th CPC National Congress. It was the five years after the establishment of the objectives of the socialist market economic system, during which all sectors of the national economy developed fast. The wholesale trade, the leading trade in each and all economic sectors, also developed rapidly. Next, the wholesale trade in the top 8 economic sectors in terms of the sales volume in 1997 will be chosen as the objects of the analysis of the wholesale structure in different economic sectors over the same period.[11]

The number of institutions

As can be clearly seen from the changes in the numbers of wholesale institutions in different economic sectors (see Fig. 4.67), the numbers of wholesale institutions all showed a growing trend, reflecting the rapid development of the commodity economy over the same period. Wholesale enterprises in all economic sectors all developed in this period.

Of which, the number of wholesale enterprises in the sector of food, drinks and tobacco was the largest of all and grew rapidly, increasing from 49,269 in 1994 to 64,843 in 1996, being 15,574 more within three years. The number of wholesale enterprises in the sector of metallic materials was the second largest of all in 1994, only to be caught up and surpassed by the number of wholesale enterprises in the sector of hardware, electrical appliances & accessories and chemical products in 1996. Wholesale enterprises in the sector of machinery and electronic equipment also grew fast, increasing from 12,830 in 1994 to 22,671 in 1996, before surpassing the number of wholesale enterprises in the sector of the means of agricultural production in 1996 and ranking the fourth.

Fig. 4.67. Numbers of wholesale institutions by sector (1994–1996)

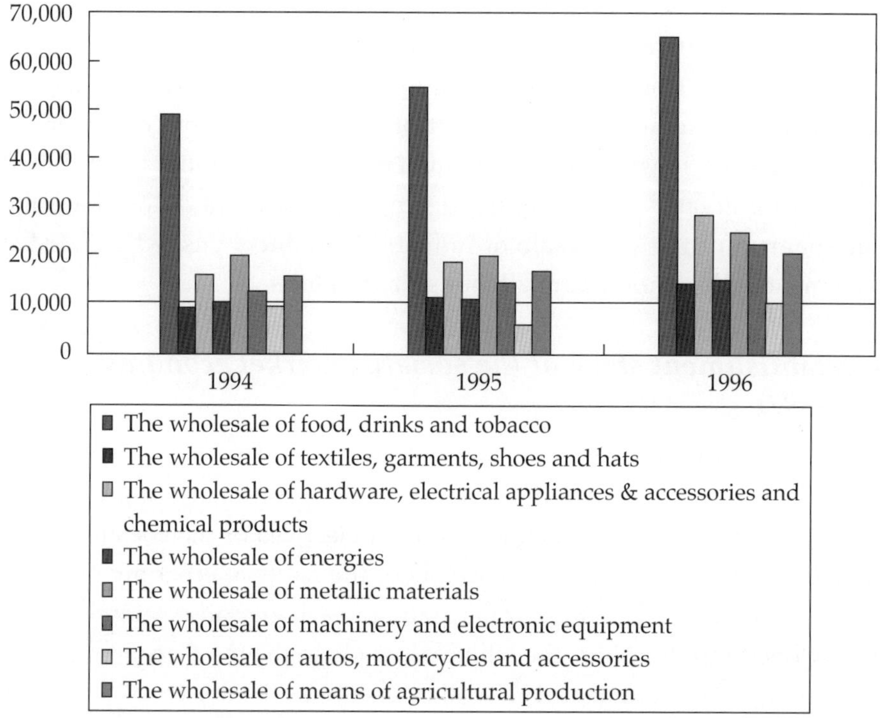

As can be seen clearly from Fig. 4.68, ratios of the numbers of wholesale enterprises in different sectors to the total number of wholesale enterprises didn't change much. Of which, the proportion of the number of wholesale institutions in the sector of food, drinks and tobacco was the highest of all, being over 20% in spite of the slight fall in 1996. There was a positive correlation between the proportions of the numbers of wholesale enterprises and the proportions of the sales of wholesale in other sectors.

Number of outlets

As can be seen clearly from Fig. 4.69, the numbers of wholesale outlets in all economic sectors all grew in this period, only to be very different, which was closely related to their respective nature. Of which, the number of wholesale outlets in the sector of food, drinks and tobacco ranked the first and showed a growing trend, increasing from 402.5 thousand in 1994 to 656.8 thousand in 1996, up 60% within two years. The growing speed was amazing. Wholesale outlets in the sector of the means of agricultural production ranked the second in terms of number, increasing from 153.3 thousand in 1994 to 210 thousand in 1996. The number of wholesale outlets in the sector of textiles, garments, shoes and hats ranked the third, growing from 137.6 thousand in 1994 to 205.4

Fig. 4.68. Ratios of the numbers of wholesale institutions in different sectors to the total number of wholesale institutions (1994–1996)

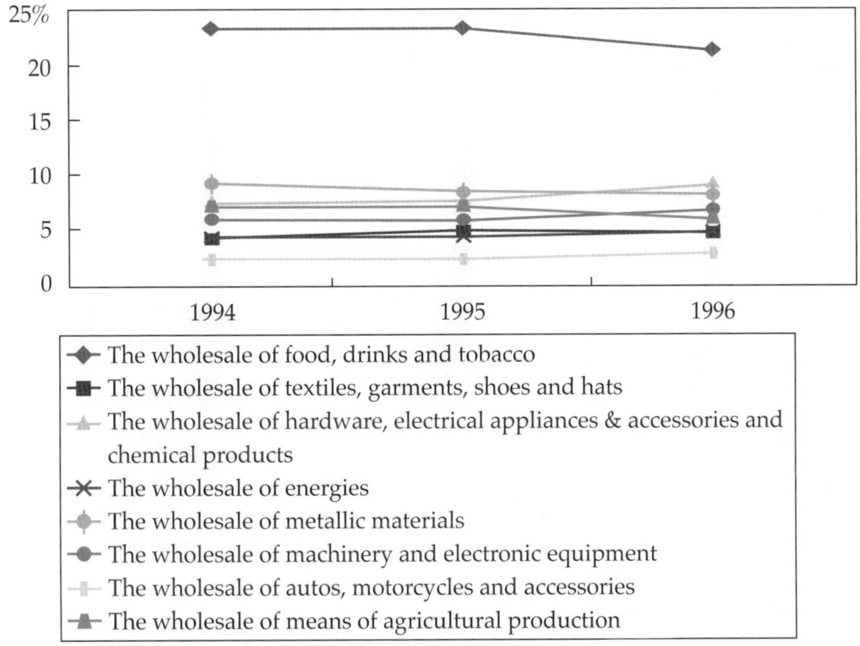

thousand in 1996; that in the sector of autos, motorcycles and accessories was the lowest among the eight sectors. The numbers of wholesale outlets in the rest sectors all grew somewhat, but their ranking didn't change.

As can be seen from Fig. 4.70, the proportions of the numbers of wholesale outlets in all sectors didn't change much; the proportion of the number of wholesale outlets in the sector of food, drinks and tobacco showed a growing trend; and the proportions of the numbers of wholesale outlets in other sectors were stable and didn't change much in the three years.

The number of practitioners

As can be seen from Fig. 4.71, the number of wholesale practitioners, wholesale institutions and that of wholesale outlets all showed the same growing trend. The number of wholesale practitioners in the sector of food, drinks and tobacco was still the highest of all, growing from 3,007 thousand in 1994 to 3,758 thousand in 1996; that in the sector of the means of agricultural production ranked the second, growing from 882 thousand in 1994 to 1,094 thousand in 1996; that in other sectors all grew to some extent, except that the number of wholesale practitioners in the sector of autos, motorcycles and accessories grew a little bit. Differences of the numbers of wholesale practitioners in different economic sectors were not great.

Fig. 4.69. Numbers of wholesale outlets by sector (1994–1996)

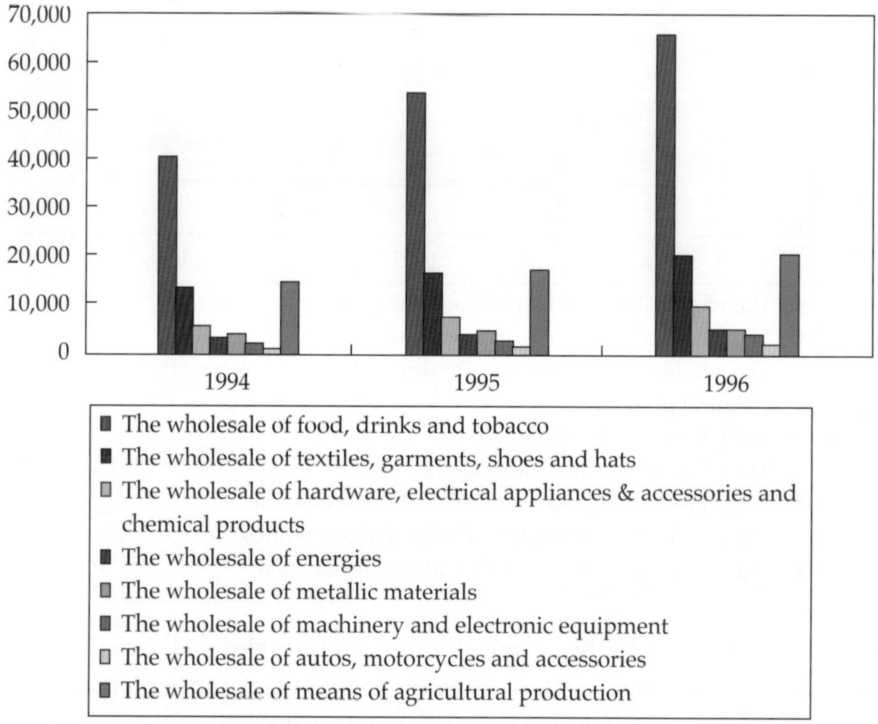

Analyzing the fundamental states of the wholesale trade in these five economic sectors, we can see that the wholesale trade in industries of life products faced retail institutions and consumers showed a relatively high level of development. For example, the number of wholesale institutions, practitioners in wholesale trade, the number of wholesale outlets of the sector of food, drinks and tobacco and that of textiles, garments, shoes and hats were the highest of all, since such economic sectors are closely related to people's daily life, individual demand of which was small, and had a great variety of products. Therefore, more wholesale institutions and outlets were needed to meet consumer demands, helping increase the number of practitioners.

Due to single product categories, easy quality appraisal, suitability for scale transaction, small numbers of transactions and large trading volume, wholesale institutions and the number of wholesale outlets in the sector of energies, machinery and other means of production were relatively small, so was the number of practitioners.

The number of wholesale outlets and practitioners in the sector of the means of agricultural production ranked ahead of the number of wholesale institutions in the same sector. It had much to do with the sales features of the means of agricultural production. China has extensive rural areas which are scattered. It needs more wholesale outlets and wholesale practitioners in the sector of the means of production in order to serve rural economy.

The number of wholesale institutions, the number of outlets and that of wholesale practitioners in the sector of autos, motorcycles and accessories were relatively small, since such sector was with a fairly high added value and related products had high values. Under the economic conditions in the then China, it was impossible for the sector of autos, motorcycles and accessories to get fully developed.

Fig. 4.70. **Ratios of the numbers of wholesale outlets to the total number of wholesale outlets (1994–1996)**

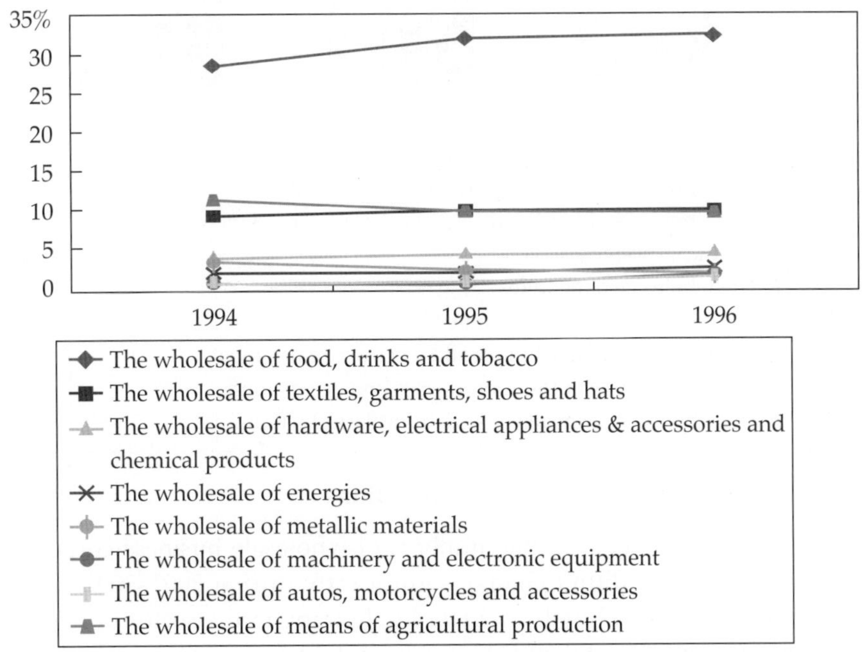

The stage of trans-century economic construction (1998–2002)

This period witnessed the rapid development of the construction of the national economy after the convening of the 15th CPC National Congress, and the tough struggle against various tests from all aspects in the cross-century economic construction. From the development progress of the wholesale trade in Chapter 2, we know that these five years was a severe test for the wholesale trade in China, since it underwent a period of sluggish development. However, wholesale enterprises in all economic sectors made their respective contribution to the development of the wholesale trade. Since *China Statistical Yearbook* didn't collect statistics of the wholesale trade by sector until 2001, we can only analyze the top 8 economic sectors in terms of sales in 2002 based on data for simply two years.[12]

Fig. 4.71. Numbers of wholesale practitioners by sector (1994–1996)

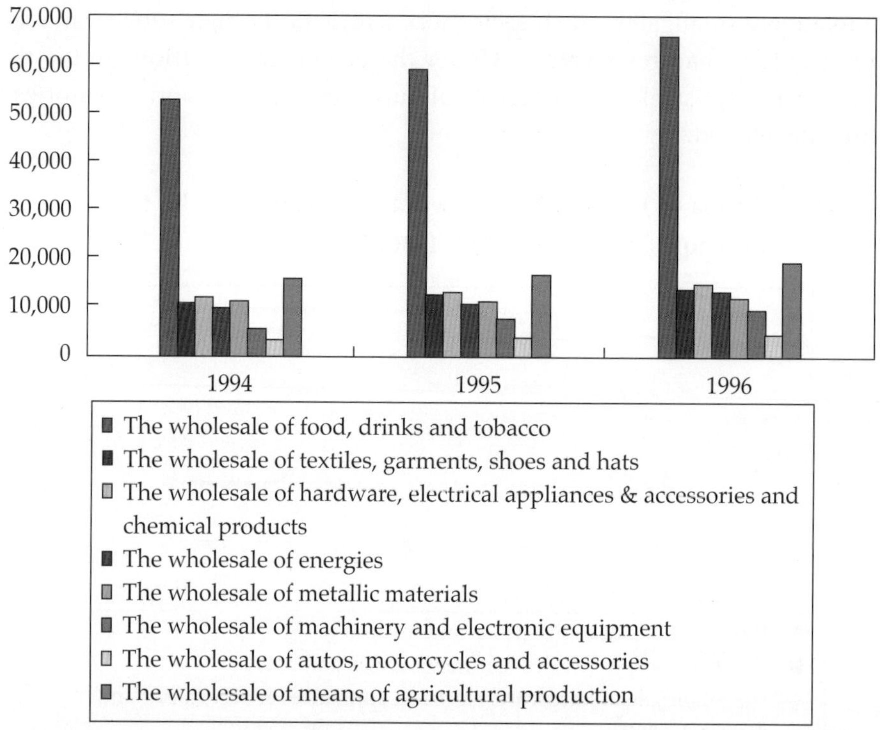

The number of wholesale business corporations

As can be seen from Fig. 4.72, the numbers of wholesale business corporations in each and all sectors didn't change significantly during 2001–2002, yet their ranking changed greatly. Firstly, the wholesale trade in the sector of drugs and medical instruments was taken into consideration in our analysis, while that in the sector of the means of agricultural production was ruled out, indicating the acceleration of the industrial process in China, and the faster development of industries than agriculture. Secondly, wholesale enterprises in the sector of energies achieved a rapid development, ranking the second; while the development of wholesale enterprises in the sector of hardware, electrical appliances & accessories and chemical products ranked the seventh, illustrating the development of the national economy and great changes in the growing speed of each and all economic sectors.

Fig. 4.72. Numbers of wholesale business corporations above the designated size in the eight sectors (2001–2002)

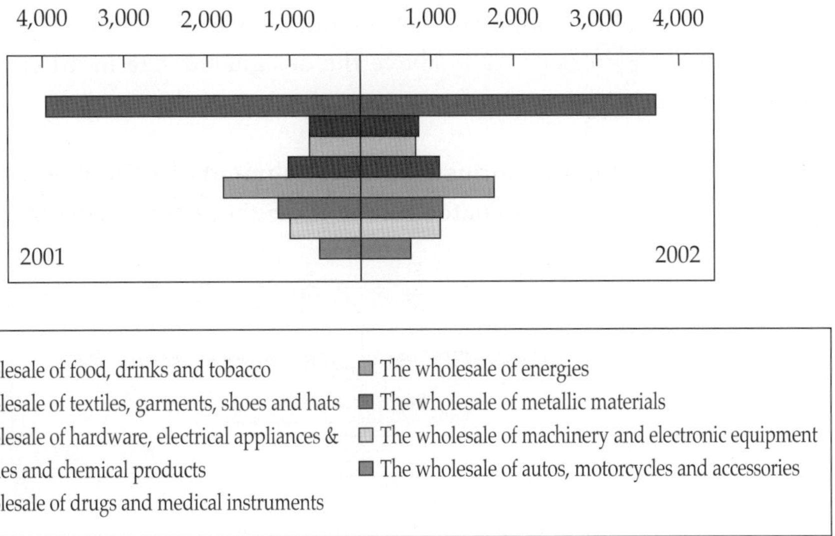

The number of wholesale business corporations in the sector of food, drinks and tobacco above the designated size was the greatest of all, being 4,073 in 2001, yet only 3,857 in 2002, falling to a certain degree. The number of wholesale business corporations above the designated size ranked the second, but also fell comparing with that in 2001. The number of wholesale business corporations in the sector of metallic materials ranked the third, and that in the sector of machinery and electronic equipment ranked the fourth.

The number of industrial establishments

As can be seen from Fig. 4.72, the ranking of the numbers of industrial establishments was different from that of the numbers of wholesale business corporations (see Fig. 4.72) in the eight sectors. Of which, the number of industrial establishments engaged in the wholesale of drugs and medical instruments ranked the third. What's significantly different from the number of wholesale business corporations, the numbers of industrial establishments engaged in the wholesale trade in each and all sectors showed a great positive growth. Of which, the number of industrial establishments above the designated size engaged in the wholesale of food, drinks and tobacco was 3,683 more in 2002 over that in 2001, growing rapidly. The number of industrial establishments above the designated size engaged in the wholesale of energies was 1,066 more in 2002 over that in 2001. Industrial establishments engaged in the wholesale of drugs and medical instruments also developed significantly, increasing by 618. It can be seen clearly that the wholesale trade encountered a crisis of industrial development, yet the numbers of industrial establishments engaged in the wholesale trade above the designated size in different sectors had all developed to some extent.

Fig. 4.73. Numbers of industrial establishments in the wholesale trade above the designated size in the right sectors (2001–2002)

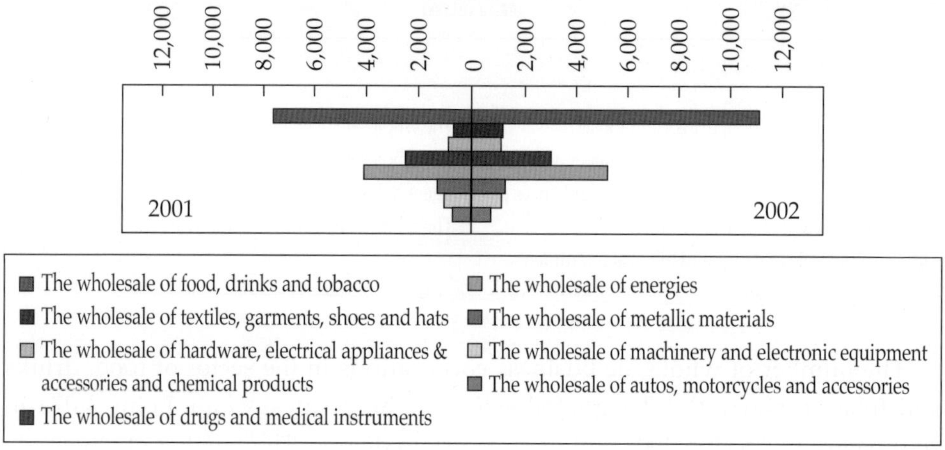

The number of practitioners

As can be seen from Fig. 4.74, the ranking of the numbers of practitioners in the wholesale enterprises in the eight sectors also changed to some extent comparing with that of the numbers of wholesale business corporations and that of the numbers of industrial establishments. The number of practitioners in the wholesale enterprises in the sector of hardware, electrical appliances & accessories and chemical products ranked the third, exceeding that in the sector of energies and that in the sector of food, drinks and tobacco. Changes in the numbers of practitioners in the wholesale enterprises in other sectors were not significant.

Great changes happened to the wholesale enterprises in each and all sectors over this period. Firstly, wholesale enterprises above the designated size in the sector of the means of production developed slowly, failing to rank among the top eight sectors. Sector of the means of production replaced that of drugs and medical instruments in terms of the development of wholesale enterprises. Secondly, changes in the basic information on the registration of wholesale enterprises in all sectors could also be seen:

Fig. 4.74. Numbers of wholesale practitioners above the designated size in the eight sectors (2001–2002)

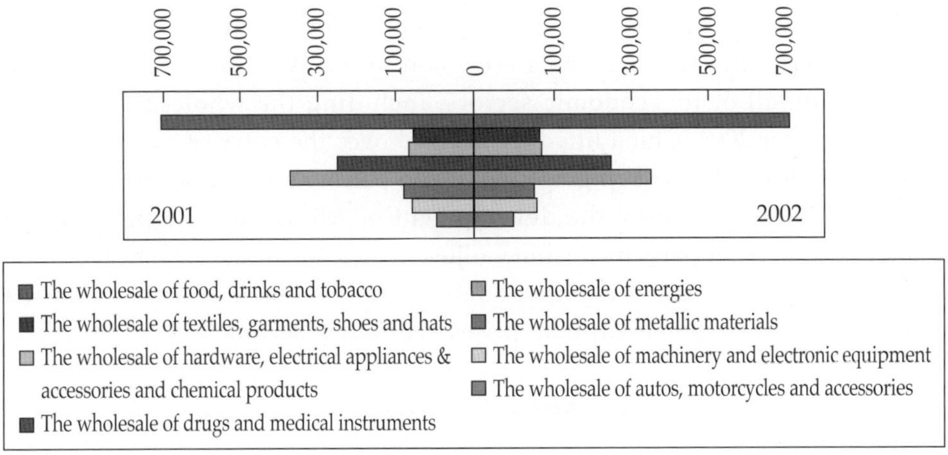

The wholesale trade in the sector of energies developed significantly, the number of wholesale business corporations, that of industrial establishments and that of practitioners of which had all ranked the second, making greater progress over the previous stage. It was closely related to the rapid development of the sector of energies in China since it implemented the Western Development Strategy in 2000. The industry of energies is a basic industry, the rapid development of which has stimulated the rapid development of other sectors of the national economy. It was followed by the wholesale trade in the sector of drugs and medical instruments which developed extremely rapidly and fully illustrated the improvement of the medical standards in China.

Wholesale enterprises in the sector of textiles, garments, shoes and hats developed slowly, the ranking of each and all indicators of which fell than before. There were two main reasons: firstly, textiles, garments, shoes and hats are consumer goods, the development of which started earlier and the development momentum and speed had all become more gentle; secondly, China's accession to the WTO had a relatively large impact on the sector of textiles, garments, shoes and hats, leading to the slow development of wholesale enterprises in the same sector.

Due to their nature, other sectors such as the wholesale of autos, motorcycles and accessories and that of machinery and electronic equipment saw the reduction of wholesale business corporations, industrial establishments and practitioners. However, due to the high values of such commodities, the total sales of these two sectors were great.

The development stage after China's accession to the WTO (2002–2007)

These five years witnessed the rapid economic development in China after its accession to the WTO. China's accession to the WTO has had significant influence on all of its economic sectors, including the wholesale trade. In particular, after 2004, China lifted the control over the entry of foreign capital into its wholesale trade, bringing fiercer competitions to the wholesale trade and objectively promoting the development of wholesale enterprises in all economic sectors. In particular, China adjusted once again the statistical criteria on the wholesale trade. A detailed analysis will be made next based on the specific states of the wholesale enterprises in different sectors.[13]

The number of wholesale business corporations

As can be seen from Fig. 4.75, the numbers of wholesale business corporations above the designated size in all sectors had all grown. In particular during 2003–2005, apart from the wholesale of drugs and medical instruments, wholesale

Fig. 4.75. Numbers of wholesale business corporations above the designated size (2003–2007)

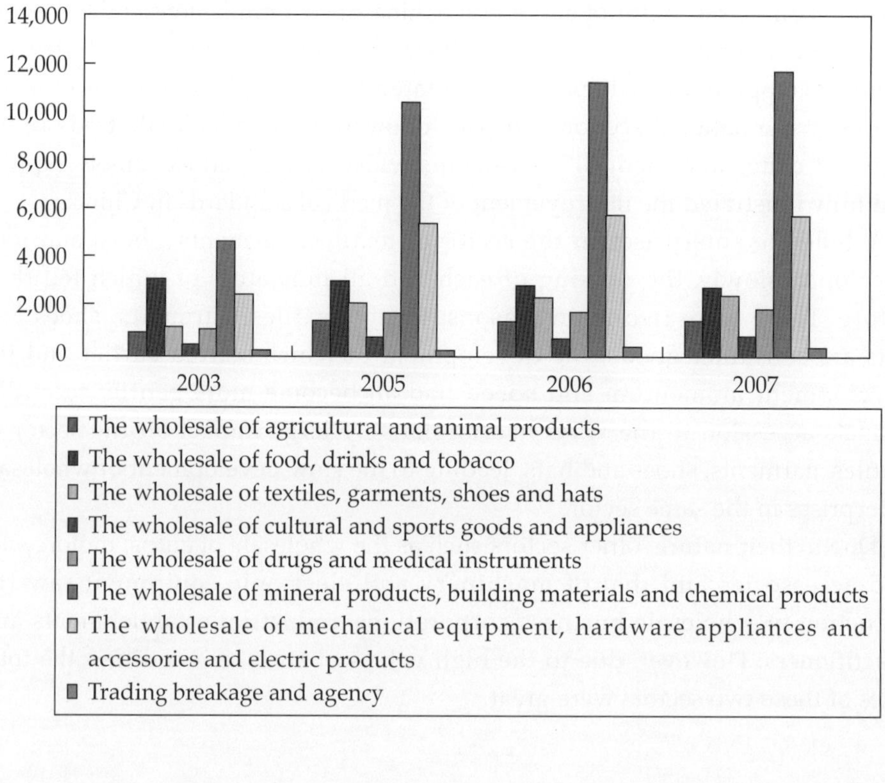

enterprises in other sectors all grew significantly. The state of development would be smooth if the missing data in 2004 were taken into consideration. Till 2007, the number of wholesale business corporations in the sector of mineral products, building materials and chemical products was the largest of all, being nearly 12,000; and that in the sector of trading breakage and agency was the smallest of all, being only 414. Now, let's check the specific ratios of each and all sectors.

As can be seen from Fig. 4.76, the ratio of the number of wholesale business corporations in the sector of food, drinks and tobacco to the total number of wholesale business corporations kept declining, falling from 23% in 2003 to 9.8% in 2007.

The ratios of the numbers of wholesale business corporations in the sector of mineral products, building materials and chemical products and that of mechanical equipment, hardware appliances and accessories and electric products to the total number of wholesale business corporations were both great, showing a growing trend. Of which, the number of wholesale business corporations in the sector of mineral products, building materials and chemical products accounted for 31% of all in 2003, which later grew to 40.6% in 2007.

Fig. 4.76. Proportions of the numbers of wholesale business corporations above the designated size (2003–2007)

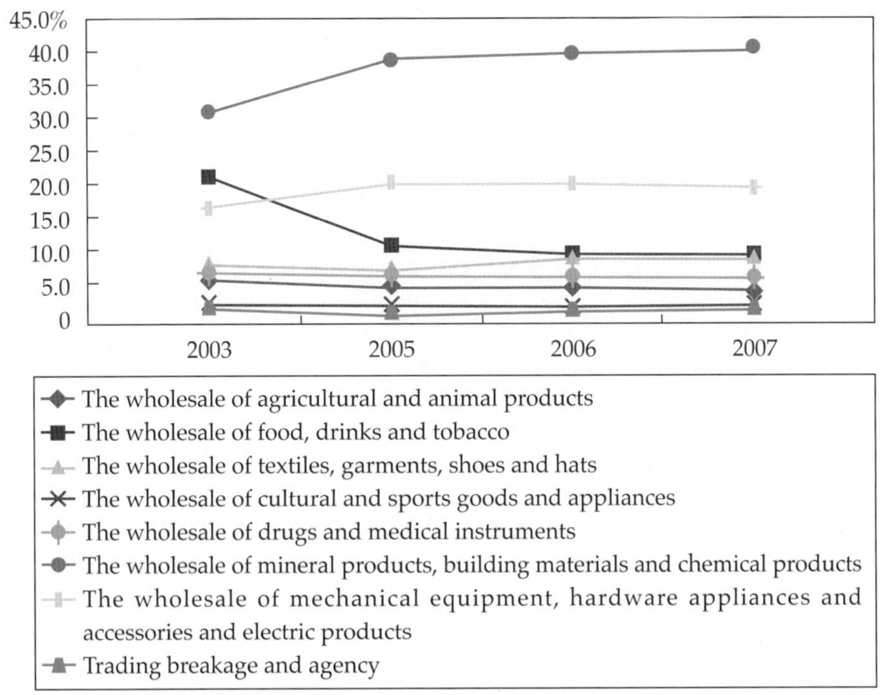

The ratio of the number of wholesale business corporations in the sector of trading breakage and agency to the total number of wholesale business corporations has always been small, being 1.9% at the highest in 2003.

The number of industrial establishments

As can be seen from Fig. 4.77, the number of industrial establishments in the wholesale of food, drinks and tobacco showed a declining trend in fluctuations, being 11,366 in 2002 which increased by nearly 50% before falling to 9,069 in 2005 and further falling nearly 9% over the previous year in 2007.

Fig. 4.77. Numbers of industrial establishments in the wholesale trade above the designated size (2003–2007)

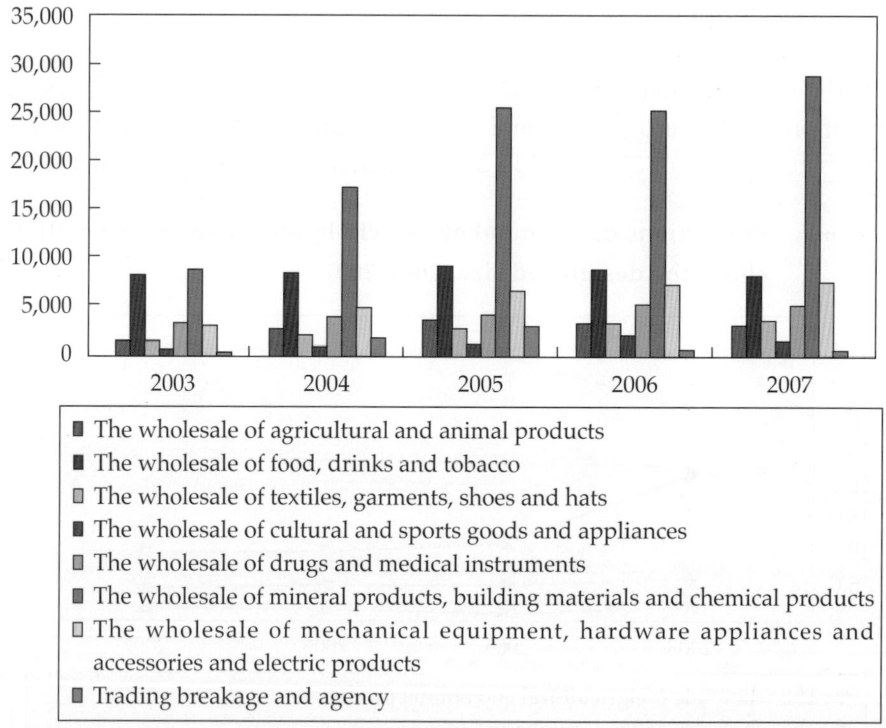

Industrial establishments in the wholesale of agricultural and animal products kept declining in number, reducing from 3,419 in 2004 to 3,172 in 2006, then to 2,954 in 2007, registering an average annual declining rate of 7%.

Wholesale enterprises in both the sector of textiles and that of drugs and medical instruments showed a growing trend in fluctuations. Take the textile industry as an example, the number of industrial establishments decreased by

18% in 2003, grew rapidly and reached 2,617 in 2005, then kept growing slowly in 2006 and 2007.

Wholesale establishments in the sector of cultural and sports goods and appliances, that of mechanical equipment, hardware appliances and accessories and electric products, and that of mineral products, building materials and chemical products all showed a significant growing trend. Wholesale establishments in the sector of mineral products, building materials and chemical products increased by 191.6% during 2003–2005. Though the number of wholesale establishments in the same sector decreased by 1.3% in 2006, it increased by 14% in 2007.

The number of wholesale enterprises in the sector of trading breakage and agency also changed greatly, increasing from 287 in 2003 to 2,912 in 2005 before declining to 463 in 2007.

Specific proportions of the numbers of wholesale establishments in different sectors are shown below in Fig. 4.78.

As can be seen from Fig. 4.78, the number of wholesale establishments in

Fig. 4.78. Proportions of the numbers of industrial establishments in the wholesale trade above the designated size (2003–2007)

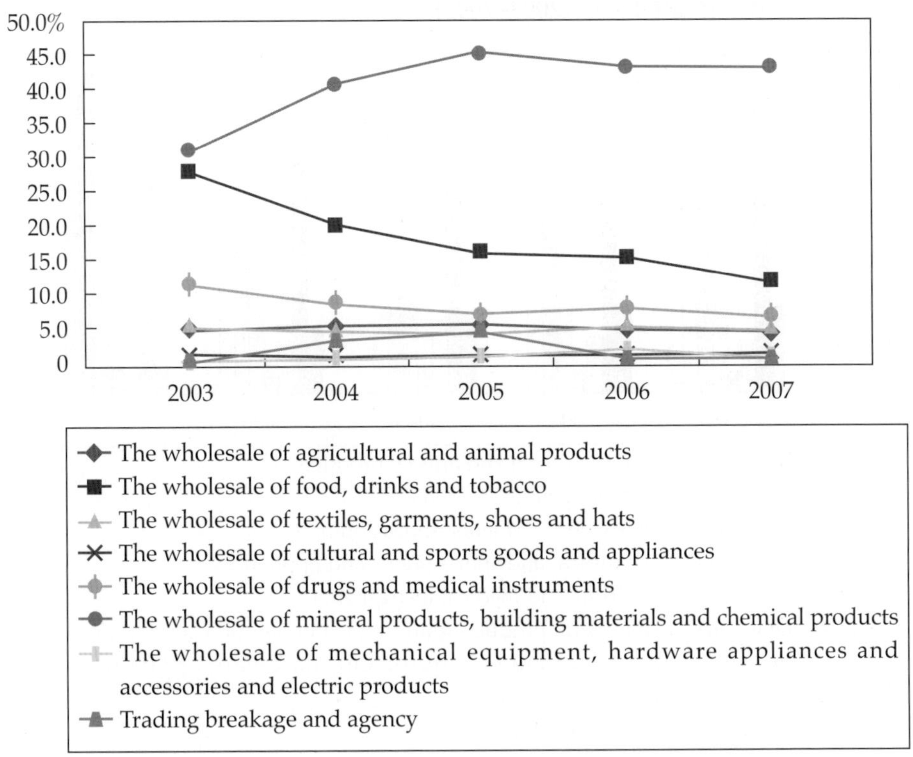

the sector of food, drinks and tobacco accounted for an increasingly small proportion, falling from 28% in 2003 to 12% in 2007.

The numbers of wholesale establishments in the sector of agricultural and animal products, that of textiles, garments, shoes and hats and that of trading breakage and agency accounted for smaller and smaller proportions. Take trading breakage and agency as an example, the number of wholesale establishments accounted for 5.2% of all in 2005, but only 0.7% in 2007.

The numbers of wholesale establishments in the sector of cultural and sports goods and appliances, and that of mineral products, building materials and chemical products accounted for large proportions and showed a steadily growing trend. Of which, the number of wholesale establishments in the sector of mineral products, building materials and chemical products accounted for 31% of all in 2003 which was later increased to 43% in 2007.

Little changes had happened to the proportion of wholesale establishments in the sector of mechanical equipment, hardware appliances and accessories and electric products which had been maintained at about 10%. The proportion of the number of wholesale establishments in the sector of drugs and medical instruments had declined slightly since 2003, from 12% in 2003 to 7.4% in 2007.

Fig. 4.79. Numbers of practitioners in the wholesale trade above the designated size (2003–2007)

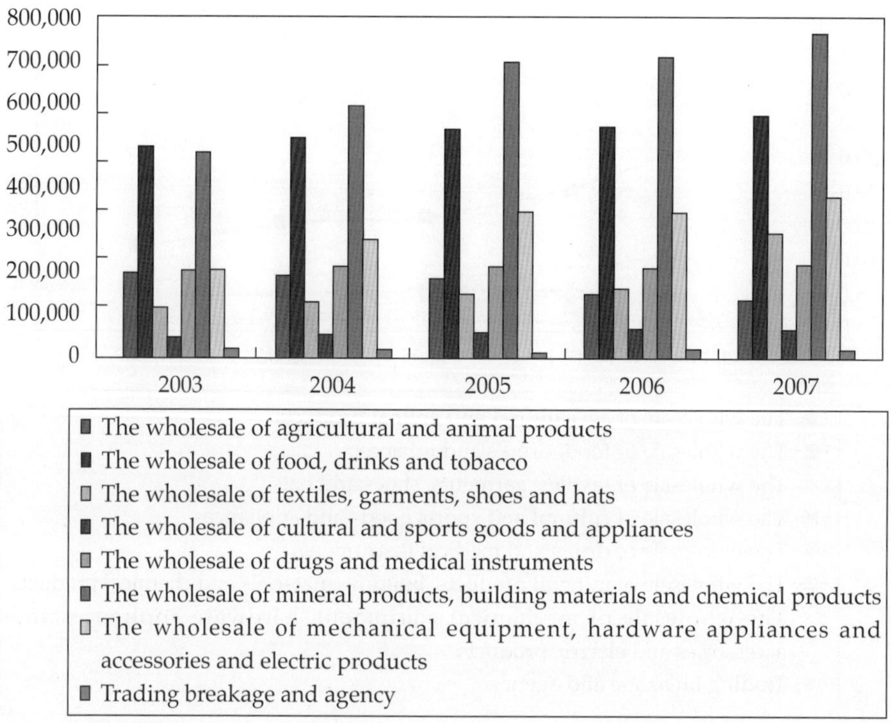

The number of practitioners

As can be seen from Fig. 4.79, the number of practitioners engaged in the wholesale of mineral products, building materials and chemical products grew quickly from 480 thousand as of the end of 2003 to 750 thousand in 2007, ranking the first of all. Practitioners engaged in the wholesale of food, drinks and tobacco had been ranking the second of all and showing a low growth rate. Though growing by 0.23% in 2006, practitioners engaged in the wholesale of mechanical equipment, hardware appliances and accessories and electric products grew progressively on the whole, being the quickest in 2005 by 66%. Practitioners engaged in the wholesale of textiles, garments, shoes and hats also grew rapidly and increased from about 100 thousand in 2003 to nearly 300 thousand in 2007, being nearly doubled. Practitioners engaged in the wholesale of agricultural and animal products reduced year on year, falling from 190 thousand as of the end of 2003 to 130 thousand in 2007. Next, let's see the specific proportions of practitioners engaged in each and all economic sectors.

As can be seen from Fig. 4.80, the ratios of practitioners engaged in the wholesale of agricultural and animal products, and that of food, drinks and

Fig. 4.80. Proportions of practitioners in the wholesale trade above the designated size (2003–2007)

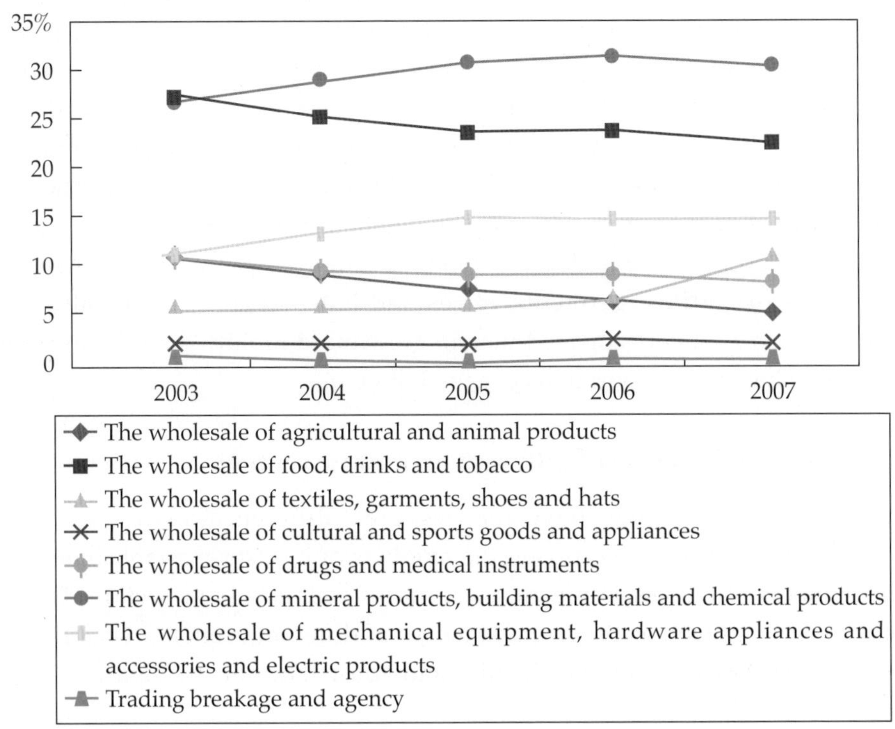

tobacco to the total number of practitioners engaged in the wholesale trade kept declining steadily.

In 2003, practitioners engaged in the wholesale of mineral products, building materials and chemical products accounted for 26.9% of the total number of practitioners engaged in the wholesale trade, second only to the proportion of practitioners engaged in the wholesale of food, drinks and tobacco which was 27.6%. Till 2005, practitioners engaged in the wholesale of mineral products, building materials and chemical products accounted for the largest proportion of all, being 30.7%, and it was kept stable in 2006 and 2007 at about 30%.

Practitioners engaged in the wholesale of cultural and sports goods and appliances accounted for an increasingly large proportion, yet the ratio of such practitioners to the all was small, being only 2.7% as of the end of 2007. Proportion of practitioners engaged in the wholesale of mechanical equipment, hardware appliances and accessories and electric products kept increasing, became stable during 2005–2007, being about 15%; and that of practitioners engaged in the wholesale of textiles, garments, shoes and hats constantly increased, too.

From the fundamental states of wholesale enterprises in different sectors, we can see that the sector of food, drinks and tobacco, that of mineral products, building materials and chemical products, and that of mechanical equipment, hardware appliances and accessories and electric products accounted for the absolute proportion in terms of the number of wholesale business corporations, that of wholesale establishments and that of practitioners engaged in the wholesale trade, being over 70% if added together. It was closely related to the statuses of such economic sectors in the national economy. The rapid development of the wholesale trade in such economic sectors played a great role in promoting the rapid development of the national economy. As for the wholesale of textiles, garments, shoes and hats, since it is typically labor-intensive, practitioners engaged therein grew more rapidly than the number of wholesale business corporations engaged therein.

The sales of wholesale of different economic sectors

As can be seen from the above analysis, great differences existed among the numbers of wholesale enterprises, the numbers of industrial establishments and the numbers of wholesale practitioners in different economic sectors. The sales of wholesale, as well as the size and tempo of different economic sectors would be analyzed based on the availability and consistence of the data in a phased way.[14]

The establishment stage of the socialist market economy (1993–1997)

Changes in the sales of wholesale of the top eight wholesale trades will be analyzed below to reflect the industrial structure during this period.[15]

As can be seen from the absolute value of the sales of wholesale (see Fig. 4.81), most economic sectors in this period showed a growing trend in terms of the sales of wholesale. Of which the sector of food, drinks and tobacco ranked the first, with the sales increasing very fast from RMB 618 billion in 1994 to 825.3 billion in 1996, up more than 30%. The sales of wholesale of energies grew rapidly, too, increasing from RMB 249.7 billion in 1994 to 327.56 billion in 1996. The sales of wholesale of the means of agricultural production also grew fast, increasing from RMB 173.6 billion in 1994 to 285 billion in 1997, up 64%. While the sales of wholesale of metallic materials showed a declining tendency, falling from RMB 316 billion in 1994 to 290.2 billion in 1996, decreased by RMB 25.8 billion. The sales of wholesale in other sectors such as the wholesale of textiles, garments, shoes and hats grew slowly during these three years, showing little changes.

As can be seen from the changes in the proportions of the sales of wholesale (see Fig. 4.82), the sales of wholesale of the top eight wholesale trades each

Fig. 4.81. **Sales of the wholesale enterprises in the top 8 wholesale trades (1994–1997)**

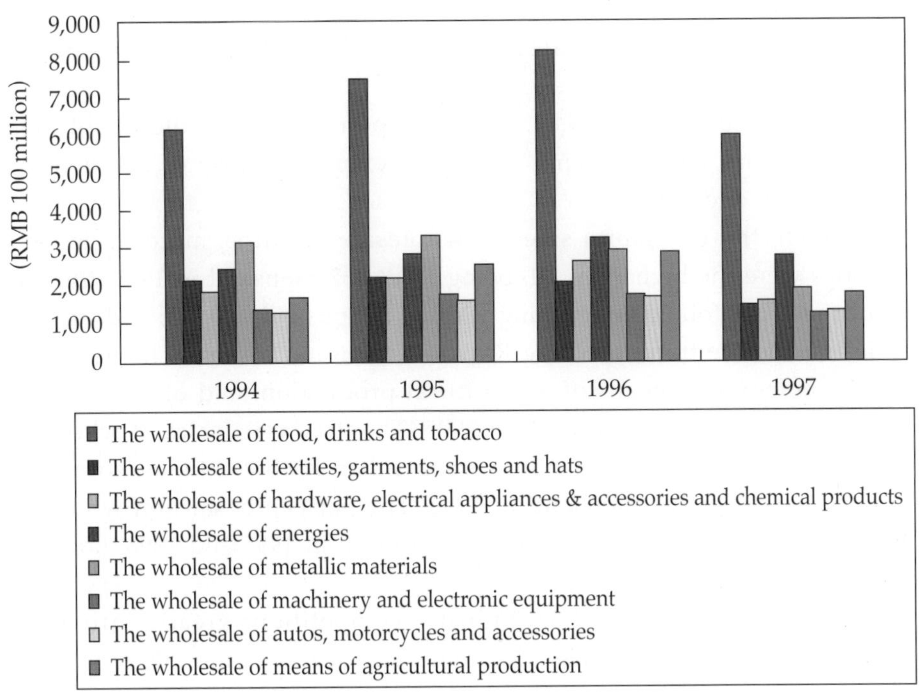

accounted for nearly 60% of the total sales of the wholesale trade as a whole during this period. Added together, the proportions of such sales of wholesale even exceeded 60% in 1997. Comparatively, changes in the sales of wholesale of different economic sectors in different years were little, with the wholesale of food, drinks and tobacco ranking the first, followed by the wholesale of metallic materials, then the wholesale of energies. The proportions were more or less the same as those in the above analysis.

Fig. 4.82. Ratios of the sales of wholesale enterprises in the top eight economic trades to the total sales of the wholesale trade (1994–1997)

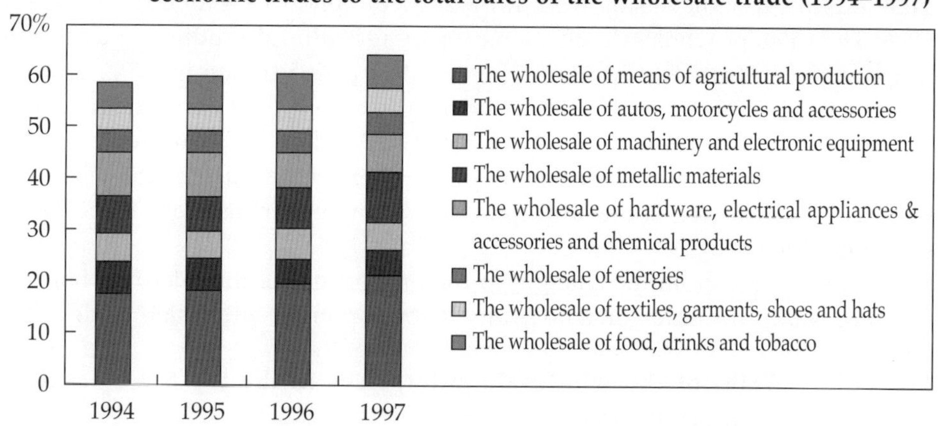

However, the per capita sales revealed the significant changes in the industrial structure.

As can be seen from Fig. 4.83, the per capita sales of wholesale of most economic sectors were growing in 1995, except for those of the textiles, garments, shoes and hats.

Of which, the per capita sales of wholesale of autos, motorcycles and accessories were the highest of all, being RMB 862 thousand in 1995; those of metallic materials followed, reaching RMB 516 thousand in 1995; and those of energies ranked the third, reaching RMB 474 thousand in 1995. The per capita sales of wholesale of means of agricultural production, and of food, drinks and tobacco were the lowest of all in 1995. The per capita sales of wholesale of means of agricultural production were less than RMB 200 thousand in 1994 before increasing to 260 thousand in 1996. The per capita sales of wholesale of food, drinks and tobacco were the lowest of all in 1995 and 1996, hovering around RMB 200 thousand.

As can be seen from Fig. 4.83, industry competitions greatly influenced the per capita sales of wholesale. The higher the degree of monopoly was, the

Fig. 4.83. Per capita sales of wholesale of the top eight wholesale trades (1994–1996)

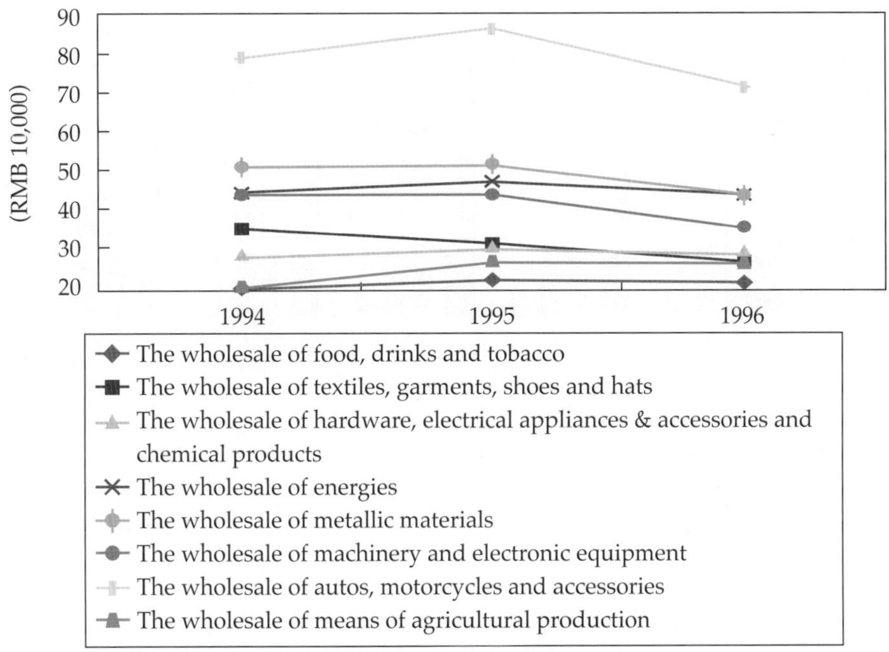

higher the per capita sales of the industry would be. The more competitive the industry was, the lower the per capita sales of the industry would be. For example, the wholesale of energies and metallic materials was mostly under the state-owned monopoly, having the highest per capita sales of all, while the wholesale of food, drinks and tobacco, and that of textiles, garments, shoes and hats belonged to the industry of consumer goods, being strong in free competitions and low in per capita sales.

The stage of trans-century economic construction (1998–2002)

The wholesale trade was finely divided in this period, making it impossible to analyze it completely and thoroughly. Therefore, the sales of the top eight economic sectors in terms of sales of wholesale will be analyzed in 2002.

As can be clearly seen from the columns of sales below (see Fig. 4.84), the ranking of the sales of wholesale in each and all economic sectors didn't change fundamentally. Of which, the sales of wholesale of food, drinks and tobacco, and of energies were far ahead of those of other economic sectors, being followed by the sales of metallic materials. The sales of wholesale of hardware, electrical appliances & accessories and chemical products, and of drugs and medical

Fig. 4.84. Sales of the wholesale enterprises in the eight sectors (1998–2002)

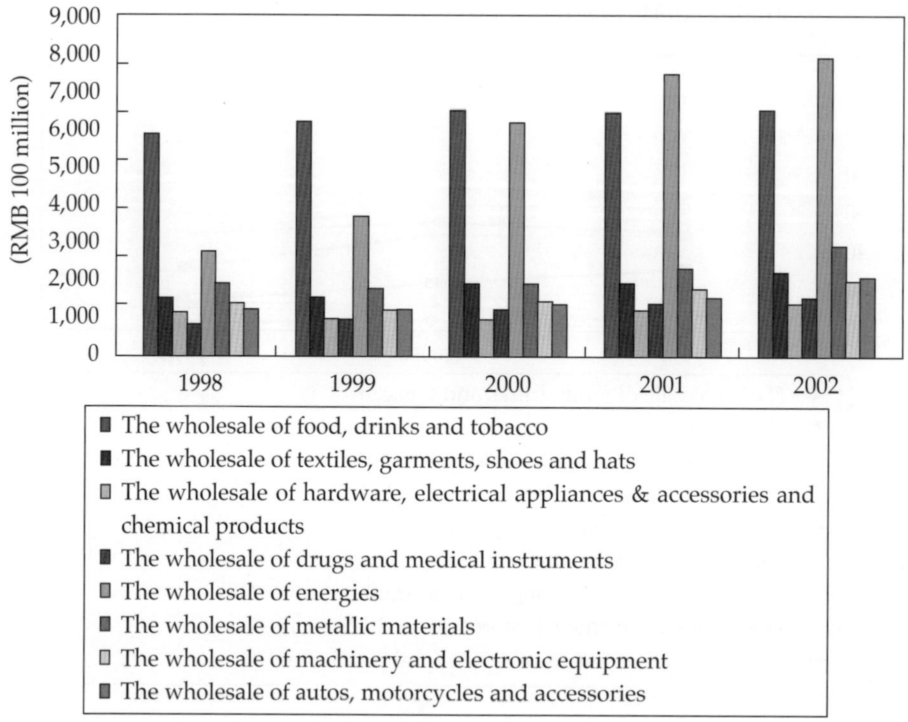

instruments changed greatly in terms of ranking, of which the latter sector rose from the eighth in 1998 to the seventh in 2002, while the former sector changed in the opposite way.

Changes in the ranking of these economic sectors can also be seen clearly from the above figure.

As can be seen from Fig. 4.85, the sales of wholesale of food, drinks and tobacco accounted for a declining proportion, being different from the rising proportions of the sales of wholesale of energies and metallic materials. Changes in other economic sectors were not that significant.

Other phenomena may also be observed from the growth rates of the sales (see Fig. 4.86).

As can be seen, great changes happened to the growth rates of the sales of wholesale of different economic sectors. Of which, the most significant changes happed to the wholesale of energies, the sales of which increased by 67% in 2000 before becoming relatively stable and about the same as the growth rate of the sales of wholesale of other economic sectors. The wholesale of textiles, garments, shoes and hats changed greatly, too, the sales growth of which increased to 27.4% in 2000, helping increase the proportion of the sales of wholesale of textiles, garments, shoes and hats. It is also worth noting that

Fig. 4.85. Proportions of the sales of wholesale of the eight sectors (1998–2002)

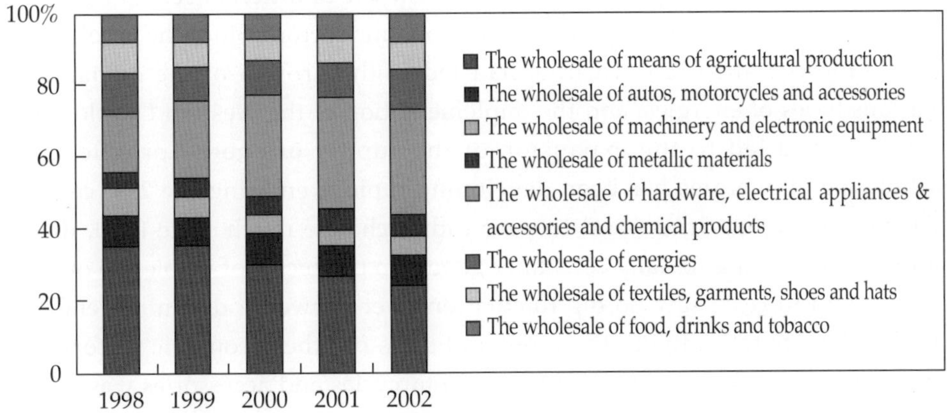

Fig. 4.86. Growth rates of the sales of wholesale of the eight sectors (1999–2002)

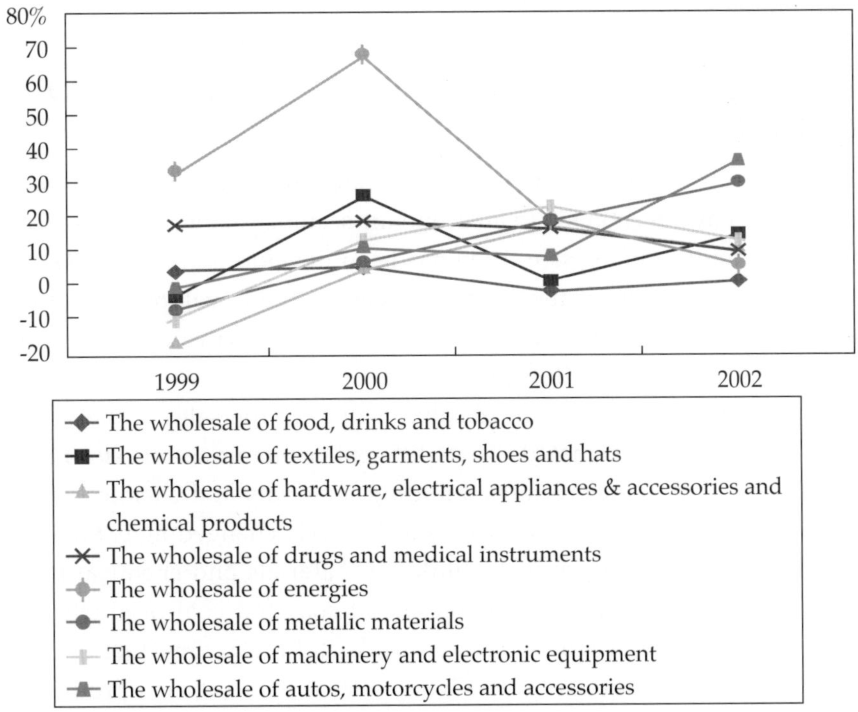

the growth of the sales of wholesale of autos, motorcycles and accessories was highly positive, being over 10% and reaching 36.1% in 2002. The wholesale of food, drinks and tobacco was relatively stable, presenting no big fluctuations during the five years.

As can be seen from the above analysis of the sales of wholesale of different economic sectors, changes in the sales of wholesale of different economic sectors had much to do with the nature of such economic sectors. Since the acceleration of the industrialization of China had led to the growth of the demand for various types of energies, and the implementation of the Western Development Strategy had led to the expansion of the supply of energy products, the wholesale of energies has been developing rapidly entering the 21st century. Demand for food, drinks and tobacco didn't change much since food, drinks and tobacco belong to daily consumer goods, so the sector of wholesale of food, drinks and tobacco saw no big fluctuations, yet showed a declining tendency in terms of its ratio due to the growth of sales of other economic sectors. The development of the wholesale of autos, motorcycles and accessories was closely related to the development of China's national economy, the improvement of the living standards of the Chinese people and the upgrading of the structure of consumption in China, showing the consumer demand for new types of transportations.

The development stage after China's accession to the WTO (2002–2007)

Economic development in China has accelerated since the new century. Great achievements have been made in all economic sectors. As the pace-setter of each economic sector, the wholesale trade has been developing fast, too. However, due to different natures of the economic sectors, the development scales and speed were different, too. A detailed analysis of the sales of nine economic sectors during this period will be made next.

As can be see clearly from the absolute values of the sales of the wholesale enterprises above the designated size in different economic sectors (see Fig. 4.87), the wholesale of mineral products, building materials and chemical products held an absolute leading position. Statistical criteria changed here. Statistics on the wholesale of mineral products, building materials and chemical products during this period included the wholesale of coal and coal products, that of petroleum and related products, that of metals and metal ores, that of building materials and that of fertilizers. The wholesale of coal and coal products, and that of petroleum and related products were included in the wholesale of energies in the previous stage. That's why the sales of wholesale of mineral products, building materials and chemical products were far higher than those of other economic sectors, and developed faster. The sales of wholesale of mineral products, building materials and chemical products were only

Fig. 4.87. Sales of the wholesale enterprises above the designated size (2003–2007)

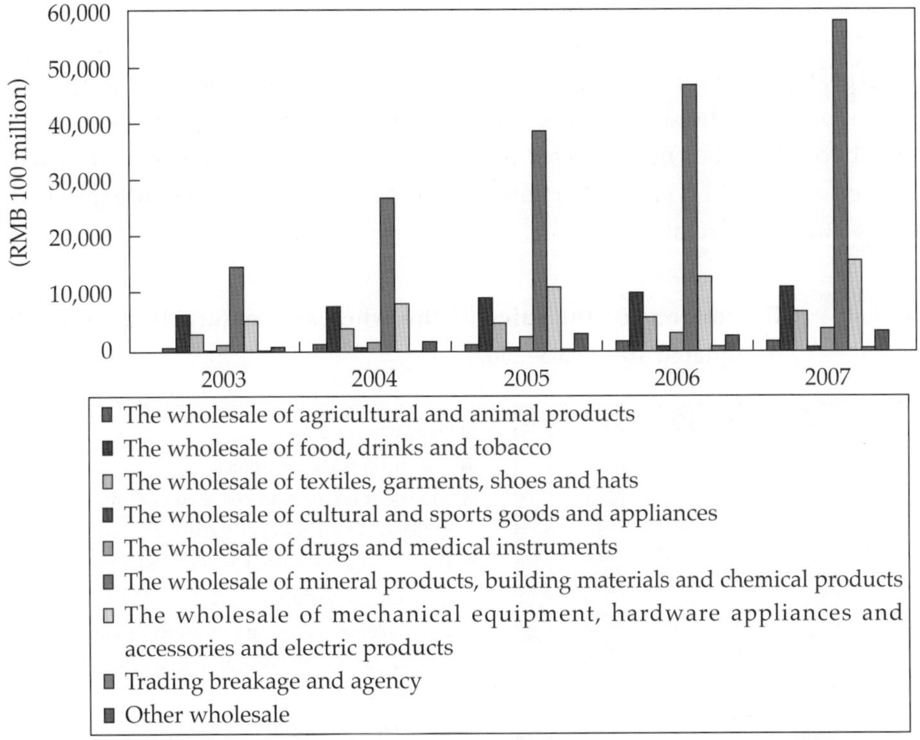

RMB 1,506.2 billion in 2003, which had grown to 5,807.3 billion in 2007, increasing by nearly three times within five years.

Of these sectors, the sector of mechanical equipment, hardware appliances and accessories and electric products changed the most significantly, the sales of wholesale of which rose from the third to the second gradually, and the number of wholesale enterprises in this sector grew rapidly. The sales of wholesale of mechanical equipment, hardware appliances & accessories and electric products was only RMB 566.8 billion in 2003, which had increased to 1,603.2 billion in 2007, being nearly tripled within five years. The sales of wholesale of food, drinks and tobacco which are closely related to people's everyday life grew slowly and increased from RMB 696.8 billion in 2003 to 1,169.6 billion in 2007, being less than doubled within five years.

The wholesale of textiles, garments, shoes and hats also showed a stunning growth rate, the sales of which increased rapidly, being more than doubled within five years. The development of sales of other economic sectors was relatively stable.

See Fig. 4.88 for the proportions of the sales of the wholesale enterprises in different economic sectors.

As can be seen clearly from Fig. 4.88, the sales of wholesale enterprises in the sector of mineral products, building materials and chemical products held the largest proportion which kept growing from 41% in 2003 to 55% in 2007; the proportion of the sales of wholesale enterprises in the sector of food, drinks and tobacco and that in the sector of textiles, garments and household articles declined relatively. The proportions of the sales of wholesale enterprises in other sectors were relatively stable.

Fig. 4.88. Proportions of the sales of the wholesale enterprises above the designated size (2003–2007)

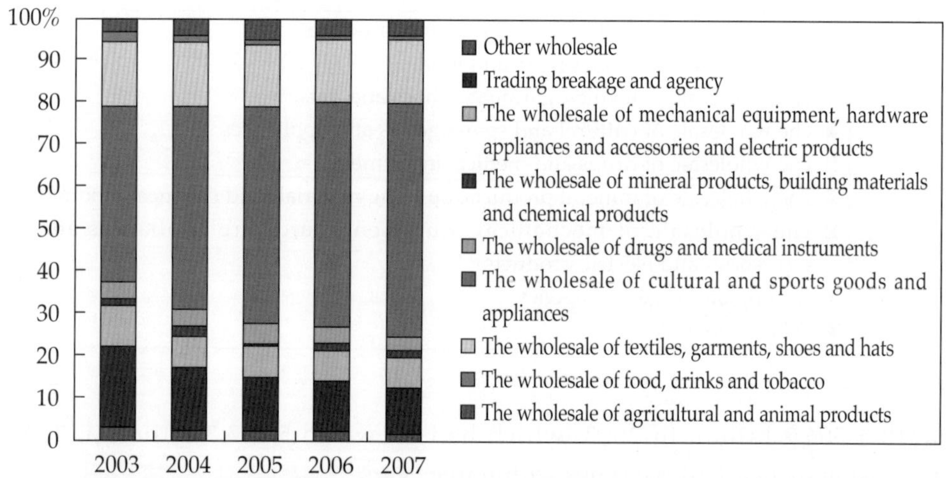

Let's check the per capita sales of wholesale of different economic sectors.

As can be seen from the per capita sales of wholesale (see Fig. 4.89), the per capita sales of the entire wholesale trade kept growing and was doubled within five years. The per capita sales of wholesale in different sectors also grew to varied extents.

The sector of trading breakage and agency had the highest per capita sales of wholesale of all, reaching RMB 7.2 million in 2005, which, though declined slightly in the two years that followed, was still higher than those in 2003. The per capita sales of wholesale of mineral products, building materials and chemical materials were also very high, showing a trend of rapid growth, increasing from RMB 3 million in 2003 to 7.66 million in 2007, being doubled. The per capita sales of wholesale of textiles, garments and daily necessities fell after 2006.

To sum up, in the analyses of the absolute values, ratios, growth rates and per capita sales of the wholesale trade in each and all economic sectors, we can see that the wholesale of mineral products, building materials and chemical products, and that of mechanical equipment, hardware appliances & accessories and electric products developed fast, accounted for larger proportions and had relatively high per capita sales. It was closely related to the rapid growth of the national economy in China, especially the rapid growth of fixed-asset investments, since the 16th National People's Congress. While the proportion of the wholesale of daily consumables such as food, drinks, tobacco, textiles, garments and articles for daily use kept declining, though it showed a certain growth, reflecting the constant upgrading of the industrial structure in China along with the development of the national economy. All in all, the growth of the sales of each and all economic sectors is intimately related to the overall development of the national economy, while different economic sectors showed different development statuses.

Fig. 4.89. Per capita sales of the wholesale enterprises above the designated size (2003–2007)

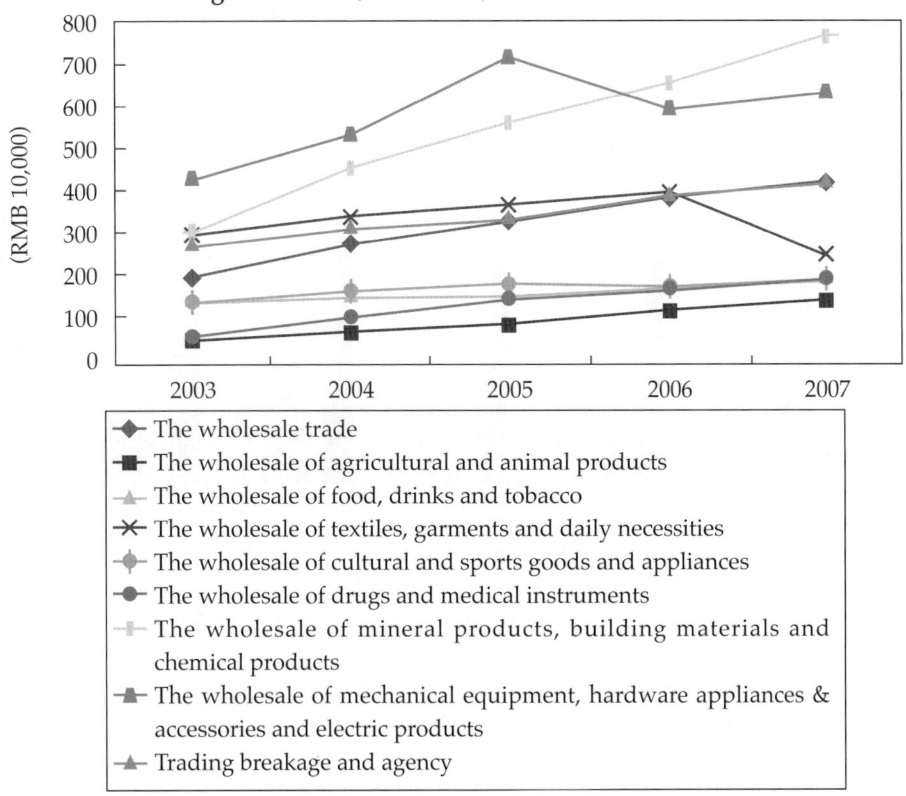

Financial states of the wholesale trade in different economic sectors

Development of and structural changes in each and all economic sectors will be analyzed below by describing the assets, liabilities and scale of profits of the wholesale trade in different sectors in different stages. The financial statuses of the wholesale enterprises above the designated size in all economic sectors will be analyzed based on availability and consistence of data.

The stage of trans-century economic construction (1998–2002)

The size of assets, the scale of liabilities and that of profits all showed a growing trend with the development of the wholesale trade during this period. See below for the specific situation of the wholesale trade in each sector.

The size of assets

As can be seen from Fig. 4.90, the size of assets of the wholesale of food, drinks and tobacco was far larger than that of the wholesale of other sectors, yet showed a declining tendency, falling from RMB 321.48 billion in 1998 to 276.46

Fig. 4.90. Sales of the wholesale enterprises in the eight sectors (1998–2002)

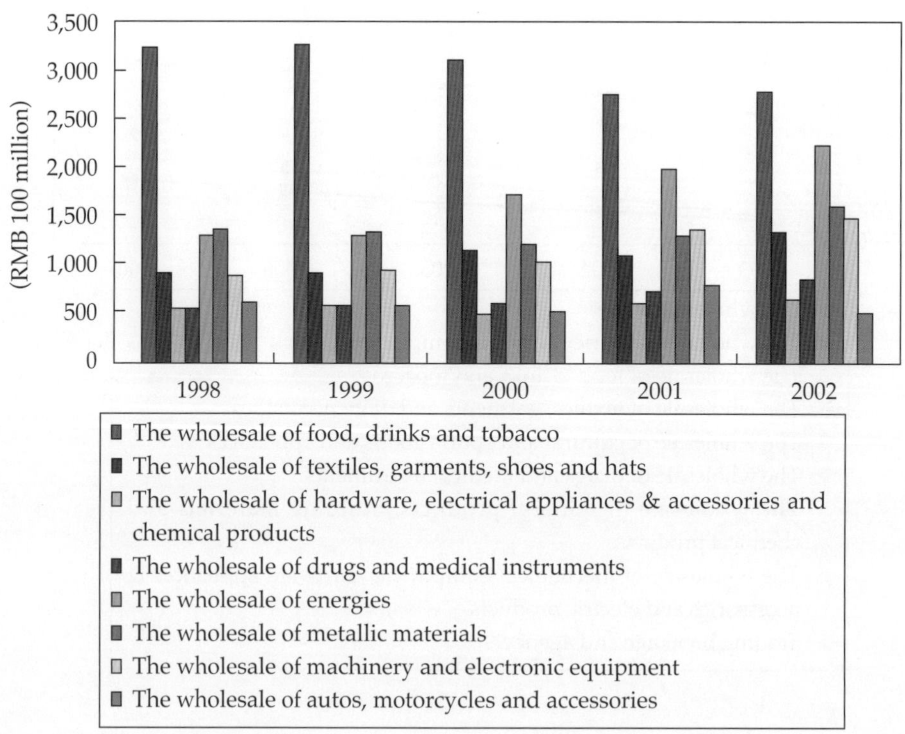

billion in 2002. Quite the opposite, the size of assets of the wholesale of energies kept growing, increasing from RMB 129.41 billion in 1998 to 222.73 billion in 2002 before ranking the second of all in the same year. The wholesale of metallic materials, that of machinery and electronic equipment, and that of textiles, garments, shoes and hats were all large in terms of the size of assets. The size of assets of each economic sector showed an increasing trend with time.

As can be clearly seen from the growth rates of assets of the wholesale trade in different economic sectors (see Fig. 4.91), the growth rates of assets of the wholesale trade in different economic sectors all showed great fluctuations during this period. Of which, the growth rate of assets of the wholesale trade in autos, motorcycles and accessories fluctuated the most significantly of all, reaching 50% in 2001 and falling by 32% in 2002. The growth rate of assets of the wholesale trade in textiles, garments, shoes and hats fluctuated greatly, being positive and more than 20% in 2000 before becoming negative and dropping by nearly 10% in 2001.

The growth rate of the assets of the wholesale of food, drinks and tobacco had been negative, falling by over 10% in 2001; that of the assets of the wholesale of energies had been positive and growing fast, reaching 32% in 2000 and being over 10% in other years.

Fig. 4.91. Growth rates of the assets of the wholesale trade in the eight major economic sectors (1999–2002)

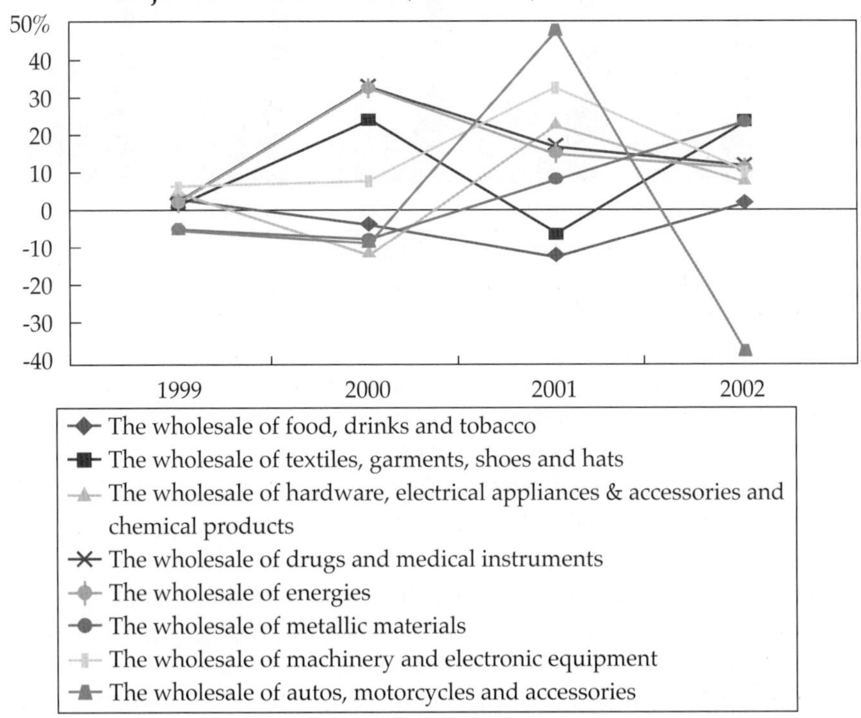

The scale of liabilities

As can be clearly seen from Fig. 4.92, the scale of liabilities of the wholesale of food, drinks and tobacco was the greatest of the wholesale trade in all economic sectors, showing a declining trend and falling from RMB 321.4 billion from 1998 to 276.46 billion in 2002. The wholesale of energies ranked the second in terms of the scale of liabilities in 2002 which escalated gradually as the size of assets and increased from RMB 89.2 billion in 1998 to 152.45 billion in 2002. In 2000, assets of the wholesale of energies exceeded those of the wholesale of metallic materials in 2000 before ranking the second. The liabilities of the wholesale of metallic materials, those of the wholesale of machinery and electronic equipment, and other of the wholesale of textiles, garments, shoes and hats all kept increasing, indicating great development of the wholesale trade in different economic sectors. Specific growths were as follows.

Fig. 4.92. Scales of liabilities of the wholesale trade in the eight major economic sectors (1998–2002)

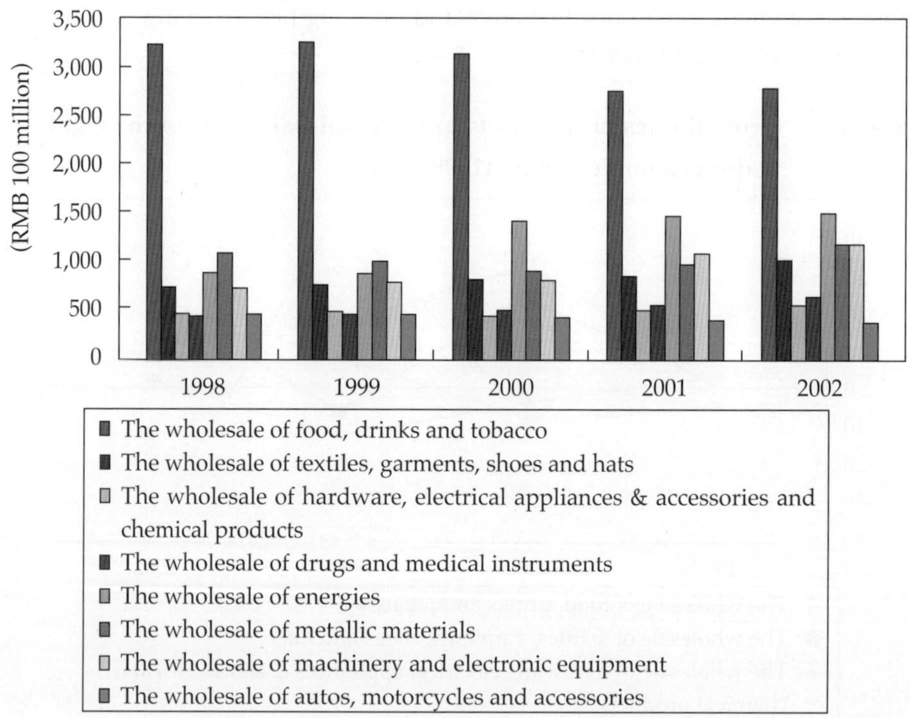

As can be clearly seen from the growth rates of liabilities (see Fig. 4.93), the growth rate of liabilities of the wholesale of energies changed greatly, reaching 56% in 2000. Similarly, the growth rate of liabilities of the wholesale of metallic materials also changed significantly, increasing from -10% in 1999 to 20% in

2002. The growth rate of liabilities of the wholesale of machinery and electronic equipment also showed a relatively high growth trend; that of the wholesale of food, drinks and tobacco showed a declining trend; and of the wholesale enterprises in other sectors was relatively stable.

Fig. 4.93. Growth rates of the liabilities of wholesale of the eight major economic sectors (1999–2002)

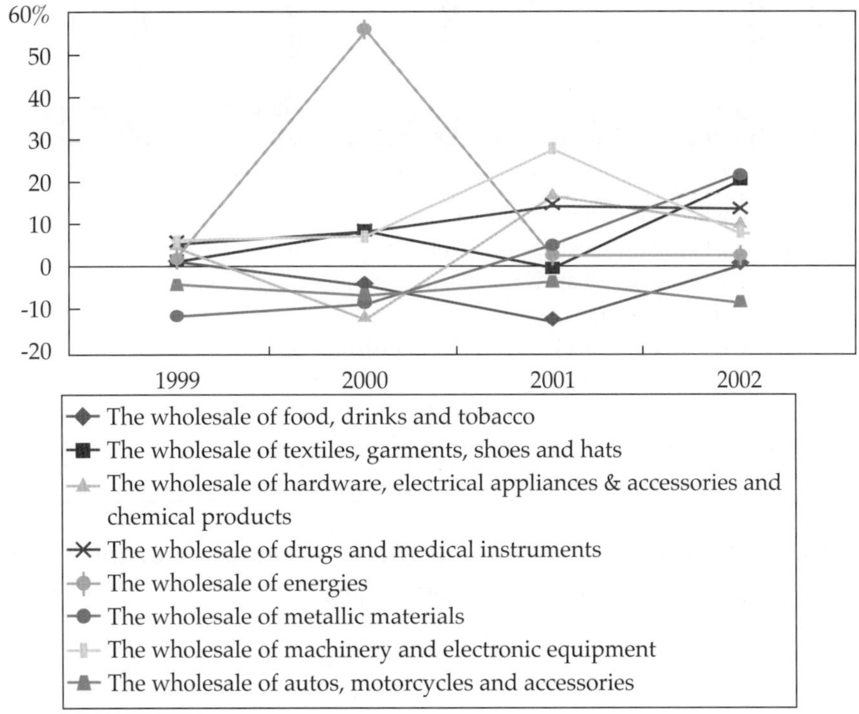

The scale of profits

As can be seen from Fig. 4.94, the sales profits of the wholesale trade in different economic sectors were more or less the same as the sizes of assets and liabilities: the sales profits of the wholesale of food, drinks and tobacco held the absolute proportion. Different from the size of assets, such sales profits increased gradually and presented a growing trend. The wholesale of energies ranked the second, the sales profits of which grew rapidly in 1999, fell in 2001, and kept more or less the same in the other several years. The wholesale of metallic materials, machinery and electronic equipment, as well as autos, motorcycles and accessories all grew rapidly. The growth of sales profits of the wholesale trade in such economic sectors can be seen more clearly from Fig. 4.95.

As can be seen from Fig. 4.95, the growth rate of sales profits of energies witnessed the most significant changes of all, reaching 67% in 1999, falling

Fig. 4.94. **The scales of profits of wholesale of the eight major economic sectors (1998–2002)**

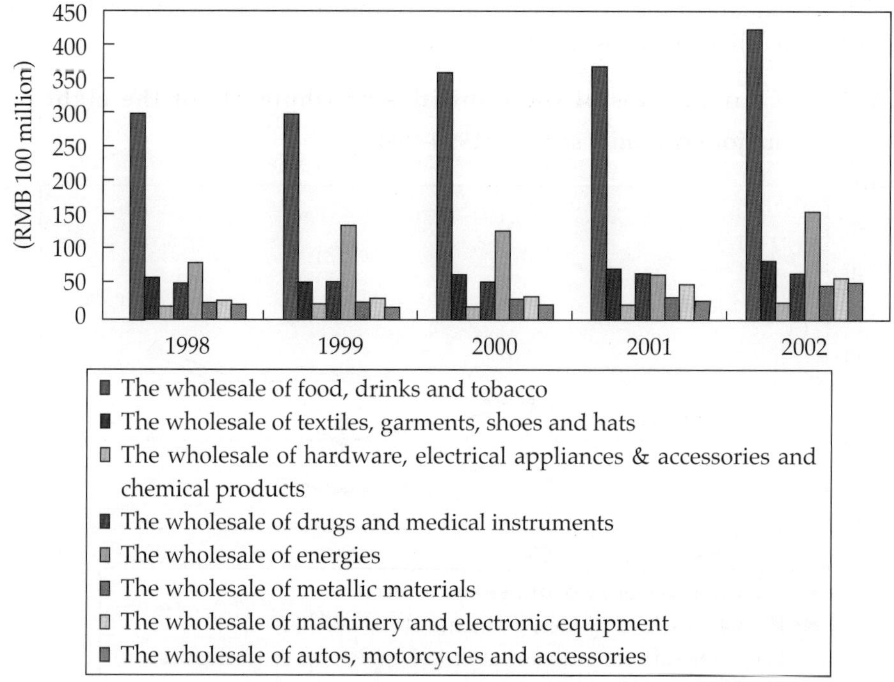

Fig. 4.95. **Growth rates of the liabilities of wholesale of the eight major economic sectors (1999–2002)**

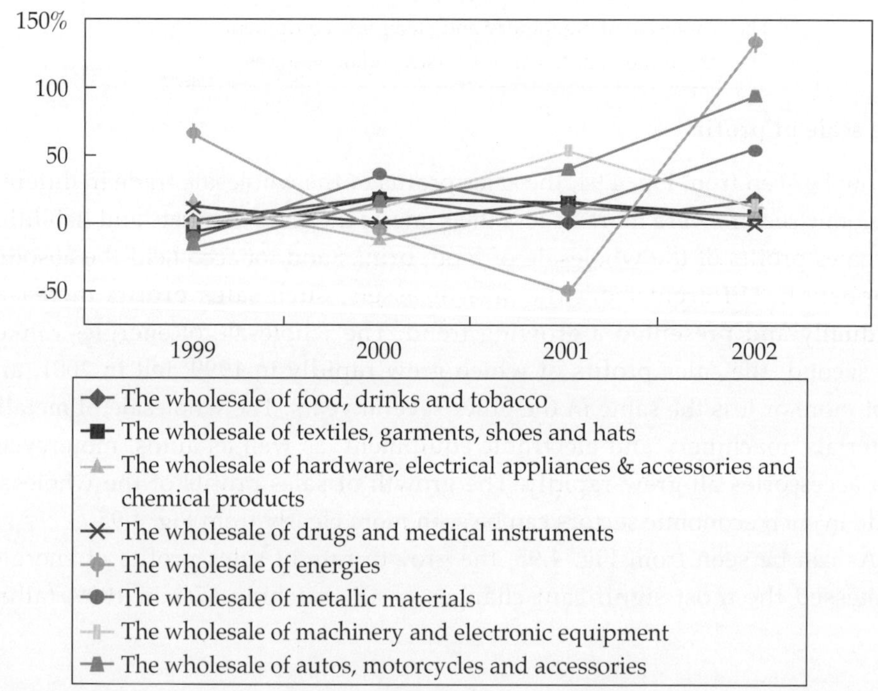

by 50% in 2001, and increasing to 132% in 2002. Growth of the sales profits of energies had much to do with the cost of energy exploitation. Thanks to the implementation of the Western Development Strategy in China in 2000, the wholesale of energies in China achieved a great development. However, since the wholesale of energies needed great amounts of fixed-asset investments, the sales profits of the wholesale of energies fell significantly in 2001.

The development stage after China's accession to the WTO (2003–2007)

The Chinese economy entered a new development stage after China's accession to the WTO. Wholesale enterprises in different economic sectors developed to varied extents during this period, and changes happened in industrial structure, the reflection of which can be seen in the size of assets, and the scale of liabilities and profits of wholesale enterprises in different economic sectors.

Size of assets

As can be seen from Fig. 4.96, the sizes of assets of wholesale enterprises in each and all economic sectors all grew to some extent during this period, of which the assets of the wholesale of mineral products, building materials and chemical products grew the most significantly of all. The assets of the wholesale of mineral products, building materials and chemical products were only RMB 582.02 billion in 2000, but increased to 1,718.1 billion in 2007. The assets of the wholesale of mechanical equipment, hardware appliances & accessories and electric products also grew rapidly, increasing by 66.8% and reaching RMB 1,112.16 billion in 2005. The assets of the wholesale of cultural and sports goods and appliances, of the wholesale of drugs and medical instruments and of the wholesale of textiles, garments and daily necessities also increased year by year. Take the wholesale of drugs and medical instruments as an example, the assets of the wholesale of drugs and medical instruments were RMB 98.37 billion in 2003, then 174.5 billion in 2007, the growth rate of which was the highest of all in 2005, reaching 38.8%.

Seen from the angle of absolute values, the assets of the wholesale of agricultural and animal products, food, drinks and tobacco increased in fluctuations. From the above analysis, we can see that the assets of the wholesale of food, drinks and tobacco declined before climbing somewhat after 2003.

As shown in Fig. 4.97, the ratio of the assets of the wholesale of mineral products, building materials and chemical products to the total assets of the wholesale trade in China grew rapidly from 32.7% in 2003 to 44.4% in 2007,

Fig. 4.96. Sizes of the assets of the wholesale enterprises above the designated size in different economic sectors (2003–2007)

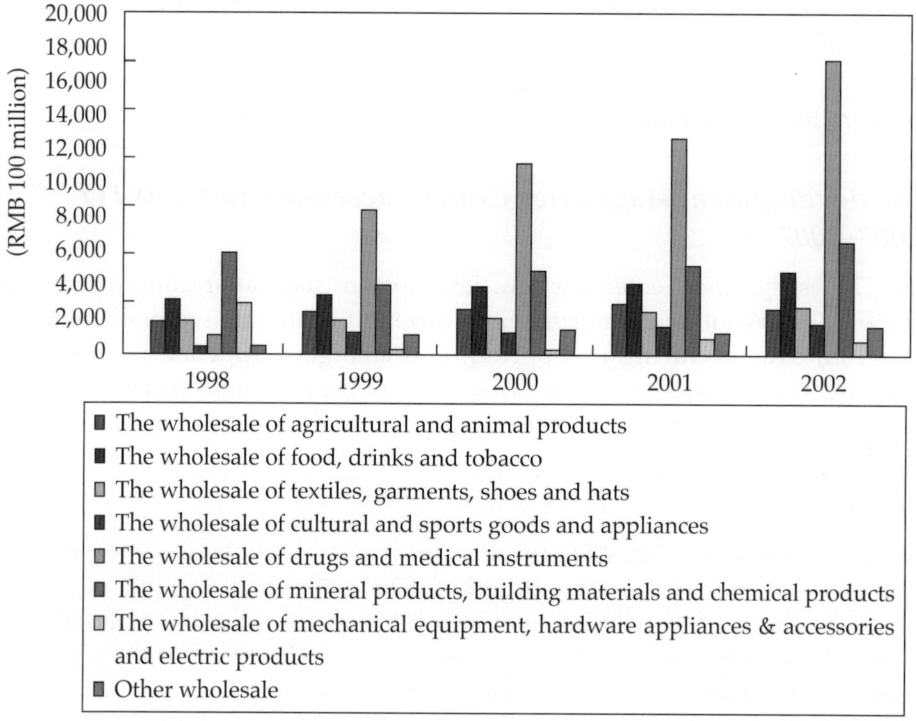

making the wholesale of mineral products, building materials and chemical products the largest of the wholesale of all economic sectors in 2003. The ratio kept increasing from 2003 to 2007. Quite the opposite, the ratio of the assets of the wholesale of food, drinks and tobacco to the total assets of the wholesale trade in China declined quickly from 26.8% in 2003 to only 12.2% in 2007, falling by half.

The assets of the wholesale of textiles, garments, daily necessities, and those of the wholesale of agricultural and animal products to the total assets of the wholesale trade both showed a declining trend in fluctuations. Seen from the wholesale of agricultural and animal products, the ratio of the assets of the wholesale of agricultural and animal products to the total assets of the wholesale trade in China was 10.5% in 2003 and dropped to 6.9% in 2007. The proportion of the assets of the wholesale of cultural and sports goods and appliances and that of the assets of trading breakage and agency were relatively small and changed little in recent years, both being about 2%.

Fig. 4.97. **Proportions of the assets of wholesale enterprises above the designated size in different economic sectors (2003–2007)**

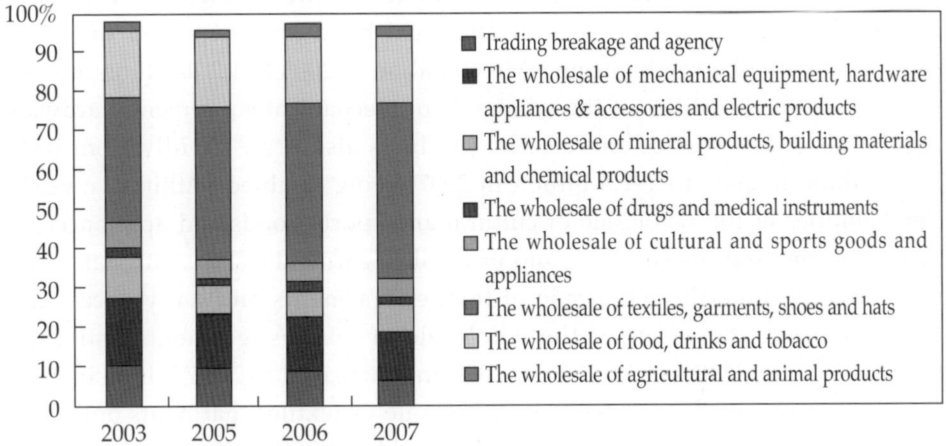

Fig. 4.98. **Scales of the liabilities of the wholesale enterprises above the designated size in different economic sectors (2003–2007)**

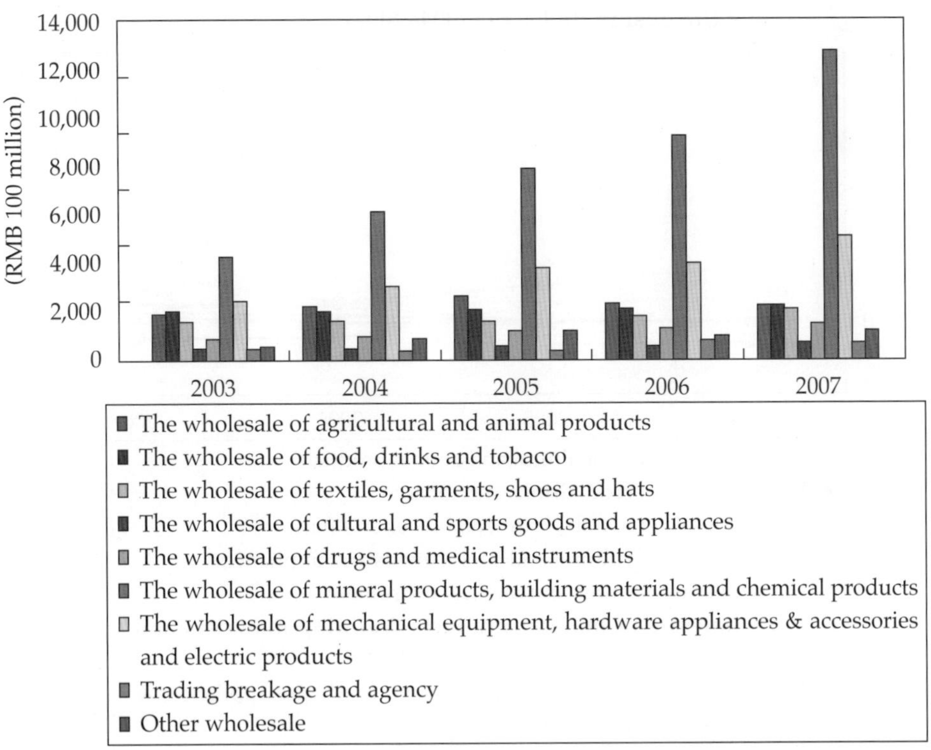

Size of liabilities

As can be seen from Fig. 4.98, the liabilities of the wholesale of mineral products, building materials and chemical products increased the most significantly of all, growing from RMB 60 billion in 2003 to 1,261 billion in 2007. In addition, the liabilities of the wholesale of mechanical equipment, hardware appliances & accessories and electric products also grew rapidly from RMB 231.1 billion in 2003 to 499.8 billion in 2007, being doubled within five years. The liabilities of the wholesale of cultural and sports goods and appliances, of drugs and medical instruments, and of textiles, garments, shoes and hats grew year on year. Take the wholesale of textiles, garments and daily necessities as an example, the assets of the wholesale of textiles, garments and daily necessities were RMB 143.5 billion in 2003 and increased to 203.7 billion in 2007. The growth rate of the assets of the wholesale of textiles, garments and daily necessities was the highest of all in 2007, reaching 16.9%. Different from it, the liabilities of the wholesale of food, drinks and tobacco reduced.

Fig. 4.99. Growth rates of the liabilities of the wholesale enterprises above the designated size (2004–2007)

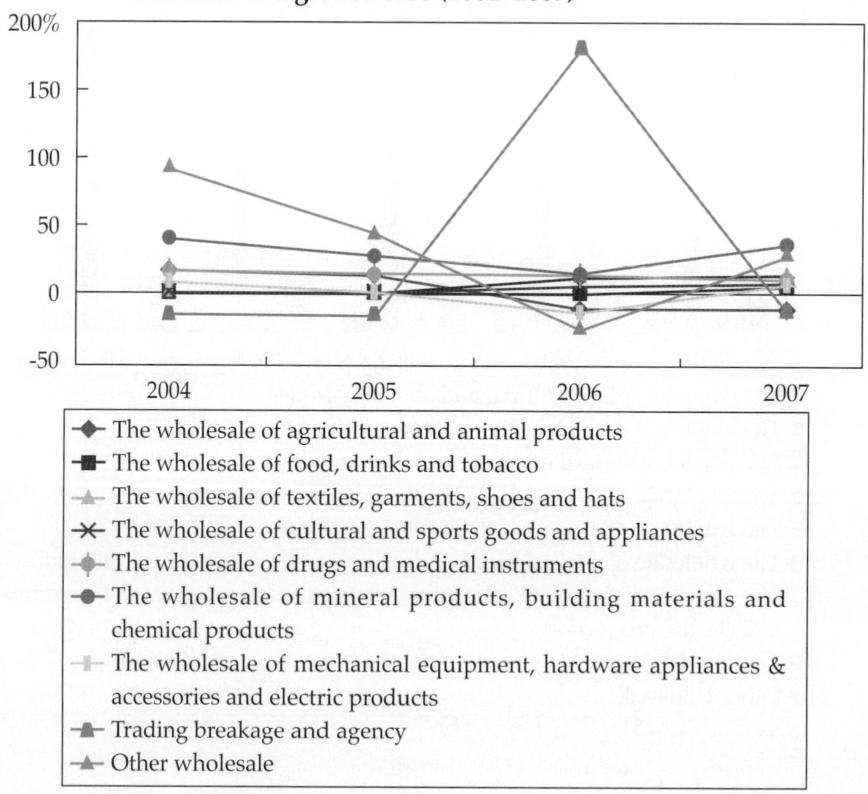

As can be seen from the growth rates of liabilities during this period (see Fig. 4.99), the growth rate of the liabilities of trading breakage and agency saw the biggest change of all, reaching 179% in 2006. The growth rates of the liabilities of other economic sectors also underwent great changes in 2006, all showing a declining trend, yet consistently rising in 2007. The growth rate of the liabilities of the wholesale of agricultural and animal products was negative in the recent two years. Comparing with those in 2006, the liabilities of the wholesale of agricultural and animal products decreased by 8.3% in 2007 and showed a trend of further declining.

Size of profits

As can be seen from the absolute values of the sales profits (see Fig. 4.100), as the same as the size of assets, the absolute value of the sales profits of the wholesale of mineral products, building materials and chemical products was the biggest of all, followed by that of the sales profits of the wholesale of food, drinks and tobacco, then that of the sales profits of the wholesale of mechanical

Fig. 4.100. Scales of the profits of the wholesale enterprises above the designated size (2003–2007)

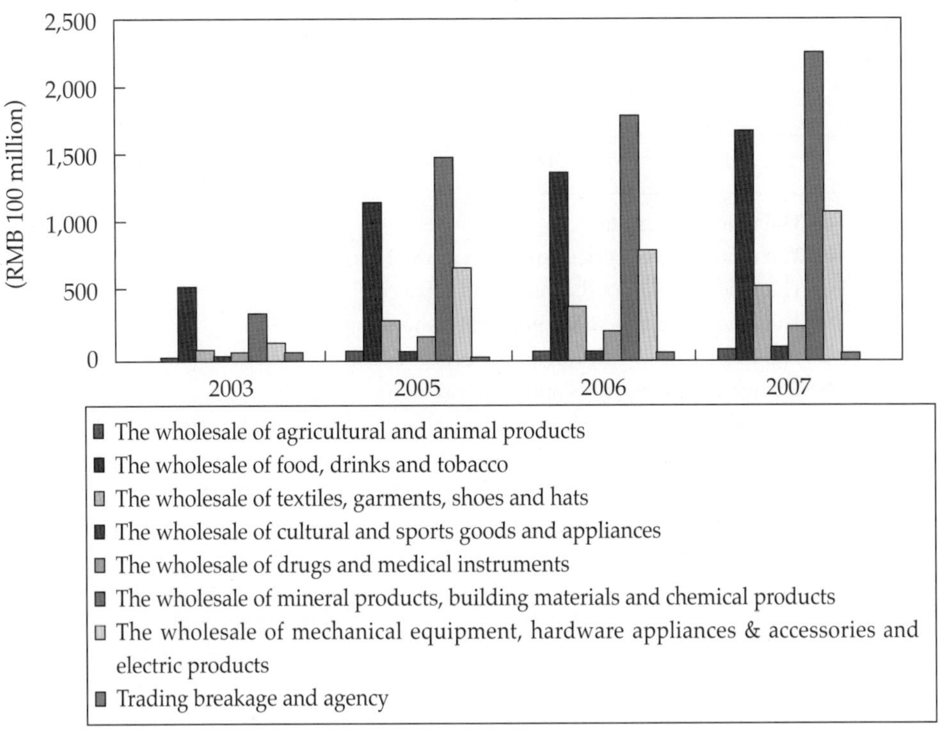

equipment, hardware appliances & accessories and electric products. All of these economic sectors are important to the development of China's national economy. Some of them are even monopolized sectors, with large scales of profits.

In Fig. 4.101, due to the lack of data, we made an average conversion of the profit margin in 2004, which reduced the degree of anomaly of growth rates. However, it could also be seen that the growth rates of profits of each and all sectors grew significantly since 2003. Apart from the wholesale of mineral products, the wholesale of mechanical equipment, hardware appliances & accessories and electric products had the highest growth rate of profits which reached 175% in 2004.

Fig. 4.101. Growth rates of the profits of the wholesale enterprises above the designated size (2004–2007)

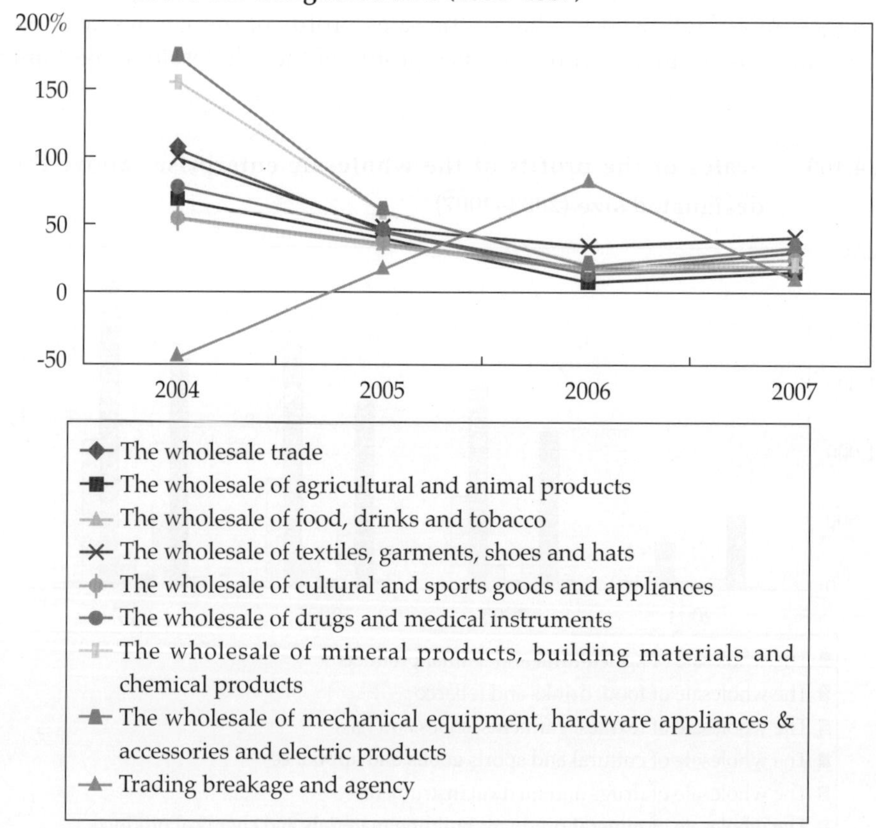

From the analyses of the financial state of the wholesale trade in the previous two stages, we can see clearly the development states of the wholesale trade in different economic sectors in the past decade: all showed a growing trend in terms of the development scale. However, significant changes happened to the proportions of the wholesale trade in different economic sectors. The proportions of the wholesale of energies, building materials, chemical engineering, machinery, electronics and other heavy industries kept increasing, while the size of assets, the scale of liabilities and that of profits of the wholesale of food, drinks and tobacco kept declining, which was similar to the situation of the wholesale of textiles, garments, shoes and hats. It was closely related to the specific roles played by each and all economic sectors in the development of the national economy. Such industries as energies, building materials, chemical engineering and electronics have been playing important roles in the rapid development of the national economy of China since the 16th National People's Congress. The wholesale of energies developed rapidly in the first stage which was closely related to the implementation of the West Development strategy in China. West China has abundant reserves of energies, along with which the implementation of the West Development strategy enabled the wholesale enterprises in different economic sectors to usher in a spring of development. In the second stage, due to the rapid and stable development of the national economy and the increase in the fixed-asset investments, such economic sectors got developed rapidly. The sector of food, tobacco and garments, as daily consumables, showed certain growth with the development of the economy, yet at a low speed. Therefore, the size of assets and the scale of profits of the wholesale trade were greatly different in the two stages.

5

Chapter

Emergence and Development of the Wholesale Markets

The wholesale market in China is an organizational form of commodity wholesale developed by borrowing the experience of trade markets, mainly the trade markets of agricultural and sideline products. In the early days of the reform and opening up, with the advance of the institutional reform in urban areas and the enlargement of enterprises' autonomy, the circulation pattern of commodities under the traditional planned economic system was broken; the stiff system of commodity wholesale featured by product deployment was unable to continue surviving; and a new system of commodity circulation and operation which was in line with the development requirements of the market economy was badly needed by the wholesale society. Under such circumstances, the wholesale market was born as a new-type organization of wholesale of means of production, some of the industrial and agricultural products and other commodities. Objectively, in the transition of China from the planned economic system to the socialist market economic system, the wholesale market, following market relations, had been playing a very important historical role in achieving the rational allocation of resources, pushing forward the information-based and networked commodity circulation, and promoting the formation of the unified big market across China. Even today, in Midwest China and the vast urban and rural areas in China, the wholesale market is still the mainstay mode of commodity wholesale and trading. Therefore, it can be said that in nature, the commodity market should be treated as an important organizational form of commodity wholesale that has an intimate relationship with the wholesale trade. It is an important component of the commodity market system in China.

In the three decades of reform and opening up, with the reform of the circulation system in China, the wholesale markets in China underwent different stages of development and played an important role in the commodity circulation in China. However, with the further development of the reform in the field of commodity circulation in China, the wholesale trade was extruded by the upstream production enterprises and the downstream retail businesses and began to dwindle. The economic foundation for the existence of the wholesale market was gradually weakened, too. In particular, after China's accession to the WTO, the distribution trade in China would be gradually opened and foreign capital would be allowed to enter the wholesale trade that has been well protected for long. Such foreign enterprises, being mature in market operations and strong in capital, would sure bring about great impacts on the domestic wholesale trade, especially the wholesale market in China. Therefore, when reviewing the development process of the wholesale market in the past three decades of reform and opening up, we must clearly realize the changes in the environment for the development of the wholesale trade in China, find out the problems existing in and the dilemma faced by the wholesale trade before improving the wholesale markets in China, and strengthening and promoting the role of the wholesale market as a modern wholesale organization to enable it to effectively link commodity wholesale with retail in accordance with the rules of commodity circulation and modern methods of distribution. Only in doing so could we make new explorations to push forward the reform and development of the wholesale trade and effectively improve the system of commodity wholesale.[1]

Reform and Development Process of the Wholesale Markets

Seen from China's national conditions, the wholesale market has three origins: trade markets, food or agricultural products exchange markets held by the system of supply and marketing cooperatives and the food system, as well as the markets opened by local government organs at all levels. Specifically, Chinese wholesale markets have undergone the following several stages of development:

The initial stage (1978–1984)

The Third Plenary Session of the 11th CPC National Congress was held in December 1978, since when China began to implement the reform and opening-up policy and its economy entered the transitional period. With the implementation of the household contract responsibility system in rural reform, productive forces in rural areas were greatly developed, varieties of agricultural and sideline products became enriched rapidly, the commodity rate was greatly improved, and the number of agricultural products pushed to the market increased largely. To save costs and speed up commodity circulation and capital turnover, China needed a kind of very influential markets to sell products in bulk as soon as possible. Lots of wholesale businesses were gradually formed at the time before gathering in some trade markets with convenient transportation. Trade markets in urban areas recovered and developed very rapidly; a great number of businessmen specialized in trading on the trade markets appeared; long-distance transport for sale became flourishing; the naturally developed trading on the trade markets got larger and larger; and the volume of market turnover became increasingly higher, all contributing to the birth of naturally developed wholesale markets for agricultural products given by trade markets, the matrix.

At the beginning of the reform and opening up, township enterprises sprang up, so did individual households with specialized lines of work. They were faced with high institutional barriers when their products tried to enter the state-owned sales channels. It rendered them to find the way out outside the system. Trade markets featured by autonomy in operation, flexible trade mode and little restrictions on the amount of commodities to wholesale became the main channel they relied on. Gathering of professional businesses then gave birth to some specialized professional markets or industrial goods wholesale markets.

On February 5, 1983, the State Council of China issued *Measures on the Administration of Trade Markets in Towns and Townships,* in which it recognized "trade markets in urban and rural areas are a component of the unified socialist market economy, which play an active role in promoting the development of agricultural productions and sideline occupations, activating urban and rural economy, making convenient people's life, and supplementing the state-owned sector of the commerce". Thanks to the name rectification of the trade market made and the legal status given to it by China, trade markets developed rapidly within 6 years from the first widely-recognized wholesale market in Qiaotou County, Zhejiang Province. The small commodities market in Hanzheng Street, Wuhan City (1979) and that in Yiwu City, Zhejiang Province (1982) were born during this period one after another. Wholesale markets gradually entered the start-up and development stage. In particular, wholesale markets for agricultural products developed well. Shouguang Vegetables Wholesale Market established in March 1984, an epoch-making turning point in the course of construction of the wholesale market for agricultural products in China, marked the official start of the construction of the wholesale markets for agricultural products in China.

As of the end of 1984, 2,248 trade centers had been established in urban areas across China, of which 753 were trade centers for agricultural products and 241 were integrated trade centers. Trade markets in urban and rural areas increased from 33,302 in 1978 to 56,500 in 1984, growing by 69.7%. The turnover of trade markets in urban and rural areas increased from RMB 12.52 billion in 1978 to 45.7 billion in 1984, growing by 265.0%. In 1983, China had 200 wholesale markets for agricultural and sideline products, the number of which increased to 1,000 in 1984, being five times larger. The wholesale markets for agricultural and sideline products developed rapidly.

Development of trade markets during this period was as shown in Fig. 5.1.

Fig. 5.1. Overview of the development of the trade market (1978–1984)

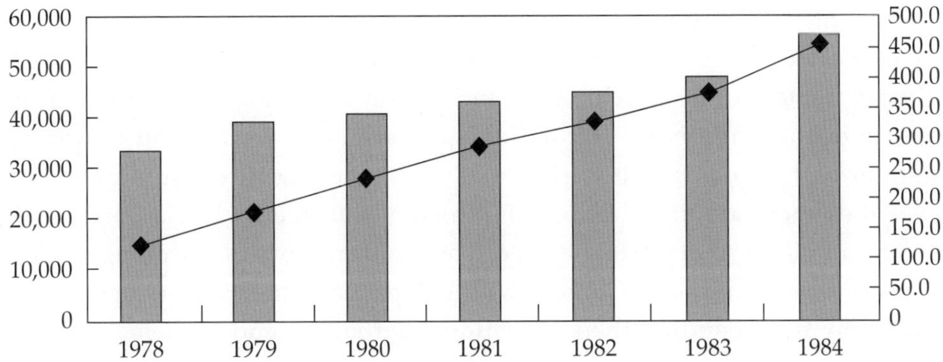

	1978	1979	1980	1981	1982	1983	1984
Number	33,302	38,993	40,809	43,013	44,775	48,003	56,500
Turnover (RMB 100 million)	125.2	183.0	235.0	287.0	328.0	379.0	457.0

Since most wholesale markets were naturally developed from trade markets at this stage, they were closely related to the development status of trade markets while showing the following characteristics:

(1) Most wholesale markets were gathered in rural areas.

(2) Operators were mostly self-employed farmers, which was intimately related to the locations of and product varieties of the wholesale markets.

(3) Wholesale markets for agricultural and sideline products achieved rapid development. The number of wholesale markets for agricultural and sideline products was 200 in 1983, which then increased to 1,000 in 1984, being five times greater. However, the wholesale markets for industrial consumables developed slowly and commodities on the market were mainly industrial consumables each with low unit values and low grades. Wholesale markets for industrial consumables established during this period were mainly wholesale markets for small commodities.

(4) Most of the traders were commune- or brigade-run enterprises. Some were newly-emerged private enterprises.

(5) It influenced the overall orientation of industrial products and solved the problem of distributing industrial products in rural areas. During this period, industrial products were sold well in urban areas with the help of a relatively developed network and great markets, yet they were in great shortage in rural areas. Therefore, the emergence of the wholesale markets solved the problem of selling industrial products in rural areas, while the supply and marketing cooperatives basically solved the problem of supplying agricultural products in urban areas.

The stage of overall construction (1986–1991)

The reform of the commodity circulation system launched in 1984 gradually gave space for the development of commodity circulation. Measures that were directly related to the development and reform of the wholesale trade in the reform of the commodity circulation system mainly focused on reforming state-owned wholesale enterprises and on weakening direct administration over the wholesale distribution. Of which, the former, while adjusting the organizational system of state-owned wholesale enterprises, encouraged them to transform into new-type entities with independent interests and operational autonomy by expanding their operational autonomy and implementing the two-step substitution of tax payment for profit delivery, the contract system and the shareholding system. The latter was reflected by the gradual reduction of commodity varieties under government planning and administration, the substitution of centralized purchase and contracted marketing of industrial products and the unified and fixed state purchase of agricultural products by the sale on credit which was in line with market rules, the lift of restrictions of fixed purchase and sale relations, the permission of free trade among market entities, the gradually strengthened role of the market mechanism for pricing in wholesale activities, and the opening up of the wholesale trade to the non-state-owned economic sector. The emerging wholesale markets capable of free production and marketing replaced the traditional closed wholesale network composed of state-owned and cooperative commerce before becoming the main distribution channel and being widely recognized by the society.

The wholesale markets for agricultural products, except for a very small number of individual products, were developed fast in terms of the number of the markets, product varieties and amounts, market turnover, as well as the opening-up degree of prices. At the same time place-of-origin wholesale markets got developed, the place-of-sales wholesale markets rose and developed gradually and the system of products wholesale markets came into being in general. During this period, the growth and development of wholesale markets accelerated and local wholesale markets for agricultural products were established one after another. Local governments began to pay attention to fostering commodities wholesale and exchange markets. Wholesale markets in China entered the stage of all-round construction.

Reform of the commodity circulation system in 1984 had not only transformed state-owned wholesale enterprises into market entities with independent interests and under hard budget constraints, but also given birth to a great number of new market entities led by individual, private and foreign-funded enterprises which were less constrained by the traditional system. After a large amount of new-type market entities entered the field of production circulation, the cost advantage of the centralized transactions on the visible market became increasingly prominent due to the yet-to-be perfect market system, incomplete market information, trading risks and the increase in trading costs. The wholesale market gradually became the main circulation channel of great numbers of small and medium-sized private enterprises, which greatly promoted the construction of wholesale markets in an all-round manner.

Wholesale markets achieved all-round development in this stage. Take the wholesale market for agricultural products as an example; there were altogether 892 wholesale markets for agricultural products in China with the aggregate market turnover valuing RMB 2.835 billion in 1986. In the several years that followed, the number, the total market turnover and the average turnover per market of the wholesale markets for agricultural products kept growing year after year. Till 1991, the number of wholesale markets for agricultural products reached 1,509, up 12.6% year on year and being 1.7 times greater than that in 1986. The total market turnover of such wholesale markets was RMB 15.309 billion, being 5.4 times greater than that in 1986 (see Fig. 5.2).

Fig. 5.2. Development of the wholesale markets for agricultural products (1986–1991)

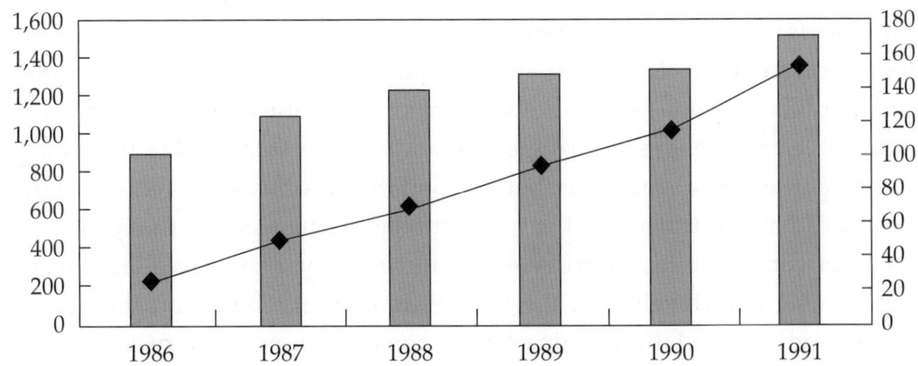

	1986	1987	1988	1989	1990	1991
Number	892	1,095	1,224	1,313	1,340	1,509
Turnover (RMB 100 million)	28.35	50.34	70.59	95.23	115.79	153.09

Development of the wholesale markets at this stage was featured by:

(1) Significantly accelerated growth and development, which was more significant in the development of wholesale markets for agricultural products.

(2) The emergence of the trend of specialty development of wholesale markets. During this period, a number of active and specialized wholesale markets appeared, including the button market in Qiaotou County, Wenzhou City, Zhejiang Province, the sofa market in Xianghe County, Hebei Province, and the tooth brush market in Hangji County, Hanjiang Township, Jiangshu Province.

(3) The all-round construction of the wholesale markets and the initial formation of the wholesale market system. Not only the place-of-origin and the place-of-sales of wholesale markets for agricultural products, but also the wholesale markets for industrial products achieved great development. Till 1991, there had been 411 wholesale markets for industrial products across China, being 146 more over the previous year; and the total market turnover of such wholesale markets had reached RMB 18.123 billion, up 60% year on year.

The stage of rapid and overheating development (1992–1995)

In 1992, China set up the goals of the socialist economic reform. In 1993, the Third Plenary Session of the 14th CPC National Congress was held, at which the *Decision of the Central Committee of the Communist Party of China on the Several Issues Concerning the Establishment of the Socialist Market Economic System* was passed. In the *Decision of the Central Committee of the Communist Party of China on the Several Issues Concerning the Establishment of the Socialist Market Economic System*, it was proposed to "reform the existing commodity circulation system and further develop the commodity market; establish wholesale markets for major agricultural products, industrial consumables and means of production; and strictly standardize the trials of futures markets of a small number of commodities. State-owned circulation enterprises have to transform their operational mechanisms, actively take part in market competitions, improve economic efficacy, and play a leading role in improving and developing the wholesale markets. Based on the demand for commodity circulation, China has to construct a network of large, small and medium-sized commodity markets featured by the coexistence of various economic forms and modes of operations, as well as complete foundations in order to push forward circulation modernization." By then, fostering the market system had become a core content of the reform of the economic system.

With the setting of the goals of the reform of the socialist market economic system, the market-oriented reform of the circulation system for agricultural products was launched in an all-round manner in China, the core of which was "merge". A new system of purchase and sale subject to market regulation was carried out on agricultural products, apart from a very small number of agricultural products such as grains and cotton. During this period, focus of the reform of the circulation system for agricultural products changed from reforming the ways of purchase and sales to constructing the market system. China saw severe inflation in a few consecutive years after 1988, especially the grain-based wave of panic buying and the soaring of commodity prices. Agricultural products being in short supply was thought to be the main reason for inflation. To improve market supply, China launched the projects of "Rice Bag (food supply)" and "Shopping Basket (vegetable supply)" at the end of the 1980s while requiring local governments to strengthen the construction of wholesale markets for agricultural products and putting forward corresponding principles. During this period, the wholesale markets for agricultural products in China had formed a multi-layered and multi-category system based in large and medium cities and covering both urban and rural areas.

Meanwhile, as local governments were more and more aware of the strong industrial competitiveness generated by the industry clusters brought about by wholesale markets, they began to consciously push each and all trade markets in towns and townships forward to being specialized, contributing to the momentum of joint development of wholesale markets and specialized trade markets in towns and townships. For example, based on the specialized trade markets in towns and townships in Wenzhou, Zhejiang Province, local government paid special attention to fostering pillar industries while speeding up the development of related industries and extending the industrial chain, helping form the pattern featured by the cooperation and division of labor of production, sales and service departments and the integration of production, supply and marketing. Specialty wholesale markets were viewed as the accelerator of industrial clusters, which were capable of constantly digesting the productivity of such industrial clusters. Promoted by industrial clusters, the wholesale markets, especially some wholesale markets specialized in industrial products, achieved great development and became more and more influential.

The Chinese Government put forward the principle of "investors are beneficiaries" on the construction of small and medium-sized wholesale markets in the boom of pushing forward the construction of wholesale markets, encouraged all social fields to make investments. However, in the construction of wholesale markets, China failed to develop fundamental laws on the wholesale markets and supporting enforcement regulations, or make any scientific appraisal. Shell markets and trading chaos showed up in some places. For example, the phenomena of bullying competitors and dominating the market, as well as giving buyers short weight could be found everywhere.

The construction and development of the wholesale markets for agricultural products, especially the place-of-sales wholesale markets were somewhat blind.

During this period, both the wholesale markets for agricultural products and those for industrial products were developing fast. As can be seen from Fig. 5.3, both the number and turnover of the wholesale markets for consumables were growing rapidly. The number of wholesale markets for consumables reached 2,418 in 1992 before growing to 5,639 in 1995, being 3,221 more; the turnover of wholesale markets for consumables reached RMB 57.95 billion in 1992 before growing to RMB 458.03 billion in 1995, up 690.4%, of which the year 1995 saw a substantial increase. The number of wholesale markets for consumables in 1995 was only 2,315 more than that in 1994, and the total turnover of the same wholesale markets for consumables was RMB 458.03 billion, up 79.2% year on year (see Fig. 5.3).

Fig. 5.3. Overview of the development of wholesale markets for consumables (1992–1995)

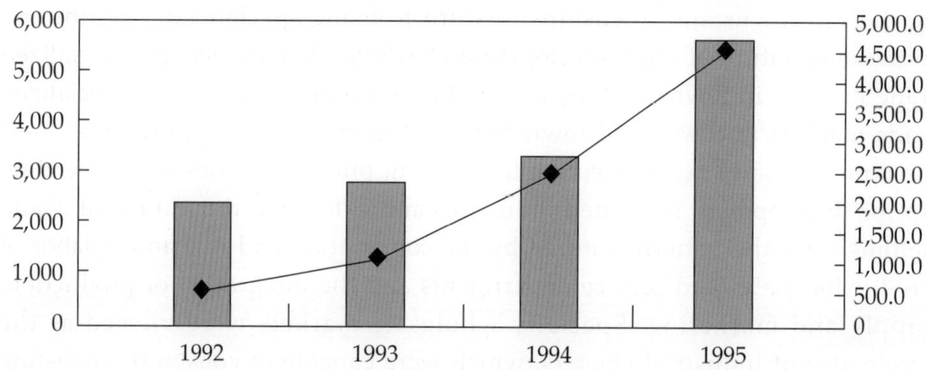

	1992	1993	1994	1995
Number	2,418	2,827	3,354	5,639
Turnover (RMB 100 million)	579.5	1,137.1	2,556.4	4,580.3

Development of the wholesale markets in this period was featured by:

(1) The rapid growth rate of the wholesale markets for agricultural products and for industrial consumables in terms of the number and the turnover.

(2) The conscious acceleration of the development of the wholesale markets by local governments compared with the spontaneous development of the wholesale markets in the past.

(3) The diversification of the wholesale market entities. Since the Chinese

Government vigorously encouraged the construction of wholesale markets during this period and put forward the principle of "investors are beneficiaries", a variety of entities chose to invest in the wholesale markets. Such entities fell inot the following several categories by origin: 1) since wholesale markets were profitable, local governments at all levels began to open such markets. In rural areas, such runners were mainly the villagers' committees, the township people's governments and the people's communes; whiles in urban areas, such runners were mainly street committees and communities. Famous wholesale markets in urban areas included Tianyi small commodities market, the market at Dongzhimen and Xiushui Street, etc. in Beijing, the development of which also brought great economic benefits for the sponsors; 2) the industrial and commercial bureaus used to be responsible for the registration of markets, but they realized the opportunity at the boom of the wholesale markets before getting engaged in opening up wholesale markets; 3) transaction entities, namely market traders; 4) entities of the shareholding system were mainly some markets.

(4) The administration of the wholesale markets being not standardized enough and related legal systems being inadequate. Plus the deviation of government policies, the administration of the wholesale markets showed certain blindness.

The stage of standardized development (1995–2001)

Though the wholesale markets had developed fast in the previous stage, the overall development of the wholesale markets showed certain blindness due to the deviation of government policies. Repetitive construction of wholesale markets led to the waste of resources and irrational resource allocation; and the chaotic market orders severely hindered the healthy development of wholesale markets, resulting in the rapid declining of the growing speed of wholesale markets. In view of the above problems, China adopted a series of measures (mainly in 4 aspects) to standardize and rectify the development of wholesale markets in order to promote the development of wholesale markets in a standardized way. (1) The separation of market administration from market building. The General Office of the State Council issued document No. 40 in 1995 entitled *Notice of the General Office of the State Council of China on forwarding the Opinion of the State Administration for Industry and Commerce of the People's Republic of China on the Soon Decoupling of Administrative Authorities for Industry and Commerce with the Markets Held by Them,* requiring industrial and commercial bureaus to decouple with the markets held by them in order to eliminate the unfair phenomenon of industrial and commercial bureaus serving as both the "players" and the "judges", and both "opening the markets" and "enforcing the laws". (2) The implementation of the system of market registration and annual check system. A number of unqualified wholesale markets were closed down, including those having terminated operation for consecutively 6 or more months or having been inactive for over a year, in order to promote rational market distribution. (3) Rectification of the market order. Such illegal behaviors as road robbers, bullying the competitors and dominating the market, etc. were cracked down upon. Some policies and measures aiming at sealing off the markets or achieving local protectionism that were adopted by local governments at all levels were cleared up and eliminated. (4) The adjustment of the belongings of grassroots administration for industry and commerce. Provincial departments for the administration of industry and commerce became the direct leaders, reducing the disturbance of grassroots governments of market administration and law enforcement. The above measures promoted the level of standardization of the operation of wholesale markets and basically eliminated the nationwide barriers for product circulation, truly laying a foundation for truly forming a unified wholesale market across China.

Fig. 5.4. Development of the wholesale markets for consumables (1995–2001)

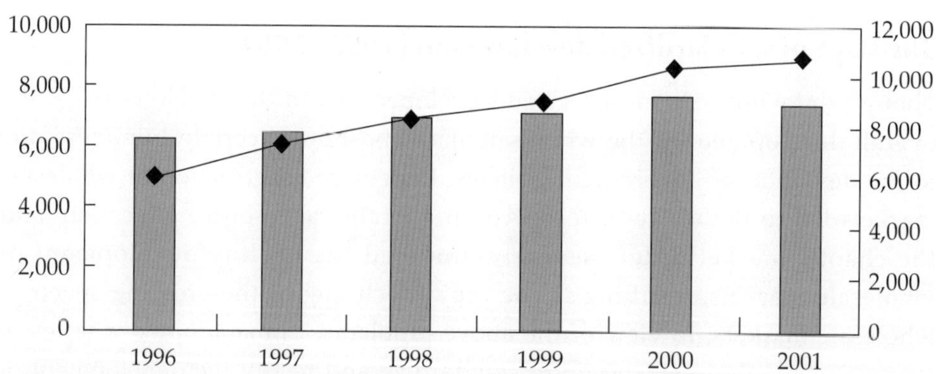

	1996	1997	1998	1999	2000	2001
Number	6,319	6.531	6.953	7,133	7,228	7,394
Turnover (RMB 100 million)	6,067.5	7,427.5	8,393.7	9,015.4	10,518.6	10,794.6

During this period, the number and turnover of wholesale markets in China were on the rise in general. In 1996, the number of wholesale markets for consumables was 6,319, and the total market turnover was RMB 606.75 billion.

Till 2001, the same number had increased to 7,394, being 1,075 more than that in 1996; and the same total market turnover had reached RMB 1,079.46 billion, up 77.9% over that in 1996. A significant trend during this period was the slowing down of the development and the declining growth rate, even negative growth of the wholesale markets. The wholesale markets for consumables reduced by 334 in number in 2001 comparing with that in 2000, showing a negative growth for the first time; and the market turnover simply grew by 2.6% year on year, showing a small margin of growth. It indicated that the quantitative development of the wholesale markets had become more stable and the wholesale markets had entered the stage of standardized development (as shown in Fig. 5.4).

Fig. 5.5. Growth of the wholesale markets for consumables (1995–2001)

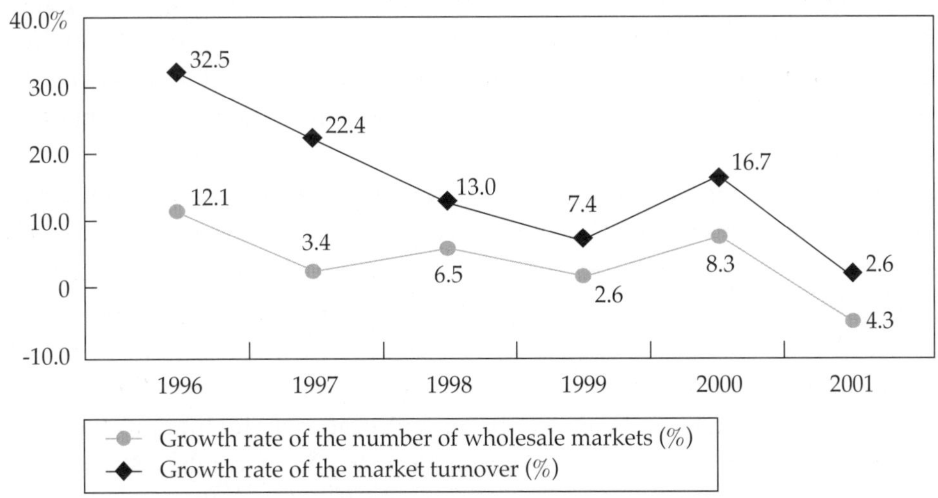

Development of the wholesale markets during this period was featured by:

(1) The slowing down of the growth, even the negative growth of the wholesale markets in terms of their number and total market turnover, which indicated the improvement of the overheating development of the wholesale markets.

(2) The gradual standardization of the administration over the wholesale markets and the gradual amelioration of the market order. China adopted a series of measures to rectify the development of the wholesale markets and made great achievements. The wholesale markets in China had entered a stage of standardized development.

(3) The better display and gradual improvement of the functions of the wholesale markets. For example, the function of trading and distributing

commodities, the formation and discovery of prices, the function of settlement, the function of risk disperse, the function of collecting, processing and distributing information, the function of proving market services, to name a few, had all been displayed to a certain extent, playing an important role in the rational allocation of commodity resources in the society.

The stage of polarized development (2002 to present)

After its accession to the WTO, China has accelerated opening up its wholesale markets to the world. Wholesale markets in China were once faced with domestic pressures and the increasingly fiercer competitions from overseas. To maintain the position of the wholesale markets in the field of circulation and help them achieve greater development, China further standardized, institutionalized and legalized the wholesale markets before upgrading their quality and helping them enter the stage of second start-up. Meanwhile, China issued a number of laws and standards to try to speed up achieving the standardization, institutionalization and legalization of the wholesale markets. For example, in December 2002, 6 ministries and commissions, including the State Planning Commission (now known as the National Development and Reform Commission), issued *Several Opinions on Accelerating the Construction of Circulation Facilities for Agricultural Products*, clearly making the circulation facilities for agricultural products an important component of social infrastructure. In June 2003, national standards on green wholesale markets for agricultural and sideline products were issued and China began to build green wholesale markets for agricultural and sideline products and further push forward the Three-green Project. On December 8, 2004, the Ministry of Agriculture issued *Opinions on Further Strengthening the Safety Management of the Quality of Agricultural Products*. During this period, a group of large wholesale markets each valuing more than RMB 100 million and with large scales of transactions and great influence emerged. The number of such wholesale markets, the number of stands, their business area and turnover were all increasing. In 2002, there were 1,235,070 stands in 1,734 wholesale markets each valuing over RMB 100 million in China, covering 70.51 million m^2 and achieving a total business volume of RMB 1,545.09 billion. Till 2007, there had been 1,674,768 stands in 2,366 wholesale markets, the total business area of which had been 150.687 million m^2 and the total turnover of which had been 35,871.5, up 36.4%, 35.6%, 113.7% and 132.2%, respectively, over 2002.

As for the development of the wholesale markets during this period, a group of large wholesale markets with large scales of transactions and great influence

Fig. 5.6. Number and the turnover of wholesale markets each valuing more than RMB 100 million (2002–2007)

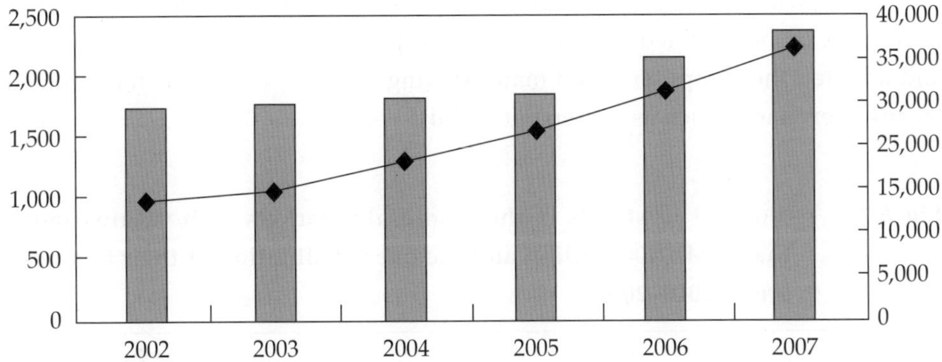

	2002	2003	2004	2005	2006	2007
Number	1,734	1,759	1,821	1,851	2,161	2,366
Turnover (RMB 100 million)	15,450.9	16,832.6	21,116.9	24,544.2	29,679.9	35,871.5

emerged on the one hand, a great number of small and medium-sized low-end wholesale markets were stuck in operational dilemma and became smaller and smaller in size and weaker and weaker in functions, showing a trend of being replaced by modern circulation organizations, on the other hand. Wholesale markets began to shrink, leading to obvious features of polarization. Apart from the features of polarization, development of the wholesale markets in this period also showed the following characteristics:

(1) Changes happened to the market environment. As can be seen from the operational situation of the wholesale markets in China in recent years, after more than 10 years of high-speed growth and scale enlargement, the wholesale markets had gradually transformed from being large in number to being great in quality. Market outlets had become increasingly centralized, the operation of which had become increasingly standardized. Hardware facilities were significantly improved; the scales of wholesale markets became expanded; the grade of commodities became improved; and the quality of market operation became increasingly optimistic. Great changes had happened to the market environment.

(2) Forms of commodity trading became diversified and the modes of transactions had been somewhat improved. For example, in the wholesale markets for small commodities, the single stand-based trading had been changed into the combination of stand-based trading, specialty shops and

specialized streets, forming specialized cities, street or shops for some commodities. In addition, the modes of transactions had been improved all the way. Some wholesale markets introduced modern way of transaction such as settlement by bill, carried out the membership system and the deposit system, and adopted the computer-aided matchmaking tradeoff, as well as modernized means of exchange such as settlement by bill.

Fig. 5.7. Number of stands in the wholesale markets each valuing more than RMB 100 million and the overall situation of their business areas (2002–2007)

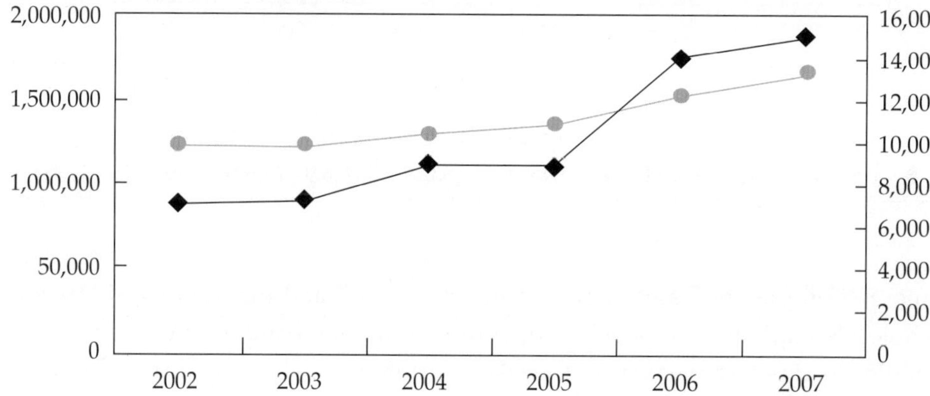

	2002	2003	2004	2005	2006	2007
Number of stands	1,235,070	1,217,734	1,303,838	1,366,064	1,533,679	1,674,768
Business area (10,000 m^2)	7,051	7,299	8,909.7	8,943.6	13,933.1	15,068.7

Organizational Evolution of the Wholesale Markets

Since the reform and opening up, the wholesale markets in China have undergone the start-up stage, the stage of all-round construction, the stage of rapid and overheating development, the stage of standardized development and the stage of polarized development, resulting in corresponding changes in the organization of the wholesale markets. In the early days of the reform and opening up, most wholesale markets came into being in trade markets. Such wholesale markets were small in size, segmented in organization and low in the degree of market concentration ratio. With the establishment and development of the market economy, the wholesale markets had been expanding in size and become increasingly centralized before forming a group of large wholesale markets with large scales of transactions and great influence. With a large share among all wholesale markets and the constantly improved market concentration ratio, these large wholesale markets brought about changes in the structure and performance of the wholesale markets as a whole.

Concentration ratio of the wholesale markets

The wholesale market is the most influential type of management over the wholesale of consumables that has been developing the fastest of all since the reform and opening up, when runners of the wholesale markets began to be diversified and the concentration ratio of the wholesale markets began to be gradually improved in China. With the acceleration of the modernization drive of the wholesale markets, wholesale markets in China have become increasingly expanded, their concentration ratio has become gradually improved, and large wholesale markets have been playing an increasingly strengthened role in leading and stimulating the development of the wholesale markets as a whole. In particular, the great numbers of wholesale markets each valuing more than RMB 100 million in recent years have had profound effects on the changes in the overall market structure. Next, the CR_4 and CR_8 of large wholesale markets[2] will be measured to describe and analyze the changes in the market concentration ratio.

Concentration ratio of the commodity exchange markets

Through the measurement, the concentration ratio and changing trend of commodity exchange markets each valuing more than RMB 100 million can be seen as follows:

From Fig. 5.8, we may find that the concentration ratio of commodity exchange markets each valuing more than RMB 100 million had been improved in general. In 2007, the CR_4 and CR_8 of such commodity exchange markets were 5.24% and 8.41%, respectively, up 20.0% and 5.4%, respectively, over 4.37% and 7.89%, respectively, in 2001. It had much to do with the gradual standardization of the means of exchange and ways of settlement on the commodity exchange markets, the further improvement of streamlined supporting services and the further extension of market functions. As the commodity exchange markets were constantly standardized, legalized and modernized, the organizational level of such markets were improved, too, which was manifested by the increase in market concentration ratio. See Fig. 5.8 carefully and you will find that in the overall increasing trend of the markets, the CR_4 and CR_8 of such markets reduced in 2005, decreasing by 2.9% and 12.7%, respectively. It had much to do with the opening up of the wholesale trade in China. After December 11, 2004, commodity exchange markets in China have entered a stage of all-round opening up. Newly-approved foreign-funded enterprises in China grew significantly in 2005, leading to the aggregation of domestic market competitions and the decrease in market concentration ratio.

Fig. 5.8. Concentration ratios of commodity exchange markets each valuing more than RMB 100 million across China (2001–2007)

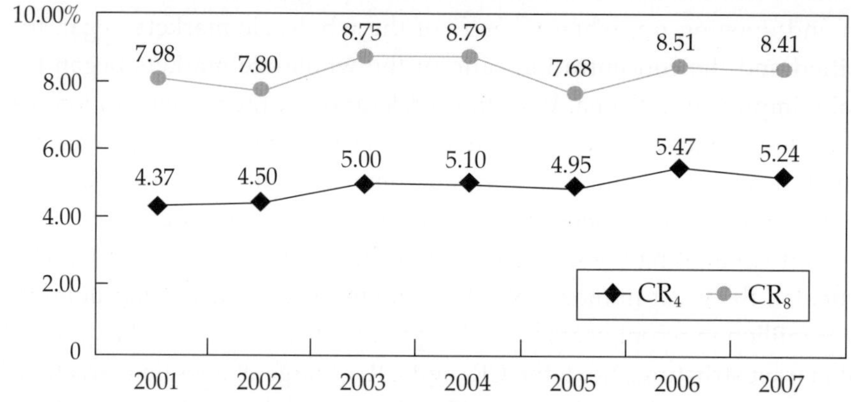

Concentration ratios of various types of commodity exchange markets

Commodity exchange markets fall into two categories-comprehensive markets and specialty markets, inside each of which are different ways of classification. To better reflect the market structure of the entire commodity exchange markets, we will measure the concentration ratios of different types of commodity exchange markets.

Concentration ratio of the various types of comprehensive markets

As can be seen from Table 5.1 and Fig. 5.9, the concentration ratio of comprehensive markets for industrial products and that of comprehensive markets for agricultural products were improved in general. Of which, the former was obviously higher than the latter, which had much to do with the natures of two different types of products. Industrial products, especially the means of production and like products are featured by unified specifications, easier identification of qualities, long cycles of wholesale and large amounts of orders and wholesale, so the centralized transaction was mainly adopted. Agricultural products are quite the opposite in nature. That's why wholesale markets for industrial products are usually larger and more concentrated than wholesale markets for agricultural products. As can also be seen from Fig. 5.9, different from the growing trend of the concentration ratio of the comprehensive markets for industrial products, the comprehensive markets for agricultural products showed great fluctuations in 2005, the CR_4 and CR_8 of which were 17.43% and 28.09%, respectively, being far higher than the levels in 2004 and 2006 (CR_4 was 11.28% and 11.43%, respectively, in 2004; while CR_8 was 18.00% and 18.68%, respectively, in 2006). The phenomenon had something to do with the annual meeting on the wholesale markets for agricultural products held in 2005. The said meeting ranked the comprehensive and specialty wholesale markets for agricultural and sideline products across China before recognizing them, which played a certain role in encouraging some wholesale markets in China. Many super-large markets strived hard to rank among the best, get recognized, and further promote their reputations. So they made great efforts to facilitate market transactions and improve market turnover, resulting in the increase in the turnover of the top four or top eight comprehensive markets for agricultural products and corresponding improvement of the market concentration ratio.

Table 5.1. Concentration ratio of the comprehensive markets of commodity exchange markets each valuing more than RMB 100 million during 2001–2007 in China (%)

Year	Comprehensive markets for industrial products		Comprehensive markets for agricultural products	
	CR_4	CR_8	CR_4	CR_8
2001	17.17	27.83	11.05	16.32
2002	17.53	29.08	10.64	16.66
2003	20.19	31.10	10.91	16.40
2004	22.23	34.02	11.28	18.00
2005	27.76	43.85	17.43	28.09
2006	31.95	47.95	11.43	18.68
2007	29.40	45.72	11.77	19.92

Concentration ratio of the various types of specialty markets

In order to analyze the differences among various types of markets inside the specialty markets for agricultural products and those for industrial products, several types of markets will be chosen from the specialty markets for agricultural products and those for industrial products next to make a comparative analysis. Markets are chosen mainly based on their features, representativeness and availability of data. CR_4 will be adopted. Let's take a look at the concentration ratio of several types of specialty markets for agricultural products.

Fig. 5.9. Concentration ratio of the comprehensive markets of commodity exchange markets each valuing more than RMB 100 million across China (2001–2007)

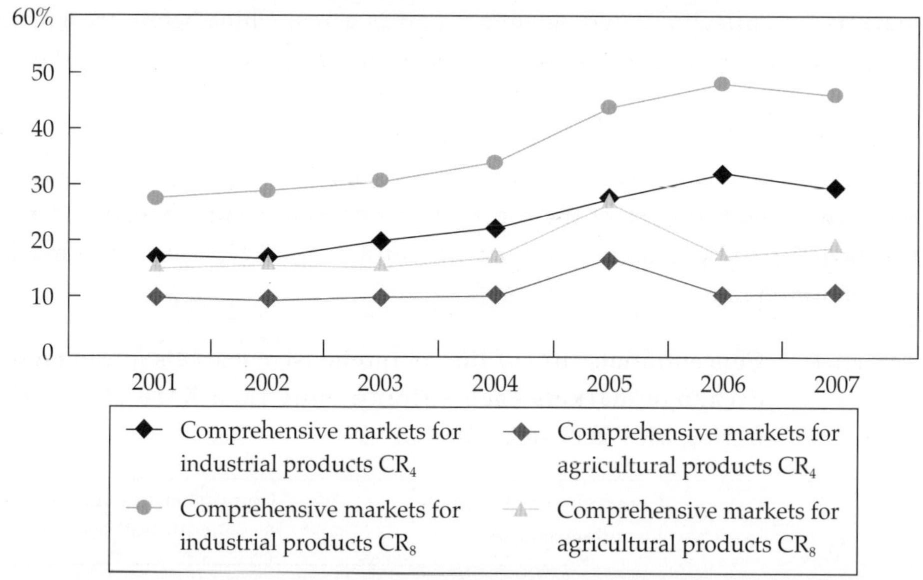

As can be seen from Table 5.2 and Table 5.10, the concentration ratios of different types of specialty markets for agricultural products showed varied development trends. The wholesale markets for grains and edible oil showed a declining trend during 2001–2007, the CR_4 of which fell from 46.91% in 2001 to 19.12% in 2007, down 59.2%; the wholesale markets for vegetables, fresh and dried nuts, fruits, food, drinks, tobacco and wines developed stably with little fluctuations. The concentration ratio of the wholesale markets for fresh and dried nuts and fruits was maintained somewhere between 20–30%; that of the wholesale markets for vegetables was 23.99% in 2001, but somewhere between 10–20% in the other few years; that of the wholesale markets for food, drinks, tobacco and wines was 14.14% in 2007, but basically about 20% in the other few years. As for the wholesale markets for meat, poultry and eggs, the concentration ratio of such markets was the most fluctuating of all. CR_4 of the wholesale markets for meat, poultry and eggs reached the highest in 2004, being 71.95%; fell to the lowest in 2005, being 27.66%; and was somewhere between 30–60% in the other few years. The wholesale markets for native products and animal by-products also fluctuated greatly, the CR_4 of which was the lowest in 2002, being 56.91%, and the highest in 2005, being 82.84%. Different development trends and fluctuations of the concentration ratios of the above specialty markets for agricultural products were largely because of the unique characteristics of each and all types of specialty markets for agricultural products and the features of the historical development of each of the markets. Specifically, grain and oil products were long been monopolized by the state and underwent a slow process before being lift state monopoly. With the devolution of powers, investment entities in the wholesale markets for grains and oil became gradually diversified, which aggregated the competition and led to smaller shares of each specialty market. The concentration ratio of the wholesale markets for grains and oil showed a declining trend on the whole. The wholesale markets for fresh and dried nuts and fruits and the wholesale markets for vegetables each showed a stable turnover and stable changing trends of concentration ratios due to the relatively short growing cycles of corresponding products, small fluctuations in supply and prices, and distinct features of being regional of the products in their growth (in particular in the place-of-origin markets). Meanwhile, since products on such markets didn't have a great scale effect, competitions were relatively fierce and concentration ratios of such markets were also relatively low. As for the wholesale markets for meat, poultry and eggs and those for native products and by-products, their turnovers were unstable since products on such markets in themselves were vulnerable to all external factors and highly regional. For example, an epidemic disease in poultry in some place may affect the trading of such products on the markets across the whole district. Therefore, concentration ratios of such markets for meat, poultry and eggs showed great fluctuations. The wholesale markets for food, drinks, tobacco and wines were very different from the previous several types of markets. Since agricultural products were further processed on the market, such markets belonged to the wholesale markets for agricultural and sideline products, each showing a high degree of competitions and low concentration ratio.

As can be seen from Table 5.3 and Fig. 5.11, during 2001–2007, the concentration ratios of various types of specialty markets for industrial products were quite different, which had much to do with the characteristics of the products on each market and the overall development trend and openness of the entire industry. Of which, in 2001, the concentration ratio of the wholesale

Table 5.2. Concentration ratios of various types of specialty markets for agricultural products each valuing more than RMB 100 million across China during 2001–2007 (%)

Year	Markets for Grains & Oil	Markets for Meat, Poultry and Eggs	Markets for Vegetables	Markets for Fresh and Dried Nuts and Fruits	Markets for Native Products and Animal By-products	Markets for Food, Drinks, Tobacco and Wines
2001	46.90	43.48	23.99	26.78	64.72	21.03
2002	235.41	45.84	16.22	23.74	56.91	19.02
2003	26.79	65.98	17.52	26.94	58.55	19.60
2004	24.22	71.95	16.83	28.20	57.38	19.54
2005	20.25	27.66	12.11	19.81	82.84	21.74
2006	17.03	33.72	14.65	30.24	64.11	17.15
2007	19.12	37.15	10.63	26.28	58.29	14.14

Fig. 5.10. Concentration ratios of various types of specialty markets for agricultural products each valuing more than RMB 100 million across China during 2001–2007 (CR_4)

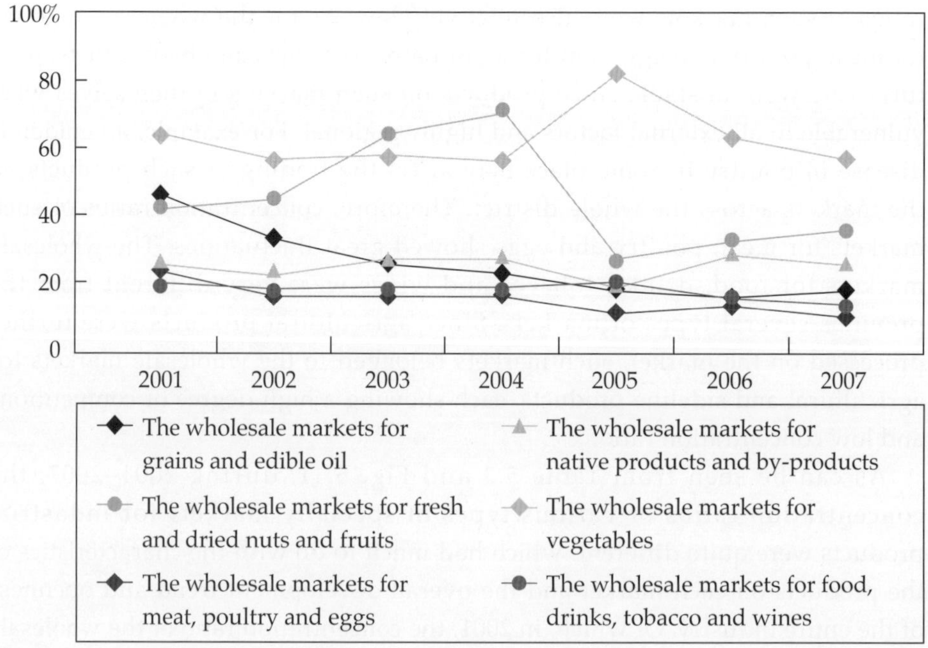

Table 5.3. Concentration ratios of various types of specialty markets for industrial products each valuing more than RMB 100 million across China during 2001–2007 (%)

Year	The wholesale markets for textiles, garments, shoes and hats	The wholesale markets for motor vehicles	The wholesale markets for building and decoration materials	The wholesale markets for coals	The wholesale markets for means of agricultural production
2001	20.85	38.63	22.80	54.15	76.51
2002	27.36	36.99	18.72	44.51	67.67
2003	29.26	30.27	16.64	—	—
2004	27.52	26.10	16.51	—	—
2005	20.14	20.91	23.62	80.18	47.50
2006	18.21	20.24	15.55	78.85	45.23
2007	22.39	16.49	12.43	74.71	41.69

Fig. 5.11. Concentration ratios of various types of specialty markets for industrial products each valuing more than RMB 100 million across China during 2001–2007 (CR_4)

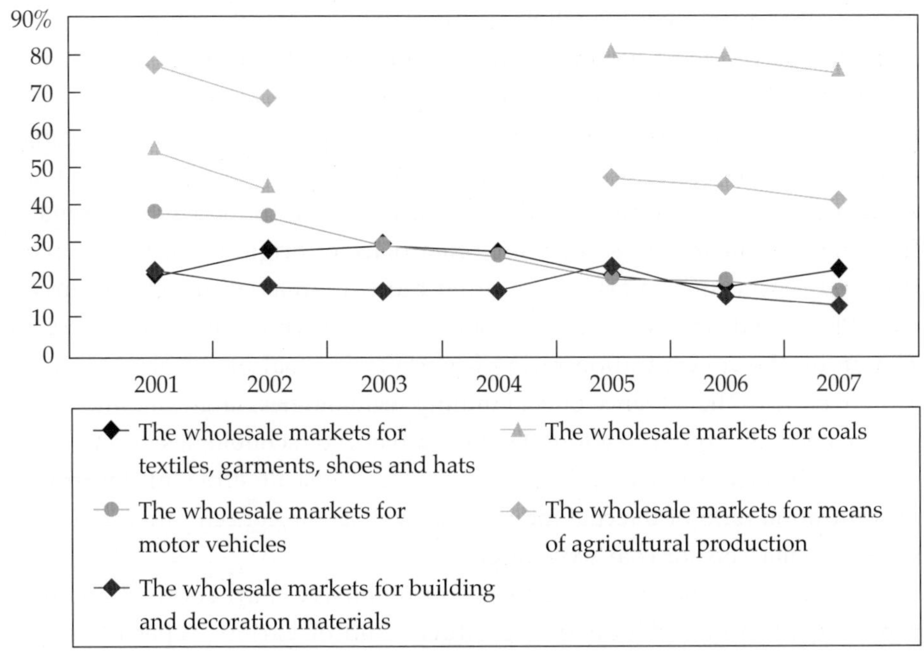

markets for means of agricultural production was the highest of all, with the CR_4 reaching 76.51%, followed by that of the wholesale markets for coal, whose CR_4 reached 54.15%; and the concentration ratio of the wholesale markets for textiles, garments, shoes and hats was the lowest of all, being 20.85%. In 2007, the concentration ratio of the wholesale markets for coal was the highest of all, with the CR_4 reaching 74.71%; that of the wholesale markets for building and decoration materials was the lowest of all, being 12.43%; the CR_4 of the wholesale markets for the means of agricultural production was 41.69%; and the CR_4 of textiles, garments, shoes and hats was 22.39%. From the above description, we can see that concentration ratios of specialty markets for means of production were usually higher than those of specialty markets for industrial consumables. It was consistent with the natures of products. The means of production and like products were featured by unified specifications, easier identification of qualities, long cycles of wholesale and large amounts of orders and wholesale. Centralized trading was mainly adopted, so the concentration ratio of such markets was high. For example, the wholesale markets for means of agricultural production and for coal having the highest CR_4 in Fig. 5.11 all belonged to such kind of markets. As for industrial consumables, especially textiles, garments, shoes and hats, due to the quite different products and small volumes of transaction, it would be more conducive for them to be scattered in different markets before satisfying consumption diversification. So the concentration ratio of such markets was often low. It can also be seen from Fig. 5.11 that apart from the wholesale markets for coal, other types of specialty markets also showed a declining tendency in terms of the concentration ratio. It was mainly because that many types of specialty markets were faced with the pressure of foreign competitions along with the acceleration of the opening up in China. Reduction in the concentration ratio was the result of fierce market competitions. The wholesale markets for coal belong to the wholesale markets for major raw materials, so they are often place-of-origin markets. To save the transport costs, such markets are often built in areas with rich resources of coal. Plus, the distribution of coal resources is relatively concentrated in China. Therefore, the concentration ratio of markets for coal has always been high. Moreover, with the advance of coal mining technologies, large amounts of costs will be needed in order to adopt the most advanced technologies in coal mining, which will make the coal mining industry more scale-efficient, improve the concentration ratio of the coal industry, as well as the concentration ratio of the wholesale markets for coal accordingly.

The concentration ratios of the comprehensive markets for agricultural products, of those for industrial products, and of various types of specialty markets measured and analyzed above could reflect certain market features. However, due to the characteristics of the circulation industry in itself, development levels in different regions were quite different. To better observe the organizational level of wholesale markets, we will next measure and analyze the concentration ratios of the commodity exchange markets each valuing more than RMB 100 million by region.

Concentration ratios of the commodity exchange markets in the six major regions

Economic development was extremely unbalanced in the six major regions. Development of the commodity exchange markets in each of the six major regions also showed different characteristics and development trends. Next, we'll measure the concentration ratio of markets in each of the six major regions. Limited by data available, we could only get related data in 2004, 2006 and 2007. Considering that too many occasional factors would make it difficult to show the changing trends, we will simply compare the absolute values of the indicators of concentration ratios instead of analyzing their changing trends. Specific indicators were as shown in Table 5.4 and Fig. 5.12.

Table 5.4. Concentration ratios of the commodity exchange markets each valuing more than RMB 100 million in the six major regions in China during 2001–2007 (%)

Region		2004	2006	2007
Northeast China	CR_4	29.84	31.26	28.29
	CR_8	41.04	44.76	41.93
North China	CR_4	19.97	22.91	35.43
	CR_8	28.86	31.41	53.62
East China	CR_4	8.59	8.98	8.74
	CR_8	14.54	13.83	13.59
South Central China	CR_4	13.61	11.79	11.48
	CR_8	19.59	19.07	18.95
Southwest China	CR_4	20.86	13.12	18.68
	CR_8	31.32	23.67	30.67
Northwest China	CR_4	27.19	20.48	25.43
	CR_8	42.33	33.38	38.19

Fig. 5.12. Concentration ratios of the commodity exchange markets each valuing more than RMB 100 million in the 6 major regions in China during 2001–2007 (CR_4)

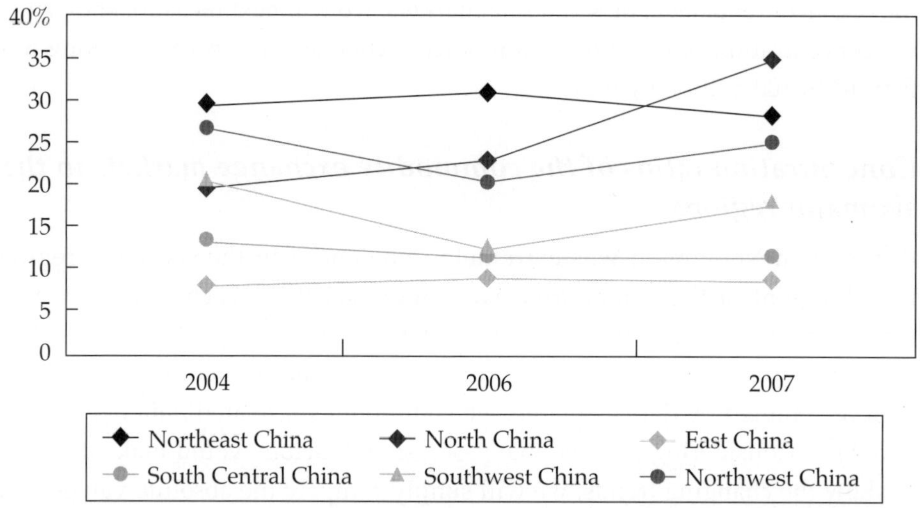

As can be seen from Fig. 5.13, CR_4 and CR_8 of the markets in each region were greatly consistent. Specifically, the concentration ratios of the markets in East China and South Central China were the lowest of all. In particular, the CR_4 of the markets in East China was basically somewhere between 8–9%, and the CR_8 of markets in East China was only slightly more than 10%. The CR_4 of markets in South Central China just exceeded 10%, and the CR_8 of markets in South Central China was less than 20%. Markets in Northeast China and Northwest China had the highest concentration ratios of all, the CR_4 of which exceeded 30% at the highest and the CR_8 of which reached 44.76% at the highest. North China and Southwest China ranked in between in terms of the concentration ratio of local markets. The levels of concentration ratios of wholesale markets in each and all regions were clearly associated with the development levels of local commerce. In terms of the above geographical scopes and administrative divisions, we can see that East China and South Central China were the two regions with the most developed commerce in China. In particular, in Shanghai and Guangdong, the market economy was fully developed, so was local commodity circulation, local market competitions were fierce, and the concentration ratio of local markets was relatively low. While Northwest China and Southwest China were relatively backward, with low levels of market economy, insufficient competitions, and high concentration ratios. Northeast China, as the main old industrial base in China, was strong in traditional industries, yet the development of commerce and the wholesale trade was insufficient in Northeast China. Therefore, market competitions were not fierce, either, and the concentration ratio of local markets was also very high.

Fig. 5.13. Concentration ratios of the commodity exchange markets each valuing more than RMB 100 million in the six major regions in China during 2001–2007 (CR_8)

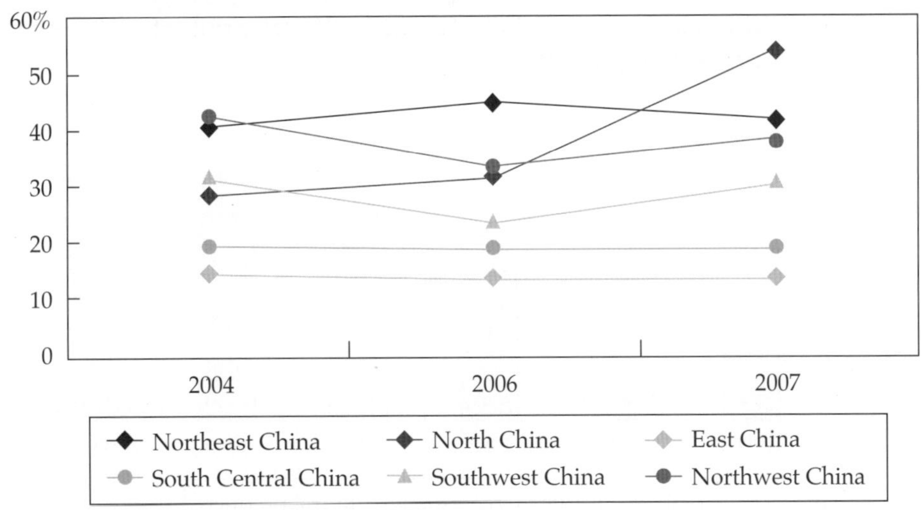

Of course, the concentration ratio of wholesale markets is not simply related to the degree of local commercial development. It also has something to do with such factors as geological location, policy supports from the local government and local traditions. Factors of this kind interact among one another before having complicated influences on the concentration ratio of wholesale markets.

Performance of wholesale markets

As can be seen from the above description and analysis, the overall scale of wholesale markets has kept enlarging all the way, and the concentration ratios of such markets have kept increasing, too. How is the performance of the wholesale markets? Will it be improved along with the extension of the scale of wholesale markets and the increase in the concentration ratio? Next, such indicators as the turnover per market, the turnover per stand, the turnover per unit of business area and the occupancy rate of market stands will be adopted in order to make a specific analysis.

The turnover per market

In view of the incompleteness and inconsistence of the statistical data, we could only analyze different indicators of market performance of some wholesale markets in some stages, from which we could still see the development characteristics and trends of the performance of wholesale markets in China since the reform and opening up.

Fig. 5.14. Overview of the development of the turnover per market of the wholesale markets for agricultural products (1986–1991) (RMB 10 thousand)

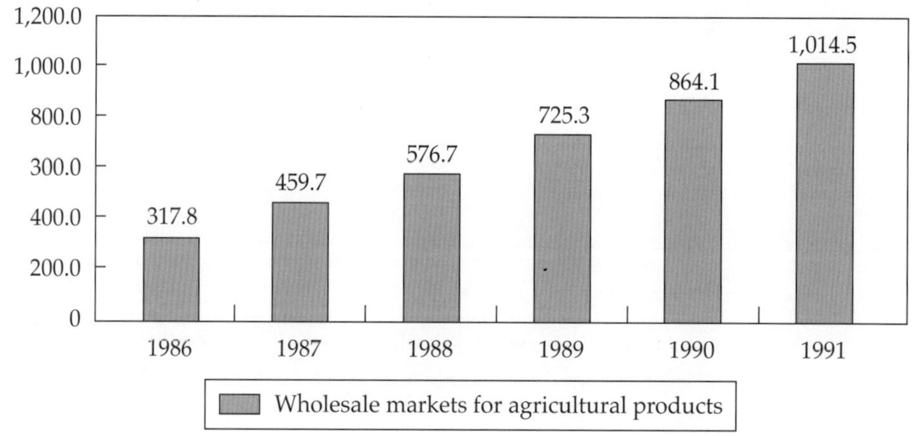

First of all, the performance of the wholesale markets for agricultural products during 1986–1991 will be analyzed with the turnover per market over the same period. See Fig. 5.14 for specific information.

From Fig. 5.14, we can see that the turnover per market of the wholesale markets for agricultural products kept increasing during 1986–1991, up nearly 220% from RMB 3,178 thousand in 1986 to 10,145 thousand in 1991. As can be seen, the market performance was constantly improved. As already mentioned, the launch of the reform of the commodity circulation system in China, along with the gradual reduction of commodity varieties under government planning and administration, the substitution of centralized purchase and contracted marketing of industrial products and the unified and fixed state purchase of agricultural products by the sale on credit which was in line with market rules, the lift of restrictions of fixed purchase and sale relations, the permission of free trade among market entities, the gradually strengthened role of the market mechanism for pricing in wholesale activities, and the opening up of the wholesale trade to the non-state-owned economic sector, the emerging wholesale markets capable of free production and marketing replaced the traditional closed wholesale network composed of state-owned and cooperative commerce before becoming the main distribution channel and being widely recognized by the society. Such reform resulted in the rapid growth of the product varieties, the number and amount of the wholesale markets for agricultural products, the constantly increased turnover per market and the great improvement of the market performance. In particular in 1988, the Chinese Government proposed to launch the Shopping Basket project, requiring local governments to strengthen the construction of wholesale markets for agricultural products. The size of single wholesale markets kept enlarging and market performance got further improved. As may also be found from Fig. 5.14, after 1988, the turnover per market of the wholesale markets for agricultural products exceeded RMB 5 million before keeping increasing to break through RMB 10 million in 1991.

With the development of the market economy in China since 1992, the collection of statistics on the markets in China has also been constantly improved. *China Market Statistical Yearbook* over this period collected relatively comprehensive statistics over the wholesale markets. Specific market performance was as shown in Fig. 5.15.

Fig. 5.15. Overview of the development of the turnover per market of the wholesale markets for consumables (1992–2001) (RMB 10 thousand)

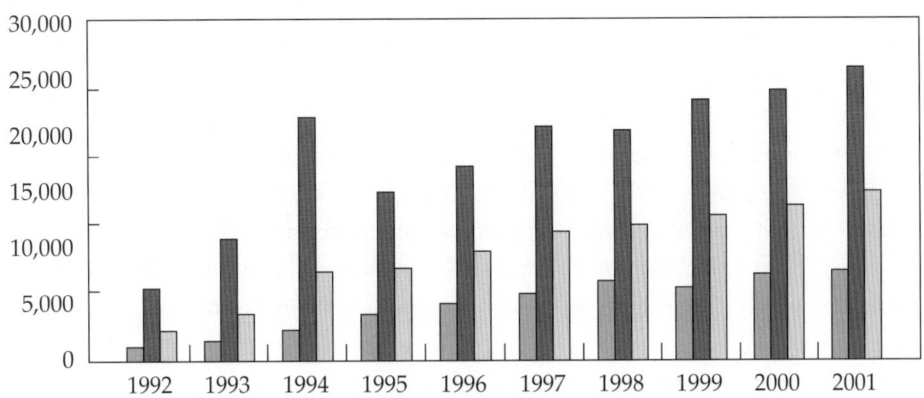

	1992	1993	1994	1995	1996	1997	1998	1999	2000	2001
Agricultural products	1,203.3	1,669.0	2,760.4	4,044.4	4,958.4	5,778.6	6,762.4	6,390.0	7,394.3	7,867.4
Industrial products	6,356.6	10,586.2	21,227.1	14,638.2	17,156.4	20,591.5	20,294.2	23,053.1	23,768.4	25,813.4
Consumables	2,396.8	4,022.1	7,622.1	8,122.5	9,602.0	11,371.9	12,072.1	12,639.0	13,611.0	14,599.1

As can be seen, during 1992–2001, the average turnover per market of the wholesale markets for consumables, that of the wholesale markets for agricultural products and that of the wholesale markets for industrial consumables all kept growing. The average turnover per market of the wholesale markets for consumables on the whole increased from RMB 23,968 thousand in 1992 to 145,991 thousand RMB in 2001, up 509.1%; the average turnover per market of the wholesale markets for agricultural products on the whole increased from RMB 12,033 thousand in 1992 to 78,674 thousand in 2001, up 553.8%. Though the wholesale markets for industrial consumables showed great fluctuations in 1994, the overall trend of the turnover per market was also on the rise, increasing from RMB 63,566 thousand in 1992 to 258,134 thousand in 2001, up 306.1%. With the setting of the goals of the socialist market economic reform in 1992 and the convening of the Third Plenary Session of the 14th CPC National Congress in 1993, fostering the market system had become the core content of the reform of the market system in this period. Local wholesale markets had also achieved great development in the wave of the market economic reform. Local governments played an important role in pushing forward the development of wholesale markets. One of the most important reasons for the substantial increase in the turnover per market of the wholesale markets was industrial supports. Development of the wholesale markets brought about highly competitive industrial clusters while the development of industrial clusters also became a solid industrial support for the development of wholesale markets. As local governments were more and more aware of the strong industrial competitiveness generated by such industrial clusters, they began to consciously push each and all trade markets in towns and townships forward to being specialized, contributing to the momentum of joint development of wholesale markets and specialized trade markets in towns and townships. Specialty wholesale markets were viewed as the accelerator of industrial clusters, which were capable of constantly digesting the productivity of such industrial clusters. Promoted by industrial clusters, the wholesale markets achieved great development, became increasingly influential, and saw a substantial increase in the average turnover per market. In 1997, the average turnover per market of the wholesale markets for consumables exceeded RMB 100 million; that of the wholesale markets for industrial consumables exceeded RMB 200 million; and that of the wholesale markets for agricultural products exceeded RMB 50 million. Though the wholesale markets were once overheating during the period, the overall market performance wasn't hence affected, but was constantly improved thanks to the timely adjustment and regulation of the Chinese Government.

Entering the 21st century, especially after its accession to the WTO, a large group of wholesale markets each valuing RMB 100 million has emerged in China. Next, the performances of such markets will be analyzed in detail with such indictors as the turnover per market, the turnover per stand, the turnover per unit of business area and the occupancy rate of market stands.

First, let's see the turnover per market of the wholesale markets each valuing more than RMB 100 million, as shown in Fig. 5.16.

Fig. 5.16. Overview of the development of the turnover per market of the wholesale markets each valuing more than 100 million RMB (2002–2007) (RMB 10 thousand)

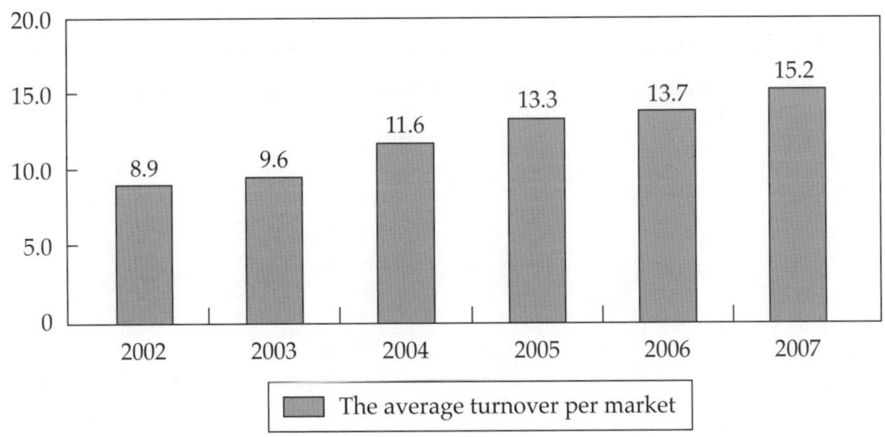

As can be seen from Fig. 5.16, the turnover per market of the wholesale markets each valuing more than RMB 100 million showed a significant growing trend, increasing from RMB 890 million in 2002 to 1,520 million in 2007, up 70.8%. The substantial increase in the turnover per market of the wholesale markets each valuing more than RMB 100 million indicated not only the extension of the overall scale of the wholesale markets, more importantly, it indicated the high rate of utilization of each and the great improvement of the market performance.

The turnover per stand

Statistical indicators of the wholesale markets each valuing more than RMB 100 million was detailed. So a more detailed observation of the market performance over such markets could be made based on the turnover per stand and the turnover per unit of business area. See Fig. 5.17 for details.

As can be seen from Fig. 5.17, during 2002–2007, the turnover per stand of the commodity exchange markets each valuing more than RMB 100 million, like the turnover per market of the same markets, showed a significant growing trend, increasing from RMB 1,251 thousand in 2002 to 2,142 thousand in 2007, up 71.2%. It was obvious that each stand in the market was more and more utilized and the market performance was increasingly better. In particular, the turnover per stand in 2007 exceeded RMB 2,142 thousand, being far higher than the turnover of the wholesale markets as a whole. The turnover of the wholesale markets for agricultural products during the 1980s and in the early 1890s was no higher than this figure. The substantial increase in the turnover per stand of the wholesale markets also showed the improvement of the efficacy and the performance of the wholesale markets.

Fig. 5.17. Overall development of the turnover per stand of the wholesale markets each valuing more than RMB 100 million (2002–2007)

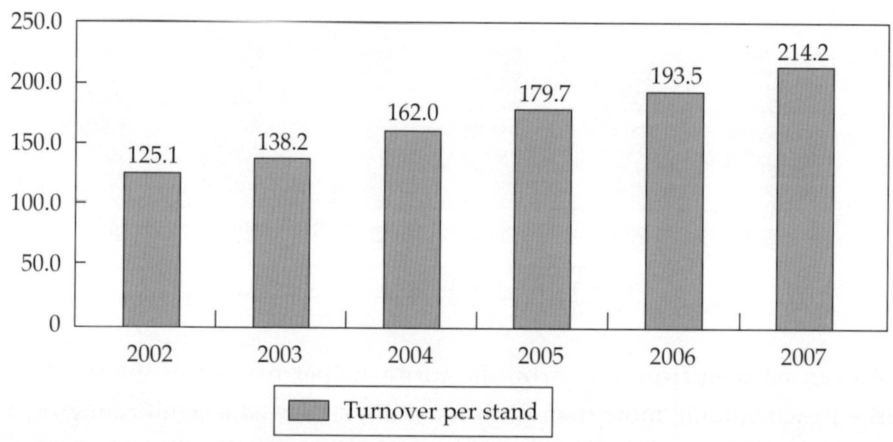

The turnover per unit of business area

As can be seen from Fig. 5.18, the turnover per unit of business area of the wholesale markets each valuing more than 100 million RMB grew stably from 2002–2005 and increased from 22 thousand RMB/m^2 to 27 thousand RMB/m^2, being five thousand RMB more per square meter. Market performance was greatly improved. Of which, the growth during 2004–2005 was the greatest of all, being three thousand RMB per square meter. Though the same turnover declined in 2006, it rose back in 2007 before recovering to the level of it in 2004. So if observed through the turnover per unit of business area, the performance of the wholesale markets was found to be improved first before declining. From the development of the overall scale of the wholesale markets each valuing more than 100 million RMB, it can be seen that the total business area of the wholesale markets had been expanding since 2002. In particular, it expanded by 55.8%, yet the turnover grew only by 20.9% in 2006 over that in 2005. That is to say, the increase in the business area hadn't contributed to the scale of wholesale markets or the improvement of the market performance. It shows that it may not be better with larger business area. The key lies in the turnover per unit of business area, the indicator of market performance.

Fig. 5.18. Overall development of the turnover per unit of business area of the wholesale markets each valuing more than 100 million RMB (2002–2007)

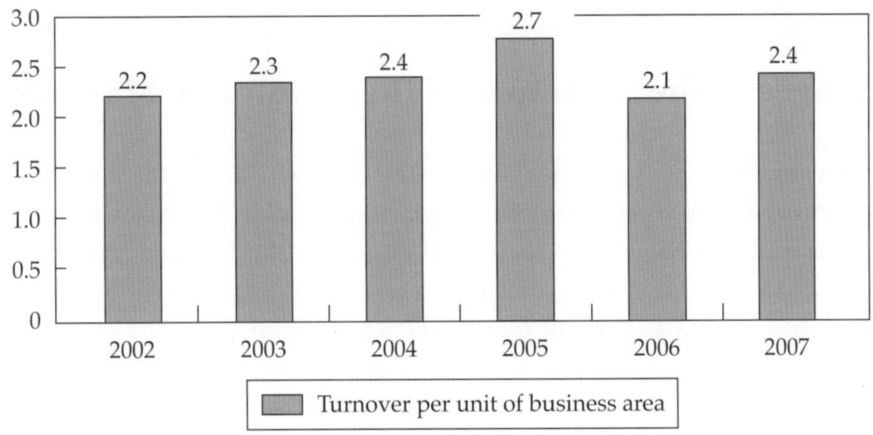

The occupancy rate of market stands

Fig. 5.19 is a detailed description of the occupancy rate of the stands of the wholesale markets each valuing more than 100 million RMB.[3]

Fig. 5.19. Occupancy rate of the stands in the wholesale markets each valuing more than 100 million RMB (2002–2007)

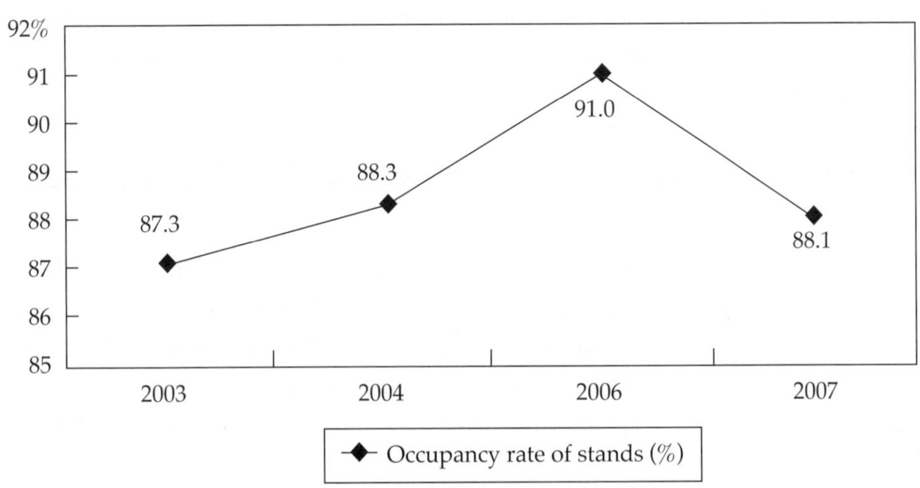

As can be seen from Fig. 5.19, the occupancy rate of the stands in the wholesale markets each valuing more than 100 million RMB was nearly 90%. It had been on the rise, growing from 87.3% in 2003 to 91.0% in 2006. The growth margin was 4% from 2003–2006. After climbing to the peak in 2006, it fell to the level similar to that in the previous several years in 2007. Though data were by no means abundant, they could still reflect the high utilization rate of stands in the wholesale markets each valuing more than 100 million RMB, which played a very important role of prerequisite in the expansion of the scale of turnover of the wholesale markets and the improvement of the above indicators of performance.

Changes in the Structure of the Wholesale Markets

The overall development of the wholesale markets in China in the three decades of reform and opening up has been described in detail in the first section of this chapter. In this section, the urban-rural structure, the regional structure and the structure of market categories of the wholesale markets will be described and analyzed so as to present the overall situation of the wholesale markets in China.

Urban-rural structure of the wholesale markets

Due to the particularity of the dual-layered economic development in urban and rural areas in China, the levels of economic development, the incomes and the levels of consumption of urban and rural residents are quite different, which can also be seen in the development history of the wholesale markets in China. Next, the development of the wholesale markets in urban and rural areas in China in the 3 decades of reform and opening up, and the characteristics of the urban-rural structure of the wholesale markets will be described, with specific data.

Structure of the numbers of wholesale markets in urban and rural areas

China launched the reform and opening up policy in 1978, since when its economy entered the transitional period. With the implementation of a series of reforms such as the implementation of the rural household contract responsibility system, productivity in China achieved a great development and the commodity rate of agricultural products was greatly improved. Industrial products produced by some township enterprises and individual households with specialized lines of work also increased constantly. To better satisfy the demand for the circulation of such products, wholesale markets came into being inside trade markets before developing rapidly. No statistical data were collected on the wholesale markets during 1978–1991. Yet wholesale markets have a natural inseparable relationship with trade markets. Therefore, related data on the trade markets in urban and rural areas will be adopted here to make an explanation. See Fig. 5.20 for details.

Fig. 5.20. Overall development of the trade markets in urban and rural areas (1978–1991)

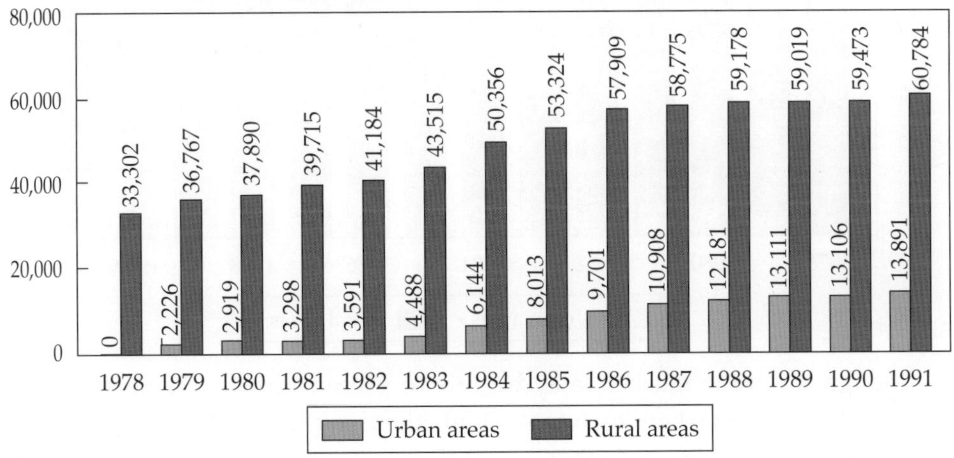

As can be seen from Fig. 5.20, the trade markets in both urban and rural areas kept growing in number. Trade markets in the rural areas grew from 33,302 in 1978 to 60,784 in 1991, up 82.5%; while trade markets in the urban areas began to develop in 1979, being only 2,226 at the beginning, yet increased to 13,891 in 1991, up 524%. However, trade markets in the rural areas far outnumbered those in the urban areas. When the number of trade markets in the urban areas was still zero in 1978, the number of trade markets in the rural areas had been developed to 33,302. In 1991, the number of rural trade markets was over 4 times larger than the number of urban trade markets. To better reflect the gap of urban and rural areas in terms of the number of trade markets, we now provide a figure of proportions. See Fig. 5.21 for details.

As can be seen from Fig. 5.21, there were two distinct features. Firstly, proportions of the numbers of trade markets in urban and rural areas were significantly different. Trade markets in the rural areas accounted for over 80% of all. Of which, the proportion had been over 90% prior to 1983. However, the proportion of the trade markets in the urban areas had been lower than 20%, and it hadn't exceeded 10% until 1984. Secondly, trade markets in urban and rural areas showed quite the opposite development trends. The proportion of trade markets in the urban areas kept growing from 0 in 1978 to 10.9% in 1984, then 18.6% in 1991; while the proportion of trade markets in the rural areas kept declining, falling from 100% in 1978 to 90.7% in 1983, later to 81.4% in 1991.

Fig. 5.21. Structure of the numbers of trade markets in urban and rural areas (1978–1991)

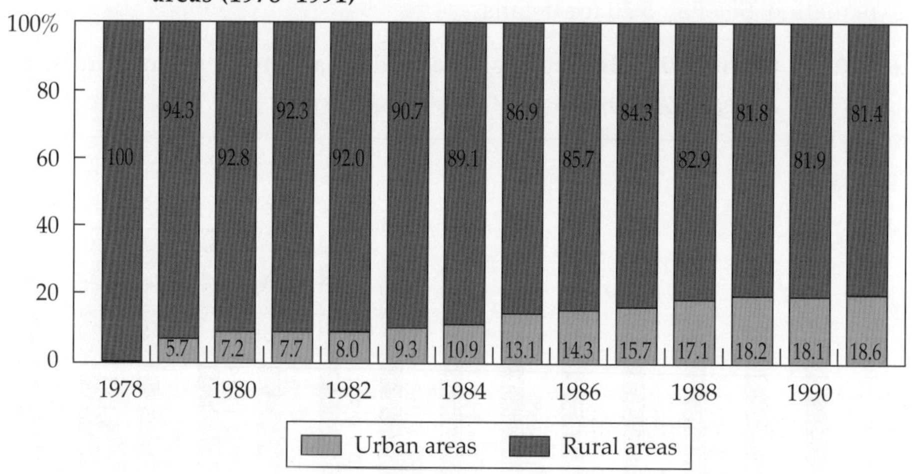

Though the trade markets may be able to present the development trend of the wholesale markets to some extent, they couldn't fully represent the wholesale markets. Since 1992, *China Market Statistical Yearbook* has been collecting detailed detail on the development of the wholesale markets. Next, let's see the structure of the numbers of the wholesale markets in urban and rural areas during 1992–2001.

Fig. 5.22 reflects the detailed development of the wholesale markets for consumables in urban and rural areas in China during 1992–2001. Such markets were growing in number in both urban and rural areas over this period. The number of wholesale markets in the rural areas grew from 1,323 in 1992 to 3,207 in 2001, being nearly 1.5 times larger; the number of wholesale markets in the urban areas grew from 1,095 in 1992 to 4,427 in 2001, being three times larger. It can be seen that wholesale markets in the urban areas grew more rapidly in terms of number, and surpassed those in the rural areas in 1996. To better reflect the specific proportions of the numbers of wholesale markets in urban and rural areas, let's see Fig. 5.23.

From Fig. 5.23, it can be seen the respective proportion of the numbers of wholesale markets in urban and rural areas and their respective development trend. Wholesale markets in urban and rural areas accounted for more or less the same proportion, being half-half on the average. The numbers were more or less the same. However, the development trends of wholesale markets in urban and rural areas were quite the opposite. The proportion of the number of wholesale markets in the urban areas kept increasing and grew from 45.3% in 1992 to 59.9% in 2001 which was more than half. On the contrary, the proportion of the number of wholesale markets in the rural areas fell from 54.7% in 1992 to 43.4% in 2001.

Fig. 5.22. Overall development of the numbers of wholesale markets for consumables in urban and rural areas (1992–2001)

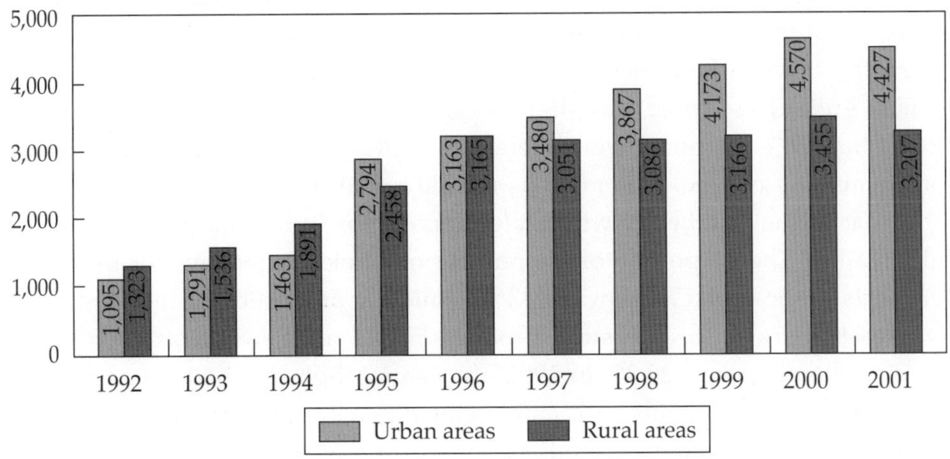

Fig. 5.23. Structure of the numbers of wholesale markets for consumables in urban and rural areas (1992–2001)

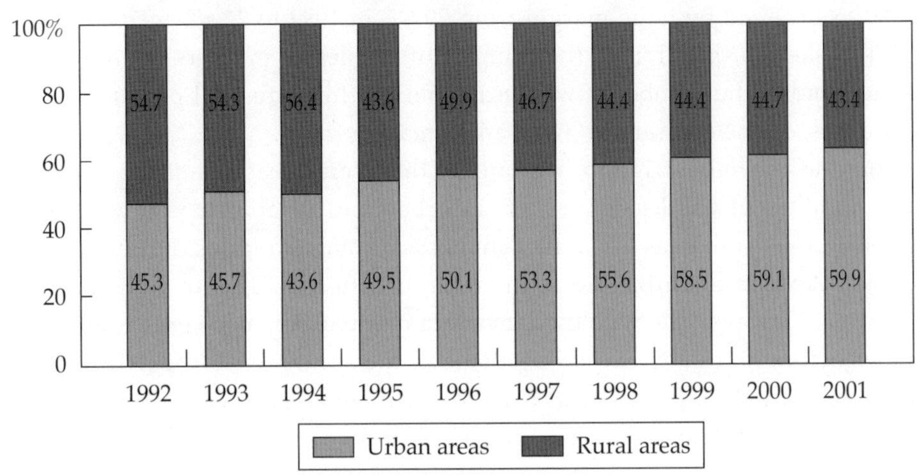

The wholesale markets for consumables include the wholesale markets for industrial consumables and the wholesale markets for agricultural consumables. The development of the above two categories of wholesale market showed different trends and characteristics in urban and rural areas. To better analyze the structure of the numbers of wholesale markets in urban and rural areas, the structure of the numbers of the above two categories of wholesale markets in urban and rural areas will be analyzed next.

Fig. 5.24 and Fig. 5.25 reflect, respectively, the urban-rural structure of the number of wholesale markets for agricultural products and that of the number of wholesale markets for industrial consumables. Seen from the absolute values of the proportions, the proportion of the number of wholesale markets for agricultural products in the rural areas was lower than that of the number of wholesale markets for agricultural products in the urban areas, yet the different wasn't great. The former was slightly higher than 50% and the latter slightly lower than 50%. Comparatively, there was a great gap between the proportion of the number of wholesale markets for industrial products in the rural areas and that of the number of wholesale markets for industrial products in the urban areas. The proportion of the number of wholesale markets for industrial products in the urban areas was 60.4%, while the proportion of the number of wholesale markets for industrial products in the rural areas was only 39.5%, making the difference 20.9% in 1992; the same proportion had become 77.4% and 22.6%, respectively till 2001, making the difference enlarged to 54.8%.

Seen from the changing trend, the proportion of the number of wholesale markets for agricultural products and that of the number of wholesale markets for industrial products in the rural areas were both declining, yet the former fell by small margin from 59.3% in 1992 to 55.3% in 2001, down simply 4%. The latter declined by large margin from 39.6% in 1992 to 22.6% in 2001, down 17%. The same proportion of the number of wholesale markets for industrial products and of the number of wholesale markets for industrial products in the urban areas, on the contrary, showed an increasing trend.

From the above description, we can get the overall features of the structure of the numbers of wholesale markets in urban and rural areas: the wholesale markets in the rural areas had a first-mover advantage in terms of number, and exceeded those in the urban areas in terms of both the absolute value and the proportion. However, the wholesale markets in the urban areas grew quickly in number before gradually exceeding those in the rural areas. In particular, the wholesale markets for industrial consumables developed faster in the urban areas, being far greater than those in the rural areas in terms of number. The difference between the proportions of the wholesale markets for agricultural products in urban and rural areas was not significant.

Fig. 5.24. Structure of the numbers of wholesale markets for agricultural products in urban and rural areas (1992–2001)

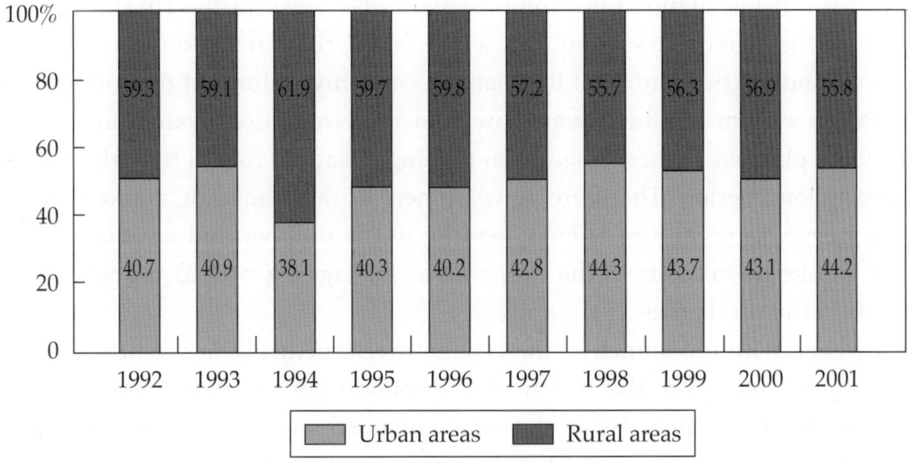

Fig. 5.25. Structure of the numbers of wholesale markets for industrial consumables in urban and rural areas (1992–2001)

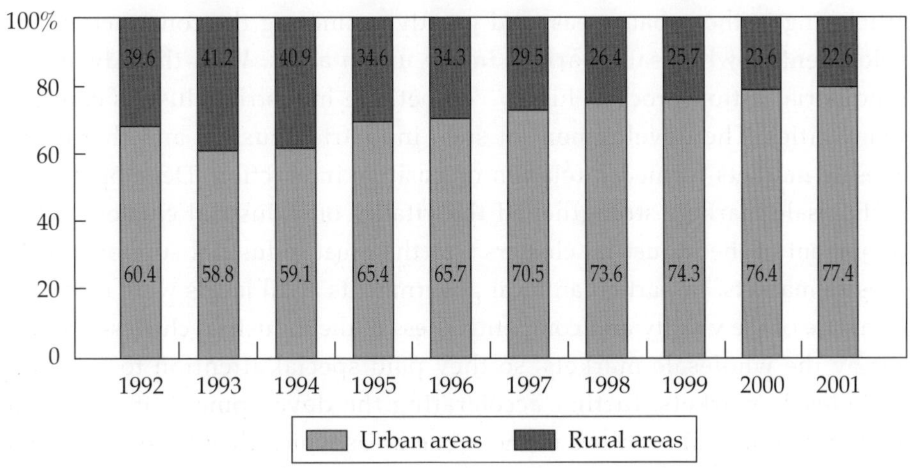

Specifically, the first-mover advantage of the wholesale markets in the rural areas was determined by the basic national conditions, the economic system and policies of China. Most Chinese people live in the rural areas, and the purchasing power parity of China also lies in the rural areas. In particular, rural areas are the largest place of origin and the most direct market of agricultural and sideline products and like products. It is safe to say that rural areas meet many requirements such as having favorable climates, favorable geographical positions and rural residents' supports. Reform of the economic system in China was initiated in the rural areas, which greatly liberalized the productivity in the rural areas and promoted the rural economy to develop rapidly. Moreover, the control of the planned economic system was weak in the rural areas, so reform of the economic system proceeded fast. Urban areas, on the contrary, were put under strict control of the planned economy. Reform of the commodity circulation system in China was slow, and the circulation system under the traditional planned economy had been playing a leading role in the urban areas in a fairly long period. Therefore, development of the wholesale markets in the urban areas was greatly restricted, leading to the number and growing speed of the wholesale markets in the urban areas far lagging behind the wholesale markets in the rural areas.

However, with the launch of the economic restructuring in the urban areas, especially the launch of the reform of the commodity circulation system after 1984, the circulation industry in the urban areas achieved a great development, witnessing the circulation entities becoming gradually diversified and the markets becoming more and more active. In 1992, China set up the goals of the reform of the socialist economic system, contributing to the substantial development of the market economy and the acceleration of the economic restructuring in the urban areas, and greatly promoting the construction and development of wholesale markets in the urban areas. With the advance of the industrialization process, highly competitive industrial clusters emerged in many cities. The development of such industrial clusters and that of the wholesale markets formed a relation of positive interaction. Development of the wholesale markets strengthened the vitality of industrial clusters, while development of the industrial clusters was the great industrial support for the wholesale markets. In particular, local governments at all levels were more and more aware of the vitality and competitiveness of the industrial clusters brought about by the wholesale markets, so they paid special attention to fostering the wholesale markets, further accelerating the development of wholesale markets for industrial products in the urban areas which then far exceeded the development of wholesale markets in the rural areas. From the demand point of view, the level of economic development in the urban areas was far higher than that in the rural areas, so were the income and level of consumption of urban residents, which stimulated the growth of urban demands. Such demands played a significant role in pulling and guiding the supply. Under the interaction of the two, the proportion of wholesale markets in the urban areas in China was improved. In particular, the gap between the wholesale markets for industrial products in the urban areas and those in the rural areas became greater and greater. As for the wholesale markets for agricultural products, they were great in number since rural areas are the largest place of origin and the most direct place of sales of agricultural and sideline products, and the proportion of such wholesale markets was half-half in urban and rural areas.

Structure of the turnover of the wholesale markets in urban and rural areas

Details on the turnover of the wholesale markets in urban and rural areas are shown in Fig. 5.26 and Fig. 5.27.

Fig. 5.26. Overall development of the turnover of trade markets in urban and rural areas (1978–1991)

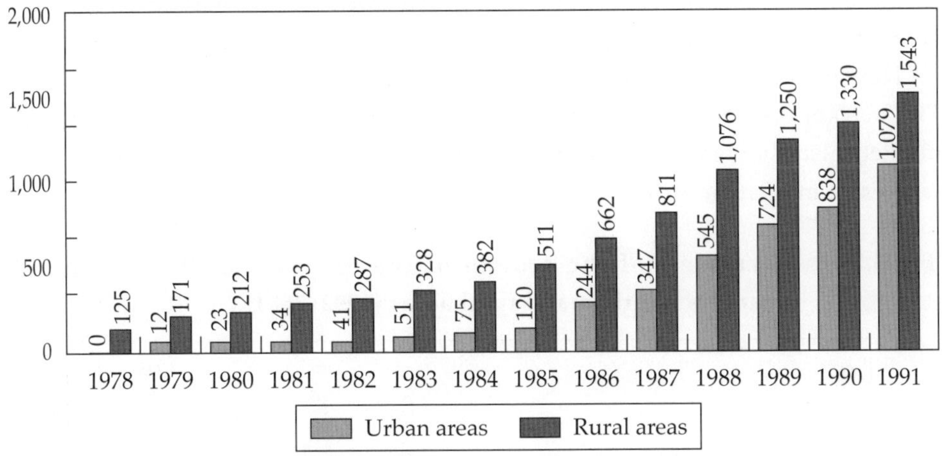

Fig. 5.27. Structure of the turnover of trade markets in urban and rural areas (1978–1991)

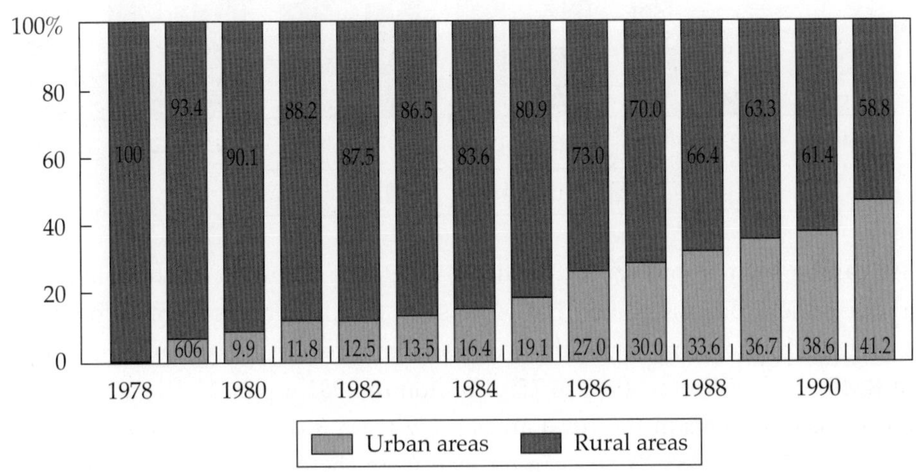

As can be seen, the turnover of the trade markets in the urban areas and that of the trade markets in the rural areas were both on the rise. The turnover of the trade markets in the urban areas reached RMB 107.9 billion in 1991, being nearly 100 times greater than RMB 1.2 billion in 1979; that of the trade markets in the rural areas also increased from RMB 17.5 billion in 1978 to 154.3 billion in 1991, being nearly 10 times greater. Seen from the development trend, the turnover of trade markets in the urban areas grew faster and its proportion became greater and greater, too, growing from less than 10% in 1980 to nearly 41.2% in 1991. The turnover of trade markets in the rural areas, on the contrary, accounted for an increasingly smaller proportion, from 100% in 1978 to 58.8% in 1991. Such development trend was constantly narrowing down the difference between the absolute values of the proportions of the turnover of trade markets in the rural areas and that of trade markets in the urban areas.

The socialist market economic structure failed to take shape until 1992. The market economy then achieved greater development and the wholesale markets also showed a significant growing trend. Details on the development of wholesale markets in urban and rural areas were as shown in Fig. 5.28.

Fig. 5.28. Overview of the growth of the turnover of the wholesale markets in urban and rural areas (1992–2001)

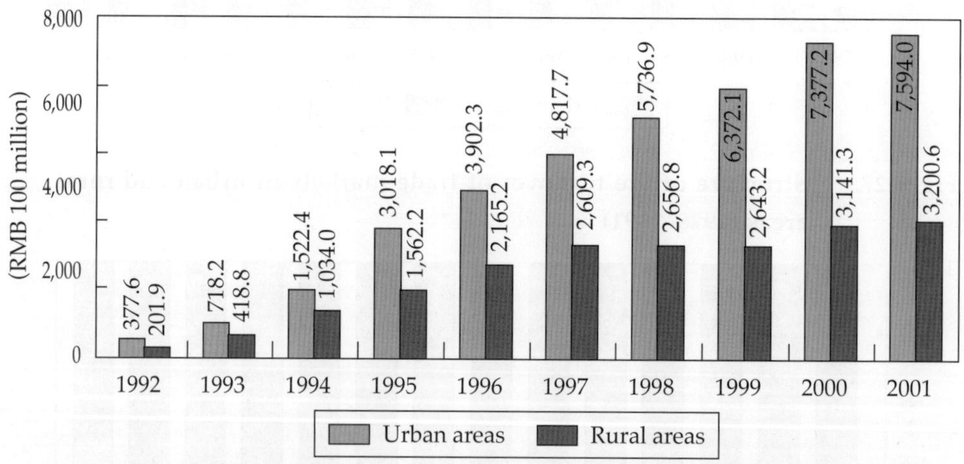

As can be seen from Fig. 5.28 and Fig. 5.29, the turnover of the wholesale markets in the urban areas and that of those in the rural areas were both on the rise. Of which, the turnover of the wholesale markets in the urban areas grew from RMB 37.76 billion in 1992 to 759.4 billion in 2001, up 1,911.1%; and that of the wholesale markets in the rural areas grew from RMB 20.19 billion to 320.06 billion in 2001, up 1,485.2%. As can be seen from the figure of proportions, the proportion of the turnover of the wholesale markets in the urban areas was far higher than that of the turnover of the wholesale markets in the rural areas, and it was on the rise. On the contrary, the turnover of the wholesale markets in the rural areas showed an opposite growth trend, the proportion of which was far lower than that of the turnover of the wholesale markets in the urban areas. The difference between the above two expanded from 30.4% in 1992 to 40.6% in 2001. Next, let's see the proportions of the turnover of various types of wholesale markets in urban and rural areas.

Fig. 5.29. Composition of the turnover of the wholesale markets in urban and rural areas (1992–2001)

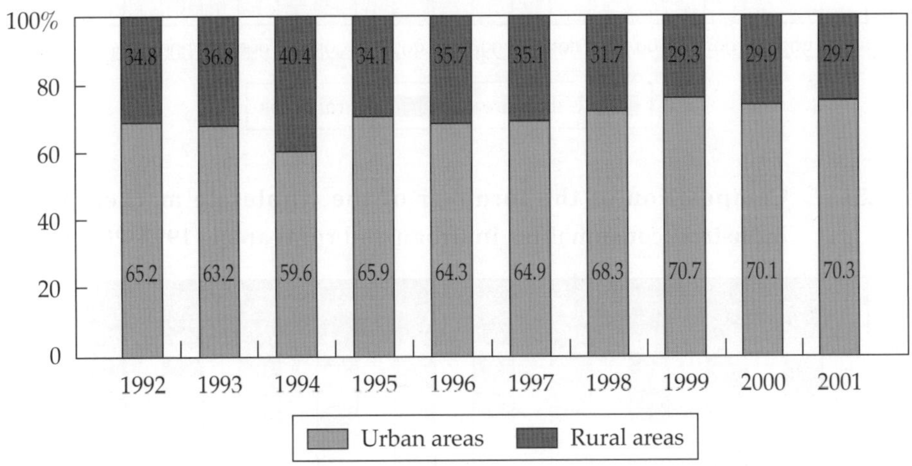

As can be seen from Fig. 5.30 and Fig. 5.31, the urban-rural structure of the turnover of the wholesale markets for industrial consumables was more or less the same as that of the turnover of the wholesale markets for agricultural products. The respective turnover of the above two categories of wholesale markets in the urban areas was about 65%, which was maintained at about 68% after 1998. The respective turnover of the above two categories of wholesale markets in the rural areas was about 35%, which was then maintained at about 32% after 1998. The urban-rural structure of the turnover of the above two categories of wholesale markets was basically the same as the urban-rural structure of the turnover of the wholesale markets as a whole.

A conclusion can be drawn from the above tables, figures and descriptions that the urban-rural structure of the turnover of the wholesale markets was similar to that of the urban-rural structure of the number of the wholesale markets on the whole. In the early days of the reform and opening up, the wholesale markets in the rural areas had this first-mover advantage and

Fig. 5.30. **Composition of the turnover of the wholesale markets for agricultural products in urban and rural areas (1992–2001)**

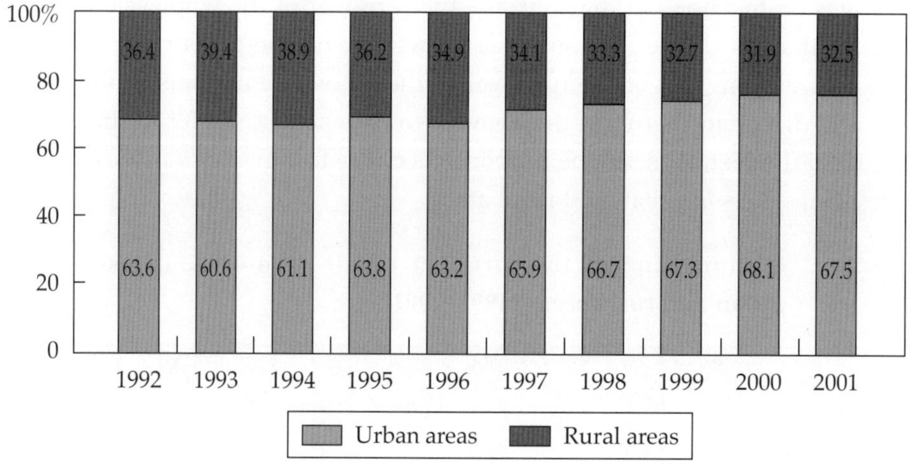

Fig. 5.31. **Composition of the turnover of the wholesale markets for industrial consumables in urban and rural areas (1992–2001)**

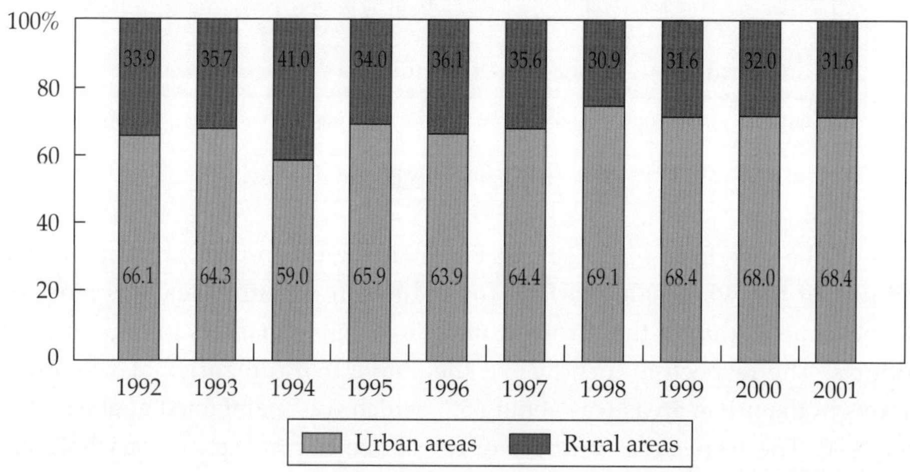

far exceeded those in the urban areas in terms of the absolute value and the proportion. However, the turnover of the wholesale markets in the urban areas grew very fast before gradually exceeding that of the wholesale markets in the rural areas. Difference between the two became greater and greater. It was the case for the wholesale markets for agricultural products and those for industrial products: the difference of the wholesale markets in urban and rural areas in terms of turnover was far greater than the difference of the two in terms of number. We may analyze the last point from the following several aspects: from the angle of supply, the wholesale markets in the urban areas had a certain industrial foundation as their backup. In particular, most wholesale markets supported by industrial clusters were large; from the angle of demand, the levels of income and consumption of urban residents were relatively high, and the market demands were large, stimulating the expansion of the market scale; lastly, developed infrastructure for transportation in the urban areas, guidance and supports of the government with policies, etc. would all contribute to the expansion of the scale of the wholesale markets.

Structure of the wholesale markets each valuing more than RMB 100 million in big, small and medium-sized cities

China mainly collected statistics on the wholesale markets each valuing more than RMB 100 million since 2002, collecting statistics on the development of the wholesale markets in big, small and medium-sized cities, yet failing to classify the urban and rural structures of the wholesale markets. Next, statistical indicators of the wholesale markets each valuing more than RMB 100 million in big, small and medium-sized cities are chosen as the objects of the analysis in order to reflect the development of the wholesale markets in recent years in cities of different sizes.

Fig. 5.32. Overall development of the numbers of the wholesale markets each valuing more than RMB 100 million in big, small and medium-sized cities (2002–2007)

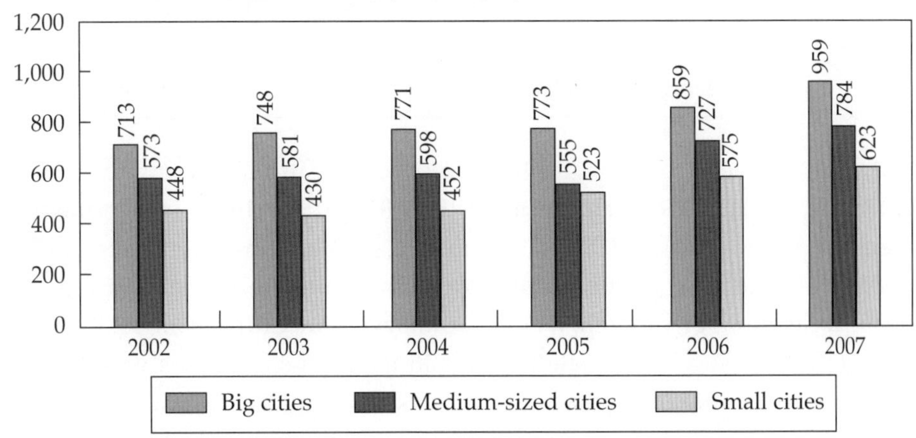

Structure of the numbers of the wholesale markets in big, small and medium-sized cities

As can be seen from Fig. 5.32, in big cities, medium-sized cities or small cities, the numbers of the wholesale markets each valuing more than RMB 100 million all kept growing. Of which, the number of the wholesale markets each valuing more than RMB 100 million in big cities grew from 713 in 2002 to 959 in 2007, up

34.5%; that of such wholesale markets in medium-sized cities grew from 573 in 2002 to 784 in 2007, up 36.8%; and that of such wholesale markets in small cities grew from 448 in 2002 to 623 in 2007, up 39.1%. From the above description, it can be seen that commodity exchange markets each valuing more than RMB 100 million developed fast in China, and were born and developed in a wide range of environments. In big, small and medium-sized cities, such markets all achieved rapid development. Specific proportions of the numbers of the wholesale markets each valuing more than RMB 100 million in cities of different sized are shown below in Fig. 5.33.

Fig. 5.33. Structure of the numbers of the wholesale markets each valuing more than RMB 100 million in big cities, medium-sized cities and small cities (2002–2007)

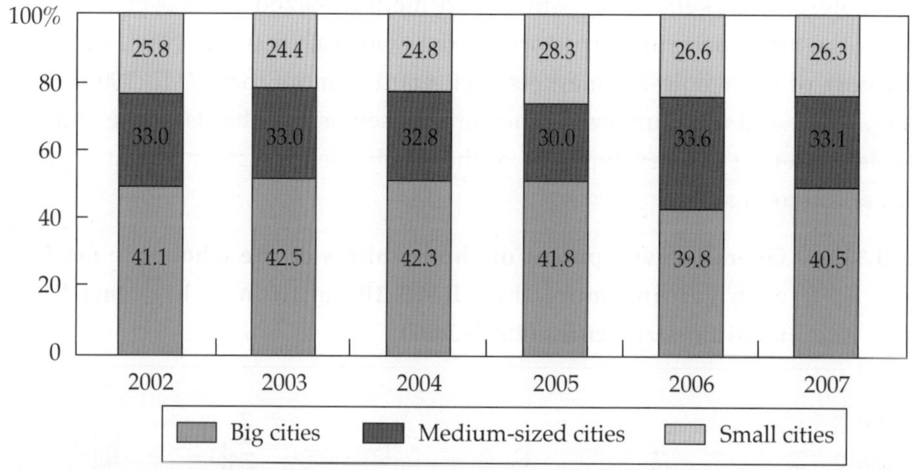

As can be seen from Fig. 5.33, the respective ratio of the numbers of the wholesale markets each valuing more than RMB 100 million in big, medium-sized and small cities to the total number of such wholesale markets in China was stable. The ratio of the number of such wholesale markets in big cities to the total number of such wholesale markets in China was 41.3% on the average; that of such wholesale markets in medium-sized cities was 32.6% on the average; and that of such wholesale markets in small cities was 26.1% on the average. Seen from their development trends, compared with that in 2003 and 2004, the ratio of the number of the wholesale markets each valuing more than RMB 100 million in big cities to the total number of such wholesale markets in China fell slightly in recent two years. The difference between the highest of it (being 42.5% in 2003) and the lowest of it (being 39.8% in 2006) reached 2.7%. The ratio of the number of the wholesale markets each valuing more than

RMB 100 million in medium-sized cities to the total number of such wholesale markets in China fell to 30% in 2005, but was maintained at about 30% in other years. The ratio of the number of the wholesale markets each valuing more than RMB 100 million in small cities to the total number of such wholesale markets in China was quite the opposite, reaching the highest level of 28.3% in 2005, yet being stabilized at slightly more than 26% in recent two years, which was about 2% higher than the 24% in 2003 and 2004.

Structure of the turnover of the wholesale markets in big, small and medium-sized cities

As can be seen from Fig. 5.34, as the same as the number of wholesale markets, during 2002–2007, the turnover of the wholesale markets each valuing more than RMB 100 million in big, small and mediums-sized cities kept growing, of which the turnover of such wholesale markets in big cities grew from RMB 713,721.84 million in 2002 to 1,765,717.41 million in 2007, up 147.4%; that of such wholesale markets in medium-sized cities grew from RMB 458,657.37 million in 2002 to 891,501.3 million in 2007, up 94.4%; and that of such wholesale markets in small cities grew from RMB 372,708.23 million in 2002 to 929,927.18 million in 2007, up 149.5%. The growth of the turnover of the wholesale markets each valuing more than RMB 100 million in small cities was the greatest of all. The same turnover even exceeded that of such wholesale markets in medium-sized cities in 2007. The proportions and changes in the respective turnover of such wholesale markets in big, small and mediums-sized cities can be seen more clearly from Fig. 5.35.

Fig. 5.34. Overall development of the respective turnover of the wholesale markets each valuing more than RMB 100 million in big, small and medium-sized cities (2002–2007) (RMB 10,000)

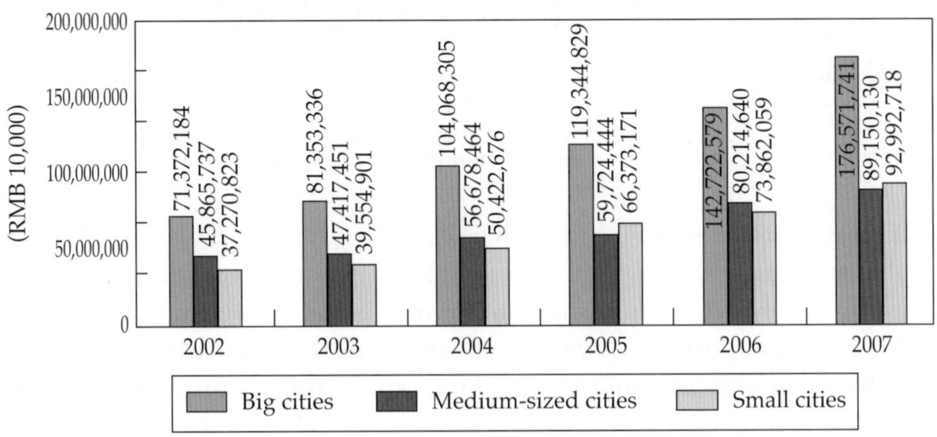

Seen from the average value over the past years, the turnover of the wholesale markets each valuing more than RMB 100 million in big cities accounted for 48.3% of the total turnover of such wholesale markets in China; the turnover of such wholesale markets in medium-sized cities accounted for 26.8% of the total turnover of such wholesale markets in China; and that of such wholesale markets in small cities accounted for 24.9% of the total turnover of such wholesale markets in China. The proportion of the turnover of the wholesale markets each valuing more than RMB 100 million was basically consistent with the scale of economic development of the city. Seen from the development trend, the proportion of the turnover of such wholesale markets in big cities grew on the whole, reaching 49.2% in 2007, being 3% higher than that in 2002 (being 46.2%); that of the turnover of such wholesale markets in medium-sized cities fell in general, being simply 24.9% in 2007 which was even lower than the proportion of the turnover of such wholesale markets in small cities (being 25.9%). The proportion of the turnover of such wholesale markets in small cities grew on the whole. In particular, in 2005 and 2007, it exceeded the proportion of the turnover of such wholesale markets in medium-sized cities.

Fig. 5.35. Structure of the respective turnover the wholesale markets each valuing more than RMB 100 million in big, small and medium-sized cities (2002–2007)

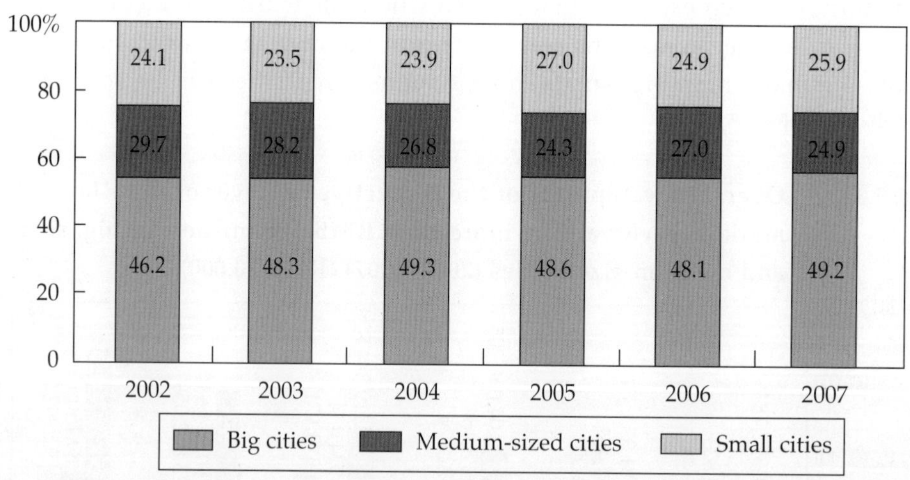

It is easy to understand the rapid development of the wholesale markets each valuing more than RMB 100 million in big and medium-sized cities. The larger the city is, the better the infrastructure for transportation and communications will be. The adoption of advanced technologies coupled with developed logistics greatly accelerated the modernization process of the circulation businesses and pushed forward the modernization, standardization and legalization of large-scale wholesale markets, enabling large wholesale markets with large scales of transactions and great influence to keep growing in terms of the number and turnover. If the rapid development of the wholesale markets each valuing more than RMB 100 million in big cities was consistent with the size of the city and the level of the city's economic development, why did such wholesale markets develop so fast in small cities, even at a speed higher than that of such wholesale markets in medium-sized cities? Specific reasons are as follows:

First of all, as has mentioned above, one of the most important reasons for the emergence of the wholesale markets was the emergence of a great number of township enterprises at the beginning of the reform and opening up. Products of such township enterprises were extruded by the institutional barriers set by the traditional sales channels of state-owned enterprises, so most of these township enterprises turned to the wholesale market, making the wholesale market the main channel of their commodity circulation. Many of the towns with well developed township enterprises at the time have developed into small cities today. Therefore, small cities had already occupied the advantages for development since the birth of the wholesale markets.

Secondly, the flourishing development of the wholesale markets in small cities had much to do with the levels of income and consumption of the residents' in small cities. The wholesale markets in themselves have the competitive advantage of being inexpensive due to the enormous numbers of transactions and low-end product quality, which rightly met the consumption level in small cities. Therefore, the wholesale markets enjoyed greater space for survival and development in small cities. In particular, some first-grade small commodities exchange market such as the wholesale market in Yiwu, Zhejiang Province all had great development potential.

Lastly, the types of commercial operations in small cities were neither complete nor developed. Since the reform and opening up, the development of the commodity circulation in China, especially that of modern retail organizations, failed to catch up with the industrialization process in China. In particular, in small cities, faced with the enormous commodities entering the field of circulation, warehouse stores and large-scale comprehensive supermarkets having the same functions as wholesale markets started late and developed slowly. Stagnation of the development of the types of commercial operation with similar structures of commodities enabled the wholesale markets to dominate in small cities, which provided opportunities and created favorable conditions for the development of wholesale markets in small cities.

Regional structure of the wholesale markets

Though China boasts a vast territory, its economic development is extremely unbalanced in different regions due to different natural environments, geological positions, policies and some historical factors, so is the development of the wholesale markets, especially large the wholesale markets each valuing more than RMB 100 million. To better reflect the development of the wholesale markets in China, we will next make a description and analysis of the regional development and structure of the wholesale markets each valuing more than RMB 100 million.

Fig. 5.36. Overview of the development of the numbers of the wholesale markets each valuing more than RMB 100 million in East China, Central China and West China (2002–2007)

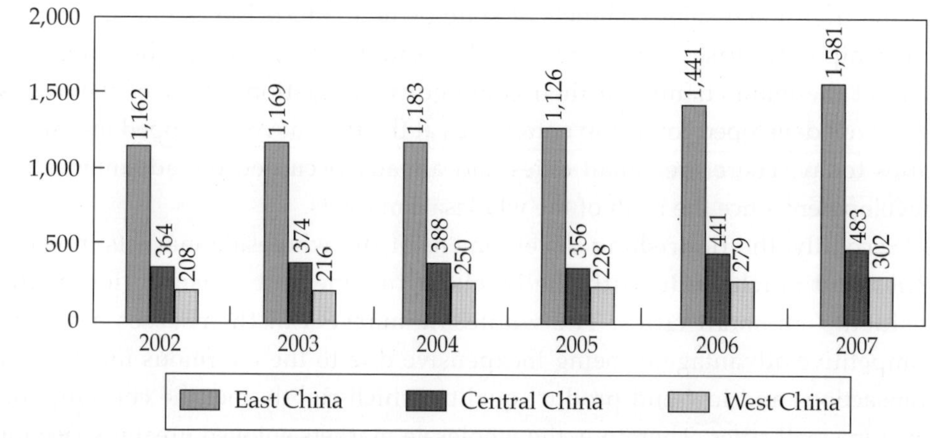

Fig. 5.37. Overview of the development of the numbers of stands in the wholesale markets each valuing more than RMB 100 million in East China, Central China and West China (2002–2007)

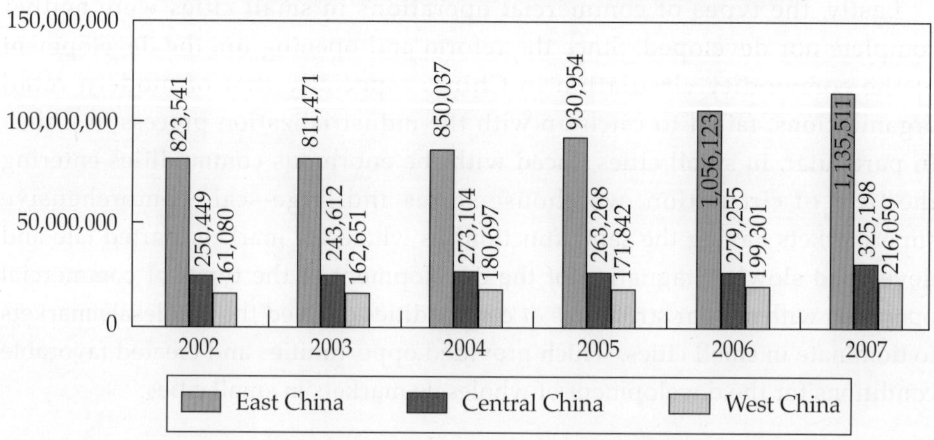

Regional structure of the wholesale markets

There are significant differences among East China, Central China and West China in politics, economy, culture and other aspects, leading to great differences in the development of wholesale markets in the above three regions. Next, the development of the wholesale markets each valuing more than RMB 100 million in each of the above three regions will be overviewed before a detailed analysis of the regional structure of such markets in East China, Central China and West China and the reasons for such regional structure.

Overview of the development of wholesale markets in East China, Central China and West China

The overall development of the wholesale markets each valuing more than RMB 100 million in East China, Central China and West China can be seen from the following indicators: the number of markets, the number of stands in the markets, business area and the market turnover.

As can be seen from Fig. 5.36, the numbers of the wholesale markets each valuing more than RMB 100 million all kept growing in East China, Central China and West China. Of which, the number of such wholesale markets in East China grew from 1,162 in 2002 to 1,581 in 2007, up 36.1%; that of such wholesale markets in Central China grew from 364 in 2002 to 483 in 2007, up 32.7%; that of such wholesale markets in West China grew from 208 to 302, up 45.2%. As can be seen, the margin of growth of the wholesale markets in West China was the greatest of all.

The numbers of market stands showed the same feature as the numbers of the wholesale markets each valuing more than RMB 100 million: numbers of market stands in the wholesale markets each valuing more than RMB 100 million in East China, Central China and West China all kept growing. During 2002–2007, the number of market stands in East China grew from 823,541 to 1,135,511, up 37.9%; that in Central China grew from 250,449 to 323,198, up 29.0%; and that in West China grew from 161,080 to 216,059, up 34.1%. Of the 3 regions, East China ranked the first in terms of the growth margin of market stands.

Business areas of each region were as follows:

As can be seen from Fig. 5.38, business area of the wholesale markets each valuing more than RMB 100 million in East China, Central China and West China kept increasing on the whole during 2002–2007. Of which, the business area of the wholesale markets each valuing more than RMB 100 million in East China grew by 93.6%; that of such wholesale markets in Central China grew by

112.9%; and that of such wholesale markets in West China grew by 298.7%. The growth margin of the business area of the wholesale markets each valuing more than RMB 100 million in West China was the greatest of all.

Fig. 5.38. Overview of the growth of the respective business area of the wholesale markets each valuing more than RMB 100 million in East China, Central China and West China (2002–2007)

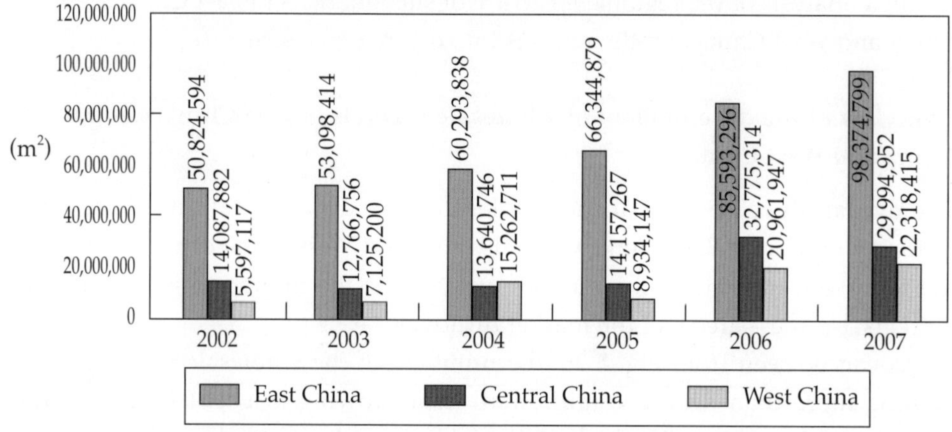

Fig. 5.39. Overview of the respective turnover of the wholesale markets each valuing more than RMB 100 million in East China, Central China and West China (2002–2007)

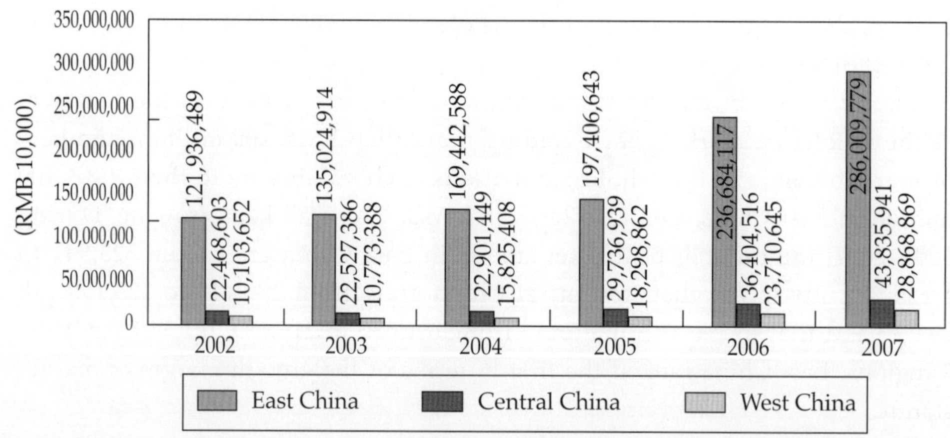

To better reflect the development of the wholesale markets, the value indicator of market turnover will be adopted next to reflect the level of development of the wholesale markets in each of the three regions.

During 2002–2007, the total turnover of the wholesale markets each valuing more than RMB 100 million in East China, Central China and West China kept increasing, of which the turnover of such wholesale markets in East China had exceeded RMB 2,860 billion in 2007, up 134.6% over that in 2002; the turnover of such wholesale markets in Central China grew by 95.1%; and that in West China grew by 185.7%. The growth margin of the turnover of the wholesale markets each valuing more than 100 million RMB in West China was the greatest of all.

Structure of the wholesale markets in East China, Central China and West China

The above table and figure reflect the overall development of the wholesale markets in each of the three regions. Composition of the above indicators of the wholesale markets in East China, Central China and West China will be provided in detail in order to reflect the differences among the development of the wholesale markets in the three major regions more clearly.

As can be seen from Fig. 5.40 and Fig. 5.41, the proportions of the numbers of the wholesale markets each valuing more than RMB 100 million were highly consistent with the proportions of the market stands in East China, Central China and West China, of which the proportion of the number of such wholesale markets in East China was the highest of all, being around 67%; that of the number of such wholesale markets in Central China ranked the second, being around 20%; and that in West China was the lowest o fall, being somewhere between 12–13%. Seen from their changing trends during 2002–2007, proportions of the three regions in terms of the above two indicators were basically stable, with few changes, or significant changing trends.

Fig. 5.40. Structure of the numbers of the wholesale markets each valuing more than RMB 100 million in East China, Central China and West China (2002–2007)

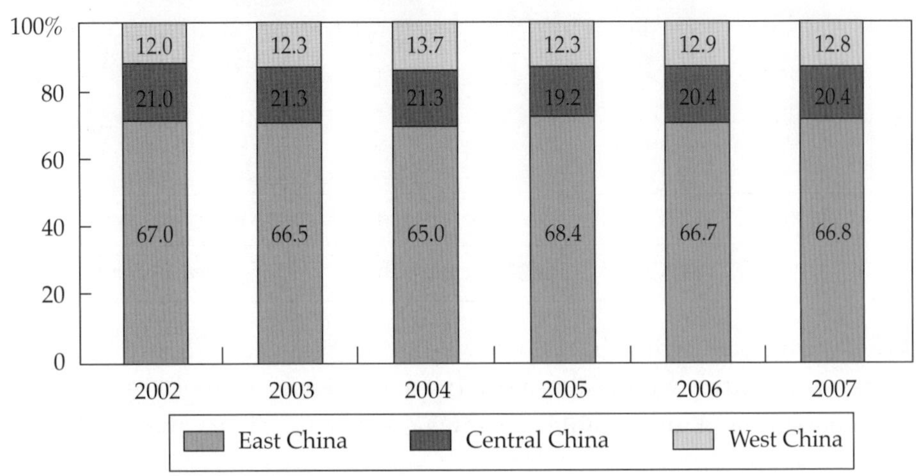

Fig. 5.41. Structure of the numbers of stands in the wholesale markets each valuing more than RMB 100 million in East China, Central China and West China (2002–2007)

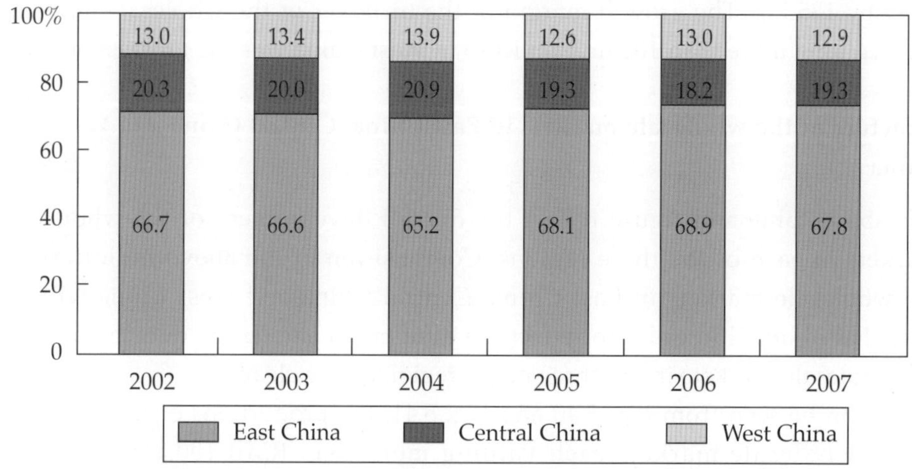

Composition of the business areas of the wholesale markets each valuing more than RMB 100 million in East China, Central China and West China was as shown in Fig. 5.42.

Fig. 5.42. Structure of the business areas of the wholesale markets each valuing more than RMB 100 million in East China, Central China and West China (2002–2007)

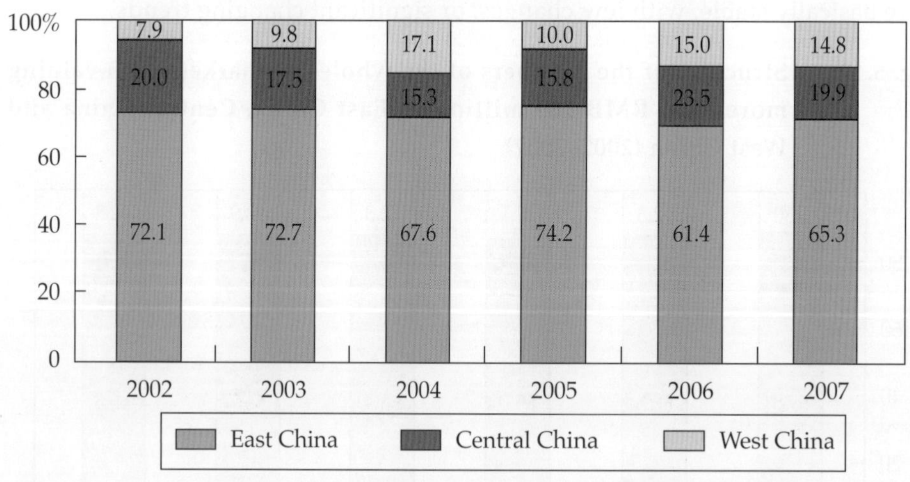

What's consistent with the above two figures was that proportion of the business area of the wholesale markets each valuing RMB 100 million in East China still held an absolute advantage, being far higher than 50%; that of the business area of such wholesale markets in Central China and that in West China were low. In particular, the proportion of the business area of the wholesale markets each valuing RMB 100 million in West China was less than 10% at its lowest level. Different from the above two indicators, composition of the business area of the wholesale markets each valuing RMB 100 million in East China and that of the business area of such wholesale markets in West China showed significant changing trends: the proportion of the business area of the wholesale markets each valuing more than RMB 100 million in East China kept declining, falling from 72.1% in 2002 to 65.3% in 2007 in spite of the fluctuations in between. Quite the opposite, the same proportion of the business area of such wholesale markets in West China increased from 7.9% in 2002 to 14.8% in 2007, even reaching 17.1% in between, showing great growth margin. It can be seen that the wholesale markets each valuing more than RMB 100 million in West China grew significantly in terms of the business area. It will be explained next with the indicator of the composition of market turnover. See Fig. 5.43 for details.

Fig. 5.43. Structure of the turnover of the wholesale markets each valuing more than RMB 100 million in East China, Central China and West China (2002–2007)

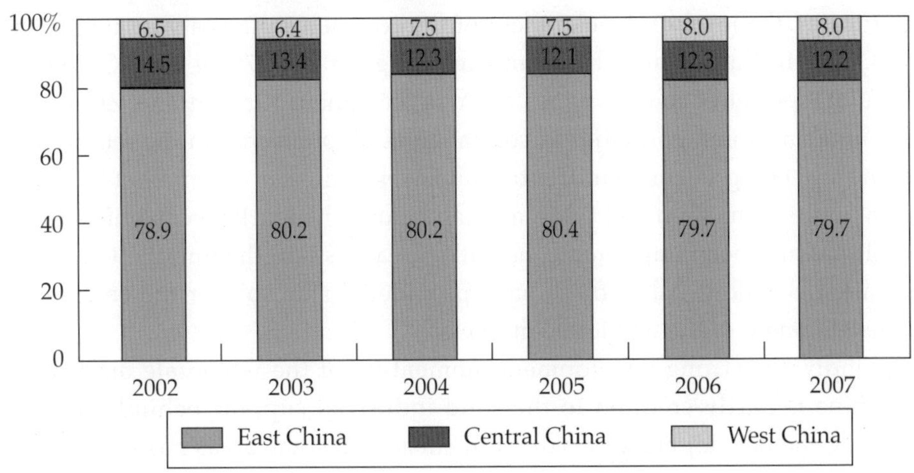

The ratio of the turnover of the wholesale markets each valuing more than RMB 100 million in East China to the total turnover of such wholesale markets across China had a more significant absolute advantage comparing with the above several indicators, being as high as around 80% which was far higher than that of the turnover of such wholesale markets in Central China and West China, as well as than the ratios of the above several indicators. It can be seen that the scale of the wholesale markets in East China, especially the scale of single wholesale market, was far greater than that of the wholesale markets in Central China and West China. As the same as the business area, the proportion of the turnover of the wholesale markets in West China was small in terms of its absolute value, yet it showed a growing trend, increasing from 6.5% in 2002 to 8.0% in 2007, up 1.5%. It was a great progress made in West China. The proportion of the turnover of the wholesale markets in West China showed an opposite trend, falling from 14.5% in 2002 to 12.2% in 2007, down 2.3%.

Summed up, the above several indicators reflected the following features of the regional structure of the wholesale markets in East China, Central China and West China: the total numbers of the wholesale markets, the total numbers of the wholesale market stands, the business areas and the turnover of the wholesale markets all kept growing in East China, Central China and West China, yet at varied rates. East China accounted for the highest proportion in each of the above indicators, holding an absolute dominance.

Many reasons have contributed to the above features of the regional structure of the wholesale trade in East China, Central China and West China. Specially, they are as follows:

First of all, the wholesale trade is included in the field of circulation. A favorable economic foundation is inevitable for a developed wholesale market. In particular, the level of development of the commerce plays a very important role. China initiated the reform and opening up in 1978 in East China. In particular, special economic zones such as Shenzhen, Xiamen and Zhuhai in East China and some port cities in coastal areas all pioneered in the reform and opening up, being faster than Central and West China in the market-oriented reform, industrialization and internationalization. The market economic system in itself has also been improved constantly, greatly strengthening the vitality of the market economy. All of these have provided fertile soil for the emergence and development of the wholesale markets.

Secondly, the strong development momentum of the wholesale markets in East China is partly credited to the solid industrial support behind them. In particular, the development of industrial clusters in some areas has become the most important industrial basis for the development of the wholesale markets. According to Michael Porter, an industrial cluster includes a series of related industries and other competition-related entities. Industrial clusters may emerge spontaneously by market forces, or through government investments or the co-action of the government and the market. After the market-oriented reform in East China, the proportion of state-owned enterprises has declined and a great number of small and medium-sized enterprises have showed strong development momentums. Since most of the small and medium-sized enterprises were private, they were small in scale, and had weak foundations and a relatively weak ability to make technical innovations. Industrial clusters could endow enterprises with the following three advantages in their development: capable of sharing external economy and having the amplification effect of 1+1>2; reducing the cost of transactions; and promoting enterprises to innovate, which could rightly make up for the deficiencies of small and medium-sized enterprises in their development. Therefore, taking the path of industrial clusters has become an inevitable choice for small and medium-sized enterprises. Most of the early industrial clusters in China were formed spontaneously by small and medium-sized enterprises. With the deepening of the awareness of the importance of industrial clusters, local governments at all levels began to adopt some industrial policies to guide the construction of local industrial parks, including improving the construction of infrastructure, creating a favorable investment environment, and positively introducing related enterprises into the industrial parks, in order to push forward the development of industrial clusters.

There is a good interaction between the development of the industrial clusters and specialty wholesale markets: development of the industrial clusters promotes before being pushed forward by the booming of specialty wholesale markets. While in China, horizontal industrial clusters have been playing the most significant role in the development of the wholesale markets. At the beginning of the formation of industrial clusters, there was this competitive relationship among enterprises. That is, products usually fell into the same categories. Of which, the first enterprises had a great demonstration effect, attracting more enterprises to follow suit and helping form such advantages as the sharing of infrastructure, specialized suppliers, and specialized supply of labor force, etc. A favorable strengthening was thus achieved, so were product brands named after certain places (e.g. leather shoes produced in Wenzhou, Zhejiang Province), contributing to the formation of industrial clusters. However, due to competitions, products are quite different in varieties, specifications, styles, shapes, colors, materials used, grades, brands, even internal qualities, creating conditions and bases for the emergence of specialty markets. Many industrial clusters in the coastal areas in China fall into the said category, greatly promoting the development of local wholesale markets.

Due to the influence of the reform and opening up policy, Central China and West China saw a late start of reform and opening up, slow industrialization and relatively backward economic development. In particular, in West China, the level of marketization was low. All of the above were not conducive to the development of the wholesale markets. Similarly, development of local wholesale markets was not based on industrial clusters or solidly supported like that of the wholesale markets in East China, so local wholesale markets in East China and West China, especially large wholesale markets, developed slowly. It resulted in the great differences among the wholesale markets each valuing more than RMB 100 million in East China, Central China and West China in terms of the number of such markets, the numbers of market stands, business areas and the market turnover.

Lastly, a very important condition for the growth of wholesale markets is superior geological position and regional transportation capable of radiating surrounding areas. Similar to any form of the circulation organizations, geological position also becomes an important factor that influences the development of wholesale markets. If the geological position of a wholesale market became a barrier against its radiation of the surrounding areas, it would soon be replaced by other wholesale markets of the same category. Though having a superior geological position is very important for a wholesale market, the wholesale market could also maintain its competitive edge if it pays enough attention to improving supporting services, including improving transportation infrastructure and facilities for logistics and distribution. Superior transportation conditions and a superior distribution system will provide strong and powerful supports for the rapid and sustained development of a wholesale market.

East China enjoys convenient external communications since more areas in East China are coastal areas, and has relatively complete transportation infrastructure. Comparatively, Central China and West China are closed. In particular, many places in West China were once faced great difficulties in building railways and other infrastructure due to terrains and other natural reasons. Therefore, East China has an upper hand in terms of regional transportation, which once greatly influenced the development of wholesale markets, especially large wholesale markets.

The above several factors are all very important in the emergence and development of the wholesale markets. There are other factors that may either greatly promote or hinder the development of the wholesale markets, such as saving the comprehensive cost of transactions and reducing the concentration ratio of wholesale markets, or whether the market credit system is sound, whether information communication is smooth, or whether the environment for market operations was standard, etc., to name a few. All these factors will become more and more important for a wholesale market to finally grow into an internationalized commodity exchange center.

Structure of the wholesale markets in the six sub-regions in China

Regional structure of the wholesale markets in East China, Central China and West China has been analyzed just now. Since the areas covered by East China, Central China and West China are general, a few indicators will be chosen to analyze the development and structure of the wholesale markets each valuing more than RMB 100 million in the six sub-regions in China.

Overview of the development of wholesale markets in the six sub-regions

As can be seen from Fig. 5.44, apart from that in Northeast China, the number of wholesale markets in each of the other five sub-regions was on the rise, of which, from 2002–2007, that of wholesale markets in North China grew by 42.4%; that of wholesale markets in East China grew by 37.3%; that of wholesale markets in South Central China grew by 40.1%; that of wholesale markets in Southwest China grew by 52%; and that of wholesale markets in Northwest China grew by 39.1%. The number of wholesale markets in Northeast China declined to some extent in 2005 and 2006 before rising back greatly in 2007. The number of wholesale markets in East China was the largest of all, having exceeded 1,000 till 2006; that in Northwest China was relatively small, being always lower than 100.

See Fig. 5.45 for the numbers of market stands. As the same as the changing trend of the numbers of the markets, apart from Northeast China, the number of market stands in the rest five regions all kept growing during 2002–2007,

Fig. 5.44. Overview of the development of the numbers of the wholesale markets each valuing more than RMB 100 million in the six major regions (2002–2007)

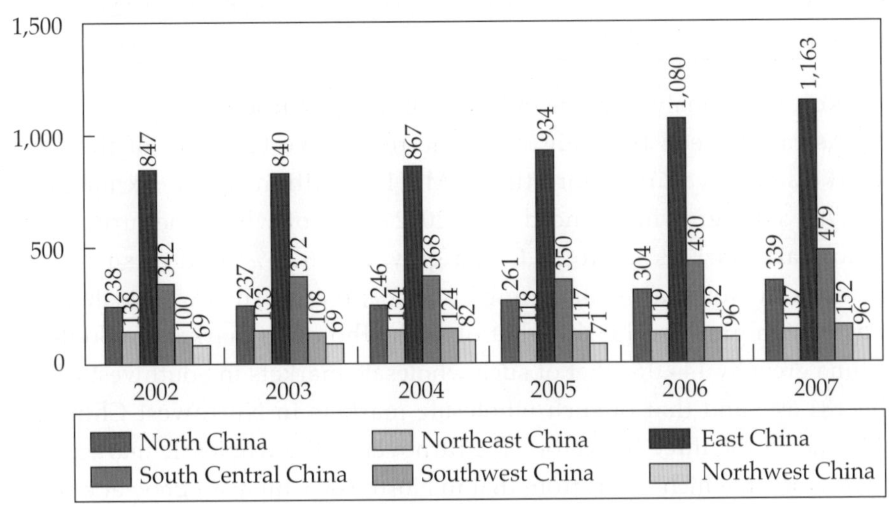

of which that of market stands in North China grew by 35.8%; that of market stands in East China grew by 40.4%; that of market stands in South Central China grew by 48.4%; that of market stands in Southwest China grew by 33.3%; that of market stands in Northwest China grew by 36.9%; and that of market stands in Northeast China fell by 1.4%. As the same as the number of wholesale markets, the number of market stands in East China was also the biggest of all, and that in Northwest China was the smallest of all.

Fig. 5.45. Overview of the development of the numbers of stands in the wholesale markets each valuing more than RMB 100 million in the six major regions (2002–2007)

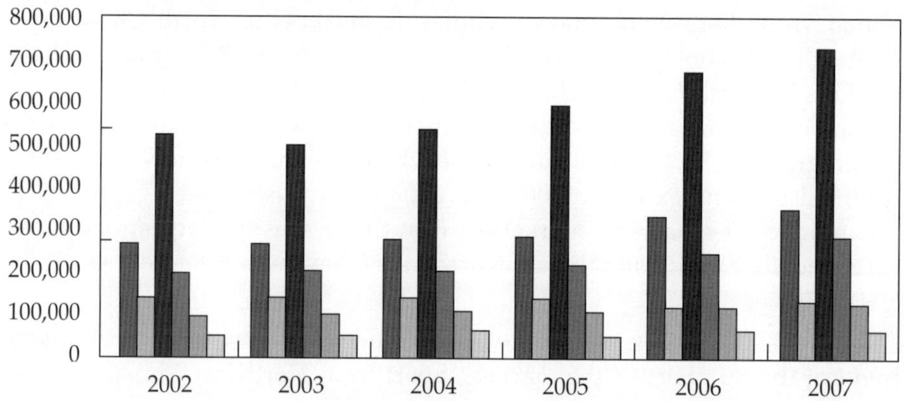

	2002	2003	2004	2005	2006	2007
North China	259,762	258,482	274,989	281,135	328,193	352,648
Northeast China	130,637	131,073	133,736	133,937	117,102	128,763
East China	521,849	494,014	537,842	592,593	675,705	732,921
South Central China	189,402	195,666	199,207	199,207	199,207	280,999
Southwest China	89,496	93,109	103,565	99,305	113,220	119,323
Northwest China	43,924	45,390	54,500	47,445	59,105	60,114

Next is the analysis of the indicator of market turnover.

As can be seen from Fig. 5.46, the respective turnover of the wholesale markets each valuing more than RMB 100 million in the six major regions all showed a growing trend during 2002–2007, of which the turnover of such wholesale markets in North China grew by 161.6%; that of such wholesale markets in Northeast China grew by 36.8%; that of such wholesale markets in East China grew by 133.6%; that of such wholesale markets in South Central China grew by 144.0%; that of such wholesale markets in Southwest China grew by 181.6%; and that of such wholesale markets in Northwest China grew by 138.9%. Of the three indicators, the turnover of the wholesale markets grew the fastest of all, which, apart from that in Northeast China, all grew at a rate higher than 100% in the rest regions. East China ranked the first, while Northwest China ranked the last in terms of the volume of turnover, which was the same as the above two indicators.

Fig. 5.46. Overview of the development of the turnover of the wholesale markets each valuing more than RMB 100 million (2002–2007) (RMB 10 thousand)

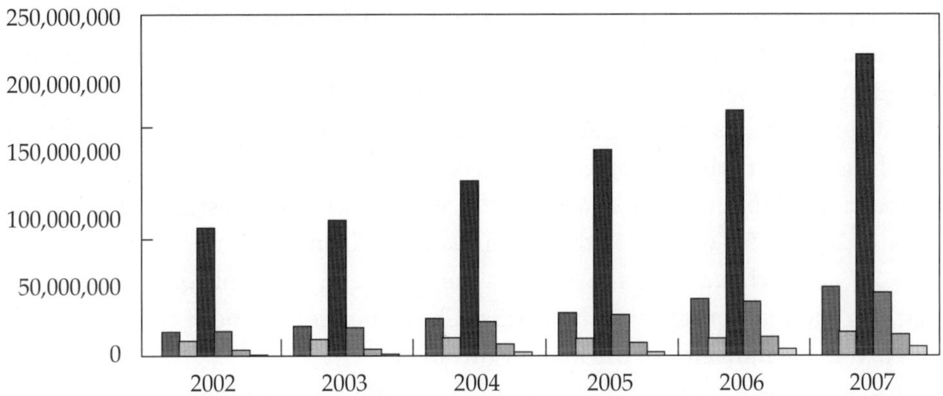

	2002	2003	2004	2005	2006	2007
North China	19,340,242	22,045,678	28,478,343	32,864,188	42,032,806	50,593,058
Northeast China	13,029,611	12,961,078	13,989,510	14,438,791	13,538,660	17,830,667
East China	94,347,139	100,827,087	129,589,664	151,987,953	180,442,724	220,429,168
South Central China	18,945,448	23,029,932	25,657,723	31,422,733	41,606,620	46,234,432
Southwest China	5,838,013	7,074,512	9,895,615	10,942,204	13,671,438	16,440,120
Northwest China	3,008,291	2,459,310	3,558,590	3,786,575	5,507,030	7,187,144

Structure of the wholesale markets in the six major regions

The totals of the wholesale markets in each and all regions have been described just now, from which it can be seen that with the economic development in China, the circulation industry became increasingly developed, the development of the wholesale trade was also accelerating, and the number and turnover of the wholesale markets in each region all kept growing by a big margin. From such totals, it is clear that differences among all regions were great. To better demonstrate the structure of proportions of each and all regions, the specific composition of each of the three indicators of the wholesale markets in the 6 regions will be provided next.

As can be seen from Fig. 5.47 and Fig. 5.48, the numbers of the wholesale markets and the numbers of markets stands in the regions were significantly different. Of which, East China accounted for the largest proportion, the number of the wholesale markets in which accounted for about 50% and the number of market stands in which accounted for about 43%, holding the absolute dominant position in terms of proportions; South Central China ranked the second, with the number of the wholesale markets and that of market stands accounting for about 20% and 15%, respectively; North China followed it, with the number of the wholesale markets and that of market stands accounting for about 13% and 20%, respectively; Northeast China, Southwest China and Northwest China ranked at the bottom, with the proportions being less than 10%. Of Northeast China, Southwest China and Northwest China, Northwest China ranked the last in terms of both the number of the wholesale markets and the number of market stand, being only about 3–4%. Seen from the changing trend, proportions of each and all regions kept basically stable, except for Northeast China which showed a relatively significant declining tendency. The proportion of the number of wholesale markets in Northeast China fell from 8.0% in 2002 to 5.8% in 2007; that of market stands in the same region fell from 10.6–7.7%, which was also the same as the change in the totals of the wholesale markets and market stands in Northeast China mentioned above.

Next is the indicator of the market turnover.

As can be seen from Fig. 5.49, what's consistent with the above two figures of composition was the ranking of the proportions of the turnover of the wholesale markets in each and all regions. What's different was that compared with the number of wholesale markets and that of market stands, the turnover of the wholesale markets in East China accounted for a higher proportion, being over 60%. Correspondingly, proportions of the turnover of the wholesale markets in

Fig. 5.47. Structure of the numbers of the wholesale markets each valuing more than RMB 100 million in the six major regions (2002–2007)

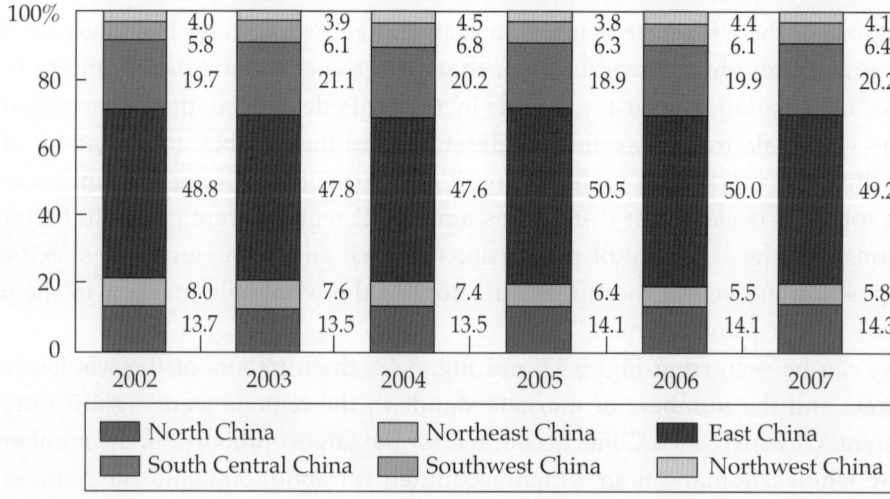

Fig. 5.48. Structure of the numbers of stands in the wholesale markets each valuing more than RMB 100 million in the six major regions (2002–2007)

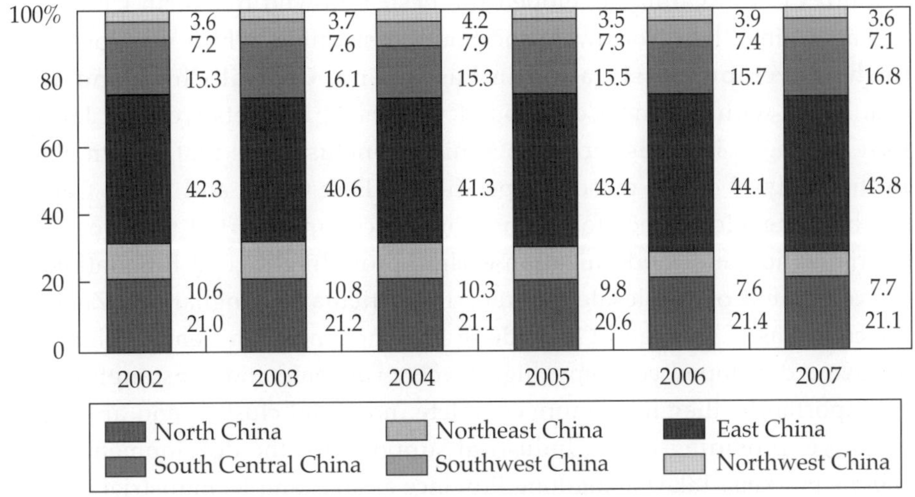

Fig. 5.49. Structure of the turnover of the wholesale markets each valuing more than RMB 100 million in the six major regions (2002–2007)

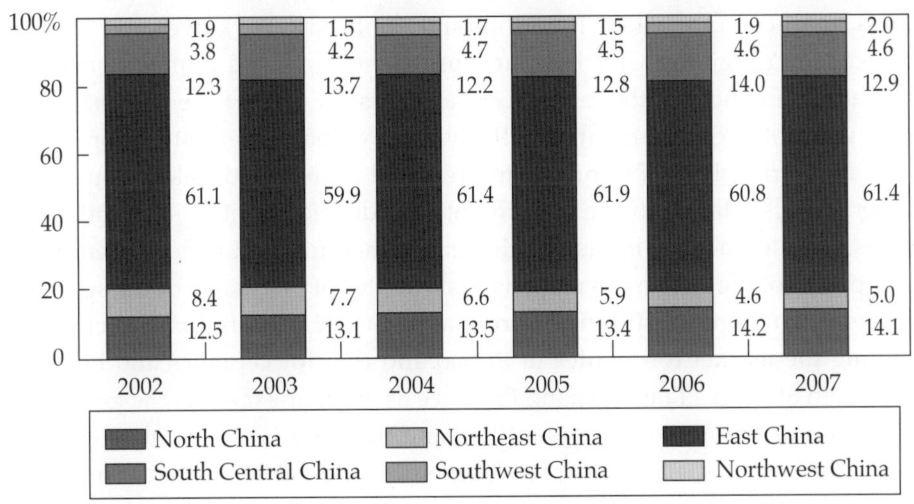

other regions were all compressed, all being smaller than the proportions of the above two indicators. In particular, the proportion of the number of wholesale markets and of the number of market stands in Northwest China were about 4%, yet that of the turnover of the wholesale markets in Northwest China was less than 2%. It indicated that the scale of single wholesale markets in East China was larger than those in other regions, and the organizational level of the wholesale markets in East China was even higher, while wholesale markets in

Northwest China were mostly small and decentralized in scale.

As can be seen from the above figures, the wholesale markets in East China and South Central China developed the best, followed by North China and Northeast China, then Northwest and Southwest China, which was consistent with the development situation in East China, Central China and West China. Areas with the most developed wholesale markets were all located in East China, so it is easy to get a similar conclusion as that drawn above from the analysis of the reasons. Specifically, East China and South Central China have developed economy and commerce, and started the process of industrialization and modernization earlier, providing a good foundation for the development of wholesale markets. In particular, Shanghai and Zhejiang Province in East China, and Guangdong Province in South Central China not only have a developed economy, high levels of income and consumption, but more importantly, they have more complete industrial clusters and are highly competitive, providing strong industrial supports for the development of the wholesale markets. Take Guangdong Province as an example, industrial clusters have become an important pillar for local economic growth. Products of some industrial clusters in Guangdong have not only been exported, some of them even hold half of the domestic market. For example, the decorative lighting fittings produced in Guzhen Township and the hardware, knives and scissors produced in Yangjiang City both account for 60% of the domestic market, the volume of export of the latter even accounts for 80% of the national total. That's why local governments at all levels have paid great attention to the role of industrial clusters in promoting regional economic development before issuing various related policies to promote the development of such industrial clusters. Development of industrial clusters pushed forward the emergence and development of the wholesale markets. As a matter of fact, some of the specialty markets in Guangdong Province grew along with local industrial clusters, including the market for textiles in Xiqiao and that for ceramics and building materials in Shiwan.[4] Take Zhejiang Province as another example, the geological distribution of industrial clusters in Zhejiang province is amazingly similar to the distribution of specialty markets. Generally, industrial cluster of one kind is located in the same area with related supporting specialty markets. Since most industrial clusters are engaged in the production of industrial products, the specialty wholesale markets for industrial products are more developed accordingly. For example, household textiles, daily commodities, hardware, magnetic materials are the major industries in Jinhua City, Zhejiang Province, which are matched with such specialty markets as the small commodities markets in Yiwu, the hardware city in Yongkang, the knitting-ware market in Yiwu, etc. Chemical fiber, knitting, leather, bags, silk are the major industries in

Jiaxing City, which are matched with such specialty markets as China cocoon silk trade market, Zhejiang leather clothes market, China leather market, etc. Industrial clusters and the wholesale markets have formed an effective mode of interaction in these areas.[5] The interactive development of industrial clusters and the wholesale markets explained the development structure of the wholesale markets each valuing more than RMB 100 million in the six major regions in China to a great extent.

In addition, most areas where the wholesale markets each valuing more than RMB 100 million develop well have a superior geological position, complete transportation infrastructure, rational government policies, a sound market credit system, smooth information exchange, a standard environment for market operations, etc. Quite the opposite, severe deficiencies in such aspects exist in other areas, especially Southwest China and Northwest China, which will also hinder the development of local wholesale markets. It is the synthetic action of the above factors that led to the structure and characteristics of the development of the wholesale markets each valuing more than RMB 100 million in the six regions in China.

Structure of all types of markets

Wholesale markets fall into two major categories-comprehensive markets and specialty markets. Specialty markets can be further divided into specialty markets for agricultural products and specialty markets for industrial products. To display the development of various categories of markets inside the wholesale markets in China, the structure of the specialty wholesale markets for agricultural products and industrial products, and the structure of comprehensive markets and specialty markets will be described and analyzed.

Structure of the specialty wholesale markets for agricultural and industrial products

Wholesale markets have been developing rapidly in China since the reform and opening up. However, development of the wholesale markets for agricultural products is not always synchronous with that of the wholesale markets for industrial products. In the start-up stage and later development, the numbers and turnover of the wholesale markets for agricultural products and of those for industrial products accounted for different ratios and presented different development trends. A detailed analysis will be made next to the structure of the wholesale markets for agricultural and that of the wholesale markets for industrial products through two indicators-the number and the turnover.

Structure of the numbers

In the early days of the reform and opening up, the wholesale markets for agricultural products started earlier and developed fast, yet those for industrial products started relatively late and developed slowly. Specifically speaking, the wholesale markets for agricultural products had reached 892 in 1986 before growing to 1,313 in 1989. The wholesale markets for industrial consumables were small in number, being only 265 in 1990. With the advance of the reform and opening up, these two categories of wholesale markets began to develop at different rates. See Fig. 5.50 for details.

As can be seen from Fig. 5.50, the number of the wholesale markets for agricultural products and that of the wholesale markets for industrial consumables were on the rise in general. Of which, the wholesale markets for agricultural products grew from 1,340 in 1990 to 4,351 in 2001 in number, up 224.7%; and the wholesale markets for industrial products grew from 265 in 1990 to 2,380 in 2001 in number, up 798.1%.

Fig. 5.50. Overview of the development of the number of the wholesale markets for agricultural products and that of the wholesale markets for industrial consumables (1990–2001)

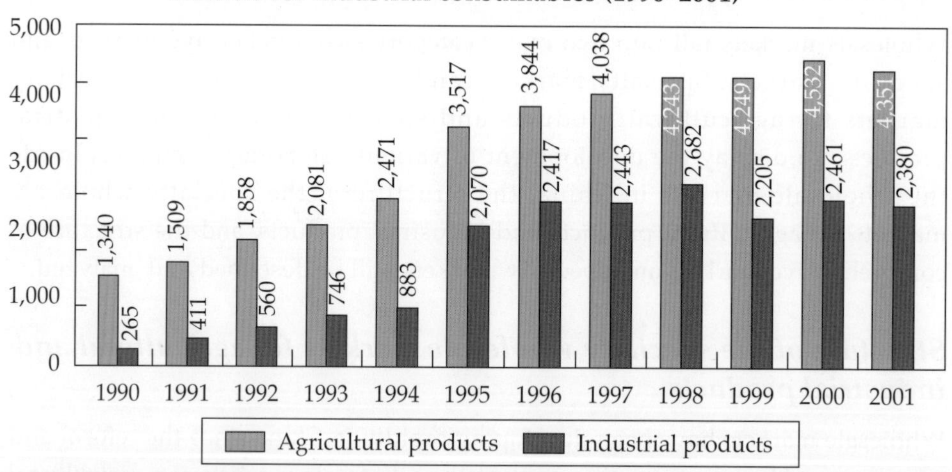

Wholesale markets for industrial products grew faster in number than those of the wholesale markets for agricultural products, yet lower than those of the wholesale markets for agricultural products in number. Fig. 5.51 reflects, in a clearer way, the proportional relation between the two.

As can be seen from Fig. 5.51, the proportion of the number of the wholesale markets for agricultural products was far greater than that of the number of the wholesale markets for industrial products, being over 50% and holding an absolute dominance. The proportion of the number of the wholesale markets for industrial products, on the contrary, was 38.7% even at the highest level. Seen from the development trend, the proportion of the number of the wholesale markets for agricultural products kept declining, falling from 83.5% in 1990 to 64.6% in 2001, down nearly 20%; that of the number of the wholesale markets for industrial products, on the contrary, kept growing, increasing from 16.5% in 1990 to 35.4% in 2001, up nearly 20%.

Fig. 5.51. Structure of the numbers of the wholesale markets for agricultural products and industrial consumables (1990–2001)

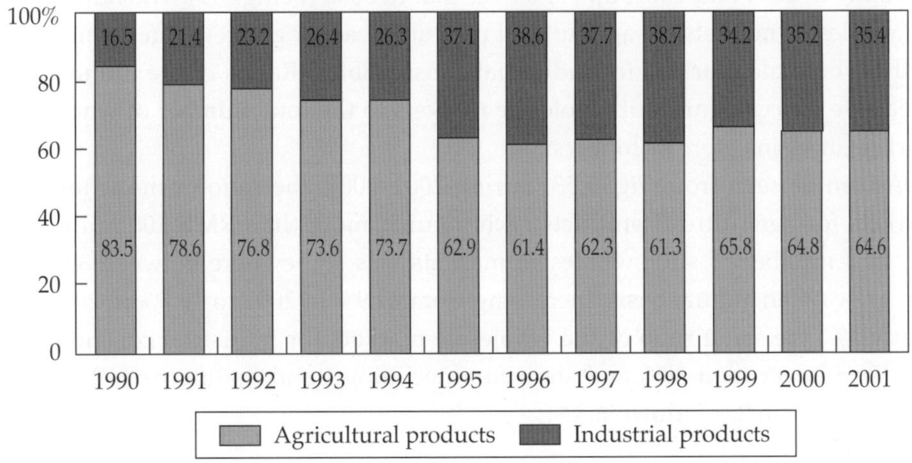

Fig. 5.52. Overview of the development of the numbers of the wholesale markets for agricultural products and for industrial consumables each valuing more than RMB 100 million (2002–2007)

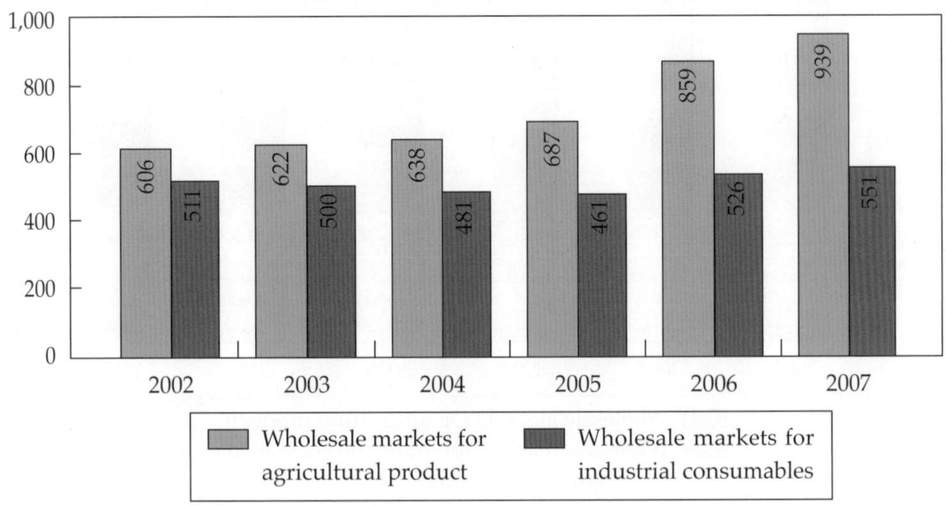

China began to collect statistics on the commodity exchange markets each valuing more than RMB 100 million after 2002. A description and analysis of the development and structure of the wholesale markets for agricultural products and those for industrial consumables each valuing more than RMB 100 million[6] will be made below.

As can be seen from Fig. 5.52, the number of the wholesale markets for agricultural products each valuing more than RMB 100 million showed a significant growing trend, from 606 in 2002 to 939 in 2007, up 55.0%; that of the wholesale markets for industrial consumables grew to 551 in 2007 after the declining in 2004 and 2005, up 7.8% over that in 2002 (being 511). The number of the wholesale markets for agricultural products was far greater than the number of the wholesale markets for industrial consumables. Ratios of the numbers of the above two categories of wholesale markets to the total number of wholesale markets in China were as follows:

As can be seen from Fig. 5.53, during 2002–2007, the ratio of the wholesale markets for agricultural products each valuing more than RMB 100 million to the total number of such wholesale markets was somewhere between 30–40% and grew on an annual basis, increasing from 34.9% in 2002 to 39.7% in 2007, up nearly 5%; the same ratio of the wholesale markets for industrial consumables had been lower than 30% and showed a declining trend, falling from 29.5% in 2002 to 23.2% in 2007, down 6.3%.

Fig. 5.53. Structure of the numbers of the wholesale markets for agricultural products and for industrial consumables each valuing more than RMB 100 million (2002–2007)

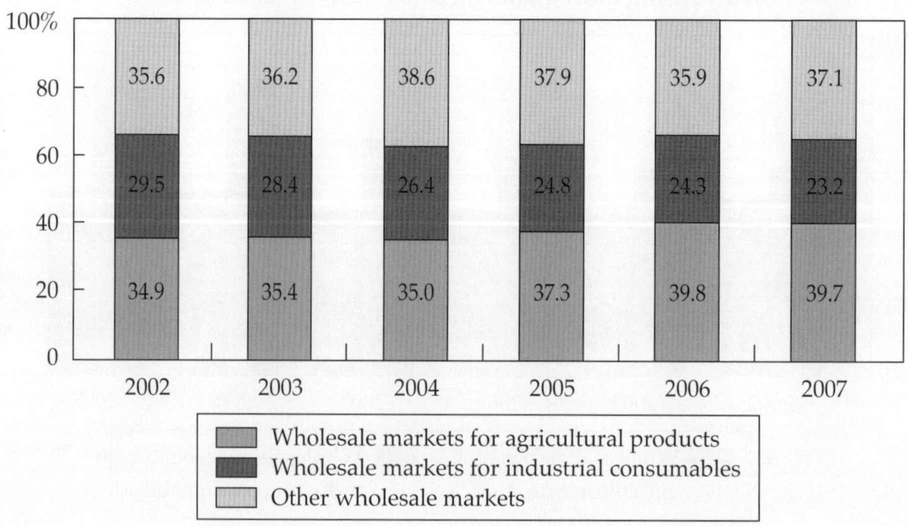

Fig. 5.54. Overview of the turnover the wholesale markets for agricultural products and for industrial consumables (1990–2001)

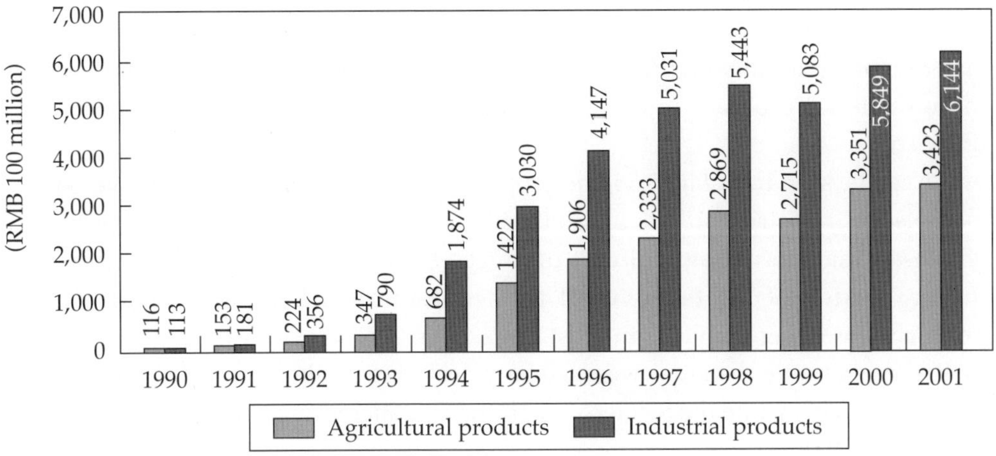

Fig. 5.55. Structure of the turnover of the wholesale markets for agricultural products and for industrial consumables (1990–2001)

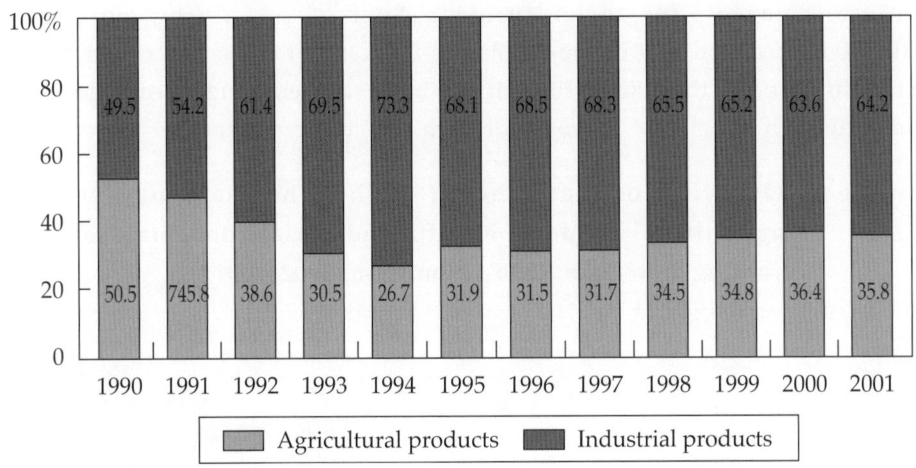

Structure of turnover

In the early days of the reform and opening up, the wholesale markets for agricultural products grew rapidly, and their turnover kept growing from RMB 2.84 billion in 1986 to 9.52 billion in 1989, up 235.9%. Quite the opposite, the wholesale markets for industrial consumables developed slowly, far lagging behind the wholesale markets for agricultural products. With the development of the market economy, such trends changed. See Fig. 5.54 for details.

As can be seen from Fig. 5.54, during 1990–2001, the turnover of the wholesale markets for agricultural products and that for industrial products kept growing, of which the former grew by 2,850.9% and the latter grew by 5,337.2%. In particular, the wholesale markets for industrial products grew even faster before gradually catching up with then surpassing the wholesale markets for agricultural products in terms of turnover. Fig. 5.55 is about their specific proportions.

As can be seen from Fig. 5.55, the proportion of the turnover of the wholesale markets for industrial products was far higher than that of the turnover of the wholesale markets for agricultural products, being nearly 70% at the highest; the proportion of the turnover of the wholesale markets for agricultural products was lower than 50% in most cases, even 26.7% at the lowest. Seen from the changing trend, the latter was basically declining, falling from 50.5% in 1990 to 35.8% in 2001; while the former was on the rise, increasing from 49.5% in 1990 to 64.2% in 2001.

Next is the overall growth of the respective turnover of the above two categories of wholesale markets.

As can be seen from Fig. 5.56, during 2002–2007, the turnover of the wholesale markets for agricultural products each valuing more than RMB 100 million and that of the wholesale markets for industrial consumables each valuing more than RMB 100 million both showed a significant growing momentum. Of which, the turnover of such wholesale markets for agricultural

Fig. 5.56. Overview of the turnover of the wholesale markets for agricultural products and for industrial consumables each valuing more than RMB 100 million (2002–2007)

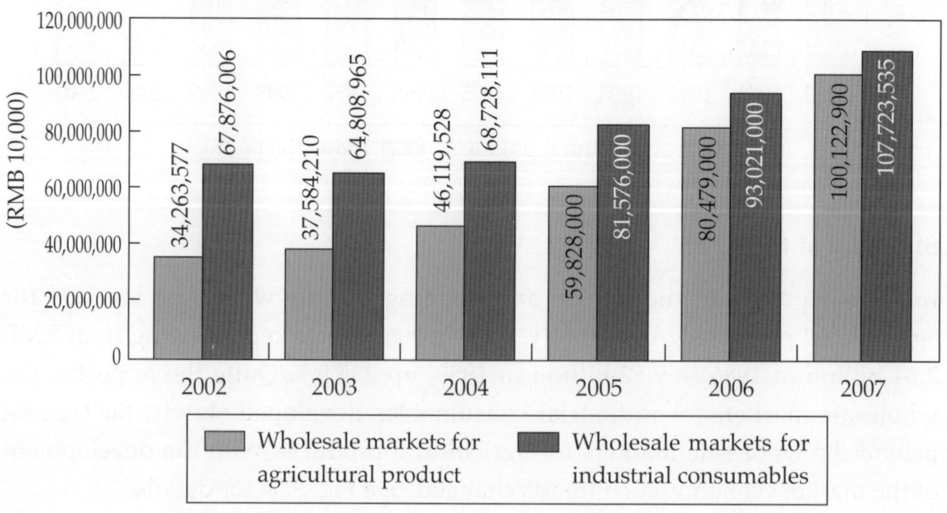

products grew by 192.2%; and that of such wholesale markets for industrial products grew by 58.7%. Opposite to the indicator of number, the turnover of the wholesale markets for industrial consumables was significantly higher than that of the wholesale markets for agricultural products. See Fig. 5.57 for the specific correlation.

Fig. 5.57. Structure of the turnover of the wholesale markets for agricultural products and for industrial consumables each valuing more than RMB 100 million (2002–2007)

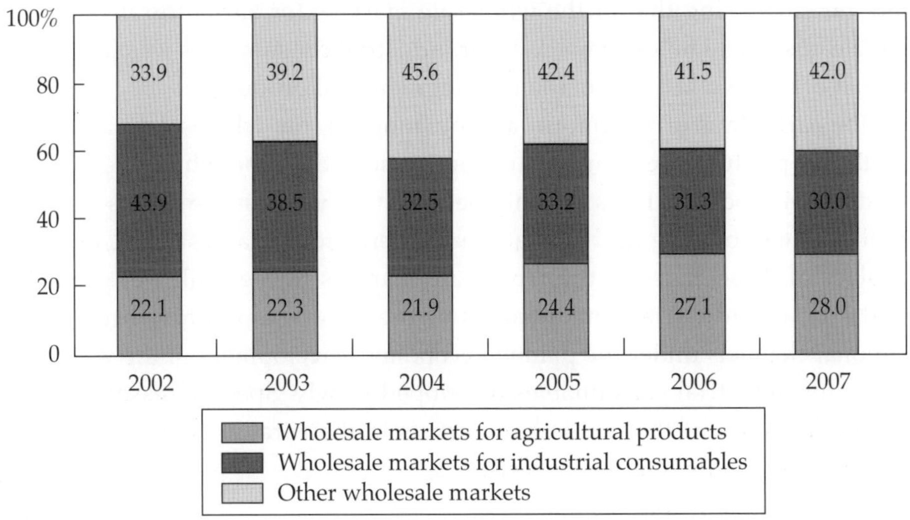

As can be seen from Fig. 5.57, the proportion of the turnover of the wholesale markets for industrial consumables each valuing more than RMB 100 million was higher than that of the turnover of the wholesale markets of the same size for agricultural products. In particular, in the first few years, it even reached 43.9% in 2002, being 21.8% higher than that of the turnover of the wholesale markets of the same size for agricultural products over the same year. The turnover of the wholesale markets for agricultural products had been accounted for less than 30% of the total. Yet with time, both proportions showed quite the opposite changing trends: the proportion of the turnover of the wholesale markets for agricultural products was on the rise, while that of the turnover the wholesale markets for industrial consumables declined. Till 2007, the difference between the two had been narrowed to 2%.

As can be seen from the above description, the structure of the wholesale markets for agricultural products and those for industrial consumables in China presented the following features: since the reform and opening up, both categories of the wholesale markets have been developing fast, keeping growing in terms of number and market turnover; in the early days of the reform and opening up, the wholesale markets for agricultural products developed rapidly, being far greater than the wholesale markets for industrial consumables (which developed a few year later) in terms of number and market turnover; with the advance of the reform and opening up, the wholesale markets for industrial consumables grew faster and faster. Though the number of such wholesale markets had been lower than that of the wholesale markets for agricultural products, the turnover of such wholesale markets gradually caught up with before far surpassing that of the wholesale markets for agricultural products. The scale of single wholesale markets for industrial consumables was far greater than that of single wholesale markets for agricultural products.

In the early days of the reform and opening up, the wholesale markets for agricultural products developed far more rapidly than the wholesale markets for industrial products. It was mainly because that wholesale markets in China initially came into being in the rural areas where are the largest place of origin and place of direct sales of the wholesale markets for agricultural products. Circulation of industrial consumables at the time was mainly through the traditional channels under the planned economy. Development of the wholesale markets for industrial consumables developed slowly. Specific reasons for the earliest emergence of the wholesale markets in the rural areas may be found mainly from the following two aspects:

(1) Origin of the wholesale markets

The wholesale market in China is an organizational form of commodity wholesale developed by borrowing the experience of trade markets, mainly the trade markets for agricultural and sideline products. Trade markets firstly appeared in the vast rural areas in China, because most Chinese people lived in the rural areas, and the purchasing power parity of China also lied in the rural areas. In particular, rural areas are the largest place of origin and the most direct market of agricultural and sideline products and like products. It is safe to say that rural areas meet many requirements such as having favorable climates, favorable geographical positions and rural residents' supports. Therefore, it was inevitable that the wholesale markets coming into being inside trade markets emerged firstly in the rural areas.

(2) Institutions and reforms

That the reform of the economic system in China was initiated in the rural areas served as another main reason for the birth of the wholesale markets in the rural areas. In the early days of the reform and opening up, with the advance of the institutional reform in the urban areas and the enlargement of enterprises' autonomy, the circulation pattern of commodities under the traditional planned economic system was broken; the stiff system of commodity wholesale featured by product deployment was unable to continue surviving; and a new system of commodity circulation and operation which was in line with the development requirements of the market economy was badly needed by the wholesale society. Under such circumstances, the wholesale market was born as a new-type organization of wholesale of means of production, some of the industrial and agricultural products and other commodities. Due to the weak control of the planned economy in the rural areas, the wholesale markets firstly developed in the rural areas at the beginning of the reform and opening up.

It can be seen from the above discussion that in the early days of the reform and opening up, the wholesale markets were born in the rural areas, and the economic features of the rural areas determined that the development of the wholesale markets for agricultural products would be definitely faster than that of the wholesale markets for industrial products. Therefore, the wholesale markets for agricultural products achieved a great development over this period; those for industrial products developed relatively slowly, the number of which in the urban areas was far smaller than that in the rural areas.

With the acceleration of the reform and opening up in China, the wholesale markets for industrial consumables grew faster and faster. Though the number of such wholesale markets had been lower than that of the wholesale markets for agricultural products, the turnover of such wholesale markets gradually caught up with before exceeding that of the wholesale markets for agricultural products. What's more, the scale of single wholesale market for industrial consumables was far greater than that of single wholesale market for agricultural products. Most wholesale markets in Western developed countries are engaged in agricultural products, while China has a great number of wholesale markets for industrial products which are developing increasingly faster and holding an important position in the field of circulation in China. Main reasons for this phenomenon may be found from:

(1) Reasons for the emergence of the wholesale markets

After the launch of the reform and opening up, a great number of township enterprises, individual and privately-run enterprises emerged in China. Such enterprises were numerous in number, small in size and low in output and efficiency, and had unstable production relations. Products produced by them were often extruded on the market, making it hard for such products to enter the field of state-owned circulation through the traditional channels of circulation. They had to seek for other channels for distribution. The emergence of the wholesale markets for industrial products conformed to the booming of the rural economy and the private sector of the economy, and solved the problem of circulation channels for related products. These being coupled with the supports of government policies later contributed to the "wholesale market fever" across China, giving birth to a group of highly-popular and large wholesale markets such as the small commodities market in Yiwu, Zhejiang Province, Hanzheng Street market in Wuhan, Hubei Province, the market for light textiles in Shaoxing, Zhejiang Province, etc.

(2) Objective conditions for commodity transactions

Generally speaking, the wholesale of industrial products, means of production, major agricultural products, wheat, cotton, etc. are all carried out in exchanges in developed countries, since developed countries have very complete infrastructure for transportation and communications and fairly sound rules and regulations on commodity exchange, plus such products are easy to be normalized, standardized and stored. With all of the above conditions ripe, it will be unnecessary to gather such products in the wholesale markets before distributing them, but simply need the manufacturers of such products to deliver the products directly to the consumers after both sides sign the purchase and sales contract at the exchanges. However, in China, the said conditions are yet to become mature, making the wide range of agricultural products (from farming, forestry, animal husbandry, side occupation and fishery), great part of the industrial products, means of agricultural production, etc. to have to be traded on the wholesale markets before entering the field of circulation.

The rapid development of the wholesale markets for industrial products, especially those each valuing more than RMB 100 million, had much to do with the development of the industrial clusters mentioned above. The interaction between industrial clusters and the wholesale markets improved the competitiveness of the industrial clusters while greatly promoting the development of the wholesale markets. Details which have been so lately said will not be repeated here.

Structure of the comprehensive wholesale markets and the specialty wholesale markets

As already mentioned, the wholesale markets fall into two major categories — the comprehensive wholesale markets and the specialty wholesale markets. With the acceleration of the economic development in China and the improvement of the specialization level of the production since the reform and opening up, the said two major categories of the wholesale markets showed different development trends. The number of specialty wholesale markets grew constantly, so did their respective turnover. Comprehensive wholesale markets, especially those each valuing more than RMB 100 million, showed an opposite development trend. A detailed description and analysis of the structure of comprehensive wholesale markets and specialty wholesale markets each valuing more than RMB 100 million during 2002–2007 will be made below, beginning with the overall development of such markets.

Overall development

As can be seen from Fig. 5.58, the number of the specialty wholesale markets each valuing more than RMB 100 million was far greater than that of the comprehensive wholesale markets of the same size. Plus, it showed a growing trend, increasing from 1,196 in 2002 to 1,852 in 2007, being 656 more; the number of the comprehensive wholesale markets each valuing more than RMB 100 million kept declining, falling from 533 in 2002 to 372 in 2007, being 161 less.

Next is the overall development of the turnover of such wholesale markets.

Fig. 5.58. Overview of the development of the numbers of the comprehensive wholesale markets and the specialty wholesale markets each valuing more than RMB 100 million (2002–2007)

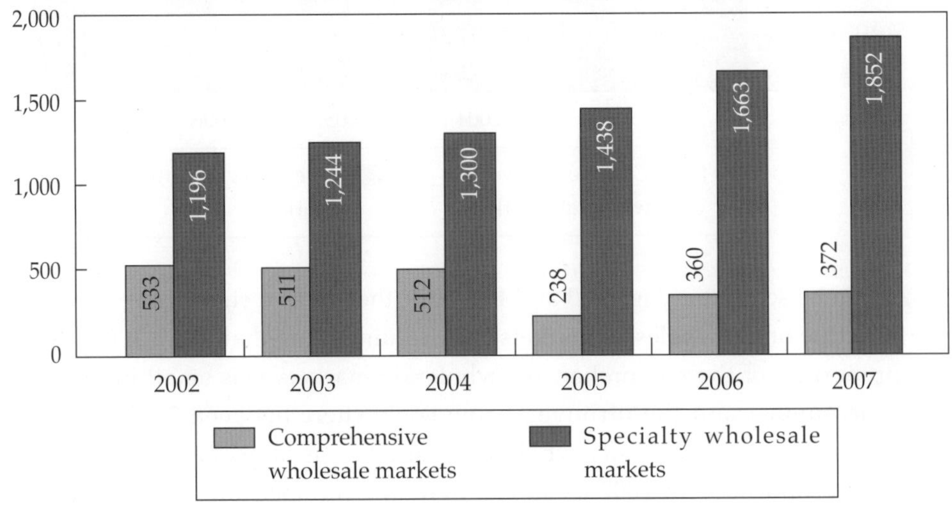

As can be seen from Fig. 5.59, the turnover of the comprehensive wholesale markets that that of the specialty wholesale markets both kept growing, yet the former grew by a smaller margin than the latter. The turnover of the specialty markets was more than doubled from 2002–2007, while that of the comprehensive markets grew only by 37.9% on the average. Seen from their absolute values, the absolute value of the turnover of comprehensive markets was far smaller than that of the turnover of specialty markets. Plus the difference between the two kept enlarging.

Structure of the numbers and the market turnover

The overall development of the comprehensive and specialty wholesale markets each valuing more than RMB 100 million has been discussed above. Next is a detailed analysis of the structural characteristics of the said two major categories of the wholesale markets.

Fig. 5.59. Overview of the growth of the turnover of the comprehensive and specialty wholesale markets each valuing more than RMB 100 million (2002–2007)

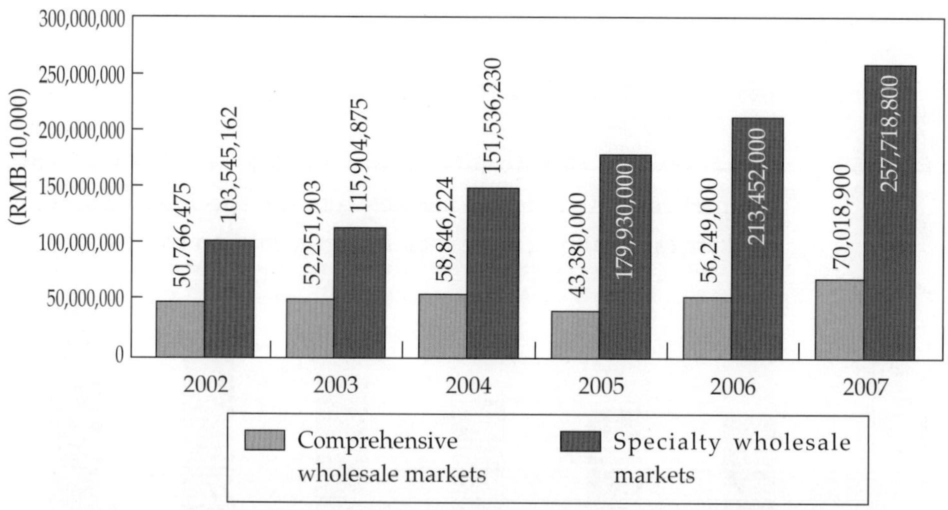

As can be seen from Fig. 5.60 and Fig. 5.61, there was a significant feature of the structure of the wholesale markets each valuing more than RMB 100 million: the proportion of the comprehensive wholesale markets was small in terms of both the number and the turnover, being somewhere between 20–30%; while the proportion of the specialty wholesale markets was large, being nearly 80%. Take the proportions in 2007 as an example, the number and turnover of the comprehensive wholesale markets accounted for 15.7% and 19.5%, respectively of all; while those of the specialty wholesale markets accounted for 8.3% and 1.8%, respectively, of all.

The rapid development of the specialty wholesale markets had had a good foundation at the emergence of the wholesale markets. The township enterprises and individual households specialized in production growing up

Fig. 5.60. **Structure of the numbers of the comprehensive wholesale markets and specialty wholesale markets each valuing more than RMB 100 million (2002–2007)**

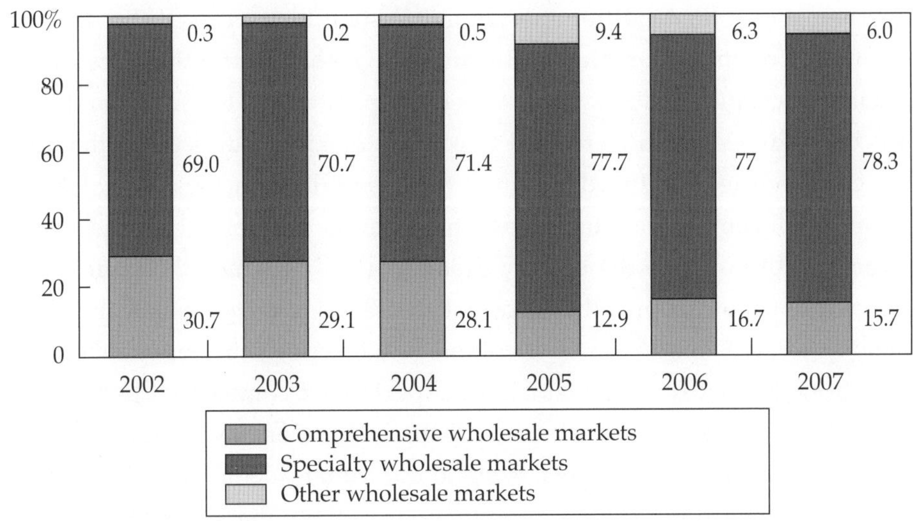

Fig. 5.61. **Structure of the turnover of the comprehensive and specialty wholesale markets each valuing more than RMB 100 million (2002–2007)**

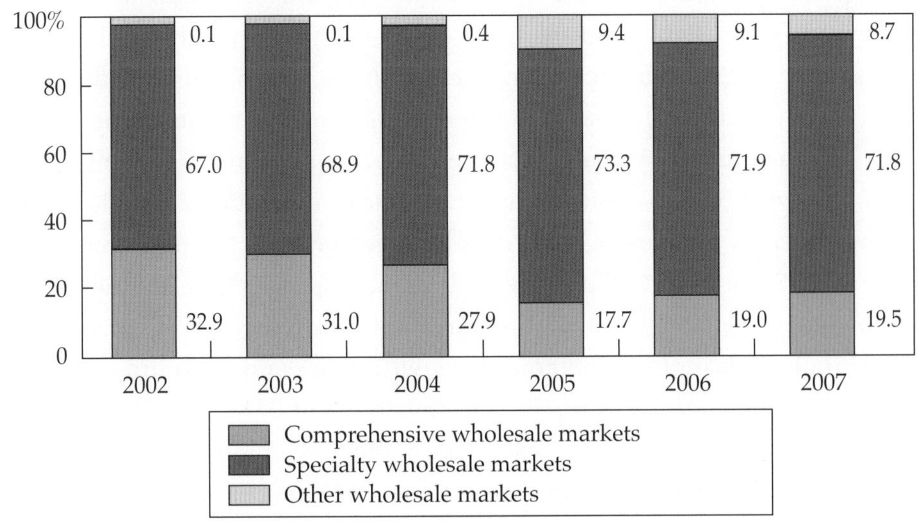

in the early days of the reform and opening up purchased, based on their weak capital and technical strength, off-cuts and odd-sized portions of materials from large and medium-sized enterprises before producing and manufacturing some small commodities. They gradually got an upper hand in terms of the cost of production and product competitiveness. However, reform of the economic system in China failed to be carried forward synchronously. Commercial enterprises under the traditional economic system hence closed the door on the products of small commercial businesses in the strict adherence to the traditional circulation policies, or distained to operate such low-value and low-profit commodities which were hard to control, making it difficult of the sales of the commodities produced by small commercial businesses. To solve the problem, small commercial businesses which started in informal sectors had to find the way out outside the system. Trade markets in which the traders had great operational autonomy, the modes of transactions were flexible and there were no restrictions on the smallest volume of wholesale thus became the main distribution channel for many small and specialized commercial businesses. The gathering of specialty businesses enabled some of the unique specialty markets, or the wholesale markets, to stand out from trade markets. Since then, the economic pattern of "specialty production-specialty market" in China kept developing along the healthy track, laying a good foundation for the subsequent booming of the specialty wholesale markets.

This pattern of specialty production-specialty markets later developed into the interactive development of industrial clusters and wholesale markets. In the recent years, small and medium-sized enterprises in China showed a strong growth momentum, becoming the new force to promote the sustained development of the Chinese economy. Most small and medium-sized enterprises were privately-run, which were usually poor in foundation, small in size, and weak in the ability to make technical innovations. So taking the path of industrial clusters in their development became the prerequisite of their success. Since industrial clusters achieve the sharing of core abilities using the knowledge exchange among all enterprises inside regional organizations and maintain such regional organizations with trust and commitment, they are capable of pushing forward the self-development of small and medium-sized enterprises. Just as has discussed above, there is an intimate relationship between the development of industrial clusters and that of specialty wholesale markets, and the development of industrial clusters promotes the booming of specialty wholesale markets. That's why the structure of the specialty wholesale markets and comprehensive wholesale markets show the specific states in the above figures.

6

Chapter

Emergence and Development of the Wholesale Logistics

The wholesale trade was born to solve the contradiction between production and consumption. Of which, the logistics functions of the wholesale trade such as storage and transportation play an irreplaceable role in regulating the time or space contradictions between production and consumption. Logistics can be said one of the most important functions of the wholesale trade at the very beginning. With the rapid development of the socialization of production, especially entering the 21st century, the wholesale trade was extruded by both ends of the industrial chain and seized by foreign capital, plus the limited improvement of its operational performance, it saw an increasingly smaller profit margin. In the rectification and reshaping, the wholesale trade shifted the focus of making profits and reducing costs on logistics, viewing logistics as "a virgin land" and "the third profit fountainhead". The establishment of and innovations on the logistics system are playing an increasingly important role in the development of the wholesale trade.[1]

Three Decades of the Reform of Wholesale Logistics

Wholesale logistics is a kind of industrial logistics based on wholesale. It refers to the planning, management and controlling process carried out by all enterprises engaged in the wholesale trade through mutual cooperation and with the help of modern information technologies, unified logistics standards and effective integration and utilization of resources of industrial logistics in order to achieve efficient and low-cost flow and storage of commodities and related information from the place of origin to the place of sales on consumers' demands.[2] The level of development of wholesale logistics, such as the levels of the transportation, handling, packaging and storage capacities, directly determines the scale and speed of the circulation of wholesale commodities. Reform of wholesale logistics is one aspect of the reform of the wholesale trade. In the three decades of the reform of the wholesale trade, wholesale logistics underwent a series of progressive reforms, from micro-reforms to macro-reforms.

Reform course of wholesale logistics

The wholesale trade was an important link in the economic system under the planned economy, playing both the economic role in commodity circulation and the political role in commodity distribution, so in a fairly long period of time, it controlled not only the shift of the property in the goods (business flow), but also the space shift of commodities (logistics). The part of the logistics that was turned into commodity circulation wasn't taken seriously. With the development of the wholesale trade and the constant deepening of the division of the wholesale functions, the functions of wholesale logistics also started to develop before being gradually strengthened.

The first stage: introduction of the concept of Wholesale Logistics (1978–1992)

The reform of wholesale logistics lagged behind not only the reform of the economic system, but also that of the wholesale system. In the early days after the founding of the People's Republic of China, commodity production was mainly carried out in a few big cities, and the storage and transportation of commodities were done by commercial wholesale, storage and transportation enterprises. In particular, about 80% of the commodities were stored and transported by various types of wholesale companies at the time. Though logistics had existed in wholesale activities, the concept of wholesale logistics failed to appear, but was demonstrated more as the circulation of logistics. Wholesale logistics only served as part of commodity allocation, which was allocated in wholesale institutions at all levels in order to make up for the time and space inconsistence of materials and carry out planned production, storage and transportation, as well as planned allocation and supply. Most organizations engaged in wholesale logistics existed in a non-independent form (e.g. inside wholesale enterprises) and subject to other functional departments (e.g. the purchase department, the sales department, etc.). They were a series of incompatible and fragmented activities in different functional departments inside an organization, existing in the form of decentralized management in terms of the mode of organizational management. Yet their functions and roles hadn't been recognized by people.

The reform of the wholesale system started since the Third Plenary Session of the 11th CPC National Congress in 1978 made requirements on the wholesale enterprises on the micro-level while reforming the traditional "three fixeds" (fixed circulation channels, fixed supply objects and fixed price rebates) circulation system, requiring wholesale enterprises to fully explore their potential at the business level in order to face the challenges brought about by social development, the improvement of the level of productivity and the expansion of the scale of wholesale businesses. When the wholesale enterprises encountered bottlenecks in reducing production costs, the role of logistics in improving the working efficiency and improving the operational performances of wholesale enterprises began to attract people's attention. In 1981, Prof. Wang

Zhitai from Beijing Wuzi University published an article entitled *On Materials* in *Newsletter on the Study of Materials Economics*, the professional publication of the materials departments in China, in which he introduced the concept of logistics into China completely for the first time. The introduction of the concept of logistics was soon extended to the field of wholesale. Starting from the 1980s, a few wholesale enterprises changed the line management of their own functional departments and organizations, and set up materials distribution departments and raw materials management departments to be responsible for wholesale logistics businesses. Wholesale logistics activities began to focus on systematic operations instead of being limited to passive warehouse and transportation, and comprehensive benefits of wholesale logistics system composed of packaging, handling, circulation, processing and transportation was also taken into consideration.

During this period, the concept of wholesale logistics emerged and certain achievements were made by China in wholesale logistics in practice and policies. But in general, wholesale logistics was still in the primary stage at the time, and hadn't got rid of its role as the subsidiary functions of wholesale. Restructuring of wholesale enterprises and organizations rarely changed the traditional departments and organizational levels of the wholesale enterprises'. Logistics management was still fragmented in the traditional manufacturing, sales and financial departments, the operation of which was also backward.

The second stage: establishment of the position of wholesale logistics (1993–2000)

Wholesale logistics failed to attract enough attention in the first few years over this period, so it was basically in the traditional stage without a modernized and large-scale wholesale logistics and distribution system. Moreover, in the late stage of the reform, under the influence of the chaotic order in the wholesale circulation, the reform of the wholesale system once again focused on the status of the state-owned wholesale enterprises as the main channel. Wholesale logistics gradually passed from people's sight and fell into silence. Even though, the concept of wholesale logistics had been deeply rooted into people's mind. In the early 1990s, it had been widely recognized by the Chinese people that wholesale logistics was superior in "import and export on a large scale", as well as in mastering market information before guiding production, pre-screening marketable products, and optimizing the allocation of resources. When no significant effects were achieved in the reform of the system of modern wholesale enterprises, wholesale logistics once again became a good medicine for bringing the dying wholesale enterprises back to life, being widely proposed. In the reform, wholesale enterprises unified all of the logistics functions and operations by setting up the logistics department, the logistics management department and the office of logistics strategies, etc., combined each field of wholesale logistics such as purchase, storage, transportation and materials management into an organizational unit of integrated operations, formed the general integrated logistics framework inside the enterprises, and achieved the shift of wholesale logistics organizations from fragmented management to integrated management. In addition, wholesale enterprises themselves also set up the planning and control department at the highest organizational level to be responsible for positioning logistics development strategies, optimizing and reorganizing the logistics system, and controlling and measuring logistics costs and the performance of consumer services. All of such reform measures had had great effects on reducing the logistics cost and improving the logistics efficiency and wholesale enterprises' performance. As for policies, the Chinese Ministry of Domestic Trade proposed to set up 10 national logistics centers and 50 regional distribution centers in the *Ninth Five-year Plan* of China in 1996, taking ameliorating logistics infrastructure as an important means of stimulating wholesale enterprises' vitality. The proposal greatly encouraged wholesale enterprises to make effective use of various means of transportation on the basis of mutual cooperation, build common warehouses, implement common distribution, and construct common circulation and technical centers. From being simply a concept to being supported in the organizational management of wholesale enterprises' and by the macro-policies of the state, wholesale logistics had been recognized of its status. Carrying out wholesale logistics distribution will be an inevitable trend in order to improve the competitiveness of the wholesale trade in China, as well as an ideal choice for the Chinese wholesale trade to get rid of the dilemma that many of their functions of business flow are internalized by production or retail enterprises.

The status of wholesale logistics was widely recognized in this stage. Theoretically, wholesale logistics was different from general logistics in that it had its unique features and was of special importance. It achieved considerable development in business practice with the support of related policies. Wholesale logistics functions began to be strengthened. However, in general, the overall cost of logistics in China wasn't reduced significantly during this period, since China failed to make a systematic exploitation in the reform of wholesale logistics. The level and efficiency of wholesale logistics was still to be improved.

The third stage: reshaping of wholesale logistics (2001 to present)

Establishment of the status of wholesale logistics in the previous stage set off a fever of building distribution centers across China. That logistics was carried out in the wholesale trade before providing services for retail enterprises became one of the main contents of the reform of the wholesale trade. Most wholesale enterprises initiated reorganization and introduced corporate governance. Some even expanded their businesses to the field of retail before establishing such types of retail operations as hypermarkets and supermarkets. But in general, wholesale logistics had failed to get fully developed and businesses of wholesale logistics had been still limited to a city or district in the previous stages. Entering the new century, wholesale logistics was faced with more new challenges: on the one hand, foreign-funded storage and logistics enterprises emerged, and on the other, the leading role of retail enterprises and chain-store commercial businesses in the market got further strengthened. In addition, since entering the 21st century, wholesale logistics has faced with more challenges brought about by the rapid development of the new economy and modern information technologies, especially network technologies. In particular, after China's accession to the WTO in 2001, international logistics enterprises have entered the enormous logistics market in China on a large scale. With rich industry knowledge and operating experience, advanced concepts and complete facilities, they have had an enormous impact on the growing wholesale logistics in China. The Chinese wholesale enterprises, as a traditional circulation industry, have to make necessary transformation and construct their own types of logistics, failing to do which will lose them their position in the market and narrow down the space for their survival.

With the deepening of the Chinese people's awareness of wholesale logistics and the development of wholesale logistics itself, especially the increase in domestic and foreign exchange brought about by China's accession to the WTO, the traditional Chinese wholesale enterprises sped up reorganizing and transforming into wholesale logistics. Most Chinese wholesale enterprises have begun to pay attention to adopting a variety of advanced logistics technologies such as new techniques and equipment. It is safe to say that under the positive influence of China's accession to the WTO, enterprises engaged in wholesale logistics in China have undergone great changes both in attitude and in action. Logistics organizations are no longer limited to the aggregation or segmentation of functions, but begin to introduce the concept of supply chain management. It has become an important direction in the modeling of wholesale logistics that specialty wholesalers provide logistics supports for retailers. In particular, the rapid development of the information and network technologies since the 21st century has provided external supports for wholesale logistics to integrate the resources, technologies, customers, markets and opportunities of each and all of its members, break through the physical boundary of the original organization, achieve the unified and coordinated logistics operation on the basis of virtualization and networking, and achieve the greatest logistics capabilities with the smallest organizations. At the meantime, six ministries and commissions, including the State Economic and Trade Commission of China, issued *Several Opinions on Accelerating the Development of Modern Logistics in China* in 2001. Nine ministries and commissions, including National Development and Reform Commission of China, issued *Opinions on Promoting the Development of Modern Logistics in China* in August 2004. The adoption of a series of policies and measures provided policy supports for the development of wholesale logistics. In addition, the establishment and operation of the national inter-ministry joint conference system for modern logistics, the development of related standards on the standardization of logistics in China, as well as local planning for logistics development made by some cities and districts all mark that a comprehensive and coordinated system for the Chinese Government to push forward the development of modern logistics has taken shape.

In 2006, the Chinese Ministry of Commerce made requirements on the development of the wholesale trade in China in the *Planning for the Development of Domestic Trade during the 11th Five-year Plan Period*. Specifically, the requirements included: pushing forward the innovation of the mode of operation and services of the wholesale trade, and promoting the upgrading of the commodity exchange markets to enable them to transform in the direction of modern market patterns such as commodity exhibition and order center, wholesale purchase center, information service center and wholesale logistics distribution center, etc. All in all, to develop the wholesale trade, China must develop comprehensive wholesale logistics in the fields of production and circulation, make full use of the constant improvement of social productivity and the rapid development of science and technologies, enable wholesale logistics to be able to provide multi-functional services and achieve functional transformation, and improve the level of modernization of wholesale logistics. It is the goal of the reform of wholesale logistics in not only the reshaping stage, but in the future.

Achievements of the reform of wholesale logistics

In the early days of the reform, the links inside wholesale logistics system were isolated from one another, making the overall efficiency of the system poor. With three decades of reform, wholesale logistics has had a constantly improved legal system, a gradually expanded overall scale, significantly improved organizational performance, and an increasingly balanced structure.

Applicable policies for wholesale logistics have been gradually improved

Since the introduction of the concept of logistics into China at the end of the 1970s, with the deepening of the reform and opening up in China and the transformation of its mode of economic growth, local governments at all levels in China, the industrial circles and the theoretical circles began to pay great attention to and effectively push forward the development of modern logistics in China, making significant achievements in the construction of the policy environment for logistics. The National People's Congress of China, the State Council and all departments under its administration, as well as local governments at all levels issued a series of policies, laws and regulations related to logistics, providing applicable policies for the development of wholesale logistics. Related national documents included *Several Opinions on Accelerating the Development of Modern Logistics in China* printed before being distributed by six ministries and commissions of China in 2001, including the State Economic and Trade Commission; and *Classification and Evaluation Indicators for Logistics Enterprises* issued in 2005. Related local documents included *Opinion on Accelerating the Development of Modern Logistics* issued the Fujian Provincial People's Government in 2005, *Opinion on Accelerating the Development of Modern Logistics in Xiamen* issued by Xiamen Municipal People's Government in 2003. In addition, there were also special policies for some specific logistics link such as special policies, laws and regulations on the adjustment of highways, railways, sea transportation and air transportation. One example of such policies, laws and regulations would be *Maritime Code of the Peoples Republic of China* (1992) developed and passed by the Standing Committee of the National People's Congress. The system of logistics policies, from state logistics policies, local logistics policies to special logistics policies for some related fields, has been gradually improved in the reform. Such policies, laws and regulations are the highest guiding principle and guide for the development of wholesale logistics, which will push forward the healthy development of wholesale logistics in China.

Wholesale logistics has made great contribution to the development of China's national economy[3]

The Chinese economy has been developing rapidly in the three decades of reform. The development of wholesale logistics has made significant contribution to the development of the national economy of China. As can be seen from Fig. 6.1, during 1991–2006, the ratio of the added value of trade logistics to GDP in China had been over 0.7%, indicating that the trade logistics played an indispensable role in the development of the Chinese economy. Seen from the development trend, the ratio of the added value of trade logistics to GDP in China has always been stable in spite of the slight fall in 1993 which was only 0.1–0.2%. What's more, since 2005, the same ratio has begun to show a growing trend, being kept at about 0.8%, up 14.3% comparing with that in 2004. It indicates that wholesale logistics has made greater contribution to the national economy of China while expanding itself, demonstrating that the growing reliance of the economic development in China on wholesale logistics.

Fig. 6.1. Ratio of the added value of trade logistics to GDP

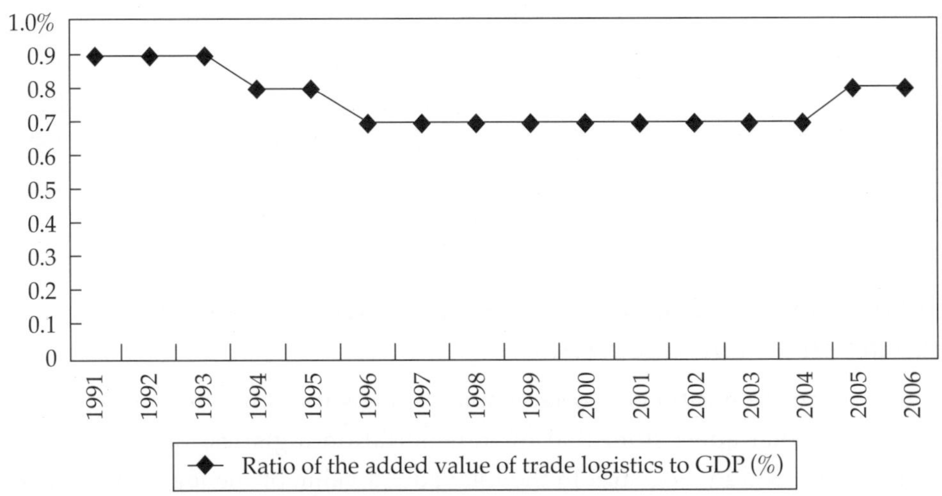

Wholesale logistics has made great contribution to the development of the tertiary industry

Development of wholesale logistics plays a pivotal role in the development of the tertiary industry in China. It has promoted the development of the tertiary industry, made great contribution to the industrial restructuring in China, and conformed to the trend of the times and the historical law of economic development. As can be seen from Fig. 6.2, during 1991–2006, the average ratio of the added value of trade logistics to the GDP of the tertiary industry in China was 2.1%, which was relatively stable in spite of its declining trend before 2004. After 2005, the said ratio began to grow, reaching 2.1% in 2006 which was 16.7% higher than that in 2004. It indicates that wholesale logistics in China is growing constantly after the reform, accounts for an increasingly proportion in the tertiary industry, and plays an increasingly prominent role in promoting the development of the tertiary industry and upgrading and optimizing the industrial structure in China.

Fig. 6.2. Ratio of the added value of trade logistics to the GDP of the tertiary industry

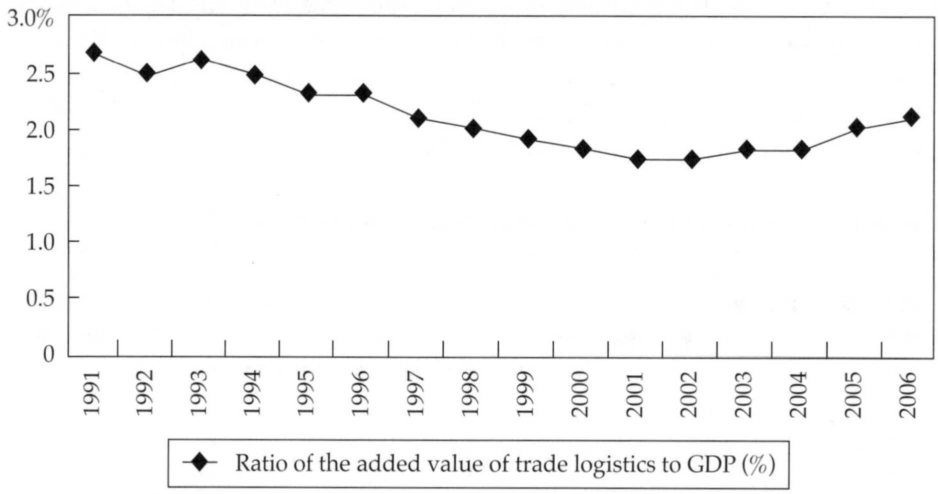

Wholesale logistics has made great contribution to the development of logistics

If to analyze the position of social wholesale logistics in the logistics industry, we can see that apart from that of transportation logistics, the ratio of the added value of trade logistics to the total added value of the logistics industry is the highest of all. Seen from its development course (see Fig. 6.3), during 1991–2001, the ratio of trade logistics to the logistics industry as a whole changed little, but being maintained at about 10.4%. With the development of the Chinese economy, trade logistics became more and more important. Since 2002, the ratio of the added value of trade logistics to the total added value of the logistics industry as a whole has exceeded that in 1991, growing at a high speed. In 2006, the above said ratio was 12.4%, indicating that of RMB 10 billion of the added value of logistics, RMB 1.24 billion was created by trade logistics. The ratio of the added value of trade logistics to the total added value of the logistics industry as a whole grew by 21.9% comparing with that in 2005 and about 20% comparing with that in 1991, indicating the great improvement of the status of trade logistics in the logistics industry, also the great improvement of the status of wholesale logistics in the logistics industry. As the result of the accelerated development of wholesale logistics in China, it also indicates that wholesale logistics will continue being the main content of the development of the wholesale trade in China.

Fig. 6.3. Composition of the added values of logistics

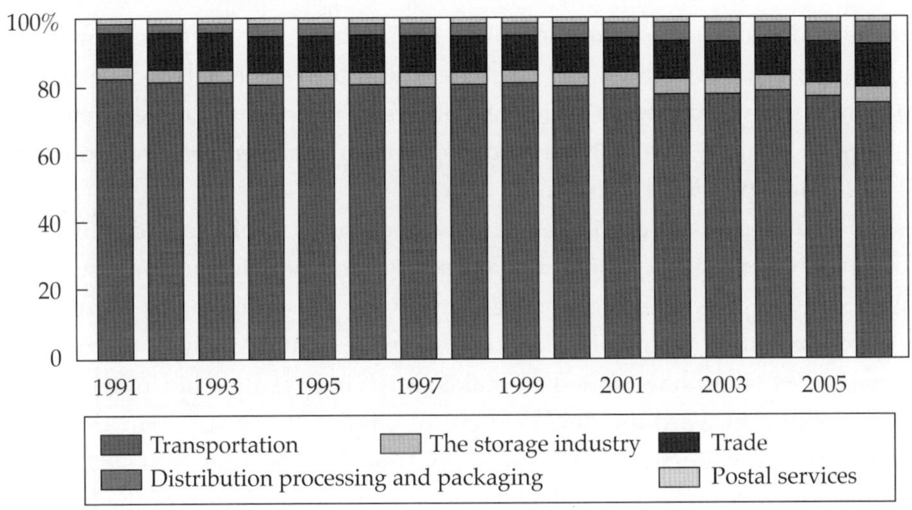

In short, since the reform, wholesale logistics has become increasingly larger in scale. With a favorable policy environment for its development, wholesale logistics plays an increasingly strengthened role in the overall economy. It has developed because people's awareness over logistics was enhanced, and the wholesale trade gave play to the role of wholesale logistics. Firstly, cities or districts featured by a convenient transportation, great commodity flow and flourishing production and sales are often chosen as locations of wholesale outlets in the construction of wholesale enterprises, providing advantaged conditions for developing logistics; secondly, wholesale enterprises have large areas of lands, great numbers of warehouses, adequately-equipped vehicles and other mechanical equipment for storage, transport, handling and transportation, providing a well developed foundation for wholesale logistics; thirdly, a large group of professionals with rich experience in purchase, storage and transportation management and equipped with modern economic theories and information technologies who are grown up in the wholesale business are the backbone of wholesale logistics in its development. In addition, in their cooperation in the past several decades, a relatively intimate relationship of mutual trust has been developed between wholesale enterprises and production enterprises, among wholesale enterprises, and between wholesale enterprises and retail enterprises, which has also laid an organizational foundation for the development of wholesale logistics. It is because of the above mentioned advantages for the wholesale trade to develop logistics that wholesale logistics became unique and made prominent achievements.

Problems existing in the reform of wholesale logistics

With three decades of reform, the policy environment for the development of wholesale logistics in China has been greatly improved. Related government departments have adopted a series of policies to support the development of the logistics industry, which have made significant achievements. Yet problems still exist. Main problems include:

(1) The already issued policies haven't been fully implemented. Since the reform and opening up, China has adopted many policies and measures in order to develop its wholesale trade, improving the policy environment for the development of wholesale logistics to some extent. However, the policies and measures taken have failed to make satisfying results, and played little role in pushing forward the development of wholesale logistics. For example, on the repeated collection of business tax from the logistics industry, many enterprises have been benefited. However, of the trial enterprises of the logistics tax, holding companies and subsidiaries can't fully enjoy the policies on trial enterprises, and wholesale logistics can only enjoy limited tax preference since its nature of business is not as significant as those professional logistics companies that forward the transportation of goods, all because of the vague definition of "subordinate enterprises". For another example, *Opinion on Promoting the Development of Modern Logistics in China* issued by the nine ministries and commissions in China, including State Development and Reform Commission, played a certain role in guiding the development of wholesale logistics, yet it hasn't been thoroughly implemented. In addition, financial policies and measures in support of the logistics industry are still absent in China. Wholesale logistics enterprises led by small and medium-sized enterprises don't have much fixed assets, or any enterprise that would like to secure them, so it's hard for them to get bank loans or to receive financial supports. Wholesale logistics has long been bothered by the problem of financing.

(2) Appropriate policies and measures are in absence when new problems emerge in the development of the logistics industry. Generally speaking, policies

lag behind physical needs, which is extremely significant in the field of wholesale logistics. On the one hand, logistics is becoming more and more crucial for the wholesale trade to get rid of its plight, but on the other hand, wholesale logistics develops spontaneously and receives few supports from corresponding policies for solving the many problems emerged in its development. For example, there have been no accommodative government policies aiming at promoting the separation and outsourcing of wholesale logistics. Such problems as the increased tax burden of wholesale logistics companies after the establishment of specialty companies by separating main logistics industries, which turns part of the original manufacturing cost into business income, as well as the way out of redundant personnel after the separation and outsourcing of wholesale logistics, etc. all need the supports of corresponding policies. In addition, guiding policies for domestic enterprises to "go global" when wholesale logistics has been developed are in absence.

(3) The contradiction between the integration of modern logistics and administrative division is prominent. The logistics industry is a trans-department and trans-industry service trade. It touches upon not only a variety of modes of transportation, but also a multiple of business lines. Since logistics touches upon the authorities of many industries, logistics enterprises would often encounter great difficulties in the integration of all resources. Plus, China saw a late start of modern wholesale logistics, so it hasn't succeeded in rationalizing the market management and industry management of wholesale logistics. Related state ministries, commissions and bureaus share the function of wholesale logistics management. Though 15 ministries, commissions and associations, including the National Development and Reform Commission, the Ministry of Commerce, the Ministry of Railways, the Ministry of Transport, the Ministry of Industry and Information Technology, Civil Aviation Administration of China and China Federation of Logistics & Purchasing, set up the national inter-ministry joint conference system for modern logistics, a high-end coordination system for mutual exchange among the authorities of the logistics industries in 2005, the said system failed to change the separated and isolated management of various departments'. Locally, economic development is unbalanced and local protectionism still exists. So, wholesale logistics in China is obviously departmentalized and regional in its development, making the allocation of resources difficult. Under the system of overlapping and segmented management, existing policies, laws and regulations on wholesale logistics, though enormous in number, sometimes contradict with one another and the contradiction is hard to reconcile for being tied up by department or local interests.

(4) Laws and mechanisms are not complete enough. China is a country that is in multiple transitions now. Of which, the most crucial one is the transformation of the economic system, that is, the transition from the traditional planned economic system to the modern socialist economic system. Since China adopts gradualism in its reforms, some characteristics and functions of the planned economy have to withdraw or disappear gradually. In a fairly long period, the disharmony even conflicts between the two systems are inevitable, making it hard for the macro-institutional environment to have this synergistic effect. The "soft" constraints of the institutional and policy environment have led to the weak ability of wholesale logistics to make comprehensive coordination. On the one hand, modern wholesale logistics needs a relatively comprehensive coordination and management system in order to get developed, but on the other hand, the existing traditional system has led to segmentation and the difficulty in making coordination, restraining the development of wholesale logistics. Industrial policies and planning necessary for the development of modern wholesale logistics haven't been introduced, so there are no effective external restraints over the social services of wholesale logistics, leading to unfair competitions inevitably and restraining the further development of the third-party wholesale logistics.

Organizational Evolution of Wholesale Logistics

Wholesale logistics organizations analyze wholesale logistics from the angle of organization. In this section, the scale of the wholesale logistics organizations and the operational performance of the wholesale logistics enterprises will be analyzed in order to reflect the organizational situation of wholesale logistics.

Scale of wholesale logistics organizations

In the early days of the reform and opening up, wholesale logistics was mainly undertaken by the storage and transportation functions of wholesale enterprises'. In face of "large and all-inclusive" and "small and all-inclusive" wholesale organizations, logistics was simply a subsidiary function of wholesale, with a limited development scale. With the advance of the reform, the logistics industry began to attract more and more attention and expand rapidly. Wholesale logistics also underwent a process of growing from small to large, witnessing the gradual expansion of the scale of logistics. The added value of wholesale logistics and the fixed-asset investment in wholesale logistics will be adopted next to reflect the organizational scale of wholesale logistics.

Added value of wholesale logistics

The added value of wholesale logistics is an important measurement for the scale of wholesale logistics. The higher the added value is, the larger the scale of wholesale logistics will be.

As can be seen from Fig. 6.4, the added value of trade logistics in China kept growing. During 1991–2006, the added value of trade logistics in the whole society grew from RMB 19.3 billion to 174.9 billion, being 8 times greater and presenting an annual growth rate of about 16%. The growth rate of the added value of trade logistics began to grow year by year since 1998, demonstrating the accelerated development of wholesale logistics in China. The same growing trend emerged in the development of wholesale logistics. The expansion of the scale of wholesale logistics indicated the increase in the commodities in circulation in the whole society from another angle, also the unceasing expansion of the economic aggregate in China indirectly. Domestic and foreign experience in developing wholesale logistics has shown that development of wholesale logistics in a country is always in direct proportion to that of the economic aggregate, and to the level of economic development of the country. Since the 1990s, the Chinese economy has maintained a rapid development, and its GDP has been growing at a rate of about 10% each year. Such an enormous scale of economic growth would be impossible without the powerful support of the logistics industry.

Fig. 6.4. Added value of trade logistics and its growth rate

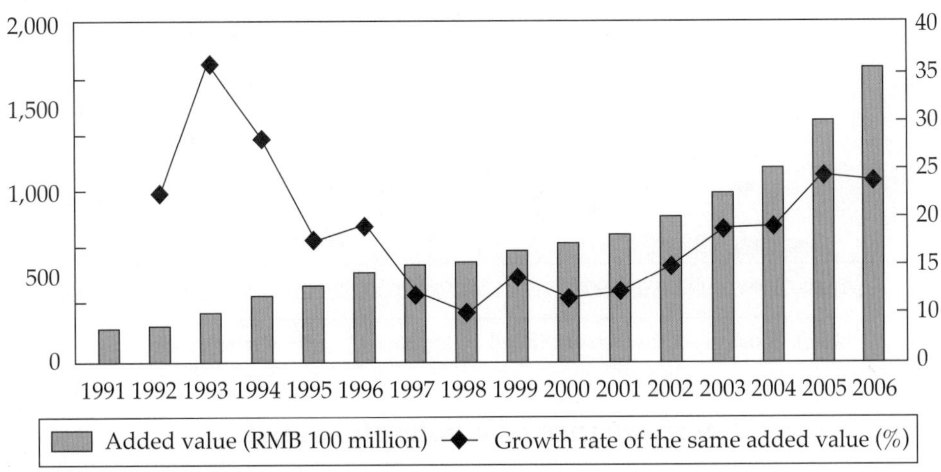

Fixed-asset investment in wholesale logistics

Fixed-asset investment in wholesale logistics could reflect the development level of wholesale logistics indirectly. Generally speaking, the higher the development level of wholesale logistics is, the more the fixed-asset investment in wholesale logistics will be.

As can be seen from Fig. 6.5, during 1991–2006, the total amount of fixed-asset investment in trade logistics kept growing, increasing from RMB 4.27 billion in 1991 to 182.7 billion in 2006, up 4,178.7%. Of which, fixed-asset investment in trade logistics in 1992 was RMB 12.27 billion, up 187.4% over that in 1991, which was the highest growth rate of all in the three decades of reform. After 1992, growth of the amount of fixed-asset investment in trade logistics could be divided into two stages: 1993–2002, during which it grew stably at a rate lower than 30%; 2003–2006, during which it was doubled and redoubled sharply. In 2003, the amount of fixed-asset investment in trade logistics was RMB 51.02 billion, up 120.2% over than in 2002. In the three years that followed, it maintained a high growth rate, being over 70% on the average annually, indicating the constantly expansion of the scale of wholesale logistics. In the reform and reshaping, the wholesale trade was faced with multiple challenges, wholesale businesses were extruded, and the size of professional wholesalers reduced. As an important direction of the reform of the wholesale trade, wholesale logistics became increasingly favored.

Fig. 6.5. Fixed-asset investment in trade logistics

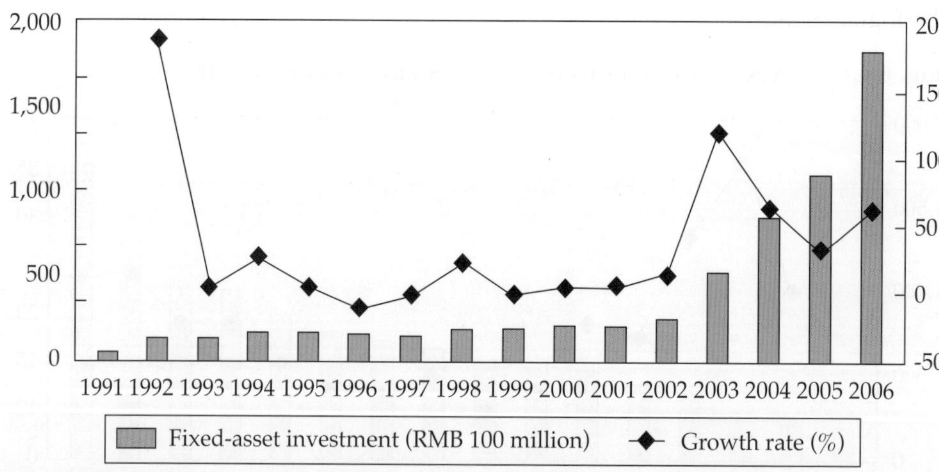

Organizational performance of wholesale logistics

With the expansion of the organizational scale of wholesale logistics, the performance of wholesale logistics has also been improved greatly. Since the reform and opening up, wholesale logistics has achieved unprecedented development at both the micro-level (in terms of the corporate system, mode of operation, level of management, facilities and equipment, technical level, etc.) and the macro-level (in terms of market size, structure of competitions, economic environment, industrial policies and the level of marketization), making ready all preconditions for improving the performance of wholesale logistics. The performance of wholesale logistics in China will be analyzed briefly as follows from the cost of logistics, technical level, the quality of practitioners, as well as enterprises' level of informationalization.

Cost of wholesale logistics

As can be seen from Fig. 6.6, in general, the growth rate of the cost of logistics in China declined in fluctuations during 1991–2002. Though the cost of wholesale logistics showed a growing trend after 1998 and reached 12.4% in 2002, it fell by 2% annually comparing with that in 1992, indicating that the efficiency of wholesale logistics was improved. Compared with the growth rate of the national economy, the growth rate of the cost of wholesale logistics was always lower than the concurrent growth rate of GDP. It further indicates that the higher the efficiency of logistics is, the greater the added value of the economic aggregate brought about by unit cost will be. According to the results of the survey on the wholesale logistics of enterprises engaged in national key circulation industries carried out by the National Development and Reform Commission, National Bureau of Statistics of China and China Federation of Logistics and Purchasing in 2006, the expense ratio of wholesale logistics of the investigated enterprises engaged in the wholesale of agricultural products was 7.44%, down 0.93% over that in 2005; the volume of sales of the above enterprises increased by 65.3%; the freight volume of the above enterprises increased by 104.1%; the expenses of such enterprises on wholesale logistics grew by 47%; and the growth rate of the expenses on wholesale logistics was 18.5% lower than that of the sales, and far lower than that of the freight volume of such enterprises.

Technical level of wholesale logistics

Seen from the technical grades of talents in wholesale logistics (see Fig. 6.7), there were 2,972 senior technicians and 13,945 senior workers in the wholesale trade in 2004, accounting for 0.23% and 1.1%, respectively of the practitioners in logistics. It meant that every 1% up of the practitioners in logistics practitioners equaled the increase of 0.23 people in senior technicians engaged in wholesale logistics. Though the proportion of senior workers was simply 1.1% in 2004, which was the lowest of all, the proportion of senior technicians ranked the second along with that of postal services. Compared with other trades, the wholesale trade was second only to the retail trade, accounting for a relatively high proportion in the logistics industry in terms of technicians.

Fig. 6.6. Growth of the cost of wholesale logistics

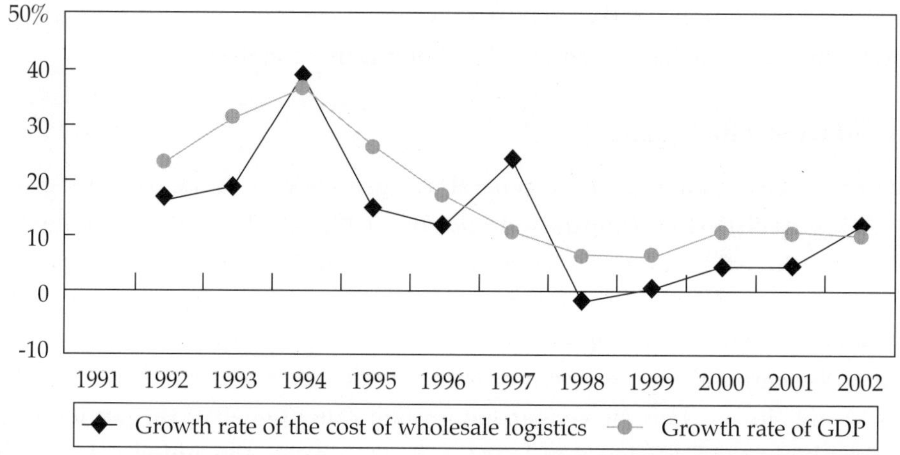

Fig. 6.7. Structure of the resources of human talents in logistics by technical grade

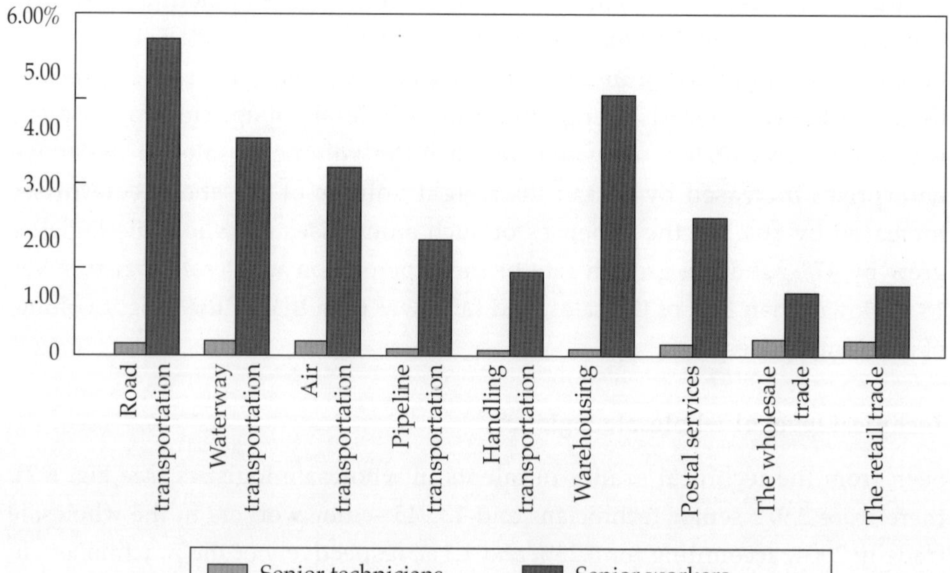

Source: Department of Higher Education, Ministry of Education. 2007. *Research Report on the Development and Demand for Talents of the Chinese Logistics*. Beijing: China Logistics Publishing House.

Quality of practitioners in wholesale logistics

Quality of wholesale practitioners refers to the ratio of professionals and technicians of all specializations and the personnel with junior college or above degrees to the total number of wholesale logistics practitioners within a certain period (usually one year). By comparing the indicators of the quality of practitioners engaged in wholesale logistics, we can measure the status quo and gap of the quality of talents in the field of wholesale logistics, and the priorities and direction of talent cultivation and education in the future in China.

As can be seen from Fig. 6.8, practitioners with secondary technical school or junior college or above education and degrees engaged in wholesale logistics were 361,796 in 2004, accounting for 28.5% of the practitioners in the logistics industry. Seen from the structure of educations received by the practitioners engaged in wholesale logistics, 14,433 were with postgraduate or above degree, accounting for only 1.1%; and 102,330 were with bachelor degree, accounting for 8.1%, second only to those engaged in air transportation.

Fig. 6.8. Indicators of the quality of practitioners in wholesale logistics in 2004

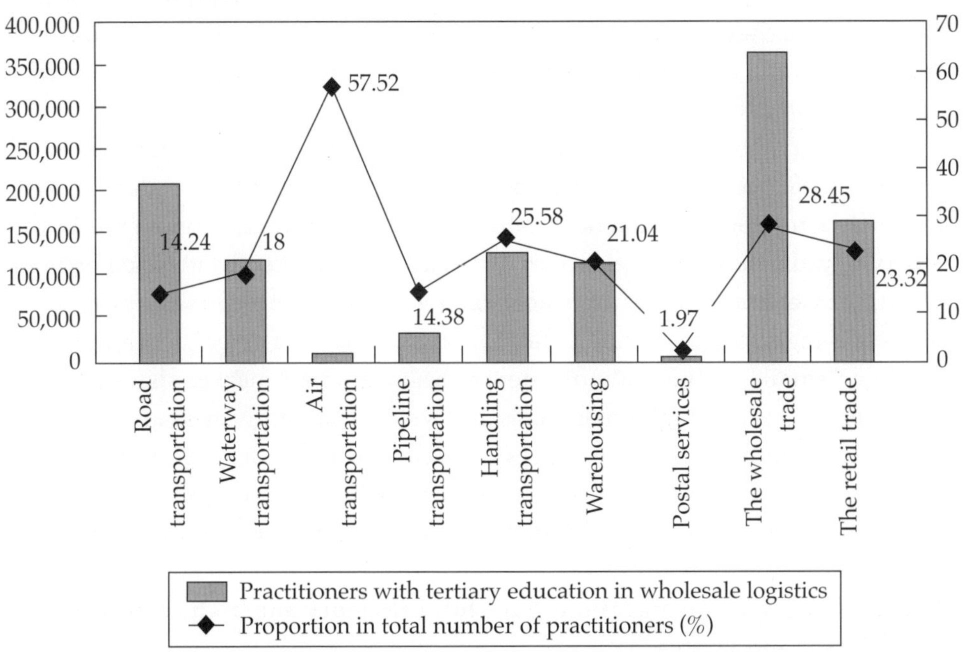

Source: Department of Higher Education, Ministry of Education. 2007. *Research Report on the Development and Demand for Talents of the Chinese Logistics*. Beijing: China Logistics Publishing House.

Level of informationalization of enterprises engaged in wholesale logistics

In 2003, the overall market size of IT products applied in the wholesale logistics trade in China reached RMB 1.63 billion, up 18.1% over that in 2002. A few number of enterprises engaged in wholesale logistics (about 15%) each with a high level of informationalization began to upgrade the level of application of information, and promote the optimization of their management and service process through information-based construction. Another few enterprises engaged in wholesale logistics (about 5%) began to enter the stage of constructing a system of nationwide supply chain. Seen from the investment structure of the enterprises engaged in wholesale logistics, hardware investment accounted for a predominating proportion. Of the total market size of RMB 1.63 billion of IT products applied in the wholesale logistics trade in China, RMB 1.19 billion was invested in hardware products, accounting for 72.8% of all; RMB 0.32 billion was invested in software products, accounting for 19.6%; and the rest RMB 0.12 billion was invested in information service products, accounting for 7.6% of all. That investment in hardware accounted for a large proportion was mainly because the Chinese wholesale logistics was still in the primary stage of information-based construction on the whole. Though the investment in software accounted for only 19.6% of the total investment in IT products applied, the ratio exceeded that of most other industries in China in their early stage of information-based construction.

To sum up, the organizational scale and performance of wholesale logistics in China have been improved. But it should also be noted that under the new economic situation, the functions and role of the wholesale commerce in the closely combination with logistics or distribution haven't truly attracted enough attention. Generally speaking, most of the Chinese enterprises engaged in wholesale logistics are "small", "few", "weak" and "scattered", meaning that they are "small" in the scale of operation, have small market shares, "few" service functions and high-quality talents, "weak" competitiveness and financial capabilities and "scattered" resources or networks available, and are in lack of necessary networks or faced with chaotic operational order. Specifically, major problems existing among the Chinese wholesale logistics organizations include:

Wholesale logistics organizations have low efficiency and high costs, with severe losses and wastes

The process of business flow and that of logistics in the existing system of wholesale logistics in China haven't been completely separated. Since commodities are bought and sold and the property in the commodities changes constantly in the process of business flow, the process of business flow is also segmented into several stages artificially. From the manufacturers to the first-level wholesalers to the second-level wholesalers to various types of intermediaries to the retail terminals, finally to consumers, commodities would go through many links, which prolongs the logistics cycles of commodities, greatly increases their logistics costs in the many times of handlings, storage and transportation, and leads to great amounts of losses and wastes.

Entities of wholesale logistics are yet to be matured and well organized

Seen from the development status quo of different wholesale logistics organizations, the original state-owned wholesale enterprises are still the core of commodity logistics (in particular major agricultural or resource products), yet most of them are with backward corporate system and single logistics function, so are nothing more than traditional storage and transportation enterprises. Though individual and private enterprises engaged in commodity storage and transportation are becoming an important force in commodity logistics, they are small in scale and scattered, and yet to be well organized. As for the third-party wholesale logistics enterprises capable of providing integrated wholesale logistics services and personalized solutions, they are usually small, with backward technologies and equipment, as well as fewer than needed talents in wholesale logistics. The wholesale logistics services and labors provided by them are unable to meet customers' demand. Moreover, for reasons regarding institutions, operating habits, etc., many Chinese enterprises are not quite dependant on professional wholesale logistics enterprises, but rely on their own wholesale logistics services. Seen from the unified level among wholesale logistics organizations, wholesale logistics is still separated and with decentralized operations. Though new types of organizations of wholesale logistics such as cooperative, associated and networked organizations have emerged under the integration of supply, production and sales, chain retail stores, they are small in number, and mostly in the primary stage of growth. So their logistics functions are yet to be improved; the division of work and coordination among organizations are yet to be improved, too; and the supply chain-based competitive mechanism hasn't been formed.

The levels of wholesale logistics services are uneven and the overall working efficiency is yet to be improved

There is still large room for the Chinese enterprises engaged in wholesale logistics to improve in such aspects as service concept, service facilities, service standards, service contents, service marketing and service quality control. In particular, they are not competitive enough with the services of the modern wholesale logistics system in such aspects as the design of comprehensive wholesale logistics services, socialized wholesale logistics services, the connection with the supply chain of industrial and commercial enterprises, the examination of the performance of wholesale logistics, etc. There are three specific reflections: firstly, the phenomenon of roundabout transportation and low efficiency under the influence of resource distribution, circulation system, industrial layout and the production organization of the enterprise is still prevailing; secondly, it is slow. Since the average operating speed of railway wagons and highway vehicles is only about 50 km/h and most ways of storage and handling are not efficient enough, the turnaround time of raw materials, semi-finished products and finished products in the warehouse is somewhere between 3–6 months; and thirdly, the losses are great. According to related data, the annual loss of China caused by packaging is about RMB 15 billion; that caused by handling and transportation is about RMB 50 billion; and that caused by improper maintenance is about RMB 3 billion.

The level of inforamtionalization of enterprises engaged in wholesale logistics is not high

Though the level of informationalization of the Chinese enterprises engaged in wholesale logistics has been improved to some extent, as can be seen from the above analysis, most of such enterprises now are engaged in traditional and regular physical services, such as storage, warehousing and distribution. Most investments focus on rebuilding equipment for wholesale logistics. Though some enterprises have adopted related management software on wholesale logistics, it is nowhere from near the goals of information-based management in the entire process of wholesale logistics. In general, the level of informationalization of Chinese enterprises engaged in wholesale logistics is still in the primary stage, the development of information-based construction of such enterprises is imbalanced. "Information islands" and "information gap" exist in many enterprises. It can be said that the backward construction of the information system for wholesale logistics is becoming the "bottleneck" of enterprise development. The ability to integrate the information resources of wholesale logistics has become an important factor that would be taken into consideration by enterprises in choosing suppliers of wholesale logistics. Therefore, as the advantage in traditional storage and hardware facilities has been replaced by the informationalized management-based ability to integrate resources, accelerating the construction of informationalization has become the breakthrough point of the development of Chinese enterprises in the future. Enterprises capable of carrying out management over modern wholesale logistics organizations and achieving informationalized management internally will become winners in the competition.

Changes in the Structure of Wholesale Logistics

In the past three decades since the reform and opening up, wholesale logistics has not only seen the constant expansion of its scale, but also a process of its structure becoming more and more improved. Structure of wholesale logistics refers to the internal composition and proportional relation of the wholesale logistics industry, and is composed of the added values, employment and the amount of wholesale logistics with different ownerships in different industries in different districts. Studying the structure of wholesale logistics is of great significance to understanding the development rules of wholesale logistics, grasping the development trends of wholesale logistics, developing related development policies on wholesale logistics, and promoting the competitions on the market of wholesale logistics. Limited by data availability, only the stock-sales ratio of the wholesale trade is chosen in this section as a measurement for the structure of wholesale logistics.[4]

Ownership composition of wholesale logistics

Development of wholesale logistics with different ownerships was consistent with that of the reform of economic system. In the early days of the reform, wholesale logistics was basically controlled and predominated by state-owned wholesale enterprises; wholesale was the main channel of commodity circulation, while the role of logistics in promoting the operating capacity of wholesale enterprises failed to attract enough attention. More commodities in circulation contributed to higher stock-sales ratio and lower level of wholesale logistics. Seen from the stock-sales ratio of the state-owned commerce and supply and marketing cooperatives, it was 63.2% in 1978, requiring high logistics costs accordingly and leading to low efficiency of wholesale logistics. With the deepening of the reform, the efficiency of wholesale logistics was gradually improved. The stock-sales ratio of the state-owned commerce and supply and marketing cooperatives was 51.2% in 1986, down 19% over that in 1978, falling by 2% annually. The stock-sales ratio of social commerce was 48.1% in 1987, which fell to 40% in 1992, down 16.8%, falling by 1.9% annually.[5] As can be seen, in the early days of the reform, the development level of the logistics of the state commerce and supply and marketing cooperatives was improved, yet the efficiency was low, growing at a low rate. It was because the state-owned sector of the wholesale trade had to play its economic role and social role in product distribution. Product storage became one of the main functions of the state-owned sector of the wholesale trade, so state-owned wholesale logistics was inefficient. State-owned enterprises dominated the commerce in China over this period, and other forms of the wholesale trade were negligible. Though diverse forms of ownerships had developed to some extent since 1987 with the advance of the reform of the pattern of wholesale circulation, which somewhat shook the dominance of state-owned enterprises in wholesale logistics and allowed different forms of ownerships to get engaged in wholesale logistics, the changes were not significant at all.

The coexistence of diverse forms of ownerships has been consolidated since 1993. Apart from the traditional state-owned and collective wholesale enterprises, private and foreign-funded wholesale enterprises all delved into the field of wholesale logistics before undergoing a period of rapid growth, breaking through the dominance of the state-owned and collective wholesale enterprises in the same field with an efficiency higher than that of state-owned and collective wholesale enterprises, and becoming one of the most active part of enterprises engaged in wholesale logistics. For example, the stock-sales ratio of the means of production of the wholesale and retail trade in 1993 was 22% in the state-owned sector, 20% in the collective sector, 10.5% in the private sector, and 10% in the foreign-invested sector.[6] After that, wholesale logistics with diverse forms of ownerships was further improved. Of the logistics of large and medium-sized enterprises engaged in the wholesale and retail trade in 1997, the stock-sales ratio of such enterprises in the state-owned sector was 18.34%; that in the collective sector was 16.84%; that in the foreign-invested sector was 12.7%; and that in the private sector was 11.6%. It can be seen, in the comparison of such figures with those in 1993, that the 4 forms of ownerships kept adjusting. The stock-sales ratio of the enterprises engaged in the wholesale and retail trade above the designated size in 2000 was 10.9% in the state-owned sector, down 12.8% over that in 1998 (which was 12.5%), 20.2% in the collective sector, down 8.8% over that in 1998 (which was 24%), 10.4% in the private sector, down 18.8% over that in 1998 (which was 12.8%), and 9.4% in the foreign-invested sector, down 18.3% over that in 1998 (which was 11.5%).

After 2001, the wholesale logistics industry entered the stage of standard development. Meanwhile, the wholesale trade was no longer combined with the retail trade in the collection of statistical data, but had its own accounting criteria. By observing the statistical data collected, we can see the development of wholesale logistics more clearly. As shown in Fig. 6.9, the development level of logistics of the private wholesale enterprises was the highest of all. The stock-sales ratio of logistics of such wholesale enterprises was 9.1% in 2001, being the lowest among all enterprises with different ownerships. Though the same ratio declined to 6.5% in 2007, the level of logistics of private wholesale enterprises was still the highest of all, being followed by that of foreign-invested wholesale enterprises. The stock-sales ratio of foreign-invested wholesale enterprises was high in 2001, being 12.4% and ranking the second, yet it began to fall rapidly since 2002 and was even lower than that of private wholesale enterprises during 2002–2005, making the foreign-invested wholesale enterprises having the lowest stock-sales ratio and the highest development level of logistics of all. The collective wholesale enterprises had the highest stock-sales ratio and the lowest development level of logistics among all wholesale enterprises. Since exceeded that of state-owned wholesale enterprises in 1998, the stock-sales ratio of collective wholesale enterprises has been ranking the first, being 23% in 2001 which was 12% higher than that of state-owned wholesale enterprises and 14% higher than that of private wholesale enterprises in the same year. However, seen from its growth trend, the stock-sales ratio of the collective wholesale enterprises declined the fastest during 2001–2007, falling to 11.9% in 2007, down nearly 50% over that in 2001. Its difference with that of wholesale enterprises with other ownerships kept narrowed down, being only 4.5% compared with that of state-owned wholesale enterprises, and only 5.5% compared with that of private wholesale enterprises in 2007. The stock-sales ratio of state-owned wholesale enterprises was second only to that of collective wholesale enterprises, and has been ranking the second since being exceeded by that of foreign-invested wholesale enterprises in 2002. Though it fell by 33% from 2001 to 2007, its declining rate was still lower than that of the stock-sales ratio of foreign-invested wholesale enterprises.

Seen from its development track, the ownership structure of wholesale logistics could be generalized this way: the development level of wholesale logistics in the state-owned and collective sectors is low and there is still large room for it to decline. In particular, the development level of logistics of collective wholesale enterprises grows slowly at a rate which is not only lower than that of the growth of the development level of logistics of private and foreign-invested wholesale enterprises, but also far lower than that of the growth of the development level of logistics of state-owned wholesale enterprises. Though the logistics of private and foreign-invested wholesale enterprises grow actively and have great growth potential, there is also room for both to decline. Seen from the change trend, the stock-sales ratio of private wholesale enterprises has been low among that of all other enterprises since its birth, yet it has been declining by 4.1% annually during 2001–2007, the declining rate of which was the lowest among all enterprises. Moreover, in some years, the stock-sales ratio of private wholesale enterprises was higher than that of foreign-invested wholesale enterprises, demonstrating that private wholesale enterprises in China is small in scale and that there is still a gap between it and that of foreign-invested wholesale enterprises.

Fig. 6.9. Changes in the stock-sales ratio of wholesale enterprises with different ownerships

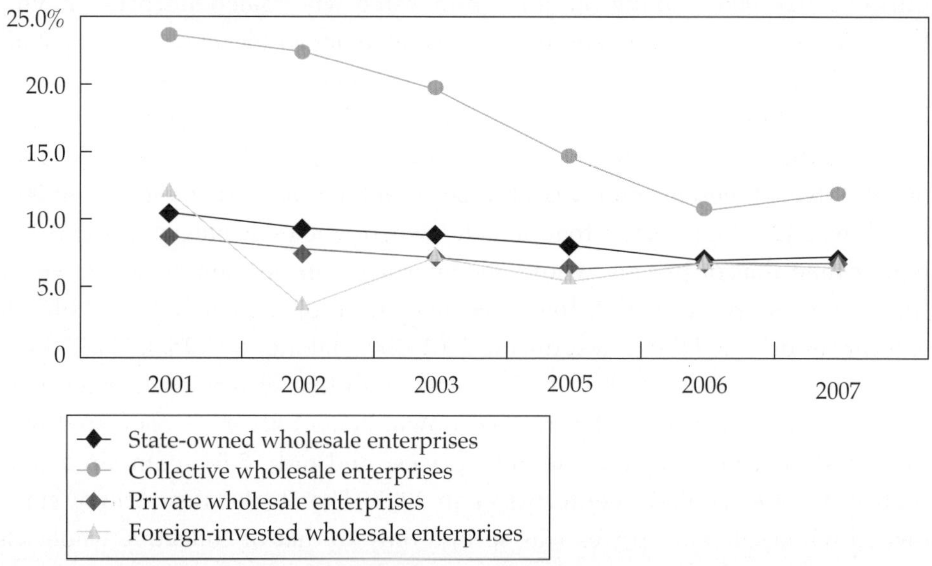

Structure of the wholesale logistics industry

Wholesale logistics is the logistics industry based on wholesale. Wholesale logistics and the wholesale trade are composed of the same sectors. In view of the availability of data, the wholesale logistics of seven major industries, namely agricultural products, textiles and garments, cultural appliances, food, scraps, machinery and mineral products, are chosen here to analyze the industrial structure of wholesale logistics.

After the foundation of New China, China followed the Soviet pattern of economic management before carrying out planned management over consumer goods and the means of production in circulation in an all-round manner, and established a materials management system led by the planned distribution and allocation of products. Most products included in wholesale logistics were the means of subsistence, while major means of production that were of pivotal importance to the national economy and the people's livelihood were viewed as "non-commodity", most of which were put under administrative allocation and not allowed to be traded on the market. With economic development and the launch of the reform and opening up in China, wholesale logistics in different trades were all increased, and the original industrial structure of wholesale logistics gradually reflected the law of economic development and changes. As for the means of subsistence, the total volume of retail sales of social consumables grew from RMB 126.49 billion in 1978 to 824.57 billion in 1991, registering an average annual growth of 39.4%. The total volume of retail sales of social consumables grew rapidly, so did the scale of wholesale logistics of social consumables correspondingly. As for the specific means of subsistence, the ratio of the total volume of retail sales of food to the total volume of sales of the means of subsistence grew by 6% in 1991 compared with that in 1978, apart from which the same ratio of the total volume of retail sales of survival-specific consumables such as clothes and medical supplies all declined. Of which, the ratio of the total volume of retail sales of clothes to the total volume of retail sales of social consumables fell from 22% in 1978 to 16.4% in 1991, down 25.5%; the same ratio of drugs and medical supplies fell from 5.1% in 1978 to 4.3% in 1991, down 15.7%. The sales of the means of subsistence for personal development or recreation grew rapidly at a rate higher than the overall growth of the sales of social consumables as a whole. For example, the proportion of the sales of culture and recreation articles was 6% in 1991, up 81.8% over that in 1978 which was 3.3%; that of the sales of books, newspapers and magazines was 1.6% in 1991, up 60% over that in 1978 which was 1%. As for the retail sales of the means of production, the sales of the means of agricultural production grew from RMB 29.37 billion in 1978 to 116.99 billion in 1991, registering an average annual growth rate of 21.3% which was lower than the growth rate of the sales of consumables. The sales of the means of other production grew slowly, too. In particular, the sales of articles for daily use such as house and building materials, and the sales of fuels declined, falling by 9.7% and 29.5%, respectively. Changes in the retail sales of social consumables in different trades reflected that wholesale logistics of related products also showed similar features. From the above data, we can conclude that over this period, the scale of wholesale logistics of the means of subsistence and the means of production was improved to some extent. However, under the influence of the traditional circulation system, the scale of wholesale logistics of the means of production was smaller than that of the means of subsistence; the scale of wholesale logistics of basic survival-specific means of subsistence reduced, while that of wholesale logistics of the means of subsistence for personal development or recreation expanded.

In its reform the economic system after 1992, China put forward such theoretical patterns as "maintaining a planned economy as the mainstay if the economic system and market regulation as the supplement", "planned commodity economy", "the inner unification of the planned economy and the socialist market economy", "the combination of the planned economy and the regulation of the market economy" and "the market economy", etc. in succession. Since then, wholesale logistics led by retailers and the operation of consumer goods began to shift its focus from the means of subsistence for survival to the means of subsistence for personal development and recreation. The theoretical restraint that means of production were not commodities was broken completely. Wholesale logistics of the means of production gradually broke through, in practice, the pattern of major means of production relying mainly on planned allocation, allowing the varieties of the means of production to be increasingly enriched and wholesale logistics of the means of production to gradually highlight its advantages. As shown in Fig. 6.10, of the wholesale logistics of the means of subsistence for retailers led by the operation of consumables, the stock-sales ratio of the wholesale of autos, motorcycles and accessories dropped the fastest of all. It was 12.5% in 1994 and 1.1% in 1998, down 91.2%. The stock-sales ratio of the wholesale of industrial art works used for meeting consumers' demand for personal development and recreation also dropped rapidly, falling from 9.2% in 1994 to 0.9% in 1998, down 90.2%. The same declining trend could also be seen in the stock-sales ratio of the wholesale of textiles, garments, hats and shoes used for meeting consumers' demand for basic survival. It fell by 6% in 1998, down 53.3% over that in 1994. The stock-sales ratio of the wholesale of other means of subsistence fell at more or less the same ratio, of which that of the wholesale of books, newspapers and magazines dropped at the lowest rate of all, down 12.3% within five years from 1994 (16.2%) to 1998 (14.2%). The stock-sales ratio of the wholesale of food, drinks and tobacco was 14.7% in 1998, down 25.6% over that in 1994. The stock-sales ratio of the wholesale of textiles, garments, shoes and hats also fell by 53.3%. Of wholesale logistics for enterprises led by the wholesale of the means of production, apart from that of the wholesale of cotton, flax, native products and animal by-products, the stock-sales ratio of the wholesale of other means of production was more or less the same, being around 15% in 1994 and 10% in 1998. Of which, the stock-sales ratio of the wholesale of cotton, flax, native products and animal by-products didn't fall, but increased, reaching 64.4% in 1998 which was nearly 1.6 times greater than that in 1994. The stock-sales ratio of the wholesale of the recycle of renewable materials fell at the highest rate. It was 5.3% in 1998, down 69.2% over that in 1994, registering an average annual fall of 13.8%. It indicated that the demand of renewable materials for wholesale logistics increased. The stock-sales ratio of the wholesale of hardware, electrical appliances & accessories and chemical products also declined at a high rate and fell from 17% in 1994 to 8.7% in 1998, decreasing by nearly 50% and registering an average annual fall of about 10%. In addition, the stock-sales ratio of the wholesale of building materials, metallic materials, wood and energies also declined rapidly, indicating the enhanced development level of wholesale logistics in these trades. The wholesale of chemical materials saw the smallest fall of the stock-sales ratio of all. During 1994–1998, the stock-sales ratio of the wholesale of chemical materials fell by simply 3.1%, indicating that the development level of wholesale logistics was relatively low in the trade.

Fig. 6.10. Stock-sales ratios of different sectors of the wholesale and retail trade in 1994 and 1998

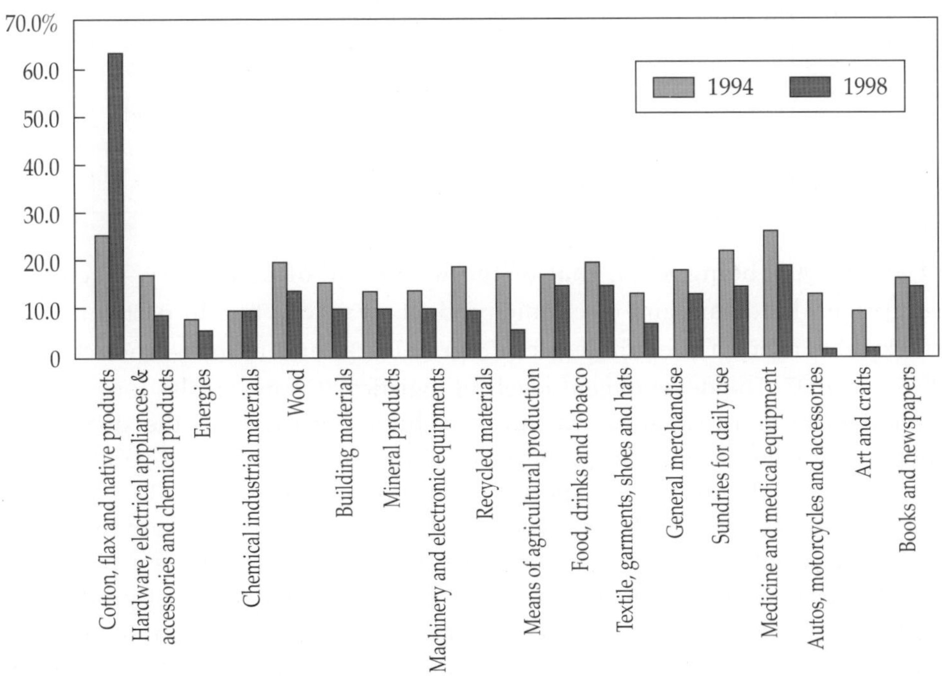

After 2000, the stock-sales ratio of the wholesale of the means of production was lower than that of the wholesale of the means of subsistence. That is to say, the development level of wholesale logistics of the means of subsistence was lower than that of the means of production, indicating that the wholesale logistics trade in China mainly served for the circulation of the means of production. As shown in Fig. 6.11, the stock-sales ratio of the wholesale of mineral products, building materials and chemical products was the lowest

Fig. 6.11. Stock-sales ratios of different wholesale trades (2000–2007)

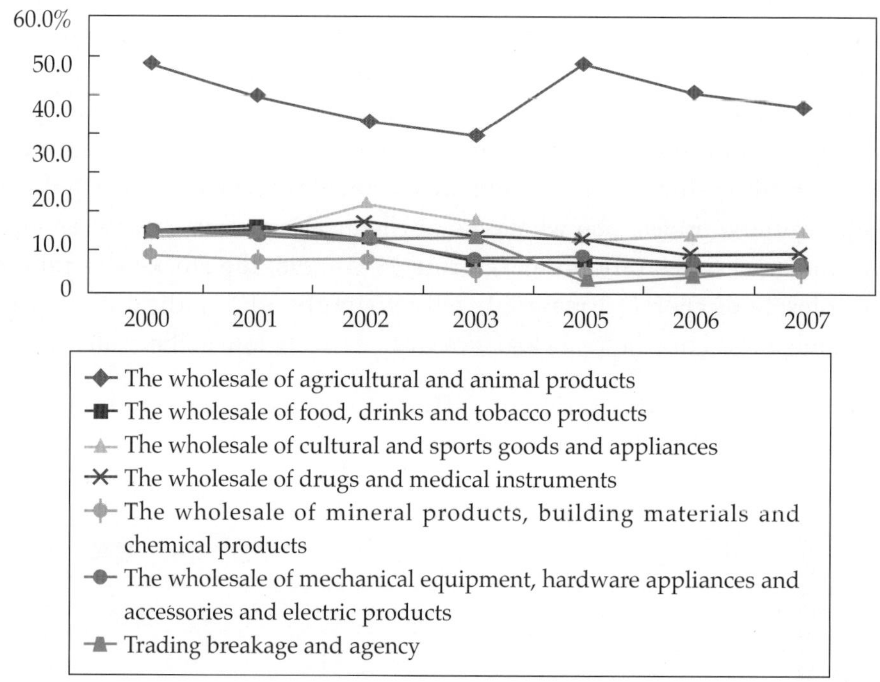

of all in 2007, being 4.6%; that of the wholesale of machinery, electronic equipment, hardware and electronic products was low, too. In particular, the stock-sales ratio of the wholesale of agricultural and animal products was 39.5% in 2007. The development levels of logistics of consumables for personal development and recreation was not very high. For example, the stock-sales ratio of the wholesale of drugs and medical instruments was 9.3%; and that of the wholesale of cultural and sports goods and appliances was 13.7% in 2007. The stock-sales ratio of the wholesale of food, drinks, tobacco products and that of the wholesale of textiles, garments and articles for daily use were low, even lower than the concurrent stock-sales ratio of such means of production as mineral products, building materials and chemical products, indicting the improvement of the quality of consumption and structural upgrading of such kind of consumer goods. Seen from the changing trend, the development level of wholesale logistics of the means of production and the means of subsistence for personal development and recreation was gradually improved. In particular, the development level of wholesale logistics of drugs and medical instruments was improved at the highest rate of all. During 2003–2007, the stock-sales ratio of the wholesale of drugs and medical instruments registered an average annual fall of 5%. While of the wholesale logistics of the means of production, the stock-sales ratio of the wholesale of mechanical equipment, that of hardware appliances and accessories and electric products, and that of mineral products all fell at a rate lower than that of the fall of the stock-sales ratio of the wholesale of the means of subsistence for personal development and recreation, registering an average annual fall of about 2%. It is worth mentioning that of the wholesale logistics trade, the wholesale logistics of trading breakage and agency started late and saw a high stock-sales ratio of 10.9% in 2003, its development momentum was extraordinarily strong and had fallen to 6.7% in 2007, registering an average annual fall of 8%.

Summing up the structural characteristics of the wholesale logistics trades mentioned above, we can get that wholesale logistics of the means of production and the means of subsistence for personal development and recreation developed well, while the development momentum of wholesale logistics of those products for basic survival was weak, reflecting the trend of economic development and constant upgrading of the pattern of consumption in China. In addition, the strong development momentum of trading breakage and agency of wholesale logistics trades demonstrates that the agency and agency for transportation of capable manufacturers will become an important development direction of wholesale logistics.

Regional structure of wholesale logistics

Regional structure is also an important content of the structure of wholesale logistics. Analysis of the regional structure of wholesale logistics can help people understand the regional features of wholesale logistics, thus is of great significance to developing regional policies for the development of the wholesale logistics trade and promoting the balanced development of the wholesale logistics trade in different regions. Seen from China's reality, the development of wholesale logistics is quite unbalanced in the six major regions. Regional development of wholesale logistics in China will be analyzed below. Limited to data available, the stock-sales ratio in each region will still be chosen as the measurement indicator.

Take an overview of the development of wholesale logistics in the three decades of reform, the stock-sales ratio of the wholesale trade has been declining year by year on the whole, indicating that the overall efficiency of wholesale logistics in China was constantly improved. However, regional differences of wholesale logistics still exist. Development of logistics can be divided into the following three stages in China based on the regional differences of its development.

The firs stage: balanced regional development (1987 and before)

From the foundation of New China to 1978, the wholesale trade, under the highly-centralized traditional planned economic system, strictly followed fixed scope of supply, fixed supply objects and scope of pricing before supplying commodities after layers of allocations through the 1st-, 2nd- and 3rd-level of distribution channels. What's more, due to the severe regional restrictions in social and economic running, China set up wholesale institutions by classifying wholesale channels into three levels by administration level, the practice of which was followed in wholesale logistics. Regional differences were not great. Seen from the data on the stock-sales ratios of social commerce, apart from the stock-sales ratio of social commerce in Northwest China which was slightly higher, being 60%, the stock-sales ratios in the other five major regions were not significantly different, but relatively balanced, all being somewhere between 45–50%.

Fig. 6.12. Respective stock-sales ratio of social commerce in the six major regions in 1987

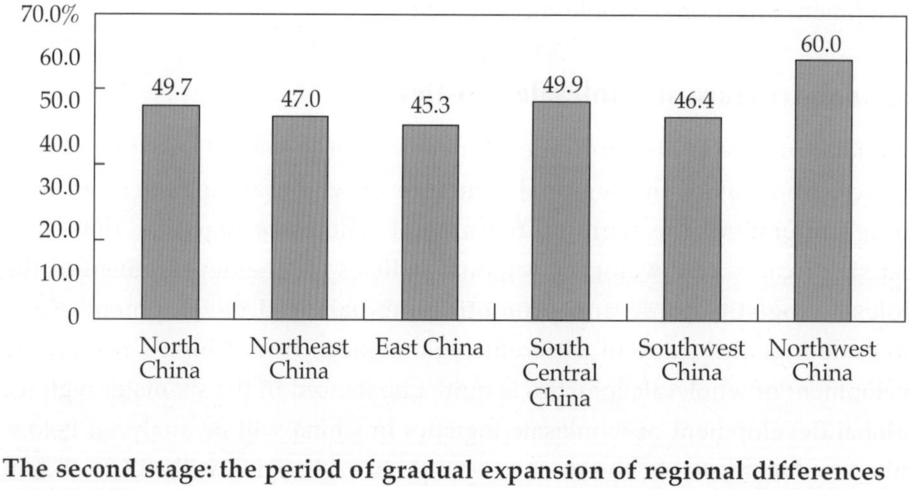

The second stage: the period of gradual expansion of regional differences (1988–1998)

After 1987, with the advance of the reform of the traditional wholesale channels and economic development, the overall efficiency of wholesale logistics was improved to some extent, yet the stock-sales ratio of wholesale logistics declined. However, regional differences of wholesale logistics emerged. See Fig. 6.13 below for details.

On the whole, in terms of the stock-sales ratio, Northwest China ranked the first, being followed by Northeast China and Southwest China, and North

China ranked the fourth, being followed by South Central China, then East China in this period. It is hence safe to say that the development level of the logistics trade in each of the regions was ranked quite the opposite way. East China and South Central China had the most developed wholesale logistics, and Northwest China had the least developed wholesale logistics. The development level of wholesale logistics in Northeast China and that in Southwest China were relatively low. It had much to do with the development level of commerce in each region, being basically the same with the development situation of the wholesale trade in each region in analyzed in the above section on regional structure.

Seen from the growth trend, the respective stock-sales ratio in each of the regions was more or less the same and all showed significant declining features, indicating that the development levels of wholesale logistics in the six regions all kept increasing, which was consistent with the overall development trend of wholesale logistics in China.

As for the regional gap of the stock-sales ratio, it was significantly enlarged in 1993 before being narrowed down in 1994. With the development of the market economy, the regional gap of the stock-sales ratio showed a trend of further expansion in 1997 before declining slightly in 1998. All in all, the expansion and declining trends of the regional gap of the stock-sales ratio appeared alternatively during this period.

Fig. 6.13. Stock-sales ratios of different wholesale trades (2000–2007)

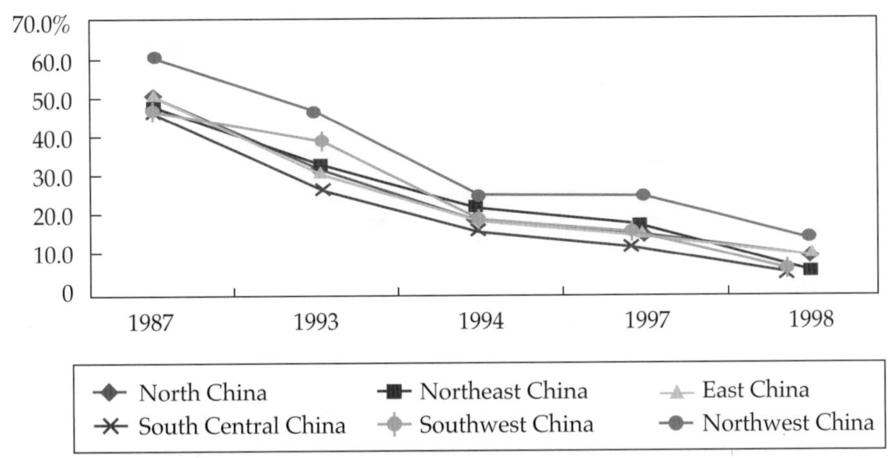

Source: *China Market Statistical Yearbook*, of which data during 1987–1993 were the stock-sales ratio of social commerce; and those during 1994–1998 were the stock-sales ratio of the wholesale and retail trade.

The third stage: Regional gap reduced gradually, yet there was still room for further declining (2001–2007)

After the short period of economic recession brought about by the financial crises in 1998, wholesale logistics in each major region began to enter the adjustment stage (see Fig. 6.14) since 1999. In 1999 and 2000, they gradually got rid of the impact of financial crises and returned to normal. Generally speaking, the stock-sales ratio of each region still kept declining over this period, indicating the further improvement of the overall development level of wholesale logistics in China. The ranking of the 6 major regions in terms of the stock-sales ratio was basically unchanged over that in the previous stage, except 2005 in which the stock-sales ratio of Northwest China was the highest of all, that is, Northwest China registered lowest development level of wholesale logistics. East China and South Central China still had a low stock-sales ratio, being the two regions with the most developed wholesale logistics of all. Seen from its regional gaps, the development level of wholesale logistics as of the end of 1999 was basically unchanged comparing with that in 1997, and became more stable in 2000. Since 2001, regional gaps of the development level of wholesale logistics had been gradually reduced, which was extraordinarily significant in 2003, and apart from the exception of Southwest China in 2005, maintained the trend of narrowing before reached the lowest level in 2007.

Fig. 6.14. Stock-sales ratio of the wholesale trade in different regions during 1999–2007

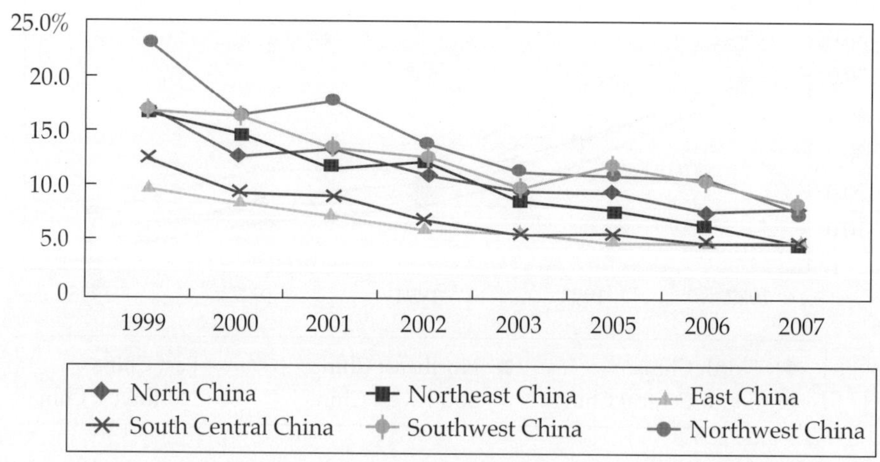

Since the reform, wholesale logistics in each of the six major regions has all achieved great development, and the regional structure has got improved.

Generally speaking, the regional structure of wholesale logistics has showed the following characteristics in its development:

(1) The development levels of wholesale logistics in East China and South Central China are the highest of all, because both regions are economically developed with highly developed wholesale trades. In addition, both regions are with more developed foreign trade processing and developed logistics systems, and local logistics demands are thus highly export-oriented.

(2) The development levels of logistics in North China and Northeast China rank in between, showing a trend of rapid growth. Both regions, especially Northeast China, are industrial bases, so local commerce is not as developed as that in East China and South Central China, and the development levels of wholesale logistics can't compete with those in East China and South Central China, either. However, thanks to their relatively good economic foundations coupled with the supporting policies made by China, the stock-sales ratios in both regions have kept declining, and the development levels of wholesale logistics have been constantly improved.

(3) Wholesale logistics in Southwest China and Northwest China have been improved to a limited extent. In the recent years, the West Development Strategy has promoted the great economic development in West China and given local wholesale logistics trades enormous development space before expanding their scales, making significant achievements. As can be seen from the analysis of the indicators regarding logistics capacity, logistics in West China is developing gradually; the West Development Strategy has played a certain role in promoting the development of local logistics; and many provinces and cities in West China have made or are making planning for the development of local logistics, laying a foundation for the further scientific development of modern logistics. However, comparing with the national average level, the stock-sales ratios of wholesale in western areas are all significantly higher. It has much to do with local characteristics. Firstly, the geological foundation for developing wholesale logistics in West China is far from being satisfying, and the urbanization rate of the development of wholesale logistics is low. Some areas are wastelands and deserts featured by abominable ecological environment, and others are barely inhabited, making it hard to develop the logistics industry. Secondly, logistics infrastructure is not adequate in West China. Comparing with its vast territory, West China has a low density of operational mileage of national railways, inland shipping, highways and public roads. Some areas have even had no access to public roads and railways. Thirdly, local logistics in West China are severely segmented. Barriers between different departments and areas in West China under the long influence of

the planned economic system are serious. Management of the development of logistics is also segmented. Therefore, vigorously developing modern logistics is the primary concern in promoting the economic development in West China.

7

Chapter

Development Prospects of the Wholesale Trade

With economic development and the reform of the circulation system, the wholesale trade in China is faced with severe internal and external challenges: on the one hand, manufacturers pay great attention to marketing, try hard to maintain their initiative in selling products, and spare no cost to establish their own distribution system, on the other hand, supermarkets, hypermarkets and other retail enterprises adopt unified purchase and order across China, place orders with manufacturers directly, and establish their own logistics distribution center. These coupled with the establishment of the foreign-invested distribution system and the emergence of the private sector of the wholesale trade, full-time wholesalers used to be the central link of the circulation system and the market network have gradually lost the original commodity, channel and market resources; the status of the wholesale trade as the main channel has been increasingly weakened and its market share has been reduced, too. The wholesale trade has begun to shrink, being stuck in a plight.

Though the status of the wholesale commerce in China has been somewhat weakened, it doesn't deny the significance to develop the wholesale commerce. Seen from its development history in the West, the wholesale commerce has experienced the initial stage, the dominating stage, the declining stage and the recovery stage. Though it develops differently in different countries and holds different statuses in different stages, the wholesale commerce, as an important link in the circulation channel, has never disappeared, but kept improving and renewing itself in historical changes. In particular, small trade markets in towns and townships and the geologically scattered existence of retail stores make direct marketing uneconomical, and make it necessary to meet the scattered demand for consumption relying on wholesale. Most manufacturers and retail enterprises in China are small or medium-sized, and less organized. Direct trading between manufacturers and retail enterprises demands a mass of manpower and material recourses, which is a great burden for both sides, thus inefficient. Their commercialized management has to be supported by the wholesale commerce. That's why the wholesale commerce will continue playing an indispensable role in the commodity market system in China in a fairly long period. The shrink of the wholesale trade just shows that reform of the wholesale trade needs to be further deepened, but by no means denies the necessity of its existence. In the days to come, China has to make efforts to overcome the disadvantages of the wholesale commerce, expand and better organize the wholesale commerce, actively foster and make use of the information superiority in the times of network, vigorously promote modern ways of wholesale operations, keep exploring the pursuits of efficiency, rights and legality, push forward the development of the wholesale commerce before getting a favorable position in the evolution of circulation channels, and achieve the modernization of the wholesale commerce in the process of industrialization. In this chapter, the goals, contents and specific measures for the development of the wholesale commerce in the days to come will be discussed from four aspects: wholesale organizations, wholesale structure, wholesale markets and wholesale logistics. Generally speaking, the development direction of the wholesale trade in the future is to further optimize industrial organizations, adjust industrial structure, build wholesale markets, achieve the modernization of logistics, and push forward the Chinese wholesale trade to transform into modern wholesale commerce adaptive to the requirements of mass production, big market and great circulation.

Optimization of the Wholesale Organizations

In the three decades since the reform and opening up, some achievements have been made to the wholesale organizations in China: wholesale organizations in China have become greater in scale, their market performance has been improved, and their market structure is more rationalized. However, comparing with that in Western developed countries, the wholesale trade in China is still less organized and far from becoming the modern wholesale commerce adaptive to the requirements of mass production, big market and great circulation. Therefore, China needs to keep optimizing its wholesale organizations in a fairly long period in the future.

The status quo of wholesale organizations

As can be seen from the analysis of the wholesale organizations in chapter 3, wholesale organizations have made a great progress in the three decades since the reform and opening up. Entering the 21st century, the scale of wholesale organizations has been expanded rapidly. In 2007, corporate wholesale enterprises above the designated size reached 80,778 in number, up increased by 165.9% comparing with that in 1999 (which was 30,381), registering an average annual growth of over 15% which was even higher than that of the concurrent GDP; the market performance of the wholesale trade got improved significantly, with the average assts increasing from RMB 88,758 thousand in 1999 to 133,440 thousand; the wholesale markets were fully competitive instead of highly monopolized as it had been, and the wholesale structure became more rationalized. The concentration ratio of the top eight large wholesale enterprises prior to 1992 was 30.12%, which had been further declined to 8.34% in 2007. Comparing with the state monopoly of the purchase and marketing of products under the planned economic system, the reduction of intermediate links and the connection of production and supply based on market demands in the past reform of the wholesale trade under the market economic system was a great step forward. However, comparing with the modernized wholesale trade, the market-oriented reform of the economic system in China hasn't been completed, an open market system with orderly competitions hasn't been formed on the domestic market, the size and organizational level of wholesale enterprises in China have been far lower than required, the modernization level of the wholesale enterprises in China has still be low, and there have existed many problems.

(1) There is still a distance between the overall size of the wholesale trade in China and that in developed countries. The overall size of the wholesale trade can be reflected by the ratio of the sales of the wholesale trade to the total volume of retail sales of social consumables. The higher the said ratio is, the greater the organizational scale of the wholesale trade and the higher the level of modernization of the wholesale trade will be. In developed countries, the sales of the wholesale trade are greater than the retail sales of social consumables, being 3–4 times in the Unite States and 2–3 times in Japan, for example. However, in China, the sales of the wholesale trade accounted for less than 60% of the total volume of retail sales of social consumables in 2003 and before. Though the sales of the wholesale trade exceeded those of the total volume of retail sales of social consumables for the first time in 2005, they exceeded by simply 12.4%. While in Japan, in the decade during 1981–1991, the ratio of the sales of the wholesale trade to the total volume of retail sales of social consumables had been over 40%. Seen from this indicator, there is still large room for the Chinese wholesale organizations to grow in scale.

(2) Wholesale enterprises are scattered and the concentration ratio of them is low. The 500 wholesale enterprises being elected into the top 100 most competitive in China in 2007 registered great a great distance with foreign wholesale enterprises in terms of the overall scale. In particular, the same distance was more significant among large enterprises each valuing more than RMB 1 billion. The size of wholesale enterprises in China is significantly smaller than that of foreign wholesale enterprises, equaling to the size of foreign wholesale enterprises in 1987. As can also be seen from the above analysis, the level of scale economy of the Chinese wholesale trade is significantly lower than that of the wholesale trade in developed countries. What's more, the scale

structure of the Chinese wholesale enterprises is not rational, either. Of the Chinese wholesale enterprises, "small and all-inclusive" ones account for a large proportion, yet such wholesale enterprises are small in organizational scale and low in the degree of specialization and coordination, making the wholesale trade in China unable to play the role of scale economy or effectively reduce the cost, and being unfavorable to the technical development of the whole industry, the improvement of the organizational and operational performance of wholesale enterprises in China, as well as the labor-intensive growth of the economy. According to the concentration ratio previously calculated, the CR_8 of the Chine wholesale trade, namely the ratio of the sales of the top 8 large wholesale enterprises to the sales of the overall wholesale trade, was only 8.34%, and CR_4, namely the ratio of the sales of the top four large wholesale enterprises to the sales of the overall wholesale trade in China, was simply 5.89%, being far lower than the standard on being competitive ($CR_8 \leq 40\%$, $CR_4 \leq 30\%$) according to Bain's classification of industrial monopoly and competition. Low concentration ratio and the extreme decentralization of production will definitely affect the intensive growth of the Chinese wholesale economy.

(3) The role of economic barriers to entry is not significant, and structural and strategic barriers to entry are low in the wholesale trade. The traditional wholesale trade was labor-intensive, requiring small capital input and having low economic barriers to entry. With the development of the market economy, and the acceleration of the reform of the circulation system and the opening up process in China, the wholesale trade became more and more information-based, the level of capital exclusiveness kept growing, and economic barriers to entry became strengthened to some extent. However, the development level, capital and technical input, scale economy, product differentiation and administrative policies and laws were yet to be improved, leading to the result that economic barriers to entry, structural barriers to entry and strategic barriers to entry were still a major reason for the organizational decentralization of the wholesale trade. From the numbers of enterprises getting engaged in or exiting the wholesale trade, we can see the role of the barriers to entry. According to statistics, the total number of enterprises getting engaged in the wholesale trade was greater than that exiting the wholesale trade in China since 1978, except individual years. For example, the number of wholesale enterprises above the designated size was 15.8 thousand more than that in 2003, and 1.2 thousand and 0.9 thousand more, respectively, in 2006 and 2007 over that in 2005 and 2006. The steady increase in the number of enterprises getting engaged in the wholesale trade in China since the reform and opening up is the demand of economic growth on the one hand, and shows the low barriers

to entry of the wholesale trade in China. Barriers to entry are mainly policy-induced, and economic barriers to entry play little role in inhibiting the entry of new enterprises, leading to a numerous number of wholesale enterprises and the phenomenon of different levels of excessive competitions, which was unfavorable to achieving the scale economy of the wholesale trade and the optimized allocation of resources.

(4) Not more advanced technologies have been applied and the level of informationalization is relatively low. Seen from the application of advanced technologies in the wholesale trade in developed countries, the negotiation, conclusion of a deal, settlement, delivery of samples needed by the market, order of commodities, and the instructions on purchasing, assembly and shipping sent to warehouse managers have all been electronic, so the wholesale trades in developed countries are capable of mastering the information on consumer demands at the very first moment, greatly improving their own functions, and promoting the development of wholesale businesses. Seen from the situation in China, though the wholesale trade has been more informationalized and standardized, there is still a great gap in the application of modern electronic information technologies, technical development of the wholesale trade is limited, and few wholesale enterprises choose to develop businesses with modern technologies or through the network, thus are unable to meet China's requirement on pushing forward the modernization of the wholesale trade and vigorously develop modern ways of wholesale.

(5) Most practitioners in the wholesale trade have little or no professional education, and wholesale talents are badly needed. Under the modern market economy, the wholesale trade gets its competitive edge relying mainly on talents that are with professional knowledge and capable of carrying out production on sales prospects and implementing new ways of marketing and management based on market demand. Though both the professional skills and the level of knowledge of wholesale practitioners in China have been improved to some extent, the improvement is far from being enough comparing with that of other industries or the average level in foreign countries.

On the whole, wholesale organizations keep growing in China, yet they are growing at a low rate and there is great room for their development in the future; market structure is overly scattered, which is not conducive to the optimization of resources and the display of scale advantages; structural barriers to entry in the wholesale trade are strong; and the application of electronic information technologies and practitioners' quality are yet to be improved. In a word, many problems still exist among wholesale organizations, requiring for solutions and further optimization.

Overall goals of the organizational optimization of the wholesale trade

Modernized mass production requires modernized great circulation. If the Chinese wholesale trade failed to get rid of the misunderstandings in the traditional patterns of trading and optimize its organizational structure, it would be hard to meet the needs of modern economic development. Optimizing wholesale organizations is a requirement of building modern wholesale commerce and adapting to mass production, big market and great circulation, as well as an objective requirement for achieving economic growth and improving the level of productive forces in China. The core problem in optimizing wholesale organizations is to save the time of circulation and reduce the cost of commerce to the maximum extent. Hereby, the specific goals of the optimization of wholesale organizations in the future should be:

(1) Further expansion of the scale. The scale of the wholesale trade is a direct reflection of the development level of the wholesale trade. Expanding the scale of the wholesale trade is conducive not only to improving the effect of scale economy, but also to adopting advanced technologies, thus is conducive to pushing forward the further development of the wholesale trade in China.

(2) Further improvement of the efficiency. Scale expansion can't necessarily improve the efficiency. Only cost-effective improvement could demonstrate that wholesale organizations are more rationalized before accelerating the development of the wholesale trade and speeding up achieving the modernization of the wholesale trade.

(3) Further perfection of functions. Basic functions of modern wholesale enterprises mainly include: gathering commodities, distributing commodities, making planning on and developing commodities, collecting information, financing, and supporting retail.

(4) Further extension of the industrial chain. The wholesale trade could extend its businesses toward both ends of the industrial chain. On the one hand, self-invested wholesale enterprises may be set up, on the other hand, the wholesale trade could develop toward retailers, strengthen its functions for providing services for the retail trade, and push forward the process of vertical integration.

Main contents of the organizational optimization of the wholesale trade

To deal with the impact brought about by the penetration of manufacturing enterprises and retail enterprises into the field of wholesale, wholesale enterprises must re-develop and re-construct its function of social existence, abandon the traditional definition of and stereotype ideas on the wholesale trade, redefine the wholesale trade based on the new circulation service industry, and further develop and improve wholesale organizations. To achieve the above objective and optimize wholesale organizations, the wholesale trade has to develop itself in the following several aspects in the future:

(1) Establishing modern wholesale enterprises and adopting modern ways of operation and management. Optimizing wholesale organizations and carrying out modernized operation is the prerequisite. Modernized operation of wholesale enterprises is achieved by improving the efficiency of circulation, the nature of which is "reducing relays or suspensions". "Reducing relays and suspensions" refers to the appropriate solution to the contradiction between production and consumption in time and space induced by social or industrial division of work in order to send products into the fields of consumption or re-production with least resources in the shortest possible time. Therefore, establishing modern wholesale enterprises aims at promoting such enterprises to adopt advanced technologies, reasonable forms of operation and highly-effective modes of management, improving the efficiency of the wholesale trade, even the entire field of circulation, ensuring the smooth circulation of products in the development of the national economy, and providing a good foundation and guarantee for the development of manufacturing enterprises.

(2) Carrying out strategic reorganization and developing scale economy. At present, major problems existing in wholesale enterprises in China can be generalized as being "small, scattered, chaotic and unsatisfying", that is, numerous wholesale enterprises small in size and low in efficiency develop separately for their own survival; financial, material and human resources are scattered, making it difficult to form scale and collective advantages; disorderly competitions lead to chaotic market order and deficiency in economic performance. After China's accession to the WTO, faced with the competitions brought about by many foreign companies, China has a new and extremely urgent mission-improving the competitiveness of its wholesale enterprises and helping the wholesale trade to speed up organizational innovation. To adapt to the market competitions under the new situation and complete the above mission, wholesale enterprises in China must expand their scale, take the path of scale operation, and improve the organizational level of wholesale enterprises. Specifically, it requires wholesale enterprises to gradually take the road of combination and include all operational resources into the same organization in order to expand their operational scale. What's more, it calls for mutually independent wholesale organizations to achieve mutual

complementarity with their respective advantages, and to strengthen mutual coordination before expanding their scale and improving their competitiveness. The said practices are very important ways of changing the status quo of the Chinese wholesale enterprises being small in scale and low in industrial concentration and helping them get scale economy advantages and improve their industrial competitiveness.

(3) Strengthening vertical integration and optimizing the structure of industrial organizations. The vertical integration of the wholesale trade aims at allowing the wholesale trade to play its important role as a connecting link (between production and consumption) in the national economy. In the process of economic development, special attention should be paid to optimizing the structure of the production and retail links, strengthening vertical integration, and giving full play to the connecting role of wholesale circulation in the process of economic development.

Specific measures for the optimization of wholesale organizations

Wholesale enterprises in China are generally small in operational scale and highly subordinate to local systems or regions, and have limited operating regions. In particular, most state-owned wholesale enterprises haven't got rid of administrative intervention, or backward business philosophy or poorly-performed operation mechanism, their further development is hence affected, making it hard for them to play the leading role in optimizing commodity circulation. An enormous number of wholesale enterprises with backward business philosophy and outdated business practices will result in the shrink of the functions of the entire wholesale trade, which the "offside" of manufacturing enterprises and retailers will become inevitable, so does the "short circuit" of the distribution channels. Therefore, to build a sound and efficient circulation highway, it is urgent to rebuild the functions of the wholesale organizations. In the future development of the wholesale trade, not only the reform and transformation of wholesale organizations will be carried out, but also a series of related policies and measures will be adopted to ensure the favorable macro-environment for the operation and development of the wholesale trade.

Measures for setting up modern wholesale enterprises

To optimize wholesale organizations and achieve the sustained development of the wholesale trade, the Chinese wholesale enterprises, especially those in the state-owned sector, should change the traditional concept on the wholesale trade and build modern wholesale enterprises starting with the internal and external environments of the wholesale trade.

Major moves on the internal environment of the wholesale enterprises

The internal environment of the wholesale enterprises is the foundation of their operation, and the starting point, basis and condition for optimizing wholesale organizations, being fundamental for them to outcompete. Only when wholesale enterprises move closer to modern enterprises could the modernization of wholesale organizations have a foothold and a sustained development capability, and wholesale organizations truly become modernized organizations. Moves to establish wholesale enterprises mainly include:

(1) Optimizing internal organizations. Wholesale enterprises have to change the original management structure of pyramid-like chain of command, adopt the pattern of flat management, highlight networked organization and management of modules, make active efforts to try to go public, and achieve great development by direct financing and accelerating mechanism transformation.

(2) Setting up the modern "customer-based" business philosophy and enhancing the service functions of the wholesale trade. The competitiveness of modern commerce is reflected directly as its service ability. The modern wholesale trade should expand its services for manufacturing and retail enterprises targeting at its service objects. Specifically speaking, modern wholesale enterprises should promote supports for the retail trade and provide comprehensive services such as purchasing and matching goods, buying wholesale and selling retail, warehousing, transportation, providing financial credits, simplifying the purchase function, and providing information and consultation services; and should enhance the functions for serving manufacturing enterprises, play an actively role in information collection and feedback, product planning, in-depth development and expansion of the market, etc., and make vigorous efforts to develop such functions as agency, the purchasing and selling, storage and delivery of goods on a commission basis, and marketing. Modern wholesale enterprises also handle financial credits for manufacturing enterprises and help them in financing.

(3) Adopting a variety of modes of business operation. For those capable manufacturing enterprises having their own brands, general agency and exclusive distribution may be adopted. In the modern society, general agency and exclusive distribution are the trends of the modern wholesale trade, being conducive to the establishment of a long-term stable cooperative relationship between industry and commerce, and helping avoid the many defects of commercial enterprises, small or big, all purchasing goods from manufacturers. To implement general agency and exclusive distribution, wholesale enterprises

are required to do well in the operation of brand-name commodities and the discovery of commodities with market potentials; stick to the principle of "interest participation and risk sharing", pay great attention to their prestige, and avoid short-term behaviors when cooperating with manufacturers; adopt equity participation and joint-venture cooperation, if they are qualified wholesalers, before serving as the general agent or exclusive distributor of the manufacturers; actively explore various modes of business operation such as agents, etc. Or for those capable wholesale enterprises, they are suggested to transform into general trading companies. As a kind of large-scale trade organizations integrating domestic and foreign trades, production, processing and financing into one and being featured by large in scale, multi-layered and strong in comprehensive strength, general trading companies not only hold a pivotal position in domestic commodity circulation, but also are conducive to tapping international markets. Some state-owned wholesale enterprises could extend to a variety of fields, establish a nationwide network for commodity circulation, form the ability to control the two markets of domestic and foreign trades, and gradually develop into general trading companies through alliance, M & A, equity participation, shareholding or chain stores with government supports. In addition, to survive in fierce competitions, some regional wholesale enterprises with weak strength could learn from foreign experience, and develop in the direction of wholesalers with limited functions such as cash and carry wholesalers, drop shipping wholesalers, truck wholesalers, storage rack wholesalers, mail-order wholesalers, etc. which provide part of the functions or services of wholesalers, get an edge in the competition with low gross profit, low costs and low prices, and provide more economic supplies of goods for retailers.

(4) The internationalization of the business mode of the wholesale trade must be achieved in order to establish modern wholesale enterprises and promote the modernization of their modes of business management. Specifically speaking, the wholesale trade in China has to adapt to the operation integration of domestic and foreign trades, strengthen the coordination and connection of policies on domestic and foreign trades, do a good job in the communication between related departments, and gradually complete the integration of the organizational forms and modes of business operation of domestic and foreign trade circulation with internationally-accepted practices. With the above efforts made, China aims at serving the establishment of a modern circulation system featured by the integration of domestic and foreign markets and unified planning, providing fast, attentive and efficient services to the maximum extent for manufacturing enterprises to open the domestic and foreign markets.

Major moves on the external environment of the wholesale enterprises

The external environment of wholesale enterprises refers to the sum of various objective factors and forces surrounding the enterprises and affecting their operations and developments. It touches upon policy, market, institutional, legal, financial and industrial environments. Related policy supports and better market supports are necessary in the establishment of modern wholesale enterprises. The following specific measures may be taken in order to establish modern wholesale enterprises and achieve the organizational modernization of wholesale enterprises:

(1) Regulating government behaviors and enhancing the service functions of the government. Reform of the government management system must be sped up and effectively transform government functions. The government has to give play to the fundamental role of the market in the allocation of resources, return the autonomy of operations back to enterprises. The government is responsible only for the fields in which the market may fail to play its role, regulate the economic operations of private enterprises and among private enterprises with economic, legal and necessary administrative means, and provide a favorable social environment for private enterprises, as well as favorable infrastructure, public services, social securities and safety security.

(2) Regulating government policies. The practice after China's accession to the WTO has proven that the Chinese Government is faced with a gradually expanding before integrating into the world domestic market and a world market that focuses on free circulation, fair competitions, regulated trading, the survival of the efficient and openness. Obviously, most wholesale enterprises cannot compete with their foreign counterparts at present and in a fairly long period. Faced with the pressure of competitions, the government is required to make more scientific policies. Lastly, efforts have to be made to enhance policy guidance, and do a good job in providing services for wholesale enterprises. Local governments and functional departments at all levels have to communicate with wholesale enterprises from now and then, timely inform such enterprises with related policy information, concern about the difficulties of enterprises, carefully implement various preferential and supporting policies, and try to work effectively within the limits of policies. The performance and problems existing in private enterprises should be treated with a forgiving, kind and helpful attitude. Illegal behaviors and behaviors that disturb the order of the market economy have to be dealt with in strict accordance to law. Special attention should be paid to overcoming prejudice and arbitrariness in order to create a favorable policy, public opinion and social environment for the

sustained, rapid, stable and healthy development of wholesale enterprises.

(3) Enhancing the building of the market environment, making more efforts to guide the development of wholesale enterprises, singling out the best for supports, and speeding up the upgrading and updating of wholesale enterprises. For historical reasons, there hasn't been an objective environment for the good and smooth development of wholesale enterprises. Plus wholesale enterprises themselves have problems in subject consciousness, main force and main mechanism, etc. All of the above situations require the government to make effective macro-planning and administration in accordance with the laws of economics, guide and regulate the development of wholesale enterprises, and positively guide the upgrading and updating of wholesale enterprises.

(4) Paying great attention to financial supports. In view of the financing difficulties, focus should be on making breakthroughs in breaking the high degree of monopoly of national banks and the acute shortage and small scale of private banks, making efforts to speed up the legal recognition of non-government financial institutions serving mainly for small and medium-sized enterprises, and fully borrowing and absorbing the advanced experience in financial management from the West before creating a good financial environment for private wholesale enterprises.

Specific measures for expanding the scale of wholesale enterprises

In the present economic environment, it is unreal to let most wholesale enterprises engaged in production and circulation to accept the guiding ideology of competition and cooperation. Under such a situation, wholesale enterprises should be encouraged to extend their scale, appropriately enhancing industrial concentration, and form some wholesale enterprises capable of playing a leading role in the supply chain through legitimate market competitions. To enable the wholesale trade to develop in the direction of being large in scale, integrated and grouping before getting an edge in scale, the following several measures may be taken into consideration:

(1) Implementing the large group strategy, reorganizing assets, adjusting the structure, and optimizing resource allocation by pushing forward enterprise merger and restructuring. In the broad sense, enterprise merger refers to the annexation of two or more enterprises, so it also includes enterprise annexation. In the narrow sense, enterprise merger also includes acquisition. It is in nature a form of transformation of enterprise ownership, which can also be viewed as a special way of investment. It is the main way of asset reorganization, structural adjustment and the optimized allocation of resources. Pushing forward

enterprise merger and reorganization needs to firstly, develop the capital market vigorously; secondly, enhancing ownership management; thirdly, improving the legal system for enterprise merger and reorganization; and fourthly regulating government behaviors in the process of enterprise merger and reorganization. In addition, due attention should be paid to the integration of enterprises after the merger and reorganization.

(2) Identifying the division of work on the basis of identifying the responsibilities, rights and interests of different enterprises with the help of the government or industrial associations, reorganizing the wholesale trade following the principles of network organizations, making full use of the existing state-owned assets, and getting the benefits of scale economy by sharing resources.

(3) Combining the reform of domestic wholesale enterprises, encouraging capable and large-scale wholesale enterprises to be conglomerated. A few capable and large-scale domestic wholesale enterprises should be encouraged to expand to more fields by association, merger, equity participation and share-holding, and establish a nationwide commodity circulation network, on the basis of which to develop toward the international market.

(4) Establishing the chain-store retail organizations led by the wholesale trade by association, acquisition or self-marketing. Chain-store operation is an important form of organization of modern commerce, the basic features of which lie in applying the principles and awareness of the modernized mass production to the retail commerce, adopting standardized commodities, services, advertisements, trade names and shop appearances, implementing professional purchasing, delivery, sales and information treatment, ensuring the advantages of large-scale business groups, and maintaining the competitive advantages of being low-cost and low-price based on "import and export on a big scale" and "FIFO (fast in fast out)". Therefore, to build an efficient chain-store operational system without losing its true intention and make it a reliable economic growth engine, China must highlight and make vigorous efforts to support scale operation in terms of the policies on the circulation industry, change the traditional situation of each industry opening up chain stores within the system, yet failing to develop the industry greater and better, implement the trans-industry, trans-department, trans-system, trans-region and trans-ownership development strategy bonded with the of demutualization of capital and cored with capable commercial undertakings, and solve such problems as capital, scale, standardization, management, commodity supply, delivery,

efficacy, cost-price, operational efficiency, etc.

(5) Developing both the "large" and the "small" wholesale enterprises. That is, some advanced large-scale or huge enterprises are advanced in the wholesale trade, while a great number of wholesale enterprises develop into the direction of being small and medium-sized. Since small wholesale enterprises are flexible in management, enormous numbers of small and medium-sized retail enterprises need small wholesale enterprises, so the role of small and medium-sized wholesale enterprises cannot be ignored. Seen from its reality, China should push forward the great numbers of small and medium-sized wholesale enterprises to grow into general trading companies, enable such wholesale enterprises to integrate commodity purchase and wholesale, import and export, warehousing and transportation, market information collection and treatment, financing, insurance and leasing, and enable them to develop into three-dimensional multi-layered enterprises with comprehensive functions with modernized tools and means of management. In addition, for those qualified large-scale state-owned wholesale enterprises, they should be encouraged to combine with large enterprises in other industries before growing into wholesale business groups by way of conglomeration and getting certain benefits of the scale economy. All in all, seen from the scale of the wholesale enterprises in China, the path of "large" and "small" wholesale enterprises should be taken.

Specific measures for vertical integration

Establishing modern wholesale enterprises, strengthening the link among enterprises, and achieving the scale economy from inside enterprises and that brought about by the horizontal organizations among enterprises is just a part of optimizing wholesale organizations. To improve the organizational optimization of the wholesale trade, the extension of the wholesale trade to the fields of production and retail before achieving the vertical integration in terms of the industrial chain is a must. Vertically-integrated organizations are a kind of highly-coordinative comprehensive operational organizations based on a high degree of work division. Implementing the vertically-integrated strategy on the basis of the industrial chain is the basis of the survival and development of modern wholesale enterprises. Considering the competing relationships between wholesalers, producers and retailers, it is necessary to adopt forceful measures to rebuild the many links of the circulation channels for wholesale commodities, enabling wholesalers and other related enterprises to form intimate partnerships and changing direct competitions into complementary competitions.

Forming a competitive cooperation relationship up to market demands

At present, wholesale enterprises in China are shocked by large-scale and integrated international companies. The system of leaving single enterprises combating by themselves and competing against each other and the dynamic mechanism under which micro-units pursues benefit maximization relying on "zero game" conditions requires too long a cycle, too great a cost of resources, and too low a probability of out-competing in realizing the optimization of the structure between wholesale and production, and wholesale and retail. Therefore, the vast wholesale enterprises along the industrial chain should change the existing mindset, and deny the "zero game" which defines the total value created by the industrial chain as being fixed, but realize that all economic entities inside the industrial chain could optimize the system of business logistics and the actual capital flow, information flow and logistics process by cooperation and the concept of early popularization of competitions and cooperation.

Rationalizing the system of government administration over wholesale, producers and retailers

Seen from the development status quo of the industrial chain, an incentive system and development trend aiming at high efficiency and coordination have been formed inside wholesale and production and retail. Therefore, policies made on the vertical integration of wholesale and production and retail should focus more on "regulation", but less on "controlling". Certain attention should be paid to promoting the early shaping of the modern wholesale circulation system which matches and adapts to the new mechanism, and guiding the dynamic coordination between wholesale, production and retail. In addition, the management over wholesale has to follow the principle of "doing things by commissions and omissions", in which the government should firstly, identify the trading identity and eligibility, safeguard and supervise the trading order; secondly, develop various laws, regulations and systems related to wholesale trading; thirdly, directly control the wholesale of a few major commodities having vital bearing on the nation's economy and the people's livelihood. Institutional adjustment and the setting of functions of related government administrations should be also carried out in the above few directions instead of being "offside" and serving as both the "judge" and the "player".

Correcting the traditional policy orientation on adjusting the relationship among wholesale, production and retail

Since an incentive mechanism and development trend aiming at efficiency and coordination have been formed inside the production and retail of the wholesale trade in terms of the industrial chain, government regulations in the formation of the self-adaptation relationship between wholesale and production and retail should never stick to the definition of the ratio between wholesale, production and retail. Setting a fixed structure between wholesale and production and that between wholesale and retail artificially and mechanically will only deepen the structural contradictions on the market. In making regulations on the structure between wholesale and production and that between wholesale and retail, the government should pursue the efficiency of wholesale coordination, and pay special attention to creating a good external market environment for wholesale and production, wholesale and retail in the coordination.

Promoting the overall coordination and wholesale innovation of the supply chain of the circulation industry

Policy supports from the government to the wholesale system cannot be provided statically or independently, but should be put into the supply chain of the commodity circulation industry in which the production system, the retail system and the market system coexist, by so doing, to facilitate policy supports to maneuver all resources in the system of commodity circulation to achieve the innovation of the managerial forms, organizational forms and economic functions. Specifically, innovation of the wholesale link may be carried out along three dimensions: firstly, extending in the direction of general distributors and general agents of manufacturing enterprises; secondly, transforming into retail-backed service providers; and thirdly, developing into the managers of resources of the commodity circulation system.

Structural Adjustment of the Wholesale Trade

With the advance of the reform and opening up, the wholesale trade in China had been developed substantially. Great changes have been happened to the structure of the wholesale trade. The ownership structure, the industrial structure and the regional structure have been optimized gradually. However, many problems still exist which hinder the rationalization process of the wholesale trade. The structural evolution of the Chinese wholesale trade is relatively slow. To build a modern wholesale commerce that is in line with the mass production, big market and great circulation and better play its role in the process of economic development, China must speed up the adjustment of the structure of the wholesale trade.

Status Quo of the Structure of the Wholesale Trade

As can be seen from the development of the structure of the wholesale trade, the ownership structure, industrial structure and regional structure of the wholesale trade in China have been adjusted constantly, but the wholesale trades of different ownerships are greatly different in terms of development levels. The structure of the wholesale trade is unbalanced in many aspects, greatly affecting the future development of the wholesale trade in China.

(1) Seen from different ownership structures, the development levels of private and foreign-funded wholesale enterprises are the highest of all, but the development of state-owned and collective wholesale enterprises lags behind. As shown in Table 7.1, the employment index of staff and workers in state-owned and collective wholesale enterprises reduced, so did the stock-sales ratio and the proportion of sales of such wholesale enterprises. However, the declining rate of the sales was not as fast as the employment index and the stock-sales ratio, indicating that state-owned and collective wholesale enterprises had made certain achievements; the employment was simplified; and the efficiency of wholesale circulation had been improved. What's worth noting is that, the declining rate of the sales of collective wholesale enterprises an that of the employment index were more or less the same, being about 82%, indicating that no better results had been made by collective wholesale enterprises in the development of the entire wholesale trade, and that the status of collective wholesale enterprises seemed to have already gone. On the contrary, private and foreign-invested wholesale enterprises showed significant upward trends in terms of the labor force employment index and the ratio of the sales volume to GDP. In 2007, the sales proportion of private enterprises was 8.15%, being more or less the same with that of state-owned wholesale enterprises which was over 40 times greater than that in 1998, registering an average annual growth of 4.3%. The foreign-invested wholesale enterprises leaped to the third in terms of the sales proportion which also reached 3.52%, registering an average annual growth of about 1%. Though the stock-sales ratios of wholesale enterprises with the above two different ownerships grew comparing with that in 1999, it grew in proportion to their scales of sales. What's more, their growth rate was far lower than that of the sales proportion and that of the employment index, further indicating that private and foreign-invested wholesale enterprises were full of vitality and their modernization process was relatively fast.

Table 7.1. Labor force employment indexes of wholesale enterprises with different ownerships in 1998 and 2007 (%)

Ownership	Labor force employment index		Sales ratio to GDP	
	1998	2007	1998	2007
State-owned enterprises	0.238	0.087	18.44	10.34
Collective enterprises	0.063	0.010	3.56	0.67
Private enterprises	0.002	0.064	0.19	8.15
Foreign-invested enterprises	0.001	0.026	0.34	3.52

Source: *China Statistical Yearbook* in 1999 and 2008.

Private and foreign-invested wholesale enterprises were the most developed and active of all, which has to be guided in the future reform in order to give play to their roles and facilitate the improvement of the development of wholesale enterprises with other forms of ownerships across China. State-owned and collective wholesale enterprises had developed to some extent, but the development was brought about largely by power decentralization and interest concessions. They were not well equipped with modern technologies and talents, the aspect of which deserves more attention in future reform. In particular, the development of collective wholesale enterprises was backward.

(2) Seen from different industries (see Table 7.2), the wholesale of mineral products, that of building materials and that of chemical products firmly held the first place. In particular, the ratio of the sales volume to GDP was 23.27% in 2007, up 96.7% within a short period of 4 year and registering an average annual growth rate of about 20%. It was not only far higher than that of other industries, but the growth rate was far higher than the concurrent economic growth rate, fully indicating that the wholesale of mineral products, that of building materials and that of chemical products are the vanguard of the fast developing wholesale trade in China. The wholesale of machinery equipment, hardware and electric products also developed fast, the sales volume of which increased by 37.8% from 2003 to 2007. The wholesale of drugs and medical instruments ranked the third, the sales volume of which grew while the stock-sales ratio of which declined. The wholesale of food, drinks and tobacco products, and that of textiles, garments and daily necessities are the traditional wholesale trades, though the labor force employment indexes were high in such trades and showed a growing trend, the circulation efficiencies of such trades were not high combining their sales proportion and stock-sales ratio. Comparing with the sales proportion, their stock-sales ratio was far too large. What's more,

the sales volume of the wholesale of food, drinks and tobacco products was as same as the wholesale of agricultural and animal products, showing a declining trend. The sales volume of the wholesale of trading breakage and agency had been declining all the way. Though the wholesale of agricultural and animal products, food, drinks and tobacco products, as well as trading breakage and agency were not high, their respective labor force employment index was high, being over than 6% on the average. Therefore, appropriate measures have to be taken in the modernization of such industries.

Table 7.2. Modernization of different industries in 2007 (%)

Industries	Labor force employment index		Sales ratio to GDP	
	2003	2007	2003	2007
The wholesale of agricultural and animal products	0.027	0.17	0.98	0.83
The wholesale of food, drinks and tobacco	0.066	0.73	5.26	4.69
The wholesale of textiles, garments, shoes and hats	0.015	0.38	2.54	2.98
The wholesale of cultural and sports goods and appliances	0.006	0.09	0.54	0.54
The wholesale of drugs and medical instruments	0.027	0.28	1.47	1.69
The wholesale of mineral products, building materials and chemical products	0.064	0.98	11.83	23.27
The wholesale of mechanical equipment, hardware appliances and accessories and electric products	0.027	0.49	4.66	6.42
Trading breakage and agency	0.002	0.02	0.59	0.46

Source: *China Statistical Yearbook* in 2004 and 2008.

As can be seen from above, the development level of the wholesale of mineral products, building materials and chemical products and that of the wholesale of mechanical equipment, hardware appliances and accessories and electric products were high; the wholesale of cultural and sports goods and appliances and that of drugs and medical instruments were very potential; the development level of the wholesale of food, drinks and tobacco and that of the wholesale of textiles, garments and essential of life were not very high. In particular, the sales of wholesale of agricultural and animal products declined, being less modernized. Improvement is badly needed. In addition, trading breakage and agency used to be the focus of the reform of the wholesale trade. Yet seen from its level of modernization, its development is less than satisfying. Unique features should be highlighted in future reform and the advantages of trading breakage and agency should be fully displayed.

(3) Seen from different regions (see Table 7.3), the development level of the wholesale trade in East China was the highest of all. Its sales volume accounted for 16.92% of local GDP in 2007, being nearly 80% higher than that of North China which ranked the second in China and being the highest of all. The labor force employment index in East China was relatively high. Though the ratio of the sales of wholesale in North China to local GDP was lower than that in East China, it grew the fastest of all. During 1998–2007, the ratio of the sales of wholesale in North China to local GDP increased from 2.53% to 9.45%, being 2.7 times greater. Meanwhile, the employment index of the wholesale trade grew by 10.2 times. South Central China ranked the third in terms of the development level of the ratio of the sales of wholesale to local GDP which grew from 5.41% in 1998 to 8.56% in 2007, being 5.8 times greater. Local labor force employment index grew by 6.2 times. The same ratio in Northeast China, that in Southwest China and that in Northwest China were all lower than 5% in 2007, all registering a low average annual growth. In Southwest China, the same ratio even declined. Though local labor force employment index grew substantially, its level was still lower than that of the other three regions.

Table 7.3. Modernization of the wholesale trade in different regions in 2007 (%)

Region	Labor force employment index		Sales ratio to GDP	
	1998	2007	1998	2007
North China	0.05	0.56	2.53	9.45
Northeast China	0.03	0.17	1.78	2.89
East China	0.12	1.32	10.93	16.92
South Central China	0.10	0.72	5.41	8.56
Southwest China	0.03	0.31	2.62	2.50
Northwest China	0.02	0.16	1.18	2.02

Source: *China Statistical Yearbook* in 1999 and 2008.

The degree of development of modernization of the wholesale trade in different regions was more or less the same with local economic growth rate. The wholesale trade in East China, that in North China and that in South Central China were more modernized; the wholesale trade in Northeast China, Southwest China and Northwest China were less modernized, showing significant regional gaps.

Overall objectives of the structural adjustment of the wholesale trade

The structure of the wholesale trade in the future must be scientific and rational. Components, members and the system, and the system and the macroeconomic development will all be mutually coordinative. The rationalization of the wholesale structure plays a vital role in the development of the wholesale trade and that of the entire national economy. Specifically, adjustment of the structure of the wholesale trade in the future has to aim at being systematic and of overall importance, accommodating the interests of all parties.

(1) Being systematic. The entire wholesale trade is an organic whole with each part being mutually connected. All activities among different system levels have to be carried out on an overall and holistic basis. Therefore, the integrative principle has to be followed in the adjustment of the structures of different parts before combining all parts into an effective whole of operation through market bond. It is a huge and complicated system engineering which is hard to be completed or achieved by an individual or some enterprise, but calls for the government to provide policy, capital and technical supports.

(2) Being holistic. Local economic development and direction have to be taken as the basis of the distribution of the wholesale trade. The government should make efforts to support the development of the wholesale trade in the less developed areas in West Central China while promoting the development of the wholesale trade in the developed areas in East China, give equal treatment to private capital when developing the state-owned sector of the wholesale trade, and take into full consideration of all factors in the development of the national economy when making industrial distribution.

(3) Accommodating the interests of all parties. The adjustment of various structures of the wholesale trade is closely related to the interests of the government, enterprises and individuals. In the adjustment process, attention should never be paid to one party, but all parties. It is a big issue having vital bearing on the nation's economy and the people's livelihood.

Main contents of the structural adjustment of the wholesale

Adjustment of various structures of the wholesale trade must be carried out in order to achieve the above goal and make the various structures of the wholesale trade more scientific and coordinative. Specifically, it includes the following contents:

(1) Introducing diverse forms of ownerships and forming various types of competition entities in accordance with the requirements of the socialist market economy: firstly, carrying out strategic reorganization and transformation of the state-owned sector of the wholesale commerce in order to improve the competitiveness of wholesale enterprises, denationalizing the property right of state-owned wholesale enterprises, forming diversified corporate property rights, and initially establishing the modern corporate system; secondly, vigorously pushing forward the development of private and foreign-invested wholesale enterprises, and forming effective competitions among multiple entities.

(2) Developing the national economy in a planned and proportionate way and paying special attention to the structure of the wholesale trade. The structure of the wholesale trade should be balanced with that of the national economy and based on consumer demands, serve downstream retail enterprises, and satisfy the unique and diversified consumer demands. The structure of industrial enterprises should be balanced internally, which is also the requirement of the rational and orderly development of the internal industrial structure of the wholesale trade. It is conducive to improving the economic benefits of the wholesale circulation, and avoiding the abnormal development inside the wholesale trade which may lead to the excess of supply over demand, the excess of demand over supply and the waste of resources, and conducive to the upgrading of the wholesale trade.

(3) Achieving a balanced regional development according to the differences in regional economic development. The wholesale trade in Southwest China and that in Northwest China are expanded and their benefits are improved. Their gaps with the wholesale trade in East China and that in South Central China are narrowed down. Each and all regions fully display their regional advantages according to their own characteristics, achieving the pattern of complementary strengths and mutual benefits.

Specific measures for the adjustment of the structure of the wholesale trade

The structure of the wholesale trade in divided into different layers, so main measures for the adjustment of the structure of the wholesale trade are also divided into adjustment of the ownership structure, adjustment of the industrial structure and adjustment of regional structure.

Measures for adjusting the ownership structure

Wholesale enterprises in China mainly fall into three categories: state-owned and collective wholesale enterprises, individual and private wholesale enterprises and foreign-invested wholesale enterprises. Correctly dealing with the relationships among them is of great economic and political significance to deepening the reform of the market economy in China and consolidating the socialist system.

(1) Further deepening the reform of the circulation system, adhering to the reform of the state-owned circulation enterprises in competitive fields, allowing them to "advance in some aspects while retreat in others", while allowing the co-existence of multiple forms of ownerships, giving equal development opportunities to private and foreign-invested enterprises. Bankruptcy liquidation must be carried out to eliminate those enterprises that should be eliminated.

(2) Improving the intellectual property rights protection system. The development of specific laws and regulations must be accelerated under the premise of "improving the legal system for private properties" put forward at the 16th CPC National Congress in order to protect the legal properties of the wholesale enterprises, especially private wholesale enterprises, against encroachment of any form. Meanwhile, great efforts must be made to vigorously develop various types of service institutions for wholesale enterprises with market forces in order to provide effective services such as the transaction of property rights, talents, information intermediaries, technical consultation and management diagnosis, etc. for wholesale enterprises and their employees. The antiquated ideas on private and foreign-invested wholesale enterprises must be changed and the building of a favorable social environment for wholesale enterprises must be accelerated with the above mentioned laws and regulations and services.

(3) Keeping deepening the reform of the modern corporate system featured by "clearly established ownership, well-defined power and responsibilities, separation of enterprise from administration, and scientific management",

transforming large and medium-sized wholesale enterprises into new-type enterprises up to the standards of modern corporate system. Limited liability companies or corporations should be taken as the main form to accelerate the transformation of the operational mechanism and the innovation of enterprise system.

(4) Encouraging large and medium-sized state-owned wholesale enterprises to merge or reorganization, developing a batch of trans-regional, trans-industrial (department), trans-economic sector and trans-national large-scale modern wholesale enterprise groups led by the public ownership and bonded by property rights. Of course, certain attention should be paid to regulating the behaviors of transferring property rights and strengthening supervision and management of state-owned assets in the merger or reorganization.

(5) Actively implementing the transformation and reorganization of small state-owned and collective wholesale enterprises, promoting the rational flow and reorganization of the inventory capital. Small state-owned wholesale enterprises can be transferred, reformed, leased and sold. For insolvent small and medium-sized enterprises having suffered losses for a long term, and with no hope of revival, bankruptcy must be carried out in accordance with laws. For small collective wholesale enterprises, the joint-stock cooperative system may be carried out actively.

(6) Rationally guiding and making full use of foreign-invested enterprises. The entry of foreign-invested enterprises could create more job opportunities for China, promote China's economic development, and play a role in stimulating and promoting the development of domestic wholesale enterprises to some extent. Therefore, foreign capital may be introduced rationally.

Problems that deserve certain attention in the adjustment of the ownership structures include:

(1) For collective enterprises, they were developed based on the planned economy, thus were featured by "congenital deficiency and lack of proper administration since emergence". Reform of collective enterprises was slower than that of state-owned wholesale enterprises. Therefore, in the process of adjusting the ownership structures, certain attention must be paid to practical results; multiple ownerships should be adopted to transform enterprises' operational mechanisms; "one-size-fits-all" must be avoided; and the reform of collective enterprises and regrouping and reformation should be combined together.

(2) National industrial security must come first when encouraging foreign-invested wholesale enterprises to enter China. The entry of capable foreign-invested wholesalers touches upon not only the destiny of the wholesale

trade and the circulation trade in China, but also the problem of the production, supply and marketing of products manufactured by small and big manufacturers, even the entire industrial chain being controlled by foreign capital. Therefore, the Chinese Government has to look ahead into the future before developing prudent and sure policies to promote the development of the domestic and foreign-invested wholesale trades, especially principles and policies on the ways of opening up the wholesale markets orderly, so as to ensure the healthy and orderly development of the circulation trade in China.

Measures for adjusting the industrial structure

The wholesale trade is the middle link in product circulation, the downstream service objects of which include not only the retail enterprises aiming at meeting consumer demands, but also manufacturing enterprises aiming at meeting the demand for reproduction. Therefore, adjustment of the structure of the wholesale trade has to enable the wholesale trade to provide not only final consumer goods according to the structure of consumer demands, but also means of production for reproduction according to the demands of manufacturing enterprises. Specific measures for adjusting the industrial structure include:

(1) The wholesale trades are multi-layered and diversified. Rational adjustment of the scale and structure of the wholesale trades may be carried out in accordance with the requirements of production and people's livelihood so as to enable the wholesale trades to satisfy the needs of national economic development.

(2) The wholesale trades play a dynamic role in the coordination with the adjustment of industrial structure. Many factors have to be taken into consideration in the adjustment of the industrial structure such as the satisfaction of consumer demands, the development prospects of the industries, the optimization and upgrading of the national industrial structure, international competitiveness, etc. Supports may be given to some major industries with market prospects and relatively long lifecycles in order to achieve the adjustment of the wholesale structure, enable the wholesale structure to guide the consumption structure instead of being adjusted passively under the influence of the consumption structure.

(3) Key industries may be developed in a selective way. With economic development, the wholesale trade should retreat from those industries in which the direct link of manufacturing enterprises and retailers could improve the circulation efficiency of the industry, especially the circulation fields of major commodities such as autos and mechanical and electrical products. The future

status of the wholesale trade relies on its competitiveness and service ability instead of how many industries it controls.

(4) Adjusting the ability to allocate commodities and organizing the sources of goods scientifically. Wholesale enterprises in China should pay attention to improving the ability to develop commodities, rationally organize sources of goods, and promoting their ability to allocate commodities before enabling them to effectively organize the link of commodity wholesale and retail, speed up the reform, and revive the Chinese wholesale trade following the rules of modern commodity circulation and the requirements of the modern ways of circulation. Specifically, when providing integrated services, wholesale enterprises should highlight building an operating system integrated with retail, and develop different services targeting at the characteristics of different types of operation, different trading conditions of different types of operation and different requirements on commodity delivery.

(5) Making overall planning for the selected varieties before pushing them forward in a gradual way. Commodity delivery must be conditioned instead of enterprises rushing to mass action. Overall planning must be made.

Measures for the adjustment of regional structure

China boasts a vast territory. Economic development among different major regions is quite different, so is the regional development of the wholesale trade. Therefore, adjustment of the regional structure of the wholesale trade must be carried out to promote the coordinated development of the economy in rural and urban areas and in different regions.

(1) Keeping enhancing the development of the wholesale trade in East China, South Central China and North China, making it stronger, more internationalized and global, and giving full play to the exemplary role of East China. Local economy is relatively developed in these three regions, so is the utilization rate of technologies. Development of local wholesale trade on the whole is far higher than that in West Central China. However, internationally, there is still a great gap between the development of local wholesale trade in East China, South Central China and North China and that in developed countries. The former is still less developed. Therefore, these three regions are suggested to take the path of internationalization in the future and push forward the modernization of the wholesale trade with advanced technologies.

(2) West China and Central China make use of their own advantages before promoting the status of local wholesale trade. Firstly, improving the investment environment and strengthening the building of the market system. To get

developed, the wholesale trade in West China and Central China has to attract more wholesale establishments. Under modern economic conditions, industrial establishments are most significantly restraint by capital. So local governments in West China and Central China should made policies on tax preference for newly-built enterprises, stimulate the initiative of various types of investors in the form of policy supports, and attract the capital of the wholesale trade to flow in. Secondly, the comparative advantages of West China and Central China are suggested to be vigorously developed. West China and Central China are rich in natural resources, so they should make use of their abundant natural and labor force resources before giving play to their competitive advantages in terms of the vast territory, abundant animal and plant resources and low cost of labor force, vigorously developing wholesale trades with special features, and completely changing resource advantage into industrial and competitive advantages. Thirdly, West China and Central China is suggested to actively carry forward the wholesale trade transferred from East China. With economic development and the deepening of the reform of the wholesale trade, some labor-intensive wholesale trades in East China have approached the point of "saturation" and begun to transfer outward. West China and Central China should make active efforts and go all out to attract investment and investors, and carry forward the transfer of labor-intensive and other types of wholesale trade groups form the Pearl River Delta. Fourthly, West China and Central China are suggested to actively develop the processing industry, change the natural and human resources advantages in into competitive edges, and stimulate the rapid development of local enterprises by the wholesale trade.

(3) East China supports West and Central China and promotes the rational flow of all kinds of resources. When giving supports to West China, East China has to make a good use of the opportunity of industrial structure transformation and upgrading. China has to maintain appropriate control, provide supplements and guarantee for spontaneous market allocation with some economic means such as capital and credits, as well as legal means. It can also strengthen macroeconomic regulation with administration, if necessary. There are corresponding requirements: firstly, breaking conceptual barriers and completely getting rid of the concept of "every miller drawing water to his own mill"; secondly, establishing a regulated and legalized system, ensuring the existence of specific service institutions and management methods, and providing effective services for investors; thirdly, making more investment in infrastructure, and focusing on solving such problems as narrow circulation channels and the difficulty in getting bank loans.

Building of the Wholesale Markets

As can be seen from the analysis of the wholesale markets in Chapter 5, great achievements have been made in the development of the wholesale markets in China in the three decades of reform and opening up. Both the number and the turnover of the wholesale markets have grown significantly. Investment entities of the wholesale markets have been diversified. Means of trading and technologies have been improved constantly. However, there are still many problems existing in the development of the wholesale markets in China. Low organizational level, market order chaos and irrational market structure are all seriously restricting the development of wholesale markets. Therefore, in a fairly long term in the future, efforts have to be made to keep strengthening the construction of wholesale markets, reforming such markets in such aspects as management and system, and adjusting them in terms of organization and structure.

Status quo of the wholesale markets

In the early days of the reform and opening up, under the influence of the traditional planned economy, commodities were not allowed to circulate freely. Though there were some spontaneous and fragmented trade markets, they were less developed and small, and usually took the traditional mode of doing business-through stands, being almost negligible in the circulation of commodities under the socialist system. With the launch and deepening of the market economic reforms in China, the functions of wholesale markets in the distribution of commodities and price formation have been increasingly strengthened, attracting great numbers of manufacturing enterprises and consumers. The wholesale markets have been developed substantially. Data show that wholesale markets each valuing more than RMB 100 million across China were 2,366 and stands in such markets were 1,674,768 in 2007, up 36.4% and 35.6%, respectively, over 2002. The number of wholesale markets and market stands kept increasing year by year. In particular, the growth rate of market turnover was far greater than that of the number of wholesale markets. The turnover of wholesale markets in 2007 was 2.32 times greater than that in 2002, registering an average annual growth of 22%. It indicated that since the reform and opening up, both the scale and the efficacy of the wholesale markets in China have been improved significantly. Even though, there are still some problems existing in wholesale markets. The order of the wholesale markets is yet to be adjusted and wholesale organizations and structures are yet to be optimized. Specifically, such problems are shown in the following several aspects:

(1) Wholesale markets are small in scale, and the improvement of market performance is limited. For a long time, wholesale markets in China have been featured by poor infrastructure and economic benefits. In particular, they have significantly lagged behind comparing with shopping centers, supermarkets and chain stores and other new types of retail operation. Comparing with the demand for industrial and agricultural production, they lack market supports and fail to truly play a leading role. During 2002–2007, the average annual growth rate of the turnover of wholesale markets each valuing more than RMB 100 million was 22%, which was only about 10% if averaged to single markets, being far lower than the growth rate of the turnover of wholesale markets as a whole. Seen from unit business area, during 2002–2007, the growth was more limited which failed to reach even 2% each year on the average, indicating little improvement of the performance of the wholesale markets and great room for the improvement of the performance of the wholesale markets.

(2) The concentration ratio of wholesale markets on the wholesale is low and capable wholesale markets are in short. Most wholesale markets in China are small and conduct both wholesale and retail businesses, affecting the normal display of the functions of the wholesale markets. Wholesale markets are small in scale is directly reflected by their low concentration ratio on the whole. As can be seen from the analysis in Chapter 3, the concentration ratio of the top eight wholesale markets was only 8.41%; that of the top 4 wholesale markets was only 5.24% in 2007. Comparatively, in Japan, the sales concentration of Kao Corporation reached 35% in the same year. Therefore, comparing with that in developed countries, the concentration ratio of the wholesale markets in China was low, far lagging behind the requirements of scale economy. It also reflected the vague layers of the scale structure of the wholesale markets in China and the lack of driving demonstration wholesale markets.

(3) Legal construction of the wholesale markets is inadequate and the trading environment is yet to be improved. Construction of the system of rules and regulations on the wholesale markets in developed countries has come a long way. However, in China, there haven't been any effective trading laws or regulations concerning the circulation on the wholesale markets; and the legal construction of wholesale markets has lagged far behind. For example, China fails to develop a series of necessary laws and regulations such as the wholesale market law, fair trade laws, the antimonopoly law, etc.; or such laws and regulations haven't been issued for a long time or effectively implemented, making the important status of the wholesale markets unable to be completely

protected by national laws and their implementation unable to get the correct instruction of national laws; some related laws and regulations in China such as the economic contract law, measures for the administration of the urban and rural trade markets and some laws, regulations and industry regulations made by local governments or departments are yet to be improved, because some of them are ambiguous and others are contradictory, making it a catch 22 situation. The legal construction of wholesale markets having lagged far behind can also be told from the insignificant public welfare role of the wholesale markets. At present, many of the investors on the wholesale markets are managers, who even get involved in the trading as operators or operators in disguised form. The phenomenon is more popular in the wholesale markets held under government administration or by government administration and other units jointly, harming fair trading and the principle of fair competitions. Due to the lack of related market laws and regulations, some operational organizations on the market, driven by short-term interest, harm consumer interests and social benefits.

(4) The utilization rate of modern and advanced technologies is not high, so is the overall quality of practitioners. Currently, most wholesale markets are lack of instant information and fail to make a full use of network facilities, being deficient in the information treatment system, information collection and release system, the e-settlement system, the online trading system and other advanced information treatment facilities and technologies. In terms of the hardware construction of the information network, the internal information system of the wholesale markets is still at the stage of manual processing. In terms of the application of information software, there haven't any application programs on logistics delivery, market management and market trading appropriate to the wholesale markets, leading to a low operational efficiency of the already built network. Besides, practitioners engaged in the wholesale trade are low in knowledge structure, and the overall quality of them is yet to be improved. The overall quality of market traders focus only on immediate interests, lack the vision of long-term development. Even market managers know less about the modern modes of circulation and modern way of corporate management.

(5) The structure of the wholesale markets is irrational and the layout is unbalanced. Seen from product varieties on the market, they are not diversified. The wholesale markets in China mainly operate staple goods right now. Most of them pay little attention to the branding, specialization and serialization of commodities, or well highlight the unique tourism, cultural and folk customs features of each city. Faced with the increasingly fierce market competitions, the wholesale markets are less adaptive, failing to timely adjust product varieties.

Seen from the programming and layout of the wholesale markets, they are not managed or coordinated in a unified manner. The distribution of the wholesale markets among different regions or between East China, Central China and West China is unbalanced. Wholesale markets in urban areas develop faster than those in rural areas, and those in East China develop faster than those in Central and West China. Take East China, Central China and West China for example. The turnover of the wholesale markets each valuing more than RMB 100 million accounted for 78.9% in 2002 and 79.7% in 2007 of that of the wholesale markets as a whole, further aggregating regional differences among East China, Central China and West China.

Overall objective of the construction of the wholesale markets

Future construction of the wholesale market must be carried out on the basis of the existing problems. Specifically, the objectives include:

(1) Consolidating the service concept on the wholesale markets. The wholesale markets will become more and more rational in competitions. For example, in choosing the mode of competitions, they will not attract clients by giving excessive preferences or carrying out excessive competitions, but with quality services and a better trading environment.

(2) Expanding the scale of the wholesale markets. The wholesale markets in China will develop into large and modern wholesale markets, and reduce in number, yet the overall scale will be improved, so will be the organizational level.

(3) Specializing the operation on the wholesale markets. A group of modern and specialized wholesale markets featured by large scales and great influences will be built relying on the development of some industrial clusters.

(4) Narrowing down regional difference of the wholesale markets. With their respective development, wholesale markets in urban and rural areas, in East China, Central China and West China, and in the six major regions will have clearer division of work. The ones getting developed on the basis of modernization.

(5) Strengthening the functions of the wholesale markets. The wholesale markets will show more and more functions, such as the trading function, the pricing function, the information function, the distribution function, the settlement function, the measurement function, the logistics distribution function, the import and export function and the travel function, forming relatively significant market features.

Main contents of the construction of the wholesale markets

Building wholesale markets calls for standardizing the market order, improving market management, expanding and grouping market organizations, narrowing down the regional differences of such markets, and coordinating their development in urban and rural areas. Specifically, main contents of building the wholesale markets include:

(1) Building wholesale markets of public welfare and self-administration nature. Wholesale markets are nonprofit and self-administered circulation service organizations, and nonprofit economic organizations in wholesale trading. However, in the wave of building the wholesale markets in China, people more than often treat such trading organizations as profitable investment objects, trying to get high incomes by collecting high rents, high commission charges and high management fees instead viewing them as nonprofit economic organizations, which led to the emergence of the some abnormal phenomena in the building and operation of the wholesale markets.

(2) Achieving the transformation of market regulation from being "spontaneous" to being "market + regulation". The spontaneous development of the wholesale markets has to be changed completely. Attention should be paid to giving play to the role of the market mechanism and that of the macroeconomic regulation of the government. With the "visible hand" and the "invisible hand", China has to guide the traditional wholesale markets to become two centers, which is of special importance to the development of the wholesale markets at the stage of overall transition.

(3) Achieving the change from direct regulation and management to the regulation and management by law. The government has to change the past "blood-transfusion" way of direct support, gradually implement indirect management centered with the system of laws and regulations, strengthening market development planning, establishing the macroeconomic management and regulation mechanism, improving the laws and regulations on market management, standardizing the behaviors of market entities, and guiding the development direction of the wholesale markets.

(4) Extending the functions of the wholesale markets. To become an important component of the modern circulation organizations, wholesale markets are required more than simply having the trading function. They have to become multi-functional and have the trading function, the exhibiting function, the information function, the pricing function and the logistics distribution function before truly developing into modern wholesale markets.

(5) Expanding the scale of wholesale. Quality of market operators

determines that of the entire market, scale of the operators determines the range of influence of the entire market, and growth of the operators determines the development height of the wholesale markets in the future. The traditional wholesale markets in China cannot be changed into modernized circulation organizations simply relying on the stand-style small scale wholesale operation. Modern wholesale markets shall never be the gathering of individual stands in the future, but the gathering of large and medium-sized wholesale enterprises. Market competitions have to be gathered, too. The law of developing the superior and weeding out the inferior is firstly reflected on the competition of the scale of operators and economic benefits. Competitions will inevitably result in the exit of many small operators from the wholesale markets for being unable to survive. The wholesale trade will be gathering and with a large operational structure in the end.

(6) Standardizing the order of the wholesale markets, enhancing the supervision and service system on various types of markets, cracking down upon various illegal trading behaviors, actively developing multiple agency and agent intermediaries, as well as storage, insurance and financing and economic organizations serving circulation, narrowing down the distance between small scale production and circulation and the visible markets of the wholesale trade, expanding the size of the wholesale markets, and achieving modernized operation.

(7) Enhancing the building of the information-based management system inside the wholesale markets, helping develop the wholesale markets into authoritative centers specialized in information collection and processing. The necessity of the existence of the wholesale markets in the future depends largely on the indispensable function of information distribution. Building a sound information management system and monitoring the operations on the markets through the e-network is an important measure for the wholesale markets to improve their own management levels, the premise for the wholesale markets to create information centers, and an inevitable requirement of modernization.

Specific measures for the building of the wholesale markets

The achievement of the future development goals and main contents of the construction of the wholesale markets calls for specific measures. Such measures include regulating the wholesale markets, improving the wholesale organizations and optimizing the wholesale structure.

Regulating the order of the wholesale markets

Alternation of the environment of the wholesale markets cannot be simply understood as ameliorating the hardware environment of the wholesale markets in the process of regulating the order of the wholesale markets, but shall focus more on the improvement of the soft environment. Specifically, it includes the management, operation, related laws and regulations on the wholesale markets.

Identifying the entities of the wholesale markets and ensuring the wholesale markets to be nonprofit

Currently, there are many investment entities on the wholesale markets in China, and few wholesale markets are built by trading entities. Of which, some are built with the appropriation from local governments, some with the investment of industrial and commercial administrations, some in the name of a village or a township, and some even by administration departments of the real estate, the army or public entities. No matter who makes the investment, the wholesale markets will be treated as profit-making units. The result of "investors are beneficiaries" will not only stimulate blind investment, leading to repeated building of the wholesale markets, excess market outlets, or inactive markets, and causing a waste of social wealth, but also will greatly increase the sales cost of sellers and price expenses of buyers, increase the cost of trading, and improve wholesale price artificially. Wholesale markets are a kind of organized trading markets. Such economic organizations should be non-governmental and autonomous organizations serving commodity circulation. To insist on treating wholesale markets as public welfare, one of the measures would be building wholesale markets in places suitable for the development of wholesale markets, create conditions to establish trade associations, which will be responsible for raising money before building, operating and managing wholesale markets. To well carry out the above measure, China must resolutely abandon the practice of government department building trade associations, but construct such autonomous organizations democratically based on the immediate interests of the trading entities on the wholesale markets. For those profit-making wholesale markets having been built following the principle of "investors are beneficiaries", appropriate conditions must be created as soon as possible to restore them into non-profit autonomous service organizations. For their vested interests, especially the interests got by differential rents, their irrationality should be clearly pointed out, the means of redemption may be adopted, and part of the rent, service charges and management fees of the wholesale markets over a certain period may be used to repay the original investment before segmenting the relationship between investors and the wholesale markets at maturity, enabling the wholesale markets to truly become public service organizations serving for the society.

Reforming the management system of the wholesale markets and establishing wholesale market administrative organizations in line with international practices

The basic pattern of the administration of the wholesale markets at present was formed under the planned economic system. In spite of the reform of government organs, the problems such as policies from different department, overlapping functions, etc. haven't been solved completely. International practices should be followed in order to rationalize various administrative management systems in China. In addition, the wholesale market administrative organizations up to the standards of international management may also pay attention to building a fair and standard competitive order and a detection monitoring system when administering the wholesale markets. At the meantime of ensuring trading convenience, trading on the wholesale markets should be transparent, fair and legal as much as possible in order to enhance the cohesion of traders on the wholesale markets, be more attractive to consumers, and constantly improve the special radiation of the wholesale markets.

Accelerating the construction of the system of laws and regulations on the wholesale markets in China

China once developed *Measures for the Administration of the Wholesale Markets and Outline of the Planning on Commodity Markets in China* during 1984–1999, the growing period of the wholesale markets. Both were department regulations which were inadequate in terms of their capability of legal coverage. Plus the Ministry of Commerce was later repealed, further weakening their legal force. It is safe to say that up to now, there hasn't been any national law on the commodity exchange markets, and the construction of the system of laws and regulations has far lagged behind. To build its system of laws and regulations on the wholesale markets, China must, based on its national conditions, accelerate the legislation for the opening of the wholesale trade, standardizing market development, trading and management, forming a series of laws and regulations on market entry, trading behaviors, trading norms, trading criteria, etc. that are up to the requirements of the market economic development, build sound laws and regulations on market management and regulation, enforce such laws and regulations strictly, form a market environment of fair competitions, and promote the orderly development of market construction, enabling the market mechanism to truly play a leading role in the operation of the wholesale markets.

Improving the wholesale market organizations

To get an upper hand in the fierce struggle for the dominance[1] of commodity circulation channels, the wholesale markets will have to improve their comprehensive economic, information and organization abilities, and improve the wholesale market organizations. Theoretically, the two major ideas of horizontal integration and vertical integration must be followed in promoting the organizational ability of the circulation link. In view of the own characteristics of the commodity circulation channels and the wholesale markets in China, promoting the dominance of the wholesale markets of the circulation channels may carry out the above two major ideas in the following three aspects:

Encouraging the development of leading markets

Integrating market resources with the purpose of getting scale benefits, breaking institutional, system or regional restrictions, adopting various means of integration such as powerful alliances, share participation and share holding, M & A, reorganization and chain-store operation, building a batch of large and capable leading markets to serve as the core before stimulating the development of small and medium-sized wholesale markets and making such markets the satellite markets of large and capable leading markets. For example, the small commodities wholesale market in Yiwu, Zhejiang Province and the wholesale market for vegetables in Shouguang, Shandong Province have basically achieved the large-scale operation of "national purchase, national selling, on a large scale", becoming the centers for price formation and information release of commodities. In addition, for the many small and medium-sized markets, taking the road of cooperation, integration or commission, involving all resources into the same organization, and achieving mutual supports is an effective measure for developing the market greater and better.

Firstly, active efforts have to be made to support leading traders in the markets to grow stronger rapidly, help them constantly improve their operation and management, vigorously publicize and promote leading enterprises to the outside world and customers, and take vitalizing the development of leading wholesale enterprises as a major task of market operation and management. Secondly, under the premise that conditions have been ripe, shareholding reform of the wholesale markets may be carried out to well solve the relationship among investors, administrators and operators; operators may be absorbed; leasing may be gradually changed into the shareholding system in order to integrate the interests of investors, administrators and operators; more markets may be opened with joint force; the modern corporate system cored with the shareholding system may be established; and wholesale markets may be encouraged to issue shares to the society and go public. Lastly, vigorous efforts should be made to introduce large wholesale enterprises, first-level agents and distribution institutions of manufacturing enterprises, especially some foreign agents, into the wholesale markets, with which to improve the organizational level of the market organizations. In addition, criteria on market entry and the mechanism of selection through competitions have to be developed. Unqualified traders or traders with lean operations have to be cleared out timely from the market.

Innovating the pattern of operation and management

Though horizontal integration could bring about scale economy and the economy of scope, under the premise that most wholesale markets in China follow the traditional modes of business operation and management mode, too large a scale would also bring about many negative influences such as repetitive construction, excessive competition, distortion of information transmission and chaotic order, etc., which further reduced the information and organizational capabilities of the wholesale markets. In reality, many large wholesale markets used to be very famous in China met difficulties in improving their benefits and competitiveness due to relatively backward operation and management modes. Therefore, when building leading wholesale markets through horizontal integration, China must make breakthrough and innovations in the modes of business operation and model, build an even closer purchase and sales relationship with upstream manufacturing enterprises and downstream customers, push forward the closely-related competitive cooperation among the vast wholesalers, and introduce advanced patterns of supply chain management, enabling the wholesale markets to become a crucial link of the supply chain and becoming the reliance of manufacturers, retailers and wholesale traders.

Integrating production with marketing

The epitome of the idea of vertical integration in the development of the wholesale markets is the construction of a market system featured by the integration of production and marketing. Currently, the integration of production and marketing led by manufacturers in the wholesale markets has become very popular, being reflected as the wide-range emergence of industrial self-marketing. It should be recognized that the emergence and existence of industrial self-marketing has an objective necessity. Judging the fact with the concept of "it is the progress of the social division of work for commerce to become independent from industries, or else it is a historical retreat" no longer works well. Though the integration of production and marketing led by manufacturers has a profound negative effect on independent wholesalers, it is a hard-won development opportunity for the wholesale markets: on the one hand, industrial self-marketing brings great numbers of suppliers, even distributors, providing a sustained driving forced for the development of the wholesale markets; on the other hand, it points out a road for the future development of large wholesale markets-developing the wholesale markets bigger and stronger could completely cater for the mindset of minimizing the cost of trading through industrial self-marketing. Taking the road of the wholesale market-led integration of production and marketing by way of actively signing purchase and sales contracts with manufacturers could not only ensure stable product suppliers, but also reduce the cost of the market itself and enhance the economic capability of the market. What's more, the wholesale markets are capable of collecting, distributing and analyzing information, so they will inevitably become forceful contenders of the dominance of the commodity circulation channels.

Taking the road of going global

With the acceleration of the globalization process, the country boundary of the wholesale markets becomes gradually vague. Globalization is the development trend of the wholesale markets. Therefore, wholesale markets in China should take going global as the yardstick before entering the purchase system of transnational companies. After China's accession to the WTO, a great number of foreign companies have entered China before engaged in trading. The wholesale markets in China should take the good opportunity, try to get the wholesale agency of big foreign companies, and be encouraged to enter the global purchase system of transnational companies. The said global purchase system falls into two categories: first, the system of local purchase and selling; second, the system of local purchase and global selling. A few Chinese enterprises have made it to enter the latter system. A successful case would be a candle manufacturer in Zhejiang Province, the candles produced by which take 70% of the global candle market. It has been involved in the global purchase system of transnational companies. Wholesale enterprises may refer to the success of this candle manufacturer and learn something from it.

Introducing modern circulation technologies and encouraging creative ways of trading

The wholesale markets, as the business entities in the traditional system of circulation, are developing flourishingly and will continue playing a dominant role in a fairly long term in the future in the link of commodity circulation channels with counterparty transactions, cash settlement, spot transactions and other traditional means of transaction. However, it is the general trend that the system of modern circulation will replace the traditional system of circulation. Modern circulation technologies shall be introduced into the wholesale markets gradually, creative ways of trading on the wholesale markets should be encouraged, and efforts should be made to develop the wholesale markets into invisible markets. Of which, the most crucial thing in innovating the circulation technologies is vigorously developing e-business, the emergence and development of which is a revolution for the traditional circulation trade, as well as a great opportunity for the wholesale markets. The wholesale markets should try to master e-business, an indispensable means of market competition in the future, actively explore online wholesale trading, extend the radius of trading and expand the scope of trading through e-business, shorten the time required for wholesale trading, and reduce the cost of wholesale trading.

Optimizing the structure of the wholesale markets

Seen from the development of different types of wholesale markets, the wholesale markets for agricultural products have always been the main component of the wholesale markets in China. Development of the wholesale markets for industrial products has also been very significant. However, in the three decades of reform and opening up, the order of the wholesale markets for agricultural products is yet to be regulated; the organizational performance is not high; the improvement of the performance of the wholesale markets for industrial products is not significant, either; and the structure of the wholesale markets for agricultural and industrial products is yet to be improved. Specifically, policies and suggestions should be made from inside the wholesale markets for agricultural products and those for industrial products.

Consolidating and improving the wholesale markets in rural areas and narrowing down regional gaps

The wholesale markets in China were born in rural areas, the development of which has helped push forward the development of rural urbanization and played an important role in changing the urban-rural dual structure. Currently, the issue concerning agriculture, Countryside and farmers and the construction of socialist new rural areas have always been hot political and economic topics in China. The wholesale markets in rural areas, especially those for agricultural and sideline products in rural areas should be further consolidated and improved. To improve the wholesale markets in rural areas in China, China has to foster marketing cooperative organizations set up by farmers, pay attention to support and guide the development of the team of farmers setting up marketing cooperative organizations, and actively encourage big manufacturers and marketers to head cooperative organizations. Agriculture production and processing enterprises should be encouraged to enter the circulation field of agricultural products, head and create professional cooperative organizations for the circulation of agricultural products. More efforts should be made to regulate and guide various types of circulation organizations and associations, encourage them to develop stronger with enhanced services, improve their ability to guard against market risks. The team of farmer brokers should be accelerated and constantly strengthened. A system to implement the training of farmer brokers has to be established to gradually improve the overall quality of farmer brokers. The environment for the development of the team of farmer brokers has to be optimized to help farmer brokers to constantly open new sales markets, expand their business scopes, improve technical means, and promote the functions as agents.

Accelerating the development of the wholesale markets in West and Central China, and promoting the upgrading of the wholesale markets in East China

Seen from their development, the wholesale markets in East China, Central China and West China are developing smoothly on the whole. Regional structure of them has been improved to some extent: the wholesale markets in East China have been increased in number; those in Central China have been decreased; and those in West China have been increased. However, in the comparison of the three regions, it is easy to find that regional gap between the wholesale markets in East China and those in West and Central China is yet to be narrowed, and wholesale markets may not be built in accordance with regional economy and planning. Wholesale markets should be distributed rationally based on the characteristics in different economic regions. National and regional wholesale markets may be built in main producing areas, distribution centers and big cities featured by centralized consumption, all enjoying convenient transportation. While giving play to the advantage of regional economy, trans-department and trans-regional market construction should be encouraged, and new trading markets in economic regions should be formed in an accelerated way. The construction of wholesale outlets may be carried out according to the overall urban and rural planning and rational layout. Wholesale outlets should be built in cities of all sizes appropriately. Efforts should be made to steadily develop types of wholesale operation that are suitable for the public. In particular, certain attention should be paid to developing social and commercial outlets and facilities in residents' communities in urban and rural areas, and to developing purchase and outlets in rural areas.

Strengthening the industrial supports for the wholesale markets for industrial products

Industrial supports could solve the problem of wholesale markets being in short of resources, while wholesale markets could solve the problem of gradient industrial development and transfer in China before promoting the upgrading and updating of the industrial structure. Therefore, it's worth it to further enhancing industrial supports for the wholesale markets, especially the wholesale markets for industrial products, to achieve which the advantage in industrial clusters has to be continued. It requires the wholesale markets to must take the road of "relying on the markets, organizing industries, developing industries greater, and supporting the markets". Industrial construction has to be strengthened relying in places where "leading wholesale markets" locate relying on local markets. Vigorous efforts have to be made to develop production bases, highlight industrial advantages and product features. In particular, several industries have to be selected before adopting effective measures such as making more investments, introducing foreign capital and advanced technologies, etc., cultivating new and characteristics industrial advantages, producing famous, special, quality and new products, and improving the overall quality and grade of commodities. Since a lot of enterprise groups of the same nature or being highly related are gathered inside industrial clusters, new products or process engineering will soon be populated, overfilled and penetrated inside the industrial cluster as long as they emerge, amplifying a single creative activity into a group of creative activities. Therefore, wholesale markets must also carry out gradient technical innovations relying on industrial clusters.

Increasing the construction of specialty wholesale markets

Currently, the operation of specialty wholesale markets is better than that of comprehensive wholesale markets. Structural adjustments will continue maintaining the existing trend before becoming more professional and wholesale-based. That is to say, the "small and all-inclusive" circulation on the wholesale markets has to be broken and specialty wholesale markets have to be developed to replace the diseconomy of wholesale markets being all-inclusive. An important thing in developing specialty wholesale markets is to develop before strengthening the connection among manufacturers based on highly specialized division of work through such strategic alliances as the integration of agriculture, industry and commerce, and that of production, supply and sales. As for the products of some small and medium-sized manufacturing enterprises, they may be sold on the wholesale markets through the agent purchase or order or trial selling by professional agents. In addition, for the existing specialty wholesale markets with rational division of work, certain attention should be paid to the development that is suitable for the field of production, and to the development new specialty wholesale markets.

Modernization of Wholesale Logistics

In recent years, modern logistics has got developed gradually. Helping achieve the management of the wholesale process of the supply chain through distribution centers, shortening the circulation time to the maximum level, and reducing the cost of circulation has become a trend. In particular, with the development of network technologies, greatly reducing the costs of commodity trading and logistics has become possible. Currently, logistics centers, distribution centers and online purchase have emerged gradually in China before achieving significant development. However, they are far from being modernized comparing with those in Western developed countries. That's why China has to further push forward the modernization of the logistics trade to enable it to better satisfy the demands of the wholesale trade, especially major commodities, for centralized commodity supply, centralized distribution, dynamic management and follow-up services.

Status quo of wholesale logistics

In the development of the wholesale trade, wholesale logistics has experienced the changes from emerging, being somewhat ignored to gradually taking the main stream. Its development and modernization level has been greatly improved. However, since logistics is a comprehensive business which requires more on technologies and management, even the development scale of logistics across China hasn't be sufficient, failing to give full play to the potential of the logistics industry. As a form of logistics inside the industry, wholesale logistics has even less developed and is far from being modernized. Specific reflections may be found in the following several aspects:

(1) Most enterprises engaged in wholesale logistics are low in technical level and weak in systematic functions. Logistics enterprises have outdated logistics equipment, low level of wholesale logistics operation, and insufficient process management. The systematic functions of wholesale logistics have failed to be fully displayed such as in the aspect of storage facilities. Few warehouses have such functions as refrigeration, insurance, etc., and most of them are ordinary flat warehouse, registering an extremely low proportion of the modernized and automatic storage facilities. Of the equipment for handling, the majority of them are porters, hand trucks and ordinary hoisting apparatus with low functions. In terms of tools for handling, ordinary vehicles account for the great majority. In terms of the systematic functions of the enterprises engaged in wholesale logistics, the storage and delivery functions are less coordinated, long-distance transportation and short-distance transportation are not effectively connected, the ways of transportation are not well integrated, and enterprises capable of providing such services as general agent, "one-station" services and "door-to-door" services are far too few.

(2) Practitioners working in enterprises engaged in wholesale logistics have low quality and professional talents are in short. Seen from the development of wholesale logistics in foreign countries, overseas enterprises engaged in wholesale logistics require practitioners to have certain knowledge on wholesale logistics and practical experience. Many countries have very developed wholesale logistics education and training, form relatively rational systems for educating and training wholesale logistics talents. Quite a lot of universities have set up the major of wholesale logistics management and opened a wide range of classes on wholesale logistics for students majoring in industrial and commercial management. Some business schools also provide postgraduate courses and degree education in the direction of wholesale logistics, forming the postgraduate educational system with a certain scale. Comparatively, the education on wholesale logistics in China is yet to be improved. Only ten or more institutions of higher education have set up the major of wholesale logistics and provided related courses, accounting for only 1% of the institutions of higher education in China; wholesale logistics education for postgraduates

just starts, and that for doctors is far from starting. Occupational education is more than inadequate. Enterprises commissioned to train practitioners are also in the initial stage. According to a headhunter company specializing in serving overseas enterprises in Beijing, the demand of some foreign companies or their parent joint-stock companies for the economy of wholesale logistics has been increased in recent years. In accordance with the statistics of related departments, professional talents on wholesale logistics have been listed as one type of urgently needed personnel in China. The gap is 600 thousand, of which Beijing needs 200 thousand and Dalian needs 90 thousand. Wholesale logistics managers that are up to the requirements of the enterprises in the markets in Beijing are extremely rare.

(3) Wholesale logistics is low in professional technical level, and the investment in the logistics assets is seriously insufficient. All commodities in wholesale circulation need not only agricultural product logistics with professional logistics technologies and equipment, but also a great amount of ordinary logistics of the means of production. However, in the existing system of wholesale logistics, due to the lack of incentive of the investment in logistics-specific and special equipment with significant asset-specific features, the application of professional assets in the logistics system in China is seriously insufficient. Seen from the ratio of the fixed assets of wholesale logistics to the fixed assets of the overall logistics trade, it was 12% in 1992, and 19% in 1993. Since 1994, the position of the fixed-asset investment of wholesale logistics in the logistics industry has been declining year by year. For example, the proportion of the fixed-asset investment in the wholesale trade was 5.4% in 1998, then 5.1% in 2002, registering a declining trend and showing a great gap when comparing with that in developed countries. Due to the severe shortage of investment in specialty assets, the technical and equipment level of the logistics industry in China is far lower than that in developed countries, seriously affecting the value maintenance and appreciation in the process of wholesale logistics in China, as well as the market competitiveness of wholesale logistics in China.

(4) China fails to form integrated systematic engineering management of wholesale logistics for mass circulation and great industries, and the overall operational efficiency of the management of wholesale logistics is low. Seen from the existing development stage of wholesale logistics in China, integrated management is an urgent need. Wholesale logistics services in China are single, most of which are still on commodity agent, storage, storage management, handling and trunk transportation. A few third-party wholesale logistics service companies are capable of providing comprehensive, overall-process

and integrated modern wholesale logistics services. Means of transportation are independent and separated, being led mainly by segment transportation and supplemented with seaways and through transport. Social wholesale logistics and distribution centers are small in number. The segmentation of the circulation industry and organizations has led to the absence of a pattern of mass circulation and great industries. There are no big enterprises engaged in wholesale logistics being capable of supporting national business flow, capital flow and information flow. Due to the irrational pattern and the lack of rational planning, the operational efficiency of wholesale logistics is low. In particular, it usually takes a long time for transporting and storage commodities. Plus, the labor capacity of infrastructure is low.

(5) Not more IT technologies have been adopted, the logistics operation of enterprises is low in terms of the informationalization level, and many enterprises know nothing about the information-based operation of logistics. Modern logistics are developed with the support of e-information technologies. Without the application of e-information technologies, there would be no development of logistics. On the whole, the application of e-information technologies in the field of logistics in China is yet to be enhanced, and that in wholesale enterprises has more lagged behind. For example, bar code, the GPS technologies, MRP and ERP and other software on the management of wholesale logistics are seldom applied in the field of wholesale logistics. There hasn't been any public platform for the exchange of information on wholesale logistics. EDI- and the network-based information system of wholesale logistics hasn't been applied widely in China.

(6) The labor force employment index of wholesale logistics industry is low. Seen from the above index, practitioners engaged in wholesale logistics were 1,271,493 in number in 2004, and the labor force employment index of wholesale logistics industry was simply 0.02% in the same year, according to the data got in the national economic census in 2005. That is to say, every 1% higher of the labor force employment index of wholesale logistics industry would increase 0.02 employees. It was not only lower than that of the industrial enterprise logistics, and the logistics of handling and other transport services, but also far lower than the average level of the labor force employment index of the logistics industry (0.16%). It demonstrates that in the modernization process of modern logistics, there is still large room for wholesale logistics to absorb labor force and provide job opportunities.

(7) The regional structure of wholesale logistics is yet to be improved. Though the respective scale of wholesale logistics in each region has been improved greatly since the reform and opening up and regional gap has been

narrowed to some extent, the gap between the scale of wholesale logistics in East China and that in West China is still large, so is that between the scale of wholesale logistics in Northwest China, Southwest China and East China. Wholesale logistics in different areas in East China is also quite different. The gap between the regional structures of wholesale logistics is still too large and yet to be optimized. Take Southwest China and Northwest China for example, most areas in these two regions are remote and isolated. Wholesale logistics of many raw materials need to rely on important coastal ports or material distribution areas. Plus, due to the special local terrains and climate conditions, these two regions are still faced with a heavy task of infrastructure construction. Meanwhile, a unified planning and effective supervising mechanism of the logistics industries among each and all provinces in West China are absent. Some local laws and regulations are against the development of modern logistics; the logistics layout is irrational; and limited resources are seriously wasted or placed idle, leading to the fairly high cost of wholesale logistics and the difficulty in meeting enterprises' demands in West China.

(8) The gap between industrial structures of wholesale logistics is also big. Though the overall level of wholesale logistics keeps growing year by year, yet from the industrial situations of different wholesale logistics trades, wholesale logistics of the means of production and means of subsistence for personal development and entertainment develops faster than that of the means of subsistence for survival. Take wholesale logistics of agricultural products for example, the cost of the wholesale of agricultural products mainly lies in the loss in the logistics process. Data show that the loss ratio of agricultural and sideline products such as fruits and vegetables is about somewhere between 25–30% in picking, transporting, storing and other logistics links. That is to say, more than 1/4 of the agricultural products are consumed in logistics links, while the loss ratio of fruits and vegetables in developed countries is controlled below 5%. As a traditional industry in China, the industry of textiles and garments has formed an intact industrial chain after more than 20 years of rapid development and become one of the pillar industries in China. Yet there still exist some problems.

Overall objectives of the modernization of wholesale logistics

The overall objective of the modernization of modern wholesale logistics has to be the improvement of the technical level and the increasing perfection of the service ability, because wholesale logistics was born to save costs of other industries.

(1) Operation and management modernization. In the operation and management of wholesale logistics in the future, there must be an enterprise system of legal and market entities featured by clearly established ownership, well defined power and responsibility, separation of enterprise from administration, independent management, and the self-assumption of profits and losses. Secondly, there must be scientific management, and a sound system of implementation and supervision. Wholesale logistics has to rely on its own facilities, technical advantages or advantages in product management, appropriately reform, expand and form a complete set of related functions. In particular, wholesale distribution centers integrating business flow, logistics and information flow into one must be set up independently. Socialized logistics distribution businesses have to be carried out widely.

(2) Improvement of the organizational level of enterprises. Future market competitions are cooperation-based competitions. Wholesale logistics must also be the organization of commodity circulation on the basis of social division of work. Therefore, both the horizontal joint among enterprises and the vertical joint of enterprises engaged in wholesale logistics, manufacturing enterprises and retailers will be strengthened.

(3) The adoption of advanced technologies. The most significant feature of the modernization of wholesale logistics in the future would be the wide application of advanced technologies, which is not only the result of social progress, but also the premise of the competitive edge of wholesale logistics.

(4) Modern logistics talents. Modernization of wholesale logistics cannot be achieved without the improvement of the knowledge deposits of the vast practitioners. Only with the existence of talents with high levels of knowledge and a strong ability to master technologies could it be truly called the modernization of wholesale logistics.

(5) Narrowing down of the industrial and structural gaps. Modernization of wholesale logistics is not only the modernization of a single industry or a single region, but the comprehensive and integrated modernization of wholesale logistics of all industries and regions on the basis of fully displaying their own advantages and complementing one another.

Main contents of the modernization of wholesale logistics

Development of wholesale logistics must be in the direction of modernization. Signs of logistics modernization include rational transportation, automated storage, standard packaging, integration of processing and distribution, mechanization of goods loading and unloading, networked management of logistics information, large-scale organizations and structural optimization. We generalize the main contents of wholesale logistics modernization as:

(1) Modernization of wholesale logistics organizations. Grasping the development trend of modern wholesale logistics, vigorously construct the four major platforms based on logistics and centered with regional logistics, namely the logistics operation platform with logistics parks as the carrier, the logistics transportation platform led by the modern integrated transportation system, the logistics information platform led by information network technologies and the logistics policy platform guided by the concept of providing guidance, coordination, regulation and supports; fostering market entities of the modern logistics trade, speeding up the planning and construction of modern logistics parks, making full use of modern information technologies, accelerating the development of e-commerce, pushing forward the networking of logistics and business flow, basically forming the great logistics circulation system composed of transportation, delivery services, processing and agency, storage management, information networking, marketing strategies, etc., and becoming one of the most important hubs and nodes of modernization in the supply chain of the development of modern wholesale logistics around the globe being geared to international standards.

(2) Optimization of the industrial structure of wholesale logistics. With the extension of the common scope of businesses of wholesalers and the diversification of enterprise marketing strategies, requirements on different commodities, different modes of sale of the same commodity, different life cycles, logistics management, stocking and delivery are different, making the optimization of the industrial structure of wholesale logistics more complicated and difficult which is not conducive to the improvement of management efficiency, or to the flexible response to different requirements on retail logistics activities and logistics services. To maintain the competitive edge of the wholesale enterprises and the entire trade on the international market while improving product profits, or to maintain the price advantage while improving the efficiency of production and operation and responding quickly to market changes, efforts must be made to improve the overall management and technical levels of wholesale logistics, optimize the industrial structure of wholesale logistics, and constructing a modern system of logistics.

(3) Optimization of the regional structure of wholesale logistics. Scientific logistics has to be achieved in accordance with the changes in the layout of major materials and resources, and that of industries. Logistics distribution depends largely on the changes in the pattern of industrial and agricultural productivities. Rational pattern of industry and agriculture can greatly salve

the cost of transportation while reducing product cost. Irrational pattern of industry and agriculture will not only cause loss to production, but also bring about pressure to the transportation industry. Currently, the industrial structure contradiction, enterprise contradiction and product structure contradiction are prominent. Economic division of work is yet to be rationalized in different regions, which not only increases the capacity of logistics and transportation, but also leads to great loss. From the angle of logistics, the urgency of adjusting regional industrial layout has to be clearly proposed.

Specific measures for modernizing wholesale logistics

A lot of measures may be taken in order to achieve the future development objective of the modernization of wholesale logistics. However, according to the main direction of logistics modernization, specific measures may include:

Modernization of wholesale logistics organizations

Modernization of wholesale logistics requires the renewal of wholesale logistics concepts, the extension of the logistics functions undertaken by the traditional wholesale trade, the innovation of the ways of operation, and certain attentions being paid to the cultivation of modern wholesale logistics talents and the adoption of modern and advanced logistics technologies.

(1) Renewal of wholesale logistics concepts and identification of the functions of wholesale logistics. In the past, the status of logistics talents held responsible in corporate organizations was not identified, though enhancing logistics was proposed constantly. In the future, wholesale logistics organizations require the separation of the staff and workers taking charge of logistics from ordinary production managers in companies before granting them greater responsibility and authority. In addition, wholesale logistics functions have to be extended. Such functions as commodity concentration, commodity distribution, commodity development, information collection and other supporting functions for retail operation have to be further expanded on the basis of further enhancing the traditional wholesale logistics functions undertaken by wholesale enterprises such as commodity distribution, resale and storage.

(2) Innovation of the modes of business operation and acceleration of the transformation into logistics distribution centers. Comparing with the traditional wholesale trade, logistics distribution centers are the main form of the modern wholesale trade. Currently, the introduction of the chain-store operation has provided broad prospects for the development of logistics distribution centers. The good reputation and great purchase channels of the

Chinese wholesale enterprises are incomparable with those of many retail enterprises. Wholesale enterprises may be developed into socialized specialty logistics distribution centers capable of reforming existing warehouses, outlets, facilities and equipment, and integrating storage, packaging, processing, distribution and transportation into one. In doing so, they can provide highly-efficient, small batches of and multiple varieties of services for other chain-store enterprises and help retail enterprises achieve zero stock.

(3) Focus on the support and cultivation of logistics management personnel. Competitions among enterprises on the earth are competitions of talents. The gap between the logistics in China and that in developed countries not only lies in equipment, technology and capital, but more importantly, in concepts and knowledge. Only when logistics management personnel and practitioners keep improving their overall quality and keep learning and applying advanced technologies and methods could they improve the management level of logistics. Through the cooperation with S & T institutions, logistic enterprises are able to combine theoretical studies with practical application, speed up the cultivation of logistics professional and management talents, and set up a team of talents familiar with the rules of logistics operation and with the pioneering spirit. While paying attention to cultivating professionals and managerial personnel, wholesale enterprises shall also highlight the training on logistics knowledge and businesses for all employees before being able to improve their overall quality.

(4) Acceleration of advanced technologies. Modernization of wholesale logistics in the future should be able to build low-cost network and achieve cost-effective good order and delivery on the basis of computer technologies and network communications technologies, improve operating efficiency and lower the cost of labor force by adopting advanced institutional equipment, and enhance audition, carefully calculate the cost of each trade competitors, and reduce or eliminate all losses and unnecessary expenses. Only in doing so could they provide low-cost commodities for joint retail stores, improve the competitive edge of such joint retail stores in price, earn retailers' trust, and finally build a low-cost operation management system in logistics centers.

(5) Intensification of administrative supports. Wholesale enterprise logistics is an indispensable part in the economic logistics system in China, the level of rationalization of which will directly affect the optimization of the entire supply chain logistics before affecting the rationalization of the circulation system of the entire national economy. Therefore, its importance is obvious. It is not enough to solve the problems of capital shortage, talent insufficient, etc. with the efforts of wholesale enterprises themselves, the government also needs to

intensify its efforts on helping small and medium-sized wholesale enterprise in their financing, guide wholesale enterprise to develop in the direction of being standardized, regulated and unified while strengthening its guidance over logistics and improving the overall quality of wholesale practitioners.

Structural optimization of wholesale logistics

Since the reform, wholesale logistics in different trades have all achieved great development; the stock-sales ratio of wholesale has been declining year by year, and the development level of wholesale logistics has been growing year by year. However, seen dynamically, wholesale logistics in different trades are different in terms of the growth rate. The industrial structure of wholesale logistics has been constantly adjusted. Here, a few representative trades in the wholesale logistics of the means of production and those of subsistence will be chosen below to analyze the problem of structural optimization of the entire wholesale logistics.

Agricultural and animal products wholesale logistics

The first thing to do to solve the problem of low efficiency of fresh agricultural and animal products wholesale logistics led by agricultural products is to, in accordance with the current basic situation of China, improve the basic conditions for the smooth operation of agricultural products logistics. It needs better infrastructure, referring not only to the construction of agricultural and animal products logistics bases, preservation warehouses and refrigeration warehouses, but also the improvement of the conditions of communication and transportation such as highways, railroads, air and sea routes. Secondly, it calls for optimizing and integrating resources, and accelerating the construction of information-based agricultural and animal products wholesale logistics. With the further improvement of the consumer requirement on foot safety and the increasingly enhanced international trade protection, integrating the segmented operation of the traditional agricultural and animal products wholesale logistics and achieving the sharing of resources through informationalization could on the one hand, ensure the production process to be carried out as planned and reduce risks, on the other hand, it could save the cost of trade and improve wholesale efficiency and the quality of services. Thirdly, efforts have to be made to strengthen the logistics supply of fresh agricultural and animal products to the supermarkets. Villages in outer suburbs have to try every means to carry out factory-based management and operation, strengthen product packaging and processing management, and carry out brand-based operation. Last but not least, green channels for agricultural products logistics have to be established by breaking regional blockade.

Wholesale logistics of textiles, garments and articles for daily use

The trade of textiles and garments is a trade with low added-value. Purchase of raw materials accounts for a great proportion. Since there are many processing links from raw materials to finished products, each of which is closely linked with another link, businesses of purchasing, storage and transporting raw materials, and those of storage and transporting semi-finished products and finished products are in a very large volume. Therefore, human input into the wholesale logistics trade has to be increased in order to reduce the operational const of logistics and the amount of capital being tied up. Specific measures may include: organizing before establishing wholesale management institutions inside enterprises engaged in textiles and garments; introducing scientific logistics management, which will reduce the cost of existing logistics; making overall planning over logistics and constructing the logistics platform for the textiles and garments trade with joint efforts.

Wholesale logistics of mineral products, building materials and chemical products

Measures for improving the wholesale logistics capability of such means of production as mineral products, building materials and chemical products mainly include: firstly, making vigorous efforts to develop e-commerce. In recent years, global e-commerce has been developing at a fast speed, the application of which has made it convenient for not only suppliers, but also purchasers, leading to the rapid growth of the trade volume. Yet it is a great challenge to wholesale logistics. The application of e-commerce has produced more opportunities for manufacturers and retailers to face each other directly, making wholesale logistics an unnecessary link, thus challenging the formation of wholesale logistics to some extent. However, the development of e-commerce has also expanded the wholesale logistics capability of such means of production as mineral products, building materials and chemical products; secondly, enhancing the distribution function of mineral products wholesale logistics. A great part of the circulation of the means of production lies in storage and transportation. Transforming wholesale logistics into distribution centers integrating fusion transactions, information and settlement into one becomes the ideal choice in order to improve the logistics efficiency of such products; and thirdly, fostering 1st- and 2nd-level large wholesale logistics enterprises. Since mineral products and other means of production are usually wholesaled in bulk, showing significant scale advantages, it is economic to narrow wholesale channels and cultivating 1st- and 2nd-level large wholesale logistics enterprises.

Trading breakage and agency

Specific measures for developing wholesale logistics of trading breakage and agency include three points: firstly, changing concepts and reaching a broad consensus. In the transition to the socialist market economy, China must abandon the old practices and create new practices, renew concepts, and unify the awareness of the significance of implementing trading breakage and agency in accordance with the requirements of the market economy; secondly, learning from foreign experience based on its own development. The system of agency has been developing for more than 100 years in Western countries, and has been gradually improved and mature with the development of commodity economy. In view of the less developed commodity economy and unbalanced development of it in different regions, China has to learn from instead of copying the advanced experience in foreign trading breakage and agency. Implementation of trading breakage and agency may not be succeeded all at once, but China's national conditions have to be taken into consideration before gradually achieving standardized operation of the system of agency; thirdly, supports from related policies and guidance. Implementing the system of agency is a voluntary choice of enterprises', as well as a systematic engineering regarding production, circulation, finance and taxation. It needs not only the cooperative efforts made by enterprises, but also a series of supporting policies.

Optimization of the regional structure of wholesale logistics

Unbalanced regional development is a significant development feature of wholesale logistics in China, which is determined by the economic levels of different regions in China. However, unbalanced regional structure of wholesale logistics is not conducive to the sustained development of wholesale logistics, making it necessary to take measures to narrow regional gaps.

(1) Promoting the upgrading and reformation of wholesale logistics in East China, North China and Northeast China. Since these three regions have a great number of seaports and airports, are located at the hubs of national highways and the national railway network, register high levels of economic development, and hold advanced logistics management concepts and technical equipment, it is safe to say that local wholesale logistics has incomparable advantages in

carrying out foreign trade and commerce. Generally speaking, developed air and sea transportation will stimulate the development of international trade, while developed port and waterway services and international trade will bring about the constant expansion of the scale of investment and the formation of industrial clusters in port areas, which will further have enormous demands for international financial services, push forward overall regional prosperity, and accelerate the process of internationalization. Wholesale logistics in East China may follow the route in order to develop itself and go global before upgrading itself.

(2) Intensifying wholesale logistics in South Central China and creating growth momentum. South Central China, the "ridgepole" that connects East China and West China, has not only a network of crisscrossed railroads and public roads, but also the artery waterway that runs through East China and West China-the Yangtze River. For quite a long time, Southeast China has been serving the development of East China and that of West China, providing diversified logistics services for the coordinated and sustained development of the national economy. Under the situation that local economy in East China and that in West China keep growing, South Central China has to create growth momentum and consolidate the status of wholesale logistics in South Central China. Therefore, the development of wholesale logistics in South Central China calls for firstly, eliminating the traditional and outdated ways of thinking such as "being large and all-inclusive" or "small and all-inclusive" or "waiting for help, relying on the help of others and asking for help", renewing concepts, completely reforming the management and economic systems, and carrying out institutional, mechanism, technical and product innovations; secondly, encouraging the development of wholesale logistics in South Central China to combine with the economy in Central and West China, even the economic development in China and Asia-Pacific region; thirdly, fully acknowledging the characteristics, difficulties and hot problems of the new economic environment from which to find the breakthrough points in line with local realities.

(3) Exploiting the potential of wholesale logistics in Southwest and Northwest China. Though the utilization rate and development level of resources in West China are relatively low, there is great room for improvement. To develop local wholesale logistics, Southwest and Northwest China have to make full use of local geological advantage and the advantage in national industrial structure adjustment: firstly, making use of their locations of being bordered with many countries and serving as the bridge that connects coastal areas with inland China, giving play to local geological advantage, and vigorously developing foreign trade; secondly, absorbing surplus labor force

created by the industrialization of West China, and providing rich and low-cost labor force resources for the construction of logistics infrastructure; thirdly, making use of the trend of mature wholesale logistics markets in developed and coastal areas being gradually saturated and transferring westward to further improve the investment environment, set a good local image, vigorously attract foreign capital to develop foreign-funded enterprises in China; and fourthly, making full use of the preferential national policies, reduction of taxes, supports for loans, administrative guidance and supports for major programs.

Attachments

Table 1. GDP and the added values of each and all trades of the tertiary industry

(RMB 100 million)

Year	GDP	The tertiary industry (current value)	Transportation and communications, warehousing and mail business (current value)	Wholesale and retail trade (current value)	Catering and accommodation trade (current value)	Financial sector (current value)	Real estate (current value)	Other trades (current value)
1978	3,645.2	872.5	182.0	242.3	44.6	68.2	79.9	255.6
1979	4,062.6	878.9	193.7	200.9	44.0	66.9	86.3	287.1
1980	4,545.6	982.0	213.4	193.8	47.4	75.0	96.4	356.0
1981	4,891.6	1,076.6	220.7	231.1	54.1	79.8	99.9	390.9
1982	5,323.4	1,163.0	246.9	171.4	62.3	114.8	110.8	456.8
1983	5,962.7	1,338.1	274.9	198.7	72.5	149.0	121.8	521.2
1984	7,208.1	1,786.3	338.5	363.5	96.8	203.9	162.3	621.2
1985	9,016.0	2,585.0	421.7	802.4	138.3	259.9	215.2	747.5
1986	10,275.2	2 993.8	498.8	852.6	163.2	356.4	298.1	824.6
1987	12,058.6	3,574.0	568.3	1,059.6	187.1	450.0	382.6	926.3
1988	15,042.8	4,590.3	685.7	1,483.4	241.4	585.4	473.8	1,120.6
1989	16,992.3	5,448.4	812.7	1,536.2	277.4	964.3	566.2	1,291.6
1990	18,667.8	5,888.4	1,167.0	1,268.9	301.9	1,017.5	662.2	1,470.9
1991	21,781.5	7,337.1	1,420.3	1,834.6	442.3	1,056.3	763.7	1,819.9
1992	26,923.5	9,357.4	1,689.0	2,405.0	584.6	1,306.2	1,101.3	2,271.3
1993	35,333.9	11,915.7	2,174.0	2,816.6	712.1	1,669.7	1,379.6	3,163.7
1994	48,197.9	16,179.8	2,787.9	3,773.4	1,008.5	2,234.8	1,909.3	4,465.8
1995	60,793.7	19,978.5	3,244.3	4,778.6	1,200.1	2,798.5	2,354.0	5,602.9
1996	71,176.6	23,326.2	3,782.2	5,599.7	1,336.8	3,211.7	2,617.6	6,778.3
1997	78,973.0	26,988.1	4,148.6	6,327.4	1,561.3	3,606.8	2,921.1	8,423.0
1998	84,402.3	30,580.5	4,660.9	6,913.2	1,786.9	3,697.7	3,434.5	10,087.3
1999	89,677.1	33,873.4	5,175.2	7,491.1	1,941.2	3,816.5	3,681.8	11,767.7
2000	99,214.6	38,714.0	6,161.0	8,158.6	2,146.3	4,086.7	4,149.1	14,012.4
2001	109,655.2	44,361.6	6,870.3	9,119.4	2,400.1	4,353.5	4,715.1	16,903.3
2002	120,332.7	49,898.9	7,492.9	9,995.4	2,724.8	4,612.8	5,346.4	19,726.7
2003	135,822.8	56,004.7	7,913.2	11,169.5	3,126.1	4,989.4	6,172.7	22,633.9
2004	159,878.3	64,561.3	9,304.4	12,453.8	3,664.8	5,393.0	7,174.1	26,571.2
2005	183,084.8	73,432.9	10,835.7	13,534.5	4,193.4	6,307.2	8,243.8	30,318.1
2006	209,407.0	84,721.4	12,481.1	15,471.1	4,792.1	8,490.3	9,664.0	33,822.7
2007	246,619.0	100,053.5	14,604.1	18,169.5	5,705.4	11,057.0	11,854.3	38,663.2

Source: *China Statistical Yearbook (1979–2008).*

Table 2. Year-end number of on-post staff and workers of all trades of the tertiary industry

Unit: 10 thousand people

Year	Nationwide	Transportation and communications, warehousing and mail business	Wholesale and retail trade	The financial sector	Real estate
1985	12,358	766	1,576	126	36
1986	12,809	775	1,616	138	38
1987	13,214	780	1,658	154	39
1988	13,608	788	1,729	174	42
1989	13,742	784	1,765	184	43
1990	14,059	797	1,813	195	44
1991	14,508	814	1,888	208	48
1992	14,792	819	1,946	223	54
1993	14,849	826	1,796	239	66
1994	14,849	835	1,833	261	72
1995	14,908	824	1,828	273	77
1996	14,845	830	1,807	288	82
1997	14,668	824	1,774	298	84
1998	12,337	701	1,256	301	89
1999	11,773	682	1,110	300	90
2000	11,259	659	977	294	93
2001	10,792	629	840	292	97
2002	10,558	613	733	287	107
2003	10,492	610	592	286	108
2004	10,576	598	551	287	120
2005	10,850	579	508	295	133
2006	11,161	579	486	300	140
2007	11,427	584	479	311	151

Source: *China Statistical Yearbook (1979–2008).*

Table 3. Investment in the fixed assets of the tertiary industry

(RMB 100 million)

Year	Total social investment in fixed assets	Wholesale and retail trade	Transportation and communications, warehousing and mail business	The financial sector	The financial sector
1996	22,913.5	529.9	3,197.2	167.2	3,445.2
1997	24,941.1	580.4	3,753.4	188.4	3,440.7
1998	28,406.2	638.8	5,422.3	195.8	3,896.9
1999	29,854.7	559.2	5,587.6	155.5	4,342.1

(Con'd)

Year	Total social investment in fixed assets	Wholesale and retail trade	Transportation and communications, warehousing and mail business	The financial sector	The financial sector
2000	32,917.7	616.1	5,898.6	118.6	5,194.4
2001	37,213.5	718.1	6,631.5	126.9	6,644.6
2002	43,499.9	798.3	6,818.8	100.2	8,154.4
2003	55,566.6	922.7	6,289.4	90.2	13,143.4
2004	70,477.4	1,273.0	7,646.2	136.0	16,678.9
2005	88,773.6	1,716.4	9,614.0	109.5	19,505.3
2006	109,998.2	2,265.3	12,138.1	121.4	24,524.4
2007	137,323.9	2,880.3	14,154.0	157.6	32,438.9

Source: *China Statistical Yearbook (1979–2008).*

Table 4. Total volume of retail sales of social consumables in commerce and all trades

(RMB 100 million)

Year	Total volume of retail sales of social consumables	The wholesale and retail trade	Total volume of retail sales of social consumables	Total volume of retail sales of social consumables of the catering trade
1978	1,558.6	1,363.7	54.8	140.1
1979	1,800.0	1,540.5	63.7	195.8
1980	2,140.0	1,768.0	80.0	292.0
1981	2,350.0	1,915.4	87.6	347.0
1982	2,570.0	2,068.1	98.4	403.5
1983	2,849.4	2,269.1	112.1	468.2
1984	3,376.4	2,645.5	137.1	593.8
1985	4,305.0	3,272.2	196.9	835.9
1986	4,950.0	3,717.8	232.8	999.4
1987	5,820.0	4,343.5	283.0	1,193.5
1988	7,440.0	5,544.6	366.5	1,528.9
1989	8,101.4	6,009.5	405.1	1,686.8
1990	8,300.1	6,127.4	419.8	1,752.9
1991	9,415.6	6,903.9	492.0	2,019.7
1992	10,993.7	7,922.2	589.7	2,481.8
1993	14,270.4	10,892.8	817.8	2,559.8
1994	18,622.9	14,903.4	1,201.4	2,518.1
1995	23,613.8	19,454.3	1,614.7	2,544.8
1996	28,360.2	23,747.5	2,070.0	2,542.7
1997	31,252.9	26,169.9	2,488.2	2,594.8
1998	33,378.1	27,859.2	2,878.8	2,640.1
1999	35,647.9	29,708.8	3,270.3	2,668.8

(Con'd)

Year	Total volume of retail sales of social consumables	The wholesale and retail trade	Total volume of retail sales of social consumables	Total volume of retail sales of social consumables of the catering trade
2000	39,105.7	32,697.3	3,836.1	2,572.3
2001	43,055.4	36,014.8	4,465.2	2,575.4
2002	48,135.9	40,926.6	5,547.1	1,662.2
2003	52,516.3	44,659.4	6,191.4	1,665.5
2004	59,501.0	50,256.8	7,550.4	1,693.8
2005	67,176.6	56,589.2	8,886.8	1,700.6
2006	76,410.0	64,325.5	10,345.5	1,739.0
2007	89,210.0	75,040.3	12,352.0	1,817.7
2008(1-6)	51,042.7	43,068.0	7,206.9	767.8

Source: *Market Statistical Yearbook of China (1990–2004)* and *China Trade and External Economic Statistical Yearbook (2005–2008).*

Table 5. Year-end number of on-post staff and workers engaged in the wholesale and retail trade

Unit: 10 thousand people

Year	Wholesale and retail trade	The wholesale trade	The retail trade
1993	1,674.8	902.3	772.5
1994	1,743.1	972.7	770.4
1995	1,742.8	980.9	761.9
1996	1,718.5	983.7	734.8
1997	1,685.4	964.1	721.3
1998	1,188.6	673.6	513.2
1999	1,049.8	594.0	455.8
2000	783.4	384.4	399.0
2001	785.2	447.9	337.3
2002	673.4	381.6	291.8
2003	592.0	324.4	267.6
2004	550.9	298.2	252.7
2005	508.3	270.3	238.0
2006	485.6	254.9	230.8
2007	479.4	246.5	232.9

Source: *China Statistical Yearbook (1993–2008)*, the article was known to be Laborforce & Salaries for Staff and Workers, and no classified statistics were collected on the number of staff and workers employed prior to 1992.

Table 6. Investment in the fixed assets of the wholesale and retail trade

(RMB 100 million)

Year	Wholesale and retail trade	The wholesale trade	The retail trade
1994	239.5	117.7	121.8
1995	229.9	122.9	107.0
1996	233.5	121.1	112.4
1997	246.4	121.0	125.4
1998	275.3	154.3	120.9
1999	263.1	159.4	103.7
2000	258.7	174.9	118.7
2001	319.1	172.6	146.5
2002	367.0	190.7	176.2
2003	516.6	204.3	312.3
2004	1,117.2	447.4	669.8
2005	1,532.1	672.2	859.9
2006	1,896.5	826.5	1,070.0
2007	2,553.0	1,195.0	1,358.0

Source: *China Statistical Yearbook (1995–2008)*. No classified data were collected prior to 1993.

Table 7. Numbers of wholesale business corporations above the designated size by ownership

Year	1999	2000	2001	2002	2003	2005	2006	2007
Total	30,381	29,075	29,675	31,626	33,275	67,064	73,879	80,778
Wholesale trade	16,382	15,393	15,258	15,262	14,937	26,963	28,125	29,046
State-owned wholesale	10,375	9,317	7,736	6,804	5,712	4,710	4,234	3,810
Collective wholesale	2,946	2,406	1,859	1,527	1,238	1,099	1,028	925
Privately-run wholesale	387	560	1,262	1,743	2,343	10,933	12,594	13,673
Foreign-invested wholesale	100	114	200	440	531	1,016	1,019	1,207

Source: *Market Statistical Yearbook of China (1990–2004)* and *China Trade and External Economic Statistical Yearbook (2005–2008)*.

Table 8. Numbers of wholesale industrial establishments above the designated size by ownership

Year	1999	2000	2001	2002	2003	2005	2006	2007
Total	47,906	47,801	53,485	67,443	66,145	156,254	174,453	193,998
Wholesale trade	23,720	23,956	25,227	31,268	27,856	56,157	57,994	60,884
State-owned wholesale	15,628	14,428	12,509	12,192	10,029	13,618	12,859	11,665
Collective wholesale	3,964	3,641	2,806	2,463	1,898	3,448	3,322	3,065
Privately-run wholesale	391	571	1,367	1,991	2,699	13,620	16,403	17,161
Foreign-invested wholesale	169	176	256	527	675	1,332	1,552	2,094

Source: *Market Statistical Yearbook of China (1999–2004)* and *China Trade and External Economic Statistical Yearbook (2005–2008).*

Table 9. Numbers of practitioners engaged in wholesale enterprises above the designated size by ownership

Year	1999	2000	2001	2002	2003	2005	2006	2007
Total	5,583,021	5,150,084	4,825,325	5,169,139	5,200,497	8,068,191	8,555,359	9,466,938
Wholesale trade	2,543,600	2,319,248	1,982,927	1,944,793	1,786,669	2,244,131	2,248,731	2,495,863
State-owned wholesale	1,699,066	1,465,201	1,124,343	1,016,379	847,948	725,578	687,278	669,839
Collective wholesale	450,698	373,647	274,613	202,541	144,120	104,940	92,511	76,079
Privately-run wholesale	14,211	20,405	47,116	82,467	106,450	399,207	444,761	489,042
Foreign-invested wholesale	10,198	12,936	19,763	34,521	44,863	109,637	137,096	199,812

Source: *Market Statistical Yearbook of China (1999–2004)* and *China Trade and External Economic Statistical Yearbook (2005–2008).*

Table 10. **Volumes of sales of wholesale above the designated size by ownership**

(RMB 100 million)

Year	1998	1999	2000	2001	2002	2003	2005	2006	2007
Wholesale trade	22,090.8	22,055.8	25,977.9	28,131.1	31,591.9	37,974.3	74,921.3	83,030.7	100,301.5
State-owned wholesale	15,561.4	15,395.1	16,786.4	14,496.4	14,233.4	14,037.3	20,173.7	22,687.3	25,798.1
Collective wholesale	3,004.8	2,299.0	2,170.8	1,510.9	1,269.7	1,323.3	1,487.7	1,629.4	1,661.4
Privately-run wholesale	160.6	279.9	424.4	1,015.6	1,614.2	2,681.7	12,321.0	16,399.7	20,343.7
Foreign-invested wholesale	289.0	183.5	450.3	857.9	1,684.7	2,273.0	6,145.6	6,438.0	8,780.7

Note: the wholesale trade refers to the part of the wholesale sales contributed by wholesale.
Source: *Market Statistical Yearbook of China (1999–2004)* and *China Trade and External Economic Statistical Yearbook (2005–2008).*

Table 11. **Incomes of the wholesale above the designated size by ownership**

(RMB 100 million)

Year	1999	2000	2001	2002	2003	2005	2006	2007
State-owned wholesale	14,133.0	15,731.0	13,509.1	13,204.8	12,667.4	18,221.6	20,156.2	23,594.8
Collective wholesale	2,019.6	2,032.1	1,466.2	1,202.6	1,255.2	1,484.5	1,519.8	1,591.7
Privately-run wholesale	242.4	391.3	999.0	1,596.3	2,658.0	11,676.1	15,195.9	19,123.9
Foreign-invested wholesale	122.4	358.4	745.4	1,528.7	2,018.7	5,484.3	5,660.5	8,091.6

Source: *Market Statistical Yearbook of China (1999–2004)* and *China Trade and External Economic Statistical Yearbook (2005–2008).*

Table 12. Costs of the wholesale trades above the designated size by ownership

(RMB 100 million)

Year	1999	2000	2001	2002	2003	2005	2006	2007
State-owned wholesale	12,932.2	14,494.9	12,406.3	12,155.1	11,575.9	16,491.5	18,349.2	21,255.2
Collective wholesale	1,906.1	1,909.4	1,383.2	1,134.9	1,189.9	1,406.8	1,454.7	1,508.4
Privately-run wholesale	225.8	369.0	946.0	1,509.4	2,527.2	11,021.6	14,473.0	18,115.8
Foreign-invested wholesale	110.7	330.6	675.2	1,360.6	1,789.2	4,519.2	4,889.1	6,813.6

Source: *Market Statistical Yearbook of China (1999–2004)* and *China Trade and External Economic Statistical Yearbook (2005–2008).*

Table 13. Profits of the wholesale trade above the designated size by ownership

(RMB 100 million)

Year	1999	2000	2001	2002	2003	2005	2006	2007
State-owned wholesale	552.0	597.9	539.0	640.8	696.3	1,404.8	1,679.5	1,950.4
Collective wholesale	32.0	51.5	29.8	30.2	33.6	55.3	54.0	66.0
Privately-run wholesale	6.0	9.0	19.5	34.7	57.5	492.3	657.9	854.5
Foreign-invested wholesale	6.9	16.7	25.4	115.7	119.6	632.1	754.6	1,198.8

Source: *Market Statistical Yearbook of China (1999–2004)* and *China Trade and External Economic Statistical Yearbook (2005–2008).*

Table 14. Assets of the wholesale trades above the designated size by ownership

(RMB 100 million)

Year	1999	2000	2001	2002	2003	2005	2006	2007
State-owned wholesale	10,211.5	9,969.0	8,816.3	8,370.1	8,002.1	8,639.2	9,016.9	10,516.6
Collective wholesale	1,969.2	1,744.0	1,462.6	1,303.7	1,178.8	925.3	867.6	909.6
Privately-run wholesale	90.3	141.9	333.8	609.4	1,062.0	4,448.7	5,674.6	7,437.3
Foreign-invested wholesale	80.1	203.3	248.3	550.5	703.0	2,211.4	2,417.8	3,546.3

Source: *Market Statistical Yearbook of China (1999–2004)* and *China Trade and External Economic Statistical Yearbook (2005–2008).*

Table 15. Liabilities of the wholesale trades above the designated size by ownership

(RMB 100 million)

Year	1999	2000	2001	2002	2003	2005	2006	2007
State-owned wholesale	8,309.1	8,165.9	6,807.4	6,488.1	6,079.7	5,943.7	5,910.9	6,775.9
Collective wholesale	1,876.8	1,656.3	1,372.1	1,211.6	1,088.1	815.4	755.3	782.2
Privately-run wholesale	69.3	105.8	257.5	461.6	835.2	3,444.2	4,424.3	5,828.4
Foreign-invested wholesale	51.1	164.0	190.3	397.2	529.9	1,540.4	1,610.7	2,473.9

Source: *Market Statistical Yearbook of China (1999–2004)* and *China Trade and External Economic Statistical Yearbook (2005–2008).*

Table 16. Numbers of wholesale business corporations above the designated size by region

Year	2007	2006	2005	2003	2002	2001	2000	1999	1998	1996	1995	1994
Nationwide	29,046	28,125	26,963	14,937	15,262	15,258	15,393	16,382	16,945	306,235	235,486	212,494
Beijing	3,493	2,941	2,768	997	997	1,046	1,059	1,128	1,070	8,811	5,708	6,539
Tianjin	1,455	1,345	1,231	559	507	507	337	492	473	7,628	6,346	6,719
Hebei	485	517	516	576	624	647	638	660	642	9,525	8,426	7,987
Shanxi	494	450	472	312	306	301	319	323	323	4,497	4,133	4,196
Inner Mongolia	278	289	308	177	180	180	203	210	218	4,880	3,824	3,817
Liaoning	1,123	1,138	1,280	607	655	667	688	701	790	23,756	17,248	17,565
Jilin	281	272	326	156	217	230	266	287	287	5,783	5,003	4,883
Heilongjiang	428	435	473	285	289	272	365	387	375	10,551	10,044	10,026
Shanghai	2,364	2,620	1,803	758	763	505	445	463	449	18,694	7,404	5,893
Jiangshu	1,861	1,801	1,202	821	930	948	990	1,113	1,279	22,408	16,381	15,080
Zhejiang	3,207	2,883	2,757	1,481	1,473	1,480	1,389	1,527	1,483	19,068	15,103	12,334
Anhui	505	482	460	388	389	396	463	478	673	9,359	8,142	6,457
Fujian	1,398	1,441	1,496	1,060	973	866	850	806	771	9,114	5,745	5,128
Jiangxi	232	239	249	241	286	322	358	395	380	6,378	4,683	5,000
Shandong	1,921	1,524	1,440	865	911	1,037	1,047	1,131	1,076	18,130	11,747	12,681
Henan	1,265	1,216	1,383	686	708	683	752	774	847	11,113	10,617	9,896
Hubei	605	642	689	372	398	469	544	640	664	12,024	7,863	6,928
Hunan	327	354	413	414	416	469	469	513	544	10,357	12,178	9,187
Guangdong	4,012	3,949	3,928	1,722	1,821	1,804	1,582	1,537	1,533	48,037	35,339	25,998
Guangxi	433	485	481	335	335	343	407	423	432	9,850	4,701	4,309
Hainan	149	165	173	87	94	71	68	71	67	3,839	3,495	1,537
Chongqing	475	447	479	286	246	234	231	297	326	—	—	—
Sichuan	450	451	475	327	341	372	421	483	696	12,682	12,067	11,076
Guizhou	143	145	151	152	150	155	158	142	139	3,109	2,444	2,498
Yunnan	601	697	689	497	456	464	568	579	578	3,962	3,974	3,973
Tibet	12	14	12	12	8	9	8	4	10	62	74	64
Shaanxi	215	226	268	197	218	232	257	265	237	7,096	7,378	7,212
Ganshu	206	229	302	180	173	148	148	149	160	1,728	1,853	1,897
Qinghai	56	63	56	32	36	45	55	60	55	604	463	487
Ningxia	155	157	174	61	62	62	69	65	60	826	781	727
Xinjiang	517	508	509	294	300	294	239	279	308	2,364	2,322	2,398

Source: *Market Statistical Yearbook of China (1995–2004)* and *China Trade and External Economic Statistical Yearbook (2005–2008).*

Table 17. Wholesale industrial establishments/outlets above the designated size by region

Year	2007	2006	2005	2003	2002	2001	2000	1999	1998	1996	1995	1994
Nationwide	60,884	57,994	56,157	27,856	31,268	25,227	23,956	23,720	19,515	2,026,002	1,675,156	1,410,671
Beijing	4,944	3,723	3,498	1,032	1,037	1,070	1,086	1,167	1,105	21,177	10,878	10,663
Tianjin	1,636	1,520	1,233	565	514	520	585	957	1,215	9,733	8,210	7,836
Hebei	641	1,295	522	577	624	647	638	660	643	91,992	85,793	67,681
Shanxi	1,261	1,096	1,174	312	306	301	319	323	323	44,550	37,050	39,983
Inner Mongolia	706	682	757	184	246	263	362	319	219	14,676	13,429	12,684
Liaoning	2,466	2,761	3,121	626	667	678	693	708	792	107,764	91,972	83,859
Jilin	794	389	436	171	224	237	270	291	290	41,747	30,612	22,828
Heilongjiang	1,676	1,768	1,733	1,030	1,142	1,014	1,063	1,087	391	62,753	49,393	43,031
Shanghai	4,483	3,603	2,568	4,602	6,156	1,383	2,098	2,301	449	33,131	8,388	7,273
Jiangshu	2,830	2,897	3,200	1,702	2,094	1,800	1,567	1,717	1,242	92,766	83,223	79,167
Zhejiang	6,153	5,652	6,315	4,606	5,307	5,428	3,072	1,537	1,605	69,986	64,076	67,296
Anhui	1,758	1,506	1,548	2,112	2,137	2,138	2,489	2,556	680	102,784	76,524	70,694
Fujian	1,709	2,057	2,228	1,078	985	883	870	820	811	46,190	38,843	33,511
Jiangxi	1,109	1,139	1,047	260	295	329	359	399	386	60,637	59,080	43,410
Shandong	3,097	2,684	3,304	974	988	1,093	1,096	1,167	1,110	185,013	145,006	123,696
Henan	4,457	3,015	4,369	703	740	706	772	795	873	130,369	113,813	106,266
Hubei	1,937	2,205	2,632	426	722	559	632	710	689	189,528	144,461	94,120
Hunan	700	792	926	1,309	1,346	512	520	601	551	164,373	144,618	98,499
Guangdong	6,778	7,444	4,006	1,759	1,855	1,836	1,589	1,547	1,858	160,432	122,596	92,317
Guangxi	1,687	1,937	1,891	398	368	405	415	456	443	50,976	37,740	31,285
Hainan	249	234	192	87	94	72	68	71	67	19,798	15,539	15,744
Chongqing	2,694	1,583	2,203	302	260	248	235	302	326	—	—	—
Sichuan	1,638	2,256	1,856	336	344	377	428	489	697	155,900	144,131	120,580
Guizhou	728	492	413	156	153	157	158	142	139	35,894	31,941	22,638
Yunnan	1,452	1,973	1,921	1,689	1,809	1,742	1,778	1,767	1,708	28,114	22,893	21,886
Tibet	15	57	69	22	17	9	8	4	10	6,287	1,099	186
Shaanxi	519	701	478	227	225	237	257	265	237	41,758	44,167	44,430
Ganshu	619	665	857	186	181	149	150	150	160	27,611	22,626	19,139
Qinghai	94	107	260	33	37	51	62	60	55	2,225	1,473	1,570
Ningxia	266	266	287	70	70	72	70	65	60	5,248	4,812	4,404
Xinjiang	1,788	1,495	1,113	322	325	311	247	287	308	22,590	20,700	14,995

Source: *Market Statistical Yearbook of China (1995–2004)* and *China Trade and External Economic Statistical Yearbook (2005–2008).*

Table 18. Numbers of practitioners engaged in the wholesale trades above the designated size by region

Year	2007	2006	2005	2003	2002	2001	2000	1998	1996	1995	1994
Nationwide	2,495,863	2,248,731	2,244,131	1,786,669	1,944,793	1,982,927	2,319,248	2,543,600	13,099,023	11,564,890	10,761,093
Beijing	196,565	151,824	146,426	80,989	76,610	79,891	96,488	102,648	366,035	215,949	210,976
Tianjin	52,993	48,965	56,896	38,691	39,888	47,280	38,911	51,263	185,821	172,149	173,639
Hebei	70,603	75,609	72,719	76,292	80,825	84,362	93,499	99,220	574,543	533,690	485,846
Shanxi	81,197	73,142	82,707	46,736	46,420	58,982	50,787	52,500	305,062	271,502	278,765
Inner Mongolia	33,123	33,507	29,464	21,850	17,939	17,137	20,525	24,501	199,211	202,247	206,239
Liaoning	58,134	61,550	76,426	57,921	77,542	83,813	101,952	109,570	955,719	890,095	787,697
Jilin	27,925	26,730	29,028	37,362	42,367	51,336	51,422	55,190	382,130	363,829	339,376
Heilongjiang	42,205	43,639	51,765	46,713	44,377	40,511	72,525	79,001	623,638	553,970	540,292
Shanghai	179,783	181,657	165,542	99,628	105,981	76,819	132,767	113,919	507,863	333,025	275,772
Jiangshu	167,793	154,960	125,361	123,105	152,941	156,737	195,820	212,728	818,503	773,115	742,023
Zhejiang	235,124	133,779	141,928	103,939	120,029	111,991	122,624	135,510	441,596	420,518	415,147
Anhui	70,525	61,824	59,038	58,672	66,771	68,073	77,595	82,925	569,585	501,434	432,536
Fujian	83,068	72,090	74,878	65,323	59,658	60,529	61,319	61,758	256,272	232,693	199,258
Jiangxi	44,777	42,844	45,140	34,743	36,223	40,533	51,878	60,888	341,112	327,771	256,536
Shandong	234,216	167,698	166,142	130,585	155,006	163,781	189,343	207,165	1,028,023	837,850	787,443
Henan	128,844	130,589	136,741	118,419	142,527	164,730	163,686	188,461	774,820	699,129	652,118
Hubei	71,011	74,271	80,392	100,054	132,674	124,704	158,652	169,302	896,184	792,193	672,968
Hunan	47,217	52,067	55,550	59,459	62,437	74,543	95,917	110,124	730,275	736,935	606,466
Guangdong	252,622	250,624	233,783	164,578	162,125	149,642	162,242	170,817	1,121,466	862,677	713,837
Guangxi	45,569	47,845	57,488	39,735	37,807	44,775	46,371	65,987	233,223	205,686	193,088
Hainan	7,164	9,567	10,772	5,873	6,037	3,797	5,832	9,361	128,485	98,315	114,770
Chongqing	61,256	61,227	60,848	51,267	48,686	36,689	39,507	57,441	—	—	—
Sichuan	69,965	63,700	63,269	48,491	51,759	58,281	68,190	88,680	735,915	684,633	621,102
Guizhou	38,040	24,217	27,874	26,899	26,568	26,407	26,247	24,733	144,877	118,358	109,830
Yunnan	69,540	68,570	63,061	53,354	52,956	54,120	71,801	74,337	166,686	160,995	150,159
Tibet	1,313	1,841	1,429	1,136	861	884	936	379	10,079	4,184	2,199
Shaanxi	41,847	52,591	43,839	28,872	29,562	33,415	37,448	41,863	246,998	241,670	485,846
Ganshu	19,188	19,241	24,792	18,087	20,562	22,059	25,987	25,744	158,862	140,318	132,046
Qinghai	7,145	6,768	6,117	6,400	7,324	6,456	9,457	8,789	21,998	18,727	17,140
Ningxia	9,152	9,695	9,349	7,019	4,544	5,191	5,988	6,643	31,580	31,676	31,335
Xinjiang	47,959	46,100	45,367	34,477	35,787	35,459	43,532	52,153	142,462	139,557	126,641

Source: *Market Statistical Yearbook of China (1995–2004)* and *China Trade and External Economic Statistical Yearbook (2005–2008).*

Table 19. Revenues from the main businesses of the wholesale trades above the designated size by region

(RMB 10 thousand)

Year	2007	2006	2005	2003	2002	2001	2000	1999
Nationwide	954,407,850	777,244,766	677,012,657	336,898,683	286,659,317	251,330,345	241,841,349	200,999,207
Beijing	132,952,966	100,865,148	80,891,520	30,070,188	23,517,708	19,997,754	18,985,560	15,270,169
Tianjin	49,931,802	40,961,691	35,411,838	14,175,498	10,361,996	10,078,443	7,586,605	4,687,899
Hebei	19,459,460	12,272,120	10,876,826	6,946,269	6,444,148	6,542,676	6,256,188	5,938,093
Shanxi	15,723,119	10,981,498	10,211,270	3,976,742	3,226,382	2,957,505	2,510,650	2,066,333
Inner Mongolia	8,698,588	6,961,630	5,965,844	1,955,343	1,637,656	1,614,661	1,577,918	1,460,965
Liaoning	45,027,664	40,282,332	37,386,512	16,952,769	13,946,904	13,105,268	12,270,783	10,150,556
Jilin	7,644,362	5,599,425	12,122,961	3,508,447	2,853,293	2,481,917	2,470,355	1,932,870
Heilongjiang	10,694,130	9,605,255	8,111,586	4,895,862	4,226,865	3,863,862	3,760,106	3,276,606
Shanghai	121,162,453	106,723,304	93,510,066	38,278,505	40,310,959	25,983,151	26,438,097	16,822,833
Jiangshu	63,368,855	51,343,107	39,659,080	23,949,132	21,067,647	19,083,333	20,790,518	18,793,744
Zhejiang	98,513,075	80,628,468	69,036,800	40,573,168	31,154,446	27,357,471	25,803,418	21,317,305
Anhui	16,400,525	13,483,544	12,089,133	7,393,664	5,997,721	4,855,694	5,121,258	4,720,206
Fujian	32,056,984	26,896,986	22,921,962	13,552,373	11,664,771	9,392,833	10,002,777	8,169,768
Jiangxi	6,837,818	6,420,119	5,429,103	3,631,913	3,378,773	3,319,390	2,716,134	2,382,687
Shandong	40,070,798	30,564,129	27,490,005	15,016,526	14,085,779	12,942,369	12,826,896	12,282,601
Henan	21,354,333	17,748,403	15,927,719	7,753,960	6,289,025	6,586,144	7,317,763	6,684,495
Hubei	26,487,109	21,676,328	17,703,934	9,031,935	7,794,736	7,639,482	7,574,914	4,983,111
Hunan	10,434,309	7,854,649	7,808,745	7,493,710	6,125,433	5,985,888	5,105,956	4,611,183
Guangdong	122,783,177	102,105,966	88,954,335	46,495,374	38,643,386	34,913,037	27,973,969	23,563,294
Guangxi	8,253,202	7,871,241	7,972,708	3,066,388	2,685,902	2,804,727	2,794,646	3,709,591
Hainan	3,281,155	3,316,723	2,240,899	1,126,996	1,015,897	779,777	727,438	468,447
Chongqing	11,298,749	8,654,261	8,646,472	4,394,641	4,127,635	3,307,915	2,723,999	2,387,297
Sichuan	17,847,466	13,398,398	12,430,067	6,701,877	5,869,649	5,838,424	6,104,967	5,780,576
Guizhou	4,303,833	3,577,419	3,409,449	2,148,461	1,836,869	1,735,385	2,084,453	1,924,856
Yunnan	18,651,275	17,475,542	14,861,525	9,682,993	7,237,471	8,036,196	9,546,286	8,764,888
Tibet	119,265	229,900	185,777	107,971	52,293	58,637	58,497	16,731
Shaanxi	15,014,020	9,597,451	8,056,065	3,491,167	2,756,716	2,521,535	3,122,856	2,786,612
Ganshu	11,696,944	8,384,454	7,592,437	4,351,632	3,263,430	3,157,460	2,966,082	1,668,302
Qinghai	1,241,616	1,222,792	728,599	474,044	471,096	332,026	354,878	303,417
Ningxia	1,376,350	1,162,689	1,029,389	485,042	381,105	451,130	362,685	337,509
Xinjiang	16,221,045	9,379,795	8,350,034	5,216,096	4,233,627	3,606,254	3,904,698	3,736,265

Source: *Market Statistical Yearbook of China (1995–2004)* and *China Trade and External Economic Statistical Yearbook (2005–2008).*

Table 20. Costs of the main businesses of the wholesale trades above the designated size by region

(RMB 10 thousand)

Year	2007	2006	2005	2003	2002	2001	2000	1999
Nationwide	880,817,164	723,928,023	620,479,108	312,110,314	265,981,592	232,932,959	223,649,603	184,697,870
Beijing	122,739,114	93,873,453	74,792,145	28,036,763	21,939,507	18,635,036	17,790,342	14,101,797
Tianjin	47,896,376	39,216,183	33,762,834	13,572,949	9,923,990	9,575,862	7,252,655	4,398,909
Hebei	17,708,244	11,257,354	9,826,350	6,457,160	6,015,771	6,119,896	5,829,553	5,552,659
Shanxi	14,016,943	9,881,596	8,978,411	3,620,513	2,934,197	2,696,697	2,305,656	1,782,772
Inner Mongolia	7,336,636	5,947,671	4,642,718	1,764,778	1,447,685	1,496,018	1,450,491	1,334,160
Liaoning	42,557,787	38,281,199	34,190,202	16,073,014	13,249,881	12,496,264	11,574,538	9,515,294
Jilin	7,091,714	5,258,795	11,520,418	3,394,042	2,821,896	2,385,137	2,365,808	1,779,989
Heilongjiang	9,753,067	8,944,115	7,455,558	4,468,498	3,882,306	3,574,641	3,514,221	2,994,958
Shanghai	110,502,140	99,511,694	82,292,143	34,921,681	37,394,609	24,136,181	24,695,836	15,396,334
Jiangshu	58,290,904	47,645,048	36,211,122	21,996,730	19,322,617	17,422,753	18,938,084	17,196,899
Zhejiang	93,303,879	76,398,083	65,353,701	37,995,741	29,043,068	25,573,597	23,990,496	19,855,152
Anhui	14,719,370	12,403,902	11,077,660	6,804,609	5,520,563	4,459,481	4,702,392	4,313,263
Fujian	30,088,482	25,315,327	21,685,761	12,631,968	10,844,996	8,717,070	9,025,096	7,541,964
Jiangxi	6,000,831	5,697,717	4,912,223	3,295,638	3,106,249	3,071,687	2,500,310	2,197,470
Shandong	36,409,512	28,140,494	25,311,763	13,965,025	13,108,929	11,858,807	11,809,626	11,202,203
Henan	19,689,595	16,461,574	14,754,562	7,177,641	5,774,868	6,027,340	6,618,314	6,027,067
Hubei	24,674,645	20,231,254	16,113,799	8,418,129	7,298,219	7,120,217	7,047,996	4,552,769
Hunan	9,192,518	6,870,887	6,608,869	6,856,206	5,609,651	5,508,340	4,696,631	4,231,331
Guangdong	115,033,291	96,032,933	83,621,290	43,523,447	36,223,201	32,681,226	26,391,353	21,970,069
Guangxi	7,424,577	7,148,716	7,325,602	2,767,699	2,423,221	2,569,041	2,560,779	3,316,225
Hainan	3,016,916	3,014,478	2,020,671	1,016,060	15,511	718,658	663,800	430,724
Chongqing	10,339,521	7,882,771	7,815,098	4,021,853	3,767,528	2,994,384	2,456,371	2,159,661
Sichuan	15,420,793	12,080,008	10,302,743	6,063,321	5,324,286	5,275,069	5,606,051	5,297,684
Guizhou	3,515,875	2,942,454	2,788,908	1,819,088	1,562,452	1,500,224	1,853,495	1,694,886
Yunnan	16,214,302	15,405,407	12,879,093	8,442,807	6,218,319	7,027,256	8,108,901	7,541,511
Tibet	103,847	197,227	153,888	55,888	44,904	51,815	53,159	15,986
Shaanxi	13,591,482	9,077,373	7,544,448	3,250,398	2,557,753	2,331,301	2,884,962	2,552,373
Ganshu	10,608,979	7,859,632	7,159,217	4,070,119	3,056,459	2,914,724	2,778,877	1,547,114
Qinghai	1,108,029	1,126,903	645,888	411,698	418,953	296,672	301,643	268,311
Ningxia	1,248,342	1,062,903	943,420	436,610	345,232	423,980	331,330	309,836
Xinjiang	15,244,918	8,760,873	7,788,604	4,780,242	3,884,684	3,273,589	3,550,838	3,618,501

Source: *Market Statistical Yearbook of China (1995–2004)* and *China Trade and External Economic Statistical Yearbook (2005–2008).*

Table 21. Profits from the main businesses of the wholesale trades above the designated size by region

(RMB 10 thousand)

Year	2007	2006	2005	2003	2002	2001	2000	1999
Nationwide	63,361,041	49,766,899	42,312,682	13,688,204	11,115,487	8,203,844	8,623,787	7,403,986
Beijing	10,016,567	6,894,094	6,017,653	1,023,726	803,969	706,249	609,730	549,05
Tianjin	1,751,330	1,532,380	1,203,453	272,605	187,128	183,224	166,095	100,533
Hebei	1,131,581	944,919	781,558	245,765	215,050	170,836	173,413	164,334
Shanxi	1,309,558	976,123	949,442	188,278	132,941	89,042	57,795	46,633
Inner Mongolia	1,102,451	933,883	1,044,031	99,860	98,972	42,866	46,702	48,743
Liaoning	1,891,131	1,776,494	1,582,756	302,583	125,701	15,226	232,878	215,930
Jilin	461,846	331,601	429,396	-102,078	-144,244	-48,264	-61,327	53,769
Heilongjiang	785,851	592,785	518,838	188,118	143,833	105,222	79,171	84,553
Shanghai	8,684,977	6,884,824	5,502,651	1,955,992	1,872,273	958,000	1,098,026	793,758
Jiangshu	4,488,568	3,253,143	2,478,332	1,194,840	980,839	788,388	905,798	739,794
Zhejiang	5,114,954	4,155,573	3,457,481	1,561,652	1,255,346	964,649	974,288	751,972
Anhui	1,308,871	958,589	869,109	360,646	272,084	200,531	210,081	200,070
Fujian	1,916,102	1,483,956	1,233,596	507,338	455,366	301,361	409,067	309,744
Jiangxi	700,953	664,651	480,272	180,304	139,579	95,607	87,632	68,851
Shandong	3,054,803	2,129,626	1,673,246	596,193	529,244	418,453	387,764	430,865
Henan	1,628,440	1,261,720	1,151,653	320,316	296,551	240,304	347,334	362,644
Hubei	1,489,859	1,326,782	970,555	355,287	270,920	242,560	237,066	172,908
Hunan	1,099,885	963,313	749,901	394,715	306,252	238,258	200,740	171,040
Guangdong	6,993,898	5,842,067	4,488,188	1,599,149	1,236,214	1,007,952	815,913	821,809
Guangxi	671,392	606,791	634,474	161,794	134,850	86,926	104,978	154,459
Hainan	171,918	249,256	212,871	58,423	51,050	30,925	34,808	16,627
Chongqing	752,611	701,784	683,354	182,994	162,525	139,096	109,419	92,589
Sichuan	1,428,585	1,161,938	1,572,065	423,793	356,381	265,980	191,130	172,814
Guizhou	631,028	598,626	494,948	213,091	176,185	115,397	93,960	117,109
Yunnan	1,993,318	1,897,023	1,635,249	832,316	665,029	508,620	730,527	693,438
Tibet	11,630	16,636	22,570	46,530	4,789	1,308	-57	-3,726
Shaanxi	1,243,710	496,125	449,577	122,664	99,628	66,340	100,546	96,722
Ganshu	532,857	394,554	410,126	87,004	54,170	85,649	85,029	42,952
Qinghai	106,818	90,884	75,428	2,333	32,521	18,141	16,783	15,975
Ningxia	111,579	95,230	82,132	25,503	16,182	8,037	10,174	1,522
Xinjiang	774,665	551,531	457,778	246,471	184,170	156,964	168,328	-93,499

Source: *Market Statistical Yearbook of China (1995–2004)* and *China Trade and External Economic Statistical Yearbook (2005–2008).*

Table 22. Sizes of assets of the wholesale trades above the designated size by region

(RMB 100 million)

Year	2007	2006	2005	2003	2002	2001	2000	1999
Nationwide	38,697.7	31,523.0	28,105.8	17,827.6	16,356.8	15,122.5	15,141.7	14,540.4
Beijing	8,776.3	6,559.8	5,071.7	2,923.1	2,486.7	2,562.4	2,385.0	2,324.8
Tianjin	1,446.3	1,122.6	1,088.6	552.1	473.9	441.4	358.8	333.8
Hebei	552.0	462.7	446.6	369.5	377.2	376.4	361.9	344.2
Shanxi	766.9	678.0	547.5	230.2	237.6	181.6	174.9	175.8
Inner Mongolia	370.0	315.1	312.1	103.6	98.8	86.7	101.6	97.8
Liaoning	1,256.5	1,096.8	1,046.9	762.0	791.6	719.3	683.9	653.8
Jilin	258.8	230.1	378.1	246.2	240.5	221.4	216.2	194.9
Heilongjiang	453.6	416.4	445.3	292.4	249.0	198.4	332.2	321.2
Shanghai	3,698.2	3,225.3	3,023.2	1,655.7	1,550.5	1,064.5	1,236.6	1,049.9
Jiangshu	2,284.4	1,789.9	1,421.0	1,083.4	1,026.6	947.8	1,037.4	970.4
Zhejiang	3,685.4	2,910.5	2,597.8	1,612.4	1,256.9	1,104.3	1,017.2	919.3
Anhui	725.6	541.5	480.3	325.4	296.9	275.2	303.8	307.6
Fujian	1,521.4	1,102.3	936.8	692.0	611.5	506.7	518.1	485.9
Jiangxi	272.6	245.4	231.0	144.2	153.1	165.7	168.7	168.2
Shandong	1,788.8	1,386.5	1,254.1	910.0	944.6	872.9	877.4	929.8
Henan	869.0	758.9	662.1	450.0	435.3	525.3	539.4	531.1
Hubei	799.4	746.9	737.7	469.0	475.7	548.5	563.4	537.3
Hunan	400.8	383.3	375.4	416.5	412.7	411.9	371.7	357.3
Guangdong	4,279.4	3,661.5	3,352.3	2,045.6	1,934.5	1,806.6	1,507.3	1,425.4
Guangxi	342.0	306.4	306.3	143.1	146.3	154.0	168.0	187.1
Hainan	109.3	121.7	94.4	53.1	60.6	45.3	48.1	53.0
Chongqing	434.0	394.6	421.9	248.2	234.7	200.8	189.2	184.9
Sichuan	669.6	507.9	584.2	314.2	310.3	281.7	309.1	345.6
Guizhou	221.6	183.3	174.2	155.7	175.4	166.7	190.2	174.2
Yunnan	1,227.4	951.8	815.9	669.6	595.1	586.5	752.3	738.8
Tibet	9.6	16.8	15.7	11.1	5.8	5.7	6.0	2.6
Shaanxi	345.1	299.6	275.1	187.1	176.7	163.6	192.6	193.9
Ganshu	313.4	244.6	208.9	140.8	133.5	94.8	91.7	79.0
Qinghai	58.8	47.0	31.4	21.5	23.5	23.4	29.7	34.0
Ningxia	80.8	69.6	64.1	28.1	27.4	7.8	27.4	24.7
Xinjiang	684.8	746.3	705.2	571.7	414.2	354.8	382.0	393.9

Source: *Market Statistical Yearbook of China (1995–2004)* and *China Trade and External Economic Statistical Yearbook (2005–2008).*

Table 23. **Sizes of fixed assets of the wholesale trades above the designated size by region**

(RMB 100 million)

Year	2007	2006	2005	2003	2002	2001	2000	1999
Nationwide	4,504.1	4,013.2	2,658.5	2,385.8	23,979.9	22,792.0	23,032.7	23,507.6
Beijing	429.8	336.6	214.2	167.1	1,562.1	1,684.4	1,774.9	1,943.0
Tianjin	102.6	85.0	64.6	59.7	581.7	530.4	451.3	493.7
Hebei	122.2	118.3	88.2	83.3	935.8	819.6	670.9	667.5
Shanxi	139.2	144.1	79.5	48.8	818.8	344.8	408.9	401.4
Inner Mongolia	49.9	63.1	36.5	18.9	287.2	173.9	167.3	185.4
Liaoning	138.7	122.8	103.1	113.1	1,237.7	1,096.2	1,137.2	1,121.4
Jilin	55.6	45.3	34.2	33.8	341.4	337.0	357.3	361.1
Heilongjiang	79.5	79.3	63.7	51.2	414.7	348.7	462.7	478.8
Shanghai	245.3	251.7	152.3	148.6	1,437.6	1,064.8	1,573.9	1,242.5
Jiangshu	327.0	268.0	155.5	149.7	1,704.2	1,749.2	1,907.1	1,924.0
Zhejiang	365.0	316.9	225.7	195.1	1,899.6	1,836.3	1,733.2	1,724.4
Anhui	93.1	82.2	60.1	53.6	491.2	478.3	506.4	497.0
Fujian	128.7	124.8	85.7	99.3	822.0	737.6	790.5	791.4
Jiangxi	64.4	63.9	42.9	35.2	331.4	286.7	290.7	341.9
Shandong	329.7	211.7	135.9	137.7	1,493.2	1,495.0	1,578.3	1,834.3
Henan	221.7	192.7	125.1	90.8	698.5	911.3	801.5	803.6
Hubei	154.3	155.2	86.0	68.0	719.9	978.3	978.4	1,003.6
Hunan	118.7	91.2	68.7	77.6	707.3	752.9	739.7	779.4
Guangdong	581.3	519.9	369.2	296.5	3,055.1	3,318.0	2,556.6	2,533.4
Guangxi	66.8	70.0	50.1	41.0	472.3	433.3	416.8	425.2
Hainan	16.4	29.2	16.9	14.5	126.0	102.6	120.4	126.4
Chongqing	87.1	78.4	68.1	48.1	511.9	413.8	382.9	382.5
Sichuan	132.8	123.9	60.1	57.4	545.5	552.9	562.2	758.1
Guizhou	52.0	43.2	32.3	36.4	403.9	301.9	290.7	253.9
Yunnan	135.3	143.8	87.9	109.3	1,023.8	1,017.2	1,147.7	1,226.3
Tibet	3.4	4.8	3.6	2.4	13.7	11.0	10.0	4.0
Shaanxi	69.5	52.8	35.2	29.8	330.2	276.0	351.3	378.4
Ganshu	44.3	31.1	24.9	29.2	296.7	212.4	199.6	170.3
Qinghai	16.5	12.4	3.5	5.6	66.1	34.7	61.8	73.8
Ningxia	11.0	10.2	6.8	7.5	67.5	60.2	56.1	52.1
Xinjiang	122.2	140.7	77.8	76.6	582.9	432.6	546.3	528.9

Source: *Market Statistical Yearbook of China (1995–2004)* and *China Trade and External Economic Statistical Yearbook (2005–2008).*

Table 24. Sizes of floating assets of the wholesale trades above the designated size by region

(RMB 100 million)

Year	2007	2006	2005	2003	2002	2001	2000	1999
Nationwide	29,271.1	23,504.6	20,985.0	13,139.9	11,775.4	10,471.0	10,807.2	10,233.0
Beijing	6,078.7	4,479.5	3,633.6	2,217.8	1,828.5	1,649.1	1,599.9	1,595.2
Tianjin	1,228.0	947.3	897.1	449.3	379.7	331.3	278.8	248.0
Hebei	380.0	314.8	288.0	259.3	248.0	254.7	261.5	246.4
Shanxi	542.7	476.6	367.0	165.8	144.0	123.2	120.5	119.0
Inner Mongolia	256.6	231.6	234.2	78.2	71.0	57.0	71.1	71.9
Liaoning	1,017.6	880.2	826.6	643.3	573.6	535.7	493.0	470.1
Jilin	172.5	157.1	334.5	191.9	194.1	174.7	170.3	148.5
Heilongjiang	371.6	329.6	353.9	252.8	199.2	152.9	270.9	258.5
Shanghai	3,024.0	2,609.6	2,430.1	1,218.0	1,169.4	764.6	904.2	747.1
Jiangshu	1,820.7	1,385.0	1,039.1	819.7	743.5	679.9	756.6	690.5
Zhejiang	2,945.7	2,265.7	2,035.0	1,235.3	912.4	769.8	719.5	644.3
Anhui	592.7	416.7	367.4	244.7	225.4	207.1	238.5	240.1
Fujian	1,135.5	829.1	695.0	506.8	435.4	337.4	357.4	325.4
Jiangxi	188.4	161.9	165.9	97.0	107.8	122.5	122.3	116.1
Shandong	1,355.9	1,012.6	963.0	647.6	682.6	608.5	590.8	617.0
Henan	582.0	516.8	465.1	334.2	330.3	386.8	410.7	392.2
Hubei	615.9	538.5	553.8	345.2	356.2	390.1	395.1	362.4
Hunan	243.5	259.9	251.9	266.6	268.1	271.8	246.0	226.5
Guangdong	3,380.9	2,828.4	2,434.4	1,373.4	1,290.6	1,157.8	1,025.2	953.2
Guangxi	242.4	200.9	187.7	87.4	87.4	92.2	108.2	122.4
Hainan	83.1	87.9	64.2	29.2	34.6	25.3	28.6	32.7
Chongqing	326.5	285.4	349.2	175.0	162.6	146.2	139.2	129.8
Sichuan	464.6	348.5	316.4	203.8	211.6	188.3	226.4	234.2
Guizhou	153.8	131.7	126.1	113.3	118.9	128.4	150.3	138.2
Yunnan	922.9	732.5	616.0	480.4	423.7	413.9	567.1	550.2
Tibet	6.2	9.9	10.5	7.4	15.4	4.4	4.6	2.0
Shaanxi	255.1	198.8	195.6	134.8	137.4	117.3	140.0	135.2
Ganshu	253.3	193.3	151.8	92.3	83.0	65.4	61.7	56.4
Qinghai	38.9	31.8	20.1	13.0	14.6	18.1	22.2	22.3
Ningxia	60.9	56.3	48.8	17.4	17.3	20.6	20.5	18.2
Xinjiang	530.6	586.6	563.0	439.1	309.3	276.0	306.1	319.1

Source: *Market Statistical Yearbook of China (1995–2004)* and *China Trade and External Economic Statistical Yearbook (2005–2008).*

Table 25. **Scales of liabilities of the wholesale trades above the designated size by region**

(RMB 100 million)

Year	2007	2006	2005	2003	2002	2001	2000	1999
Nationwide	27,452.8	22,249.6	20,199.5	13,452.2	12,573.5	11,726.7	12,336.3	11,891.0
Beijing	6,159.64	494.6	3,616.2	2,170.2	1,820.6	1,710.1	1,702.1	1,787.3
Tianjin	1,088.6	837.9	821.0	449.5	388.4	346.0	323.7	283.0
Hebei	394.2	348.8	345.7	304.0	311.6	322.1	323.8	298.9
Shanxi	541.4	484.7	398.6	175.1	188.9	157.0	156.9	149.6
Inner Mongolia	236.6	210.1	182.5	82.3	81.8	72.2	87.9	87.3
Liaoning	974.0	844.6	905.6	664.0	687.6	622.6	589.8	546.4
Jilin	211.2	177.1	350.4	236.8	234.4	211.5	214.3	198.1
Heilongjiang	355.7	318.1	360.1	240.9	218.1	181.0	311.9	303.8
Shanghai	2,601.6	2,223.4	2,123.2	1,122.5	1,054.2	745.4	895.4	789.6
Jiangshu	1,649.2	1,264.0	959.2	790.4	760.0	729.3	821.9	781.1
Zhejiang	2,772.1	2,121.1	1,795.5	1,147.0	866.1	755.1	727.9	647.5
Anhui	538.3	397.0	349.5	256.2	258.5	249.0	279.0	280.1
Fujian	989.4	683.7	586.2	445.4	400.7	334.5	349.5	332.6
Jiangxi	175.1	166.7	159.0	111.8	127.0	150.9	166.7	159.9
Shandong	1,292.7	1,013.3	950.5	737.8	801.4	748.8	775.3	796.2
Henan	657.7	590.1	522.4	385.7	386.9	472.8	507.9	494.8
Hubei	590.0	527.5	621.6	382.5	420.6	495.1	539.9	500.8
Hunan	212.8	232.7	250.2	337.4	340.5	371.4	350.3	328.5
Guangdong	3,069.5	2,612.8	2,351.5	1,486.5	1,438.5	1,348.6	1,203.7	1,101.1
Guangxi	215.3	192.3	196.6	109.5	114.5	129.0	143.2	141.7
Hainan	65.7	74.2	57.7	27.4	38.7	31.5	38.9	43.6
Chongqing	317.9	296.5	328.8	198.1	200.8	178.3	169.1	166.7
Sichuan	422.2	334.5	310.4	223.8	233.9	222.1	263.9	280.6
Guizhou	113.2	110.5	117.8	126.0	144.5	148.7	175.2	152.7
Yunnan	693.4	602.2	519.5	458.0	397.2	401.4	555.6	563.3
Tibet	5.0	8.0	8.9	7.9	4.3	5.0	4.9	1.8
Shaanxi	261.8	231.4	223.9	167.7	160.7	148.1	178.0	174.9
Ganshu	197.5	174.1	141.9	110.8	113.2	92.3	87.0	71.1
Qinghai	32.3	25.6	14.7	13.0	17.3	19.2	26.1	30.3
Ningxia	53.2	49.0	45.3	20.8	22.3	25.1	24.0	24.8
Xinjiang	565.4	603.0	585.0	462.8	340.2	302.5	342.6	372.9

Source: *Market Statistical Yearbook of China (1995–2004)* and *China Trade and External Economic Statistical Yearbook (2005–2008).*

Table 26. The wholesale of agricultural and sideline products and the wholesale of industrial products

Year	Purchase and wholesale institutions for agricultural and sideline products in the society (10 thousand)	Wholesale institutions for of social products (10 thousand)	Practitioners engaged in the purchase and wholesale of farm and sideline products (10 thousand)	Practitioners engaged in the wholesale of social products (10 thousand)
1978	12.1	3.7	88.5	69.7
1979	13.6	4.8	121.3	89.1
1980	15.1	4.5	130.3	70.9
1981	16.6	4	142.8	73.6
1982	16.5	4.1	151.9	76.2
1983	16.9	4.3	153.7	79.2
1984	17.7	6.2	162.1	99.7
1985	22.1	6.7	165.8	106.7
1986	22.6	7.1	170.2	110.5
1987	26.3	6.7	201.7	108.9
1988	26.4	7.5	210.4	119.7
1989	22.6	9.9	187.9	155
1990	20.1	8.7	187.6	150.6
1991	19.2	10.1	203.5	151.8
1992	18.3	12.1	217.2	195.2

Source: Data during 1978–1988 come from *China Trade and External Economic Statistical Yearbook (1952–1988)*; and data during 1988–1992 come from *China Business Yearbook (1988–1993)*.

Table 27. Wholesale corporate institutions by trade (1994–1996)

Year	1996	1995	1994
Wholesale commerce of food, drinks, tobacco and household articles	145,507	118,515	106,121
The wholesale of food, drinks and tobacco	64,843	54,665	49,269
The wholesale of cotton, flax, native products and animal by-products	5,338	5,632	5,581
The wholesale of textiles, garments, shoes and hats	14,482	11,905	9,388
The wholesale of articles for daily use	19,533	17,223	15,101
The wholesale of daily sundries	5,965	4,871	5,035
The wholesale of hardware, electrical appliances & accessories and chemical products	28,659	18,794	16,444
The wholesale of drugs and medical instruments	6,687	5,425	5,303

(Con'd)

Year	1996	1995	1994
The wholesale of energies, material and machinery electronic equipment	122,430	87,080	80,411
The wholesale of energies	15,228	10,751	9,734
The wholesale of chemical materials	10,914	7,421	6,289
The wholesale of woods	6,522	4,888	5,022
The wholesale of building materials	24,978	17,077	15,345
The wholesale of mineral products	2,254	1,501	1,301
The wholesale of metallic materials	24,950	20,313	20,056
The wholesale of machinery and electronic equipment	22,671	14,574	12,830
The wholesale of autos, motorcycles and accessories	9,423	5,919	5,295
The wholesale of recycled materials	5,490	4,639	4,539
Other wholesale trades	38,298	29,891	25,962
The wholesale of artistic handicrafts	1,170	832	632
The wholesale of books and newspapers	1,317	1,144	1,013
The wholesale of means of agricultural production	20,712	17,108	15,909
Other wholesale not classified	15,099	10,807	8,408

Source: *China Market Statistical Yearbook (1993–2008).*

Table 28. The numbers of wholesale outlets by trade (1994–1996)

Year	1996	1995	1994
Wholesale commerce of food, drinks, tobacco and household articles	1,366,870	1,150,359	913,107
The wholesale of food, drinks and tobacco	656,791	535,638	402,549
The wholesale of cotton, flax, native products and animal by-products	34,549	41,832	32,270
The wholesale of textiles, garments, shoes and hats	205,385	170,120	137,584
The wholesale of articles for daily use	261,467	233,426	199,006
The wholesale of daily sundries	62,993	51,567	47,382
The wholesale of hardware, electrical appliances & accessories and chemical products	100,668	78,161	58,493
The wholesale of drugs and medical instruments	45,017	39,615	35,823
The wholesale of energies, material and machinery electronic equipment	345,100	261,673	231,829

(Con'd)

Year	1996	1995	1994
The wholesale of energies	53,781	39,728	34,961
The wholesale of chemical materials	33,879	24,553	18,993
The wholesale of woods	23,311	17,676	16,746
The wholesale of building materials	71,566	53,687	42,961
The wholesale of mineral products	4,958	2,668	2,829
The wholesale of metallic materials	56,196	48,890	44,588
The wholesale of machinery and electronic equipment	44,308	29,482	25,175
The wholesale of autos, motorcycles and accessories	26,098	17,423	14,181
The wholesale of recycled materials	31,003	27,566	31,395
Other wholesale trades	314,032	263,124	256,735
The wholesale of artistic handicrafts	6,249	3,579	2,327
The wholesale of books and newspapers	11,687	9,630	9,663
The wholesale of means of agricultural production	209,978	173,611	153,322
Other wholesale not classified	86,118	76,304	91,423

Source: *China Market Statistical Yearbook (1997–2003).*

Table 29. The numbers of wholesale practitioners by trade (1994–1996)

Year	1996	1995	1994
Wholesale commerce of food, drinks, tobacco and household articles	7,708,265	6,973,805	6,313,894
The wholesale of food, drinks and tobacco	3,757,963	3,348,918	3,007,132
The wholesale of cotton, flax, native products and animal by-products	421,290	385,304	369,732
The wholesale of textiles, garments, shoes and hats	765,669	699,899	600,174
The wholesale of articles for daily use	1,159,439	1,135,355	1,045,986
The wholesale of daily sundries	317,824	298,193	264,645
The wholesale of hardware, electrical appliances & accessories and chemical products	844,541	710,485	644,829
The wholesale of drugs and medical instruments	441,539	395,651	381,396
The wholesale of energies, material and machinery electronic equipment	353,198	2,978,723	2,749,094
The wholesale of energies	748,926	598,045	555,673
The wholesale of chemical materials	286,075	225,808	207,266
The wholesale of woods	258,940	221,363	219,238
The wholesale of building materials	536,500	432,647	383,549

(Con'd)

Year	1996	1995	1994
The wholesale of mineral products	54,530	44,247	38,225
The wholesale of metallic materials	658,803	636,013	621,394
The wholesale of machinery and electronic equipment	498,513	399,174	320,810
The wholesale of autos, motorcycles and accessories	241,331	188,350	168,832
The wholesale of recycled materials	252,580	233,076	234,107
Other wholesale trades	1,854,560	1,612,362	1,406,535
The wholesale of artistic handicrafts	42,447	31,647	23,864
The wholesale of books and newspapers	62,694	52,912	52,458
The wholesale of means of agricultural production	1,093,701	956,397	882,462
Other wholesale not classified	655,718	571,406	447,751

Source: *China Market Statistical Yearbook (1997–2003).*

Table 30. Basic registrations of the wholesale trades above the designated size (2001–2002)

Year	2001			2002		
	Business corporations	Industrial establishments	Practitioners (person)	Business corporations	Industrial establishments	Practitioners (person)
The wholesale trade	15,258	25,227	1,982,927	15,262	31,268	1,944,793
Wholesale commerce of food, drinks, tobacco and household articles	7,636	13,451	1,205,151	7,467	17,994	1,183,047
The wholesale of food, drinks and tobacco	4,073	7,683	619,406	3,857	11,366	623,653
Of which: The wholesale of grains and edible oil	1,016	1,946	183,565	928	1,751	171,792
The wholesale of tobacco and its products	1,888	3,811	221,043	1,849	5,751	243,248
The wholesale of cotton, flax, native products and animal by-products	467	717	152,907	422	633	108,064
The wholesale of textiles, garments, shoes and hats	776	853	73,580	829	1,112	81,778
The wholesale of articles for daily use	465	628	61,970	463	634	55,173
The wholesale of daily sundries	87	114	8,616	79	152	8,273

(Con'd)

Year	2001			2002		
	Business corporations	Industrial establishments	Practitioners (person)	Business corporations	Industrial establishments	Practitioners (person)
The wholesale of hardware, electrical appliances & accessories and chemical products	798	993	85,499	787	1,016	86,905
The wholesale of drugs and medical instruments	970	2,463	203,173	1,030	3,081	219,201
The wholesale of energies, material and machinery electronic equipment	5,806	8,941	599,017	5,941	10,395	591,401
The wholesale of energies	1,875	4,062	316,301	1,805	5,128	302,180
Of which: The wholesale of petroleum and related products	1,530	3,641	246,829	1,471	4,692	252,335
The wholesale of coal and related products	337	412	68,813	328	428	48,920
The wholesale of chemical materials	612	732	33,716	639	809	35,998
The wholesale of woods	67	79	7,235	74	123	8,923
The wholesale of building materials	262	318	17,523	274	334	18,422
The wholesale of mineral products	77	86	5,881	73	79	4,966
The wholesale of metallic materials	1,172	1,349	80,349	1,191	1,361	74,014
The wholesale of machinery and electronic equipment	924	1,037	71,146	1,021	1,129	76,387
The wholesale of autos, motorcycles and accessories	593	707	45,561	627	776	48,287
Of which: The wholesale of autos	411	498	33,904	442	539	33,166
The wholesale of recycled materials	224	571	21,305	237	656	22,224
Other wholesale trades	1,816	2,835	178,759	1,854	2,879	170,345
The wholesale of artistic handicrafts	86	94	8,370	93	102	8,912
The wholesale of books and newspapers	168	227	26,409	182	291	30,944
The wholesale of means of agricultural production	1,204	2,129	120,769	991	1,856	94,969
Other wholesale not classified	358	385	23,211	588	630	35,520

Source: *China Market Statistical Yearbook (2002–2003).*

Table 31. Sales volume of the wholesale trade above the designated size by trade (1998–2002)

(RMB 100 million)

Year	1998	1999	2000	2001	2002
The wholesale of food, drinks and tobacco	5,919.5	6,184.4	6,517.7	6,405.4	6,482.1
The wholesale of cotton, flax, native products and animal by-products	809.3	639.2	930.3	692.7	620.8
The wholesale of textiles, garments, shoes and hats	1,553.3	1,520.0	1,932.6	1,961.8	2,264.7
The wholesale of articles for daily use	723.3	612.4	588.7	75.1	659.9
The wholesale of daily sundries	107.1	74.0	70.6	62.3	64.0
The wholesale of hardware, electrical appliances & accessories and chemical products	1,180.6	984.3	1,029.8	1,221.9	1,352.4
The wholesale of drugs and medical instruments	853.7	1,011.4	1,206.0	1,410.0	1,567.3
The wholesale of energies	2,781.5	3,713.3	6,205.7	7,460.1	7,877.1
The wholesale of chemical materials	718.3	681.7	807.4	810.3	1,006.9
The wholesale of woods	58.9	53.7	74.6	54.4	80.1
The wholesale of building materials	184.9	171.3	188.4	191.0	240.7
The wholesale of mineral products	72.7	86.3	182.2	162.1	156.5
The wholesale of metallic materials	1,916.3	1,796.9	1,930.7	2,293.2	2,986.2
The wholesale of machinery and electronic equipment	1,413.6	1,264.8	1,448.5	1,789.2	2,034.7
The wholesale of autos, motorcycles and accessories	1,262.1	1,259.6	1,411.5	1,533.6	2,087.1
The wholesale of recycled materials	172.3	154.6	150.4	198.7	235.1
The wholesale of artistic handicrafts	156.0	165.7	156.6	165.7	169.6
The wholesale of books and newspapers	290.5	303.0	284.0	311.7	337.4
The wholesale of means of agricultural production	1,510.1	1,307.1	1,059.8	886.3	879.9
Other wholesale not classified	725.7	630.9	771.9	650.2	1,318.0

Source: *China Market Statistical Yearbook (1999–2003).*

Table 32. Income from main wholesale businesses above the designated size by trade (1998–2002)

(RMB 10 thousand)

Year	2002	2001	2000	1999	1998
Wholesale trade	286,659,317	251,330,34	241,841,349	200,999,207	92,686,852
The wholesale of food, drinks and tobacco	56,022,855	55,025,188	58,636,778	54,464,009	55,102,998
The wholesale of grains and edible oil	9,327,521	8,521,469	8,382,658	8,357,208	8,423,949
The wholesale of tobacco and its products	35,891,130	35,289,929	38,679,048	33,660,428	33,708,475
The wholesale of cotton, flax, native products and animal by-products	5,741,313	6,673,129	8,850,571	6,020,069	7,402,708
The wholesale of textiles, garments, shoes and hats	21,764,822	18,347,967	17,573,535	14,017,151	13,087,386
The wholesale of articles for daily use	5,796,538	5,607,995	5,480,493	4,774,330	5,366,325
The wholesale of daily sundries	589,384	609,561	594,104	707,523	1,079,383
The wholesale of hardware, electrical appliances & accessories and chemical products	11,555,002	10,461,935	8,657,830	8,878,059	7,780,863
The wholesale of drugs and medical instruments	1,415,072	12,050,446	10,022,832	8,682,278	7,681,211
The wholesale of energies	67,493,441	63,048,514	56,792,584	34,012,882	24,604,703
The wholesale of petroleum and related products	61,381,274	57,473,857	52,094,932	29,028,437	20,182,357
The wholesale of coal and related products	5,971,066	5,485,633	4,629,385	4,939,842	3,884,500
The wholesale of chemical materials	9,627,018	7,430,942	7,633,859	6,318,751	6,374,521
The wholesale of woods	725,798	521,900	528,138	493,368	407,426
The wholesale of building materials	2,185,861	1,607,433	1,437,037	1,597,463	1,556,999
The wholesale of mineral products	1,126,965	1,200,829	1,927,829	752,047	613,826
The wholesale of metallic materials	26,758,161	20,319,469	17,494,749	15,797,813	15,515,938
The wholesale of machinery and electronic equipment	18,670,951	15,297,802	12,142,852	10,625,947	10,312,489
The wholesale of autos, motorcycles and accessories	16,888,397	12,463,990	11,218,149	10,183,870	10,382,758
The wholesale of autos	14,209,537	10,632,493	7,468,527	7,875,806	7,693,868
The wholesale of recycled materials	2,385,613	1,842,315	1,323,797	1,168,005	1,273,143
The wholesale of artistic handicrafts	1,525,463	1,433,709	1,431,523	1,525,360	1,301,209
The wholesale of books and newspapers	2,413,284	2,785,853	2,497,981	2,755,187	2,617,425
The wholesale of means of agricultural production	8,263,983	8,475,894	10,305,261	12,745,911	15,223,421
Other wholesale not classified	12,973,897	6,125,474	7,291,445	5,479,185	5,002,120

Source: *China Market Statistical Yearbook (1999–2003).*

Table 33. Cost of main wholesale businesses above the designated size by trade (1998–2002)

(RMB 10 thousand)

Year	2002	2001	2000	1999	1998
Wholesale trade	265,981,592	232,932,959	223,649,603	184,697,870	176,304,072
The wholesale of food, drinks and tobacco	49,616,554	48,883,757	52,072,850	49,006,078	49,572,069
The wholesale of grains and edible oil	9,216,098	8,312,687	7,946,045	7,994,178	8,005,874
The wholesale of tobacco and its products	30,778,662	30,602,,558	33,712,465	29,789,668	29,737,497
The wholesale of cotton, flax, native products and animal by-products	5,367,451	6,289,727	8,302,952	5,784,143	6,947,243
The wholesale of textiles, garments, shoes and hats	20,217,578	16,889,657	16,261,536	12,778,951	11,898,043
The wholesale of articles for daily use	5,384,385	5,213,020	5,094,525	4,,405,072	4,862,017
The wholesale of daily sundries	547,799	569,742	548,070	660,569	864,993
The wholesale of hardware, electrical appliances & accessories and chemical products	10,837,897	9,810,427	8,110,730	8,354,523	7,328,751
The wholesale of drugs and medical instruments	12,851,870	10,782,494	8,965,930	7,670,431	6,709,879
The wholesale of energies	63,507,937	60,198,177	53,839,873	31,242,268	22,479,117
The wholesale of petroleum and related products	58,043,912	55,100,178	49,567,910	26,739,367	18,547,912
The wholesale of coal and related products	5,329,645	5,015,281	4,205,913	4,460,369	3,406,676
The wholesale of chemical materials	9,086,664	7,073,365	7,242,797	5,934,178	6,084,735
The wholesale of woods	687,075	487,671	482,815	451,519	374,432
The wholesale of building materials	2,033,297	1,467,328	1,339,082	1,471,072	1,438,887
The wholesale of mineral products	1,049,549	1,099,180	1,794,804	644,924	533,066
The wholesale of metallic materials	25,736,212	19,556,676	16,797,382	15,193,276	14,777,891
The wholesale of machinery and electronic equipment	17,586,846	14,246,239	11,477,714	10,055,344	9,709,438
The wholesale of autos, motorcycles and accessories	15,923,590	11,869,092	10,733,177	9,719,850	9,753,282
The wholesale of autos	13,396,593	10,144,946	7,172,710	7,535,756	7,,175,099
The wholesale of recycled materials	2,336,205	1,789,716	1,277,023	1,125,603	1,221,925
The wholesale of artistic handicrafts	1,403,428	1,312,177	1,301,323	1,373,966	1,189,002
The wholesale of books and newspapers	2,072,952	1,789,132	1,643,338	1,814,210	1,755,142
The wholesale of means of agricultural production	7,851,369	7,895,330	9,735,127	12,048,849	14,298,909
Other wholesale not classified	11,882,936	5,710,051	6,628,556	4,963,046	4,505,251

Source: *China Market Statistical Yearbook (1999–2003).*

Table 34. Profits from main wholesale businesses above the designated size by trade (1998–2002)

(RMB 10 thousand)

Year	2002	2001	2000	1999	1998
Wholesale trade	11,115,487	8,203,844	8,623,787	7,403,986	7,123,885
The wholesale of food, drinks and tobacco	4,221,753	3,670,469	3,584,206	3,012,814	2,996,606
The wholesale of grains and edible oil	-360,314	-270,386	-290,934	-103,005	-165,571
The wholesale of tobacco and its products	3,999,157	3,329,562	3,322,164	2,581,582	2,645,526
The wholesale of cotton, flax, native products and animal by-products	190,637	183,366	288,866	-61,884	145,500
The wholesale of textiles, garments, shoes and hats	808,702	754,130	651,396	547,461	606,549
The wholesale of articles for daily use	149,453	140,084	152,219	125,276	171,220
The wholesale of daily sundries	15,783	13,684	15,799	16,143	22,821
The wholesale of hardware, electrical appliances & accessories and chemical products	214,571	200,186	176,872	197,640	171,521
The wholesale of drugs and medical instruments	663,418	655,954	556,265	544,301	495,591
The wholesale of energies	1,529,147	656,844	1,296,393	1,345,399	807,043
The wholesale of petroleum and related products	1,307,700	491,238	1,141,275	1,164,223	659,046
The wholesale of coal and related products	220,769	161,976	154,263	180,067	139,537
The wholesale of chemical materials	252,722	138,607	175,138	158,761	60,598
The wholesale of woods	6,377	9,931	12,341	11,355	2,625
The wholesale of building materials	69,697	40,690	36,203	48,861	41,195
The wholesale of mineral products	20,984	22,674	34,793	19,771	22,796
The wholesale of metallic materials	481,045	313,624	287,126	212,251	230,466
The wholesale of machinery and electronic equipment	585,695	504,082	329,264	290,492	281,967
The wholesale of autos, motorcycles and accessories	528,083	274,232	197,272	166,171	194,727
The wholesale of autos	453,929	224,259	126,274	115,754	162,999
The wholesale of recycled materials	14,014	3,855	12,725	12,496	16,524
The wholesale of artistic handicrafts	54,933	50,730	64,665	80,757	59,840
The wholesale of books and newspapers	201,525	162,181	152,737	152,205	133,725
The wholesale of means of agricultural production	183,638	186,990	220,673	283,099	396,488
Other wholesale not classified	923,309	221,530	378,834	240,617	266,083

Source: *China Market Statistical Yearbook (1999–2003).*

Table 35. Scale of assets of the wholesale trade above the designated size by trade (1998–2002)

(RMB 10 thousand)

Year	2002	2001	2000	1999	1998
Wholesale enterprises	163,568,388	151,224,624	151,417,114	145,404,324	145,610,239
Wholesale commerce of food, drinks, tobacco and household articles	80,869,644	76,206,191	80,341,985	79,816,754	79,509,660
The wholesale of food, drinks and tobacco	38,016,270	36,982,899	40,520,119	40,996,527	40,220,866
The wholesale of grains and edible oil	14,890,724	14,100,302	14,254,706	14,148,516	15,241,312
The wholesale of tobacco and its products	15,033,052	14,152,373	17,175,222	16,271,997	15,558,546
The wholesale of cotton, flax, native products and animal by-products	10,628,302	10,803,365	12,923,427	13,957,814	14,402,234
The wholesale of textiles, garments, shoes and hats	13,248,591	10,706,341	11,473,810	9,242,404	9,161,294
The wholesale of articles for daily use	3,693,867	3,909,519	3,791,023	3,709,604	4,056,002
The wholesale of daily sundries	437,478	392,104	414,197	472,084	804,351
The wholesale of hardware, electrical appliances & accessories and chemical products	6,418,903	5,998,675	4,938,733	5,616,761	5,409,012
The wholesale of drugs and medical instruments	8,426,234	7,413,287	6,280,676	5,821,560	5,455,901
The wholesale of energies, material and machinery electronic equipment	65,999,199	61,010,639	53,462,897	49,038,397	49,498,017
The wholesale of energies	22,272,824	19,915,165	17,277,238	13,011,654	12,941,396
The wholesale of petroleum and related products	19,007,058	16,748,297	13,828,607	9,648,759	9,640,268
The wholesale of coal and related products	3,134,044	3,034,821	3,353,395	3,300,495	3,035,609
The wholesale of chemical materials	4,099,125	3,437,244	3,935,887	4,228,077	4,492,722
The wholesale of woods	601,474	580,162	667,308	576,907	623,650
The wholesale of building materials	1,659,030	1,241,309	1,273,785	1,565,341	1,520,559
The wholesale of mineral products	728,254	911,185	2,271,026	763,132	643,787
The wholesale of metallic materials	15,938,508	13,000,586	12,064,038	13,094,552	13,758,427
The wholesale of machinery and electronic equipment	14,869,714	13,475,162	10,148,171	9,388,833	8,795,053
The wholesale of autos, motorcycles and accessories	5,293,037	7,872,474	5,255,347	5,739,382	5,968,634
The wholesale of autos	3,962,102	6,432,453	3,666,967	3,940,053	3,865,226
The wholesale of recycled materials	537,233	577,353	570,097	670,519	753,789
Other wholesale trades	16,699,546	14,007,794	17,612,233	16,549,175	16,602,562
The wholesale of artistic handicrafts	1,667,518	1,704,504	1,349,512	1,407,203	911,953
The wholesale of books and newspapers	1,935,389	1,611,164	1,320,887	1,283,210	1,070,722
The wholesale of means of agricultural production	5,089,382	5,496,046	6,914,783	7,479,069	8,583,513
Other wholesale not classified	8,007,256	5,196,080	8,027,051	6,379,693	6,036,374

Source: *China Market Statistical Yearbook (1999–2003).*

Table 36. Fixed assets of the wholesale trade above the designated size by trade (1998–2002)

(RMB 10 thousand)

Year	2002	2001	2000	1999	1998
Wholesale enterprises	23,979,911	22,792,036	23,032,712	23,507,643	25,453,032
Wholesale commerce of food, drinks, tobacco and household articles	11,254,229	11,420,774	12,080,711	12,693,078	12,961,847
The wholesale of food, drinks and tobacco	6,760,807	6,720,196	6,936,565	7,207,154	7,215,761
The wholesale of grains and edible oil	1,805,084	1,704,211	1,822,146	2,045,014	2,262,126
The wholesale of tobacco and its products	3,054,925	2,875,165	2,807,644	2,766,182	2,537,425
The wholesale of cotton, flax, native products and animal by-products	857,893	907,869	1,093,829	1,145,543	1,191,348
The wholesale of textiles, garments, shoes and hats	1,219,114	1,167,509	1,301,874	1,350,645	1,382,921
The wholesale of articles for daily use	511,754	689,917	799,113	821,122	951,080
The wholesale of daily sundries	65,145	60,111	82,661	95,658	178,618
The wholesale of hardware, electrical appliances & accessories and chemical products	644,301	682,168	792,578	993,747	1,037,715
The wholesale of drugs and medical instruments	1,195,215	1,193,005	1,074,091	1,079,209	1,004,404
The wholesale of energies, material and machinery electronic equipment	10,765,325	9,378,235	8,088,531	8,193,422	8,633,577
The wholesale of energies	6,709,646	5,289,260	3,738,012	3,226,831	3,577,417
The wholesale of petroleum and related products	6,014,765	4,687,925	3,017,065	2,445,363	2,667,928
The wholesale of coal and related products	688,533	594,189	706,496	765,757	877,127
The wholesale of chemical materials	507,886	466,894	507,575	539,625	673,455
The wholesale of woods	146,399	137,765	166,538	132,589	172,893
The wholesale of building materials	197,127	188,411	230,326	297,794	282,235
The wholesale of mineral products	56,120	63,218	187,811	54,176	63,145
The wholesale of metallic materials	1,373,140	1,325,786	1,398,924	1,657,684	1,646,017
The wholesale of machinery and electronic equipment	1,069,628	1,045,358	998,870	1,172,421	1,137,036
The wholesale of autos, motorcycles and accessories	592,750	705,038	722,985	949,624	905,162
The wholesale of autos	434,301	552,376	487,379	502,572	464,413
The wholesale of recycled materials	112,629	156,505	137,490	162,678	176,217
Other wholesale trades	1,960,357	1,993,027	2,863,470	2,621,144	3,857,608
The wholesale of artistic handicrafts	240,962	259,072	194,396	215,542	181,271
The wholesale of books and newspapers	395,169	382,227	321,365	316,741	1,464,581
The wholesale of means of agricultural production	716,484	842,631	1,100,637	1,262,030	724,657
Other wholesale not classified	607,743	509,097	1,247,072	826,831	1,487,099

Source: *China Market Statistical Yearbook (1999–2003).*

Table 37. Current assets of the wholesale trade above the designated size by trade (1998–2002)

(RMB 10 thousand)

Year	2002	2001	2000	1999	1998
Wholesale enterprises	117,753,564	104,710,432	108,072,294	102,330,465	104,557,046
Wholesale commerce of food, drinks, tobacco and household articles	61,134,781	55,240,709	57,870,696	56,337,725	57,264,055
The wholesale of food, drinks and tobacco	27,823,492	26,444,269	29,920,814	29,501,926	29,713,149
The wholesale of grains and edible oil	11,932,056	11,118,590	11,185,539	10,759,300	11,802,922
The wholesale of tobacco and its products	10,821,126	10,087,486	13,212,594	12,299,135	12,018,491
The wholesale of cotton, flax, native products and animal by-products	8,390,661	7,569,305	8,821,155	9,043,987	9,633,835
The wholesale of textiles, garments, shoes and hats	10,309,459	8,073,909	7,844,718	6,755,396	6,724,336
The wholesale of articles for daily use	2,752,979	2,710,578	2,597,017	2,329,820	2,692,935
The wholesale of daily sundries	323,048	293,889	298,747	335,380	549,399
The wholesale of hardware, electrical appliances & accessories and chemical products	5,342,564	4,651,529	3,703,435	4,056,202	3,846,093
The wholesale of drugs and medical instruments	6,192,578	5,497,231	4,684,810	4,315,014	4,104,308
The wholesale of energies, material and machinery electronic equipment	44,044,148	39,562,144	37,549,883	33,927,005	34,756,281
The wholesale of energies	10,218,627	10,581,830	10,885,895	7,872,086	7,763,732
The wholesale of petroleum and related products	7,965,279	8,427,609	8,578,231	5,699,721	5,659,927
The wholesale of coal and related products	2,148,531	2,044,404	2,240,778	2,135,885	1,912,029
The wholesale of chemical materials	2,914,754	2,471,764	2,842,329	3,134,506	3,263,662
The wholesale of woods	357,620	351,037	398,915	353,408	377,959
The wholesale of building materials	1,227,315	899,210	877,594	1,039,926	1,035,056
The wholesale of mineral products	615,256	776,267	1,696,704	619,676	497,344
The wholesale of metallic materials	12,073,208	9,280,733	8,506,900	9,258,504	10,234,705
The wholesale of machinery and electronic equipment	12,096,339	10,778,166	8,084,223	7,291,358	6,822,535
The wholesale of autos, motorcycles and accessories	4,166,254	4,064,238	3,889,717	3,922,581	4,267,085
The wholesale of autos	3,104,858	3,018,923	2,850,052	2,848,632	2,937,337
The wholesale of recycled materials	374,775	358,900	367,606	434,960	494,203
Other wholesale trades	12,574,635	9,907,579	12,651,716	12,065,737	12,536,710
The wholesale of artistic handicrafts	1,144,337	1,115,739	880,858	899,366	606,483
The wholesale of books and newspapers	1,304,710	1,026,417	882,708	854,087	766,514
The wholesale of means of agricultural production	3,952,587	4,168,963	5,272,314	5,753,255	6,658,957
Other wholesale not classified	6,173,002	3,596,461	5,615,836	4,559,029	4,504,756

Source: *China Market Statistical Yearbook (1999–2003).*

Table 38. Liabilities of the wholesale trade above the designated size by trade (1998–2002)

(RMB 10 thousand)

Year	2002	2001	2000	1999	1998
Wholesale enterprises	125,735,165	117,266,796	123,363,167	118,910,192	25,453,032
Wholesale commerce of food, drinks, tobacco and household articles	64,263,255	61,352,643	66,410,723	68,022,498	12,961,847
The wholesale of food, drinks and tobacco	27,646,179	27,484,460	31,276,927	32,461,322	7,215,761
The wholesale of grains and edible oil	3,888,173	12,987,104	13,235,512	13,307,318	2,262,126
The wholesale of tobacco and its products	8,101,790	8,384,645	11,610,401	11,241,242	2,537,425
The wholesale of cotton, flax, native products and animal by-products	10,451,683	10,791,833	13,465,663	14,619,693	1,191,348
The wholesale of textiles, garments, shoes and hats	10,308,007	8,560,522	8,487,628	7,771,408	1,382,921
The wholesale of articles for daily use	3,181,071	3,165,682	3,279,620	3,054,435	951,080
The wholesale of daily sundries	378,092	359,912	383,255	428,574	178,618
The wholesale of hardware, electrical appliances & accessories and chemical products	5,771,370	5,220,032	4,458,668	5,013,891	1,037,715
The wholesale of drugs and medical instruments	6,526,852	5,770,202	5,058,962	4,673,175	1,004,404
The wholesale of energies, material and machinery electronic equipment	48,998,581	45,133,296	43,265,925	37,827,774	8,633,577
The wholesale of energies	15,244,956	14,583,761	14,057,326	9,000,450	3,577,417
The wholesale of petroleum and related products	13,001,858	12,435,337	11,683,276	6,687,037	2,667,928
The wholesale of coal and related products	2,149,209	2,049,042	2,296,377	2,261,182	877,127
The wholesale of chemical materials	2,996,542	2,684,071	3,027,326	3,313,470	673,455
The wholesale of woods	420,609	464,490	559,234	427,674	172,893
The wholesale of building materials	1,222,742	948,878	972,239	1,191,366	282,235
The wholesale of mineral products	774,044	943,789	2,002,370	778,926	63,145
The wholesale of metallic materials	11,912,729	9,762,583	9,222,710	9,929,775	1,646,017
The wholesale of machinery and electronic equipment	11,931,794	10,923,734	8,489,595	7,911,240	1,137,036
The wholesale of autos, motorcycles and accessories	4,040,337	4,385,139	4,493,869	4,722,312	905,162
The wholesale of autos	3,105,630	3,284,971	3,389,763	3,387,398	464,413
The wholesale of recycled materials	454,829	436,850	441,256	552,561	176,217
Other wholesale trades	12,473,329	10,780,857	13,686,519	13,059,921	3,857,608
The wholesale of artistic handicrafts	1,387,293	1,510,228	1,085,287	1,102,418	181,271
The wholesale of books and newspapers	1,199,209	970,339	821,322	808,555	1,464,581
The wholesale of means of agricultural production	4,139,053	4,598,079	5,831,657	6,332,275	724,657
Other wholesale not classified	5,747,774	3,702,211	5,948,253	4,816,673	1,487,099

Source: *China Market Statistical Yearbook (1999–2003).*

Table 39. The number of wholesale business corporations above the designated size by trade (2003–2007)

Year	2003	2005	2006	2007
The wholesale trade	14,937	26,963	28,125	29,046
The wholesale of agricultural and animal products	920	1,494	1,478	1,415
The wholesale of food, drinks and tobacco	3,189	3,013	2,918	2,839
The wholesale of textiles, garments, shoes and hats	1,233	2,143	2,474	2,580
The wholesale of cultural and sports goods and appliances	442	751	772	781
The wholesale of drugs and medical instruments	1,115	1,814	1,859	1,931
The wholesale of mineral products, building materials and chemical products	4,662	10,451	11,216	11,794
The wholesale of mechanical equipment, hardware appliances and accessories and electric products	2,526	5,483	5,760	5,798
Trading breakage and agency	286	273	367	414

Source: *Market Statistical Yearbook of China (2004)* and *China Trade and External Economic Statistical Yearbook (2005–2008).*

Table 40. Number of industrial establishments of the wholesale trade above the designated size by trade (2003–2007)

Year	2003	2004	2005	2006	2007
Wholesale trade	27,856	42,006	56,157	57,994	66,084
The wholesale of agricultural and animal products	1,553	2,486	3,419	3,172	2,945
The wholesale of food, drinks and tobacco	7,917	8,493	9,069	8,790	8,018
The wholesale of textiles, garments, shoes and hats	1,549	2,083	2,617	3,173	3,429
The wholesale of cultural and sports goods and appliances	515	801	1,087	1,146	1,474
The wholesale of drugs and medical instruments	3,340	3,812	4,285	4,968	4,888
The wholesale of mineral products, building materials and chemical products	8,712	17,072	25,432	25,113	28,636
The wholesale of mechanical equipment, hardware appliances and accessories and electric products	3,016	4,760	6,504	7,268	7,360
Trading breakage and agency	287	1,599	2,912	435	463

Source: *Market Statistical Yearbook of China (2004)* and *China Trade and External Economic Statistical Yearbook (2005–2008).*

Table 41. Number of practitioners in the wholesale enterprises above the designated size by trade (2003–2007)

Year	2003	2004	2005	2006	2007
Wholesale trade	1,786,669	2,015,400	2,244,131	2,248,731	2,495,863
The wholesale of agricultural and animal products	197,328	187,952	178,576	145,299	131,417
The wholesale of food, drinks and tobacco	492,769	511,889	531,009	536,744	563,461
The wholesale of textiles, garments, shoes and hats	112,202	128,722	145,242	160,484	288,791
The wholesale of cultural and sports goods and appliances	45,347	51,687	58,026	64,907	68,353
The wholesale of drugs and medical instruments	202,795	207,250	211,704	212,225	215,633
The wholesale of mineral products, building materials and chemical products	480,011	584,560	689,108	704,925	757,422
The wholesale of mechanical equipment, hardware appliances and accessories and electric products	203,653	270,909	338,165	337,387	374,202
Trading breakage and agency	18,468	14,077	9,686	18,079	18,080

Source: *Market Statistical Yearbook of China (2004)* and *China Trade and External Economic Statistical Yearbook (2005–2008).*

Table 42. Sales volume of the wholesale trade above the designated size by trade (2003–2007)

(RMB 100 million)

Year	2003	2004	2005	2006	2007
Wholesale trade	36,365	55,938	75,511	87,594	105,620
The wholesale of agricultural and animal products	1,310	1,554	1,798	1,925	2,070
The wholesale of food, drinks and tobacco	6,968	8,239	9,509	10,548	11,696
The wholesale of textiles, garments, shoes and hats	3,392	4,405	5,417	6,461	7,448
The wholesale of cultural and sports goods and appliances	688	901	1,114	1,229	1,354
The wholesale of drugs and medical instruments	1,398	2,273	3,148	3,638	4,206
The wholesale of mineral products, building materials and chemical products	15,062	26,993	38,925	46,531	58,073
The wholesale of mechanical equipment, hardware appliances and accessories and electric products	5,668	8,644	11,621	13,211	16,032
Trading breakage and agency	794	746	698	1,068	1,144
Other wholesale trades	1,083	2,183	3,282	2,984	3,597

Source: *Market Statistical Yearbook of China (2004)* and *China Trade and External Economic Statistical Yearbook (2005–2008).*

Table 43. Incomes of the main businesses of the wholesale trades above the designated size by trade (2003–2007)

(RMB 100 million)

Year	2007	2006	2005	2003
Wholesale trade	1,920.6	77,724.5	67,701.3	33,689.9
The wholesale of agricultural and animal products	9,786.5	1,798.3	1,719.0	1,288.8
The wholesale of food, drinks and tobacco	751.6	8,793.1	8,262.6	5,905.1
The wholesale of rice and flour products and edible oil	6,418.5	645.8	643.0	634.6
The wholesale of tobacco products	7,001.3	5,944.5	5,797.2	4,228.3
The wholesale of textiles, garments and daily necessities	2,752.1	6,069.4	5,080.7	3,265.8
The wholesale of garments	1,176.0	2,407.5	1,911.9	1,071.9
The wholesale of cultural and sports goods and appliances	3,775.0	1,038.8	962.9	583.7
The wholesale of drugs and medical instruments	52,120.3	3,182.2	2,930.7	1,752.6
The wholesale of mineral products, building materials and chemical products	4,028.7	40,962.7	34,529.8	13,857.9
The wholesale of coal and related products	21,660.9	2,820.7	2,630.3	772.3
The wholesale of petroleum and related products	1,796.6	17,609.9	14,806.2	6,629.2
The wholesale of metals and metallic mines	2,362.1	13,569.3	10,829.8	3,924.8
The wholesale of building materials	1,428.3	1,618.9	1,363.8	458.0
The wholesale of fertilizers	14,496.4	1,179.8	1,056.7	677.6
The wholesale of mechanical equipment, hardware appliances and accessories and electric products	3,350.3	11,663.4	10,432.8	5,314.2
The wholesale of autos, motorcycles and accessories	2,484.7	2,317.8	2,966.7	2,032.3
The wholesale of household appliances	1,339.4	1,888.2	1,571.4	551.2
The wholesale of computers, software and auxiliaries	1,677.6	1,076.7	984.1	265.4
Trading breakage and agency	3,487.0	1,413.4	683.9	730.4
Other wholesale trades	2,803.3	3,098.8	991.5	—

Source: *Market Statistical Yearbook of China (2004)* and *China Trade and External Economic Statistical Yearbook (2005–2008).*

Table 44. Costs of the main wholesale businesses above the designated size by trade (2003–2007)

(RMB 100 million)

Year	2007	2006	2005	2003
Wholesale trade	1,798.6	72,392.8	62,047.9	31,211.0
The wholesale of agricultural and animal products	7,858.2	1,703.1	1,605.8	1,234.8
The wholesale of food, drinks and tobacco	706.7	7,285.8	6,929.4	5,132.6
The wholesale of rice and flour products and edible oil	4,879.1	617.9	614.9	609.2
The wholesale of tobacco products	6,379.5	4,731.7	4,707.9	3,586.6
The wholesale of textiles, garments and daily necessities	2,515.0	5,635.2	4,709.5	3,058.7
The wholesale of garments	1,050.5	2,239.2	1,778.5	991.8
The wholesale of cultural and sports goods and appliances	3,488.2	936.0	841.5	522.4
The wholesale of drugs and medical instruments	49,421.7	2,954.2	2,684.0	1,604.1
The wholesale of mineral products, building materials and chemical products	3,633.2	39,073.5	32,431.9	13,084.0
The wholesale of coal and related products	20,517.1	2,573.4	2,344.4	695.7
The wholesale of petroleum and related products	16,964.0	16,699.9	13,994.9	6,215.5
The wholesale of metals and metallic mines	2,252.1	13,160.1	10,284.6	3,773.7
The wholesale of building materials	1,341.7	1,547.9	1,282.2	435.0
The wholesale of fertilizers	13,266.2	1,125.6	997.7	643.7
The wholesale of mechanical equipment, hardware appliances and accessories and electric products	3,117.4	10,817.1	9,379.3	5,001.5
The wholesale of autos, motorcycles and accessories	2,264.1	2,200.2	2,583.4	1,919.7
The wholesale of household appliances	1,285.7	1,729.2	1,437.0	516.2
The wholesale of computers, software and auxiliaries	1,608.5	1,033.7	936.8	253.6
Trading breakage and agency	3,210.3	1,351.1	640.4	623.9
Other wholesale trades	2,636.9	2,826.2	948.9	—

Source: *Market Statistical Yearbook of China (2004)* and *China Trade and External Economic Statistical Yearbook (2005–2008).*

Table 45. Profits from main wholesale businesses above the designated size by trade

(RMB 100 million)

Year	2007	2006	2005	2003
Wholesale trade	98.4	4,976.7	4,231.3	1,368.8
The wholesale of agricultural and animal products	1,680.5	83.3	76.8	0.3
The wholesale of food, drinks and tobacco	32.6	1,382.6	1,173.9	561.3
The wholesale of rice and flour products and edible oil	1,353.7	22.5	20.3	1.2
The wholesale of tobacco products	564.3	1,129.9	975.3	512.8
The wholesale of textiles, garments and daily necessities	219.3	405.7	305.5	103.0
The wholesale of garments	112.4	151.5	116.6	41.9
The wholesale of cultural and sports goods and appliances	256.6	90.2	75.9	35.1
The wholesale of drugs and medical instruments	2,243.6	214.0	188.0	73.2
The wholesale of mineral products, building materials and chemical products	350.2	1,785.0	1,489.2	363.5
The wholesale of coal and related products	1,018.6	226.9	249.8	24.4
The wholesale of petroleum and related products	506.6	883.0	712.6	197.3
The wholesale of metals and metallic mines	95.9	380.2	282.0	82.1
The wholesale of building materials	68.1	64.7	54.5	9.7
The wholesale of fertilizers	1,092.5	45.5	45.3	14.3
The wholesale of mechanical equipment, hardware appliances and accessories and electric products	183.5	802.4	668.5	148.4
The wholesale of autos, motorcycles and accessories	204.6	112.5	116.3	59.1
The wholesale of household appliances	51.0	144.4	114.5	7.0
The wholesale of computers, software and auxiliaries	61.7	39.4	29.4	5.9
Trading breakage and agency	226.1,	56.3,	33.4,	63.1
Other wholesale trades	—	157.2	220.0	20.8

Source: *Market Statistical Yearbook of China (2004)* and *China Trade and External Economic Statistical Yearbook (2005–2008).*

Table 46. Size of assets of the wholesale trade above the designated size by trade (2003–2007)

(RMB 100 million)

Year	2007	2006	2005	2003
Wholesale trade	38,697.7	31,523.0	28,105.8	17,827.6
The wholesale of agricultural and animal products	2,677.1	2,811.1	2,656.4	1,878.5
The wholesale of food, drinks and tobacco	4,709.3	4,189.5	3,838.7	3,106.4
The wholesale of rice and flour products and edible oil	668.7	699.4	675.1	688.0
The wholesale of tobacco products	2,752.0	2,413.8	2,171.9	1,663.8
The wholesale of textiles, garments and daily necessities	2,765.6	2,410.1	2,058.0	1,823.6
The wholesale of garments	1,015.9	934.5	712.4	606.5
The wholesale of cultural and sports goods and appliances	761.5	672.4	582.5	484.4
The wholesale of drugs and medical instruments	1,745.8	1,538.0	1,366.0	983.7
The wholesale of mineral products, building materials and chemical products	17,181.4	12,670.4	11,121.6	5,820.2
The wholesale of coal and related products	1,358.6	1,058.4	942.2	391.0
The wholesale of petroleum and related products	4,650.0	3,574.7	3,253.0	2,003.5
The wholesale of metals and metallic mines	7,276.6	5,080.4	4,275.2	2,103.9
The wholesale of building materials	1,216.3	845.8	735.6	314.4
The wholesale of fertilizers	840.0	675.9	550.0	416.8
The wholesale of mechanical equipment, hardware appliances and accessories and electric products	6,478.0	5,162.0	4,754.3	2,850.9
The wholesale of autos, motorcycles and accessories	1,197.1	962.6	1,059.2	734.7
The wholesale of household appliances	992.6	794.2	707.3	237.1
The wholesale of computers, software and auxiliaries	407.8	346.1	400.8	130.0
Trading breakage and agency	813.1	890.8	303.4	403.7
Other wholesale trades	1,565.9	1,178.6	1,424.9	476.1

Source: *Market Statistical Yearbook of China (2004)* and *China Trade and External Economic Statistical Yearbook (2005–2008)*.

Table 47. Fixed assets of the wholesale trade above the designated size by trade (2003–2007)

(RMB 100 million)

Year	2007	2006	2005	2003
Wholesale trade	4,504.1	4,013.2	2,658.5	2,385.8
The wholesale of agricultural and animal products	297.8	302.3	213.1	175.2
The wholesale of food, drinks and tobacco	935.0	912.4	584.8	589.0
The wholesale of rice and flour products and edible oil	109.6	130.8	78.8	88.7
The wholesale of tobacco products	595.9	558.7	352.4	348.5
The wholesale of textiles, garments and daily necessities	298.7	224.1	143.9	153.8
The wholesale of garments	94.1	80.3	48.1	44.2
The wholesale of cultural and sports goods and appliances	109.9	100.7	61.1	78.7
The wholesale of drugs and medical instruments	162.8	170.8	115.1	136.8
The wholesale of mineral products, building materials and chemical products	2,121.6	1,786.3	1,195.0	966.6
The wholesale of coal and related products	176.1	136.0	75.7	63.7
The wholesale of petroleum and related products	1,341.5	1,161.2	751.5	639.7
The wholesale of metals and metallic mines	319.4	252.5	185.1	133.9
The wholesale of building materials	105.1	80.8	59.8	34.5
The wholesale of fertilizers	63.5	57.8	45.1	38.3
The wholesale of mechanical equipment, hardware appliances and accessories and electric products	399.2	346.9	260.2	222.4
The wholesale of autos, motorcycles and accessories	90.2	85.5	77.5	62.6
The wholesale of household appliances	38.7	38.1	40.8	15.1
The wholesale of computers, software and auxiliaries	16.8	15.8	8.1	6.7
Trading breakage and agency	55.6	54.2	15.4	21.5
Other wholesale trades	123.5	115.5	69.9	41.8

Source: *Market Statistical Yearbook of China (2004)* and *China Trade and External Economic Statistical Yearbook (2005–2008).*

Table 48. Sizes of floating assets of the wholesale trades above the designated size by trade (2003–2007)

(RMB 100 million)

Year	2007	2006	2005	2003
Wholesale trade	29,271.1	23,504.6	20,985.0	13,139.9
The wholesale of agricultural and animal products	1,773.3	2,018.4	2,099.2	1,536.1
The wholesale of food, drinks and tobacco	3,443.9	2,887.2	2,691.8	2,160.0
The wholesale of rice and flour products and edible oil	501.5	477.7	492.2	530.2
The wholesale of tobacco products	2,029.8	1,684.5	1,514.9	1,139.5
The wholesale of textiles, garments and daily necessities	2,150.9	1,794.7	1,591.3	1,506.7
The wholesale of garments	780.2	638.6	563.9	463.3
The wholesale of cultural and sports goods and appliances	535.8	463.8	409.8	321.1
The wholesale of drugs and medical instruments	1,397.5	1,248.5	1,101.8	737.9
The wholesale of mineral products, building materials and chemical products	12,808.5	9,324.8	7,816.4	3,845.9
The wholesale of coal and related products	999.7	809.3	681.3	292.2
The wholesale of petroleum and related products	2,728.1	1,957.1	1,648.2	825.9
The wholesale of metals and metallic mines	6,010.5	4,228.8	3,426.5	1,712.2
The wholesale of building materials	923.7	644.5	561.2	219.8
The wholesale of fertilizers	698.9	565.2	475.9	348.4
The wholesale of mechanical equipment, hardware appliances and accessories and electric products	5,258.7	4,163.0	3,884.6	2,308.7
The wholesale of autos, motorcycles and accessories	938.0	733.4	929.7	596.1
The wholesale of household appliances	824.1	636.1	536.2	213.2
The wholesale of computers, software and auxiliaries	359.9	309.4	343.3	93.4
Trading breakage and agency	656.5	723.5	246.8	365.2
Other wholesale trades	1,246.0	880.7	1,143.4	358.2

Source: *Market Statistical Yearbook of China (2004)* and *China Trade and External Economic Statistical Yearbook (2005–2008).*

Table 49. Scales of liabilities of the wholesale trades above the designated size by trade (2003–2007)

(RMB 100 million)

Year	2007	2006	2005	2003
Wholesale trade	27,452.8	22,249.6	20,199.5	13,452.2
The wholesale of agricultural and animal products	2,087.1	2,277.1	2,470.4	1,798.4
The wholesale of food, drinks and tobacco	2,107.3	1,982.8	1,960.6	1,918.0
The wholesale of rice and flour products and edible oil	560.5	544.8	557.1	589.4
The wholesale of tobacco products	633.8	695.2	708.0	797.7
The wholesale of textiles, garments and daily necessities	2,037.1	1,741.8	1,514.5	1,435.1
The wholesale of garments	743.0	640.7	513.0	439.1
The wholesale of cultural and sports goods and appliances	496.8	429.4	380.9	335.3
The wholesale of drugs and medical instruments	1,380.2	1,223.9	1,093.2	774.6
The wholesale of mineral products, building materials and chemical products	12,613.0	9,162.0	7,816.7	4,184.0
The wholesale of coal and related products	958.9	754.2	649.6	278.9
The wholesale of petroleum and related products	3,069.9	2,230.6	2,000.8	1,199.1
The wholesale of metals and metallic mines	5,669.1	3,962.1	3,193.0	1,652.4
The wholesale of building materials	911.6	643.3	557.1	244.8
The wholesale of fertilizers	648.9	542.1	442.1	351.7
The wholesale of mechanical equipment, hardware appliances and accessories and electric products	4,998.8	3,907.1	3,636.6	2,311.7
The wholesale of autos, motorcycles and accessories	916.7	731.2	842.5	594.9
The wholesale of household appliances	811.0	641.4	583.2	209.1
The wholesale of computers, software and auxiliaries	302.7	257.0	312.4	88.6
Trading breakage and agency	601.0	674.2	241.2	321.1
Other wholesale trades	1,131.5	851.2	1,085.4	374.0

Source: *Market Statistical Yearbook of China (2004)* and *China Trade and External Economic Statistical Yearbook (2005–2008).*

Table 50. Ownership interests of the wholesale trades above the designated size by trade (2003–2007)

(RMB 100 million)

Year	2007	2006	2005	2003
Wholesale trade	11,239.4	9,268.9	7,906.9	4,375.4
The wholesale of agricultural and animal products	590.0	534.0	186.0	80.1
The wholesale of food, drinks and tobacco	2,602.0	2,206.7	1,878.2	1,188.5
The wholesale of rice and flour products and edible oil	108.1	154.6	118.0	98.6
The wholesale of tobacco products	2,118.2	1,718.7	1,463.9	866.1
The wholesale of textiles, garments and daily necessities	728.4	668.4	543.4	388.4
The wholesale of garments	272.9	293.7	199.4	167.4
The wholesale of cultural and sports goods and appliances	264.7	243.0	201.6	149.1
The wholesale of drugs and medical instruments	365.6	314.1	272.8	209.1
The wholesale of mineral products, building materials and chemical products	4,562.8	3,503.8	3,305.2	1,636.2
The wholesale of coal and related products	399.7	304.3	292.6	112.0
The wholesale of petroleum and related products	1,574.6	1,339.5	1,252.6	804.4
The wholesale of metals and metallic mines	1,607.5	1,118.3	1,082.2	451.5
The wholesale of building materials	304.7	202.5	178.5	69.6
The wholesale of fertilizers	191.0	133.8	107.9	65.2
The wholesale of mechanical equipment, hardware appliances and accessories and electric products	1,479.2	1,254.9	1,117.9	539.2
The wholesale of autos, motorcycles and accessories	280.4	231.5	216.9	139.7
The wholesale of household appliances	181.6	152.8	124.1	28.1
The wholesale of computers, software and auxiliaries	105.1	89.1	88.4	41.3
Trading breakage and agency	212.1	216.6	62.2	82.6
Other wholesale trades	434.5	327.3	339.6	102.1

Source: *Market Statistical Yearbook of China (2004)* and *China Trade and External Economic Statistical Yearbook (2005–2008).*

Table 51. Turnovers of the commodity exchange markets each valuing more than RMB 100 million during 2001–2007

(RMB 100 million)

Year	Total market turnover	Total market turnover of the top 4 commodity exchange markets	Total market turnover of the top 8 commodity exchange markets
2001	17,719.1	773.6	1,413.8
2002	19,840.0	892.5	1,548.1
2003	21,514.5	1,075.8	1,883.3
2004	26,102.7	1,330.1	2,295.2
2005	30,020.9	1,486.0	2,305.5
2006	37,137.5	2,029.9	3,161.1
2007	44,085.1	2,310.2	3,707.6

Source: *Statistical Yearbook of China Commodity Exchange Market (2002–2008).*

Table 52. Total turnover of the comprehensive wholesale markets for industrial products each valuing more than RMB 100 million during 2001–2007

(RMB 100 million)

Year	Total market turnover	Total market turnover of the top 4 commodity exchange markets	Total market turnover of the top 8 commodity exchange markets
2001	3,752.3	644.3	1,044.3
2002	3,963.2	694.7	1,152.5
2003	3,873.7	782.0	1,204.8
2004	4,099.7	911.4	1,394.7
2005	3,665.0	1,017.6	1,607.2
2006	3,484.9	1,113.3	1,670.8
2007	4,474.1	1,315.2	2,045.4

Source: *Statistical Yearbook of China Commodity Exchange Market (2002–2008).*

Table 53. Total turnover of the comprehensive wholesale markets for agricultural products each valuing more than RMB 100 million during 2001–2007

(RMB 100 million)

Year	Total market turnover	Total market turnover of the top 4 commodity exchange markets	Total market turnover of the top 8 commodity exchange markets
2001	2,607.0	288.1	425.5
2002	2,740.6	291.6	456.5
2003	3,007.1	328.2	493.3
2004	3,300.1	372.3	594.1
2005	2,412.0	420.5	677.7
2006	4,339.3	495.9	810.5
2007	5,047.9	594.1	1,005.5

Source: *Statistical Yearbook of China Commodity Exchange Market (2002–2008).*

Table 54. Turnovers of the specialty markets for various agricultural products each valuing more than RMB 100 million during 2001–2007

(RMB 100 million)

Year	Turnover of the markets for grains and edible oil		Turnover of the markets for meat, poultry and eggs		Turnover of the markets for vegetables		Turnover of the markets for fresh and dried nuts and fruits		Turnover of the markets for native products and by-products		Turnover of the markets for food, drinks, tobacco and wines	
	The top 4	The top 20	The top 4	The top 20	The top 4	The top 20	The top 4	The top 20	The top 4	The top 20	The top 4	The top 20
2001	88	188	31	71	134	559	49	185	43	66	126	601
2002	66	188	35	77	102	631	52	220	39	68	137	722
2003	51	189	65	99	115	657	75	278	50	86	149	759
2004	74	306	90	125	135	801	89	315	62	109	167	852
2005	139	688	145	523	205	1,689	126	635	338	408	148	682
2006	89	520	158	469	192	1,310	249	822	443	692	146	850
2007	138	721	251	675	174	1,639	259	984	409	702	147	1,040

Source: *Statistical Yearbook of China Commodity Exchange Market (2002–2008).*

Table 55. Turnovers of the specialty markets for various agricultural products each valuing more than RMB 100 million during 2001–2007

(RMB 100 million)

Year	Turnover of the markets for textiles, garments, shoes and hats		Turnover of the markets for cultural, audio-video products, books, news papers and magazines		Turnover of the markets for furniture		Turnover of the markets for motor vehicles	
	The top 4	The top 20	The top 4	The top 20	The top 4	The top 20	The top 4	The top 20
2001	671	3,216	57	132	81	178	246	638
2002	723	2,640	64	232	93	203	337	912
2003	819	2,800	55	185	92	234	324	1,072
2004	870	3,162	60	196	84	251	361	1,383
2005	953	4,732	117	190	121	319	345	1,648
2006	1,156	6,349	124	280	176	483	396	1,958
2007	1,512	6,751	119	290	244	627	380	2,306

Source: *Statistical Yearbook of China Commodity Exchange Market (2002–2008).*

Table 56. Turnovers of the specialty markets for various agricultural products each valuing more than RMB 100 million during 2001–2007

(RMB 100 million)

Year		2004	2006	2007
North China	Total market turnover of the top 4 commodity exchange markets	708.7	1,200.9	2,269.1
	Total market turnover of the top 20 commodity exchange markets	1,024.2	1,646.5	3,433.5
	Total market turnover	3,548.7	5,242.2	6,403.6
Northeast China	Total market turnover of the top 4 commodity exchange markets	546.8	745.2	759.9
	Total market turnover of the top 20 commodity exchange markets	752.1	1,067.0	1,126.3
	Total market turnover	1,832.3	2,383.8	2,685.9
East China	Total market turnover of the top 4 commodity exchange markets	1,330.1	1,942.2	2,279.1
	Total market turnover of the top 20 commodity exchange markets	2,251.1	2,990.5	3,545.5
	Total market turnover	15,483.6	21,620.8	26,083.8
Northwest China	Total market turnover of the top 4 commodity exchange markets	122.7	135.4	212.5
	Total market turnover of the top 20 commodity exchange markets	191.1	220.7	319.0
	Total market turnover	451.3	661.2	835.3
Southwest China	Total market turnover of the top 4 commodity exchange markets	243.7	210.1	368.4
	Total market turnover of the top 20 commodity exchange markets	365.9	379.1	604.8
	Total market turnover	1,168.4	1,601.3	1,972.3

(Con'd)

Year		2004	2006	2007
South Central China	Total market turnover of the top 4 commodity exchange markets	492.6	663.7	700.7
	Total market turnover of the top 20 commodity exchange markets	708.8	1,073.3	1,156.7
	Total market turnover	3,618.5	5,628.2	6,105.2

Source: *Statistical Yearbook of China Commodity Exchange Market (2002–2008).*

Table 57. Numbers of wholesale markets each valuing more than RMB 100 million during 2002–2007

Year	2002	2003	2004	2005	2006	2007
Nationwide	1,734	1,759	1,821	1,851	2,161	2,366
Comprehensive markets	533	511	512	238	360	372
Comprehensive markets for industrial products	240	228	223	121	137	147
Comprehensive markets for agricultural products	198	191	197	117	223	225
Specialty markets	1,196	1,244	1,300	1,438	1,663	1,852
Markets for textiles, garments, shoes and hats	182	192	181	240	268	277
Markets for furniture	18	15	17	23	23	27
Markets for small commodities	47	42	42	65	67	67
Markets for cultural, audio-video products, books, news papers and magazines	24	23	18	12	31	33
Markets for food, drinks, tobacco and wines	103	99	96	88	101	114
Markets for grains and edible oil	38	39	46	103	75	84
Markets for fresh and dried nuts and fruits	53	61	62	85	100	118
Markets for aquatic products	55	56	63	57	77	93
Markets for vegetables	119	128	129	168	192	213
Markets for meat, poultry and eggs	21	28	25	53	49	51
Markets for native products and animal by-products	19	20	20	16	42	41

Source: *Statistical Yearbook of China Commodity Exchange Market (2003–2008).*

Table 58. Turnovers of the wholesale markets each valuing more than RMB 100 million during 2002–2007

(RMB 10 thousand)

Year	2002	2003	2004	2005	2006	2007
Nationwide	154,508,744	168,325,688	211,169,445	245,442,000	296,799,000	358,714,600
Comprehensive markets	50,766,475	52,251,903	58,846,224	43,380,000	56,249,000	70,018,900
Comprehensive markets for industrial products	33,019,088	32,152,021	32,152,021	33,133,494	30,264,000	27,795,000
Comprehensive markets for agricultural products	11,676,384	14,554,917	14,554,917	18,080,447	13,116,000	28,454,000
Specialty markets	103,545,162	115,904,875	151,536,230	179,930,000	213,452,000	257,718,800
Markets for textiles, garments, shoes and hats	24,333,581	26,218,282	26,218,282	28,924,417	41,854,000	54,925,000
Markets for furniture	2,026,723	1,237,367	1,237,367	1,115,244	1,728,,000	2,267,000
Markets for small commodities	6,179,375	4,125,094	4,125,094	4,276,599	6,523,000	5,671,000
Markets for cultural, audio-video products, books, news papers and magazines	2,317,239	1,076,201	1,076,201	1,278,357	1,207,000	2,363,000
Markets for food, drinks, tobacco and wines	7,215,480	7,144,660	7,144,660	8,280,849	6,420,000	7,659,000
Markets for grains and edible oil	1,877,042	1,787,828	1,787,828	2,956,843	6,035,000	4,734,000
Markets for fresh and dried nuts and fruits	2,203,935	2,697,877	2,697,877	2,949,133	5,754,000	7,320,000
Markets for aquatic products	4,136,975	4,027,154	4,027,154	4,742,481	6,739,000	9,404,000
Markets for vegetables	5,689,835	5,911,025	5,911,025	7,244,765	14,406,000	12,253,000
Markets for meat, poultry and eggs	771,628	877,200	877,200	1,122,486	3,674,000	3,796,000
Markets for native products and animal by-products	692,298	583,549	583,549	742,524	3,684,000	6,859,000

Source: *Statistical Yearbook of China Commodity Exchange Market (2003–2008).*

Table 59. Financial indicators of the top 50 large-scale wholesale enterprises

(RMB 100 million)

Year	Total sales volume	Total profits	Total assets
1999	3,688.2	88.5	—
2000	5,884.3	113.8	—
2001	5,943.7	68.2	1,496.5
2002	6,451.9	91.9	1,417.0
2003	7,455.1	3.9	619.8
2005	12,309.5	218.2	2,196.4
2006	15,787.3	274.4	2,833.0
2007	20,028.3	549.3	3,403.0

Source: *Market Statistical Yearbook of China (2000–2008).*

Table 60. Added value of the logistics industry

(RMB 100 million)

Year	Transportation	The storage industry	Trade	Distribution processing and packaging	Postal services	Total
1991	1,526	59	193	53	20	1,851
1992	1,778	73	232	68	22	2,174
1993	2,371	98	315	94	27	2,906
1994	2,935	138	399	147	35	3,654
1995	3,396	175	459	195	40	4,265
1996	4,013	187	533	217	45	4,996
1997	4,324	205	571	251	47	5,398
1998	4,732	211	602	269	44	5,858
1999	5,205	226	665	279	42	6,416
2000	5,498	274	714	335	68	6,887
2001	5,903	308	772	377	68	7,429
2002	6,195	363	861	442	65	7,927
2003	7,122	409	1,001	516	64	9,112
2004	8,466	458	1,168	596	87	10,776
2005	9,475	539	1,435	728	93	12,271
2006	10,665	648	1,749	948	109	14,120

Source: China Federation of Logistics & Purchasing. 2007. *China Logistics Yearbook (2007)*. Beijing: China Logistics Publishing House.

Table 61. Investment in the fixed assets of the logistics industry

(RMB 100 million)

Year	Transportation	The storage industry	Trade	Distribution processing and packaging	Postal services
1991	299.8	9.6	42.7	1.3	4.1
1992	496.6	11.1	122.7	3.3	16.4
1993	890.6	18.5	128.9	5.8	31.9
1994	1,284.5	24.2	163.1	9.1	46.4
1995	1,469.7	28.7	169.9	9.6	45.8
1996	1,776.3	39.5	150.1	8.1	46.8
1997	2,113.2	52.2	149.2	6.8	45.8
1998	3,082	69.9	185	6.5	58.1
1999	3,164.7	130.6	185.8	6.4	46
2000	3,194.6	95.3	194.5	7.7	62.7
2001	3,589.4	91.4	202.2	8.7	64.6
2002	4,154.9	115.5	231.7	12.0	39.4

(Con'd)

Year	Transportation	The storage industry	Trade	Distribution processing and packaging	Postal services
2003	4,861	161.5	510.2	23.5	38.2
2004	6,319.6	341.1	838.7	34.2	36.9
2005	7,749.6	356.3	1,103.8	45.5	37.9
2006	9,774.9	469.8	1,827	57.8	39.9

Source: China Federation of Logistics & Purchasing. 2007. *China Logistics Yearbook (2007)*. Beijing: China Logistics Publishing House.

Table 62. Growth rate of the cost of logistics (%)

Year	The wholesale trade	Transportation	The storage industry	Distribution processing and packaging	Postal services	Total
1992	16.6	15.9	21.6	20.9	12.2	16.3
1993	19.4	19.8	38.1	35.8	21.0	20.1
1994	38.8	19.7	62.5	56.3	29.5	30.3
1995	15.3	3.2	33.2	33.0	15.5	10.7
1996	11.8	8.5	0.8	3.3	11.1	10.0
1997	24.1	4.3	-9.3	-7.8	4.7	14.6
1998	-1.4	7.1	-8.7	-5.4	-6.7	1.5
1999	0.8	5.7	5.9	9.3	-5	2.9
2000	4.1	8.2	19	19.2	58.2	6.6
2001	5	2.2	0	8.2	3.1	3.9
2002	12.4	-0.1	12.4	21.3	-3.3	7.5

Source: China Federation of Logistics & Purchasing. *China Logistics Yearbook (2004)*. Beijing: China Logistics Publishing House.

Table 63. Total number of HR and personnel qualifications structure of logistics practitioners in China in 2004

Industries	Practitioners with the master's and above degrees		Practitioners with bachelor degree		Practitioners with junior college educational background		Subtotal	
	Number (person)	Composition (%)	Number (person)	Composition (%)	Number (person)	Composition (%)	Number (person)	Composition (%)
Road transportation	2,371	0.2	41,841	2.8	165,985	11.3	210,196	14.3
Waterway transportation	1,356	0.2	36,861	5.5	82,294	12.3	120,511	18
Air transportation	217	1.2	4,042	22.1	6,284	34.3	10,542	57.5
Pipeline transportation	371	0.2	9,373	3.8	25,346	10.4	35,090	14.4
Handling and other	2,646	0.5	38,685	7.8	85,724	17.3	127,055	25.6
transportation services	1,205	0.2	27,391	4.9	88,760	15.9	117,356	21
Warehousing	2,370	0.6	30,473	7.2	83,769	19.7	116,613	27.5
Postal services								
The wholesale trade	14,433	1.1	102,330	8.1	245,033	19.3	361,796	28.5
The retail trade	3,047	0.4	39,048	5.5	125,082	17.5	167,177	23.3

Source: Department of Higher Education, Ministry of Education. 2007. *Research Report on the Development and Demand for Talents of the Chinese Logistics.*

Table 64. Competences of logistics practitioners in 2004

Industries	Total (person)	Senior technicians		Senior workers	
		Number (person)	Composition (%)	Number (person)	Composition (%)
Logistics total	16,759,983	—	—	—	—
Railway transportation	1,204,676	—	—	—	—
Road transportation	1,475,732	2,635	0.2	82,617	5.6
Waterway transportation	669,370	1,426	0.2	25,928	3.9
Air transportation	18,329	43	0.2	604	3.3
Pipeline transportation	244,089	185	0.1	4,948	2.0
Handling transportation	496,693	559	0.1	7,252	1.5

(Con'd)

Industries	Total (person)	Senior technicians		Senior workers	
		Number (person)	Composition (%)	Number (person)	Composition (%)
Warehousing	557,747	698	0.1	25,633	4.6
Postal services	424,294	981	0.2	10,257	2.4
The wholesale trade	127,149	2,972	0.2	13,945	1.1
The retail trade	716,902	1,764	0.2	8,861	1.2
Transportation	4,768,638	—	—	—	—
Industrial enterprises	4,685,839	—	—	—	—

Source: Department of Higher Education, Ministry of Education. 2007. *Research Report on the Development and Demand for Talents of the Chinese Logistics.*

Table 65. Inventory values of the wholesale trade with different ownerships

(RMB 10 thousand)

Year	2001	2002	2003	2005	2006	2007
Total	3,618.0	3,577.9	3,898.2	7,061.0	7,629.6	9,193.2
Wholesale trade	2,843.9	2,675.6	2,865.0	5,274.8	5,632.6	6,649.9
State-owned enterprises	1,600.0	1,378.4	1,280.1	1,683.6	1,675.7	1,903.7
Collective enterprises	354.8	282.6	258.8	221.1	175.1	198.8
Private enterprises	92.3	123.5	191.6	856.8	1,041.1	1,316.2
Foreign-invested enterprises	106.2	68.2	176.6	379.5	443.1	603.3

Source: *China Statistical Yearbook (2002–2008).*

Table 66. Inventory values of different wholesale trades during 1994–1998

(RMB 10 thousand)

Year	1994	1995	1996	1997	1998
Total	61,009,092	67,054,939	72,273,449	39,461,991	37,896,856
Wholesale commerce of food, drinks, tobacco and household articles	26,032,369	30,395,647	33,134,358	19,418,619	—
The wholesale of food, drinks and tobacco	12,217,632	14,702,271	18,465,607	9,460,327	8,701,487
The wholesale of grains and edible oil	—	—	—	—	4,022,411
The wholesale of tobacco and its products	—	—	—	—	3,065,732
The wholesale of cotton, flax, native products and animal by-products	2,700,105	4,283,819	3,732,883	4,074,494	5,215,704
The wholesale of textiles, garments, shoes and hats	2,743,709	2,537,018	2,080,338	1,140,382	933,356

(Con'd)

Year	1994	1995	1996	1997	1998
The wholesale of articles for daily use	2,541,457	2,756,308	2,937,539	1,363,555	931,767
The wholesale of daily sundries	678,357	654,476	595,491	142,698	152,314
The wholesale of hardware, electrical appliances & accessories and chemical products	3,221,562	3,303,807	3,380,806	1,825,021	1,022,556
The wholesale of drugs and medical instruments	1,929,543	2,157,946	1,941,694	1,412,143	1,581,048
The wholesale of energies, material and machinery electronic equipment	14,752,512	13,634,038	13,720,439	7,290,309	—
The wholesale of energies	1,978,055	1,758,875	2,015,173	1,776,722	1,570,658
The wholesale of chemical materials	1,244,857	1,255,780	1,290,125	634,010	672,167
The wholesale of woods	542,052	399,428	359,721	97,236	81,564
The wholesale of building materials	1,121,127	1,038,294	1,076,620	251,680	197,958
The wholesale of mineral products	277,262	240,577	271,970	110,073	74,513
The wholesale of metallic materials	4380,937	3,953,537	3,625,599	1,853,286	1,870,572
The wholesale of machinery and electronic equipment	2,595,993	2,412,318	2,233,587	1,021,363	1,317,094
The wholesale of autos, motorcycles and accessories	1,664,527	1,954,010	2,290,001	1,263,140	139,369
The wholesale of recycled materials	947,698	621,309	557,643	282,798	91,759
Other wholesale trades	4,362,066	5,943,136	6,744,228	3,494,102	—
The wholesale of artistic handicrafts	218,412	279,187	167,785	77,951	14,588
The wholesale of books and newspapers	176,804	342,198	336,966	459,603	411,691
The wholesale of means of agricultural production	2,994,063	4,192,416	4,872,713	2,436,693	2,175,983
Other wholesale not classified	972,784	1,129,334	1,366,764	519,854	823,176

Source: *China Market Statistical Yearbook (1995–1999).*

Table 67. Inventory values of different wholesale trades during 2000–2007

(RMB 100 million)

Year	2000	2001	2002	2003	2005	2006	2007
Wholesale trade	2,831.1	2,843.9	2,675.6	2,865	5,274.8	5,632.6	6,649.9
The wholesale of agricultural and animal products	385.69	293.4	230.5	441.9	876.9	821.5	816.7
The wholesale of food, drinks and tobacco	890.0	939.7	827.9	539.6	693.6	714.8	754.6
The wholesale of textiles, garments and daily necessities	313.6	316.1	331.5	156.5	230.4	312.0	404.4

(Con'd)

Year	2000	2001	2002	2003	2005	2006	2007
The wholesale of cultural and sports goods and appliances	56.8	61.1	97.1	115.9	139.2	159.6	185.7
The wholesale of drugs and medical instruments	160.7	197.4	241.7	250.4	373.2	340.1	392.6
The wholesale of mineral products, building materials and chemical products	96.2	81.2	99.6	747.6	1,797.4	2,114.6	2,669.8
The wholesale of mechanical equipment, hardware appliances and accessories and electric products	330.5	362.7	401.6	476.2	878.2	905.1	1,059.7
Trading breakage and agency	—	—	—	86.4	15.2	41.8	76.2

Source: *China Statistical Yearbook (2001–2008).*

Table 68. Inventory values of the wholesale trade in different regions

(RMB 100 million)

Year	Nationwide	North China	Northeast China	East China	South Central China	Southwest China	Northwest China
1993	1,247.2	300.0	335.2	254.6	213.2	90.3	53.0
1994	6,101.0	895.8	752.8	1,983.5	1,447.0	578.6	443.3
1997	3,946.2	650.4	371.2	1,433.2	741.2	422.6	327.8
1998	3,789.7	767.6	332.2	1,237.0	712.2	393.2	347.6
1999	3,629.7	729.9	344.0	1,176.7	718.0	400.8	260.1
2000	3,569.9	698.9	364.6	1,172.6	666	439.7	228.2
2001	2,843.9	617.6	258.9	890.1	573.1	314.6	189.7
2002	2,675.6	557.9	288.2	894.0	471.0	293.0	171.6
2003	2,865.0	634.4	263.8	1,023.1	484.9	275.9	182.8
2005	5,274.8	1,492.3	508.6	1,557.0	893.9	520.4	302.6
2006	5,632.6	1,477.2	438.6	1,916.4	920.0	518.4	362.0
2007	6,649.9	1,868.9	383.5	2,390.3	1,084.7	540.9	381.6

Source: *Market Statistical Yearbook of China (1994–2000)* and *China Statistical Yearbook (2001–2008).*

Postscript

December 16, 2008 marks the 30th anniversary of the reform and opening up in China. All industries and trades are looking back at their advantages and disadvantages in the development, aiming at summarizing experience, learning lessons, and developing better in the years ahead.

2008 also marks the 30th anniversary of the restoration of the Department of Trade of Renmin University of China. In the past three decades, the Department of Trade has been developing along with the circulation and market reform in China, witnessed the tough development of the circulation industry in China, and experienced the sorrows and joys, ups and downs of the market-oriented reform in China. Therefore, it ought to sort things out and reflect the economic development in China. In view of this idea, the Department of Trade in the Business School of Renmin University of China organized the compilation of a series of monographs to focus on making comments on the development of the wholesale trade, the retail trade and foreign trade of China, as well as the evolution process of their theoretical policies. We aim at one thing-telling thoroughly the achievements and the problems as well. Experiences in success and lessons from failures are both our spiritual wealth, only from both of which could we learn the essence and clarify our direction.

We have intended to summarize nothing selectively in this book, but simply wanted to provide a "panorama" of the development process of the wholesale trade in the past three decades, trying to make the book more informative and truthful to data and the historic facts. However, by making a full exploitation, we have still got several conclusions of rules or laws in nature from large amounts of data and documented materials. From the reform and development track of the wholesale trade in China, we have found that reform is the direction. Problems emerging in the reform, opening up and development have to be solved in the reform, opening up and development. In view of the relationships of all parties, compromise is sometimes necessary in the reform. Yet reform principles cannot be compromised.

During the writing of this book, my Ph.D. candidate Gong Yingqing, Master degree candidates Chang Shuhua and Lin Wenkuan did a great deal of effective work, and the leaders and editors of China Renmin University Press offered their supports and help selflessly. I want to extend my thanks to all of them as well.

It is inevitable that this book has some careless omissions, even errors in data collection and processing, and in conclusion formation, which were all done by me. I sincerely hope that readers could provide constructive feedback.

The year 2009 will be the 60th anniversary of the founding of the People's Republic of China. I hope that researchers of the theories and practices on the development experience of the circulation industry in the past six decades could go on doing deeper researches on the basis of this book. If it could provide one or a few bases or starting points for people to think further, we'll be so relieved.

Ma Longlong

Notes

Chapter 2 Growth and Contribution of the Wholesale Trade

1. *China Statistical Yearbook (2008)*. Beijing: China Statistics Press.
2. *China Youth Daily*, March 20, 2006.
3. Part of the data were calculated in accordance with *China Statistical Yearbook* (1979–2007).
4. Calculated at current year price.
5. Year-end number of on-post staff and workers refers to the number of all staff and workers prior to 1997, but that of on-post staff and workers since 1998. In 2003, new industry classification standards were adopted. Since 1998, the wholesale and retail trade has been calculating the number of on-post staff and workers of wholesale and retail enterprises above the designated size.
6. Some materials are from China Statistical Yearbook (1981–2008). Data during January-June, 2008 were the quarterly data from the website of National Bureau of Statistics of China. Data in 1992 and before were the total amounts of retail sales of social consumables. Data of the total amounts of retail sales of social consumables in 1997 and after didn't include houses purchased by residents. The criteria on the total amount of retail sales of social consumables were adjusted in 2003, and corresponding adjustment was made to the data in 2002. Apart from the national totals, data were from the economic census in 2004, but annual reports in other years. Summation of local data doesn't equal national totals, for national data were somewhat revised.
7. Considering that the ratio of fixed-asset investment in the urban and rural wholesale trade to the social investment in fixed assets of the wholesale trade was very great and capable of representing the overall situation of the wholesale trade, fixed-asset investment in the wholesale trade is hereby used to replace the fixed-asset investment in the urban and rural wholesale trade.

Chapter 3 Evolution of the Wholesale Industrial Organizations

1. Data in this part are from *China Commerce and External Economic Statistics: 1952–1988*, China Business Yearbook (1991–1992), Market Statistical Yearbook of China (1993–2004) and China Trade and External Economic Statistical Yearbook. The statistical criteria during 1999–2007 were limited to the wholesale trade above the designated size. Wholesale enterprises above the designated size refer to those enterprises each with over 20 million RMB of annual sales volume and more than 20 practitioners.
2. Sum of the respective ratio of the realized sales volume of the top 4 wholesale enterprises in terms of sales in China to the total volume of social wholesale in the same year.
3. Sum of the respective ratio of the realized sales volume of the top 8 wholesale enterprises in terms of sales in China to the total volume of social wholesale in the same year.
4. Total assets turnover=Sales revenue/Total assets
5. Current assets turnover=Sales revenue/Total current assets
6. Rate of return on sales =Sales profit/Sales revenue
7. Return on assets (ROA)=Profits/Total assets
8. Asset-liability ratio=Total liabilities/Total assets

Chapter 4 Changes in the Structure of the Wholesale Trade

1. Most data used in this chapter are from *China Business Yearbook (1989–1991), China Business Yearbook (1991–1992), Market Statistical Yearbook* of China (1993–2004) and China Trade and External Economic Statistical Yearbook. Of which, the statistical criteria during 1999–2007 were limited to the wholesale trade above the designated size. Wholesale enterprises above the designated size refer to those enterprises each with over 20 million RMB of annual sales volume and more than 20 practitioners. For statistics reasons, individual sums of proportions are not 1.
2. *China Business Yearbook* (1988). Beijing: China Statistics Press.
3. State Commission for Economic Restructuring ed. 1988. *A Decade of China's Economic Reform*. Beijing: Economic Management Publishing House, China Reform Publishing House.
4. Hu Jun, Zhou Xincheng. Reforms of the Ownership Structure in China at the Primary Stage of Socialism. Beijing: China Economic Publishing House, 2007.
5. China Yearbook of the Private Economic Sector (1999–2001), China Statistical Yearbook (1981–1992)
6. China didn't collect data on the financial states of different sectors of the wholesale trade above the designated size until 1999.

Notes

7. China is usually divided into East China, Central China and West China according to local economic development. Of which, East China covers 11 provinces and municipalities, namely Beijing, Tianjin, Hebei, Liaoning, Shandong, Jiangsu, Shanghai, Zhejiang, Fujian, Guangdong and Hainan; Central China covers 10 provinces and municipalities, namely Shanxi, Jilin, Heilongjiang, He'nan, Hubei, Hu'nan, Anhui, Jiangxi, Chongqing and Sichuan; and West China covers 10 provinces and autonomous regions, namely Inner Mongolia Autonomous Region, Shaanxi, Gansu, Ningxia Hui Autonomous Region, Qinghai, Xinjiang Uygur Autonomous Region, Yunnan, Guizhou, Guangxi Zhuang Autonomous Region and Tibet Autonomous Region.
8. Sum of the ratios is not 100% because national data were adjusted.
9. Liu Yong. 1999. *Business Growth Pattern*. Beijing: Economic Management Publishing House.
10. The country is divided into six regions: North China, Northeast China, East China, South Central China, Southwest China and Northwest China. Specifically, North China covers: Beijing, Tianjin, Hebei Province, Shanxi Province and Inner Mongolia Autonomous Region; Northeast China covers: Liaoning Province, Jilin Province and Heilongjiang Province; East China covers: Shanghai, Jiangsu Province, Zhejiang Province, Anhui Province, Fujian Province, Jiangxi Province and Shandong Province; South Central China covers: He'nan Province, Hubei Province, Hu'nan Province, Guangdong Province, Hainan Province, Guangxi Zhuang Autonomous Region; Southwest China covers: Chongqing, Sichuan Province, Guizhou Province, Yunnan Province and Tibet Autonomous Region; Northwest China covers: Shannxi Province, Gansu Province, Qinghai Province and Ningxia Hui Autonomous Region.
11. The wholesale trade over this period was divided into three major categories by China Statistical Yearbook, namely the wholesale of food, drinks, tobacco and household articles (which can be further divided into seven categories), the wholesale of energies, materials and machinery and electronic equipment (which can be further divided into 9 categories) and the wholesale trade in other economic sectors (which can be further divided into four categories). Data on the basic information only cover those during 1994–1996. For the wholesale trade in other economic sectors that haven't been analyzed, see the attachments of this book.
12. Before 2000 in this period, statistical criteria were the wholesale trade in 20 economic sectors. Of which, the sector of food, drinks and tobacco was subdivided into the wholesale of grains and edible oil, as well as the wholesale of tobacco and its products; the sector of energies was subdivided into the wholesale of petroleum and related products, and the wholesale of coal and related products; and the sector of autos, motorcycles and accessories was subdivided into the wholesale of autos. China began to merge the above 20 sectors in 2001 into threemajor categories, namely the wholesale of food, drinks, tobacco and household articles (which can be further divided into seven categories), the wholesale of energies, materials and machinery and electronic equipment (which can be further divided into nine categories) and the wholesale trade in other economic sectors (which can be further divided into four categories). Statistics on wholesale enterprises above the designated size were collected.
13. The statistical criteria on the wholesale trade in China were adjusted into nine major categories in this period. Of which the wholesale of food, drinks and tobacco was subdivided into the wholesale of rice and flour products and edible oil; the wholesale of mineral products, building materials and chemical products was subdivided into the wholesale of coal and its products, the wholesale of petroleum and related products, the wholesale of metals and metal ores, the wholesale of building materials and the wholesale of fertilizers; the wholesale of hardware, electrical appliances & accessories and chemical products was subdivided into the wholesale of autos, motorcycles and accessories, the wholesale of household appliances and the wholesale of computers, software and auxiliary equipment. Statistics on the wholesale enterprises above the designated size were collected.
14. Economic sectors chosen here are the same as those used in the above introduction of fundamentals states.
15. What's collected in 1997 were the data on the sales of wholesale of large and medium-sized wholesale enterprises, making them incomparable.

Chapter 5 Emergence and Development of the Wholesale Markets

1. Data during 1978–2001 are extracted from China Market Statistical Yearbook, in which the wholesale markets for consumables also included the wholesale market for agricultural products, and the wholesale market for industrial consumables. Data on the commodity exchange and wholesale markets each valuing more than 100 million RMB during 2001–2007 are from Statistical Yearbook of China Commodity Exchange Market. Commodity exchange market-related data are used directly in measuring the degree of market concentration, while other indicators are based on data related to the wholesale trade by the mode of operation.
2. Statistical data on the commodity exchange markets in China are relatively complete, while most commodity exchange markets are wholesale-based. Large markets here refer to those commodity exchange markets each valuing more than 100 million RMB.
3. Statistical Yearbook of China Commodity Exchange Market failed to collect this statistical indicator in 2002 and 2005, thus no data on this indicator were available in the said two years. Analysis of the indicator in the said two years is thus skipped.
4. Ou Kaipei, Xiao Yi. 2007. *Plight and the Way Out of the Wholesale Markets in China*. Beijing: Central Compilation and Translation Press.
5. Ou Kaipei, Xiao Yi. 2007. *Plight and the Way Out of the Wholesale Markets in China*. Beijing: Central Compilation and Translation Press.

6. Wholesale markets for agricultural products refer to the big agriculture, which include farming, forestry, animal husbandry, sideline occupation and fishery. Specifically, such markets include the comprehensive market for agricultural products, the market for food, drinks, tobacco and wine, the market for grains and oil, the market for fresh and dried nuts and fruits, the market for aquatic products, the market for vegetables, the market for meat, poultry and eggs and the market for native products and animal by-products. The wholesale markets for industrial consumables include 4 types of specialty markets, namely the comprehensive market for industrial products, the market for textiles, garments, shoes and hats, the market for small commodities, the market for furniture and the market for cultural, audio-video products, books, news papers and magazines.

Chapter 6 Emergence and Development of the Wholesale Logistics

1. Zhou Changlin. 2004. *On the Competitiveness of wholesale logistics, Economic Problems*, (6).
2. Since China Logistics Yearbook adopted different statistical criteria on the logistics industries classified by sector in different years, the added value of trade logistics is chosen here to reflect the added value of wholesale logistics. It is ditto for the fixed-asset investment to be mentioned below.
3. According to Song Ze et al in Frontier of the Theoretical Development of China IV (Song Ze et al., 2006), the stock-sales ratio of wholesale refers to the ratio of the total inventory in the whole society to the sales of wholesale of the whole society within a certain period (which is usually one year). Statistical data have shown that of the composition of wholesale logistics expenses, warehouse expenses account for the largest proportion of all, so they can directly represent the cost of wholesale logistics. The stock-sales ratio is in inverse proportion to warehouse expenses, so it is safe to say that the higher the stock-sales ratio is, the higher the cost of logistics and the lower the development level of logistics will be, vise versa.
4. Data are from China Market Statistical Yearbook (1993), of which those in 1986 and before were on state-owned commerce and supply and marketing cooperatives; and those during 1987–1992 were on social commerce.
5. Data are from China Statistical Yearbook (1995–1998), of which data on the wholesale and retail trade in 1993 were the original data on materials supply and marketing cooperatives. No data are available on the private sector of the economy. The foreign-invested sector of the economy includes the foreign-invested economy where investments are made by businessmen from Hong Kong, Macao and Taiwan and that where investments are made by foreign businessmen. Data below are the same.

Chapter 7 Development Prospects of the Wholesale Trade

1. Commodity circulation channel dominance is a basic theory in circulation economics, which is based on the differences of different channel members in economic capability, information capability and organizational capability. The member with the strongest comprehensive capabilities will become the dominator of circulation channels.

Notes

Chapter 6 Emergence and Development of the Wholesale Logistics

Chapter 7 Development Prospects of the Wholesale Trade

References

Department of Higher Education, Ministry of Education. 2007. *Research Report on the Development and Demand for Talents of the Chinese Logistics.* Beijing: China Logistics Publishing House.

Hu Jun, Zhou Xincheng. 2007. *Reforms of the Ownership Structure in China at the Primary Stage of Socialism.* Beijing: China Economic Publishing House.

Jin Yongsheng. 2004. *Studies on the Organizational Innovation of the Circulation Industry in China.* Beijing: Capital University of Economics & Business Press.

Liu Yong. 1999. *Business Growth Pattern.* Beijing: Economic Management Publishing House.

Ou Kaipei, Xiao Yi. 2007. *Plight and the Way Out of the Wholesale Markets in China*. Beijing: Central Compilation and Translation Press.

State Commission for Economic Restructuring ed. 1988. *A Decade of China's Economic Reform*. Beijing: Economic Management Publishing House, China Reform Publishing House.

Song Ze et al. 2006. *Frontier of the Theoretical Development of China IV.* Beijing: Social Sciences Academic Press (China).

Zhou Changlin. 2004. *On the Competitiveness of wholesale logistics, On Economic Problems,* 31.

Index